THE OFFICIAL ACT® PREP GUIDE 2026–2027

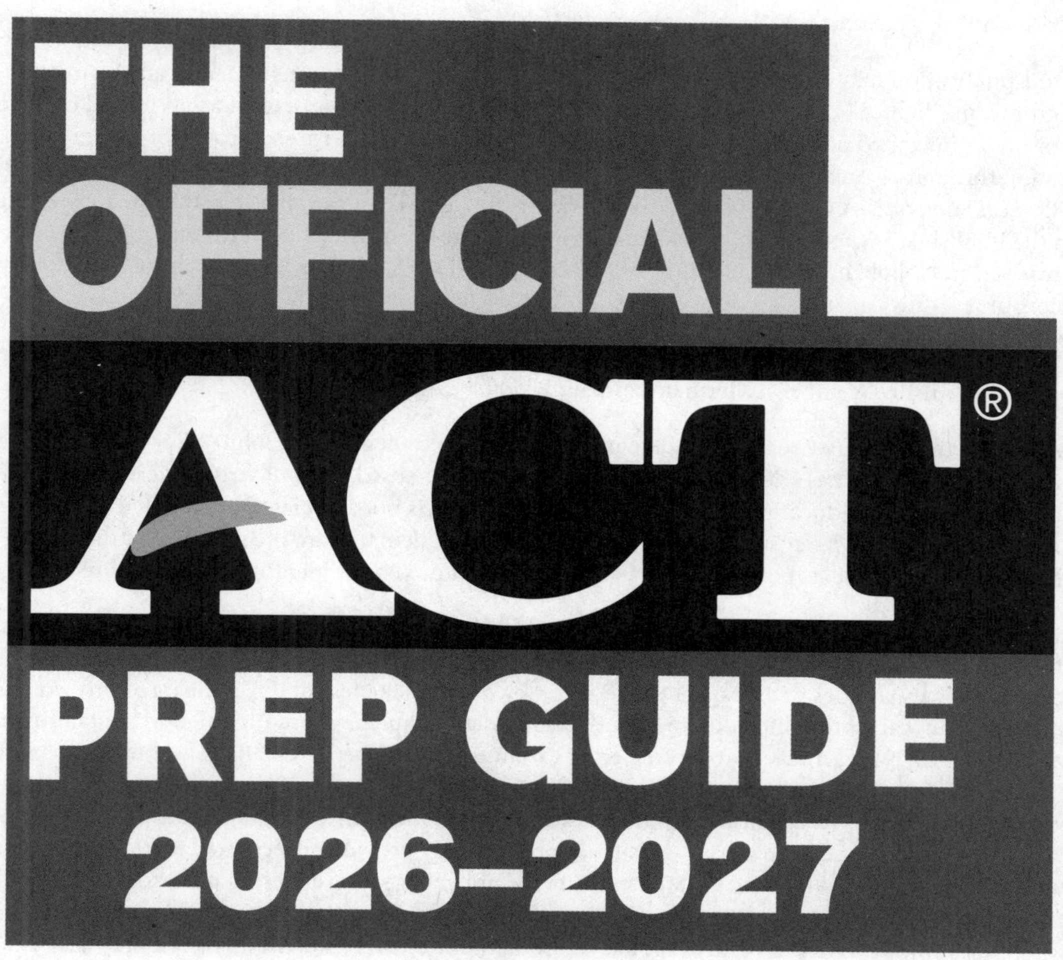

The ONLY Official Prep Guide from the Makers of the ACT

WILEY

Contents

Part Two: Taking and Evaluating Your First Practice Test 35

Chapter 3: Taking and Scoring Your First ACT Practice Test 37

Chapter 4: Identifying Areas for Improvement 170

Part Three: Improving Your Score 183

Chapter 5: Improving Your English Score 185

Preface

You want to do your best on the ACT® test, and this book can help. It supplements our free booklet, *Preparing for the ACT,* and our *ACT Online Prep*™ (a web-based preparation program for the ACT). This book features four actual ACT tests—all of which include the optional science and writing tests—which you can use for practice, and it gives detailed explanatory answers to every question to help you review.

Using this book will help you become familiar with the following:

- The content of the ACT
- The procedures you'll follow when you're actually taking the ACT
- The types of questions you can expect to find on the ACT
- Suggestions on how to approach the questions
- General test-taking strategies

This book is intended to help you **know what to expect** when you take the ACT so you can relax and concentrate on doing your best. The more you know about what to expect on any test you take, the more likely it is that your performance on that test will accurately reflect your overall preparation and achievement in the areas it measures. Knowing what to expect can help reduce any nervousness you may feel as you approach the test.

The ACT measures your understanding of what you've been taught in core high school courses that you should have completed by the time you finish high school. Because it has taken you years to learn all this material, it might take you some time to review for the ACT. You can't expect to cram for the ACT in a night or two. However, any review should be helpful to you, even if it just makes you more comfortable when you actually sit down to take the ACT. We hope this book helps you to gauge how much reviewing you feel you need to do and identify subject areas on which to focus your efforts.

Your purchase of *The Official ACT® Prep Guide* includes access to four full-length, digital practice tests via the Wiley Online Platform. Use these assets to simulate the test day experience. Detailed rationales and official explanations are provided for every question from the makers of the ACT® test.

Terms of Use: Purchase of this book offers access to the companion online course for 12 months from the date of activation for the original purchaser only. ACT and Wiley are not responsible for providing access to customers who borrow or purchase used copies of this study guide. Purchase of this study guide grants access only to the companion online course and not to other Wiley or ACT-owned password protected websites.

Online course access is subject to limitations and may not be available indefinitely. Continuity of service may be affected by various factors such as maintenance, upgrades, technical difficulties, or a change in market demand. To maximize use of all online prep materials included with your book, it is recommended that you access your practice tests on the online platform as soon as you begin your prep journey for your upcoming ACT test.

How This Book Is Arranged

This book is divided into five parts:

Part One: **Getting Acquainted with the ACT.** Chapters in this part introduce the ACT, explain how to prepare, and present general test-taking techniques and strategies for you to consider.

Part Two: **Taking and Evaluating Your First Practice Test.** This part includes a practice test along with guidance on how to use the test to identify areas where you may need to invest more time and effort.

Part Three: **Improving Your Score.** Chapters in this part present test-taking strategies tailored for each subject test—English, math, and reading—along with suggestions for taking the optional science and writing tests.

Part Four: **Taking Additional Practice Tests.** In this part, you have the opportunity to take three additional practice tests, see the results, and interpret your scores to determine how well prepared you are to take the ACT.

Part Five: **Moving Forward to Test Day.** This part prepares you for test day by explaining how to register for the ACT and describing what to expect on the day of the test, so you show up on time with everything you need.

The parts are identified by bars on the edge of their right-hand pages.

Before You Begin

There is no standardized way to prepare for the ACT. Everyone learns and prepares differently. Some people prepare best when they are by themselves. Others need to work with fellow students to do their best. Still others function best in a structured class with a teacher leading them through their work. Use whatever method works best for you. Keep in mind, though, that when you actually take the ACT, it will be just you and the test.

As you use this book to prepare for the ACT, consider working in 1-hour segments (except when you're taking the timed practice tests, of course). If you want to invest more than 1 hour a day, that's fine, but take breaks to stretch and give your mind a chance to absorb the material. Toiling to the point of burnout is counterproductive.

Part One:
Getting Acquainted with the ACT Test

In This Part

This part introduces you to the ACT, the five tests that it is composed of (English, mathematics, reading, and optional science and writing tests), and testing procedures. It also features test-taking strategies and skills that apply to all of the component tests. Specifically, you will do the following:

Find out what is covered on the tests.

Determine when you can use a calculator and the types of calculators you are permitted to use and prohibited from using.

Get a preview of what you can expect on test day.

Obtain guidance on how to prepare for test day.

Learn test-taking strategies that may improve your scores on all of the tests.

Chapter 1:
About the ACT

The ACT® measures your achievement in core academic areas important for your college and career success: English, math, reading, science, and (optionally) writing. It isn't an IQ test—it doesn't measure your basic intelligence. It's an achievement test that's been carefully designed—using surveys of classroom teachers, reviews of curriculum guides for schools all over the country, and advice from curriculum specialists and college faculty members—to be one of several effective tools for evaluating your college and career readiness.

The individual tests that make up the ACT consist of questions that measure your knowledge and skills. You're not required to memorize facts or vocabulary to do well on the ACT. Of course, all the terms, formulas, and other information you learned in your classes will be useful to you when you take the ACT. However, last-minute cramming (such as memorizing 5,000 vocabulary words or the entire periodic table of elements) won't directly improve your performance on the ACT.

Description of the Full ACT Test

The full ACT consists of four multiple-choice tests—English, mathematics, reading, and science—and an optional writing test. Topics covered on these five tests correspond very closely to topics covered in typical high school classes. Table 1.1 gives you a snapshot of all five tests.

Table 1.1: ACT Tests			
Test	**Questions**	**Time**	**Content Covered**
English	50 questions	35 minutes	Measures standard written English knowledge and skills along with English language conventions
Mathematics	45 questions	50 minutes	Measures mathematical skills students have typically acquired in courses taken up to the beginning of grade 12
Reading	36 questions	40 minutes	Measures reading comprehension
Science	40 questions	40 minutes	Measures the interpretation, analysis, evaluation, reasoning, and problem-solving skills required in the natural sciences
Writing (optional)	1 prompt	40 minutes	Measures writing skills emphasized in high school English classes and in entry-level college composition courses

Questions on the tests are intended to help assess college and career readiness. The following sections provide an overview of what you should know to perform well on each test. For additional details, check out the ACT College and Career Readiness Standards presented in chapter 12.

English Test

50 questions (40 scored), 35 minutes

The English test consists of six or seven essays or passages, each of which is accompanied by a sequence of multiple-choice test questions. The length of the passages will vary; longer passages of approximately 340 words will be accompanied by ten items, while shorter passages of approximately 185 words will be accompanied by five items. Different passage types are employed to provide a variety of rhetorical situations. Passages are chosen not only for their appropriateness in assessing writing skills but also to reflect students' interests and experiences.

You will receive four scores for the ACT English test: a total test score based on all 40 scored questions and three reporting category scores based on the following:

- Production of Writing

- Knowledge of Language

- Conventions of Standard English

Production of Writing

Production of Writing questions test knowledge and skills in two areas of English composition:

- Topic development in terms of purpose and focus
- Organization, unity, and cohesion

Topic Development in Terms of Purpose and Focus

Examples of knowledge and skills tested include the following:

- Determine the relevance of material to the topic or the focus of the passage or paragraph.
- Identify the purpose of a word or phrase (for example, to identify a person, to define a term, or to help describe an object).
- Determine whether a passage has met a specific goal.
- Use a word, phrase, or sentence to accomplish a specific purpose, such as to convey a feeling or attitude or to illustrate a given statement.

Organization, Unity, and Cohesion

Examples of knowledge and skills tested include the following:

- Determine the need for transition words or phrases to define relationships in terms of time or logic.
- Determine the most logical place for a sentence in a paragraph or in the passage as a whole.
- Provide a suitable conclusion for a paragraph or passage.
- Provide a suitable introduction for a paragraph or passage.
- Rearrange sentences in a paragraph to establish a logical flow.
- Determine the most logical place to divide a paragraph to achieve a stated goal.

Knowledge of Language

Knowledge of Language questions test your ability to clearly and succinctly express yourself in written English. Knowledge and skills tested include the following:

- Revise unclear, clumsy, and confusing writing.
- Delete redundant and wordy material.
- Revise an expression to make it conform to the style and tone used throughout the passage.

- Determine logical connections between clauses.

- Choose the most appropriate word or phrase in terms of the sentence content.

Conventions of Standard English

Conventions of Standard English questions test knowledge and skills such as the following:

- Determine the need for punctuation or conjunctions to join clauses or to correct awkward-sounding fragments, fused sentences, and faulty subordination and coordination of clauses.

- Recognize and correct inappropriate shifts in verb tense.

- Recognize and correct disturbances in sentence structure, such as faulty placement of adjectives, participial phrase fragments, missing or incorrect relative pronouns, dangling or misplaced modifiers, faulty parallelism, and run-on sentences.

- Maintain consistent and logical verb tense and voice and pronoun person within a paragraph or passage.

Note: Spelling and the rote recall of grammar rules are not tested.

Mathematics Test

45 questions (41 scored), 50 minutes

The mathematics test presents multiple-choice questions that require you to use reasoning skills to solve practical math problems. The material covered on the test emphasizes the major content areas that are prerequisites to successful performance in entry-level courses in college mathematics. Some questions may belong to a set of several questions (for example, several questions about the same graph or chart).

Conceptual knowledge and computational skills are assumed as background for the problems, but recall of complex formulas and extensive computation is not required.

Nine scores are reported for the ACT mathematics test: a total test score based on all 41 scored questions and eight reporting category scores based on specific mathematical knowledge and skills. The reporting categories are:

- Preparing for Higher Mathematics, which includes separate scores for Number and Quantity, Algebra, Functions, Geometry, and Statistics and Probability

- Integrating Essential Skills

- Modeling

Preparing for Higher Mathematics

This category captures the more recent mathematics that students are learning, starting when they begin using algebra as a general way of expressing and solving equations. This category is divided into the following five subcategories:

- Number and Quantity
- Algebra
- Functions
- Geometry
- Statistics and Probability

Number and Quantity

Math questions in this category test your knowledge of numbers and fundamental math concepts and operations, including the following:

- Perform calculations on whole numbers and decimals.
- Recognize equivalent fractions and fractions in lowest terms.
- Locate rational numbers (whole numbers, fractions, decimals, and mixed numbers) on the number line.
- Recognize single-digit factors of a number.
- Identify a digit's place value.
- Demonstrate knowledge of elementary number concepts, including rounding, ordering of decimals, pattern identification, primes, and greatest common factor.
- Write powers of 10 using exponents.
- Comprehend the concept of length on the number line, and find the distance between two points.
- Understand absolute value in terms of distance.
- Find the distance between two points with the same x-coordinate or y-coordinate in the coordinate plane.
- Add, subtract, and multiply matrices (tables of numbers).
- Order fractions.
- Find and use the least common multiple.
- Demonstrate knowledge of complex numbers and multiply two complex numbers.

- Comprehend the concept of irrational numbers, such as π.

- Apply properties of rational exponents.

- Use relations involving addition, subtraction, and scalar multiplication of vectors and matrices.

- Analyze and draw conclusions based on number concepts.

Algebra and Functions

The mathematics test contains questions that require knowledge of and skills in algebra, functions, or both. *Algebra* involves formulas and equations in which letters and other symbols are used to represent unknown or unspecified values. A *function* is a rule, equation, or expression that produces exactly one output for any given input; for example, $2x$ is a function in that any input used for x results in an output that is twice the input's value.

Algebra

Algebra knowledge and skills tested include the following:

- Demonstrate knowledge of basic expressions, such as $b + g$ to identify a total.

- Solve equations in the form $x + a = b$, where a and b are whole numbers or decimals.

- Use substitution to evaluate mathematical expressions.

- Combine like terms, such as $2x + 5x$.

- Add and subtract algebraic expressions.

- Multiply two binomials.

- Match inequalities with their graphs on the number line.

- Demonstrate knowledge of slope.

- Solve real-world problems by using first-degree equations.

- Solve inequalities.

- Match linear or compound inequalities with their graphs on the number line.

- Add, subtract, and multiply polynomials.

- Solve quadratic equations.

- Factor quadratics.

- Work with squares/square roots and cubes/cube roots of numbers.

- Work with scientific notation.

- Solve problems involving positive integer exponents.

- Determine the slope of a line from an equation.

- Solve linear inequalities when the method involves reversing the inequality sign.

- Solve systems of two linear equations.

- Solve absolute value equations and inequalities.

- Match quadratic inequalities with their graphs on the number line.

Functions

Questions that involve functions test your ability to do the following:

- Understand the concept of a function having a well-defined output value at each valid input value.

- Extend a given pattern by a few terms for patterns that have a constant increase or decrease between terms or that have a constant factor between terms.

- Evaluate linear, quadratic, and polynomial functions expressed in function notation at the integer level.

- Interpret statements that use function notation in terms of their context.

- Find the domain of polynomial functions and rational functions.

- Find the range of polynomial functions.

- Find where a rational function's graph has a vertical asymptote.

- Use function notation for simple functions of two variables.

- Relate a graph to a situation described qualitatively in terms of faster change or slower change.

- Build functions for relations that are inversely proportional or exponential.

- Find a recursive expression for the general term in a sequence described recursively.

- Evaluate composite functions of integer values.

- Compare actual values and the values of a modeling function to judge model fit and compare models.

- Demonstrate knowledge of geometric sequences.

- Demonstrate knowledge of unit circle trigonometry.

- Match graphs of basic trigonometric functions with their equations.

- Use trigonometric concepts and basic identities to solve problems.
- Demonstrate knowledge of logarithms.
- Write an expression for the composite of two simple functions.

Algebra and Functions

Questions that involve both algebra and functions test your ability to do the following:

- Solve problems using whole numbers and decimals in the context of money.
- Solve one- or two-step arithmetic problems using positive rational numbers, such as percent.
- Relate a graph to a situation described quantitatively.
- Solve two- or three-step arithmetic problems involving concepts such as rate and proportion, sales tax, percentage off, and estimation.
- Perform word-to-symbol translations.
- Solve multistep arithmetic problems that involve planning or converting units of measure (for example, feet per second to miles per hour).
- Build functions and write expressions, equations, or inequalities with a single variable for common pre-algebra settings, such as rate and distance problems and problems that involve proportions.
- Match linear equations with their graphs in the coordinate plane.
- Solve word problems containing several rates, proportions, or percentages.
- Build functions and write expressions, equations, and inequalities for common algebra settings.
- Interpret and use information from graphs in the coordinate plane.
- Solve complex math problems involving percent of increase or decrease or requiring integration of several concepts.
- Build functions and write expressions, equations, and inequalities when the process requires planning and/or strategic manipulation.
- Analyze and draw conclusions based on properties of algebra and/or functions.
- Analyze and draw conclusions based on information from graphs in the coordinate plane.
- Identify characteristics of graphs based on a set of conditions or on a general equation, such as $y = ax^2 + c$.
- Given an equation or function, find an equation or function whose graph is a translation by specified amounts up or down.

Geometry

Geometry questions are based primarily on the mathematical properties and relationships of points, lines, angles, two-dimensional shapes, and three-dimensional objects. Knowledge and skills tested include the following:

- Estimate the length of a line segment based on other lengths in a geometric figure.

- Calculate the length of a line segment based on the lengths of other line segments that go in the same direction (for example, overlapping line segments and parallel sides of polygons with only right angles).

- Perform common conversions of money and of length, weight, mass, and time within a measurement system (for example, inches to feet and hours to minutes).

- Compute the area and perimeter of triangles, rectangles, and other polygons.

- Use properties of parallel lines to find the measure of an angle.

- Exhibit knowledge of basic angle properties and special sums of angle measures (for example, 90°, 180°, and 360°).

- Use geometric formulas when all necessary information is given.

- Locate points in the coordinate plane.

- Translate points up, down, left, and right in the coordinate plane.

- Use several angle properties to find an unknown angle measure.

- Count the number of lines of symmetry of a geometric figure.

- Use symmetry of isosceles triangles to find unknown side lengths or angle measures.

- Recognize that real-world measurements are typically imprecise and that an appropriate level of precision is related to the measuring device and procedure.

- Compute the perimeter of composite geometric figures with unknown side lengths.

- Compute the area and circumference of circles.

- Given the length of two sides of a right triangle, find the length of the third side.

- Express the sine, cosine, and tangent of an angle in a right triangle as a ratio of given side lengths.

- Determine the slope of a line from points or a graph.

- Find the midpoint of a line segment.

- Find the coordinates of a point rotated 180° around a given center point.

- Use relationships involving area, perimeter, and volume of geometric figures to compute another measure (for example, surface area for a cube of a given volume and simple geometric probability).

- Use the Pythagorean theorem.

- Apply properties of 30°–60°–90°, 45°–45°–90°, similar, and congruent triangles.

- Apply basic trigonometric ratios to solve right-triangle problems.

- Use the distance formula.

- Use properties of parallel and perpendicular lines to determine an equation of a line or coordinates of a point.

- Find the coordinates of a point reflected across a vertical or horizontal line or across $y = x$.

- Find the coordinates of a point rotated 90° across a vertical.

- Recognize special characteristics of parabolas and circles (for example, the vertex of a parabola and the center or radius of a circle).

- Use relationships among angles, arcs, and distances in a circle.

- Compute the area of composite geometric figures when planning and/or visualization is required.

- Use scale factors to determine the magnitude of a size change.

- Analyze and draw conclusions based on a set of conditions.

- Solve multistep geometry problems that involve integrating concepts, planning, and/or visualization.

Statistics and Probability

Statistics is a branch of mathematics that involves the collection and analysis of large quantities of numerical data. *Probability* is a branch of mathematics that involves calculating the likelihood of an event occurring or a condition existing. Statistics and Probability questions test your ability to do the following:

- Calculate averages.

- Read and extract relevant data from a basic table or chart, and use the data in a computation.

- Use the relationship between the probability of an event and the probability of its complement.

- Calculate the missing data value given the average and all other data values.

- Translate from one representation of data to another (for example, from a bar graph to a circle graph).

- Compute probabilities.

- Describe events as combinations of other events (for example, using *and*, *or*, and *not*).

- Demonstrate knowledge of and apply counting techniques.

- Calculate the average given the frequency counts of all the data values.

- Manipulate data from tables and charts.

- Use Venn diagrams in counting.

- Recognize that when data summaries are reported in the real world, results are often rounded and must be interpreted as having appropriate precision.

- Recognize that when a statistical model is used, model values typically differ from actual values.

- Calculate or use a weighted average.

- Interpret and use information from tables and charts, including two-way frequency tables.

- Recognize the concepts of conditional and joint probability and of independence expressed in real-world contexts.

- Distinguish among mean, median, and mode for a list of numbers.

- Analyze and draw conclusions based on information from tables and charts, including two-way frequency tables.

- Understand the role of randomization in surveys, experiments, and observational studies.

- Demonstrate knowledge of conditional and joint probability.

- Recognize that part of the power of statistical modeling comes from looking at regularity in the differences between actual values and model values.

Integrating Essential Skills

Students learn some of the most useful mathematics before grade 9: rates and percentages; proportional relationships; area, surface area, and volume; average and median; expressing numbers in different ways; using expressions to represent quantities and equations to capture relationships; and other topics. Each year, students should grow in what they can accomplish using learning from prior years. Students should be able to solve problems of increasing complexity, combine skills in longer chains of steps, apply skills in more varied contexts, understand more connections, and increase fluency. In order to assess whether students have had appropriate growth, all questions in this reporting category focus on the higher-level cognitive skills, such as making decisions on how to approach a problem, comparing, reasoning, planning, applying algebra strategically, drawing conclusions, solving novel problems, and the like.

Modeling

Modeling uses mathematics to represent with a model an analysis of an actual, empirical situation. Models often help us predict or understand the actual. However, sometimes knowledge of the actual helps us understand the model, such as when addition is introduced to students as a model of combining two groups. The Modeling reporting category represents all questions that involve producing, interpreting, understanding, evaluating, and improving models. Each modeling question is also counted in the other appropriate reporting categories previously identified. Thus, the Modeling reporting category is an overall measure of how well a student uses modeling skills across mathematical topics.

Reading Test

36 questions (27 scored), 40 minutes

The reading test comprises four sections, each containing one long or two shorter prose passages that are representative of the level and kinds of text commonly encountered in first-year college curricula. Passages include literary narratives and informational texts from the humanities, natural sciences, and social sciences. One informational passage may include a mixed-information format—visual and quantitative elements (like graphs, diagrams, or tables) that acccompany the passage and contain additional information related to the passage topic. The passages vary in terms of how challenging and complex they are.

Four scores are reported for the ACT reading test: a total test score based on all 27 scored questions, and three reporting category scores based on specific knowledge and skills. The reporting categories are:

- Key Ideas and Details
- Craft and Structure
- Integration of Knowledge and Ideas

Key Ideas and Details

These questions focus primarily on identifying key details in the passage and grasping the overall meaning of the passage. Reading skills tested fall into these categories:

- Close reading
- Central ideas, themes, and summaries

Close Reading

Close-reading skills involve your ability to do the following:

- Locate and interpret facts or details in a passage.
- Draw logical conclusions.
- Paraphrase statements.

- Identify the sequence of events or place events in their correct sequence.

- Identify stated or implied cause-effect relationships.

- Identify stated or implied comparative relationships.

Central Ideas, Themes, and Summaries

Questions that focus on central ideas, themes, and summaries challenge your ability to do the following:

- Identify or infer the main idea of a paragraph.

- Identify or infer the central idea or theme of a passage.

- Differentiate key ideas from secondary ideas.

- Summarize key ideas and information.

Craft and Structure

Some reading questions go beyond the meaning of the passage to challenge your understanding of how the author crafted and structured the passage. Reading skills tested in this area are divided into three categories:

- Word meanings and word choice

- Text structure

- Purpose and point of view

Word Meanings and Word Choice

Reading questions may focus on the meaning or impact of a word or phrase, challenging your ability to do the following:

- Use context to determine the meaning of a word or phrase, including determining technical, academic, and connotative meanings.

- Understand the implication of a word or phrase and of descriptive language.

- Determine the meaning of figurative language in context.

Text Structure

Text-structure questions ask you to analyze how various structural elements function to serve a specific purpose in the passage. To answer such questions, you may need to do one of the following:

- Analyze the overall structure of a passage.

- Analyze how one or more sentences in a passage relate to the whole passage.

- Identify or infer the function of one or more paragraphs in a passage.

- Determine the function or effect of specific words or phrases in a passage.

Purpose and Point of View

The reading test may include questions that challenge your ability to do the following:

- Identify or infer the author's or narrator's purpose or intent.
- Determine how an author's or narrator's purpose or intent shapes the content and style of the passage.
- Recognize an author's or narrator's point of view.

Integration of Knowledge and Ideas

Reading questions may require that you go beyond simply reading and understanding a passage. Some questions will require analyzing two passages. Others may ask you to integrate information from different formats (like graphs, diagrams, and tables). Reading skills tested in the area of Integration of Knowledge and Ideas are divided into three categories:

- Arguments
- Multiple texts
- Mixed-information format

Arguments

Questions in this category may test your ability to do the following:

- Identify or infer the central claim being presented in the passage.
- Analyze how one or more sentences offer reasons for or support the claim.
- Differentiate between fact and opinion.
- Recognize errors in reasoning or identify information that would strengthen or weaken a claim in the passage.

Multiple Texts

Multiple-text questions involve reading two passages and may test your ability to do the following:

- Make connections between people, relationships, and ideas across the two passages.
- Draw logical conclusions using information from the two passages.
- Compare text structure, purpose, and perspective in the two passages.

Visual and Quantitative Information

Though these questions are not as common as questions about arguments and multiple texts, you may also encounter questions that ask you to understand information in visual or quantitative formats. These questions test your ability to do the following:

- Identify and interpret information represented in quantitative or graphic formats (e.g., graphs, diagrams, and tables).

- Draw conclusions and compare information across a passage and graphic element.

Science Test

40 questions (34 scored), 40 minutes

The science test measures the interpretation, analysis, evaluation, reasoning, and problem-solving skills required in the natural sciences: life science/biology; physical science/chemistry, physics; and earth and space science.

The test assumes that students are in the process of taking the core science course of study (three years or more) that will prepare them for college-level work and have completed a course in earth science and/or physical science and a course in biology. The test presents several sets of scientific information, each followed by a number of multiple-choice test questions. The scientific information is conveyed in the form of reading passages and graphic representations—graphs (charts), tables, and illustrations.

Four scores are reported for the ACT science test: a total test score based on all 34 scored questions and three reporting category scores based on scientific knowledge, skills, and practices. The reporting categories are:

- Interpretation of Data

- Scientific Investigation

- Evaluation of Models, Inferences, and Experimental Results

Interpretation of Data

Interpretation of Data involves the following skills:

- Select data from a data presentation (for example, a food web diagram, a graph, a table, or a phase diagram).

- Identify features of a table, graph, or diagram (for example, units of measurement).

- Find information in text that describes a data presentation.

- Understand scientific terminology.

- Determine how the values of variables change as the value of another variable changes in a data presentation.

- Compare or combine data from one or more data presentations (for example, order or sum data from a table).

- Translate information into a table, graph, or diagram.

- Perform an interpolation or extrapolation using data in a table or graph (for example, categorize data from a table using a scale from another table).

- Determine and/or use a mathematical relationship that exists between data.

- Analyze presented information when given new information.

Scientific Investigation

Questions that apply to scientific investigation are typically related to experiments and other research. Such questions challenge your ability to do the following:

- Find information in text that describes an experiment.

- Understand the tools and functions of tools used in an experiment.

- Understand the methods used in an experiment.

- Understand experimental design.

- Identify a control in an experiment.

- Identify similarities and differences between experiments.

- Determine which experiments use a given tool, method, or aspect of design.

- Predict the results of an additional trial or measurement in an experiment.

- Determine the experimental conditions that would produce specified results.

- Determine the hypothesis for an experiment.

- Determine an alternate method for testing a hypothesis.

- Understand precision and accuracy issues.

- Predict the effects of modifying the design or methods of an experiment.

- Determine which additional trial or experiment could be performed to enhance or evaluate experimental results.

Evaluation of Models, Inferences, and Experimental Results

Some questions on the science test challenge your ability to evaluate models, inferences, and experimental results. (A *model* is a description of an object or phenomenon intended to explain and predict its behavior.) To answer such questions, you must be able to do the following:

- Find basic information in a model.

- Identify implications in a model.

- Determine which models present certain information.

- Determine which hypothesis, prediction, or conclusion is, or is not, consistent with one or more data presentations, models, or pieces of information in the text.

- Identify key assumptions in a model.

- Identify similarities and differences between models.

- Determine whether presented information or new information supports or contradicts (or weakens) a hypothesis or conclusion and why.

- Identify the strengths and weaknesses of models.

- Determine which models are supported or weakened by new information.

- Determine which experimental results or models support or contradict a hypothesis, prediction, or conclusion.

- Use new information to make a prediction based on a model.

Writing Test (Optional)

1 prompt, 40 minutes

The writing test is a 40-minute essay test that measures your writing skills—specifically those writing skills emphasized in high school English classes and in entry-level college composition courses.

The test asks you to produce an essay in response to a contemporary issue. You will be given a prompt that presents the issue and provides three different perspectives on it. Your task is to write an essay in which you develop a perspective on the issue, providing a convincing rationale through discussion of your perspective's strengths and weaknesses, and explore how it relates to at least one other perspective, recognizing relationships between or among conflicting views.

Trained readers will evaluate your essay for the evidence it provides of a number of core writing skills. You will receive a total of five scores for this test: four domain scores (provided by two readers) based on an analytic scoring rubric and a single subject-level writing score reported on a scale of 2–12 (reflecting a rounded average of the four domain scores). The four domain scores are

- Ideas and Analysis

- Development and Support

- Organization

- Language Use and Conventions

Ideas and Analysis

Effective writing depends on effective ideas. It is important to think carefully about the issue in the prompt and compose an argument that addresses the issue meaningfully, allowing any reader to understand why your argument is worth considering. In evaluating the ideas and analysis in your essay, readers will look for your ability to do the following:

- Generate a clear main idea that establishes your perspective on the issue and the thesis that will direct your essay.

- Engage with multiple perspectives on the issue by analyzing the relationship between your perspective and at least one other perspective.

- Clarify your understanding of the issue and differing perspectives on it by providing a relevant context for discussion, describing the circumstances surrounding the issue and connecting the specific issue in the prompt to a broader situation.

- Analyze critical elements such as implications (potential effects of decisions) and complexities (factors that complicate an issue or challenge a perspective).

Development and Support

No single idea should be left to speak for itself. Even the best ideas must be developed and supported to be effective in a written argument. By explaining and illustrating your points, you help the reader understand your thinking. In evaluating this dimension of your essay, readers will look for your ability to do the following:

- Clarify your ideas by explaining your reasoning.

- Bolster your claims with persuasive examples.

- Convey the significance of your perspective by exploring reasons why your ideas are worth considering; address why your argument might be more compelling than another.

- Extend your argument by considering qualifications, exceptions, counterarguments, and complicating factors. Convey your understanding of the limitations of your argument, demonstrating to the reader that you have considered its potential weaknesses.

Organization

Organizational choices are essential to effective writing. Guide the reader through your discussion by arranging your ideas according to the logic of your argument, making sure that the connections among ideas are clear. As readers evaluate the organization of your essay, they will look for your ability to do the following:

- Unify your essay by making strategic use of a controlling idea, ensuring all ideas are working in service of the thesis, and employing other organizational techniques (e.g., theme or motif).

- Group ideas clearly, with each paragraph limited to the discussion of related ideas while still linked to the argument as a whole.

- Produce a sequence of ideas that follows a clear logic, both in terms of the argument's overall structure (e.g., introduction, body, and conclusion) and within the argument itself, with each point following logically from the last.

- Use transitions to connect ideas, both within paragraphs (e.g., relating claims to support) and across paragraphs (e.g., moving from discussion of one point to that of another).

Language Use and Conventions

Skillful language use enhances argumentative writing. Strategic choices in the vocabulary you use and the style you employ can make your essay more effective. To evaluate your use of language, readers will look for your ability to do the following:

- Make precise word choices that communicate your ideas with clarity. Use specific rather than vague terms that enhance understanding (e.g., "a lot of free music is available today" vs. "the endless volumes of free music available today can be overwhelming").

- Demonstrate control over a variety of sentence structures. Use a mixture of simple and complex sentences, exhibiting as much grammatical control over longer sentences as shorter ones.

- Match the style of your writing to the audience and purpose (e.g., more evocative language to convey emotional appeals versus a more neutral voice to convey an argument based on reason).

- Accurately apply the conventions of grammar, word usage, syntax, and mechanics.

Unscored Items

ACT is dedicated to meeting professional testing standards. To accomplish this, ACT includes additional questions on the test that do not count toward your score. This practice ensures that ACT develops questions that are fair and of the highest possible quality.

For the English, Math, Reading, and Science sections, there are questions that do not contribute to your score. For the Math section, there are four items that are not scored placed within the section. For the Reading and Science sections, one passage and the corresponding item set will not be scored. For the English section, either one long passage and its item set or two short passages and their item sets will not be scored.

ACT Test Formats: Paper and Online

The ACT is available as a paper test and as an online test for both National (weekend) and State/District testing. For National testing you may select to test on computer or paper, based on your personal preference and the available testing centers in your area. For in-school testing, the decision for computer or paper format is made by either the state or district. Some sections may look slightly different online than they do on paper. For example, English items may be indicated by highlighted text instead of underlining, or you may see highlighted asterisks in brackets in the essay instead of numbers in boxes. Likewise, reading items may refer to highlighting in the passage instead of containing line references. Regardless of format, what is most important is the knowledge and skills you have developed over your course of study. If you know the material, whether you choose answers by marking them on paper or clicking an option on a computer screen will likely make little difference.

Using a Calculator

You may use a permitted calculator only on the mathematics test, but you are not required to do so. All math problems on the test can be solved without a calculator, and you may be able to perform some of the math more quickly in your head or on scratch paper.

Note: You may use any four-function, scientific, or graphing calculator as long as it is a permitted calculator modified, if necessary, as described in the following. For additional details and ACT's most current calculator policy, visit https://www.act.org/content/act/en/products-and-services/the-act/test-day/calculator-policy.html.

Certain types of calculators, including the following, are prohibited:

- Calculators with built-in or downloaded computer algebra system (CAS) functionality, including the TI-89, TI-92, TI-Nspire CAS, HP Prime, HP 48GII, HP 40G, HP 49G, HP 50G, fx-ClassPad 400, ClassPad 300, ClassPad 330, and all Casio models that start with CFX-9970G. (Using the TI-89 is the most common reason students are dismissed from the ACT for prohibited calculator use.)

- Handheld, tablet, or laptop computers, including PDAs.

- Electronic writing pads or pen-input devices (the Sharp EL 9600 is permitted).

- Calculators built into cell phones or any other electronic communication devices.

- Calculators with a typewriter keypad (letter keys in QWERTY format). This does not apply to calculators that are provided in a secure test delivery platform. Letter keys not in QWERTY format are permitted.

The following types of calculators are permitted but only after they are modified as noted:

- Calculators that can hold programs or documents (remove all documents and all programs that have CAS functionality).

- Calculators with paper tape (remove the tape).

- Calculators that make noise (mute the device).

- Calculators with an infrared data port (completely cover the infrared data port with heavy opaque material, such as duct tape or electrician's tape). These calculators include the Hewlett-Packard HP 38G series, HP 39G series, and HP 48G.

- Calculators that have power cords (remove all power and electrical cords).

- Accessible calculators (such as audio-talking or braille calculators) may be allowed under the accessibility policies for the ACT test. (Visit www.act.org for details.)

If you choose to use a calculator during the mathematics test, follow these guidelines:

- Use a calculator you are accustomed to using. A more powerful, but unfamiliar, calculator may be a disadvantage. If you are unaccustomed to using a calculator, practice using it when you take the practice tests in this book so you are comfortable with using it in a test situation.

- Sharing calculators during the test is not permitted.

- Make sure your calculator works properly. If your calculator uses batteries, the batteries should be strong enough to last throughout the testing session.

- Bring a spare calculator and/or extra batteries.

In a computer-based testing environment:

- An on-screen calculator may be available.

- Calculators may not be connected in any way to the computer or device being used for testing.

Taking the Test

Knowing what to expect on test day can alleviate any anxiety you may feel. The following list describes the steps you will take through the testing day:

1. You must report to the test center by the reporting time.

    - If you are testing on a ***national test*** date and are taking the full ACT test, the reporting time is 8:00 AM.

        ○ You will need to bring the following for either paper or computer testing:

            – A printed copy of your ACT admission ticket, which contains important match information that cannot be found anywhere else. Failure to bring your admission ticket will delay your scores.

            – Acceptable photo ID; if you do not bring acceptable photo ID, you will not be allowed to take the test.

            – Sharpened no. 2 soft-lead pencils with good erasers (no mechanical pencils or ink pens).

            – A permitted calculator, if you would like to use one.

- If you are testing during the week day at your school through ***state and district*** testing, the reporting time will be at the same time you usually report for school.
  - You will need to bring the following:
    - Acceptable photo ID
    - Sharpened no. 2 soft-lead pencils with good erasers (no mechanical pencils or ink pens)
    - A permitted calculator, if you would like to use one

  (**Note:** You will *not* be admitted to test if you are late or if your ID does not meet ACT's requirements.)

2. When all examinees present at the reporting time are checked in and seated, wait until you are notified to start the test.

3. A short break is scheduled after the first two tests. You are prohibited from using a cell phone or any electronic device during the break, and you may not eat or drink anything in the test room. (If you take the ACT with writing, you will have time before the writing test to relax and sharpen your pencils.)

4. When time has expired, paper tests are collected. Online tests must be submitted prior to your dismissal.

Note: If you do not complete all your tests for any reason, tell a member of the testing staff whether you want your answer document or online test to be scored before you leave the test center. If you do not, all tests attempted will be scored.

Summary

This book should help you to understand how to get ready to take the ACT. Knowing the basics should get you started. By now, you should have a fair idea of what to expect at the test center and know where to find more information: on ACT's website at www.act.org. Now that you know the basic information, you should be ready to start preparing for the ACT.

Prep Online!

Want even more ways to prep? Go to https://study.learning.wiley.com/ to access our online platform and take practice tests. To get started, go to https://study.learning.wiley.com/, select your title, answer the redemption question, and start studying!

Chapter 2:
Preparation, Skills, and Strategies

Performance on the ACT is largely influenced by two factors: the knowledge and skills you acquire over your many years of formal education and your familiarity with the test format and questions.

The best preparation for the ACT is taking rigorous high school classes. If you've taken challenging courses, paid attention in class, and completed your assignments satisfactorily, you've already done much of the preparation required to do well on the ACT.

Your familiarity with the test format and questions and your comfort and confidence in tackling the ACT also play an important role in how well you do on the test. Of course, no test-taking strategy can help you choose the correct answer when you don't understand the question or don't have the knowledge and skills to answer it, but certain strategies and skills can help you avoid common mistakes that will lower your score, such as misreading an answer choice or spending too much time on any given question.

The suggestions in this chapter are designed to help you build on the preparation that you have already completed. They're taken from advice gathered over years—from education specialists, testing specialists, and people who, similar to you, have taken lots of tests. Read the advice, try it out, and see whether it helps. Realize that you can choose how you will take the ACT. Then make intelligent choices about what will work for you.

Mental Preparation

The best mental preparation for the ACT is rigorous coursework, but mental preparation also involves confidence and clear thinking. The following tips will help make you feel calmer and more confident so that you'll do your very best on the ACT.

Identify Strengths and Address Areas of Improvement

One of the best ways to prepare mentally for the test is to identify your strengths and areas of improvement, then work toward addressing the areas that may hamper your performance on the test. For example, if time expires before you have a chance to answer all the questions on a practice test, you need to work on pacing. If you struggle to comprehend word problems in math, you need to practice solving more word problems. However, if you breeze through reading comprehension questions, you might not need to spend time improving your reading comprehension skills.

The following sections explain how to identify strengths and areas of improvement and address issues that may hamper your performance on the test.

Take the First Practice Test

To evaluate your ACT readiness, take the first practice test in chapter 3 and analyze the results, as instructed in chapter 4. The test-taking experience and the results will help reveal your strengths and areas for improvement. If you do well on the first practice test, you can be confident that you know the material and are comfortable with the test format. You may decide to take additional practice tests for confirmation or review the test-taking skills in this chapter and in chapters 5 through 9 to see whether they can help you do even better.

If your performance on the first practice test falls short of your goal, you may need to do additional coursework in certain subject areas or invest additional time and effort developing effective test-taking strategies and skills. Do not be discouraged if you do not meet your goal on the practice test. Be thankful that your areas for improvement were identified before test day and that you now have the information you need to formulate your improvement plan.

Identify Subject Areas to Review

Some students do better in certain subjects than in others. The practice tests in this book will help you identify your stronger and weaker subjects. As you take and score the practice tests, create a list of the subject areas and types of questions you struggle with. For example, if you had trouble answering math questions about angles in a triangle, the circumference of a circle, the volume of a cube, the relationships among parallel and perpendicular lines, and so forth, you may need a refresher course in plane geometry. Pay attention to how you scored on each reporting category within a section to identify areas to review.

Chapter 1 includes a list of subject areas covered on each portion of the ACT to help you categorize the questions you answered incorrectly and identify subject areas you need to study or review.

Plan Your Practice and Study Time

To stay on track leading up to test day, set up a reasonable schedule to practice and study for the ACT. **Set aside small amounts of time** for studying over an extended period—days, weeks, or even months—so you won't feel the need to cram in the days leading up to the test.

Make your schedule flexible enough to allow for a surprise homework assignment or some unexpected fun. And find a way to reward yourself as you get the work done, even if it's just a checklist you can mark to show your progress. A flexible schedule with regular rewards will prevent burnout while keeping you motivated.

Develop a Positive Mental Attitude

Approach the ACT confident that you will do your best. Although confidence alone obviously isn't enough to ensure good performance on a test, doubt and fear can hurt your performance. Be confident in your ability to do well on the ACT. **You will do well!** You just need to be prepared.

Some small changes can make a surprising difference. For example, how you imagine yourself taking the exam may affect how well you actually do. Negative thoughts have a way of generating negative results. So **practice positive thinking;** imagine yourself meeting the challenge of the exam with ease. The day of the test, tell yourself you intend to do your best, and believe it.

Keep the Test in Perspective

Remembering that the ACT is only one part of the process of your education and training will help you keep it in perspective. So will remembering that the ACT and tests similar to it are designed to provide you with feedback and direction. Your scores can help make decisions about your future education and career choices. Think of the test as an opportunity to get to know more about yourself, not as a potential barrier to your future plans.

Another way to keep the ACT in perspective is to use the test as an opportunity to identify careers that match your interests, abilities, and values; explore suitable college majors; and start choosing high school courses that align with your future education and career goals.

General Test-Taking Strategies and Skills

How you approach the ACT and various types of questions, how well you manage your time, whether you change answers, and other factors may affect how well you do on the ACT. The following sections present a few test-taking strategies and skills to help you perform to the best of your ability.

Remain Calm

When you're under pressure during a test, an unexpected question or a minor incident such as breaking a pencil can be very upsetting. For many students, the natural tendency at such times is to panic. Panic detracts from test performance by causing students to become confused and discouraged and to have trouble recalling information they know.

It's a good idea to have a strategy ready for dealing with incidents that might rattle your nerves. One effective strategy is to take a brief time out to center yourself. Take slow, deep breaths and let yourself relax. Put the test temporarily out of your mind. Close your eyes if you want. Visualize yourself confidently resuming work on the test, turning in a completed answer document, and leaving the room with a feeling of having done your best work. Allow 20 to 30 seconds for your time out, which is probably all you'll need to regain your composure.

Pace Yourself

The ACT, similar to many tests, must be completed within a specific and limited amount of time. Working quickly and efficiently is one of the skills necessary for conveying how much you've learned in the subject area being tested.

To develop an effective, efficient pace, time yourself as you take the practice tests. If time expires before you have a chance to answer all the questions, you know that you need to work faster next time. If you rushed through the test, had time remaining at the end, and made careless mistakes, you know that you will need to work at a more relaxed pace and be more careful in answering questions.

Warning: Don't try to push yourself to work so fast that you make errors. Answering 40 questions carefully and correctly and leaving 5 unanswered is better than answering 45 questions too quickly and missing 15 because of mistakes.

Although you won't want to lose time by being distracted, you shouldn't obsess about time either. Use all the time available so you can do your very best on the test.

Some people suggest more formal methods for pacing yourself by allocating a certain amount of time per question or set of questions, as in the following examples:

- **Divide the available time by the number of questions.** For example, on the mathematics test, divide 50 minutes by 45 questions, and you know you have about 67 seconds (or just over a minute) per question.

- **Divide the available time into different stages of the writing process.** If you're taking the optional writing test, you may want to allocate the time to planning, writing, and revising/editing your essay. Keep in mind that you probably won't have enough time to fully draft, revise, and then recopy your essay, so spending a few minutes planning your essay before you start writing it is usually wise.

Keep in mind that these strategies are not foolproof, that some questions will take you longer to answer than others, and that doing the math to calculate your time allocations takes time. You may be better off developing a feel for the time and occasionally checking the clock to make sure you're on track to finish, perhaps with a few minutes remaining at the end to check answers you were unsure of. If you want to keep track of your pace while taking the ACT, bring a watch. Not all testing centers have wall clocks.

Know the Directions Ahead of Time

You can save yourself precious moments on the ACT by being familiar with the directions ahead of time. Then, when taking the test, you can read the directions to refresh your memory instead of having to spend time and mind power processing those directions. For example, the ACT English, reading, and science tests ask for the "best" answer, and the mathematics test asks for the "correct" answer. This simple difference in the instructions signals an important distinction to keep in mind as you're working through those tests. Because only one answer is "correct" in the mathematics test, you'll want to be sure your understanding of the question and your calculations are precise—so that your answer matches one, and only one, of the possible answers. In the other tests, more than one of the possible answers may be correct to some degree, and you'll need to be careful to select the "best" answer among those potentially "correct" ones. You'll find the directions for each test in the practice ACT tests in this book.

The directions for the writing test are also very important because they spell out the aspects of writing that will be evaluated. They also tell you where in the test booklet you can plan your essay and where you should write your final version. The directions for the writing test and a sample answer document appear in the practice ACT tests in this book.

Before you take the ACT, become familiar with the answer document. Knowing in advance how to use the answer document will save you time and prevent worry when you take the actual ACT.

Read Carefully and Thoroughly

Just as it's important to read and understand the directions for a test, it's also important to read and understand each question and answer choice on the test. As you've probably discovered somewhere along the line, you can miss even the simplest test question by reading carelessly and overlooking an important word or detail. Some questions on the ACT, for instance, require more than one step, and the answer to each preliminary step may be included as an answer choice. If you read these questions too quickly, you can easily make the mistake of choosing a plausible answer that relates to a preliminary step but is the incorrect answer to the question.

Take the time to read each question carefully and thoroughly before choosing your answer. Make sure you understand exactly what the question asks and what you are to do to answer it. You may want to underline or circle key words in the test booklet (see the later section "Write Notes in Your Test Booklet"). Reread the item if you are confused.

Watch the question's wording. Look for words such as *not* or *least*, especially when they are not clearly set off with underlining, capital letters, or bold type. Don't make careless errors because you only skimmed the question or the answer choices. Pay close attention to qualifying words such as *all, most, some, none; always, usually, seldom, sometimes, never; best, worst; highest, lowest; smaller, larger.* (There are many other qualifying words; these are only a few examples of related groups.) When you find a qualifier in one of the responses to a question, a good way to determine whether the response is the best answer is to substitute related qualifiers and see which makes the best statement. For example, if a response says, "Tests are always difficult," you might test the truth of the word *always* by substituting *sometimes* and the other words related to *always*.

If any of the words other than the one in the answer makes the best statement, then the response is not the best answer.

Pay close attention to modifying or limiting phrases in the statement. For instance, a question in the reading test might have the following as a possible answer: "Lewis and Clark, the great British explorers, began their historic trip to the West Coast by traveling up the Mississippi." The answer is incorrect because Lewis and Clark were not British but were US citizens. (You would not be expected to know from memory that Lewis and Clark were US citizens; that information would be included in the passage.)

Read all the answer choices before selecting one. Questions on the ACT often include answer choices that seem plausible but aren't quite correct. Even though the first answer choice may appeal to you, the correct or best answer may be farther down the list.

When taking the writing test, read the writing prompt carefully. Before you start to plan your essay, make sure you understand the writing prompt and the specific issue it asks you to respond to.

Choose Strategies for Answering Easier and More Difficult Questions

A strategy for taking the ACT is to answer the easy questions first and skip the questions you find difficult. After answering all the easy questions, go back and answer the more difficult questions, as time permits. When you skip a question, mark it in the test booklet (but not on the answer document) or flag it on the computer so you can quickly return to that item later. Also, make absolutely sure that on the answer document, you skip the set of answer choices that correspond to the question you skipped. When you answer the next question after skipping a question, double check that you are using the correct answer set (A through D or F through J).

Use Logic on More Difficult Questions

When you return to more difficult questions, use logic to eliminate incorrect answer choices. Compare the remaining answer choices and note how they differ. Such differences may provide clues as to what the question requires. Eliminate as many incorrect answer choices as you can, then make an educated selection from the remaining choices.

Choose a Strategy for Guessing on Multiple-Choice Questions

On some standardized tests, you're penalized for each incorrect answer. On the ACT multiple-choice tests, however, your raw score is based on the number of questions you answer correctly—nothing is deducted for wrong answers.

Because you're not penalized for guessing on the ACT, answering every question is advantageous. Here's a good way to proceed:

1. If a question stumps you, try to eliminate wrong choices. Narrowing your choices increases your odds of guessing the correct answer.

2. If you still aren't sure about the answer, take your best guess.

You don't need a perfect reason to eliminate one answer and choose another. Sometimes an intelligent guess is based on a hunch—on something you may know but don't have time to consciously recognize in a timed-test situation.

Maybe you've heard some advice about how to answer questions when you don't know the correct answer, such as "When in doubt, choose 'C,'" or "When in doubt, select the longest (or shortest) alternative," or "If 'none of the above' (or a similar response) is among the answer choices, select it." Although these bits of advice may hold true now and then, the questions on the ACT have been carefully written to make these strategies ineffective.

Choose a Strategy for Changing Answers

You think you marked the wrong answer choice on a certain question. Do you go with your original answer or change it to the new answer? Some people advise always going with your first response. And surely everyone has had the experience of agonizing over a response, trying to decide whether to change it, then doing so only to find out later that the first answer was the correct one.

However, some research by education and testing specialists suggests that you should change your answer when you change your mind. If you're like the test-takers in the study, your second answer is more likely to be the correct one.

So, how can you decide what to do? Before you change an answer, think about how you approached the question in the first place. Give some weight to the reasons why you now believe another answer is better. Don't mechanically follow an arbitrary rule just because it works for somebody else. Know yourself, then trust yourself to make intelligent, informed decisions.

Write Notes in Your Test Booklet

You're allowed to write in the test booklet, so feel free to write notes in the test booklet to flag key details or to work out a problem on paper. If you are testing on the computer, you can write notes on the scratch paper provided. You can also use tools such as the highlighter, answer eliminator, or item flag to mark up your computer-based test.

Mark Your Answers Carefully

Only answers marked on the answer document during the time allowed for a particular test will count. Carefully mark your answers on the answer document as you work through the questions on each test.

Remember that during an actual test you may not fill in answers or alter answers on your answer document after "stop" is called.

For the writing test, writing (or printing) legibly in English in the correct place in the test booklet is vital. If readers cannot read what you have written, they will be unable to score your essay. You are allowed to write in cursive or print your essay, but you must do so clearly. Keep in mind, you must write your essay **using a soft-lead pencil (not a mechanical pencil)**. You must write on the lined pages in the answer folder. If you make corrections, do so thoroughly. You may write corrections or additions neatly between the lines of your essay, but you may not write in the margins.

Plan to Check Your Answers

When you reach the end of one of the ACT tests with several minutes to spare, you may feel you've done quite enough. Resist the temptation to rest. Use the remaining time to check your work, as follows:

- For the multiple-choice tests, be sure you've marked all your answers in the proper section on the answer document.

- Be certain you've answered all the questions on your answer document, even the ones you weren't sure about. (Of course, you must stop marking ovals when time is called.)

- When you reach the end of the mathematics test, check your calculations. You may check your calculations using the test booklet or scratch paper, or using a permitted calculator (see chapter 1).

- Check your answer document for stray pencil marks that may be misread by the scoring machine. Erase any such marks cleanly and completely.

- Be sure you've marked only one answer on your answer document for each question.

- If there are too many questions for you to check all your answers, be sure to check those that you feel most uncertain about first, then any others that you have time for on that test.

- At the end of the writing test, take a few minutes to read over your essay. Correct any mistakes in spelling, grammar, usage, or punctuation. If you see any words that are difficult to read, rewrite them so they're legible. Make any revisions neatly between the lines (but do not write in the margins).

Learn Strategies for Specific Tests

In addition to the general test-taking strategies presented in the preceding sections, there are specific strategies for each of the ACT tests. For example, on the mathematics test, if a question includes an illustration, you may want to write dimensions given in the question on the illustration to help you visualize what the question is asking. In part 3 of this book, the chapters provide test-taking tips for each of the ACT tests along with additional information that reveals the types of questions you can expect to encounter on each test.

Summary

All the strategies outlined in this chapter are merely suggestions intended to give you ideas about good preparation habits and strategies for getting through the ACT in the best, most efficient manner possible. Some of the strategies will work for you; others won't. Feel free to pick and choose from among all the strategies in this chapter, as well as the more specific strategies in part 3, so that you have a test-taking plan that works best for you.

Prep Online!

Want even more ways to prep? Go to https://study.learning.wiley.com/ to access our online platform and take practice tests. To get started, go to https://study.learning.wiley.com/, select your title, answer the redemption question, and start studying!

NOTES

Part Two: Taking and Evaluating Your First Practice Test

In This Part

In this part, you have the opportunity to take, score, and evaluate your first practice test. This exercise enables you to identify your strengths and weaknesses, so you can develop an efficient study plan that focuses on areas where you need the most improvement. In this part, you will do the following:

Simulate testing conditions, so you become acclimated to the conditions you will experience on test day.

Take a complete practice test comprising all five ACT tests—English, mathematics, reading, and optional science and writing tests.

Score your test to gauge your overall performance.

Review explanatory answers to understand why you answered each question correctly or incorrectly.

Determine whether you need to work more on subject matter or on test-taking strategies and skills.

Analyze your performance on each test to gain better insight on the knowledge and skills in greatest need of improvement.

Chapter 3:
Taking and Scoring Your First ACT Practice Test

In this chapter, you take the first practice test in this book, score the test, and review the answers with explanations. We encourage you to take the test under conditions similar to those you will encounter on test day and to try your very best.

After you take and score the test and review the answers, you will be well poised to analyze your performance in chapter 4. The results of this first practice test will help you identify subject areas you may need to review and test-taking strategies, such as pacing, that you may want to work on prior to test day.

Simulating Testing Conditions

Taking the practice tests can help you become familiar with the ACT. We recommend that you take the tests under conditions that are as similar as possible to those you will experience on the actual test day. The following tips will help you make the most of the practice tests:

- The three multiple-choice tests require a total of 2 hours and 20 minutes. The optional Science test will take 40 minutes. The optional Writing test will take 40 minutes. Try an entire practice test in one sitting, with a 10-minute break between the mathematics test and the reading test. (If you are taking the writing test, you may also take a break of roughly 5 minutes after the science test.)

- Sit at a desk with good lighting. You will need sharpened no. 2 pencils with good erasers. You may not use mechanical pencils or highlight pens. Remove all books and other aids from your desk. On test day, you will not be allowed to use references or notes. Scratch paper is not needed as each page of the mathematics test has a blank column that you can use for scratch work. In some circumstances you are not permitted to write in your test booklet. In those circumstances, you'll be given scratch paper, and you can use it to jot down the numbers of the questions you skip.

- If you plan to use a calculator on the mathematics test, review the details about permissible calculators on ACT's website, https://www.act.org/content/act/en/products-and-services/the-act/test-day/calculator-policy.html. Use a calculator with which you are familiar for both the practice test and on the test day. You may use any four-function, scientific, or graphing calculator on the mathematics test, except as specified in ACT's Calculator Policy and in chapter 1.

- Use a digital timer or clock to time yourself on each test. Set your timer for 5 minutes less than the allotted time for each test so you can get used to the 5-minute warning. (If you receive accommodations through an IEP or 504 plan, you should set the timer based on the accommodations allowed in your plan. For example, 1.5 time would mean that you should set your timer to 90 minutes (60 × 1.5) for math. Students approved for self-paced extended time should set a timer for 60-minute warnings up to the total time allowed—5 hours for the multiple-choice tests. If you take the optional writing test, you will then have an additional hour to complete that test.)

- Allow yourself only the time permitted for each test.

- Detach and use one sample multiple-choice answer document.

- Read the general test directions on the first page of the practice test. After reading the directions, start your timer and begin with the English test. Continue through the science test, taking a short break between the mathematics test and the reading test. If you do not plan to take the ACT writing test, score your multiple-choice tests using the information beginning on page 99.

- If you plan to take the writing test, take a short break after the science test. Detach (or photocopy) the writing test answer document that follows the writing test planning pages. Then read the test directions on the first page of the practice ACT writing test. After reading the directions, start your timer, then carefully read the prompt. After you have considered what the prompt is asking you to do, use the pages provided to plan your essay, and then write your essay on the answer document. After you have finished, score your essay using the information beginning on page 106.

The ACT® *Sample Answer Document*

EXAMINEE STATEMENTS, CERTIFICATION, AND SIGNATURE

1. **Statements**: I understand that by registering for, launching, starting, or submitting answer documents for an ACT® test, I am agreeing to comply with and be bound by the *Terms and Conditions: Testing Rules and Policies for the ACT® Test* ("Terms").

I UNDERSTAND AND AGREE THAT THE TERMS PERMIT ACT TO CANCEL MY SCORES IN CERTAIN CIRCUMSTANCES. THE TERMS ALSO LIMIT DAMAGES AVAILABLE TO ME AND REQUIRE ARBITRATION OF CERTAIN DISPUTES. BY AGREEING TO ARBITRATION, ACT AND I BOTH WAIVE THE RIGHT TO HAVE THOSE DISPUTES HEARD BY A JUDGE OR JURY.

I understand that ACT owns the test questions and responses, and I will not share them with anyone by any form of communication before, during, or after the test administration. I understand that taking the test for someone else may violate the law and subject me to legal penalties. I consent to the collection and processing of personally identifying information I provide, and its subsequent use and disclosure, as described in the ACT Privacy Policy (www.act.org/privacy.html). If I am taking the test outside of the United States, I also permit ACT to transfer my personally identifying information to the United States, to ACT, or to a third-party service provider, where it will be subject to use and disclosure under the laws of the United States, including being accessible to law enforcement or national security authorities.

2. **Certification**: Copy the italicized certification below, then sign and date in the spaces provided.

*I agree to the **Statements** above and certify that I am the person whose information appears on this form.*

____

____

Your Signature   Today's Date

Your First Practice Test

Do NOT mark in this shaded area.

USE A NO. 2 PENCIL ONLY.
(Do NOT use a mechanical pencil, ink, ballpoint, correction fluid, or felt-tip pen.)

A   NAME, MAILING ADDRESS, AND TELEPHONE
(Please print.)

Last Name   First Name   MI (Middle Initial)

House Number & Street (Apt. No.); or PO Box & No.; or RR & No.

City   State/Province   ZIP/Postal Code

Area Code   Number   Country

ACT, Inc.—Confidential Restricted when data present

ALL examinees must complete block A – please print.

Blocks B, C, and D are required for all examinees. Find the MATCHING INFORMATION on your ticket. Enter it EXACTLY the same way, even if any of the information is missing or incorrect. Fill in the corresponding ovals. If you do not complete these blocks to match your previous information EXACTLY, your scores will be **delayed up to 8 weeks.**

ACT®

PO BOX 168, IOWA CITY, IA 52243-0168

B MATCH NAME
(First 5 letters of last name)

C MATCH NUMBER

D DATE OF BIRTH

Month	Day	Year
January		
February		
March		
April		
May		
June		
July		
August		
September		
October		
November		
December		

PAGE 2

Marking Directions: Mark only **one** oval for each question. Fill in response completely. Erase errors cleanly without smudging.

Correct mark: ○ ● ○ ○

Do NOT use these *incorrect* or *bad* marks.

Incorrect marks: ⊘ ⊗ ●
Overlapping mark: ○ ○ ●
Cross-out mark: ○ ⊗ ○
Smudged erasure: ○ ○ ○
Mark is too light: ○ ○ ○

BOOKLET NUMBER

FORM

① ① Ⓜ Ⓒ ①

Print your 5-character **Test Form** in the boxes at the right <u>and</u> fill in the corresponding ovals.

TEST 1: ENGLISH

1 Ⓐ Ⓑ Ⓒ Ⓓ	14 Ⓕ Ⓖ Ⓗ Ⓙ	27 Ⓐ Ⓑ Ⓒ Ⓓ	40 Ⓕ Ⓖ Ⓗ Ⓙ	53 Ⓐ Ⓑ Ⓒ Ⓓ	66 Ⓕ Ⓖ Ⓗ Ⓙ
2 Ⓕ Ⓖ Ⓗ Ⓙ	15 Ⓐ Ⓑ Ⓒ Ⓓ	28 Ⓕ Ⓖ Ⓗ Ⓙ	41 Ⓐ Ⓑ Ⓒ Ⓓ	54 Ⓕ Ⓖ Ⓗ Ⓙ	67 Ⓐ Ⓑ Ⓒ Ⓓ
3 Ⓐ Ⓑ Ⓒ Ⓓ	16 Ⓕ Ⓖ Ⓗ Ⓙ	29 Ⓐ Ⓑ Ⓒ Ⓓ	42 Ⓕ Ⓖ Ⓗ Ⓙ	55 Ⓐ Ⓑ Ⓒ Ⓓ	68 Ⓕ Ⓖ Ⓗ Ⓙ
4 Ⓕ Ⓖ Ⓗ Ⓙ	17 Ⓐ Ⓑ Ⓒ Ⓓ	30 Ⓕ Ⓖ Ⓗ Ⓙ	43 Ⓐ Ⓑ Ⓒ Ⓓ	56 Ⓕ Ⓖ Ⓗ Ⓙ	69 Ⓐ Ⓑ Ⓒ Ⓓ
5 Ⓐ Ⓑ Ⓒ Ⓓ	18 Ⓕ Ⓖ Ⓗ Ⓙ	31 Ⓐ Ⓑ Ⓒ Ⓓ	44 Ⓕ Ⓖ Ⓗ Ⓙ	57 Ⓐ Ⓑ Ⓒ Ⓓ	70 Ⓕ Ⓖ Ⓗ Ⓙ
6 Ⓕ Ⓖ Ⓗ Ⓙ	19 Ⓐ Ⓑ Ⓒ Ⓓ	32 Ⓕ Ⓖ Ⓗ Ⓙ	45 Ⓐ Ⓑ Ⓒ Ⓓ	58 Ⓕ Ⓖ Ⓗ Ⓙ	71 Ⓐ Ⓑ Ⓒ Ⓓ
7 Ⓐ Ⓑ Ⓒ Ⓓ	20 Ⓕ Ⓖ Ⓗ Ⓙ	33 Ⓐ Ⓑ Ⓒ Ⓓ	46 Ⓕ Ⓖ Ⓗ Ⓙ	59 Ⓐ Ⓑ Ⓒ Ⓓ	72 Ⓕ Ⓖ Ⓗ Ⓙ
8 Ⓕ Ⓖ Ⓗ Ⓙ	21 Ⓐ Ⓑ Ⓒ Ⓓ	34 Ⓕ Ⓖ Ⓗ Ⓙ	47 Ⓐ Ⓑ Ⓒ Ⓓ	60 Ⓕ Ⓖ Ⓗ Ⓙ	73 Ⓐ Ⓑ Ⓒ Ⓓ
9 Ⓐ Ⓑ Ⓒ Ⓓ	22 Ⓕ Ⓖ Ⓗ Ⓙ	35 Ⓐ Ⓑ Ⓒ Ⓓ	48 Ⓕ Ⓖ Ⓗ Ⓙ	61 Ⓐ Ⓑ Ⓒ Ⓓ	74 Ⓕ Ⓖ Ⓗ Ⓙ
10 Ⓕ Ⓖ Ⓗ Ⓙ	23 Ⓐ Ⓑ Ⓒ Ⓓ	36 Ⓕ Ⓖ Ⓗ Ⓙ	49 Ⓐ Ⓑ Ⓒ Ⓓ	62 Ⓕ Ⓖ Ⓗ Ⓙ	75 Ⓐ Ⓑ Ⓒ Ⓓ
11 Ⓐ Ⓑ Ⓒ Ⓓ	24 Ⓕ Ⓖ Ⓗ Ⓙ	37 Ⓐ Ⓑ Ⓒ Ⓓ	50 Ⓕ Ⓖ Ⓗ Ⓙ	63 Ⓐ Ⓑ Ⓒ Ⓓ	
12 Ⓕ Ⓖ Ⓗ Ⓙ	25 Ⓐ Ⓑ Ⓒ Ⓓ	38 Ⓕ Ⓖ Ⓗ Ⓙ	51 Ⓐ Ⓑ Ⓒ Ⓓ	64 Ⓕ Ⓖ Ⓗ Ⓙ	
13 Ⓐ Ⓑ Ⓒ Ⓓ	26 Ⓕ Ⓖ Ⓗ Ⓙ	39 Ⓐ Ⓑ Ⓒ Ⓓ	52 Ⓕ Ⓖ Ⓗ Ⓙ	65 Ⓐ Ⓑ Ⓒ Ⓓ	

TEST 2: MATHEMATICS

1 Ⓐ Ⓑ Ⓒ Ⓓ Ⓔ	11 Ⓐ Ⓑ Ⓒ Ⓓ Ⓔ	21 Ⓐ Ⓑ Ⓒ Ⓓ Ⓔ	31 Ⓐ Ⓑ Ⓒ Ⓓ Ⓔ	41 Ⓐ Ⓑ Ⓒ Ⓓ Ⓔ	51 Ⓐ Ⓑ Ⓒ Ⓓ Ⓔ
2 Ⓕ Ⓖ Ⓗ Ⓙ Ⓚ	12 Ⓕ Ⓖ Ⓗ Ⓙ Ⓚ	22 Ⓕ Ⓖ Ⓗ Ⓙ Ⓚ	32 Ⓕ Ⓖ Ⓗ Ⓙ Ⓚ	42 Ⓕ Ⓖ Ⓗ Ⓙ Ⓚ	52 Ⓕ Ⓖ Ⓗ Ⓙ Ⓚ
3 Ⓐ Ⓑ Ⓒ Ⓓ Ⓔ	13 Ⓐ Ⓑ Ⓒ Ⓓ Ⓔ	23 Ⓐ Ⓑ Ⓒ Ⓓ Ⓔ	33 Ⓐ Ⓑ Ⓒ Ⓓ Ⓔ	43 Ⓐ Ⓑ Ⓒ Ⓓ Ⓔ	53 Ⓐ Ⓑ Ⓒ Ⓓ Ⓔ
4 Ⓕ Ⓖ Ⓗ Ⓙ Ⓚ	14 Ⓕ Ⓖ Ⓗ Ⓙ Ⓚ	24 Ⓕ Ⓖ Ⓗ Ⓙ Ⓚ	34 Ⓕ Ⓖ Ⓗ Ⓙ Ⓚ	44 Ⓕ Ⓖ Ⓗ Ⓙ Ⓚ	54 Ⓕ Ⓖ Ⓗ Ⓙ Ⓚ
5 Ⓐ Ⓑ Ⓒ Ⓓ Ⓔ	15 Ⓐ Ⓑ Ⓒ Ⓓ Ⓔ	25 Ⓐ Ⓑ Ⓒ Ⓓ Ⓔ	35 Ⓐ Ⓑ Ⓒ Ⓓ Ⓔ	45 Ⓐ Ⓑ Ⓒ Ⓓ Ⓔ	55 Ⓐ Ⓑ Ⓒ Ⓓ Ⓔ
6 Ⓕ Ⓖ Ⓗ Ⓙ Ⓚ	16 Ⓕ Ⓖ Ⓗ Ⓙ Ⓚ	26 Ⓕ Ⓖ Ⓗ Ⓙ Ⓚ	36 Ⓕ Ⓖ Ⓗ Ⓙ Ⓚ	46 Ⓕ Ⓖ Ⓗ Ⓙ Ⓚ	56 Ⓕ Ⓖ Ⓗ Ⓙ Ⓚ
7 Ⓐ Ⓑ Ⓒ Ⓓ Ⓔ	17 Ⓐ Ⓑ Ⓒ Ⓓ Ⓔ	27 Ⓐ Ⓑ Ⓒ Ⓓ Ⓔ	37 Ⓐ Ⓑ Ⓒ Ⓓ Ⓔ	47 Ⓐ Ⓑ Ⓒ Ⓓ Ⓔ	57 Ⓐ Ⓑ Ⓒ Ⓓ Ⓔ
8 Ⓕ Ⓖ Ⓗ Ⓙ Ⓚ	18 Ⓕ Ⓖ Ⓗ Ⓙ Ⓚ	28 Ⓕ Ⓖ Ⓗ Ⓙ Ⓚ	38 Ⓕ Ⓖ Ⓗ Ⓙ Ⓚ	48 Ⓕ Ⓖ Ⓗ Ⓙ Ⓚ	58 Ⓕ Ⓖ Ⓗ Ⓙ Ⓚ
9 Ⓐ Ⓑ Ⓒ Ⓓ Ⓔ	19 Ⓐ Ⓑ Ⓒ Ⓓ Ⓔ	29 Ⓐ Ⓑ Ⓒ Ⓓ Ⓔ	39 Ⓐ Ⓑ Ⓒ Ⓓ Ⓔ	49 Ⓐ Ⓑ Ⓒ Ⓓ Ⓔ	59 Ⓐ Ⓑ Ⓒ Ⓓ Ⓔ
10 Ⓕ Ⓖ Ⓗ Ⓙ Ⓚ	20 Ⓕ Ⓖ Ⓗ Ⓙ Ⓚ	30 Ⓕ Ⓖ Ⓗ Ⓙ Ⓚ	40 Ⓕ Ⓖ Ⓗ Ⓙ Ⓚ	50 Ⓕ Ⓖ Ⓗ Ⓙ Ⓚ	60 Ⓕ Ⓖ Ⓗ Ⓙ Ⓚ

TEST 3: READING

1 Ⓐ Ⓑ Ⓒ Ⓓ	8 Ⓕ Ⓖ Ⓗ Ⓙ	15 Ⓐ Ⓑ Ⓒ Ⓓ	22 Ⓕ Ⓖ Ⓗ Ⓙ	29 Ⓐ Ⓑ Ⓒ Ⓓ	36 Ⓕ Ⓖ Ⓗ Ⓙ
2 Ⓕ Ⓖ Ⓗ Ⓙ	9 Ⓐ Ⓑ Ⓒ Ⓓ	16 Ⓕ Ⓖ Ⓗ Ⓙ	23 Ⓐ Ⓑ Ⓒ Ⓓ	30 Ⓕ Ⓖ Ⓗ Ⓙ	37 Ⓐ Ⓑ Ⓒ Ⓓ
3 Ⓐ Ⓑ Ⓒ Ⓓ	10 Ⓕ Ⓖ Ⓗ Ⓙ	17 Ⓐ Ⓑ Ⓒ Ⓓ	24 Ⓕ Ⓖ Ⓗ Ⓙ	31 Ⓐ Ⓑ Ⓒ Ⓓ	38 Ⓕ Ⓖ Ⓗ Ⓙ
4 Ⓕ Ⓖ Ⓗ Ⓙ	11 Ⓐ Ⓑ Ⓒ Ⓓ	18 Ⓕ Ⓖ Ⓗ Ⓙ	25 Ⓐ Ⓑ Ⓒ Ⓓ	32 Ⓕ Ⓖ Ⓗ Ⓙ	39 Ⓐ Ⓑ Ⓒ Ⓓ
5 Ⓐ Ⓑ Ⓒ Ⓓ	12 Ⓕ Ⓖ Ⓗ Ⓙ	19 Ⓐ Ⓑ Ⓒ Ⓓ	26 Ⓕ Ⓖ Ⓗ Ⓙ	33 Ⓐ Ⓑ Ⓒ Ⓓ	40 Ⓕ Ⓖ Ⓗ Ⓙ
6 Ⓕ Ⓖ Ⓗ Ⓙ	13 Ⓐ Ⓑ Ⓒ Ⓓ	20 Ⓕ Ⓖ Ⓗ Ⓙ	27 Ⓐ Ⓑ Ⓒ Ⓓ	34 Ⓕ Ⓖ Ⓗ Ⓙ	
7 Ⓐ Ⓑ Ⓒ Ⓓ	14 Ⓕ Ⓖ Ⓗ Ⓙ	21 Ⓐ Ⓑ Ⓒ Ⓓ	28 Ⓕ Ⓖ Ⓗ Ⓙ	35 Ⓐ Ⓑ Ⓒ Ⓓ	

TEST 4: SCIENCE

1 Ⓐ Ⓑ Ⓒ Ⓓ	8 Ⓕ Ⓖ Ⓗ Ⓙ	15 Ⓐ Ⓑ Ⓒ Ⓓ	22 Ⓕ Ⓖ Ⓗ Ⓙ	29 Ⓐ Ⓑ Ⓒ Ⓓ	36 Ⓕ Ⓖ Ⓗ Ⓙ
2 Ⓕ Ⓖ Ⓗ Ⓙ	9 Ⓐ Ⓑ Ⓒ Ⓓ	16 Ⓕ Ⓖ Ⓗ Ⓙ	23 Ⓐ Ⓑ Ⓒ Ⓓ	30 Ⓕ Ⓖ Ⓗ Ⓙ	37 Ⓐ Ⓑ Ⓒ Ⓓ
3 Ⓐ Ⓑ Ⓒ Ⓓ	10 Ⓕ Ⓖ Ⓗ Ⓙ	17 Ⓐ Ⓑ Ⓒ Ⓓ	24 Ⓕ Ⓖ Ⓗ Ⓙ	31 Ⓐ Ⓑ Ⓒ Ⓓ	38 Ⓕ Ⓖ Ⓗ Ⓙ
4 Ⓕ Ⓖ Ⓗ Ⓙ	11 Ⓐ Ⓑ Ⓒ Ⓓ	18 Ⓕ Ⓖ Ⓗ Ⓙ	25 Ⓐ Ⓑ Ⓒ Ⓓ	32 Ⓕ Ⓖ Ⓗ Ⓙ	39 Ⓐ Ⓑ Ⓒ Ⓓ
5 Ⓐ Ⓑ Ⓒ Ⓓ	12 Ⓕ Ⓖ Ⓗ Ⓙ	19 Ⓐ Ⓑ Ⓒ Ⓓ	26 Ⓕ Ⓖ Ⓗ Ⓙ	33 Ⓐ Ⓑ Ⓒ Ⓓ	40 Ⓕ Ⓖ Ⓗ Ⓙ
6 Ⓕ Ⓖ Ⓗ Ⓙ	13 Ⓐ Ⓑ Ⓒ Ⓓ	20 Ⓕ Ⓖ Ⓗ Ⓙ	27 Ⓐ Ⓑ Ⓒ Ⓓ	34 Ⓕ Ⓖ Ⓗ Ⓙ	
7 Ⓐ Ⓑ Ⓒ Ⓓ	14 Ⓕ Ⓖ Ⓗ Ⓙ	21 Ⓐ Ⓑ Ⓒ Ⓓ	28 Ⓕ Ⓖ Ⓗ Ⓙ	35 Ⓐ Ⓑ Ⓒ Ⓓ	

The ACT® *Sample Answer Document*

EXAMINEE STATEMENTS, CERTIFICATION, AND SIGNATURE

1. Statements: I understand that by registering for, launching, starting, or submitting answer documents for an ACT® test, I am agreeing to comply with and be bound by the *Terms and Conditions: Testing Rules and Policies for the ACT® Test* ("Terms").

I UNDERSTAND AND AGREE THAT THE TERMS PERMIT ACT TO CANCEL MY SCORES IN CERTAIN CIRCUMSTANCES. THE TERMS ALSO LIMIT DAMAGES AVAILABLE TO ME AND REQUIRE ARBITRATION OF CERTAIN DISPUTES. BY AGREEING TO ARBITRATION, ACT AND I BOTH WAIVE THE RIGHT TO HAVE THOSE DISPUTES HEARD BY A JUDGE OR JURY.

I understand that ACT owns the test questions and responses, and I will not share them with anyone by any form of communication before, during, or after the test administration. I understand that taking the test for someone else may violate the law and subject me to legal penalties. I consent to the collection and processing of personally identifying information I provide, and its subsequent use and disclosure, as described in the ACT Privacy Policy (www.act.org/privacy.html). If I am taking the test outside of the United States, I also permit ACT to transfer my personally identifying information to the United States, to ACT, or to a third-party service provider, where it will be subject to use and disclosure under the laws of the United States, including being accessible to law enforcement or national security authorities.

2. Certification: Copy the italicized certification below, then sign and date in the spaces provided.

*I agree to the **Statements** above and certify that I am the person whose information appears on this form.*

____

____

___________________________   ___________________________
Your Signature   Today's Date

Do NOT mark in this shaded area.

USE A NO. 2 PENCIL ONLY.
(Do NOT use a mechanical pencil, ink, ballpoint, correction fluid, or felt-tip pen.)

A   NAME, MAILING ADDRESS, AND TELEPHONE
(Please print.)

Last Name   First Name   MI (Middle Initial)

House Number & Street (Apt. No.); or PO Box & No.; or RR & No.

City   State/Province   ZIP/Postal Code

Area Code   Number   Country

ACT, Inc.—Confidential Restricted when data present

ALL examinees must complete block A – please print.

Blocks B, C, and D are required for all examinees. Find the MATCHING INFORMATION on your ticket. Enter it EXACTLY the same way, even if any of the information is missing or incorrect. Fill in the corresponding ovals. If you do not complete these blocks to match your previous information EXACTLY, your scores will be **delayed up to 8 weeks**.

ACT®
PO BOX 168, IOWA CITY, IA 52243-0168

B   MATCH NAME
(First 5 letters of last name)

C   MATCH NUMBER

D   DATE OF BIRTH

Month	Day	Year
January		
February		
March		
April		
May		
June		
July		
August		
September		
October		
November		
December		

The ONLY Official Prep Guide from the Makers of the ACT

PAGE 2

Marking Directions: Mark only **one** oval for each question. Fill in response completely. Erase errors cleanly without smudging.

Correct mark: ○ ● ○ ○

Do NOT use these *incorrect* or *bad* **marks.**

Incorrect marks: ⊘ ⊗ ⊖ ⊙
Overlapping mark: ○ ○ ◑ ◖
Cross-out mark: ○ ◉ ○ ○
Smudged erasure: ○ ○ ◔ ○
Mark is too light: ◌ ○ ○ ○

BOOKLET NUMBER

FORM

Print your 5-character **Test Form** in the boxes at the right <u>and</u> fill in the corresponding ovals.

TEST 1: ENGLISH

1 Ⓐ Ⓑ Ⓒ Ⓓ	14 Ⓕ Ⓖ Ⓗ Ⓙ	27 Ⓐ Ⓑ Ⓒ Ⓓ	40 Ⓕ Ⓖ Ⓗ Ⓙ	53 Ⓐ Ⓑ Ⓒ Ⓓ	66 Ⓕ Ⓖ Ⓗ Ⓙ
2 Ⓕ Ⓖ Ⓗ Ⓙ	15 Ⓐ Ⓑ Ⓒ Ⓓ	28 Ⓕ Ⓖ Ⓗ Ⓙ	41 Ⓐ Ⓑ Ⓒ Ⓓ	54 Ⓕ Ⓖ Ⓗ Ⓙ	67 Ⓐ Ⓑ Ⓒ Ⓓ
3 Ⓐ Ⓑ Ⓒ Ⓓ	16 Ⓕ Ⓖ Ⓗ Ⓙ	29 Ⓐ Ⓑ Ⓒ Ⓓ	42 Ⓕ Ⓖ Ⓗ Ⓙ	55 Ⓐ Ⓑ Ⓒ Ⓓ	68 Ⓕ Ⓖ Ⓗ Ⓙ
4 Ⓕ Ⓖ Ⓗ Ⓙ	17 Ⓐ Ⓑ Ⓒ Ⓓ	30 Ⓕ Ⓖ Ⓗ Ⓙ	43 Ⓐ Ⓑ Ⓒ Ⓓ	56 Ⓕ Ⓖ Ⓗ Ⓙ	69 Ⓐ Ⓑ Ⓒ Ⓓ
5 Ⓐ Ⓑ Ⓒ Ⓓ	18 Ⓕ Ⓖ Ⓗ Ⓙ	31 Ⓐ Ⓑ Ⓒ Ⓓ	44 Ⓕ Ⓖ Ⓗ Ⓙ	57 Ⓐ Ⓑ Ⓒ Ⓓ	70 Ⓕ Ⓖ Ⓗ Ⓙ
6 Ⓕ Ⓖ Ⓗ Ⓙ	19 Ⓐ Ⓑ Ⓒ Ⓓ	32 Ⓕ Ⓖ Ⓗ Ⓙ	45 Ⓐ Ⓑ Ⓒ Ⓓ	58 Ⓕ Ⓖ Ⓗ Ⓙ	71 Ⓐ Ⓑ Ⓒ Ⓓ
7 Ⓐ Ⓑ Ⓒ Ⓓ	20 Ⓕ Ⓖ Ⓗ Ⓙ	33 Ⓐ Ⓑ Ⓒ Ⓓ	46 Ⓕ Ⓖ Ⓗ Ⓙ	59 Ⓐ Ⓑ Ⓒ Ⓓ	72 Ⓕ Ⓖ Ⓗ Ⓙ
8 Ⓐ Ⓑ Ⓒ Ⓓ	21 Ⓐ Ⓑ Ⓒ Ⓓ	34 Ⓕ Ⓖ Ⓗ Ⓙ	47 Ⓐ Ⓑ Ⓒ Ⓓ	60 Ⓕ Ⓖ Ⓗ Ⓙ	73 Ⓐ Ⓑ Ⓒ Ⓓ
9 Ⓐ Ⓑ Ⓒ Ⓓ	22 Ⓕ Ⓖ Ⓗ Ⓙ	35 Ⓐ Ⓑ Ⓒ Ⓓ	48 Ⓕ Ⓖ Ⓗ Ⓙ	61 Ⓐ Ⓑ Ⓒ Ⓓ	74 Ⓕ Ⓖ Ⓗ Ⓙ
10 Ⓕ Ⓖ Ⓗ Ⓙ	23 Ⓐ Ⓑ Ⓒ Ⓓ	36 Ⓕ Ⓖ Ⓗ Ⓙ	49 Ⓐ Ⓑ Ⓒ Ⓓ	62 Ⓕ Ⓖ Ⓗ Ⓙ	75 Ⓐ Ⓑ Ⓒ Ⓓ
11 Ⓐ Ⓑ Ⓒ Ⓓ	24 Ⓕ Ⓖ Ⓗ Ⓙ	37 Ⓐ Ⓑ Ⓒ Ⓓ	50 Ⓕ Ⓖ Ⓗ Ⓙ	63 Ⓐ Ⓑ Ⓒ Ⓓ	
12 Ⓕ Ⓖ Ⓗ Ⓙ	25 Ⓐ Ⓑ Ⓒ Ⓓ	38 Ⓕ Ⓖ Ⓗ Ⓙ	51 Ⓐ Ⓑ Ⓒ Ⓓ	64 Ⓕ Ⓖ Ⓗ Ⓙ	
13 Ⓐ Ⓑ Ⓒ Ⓓ	26 Ⓕ Ⓖ Ⓗ Ⓙ	39 Ⓐ Ⓑ Ⓒ Ⓓ	52 Ⓕ Ⓖ Ⓗ Ⓙ	65 Ⓐ Ⓑ Ⓒ Ⓓ	

TEST 2: MATHEMATICS

1 Ⓐ Ⓑ Ⓒ Ⓓ Ⓔ	11 Ⓐ Ⓑ Ⓒ Ⓓ Ⓔ	21 Ⓐ Ⓑ Ⓒ Ⓓ Ⓔ	31 Ⓐ Ⓑ Ⓒ Ⓓ Ⓔ	41 Ⓐ Ⓑ Ⓒ Ⓓ Ⓔ	51 Ⓐ Ⓑ Ⓒ Ⓓ Ⓔ
2 Ⓕ Ⓖ Ⓗ Ⓙ Ⓚ	12 Ⓕ Ⓖ Ⓗ Ⓙ Ⓚ	22 Ⓕ Ⓖ Ⓗ Ⓙ Ⓚ	32 Ⓕ Ⓖ Ⓗ Ⓙ Ⓚ	42 Ⓕ Ⓖ Ⓗ Ⓙ Ⓚ	52 Ⓕ Ⓖ Ⓗ Ⓙ Ⓚ
3 Ⓐ Ⓑ Ⓒ Ⓓ Ⓔ	13 Ⓐ Ⓑ Ⓒ Ⓓ Ⓔ	23 Ⓐ Ⓑ Ⓒ Ⓓ Ⓔ	33 Ⓐ Ⓑ Ⓒ Ⓓ Ⓔ	43 Ⓐ Ⓑ Ⓒ Ⓓ Ⓔ	53 Ⓐ Ⓑ Ⓒ Ⓓ Ⓔ
4 Ⓕ Ⓖ Ⓗ Ⓙ Ⓚ	14 Ⓕ Ⓖ Ⓗ Ⓙ Ⓚ	24 Ⓕ Ⓖ Ⓗ Ⓙ Ⓚ	34 Ⓕ Ⓖ Ⓗ Ⓙ Ⓚ	44 Ⓕ Ⓖ Ⓗ Ⓙ Ⓚ	54 Ⓕ Ⓖ Ⓗ Ⓙ Ⓚ
5 Ⓐ Ⓑ Ⓒ Ⓓ Ⓔ	15 Ⓐ Ⓑ Ⓒ Ⓓ Ⓔ	25 Ⓐ Ⓑ Ⓒ Ⓓ Ⓔ	35 Ⓐ Ⓑ Ⓒ Ⓓ Ⓔ	45 Ⓐ Ⓑ Ⓒ Ⓓ Ⓔ	55 Ⓐ Ⓑ Ⓒ Ⓓ Ⓔ
6 Ⓕ Ⓖ Ⓗ Ⓙ Ⓚ	16 Ⓕ Ⓖ Ⓗ Ⓙ Ⓚ	26 Ⓕ Ⓖ Ⓗ Ⓙ Ⓚ	36 Ⓕ Ⓖ Ⓗ Ⓙ Ⓚ	46 Ⓕ Ⓖ Ⓗ Ⓙ Ⓚ	56 Ⓕ Ⓖ Ⓗ Ⓙ Ⓚ
7 Ⓐ Ⓑ Ⓒ Ⓓ Ⓔ	17 Ⓐ Ⓑ Ⓒ Ⓓ Ⓔ	27 Ⓐ Ⓑ Ⓒ Ⓓ Ⓔ	37 Ⓐ Ⓑ Ⓒ Ⓓ Ⓔ	47 Ⓐ Ⓑ Ⓒ Ⓓ Ⓔ	57 Ⓐ Ⓑ Ⓒ Ⓓ Ⓔ
8 Ⓕ Ⓖ Ⓗ Ⓙ Ⓚ	18 Ⓕ Ⓖ Ⓗ Ⓙ Ⓚ	28 Ⓕ Ⓖ Ⓗ Ⓙ Ⓚ	38 Ⓕ Ⓖ Ⓗ Ⓙ Ⓚ	48 Ⓕ Ⓖ Ⓗ Ⓙ Ⓚ	58 Ⓕ Ⓖ Ⓗ Ⓙ Ⓚ
9 Ⓐ Ⓑ Ⓒ Ⓓ Ⓔ	19 Ⓐ Ⓑ Ⓒ Ⓓ Ⓔ	29 Ⓐ Ⓑ Ⓒ Ⓓ Ⓔ	39 Ⓐ Ⓑ Ⓒ Ⓓ Ⓔ	49 Ⓐ Ⓑ Ⓒ Ⓓ Ⓔ	59 Ⓐ Ⓑ Ⓒ Ⓓ Ⓔ
10 Ⓕ Ⓖ Ⓗ Ⓙ Ⓚ	20 Ⓕ Ⓖ Ⓗ Ⓙ Ⓚ	30 Ⓕ Ⓖ Ⓗ Ⓙ Ⓚ	40 Ⓕ Ⓖ Ⓗ Ⓙ Ⓚ	50 Ⓕ Ⓖ Ⓗ Ⓙ Ⓚ	60 Ⓕ Ⓖ Ⓗ Ⓙ Ⓚ

TEST 3: READING

1 Ⓐ Ⓑ Ⓒ Ⓓ	8 Ⓕ Ⓖ Ⓗ Ⓙ	15 Ⓐ Ⓑ Ⓒ Ⓓ	22 Ⓕ Ⓖ Ⓗ Ⓙ	29 Ⓐ Ⓑ Ⓒ Ⓓ	36 Ⓕ Ⓖ Ⓗ Ⓙ
2 Ⓕ Ⓖ Ⓗ Ⓙ	9 Ⓐ Ⓑ Ⓒ Ⓓ	16 Ⓕ Ⓖ Ⓗ Ⓙ	23 Ⓐ Ⓑ Ⓒ Ⓓ	30 Ⓕ Ⓖ Ⓗ Ⓙ	37 Ⓐ Ⓑ Ⓒ Ⓓ
3 Ⓐ Ⓑ Ⓒ Ⓓ	10 Ⓕ Ⓖ Ⓗ Ⓙ	17 Ⓐ Ⓑ Ⓒ Ⓓ	24 Ⓕ Ⓖ Ⓗ Ⓙ	31 Ⓐ Ⓑ Ⓒ Ⓓ	38 Ⓕ Ⓖ Ⓗ Ⓙ
4 Ⓕ Ⓖ Ⓗ Ⓙ	11 Ⓐ Ⓑ Ⓒ Ⓓ	18 Ⓕ Ⓖ Ⓗ Ⓙ	25 Ⓐ Ⓑ Ⓒ Ⓓ	32 Ⓕ Ⓖ Ⓗ Ⓙ	39 Ⓐ Ⓑ Ⓒ Ⓓ
5 Ⓐ Ⓑ Ⓒ Ⓓ	12 Ⓕ Ⓖ Ⓗ Ⓙ	19 Ⓐ Ⓑ Ⓒ Ⓓ	26 Ⓕ Ⓖ Ⓗ Ⓙ	33 Ⓐ Ⓑ Ⓒ Ⓓ	40 Ⓕ Ⓖ Ⓗ Ⓙ
6 Ⓕ Ⓖ Ⓗ Ⓙ	13 Ⓐ Ⓑ Ⓒ Ⓓ	20 Ⓕ Ⓖ Ⓗ Ⓙ	27 Ⓐ Ⓑ Ⓒ Ⓓ	34 Ⓕ Ⓖ Ⓗ Ⓙ	
7 Ⓐ Ⓑ Ⓒ Ⓓ	14 Ⓕ Ⓖ Ⓗ Ⓙ	21 Ⓐ Ⓑ Ⓒ Ⓓ	28 Ⓕ Ⓖ Ⓗ Ⓙ	35 Ⓐ Ⓑ Ⓒ Ⓓ	

TEST 4: SCIENCE

1 Ⓐ Ⓑ Ⓒ Ⓓ	8 Ⓕ Ⓖ Ⓗ Ⓙ	15 Ⓐ Ⓑ Ⓒ Ⓓ	22 Ⓕ Ⓖ Ⓗ Ⓙ	29 Ⓐ Ⓑ Ⓒ Ⓓ	36 Ⓕ Ⓖ Ⓗ Ⓙ
2 Ⓕ Ⓖ Ⓗ Ⓙ	9 Ⓐ Ⓑ Ⓒ Ⓓ	16 Ⓕ Ⓖ Ⓗ Ⓙ	23 Ⓐ Ⓑ Ⓒ Ⓓ	30 Ⓕ Ⓖ Ⓗ Ⓙ	37 Ⓐ Ⓑ Ⓒ Ⓓ
3 Ⓐ Ⓑ Ⓒ Ⓓ	10 Ⓕ Ⓖ Ⓗ Ⓙ	17 Ⓐ Ⓑ Ⓒ Ⓓ	24 Ⓕ Ⓖ Ⓗ Ⓙ	31 Ⓐ Ⓑ Ⓒ Ⓓ	38 Ⓕ Ⓖ Ⓗ Ⓙ
4 Ⓕ Ⓖ Ⓗ Ⓙ	11 Ⓐ Ⓑ Ⓒ Ⓓ	18 Ⓕ Ⓖ Ⓗ Ⓙ	25 Ⓐ Ⓑ Ⓒ Ⓓ	32 Ⓕ Ⓖ Ⓗ Ⓙ	39 Ⓐ Ⓑ Ⓒ Ⓓ
5 Ⓐ Ⓑ Ⓒ Ⓓ	12 Ⓕ Ⓖ Ⓗ Ⓙ	19 Ⓐ Ⓑ Ⓒ Ⓓ	26 Ⓕ Ⓖ Ⓗ Ⓙ	33 Ⓐ Ⓑ Ⓒ Ⓓ	40 Ⓕ Ⓖ Ⓗ Ⓙ
6 Ⓕ Ⓖ Ⓗ Ⓙ	13 Ⓐ Ⓑ Ⓒ Ⓓ	20 Ⓕ Ⓖ Ⓗ Ⓙ	27 Ⓐ Ⓑ Ⓒ Ⓓ	34 Ⓕ Ⓖ Ⓗ Ⓙ	
7 Ⓐ Ⓑ Ⓒ Ⓓ	14 Ⓕ Ⓖ Ⓗ Ⓙ	21 Ⓐ Ⓑ Ⓒ Ⓓ	28 Ⓕ Ⓖ Ⓗ Ⓙ	35 Ⓐ Ⓑ Ⓒ Ⓓ	

Practice Test 1

EXAMINEE STATEMENTS, CERTIFICATION, AND SIGNATURE

1. **Statements:** I understand that by registering for, launching, starting, or submitting answer documents for an ACT® test, I am agreeing to comply with and be bound by the *Terms and Conditions: Testing Rules and Policies for the ACT® Test* ("Terms").

   I UNDERSTAND AND AGREE THAT THE TERMS PERMIT ACT TO CANCEL MY SCORES IN CERTAIN CIRCUMSTANCES. THE TERMS ALSO LIMIT DAMAGES AVAILABLE TO ME AND REQUIRE ARBITRATION OF CERTAIN DISPUTES. BY AGREEING TO ARBITRATION, ACT AND I BOTH WAIVE THE RIGHT TO HAVE THOSE DISPUTES HEARD BY A JUDGE OR JURY.

   I understand that ACT owns the test questions and responses, and I will not share them with anyone by any form of communication before, during, or after the test administration. I understand that taking the test for someone else may violate the law and subject me to legal penalties.

   I consent to the collection and processing of personally identifying information I provide, and its subsequent use and disclosure, as described in the ACT Privacy Policy (www.act.org/privacy.html). If I am taking the test outside of the United States, I also permit ACT to transfer my personally identifying information to the United States, to ACT, or to a third-party service provider, where it will be subject to use and disclosure under the laws of the United States, including being accessible to law enforcement or national security authorities.

2. **Certification:** Copy the italicized certification below, then sign, date, and print your name in the spaces provided.

   *I agree to the **Statements** above and certify that I am the person whose information appears on this form.*

____

____

Your Signature   Today's Date   Print Your Name

The **ACT**®   **Form 26MC1**
2026 | 2027

Directions

This booklet contains tests in English, mathematics, reading, and science. These tests measure skills and abilities highly related to high school course work and success in college. **Calculators may be used on the mathematics test only.**

The questions in each test are numbered, and the suggested answers for each question are lettered. On the answer document, the rows of ovals are numbered to match the questions, and the ovals in each row are lettered to correspond to the suggested answers.

For each question, first decide which answer is best. Next, locate on the answer document the row of ovals numbered the same as the question. Then, locate the oval in that row lettered the same as your answer. Finally, fill in the oval completely. Use a soft lead pencil and make your marks heavy and black. **Do not use ink or a mechanical pencil.**

Mark only one answer to each question. If you change your mind about an answer, erase your first mark thoroughly before marking your new answer. For each question, make certain that you mark in the row of ovals with the same number as the question.

Only responses marked on your answer document will be scored. Your score on each test will be based only on the number of questions you answer correctly during the time allowed for that test. You will **not** be penalized for guessing. **It is to your advantage to answer every question even if you must guess.**

You may work on each test **only** when the testing staff tells you to do so. If you finish a test before time is called for that test, you should use the time remaining to reconsider questions you are uncertain about in that test. You may **not** look back to a test on which time has already been called, and you may **not** go ahead to another test. To do so will disqualify you from the examination.

Lay your pencil down immediately when time is called at the end of each test. You may **not** for any reason fill in or alter ovals for a test after time is called for that test. To do so will disqualify you from the examination.

Do not fold or tear the pages of your test booklet.

DO NOT OPEN THIS BOOKLET UNTIL TOLD TO DO SO.

The ONLY Official Prep Guide from the Makers of the ACT

1 ▪ ▪ ▪ ▪ ▪ ▪ ▪ ▪ 1

ENGLISH TEST
35 Minutes—50 Questions

DIRECTIONS: In the passages that follow, certain words and phrases are underlined and numbered. In the right-hand column, you will find alternatives for the underlined part. You are to choose the best answer to each question. If you think the original version is best, choose "**No Change**."

You will also find questions about a section of the passage, or about the passage as a whole. These questions do not refer to an underlined portion of the passage, but rather are identified by a number or numbers in a box.

For each question, choose the alternative you consider best and fill in the corresponding oval on your answer document. Read each passage through once before you begin to answer the questions that accompany it. For many of the questions, you must read several sentences beyond the question to determine the answer. Be sure that you have read far enough ahead each time you choose an alternative.

PASSAGE I

Seeing Streams in a New Light

[1]

As cities grew, in the nineteenth, and twentieth
                    ——————————————
                            1
centuries, thousands of urban streams were diverted

underground into large metal or concrete pipes called

culverts. Culverting controlled the paths of urban

waterways and created space for new construction, but

its unintended consequences—increased flooding, habitat

loss, maintenance costs—far outweigh its benefits today.

To alleviate these issues, communities should invest in
—————————————————————————————
                                              2
"daylighting" long-buried waterways by uncovering and

then restoring them to more natural conditions. [A]

1. Which choice makes the sentence most grammatically acceptable?
   A. **No Change**
   B. grew in the nineteenth
   C. grew in the nineteenth,
   D. grew, in the nineteenth

2. Which choice most effectively maintains the essay's tone?
   F. **No Change**
   G. To curtail the predicaments referenced above, communities may want to contemplate investing
   H. But there's a conceivable fix if communities would only just invest their monetary assets
   J. One surefire way to remedy the culverting mess is for communities to invest

GO ON TO THE NEXT PAGE.

1 ■ ■ ■ ■ ■ ■ ■ ■ ■ **1**

[2]

Daylighting projects remove impermeable barriers (such as concrete) between waterways and the soil. Thus, daylighting reduces flooding by allowing more rainwater to be absorbed where it falls. ⟨3⟩ Furthermore, the rocky bottoms and plant life of daylighted <u>streams, which slow</u> the water's flow, giving rain more time to be absorbed. Culverts and storm sewers, by contrast, accelerate water velocity, which leads to flash floods, downstream flooding, and greater erosion.

[3]

Although it's initially expensive, daylighting ultimately saves much more money than it costs. [B] Daylighting a mile of the Bee Branch Creek watershed cost Dubuque, Iowa, $100 million; however, researchers estimate that the project will prevent $582 million in flood damages over the coming decades. [C] And daylighting saves cities money in other ways, too: open creeks are much cheaper to maintain than culverts are, and <u>daylighting projects have lessened flooding in cities across the United States.</u>

3. If the writer were to delete the preceding sentence, the essay would primarily lose information that:

A. articulates one advantage of removing barriers between waterways and the soil.
B. provides data on the effects of removing barriers between waterways and the soil.
C. describes the process through which soil absorbs rainwater where it falls.
D. explains the impact of rainwater on daylighting projects.

4. Which choice makes the sentence most grammatically acceptable?

F. **No Change**
G. streams, these
H. streams that
J. streams

5. Given that all the choices are accurate, which one provides the most relevant support for the primary claim in this sentence?

A. **No Change**
B. keeping stormwater out of sewer systems reduces water treatment costs.
C. natural streambeds actually help clean the water that flows over them.
D. accessible waterways provide habitats for fish and other wildlife.

GO ON TO THE NEXT PAGE.

1 ... **1**

[4]

Because culverting was historically used to construct buildings over waterways, early attempts at culverting required innovative construction techniques. Therefore, city officials need to plan daylighting projects in careful collaboration with residents and business

owners whom may be effected. Thoughtfully planned daylighting embellishes the quality of life for the community as a whole—creating green spaces, reintroducing wildlife, and providing public recreational amenities. [D] Nearby homes increase in value, and businesses report higher profits. Citizens far and wide should oppose future culverting initiatives.

6. At this point in the essay, the writer wants to introduce a counterclaim that an opponent of daylighting might reasonably assert. Which choice most effectively accomplishes that goal?
   F. **No Change**
   G. certain daylighting projects tear down abandoned malls and warehouses before adding bridges.
   H. many citizens have lived and worked above their cities' streams.
   J. a downside of daylighting is the loss of some usable structures.

7. Which choice makes the sentence most grammatically acceptable?
   A. **No Change**
   B. whom may be affected.
   C. who may be effected.
   D. who may be affected.

8. Which choice is clearest and most precise in context?
   F. **No Change**
   G. refurbishes
   H. enriches
   J. fortifies

9. Which choice provides the most effective conclusion for the paragraph and essay?
   A. **No Change**
   B. In the last twenty years, cities worldwide have contemplated daylighting various streams.
   C. Daylighting offers more than a view of a waterway; it brings life back to the city center.
   D. Daylighting is doable when people work together, but it isn't easy.

Question 10 asks about the preceding passage as a whole.

---

10. The writer is considering adding the following assertion to the essay:

    > (If it had happened sooner, the project might have saved $70 million more in flood damage that occurred between 1999 and 2011.)

    If the writer were to add the sentence, it would most logically be placed at:

    F. Point A in Paragraph 1.
    G. Point B in Paragraph 3.
    H. Point C in Paragraph 3.
    J. Point D in Paragraph 4.

GO ON TO THE NEXT PAGE.

1 ▪ ▪ ▪ ▪ ▪ ▪ ▪ ▪ ▪ 1

PASSAGE II

Long Distance

"I can't believe people gather to throw cell phones for fun," I scoffed, stretching my stiffened muscles. After a long drive from her place in Helsinki, my cousin Anneli and I had finally arrived at our destination—a running track in Savonlinna, Finland. A huge banner near the entrance read, "Welcome to the Mobile Phone Throwing World Championships!"

"Give it a chance," Anneli replied, grinning at me. "It's become something of a national sport."

I've definitely felt the urge, during <u>a few annoyingly irritating calls with my sister,</u> to want to hurl my phone
₁₁
across the room. But, according to Anneli, this competition wasn't inspired by annoying siblings; it was <u>ascertained as</u> an engaging reminder for Finns to dispose of their mobile
₁₂
phones responsibly. As such, after the competition, all the phones gathered for the event are recycled at appropriate facilities. Beforehand, though, contestants dig through the tubs of outdated models, <u>searching for the phone with the greatest flight potential.</u>
₁₃

As we entered the venue, athletes and spectators of all ages milled around us. I found the <u>lively, agitated</u> atmosphere (with no trace of the fierce rivalry I often
₁₄
saw at competitive events) to be a pleasant surprise. Some attendees showed off themed or zany costumes, but most people wore casual, everyday clothes. <u>However,</u> the only
₁₅
telltale signs of who was competing were the paper bib numbers pinned to the athletes' shirts.

11. Which choice is least redundant in context?
   A. **No Change**
   B. aggravating calls with my sister that make me long to throw my phone,
   C. some frustrating calls with my sister on the phone,
   D. certain exasperating calls with my sister,

12. Which choice is clearest and most precise in context?
   F. **No Change**
   G. speculated
   H. conceived
   J. supposed

13. Which choice most effectively maintains the essay's tone?
   A. **No Change**
   B. in pursuit of the phone with which an elongated lob could most likely be achieved.
   C. seeking the phone with a structural configuration most suited to being flung afar.
   D. keeping their eyes peeled for the phone that might take to the skies with gusto.

14. Which choice creates the clearest contrast between the atmosphere at this event and the fierce rivalry the narrator expected to see?
   F. **No Change**
   G. dignified, focused
   H. festive, cordial
   J. tense, wary

15. Which transition word or phrase is most logical in context?
   A. **No Change**
   B. Eventually,
   C. Besides,
   D. In fact,

GO ON TO THE NEXT PAGE.

1 ■ ■ ■ ■ ■ ■ ■ ■ ■ 1

[1] The crowd cheered as a woman rode a unicycle in a circle for a full forty-five seconds before lofting her phone to the sky. [2] The contestant after that drew whistles and whoops when, from a handstand position, he "threw" his phone—with his teeth. [3] We stopped

to watch the Freestyle event, which is judged more on

the creativity of the throws than on their distance. 18

Everyone—even competitors in the Original category, who were genuinely trying for the farthest throw—seemed to be having fun. Spectators didn't talk on their phones; they talked to each other. Following

their lead, I turned my own phone off. 20

16. If the writer were to delete the underlined portion, the essay would primarily lose a specific detail that:
    F. helps clarify that the woman on the unicycle was the most impressive contestant.
    G. helps illustrate why the woman's performance was particularly noteworthy.
    H. defines the minimum required length of the performances in this event.
    J. reveals why the woman chose to ride a unicycle before throwing her phone.

17. Which choice makes the sentence most grammatically acceptable?
    A. **No Change**
    B. at least as much
    C. primarily
    D. **Delete** the underlined portion.

18. Which sequence of sentences makes this paragraph most logical?
    F. **No Change**
    G. 1, 3, 2
    H. 3, 1, 2
    J. 3, 2, 1

19. Which choice makes the sentence most grammatically acceptable?
    A. **No Change**
    B. phones, instead, they talked
    C. phones, they were talking
    D. phones instead talking

20. Which of the following sentences, if added here, would most effectively suggest that at this moment the narrator intends to connect with others in person rather than engaging with the phone?
    F. After all, I had taken enough pictures and video to remember this experience in the years to come.
    G. Then I linked arms with Anneli and stepped further into the crowd.
    H. At that moment, I started hoping that I could come again next year.
    J. I could still feel it in my pocket, but I ignored it—mostly.

GO ON TO THE NEXT PAGE.

1 ▪ ▪ ▪ ▪ ▪ ▪ ▪ ▪ ▪ 1

PASSAGE III

Threading Connections

As a child growing up in the village of Bermeja, Cuba, artist Alexi Torres worked the land with his father, friends, and neighbors. For Torres, farming was a revelation through which he first noticed that his village, the land, and time were interconnected. He and his people planted and harvested the crops during consecutive waning moons, just as their ancestors had in centuries past. Interconnectedness eventually became the central theme of Torres's <u>art in 2016, with his *Sun Light*</u>
<u>21</u>
series, he paid homage to the people and place that first inspired him. Torres created sixteen oil portraits of friends and family from Bermeja, <u>starting and completing each portrait in the same</u>
<u>22</u>
<u>lunar phase in which the village's residents farm.</u>
<u>22</u>

To visually represent interconnectedness, Torres painted the <u>portraits—in his signature,</u> "woven" style.
<u>23</u>
The portraits appear as though they're made from strands of hemp or jute that have been <u>assembled to</u>
<u>24</u>
form lifelike faces. To achieve this effect, Torres worked from <u>photographs to draw</u> realistic renderings
<u>25</u>
of his subjects directly onto giant canvases in his

---

21. Which choice makes the sentence most grammatically acceptable?

    A. **No Change**
    B. art, and
    C. art and
    D. art,

22. If the writer were to delete the underlined portion (adjusting the punctuation as needed), the paragraph would primarily lose:

    F. a detail illustrating how Torres's approach to creating the *Sun Light* series was influenced by his personal and cultural history.
    G. an example clarifying how Torres depicted various types of moonlight in the paintings in his *Sun Light* series.
    H. a suggestion that Torres often finds inspiration for his art from a connection with friends and family.
    J. a description of Torres's upbringing and the cultural traditions that most influenced his artistry.

23. Which choice makes the sentence most grammatically acceptable?

    A. **No Change**
    B. portraits, in his signature,
    C. portraits in his signature
    D. portraits, in his signature

24. Which choice provides the most specific description of the appearance of the "strands" composing the faces in Torres's portraits?

    F. **No Change**
    G. combined in such a way that they
    H. precisely interlaced to
    J. artistically used to

25. Which choice makes the sentence most grammatically acceptable?

    A. **No Change**
    B. photographs, which would draw
    C. photographs, who drew
    D. photographs that drew

GO ON TO THE NEXT PAGE.

1 ■ ■ ■ ■ ■ ■ ■ ■ 1

studio in Atlanta, Georgia. For instance, he
26
applied thousands of thin, fiber-like dabs of

paint, mostly—whites, grays, and blacks—to give
27
the multilayered portraits the appearance of being

rough and woven.

Torres chose a unique set of textures for each of

the sixteen portraits in the series. In *Sun Light—Mario*,

an older man's skin possesses a checkered texture, so the
28
salt-and-pepper hairs of his handlebar mustache appear

sharp and wiry. In *Sun Light—Yaneisy*, a young woman's

skin has a subtle, flower-patterned texture, and her hair,

soft and silky, is tied on the top of her head in a bun. To

Torres, each brushstroke or "thread" in the work is an

integral part of the whole, final creation—a reflection of

his overarching philosophy that everything (and everyone)

is interconnected. He likens his artistic process to how

his family has, for generations, cultivated and harvested

crops: "With my works, it is as if I am planting an idea
29
and working with universal laws in their realization."
29

26. Which transition word or phrase is most logical in
context?
   F. **No Change**
   G. Consequently,
   H. Again,
   J. Then,

27. Which choice makes the sentence most grammatically
acceptable?
   A. **No Change**
   B. paint—mostly whites, grays, and blacks—
   C. paint, (mostly whites, grays, and blacks),
   D. paint—mostly whites, grays, and blacks,

28. Which choice is clearest and most precise in context?
   F. **No Change**
   G. since
   H. and
   J. for

29. Given that all the choices are actual quotations from
Torres, which one would most effectively conclude the
sentence and the essay?
   A. **No Change**
   B. "Even if it looks like a lot of effort to create my
paintings, they are effortless because it is total joy
to make them."
   C. "Most of the Cuban population is made up of
farmers who plant and harvest their crops on the
waning moon."
   D. "I started to paint objects and people made out of
natural elements, like feathers and basket weaving."

GO ON TO THE NEXT PAGE.

Question 30 asks about the preceding passage as a whole.

30. Suppose the writer's primary purpose had been to discuss paintings that represent a key theme in an artist's work. Would this essay accomplish that purpose?

  F. Yes, because it explains Torres's philosophy that childhood relationships have the most profound influence on an artist's paintings.
  G. Yes, because it explores how Torres's *Sun Light* series exemplifies his philosophy about interconnectedness.
  H. No, because although it discusses major ideas that Torres has explored throughout his artistic career, it doesn't focus on particular artworks.
  J. No, because although it describes Torres's *Sun Light* portraits in detail, it fails to discuss thematic elements in the series.

The Object of Love

[1]

[A] I was waiting at the veterinarian's office recently with my cat when a young woman came in. After she sat down next to me, she asked if I would mind if she took her pet iguana out of its carrier. It was just a baby, she said, and it liked being held. [B]

[2]

Now, I'm not fond of iguanas. [C] They're strange, unpredictable creatures that belong deep in a rain forest, walking on the ground or resting high in the trees, which are hidden in the canopy. Wishing to be polite, but with reluctance in my voice, I told the woman that I didn't mind. She thanked me as she popped open the plastic carrier and pulled the iguana out, onto her lap.

31. Which choice is least redundant in context?

  A. **No Change**
  B. into the veterinarian's office where I was.
  C. in, and there I was, waiting in the office.
  D. in while I was waiting there.

32. Which choice provides the most vivid description of iguanas on the floor of a rain forest?

  F. **No Change**
  G. scuttling through dank undergrowth
  H. living underneath the treetops
  J. moving about down low

33. Which choice makes the sentence most grammatically acceptable?

  A. **No Change**
  B. trees, they are
  C. trees,
  D. trees;

GO ON TO THE NEXT PAGE.

1 ■ ■ ■ ■ ■ ■ ■ ■ ■ 1

[3]

I guardedly examined the animal: A dinosaur-like
thing, it was the size of a cat but armored in gray-green
scales, with a black-striped, whiplike tail two feet long.
It had a spine with tiny spikes, and its muscular limbs
<u>It had a spine with tiny spikes</u>, and its muscular limbs
ended with what resembled crinkly leather gloves drawn
tightly over fine-boned human hands. When I looked more
closely, I saw a tiny claw at the tip of each slender finger.

[4]

The woman began to pet the iguana under its
chin, and the little dragon arched its neck and closed
its eyes. The reptile's calmness amazed me, as did the
<u>caress that was given tenderly from the woman to her pet</u>
and watched it peacefully rest. With a twinge of pity, I
thought how sad it was for the woman to lavish so much
affection on something that couldn't love her back.

[5]

At that moment, the iguana slowly opened its
eyes, which shone <u>large and bright, from</u> its scaly face.
[D] Head slightly cocked, it regarded me, steadily and

fixedly, like a judge <u>delivering</u> a verdict.

[6]

"Who are you," it seemed to ask me, "to name the
proper object of love?"

34. Given that all the choices are accurate, which one pro-
    vides the most precise description of the pattern of
    spikes on the iguana's spine?
    F. No Change
    G. I saw spikes that looked like they were just begin-
        ning to develop,
    H. There were small spikes on its armored back,
    J. Rows of budding spikes lined its spine,

35. Which choice makes the sentence most grammatically
    acceptable?
    A. No Change
    B. tenderness with which the woman caressed her pet
    C. woman caressing her pet tenderly
    D. tenderness the woman showed

36. Which choice makes the sentence most grammatically
    acceptable?
    F. No Change
    G. large and bright from,
    H. large, and bright from
    J. large and bright from

37. Which choice makes the sentence most grammatically
    acceptable?
    A. No Change
    B. having a delivery of
    C. in deliverance with
    D. deliver

GO ON TO THE NEXT PAGE.

[7]

The veterinary assistant called for my cat and me from the hallway that leads to the examination area. A bit unsettled, I rose and picked up my cat carrier. As I walked from the waiting room into the hall, I glanced back and saw the iguana snuggle down into the young woman's lap, <u>looking</u> as content as a kitten, and close its eyes again.
38

38. Which choice best avoids wordiness and redundancy in context?

   F. **No Change**
   G. like as if it was giving off the impression of being
   H. appearing something like
   J. sort of like it was

Questions 39 and 40 ask about the preceding passage as a whole.

---

39. Upon reviewing the essay and finding that some information has been left out, the writer composes the following sentence incorporating that information:

> She told me that her iguana especially liked attention when it was in unfamiliar surroundings, and that this was its first trip to the veterinarian.

If the writer were to add this sentence to the essay, it would most logically be placed at:

   A. Point A in Paragraph 1.
   B. Point B in Paragraph 1.
   C. Point C in Paragraph 2.
   D. Point D in Paragraph 5.

40. Suppose the writer's primary purpose had been to describe a moment in which a person notices something unexpected while observing his or her surroundings. Would this essay accomplish that purpose?

   F. Yes, because it describes what the narrator, while waiting at the vet, perceived to be a surprising bond between a woman and her pet iguana.
   G. Yes, because it recounts a moment when the narrator, while waiting at the vet, realized people often don't know when they're being impolite.
   H. No, because it instead tells the story of why the narrator doesn't like iguanas.
   J. No, because it instead focuses on providing information about the physical characteristics of iguanas and their habitat.

PASSAGE V

(Re)Defining Music

Dip hop—a growing subgenre of hip hop grounded in Deaf culture and aesthetics—<u>challenge stereotypes</u>
      41
<u>and help</u> to reshape mainstream notions of what music
41
is. Fundamental to the style are a heavy emphasis on bass beats and lyrics rapped in sign language such as ASL (American Sign Language). Audiences feel the rhythmic vibrations, see the lyrics in motion, and engage sonic imagination.

41. Which choice makes the sentence most grammatically acceptable?

   A. **No Change**
   B. are challenging stereotypes and have helped
   C. challenge stereotypes and are helping
   D. challenges stereotypes and is helping

GO ON TO THE NEXT PAGE.

1 ■ ■ ■ ■ ■ ■ ■ ■ **1**

Though rooted in hip hop, dip hop is not simply
                          42
rap songs translated into ASL but musical expression
                                    42
from a Deaf perspective; artists craft original songs
and develop individual styles. Some collaborate with

DJs, deaf or hearing, some induct visual elements
                               43
like sound-activated lights, and some use specialized
equipment to enhance sound vibrations. There are
artists who only sign their raps, and those who
                          44
incorporate both oral and sign languages to make
their music accessible to hearing audiences.

But many have yet to encounter dip hop. In 2020,
                                  45
dip hop artist Sean Forbes's "Little Victories" reached
number one in hip hop on iTunes; in 2021, Wawa's
"LOUD" was a Top 20 dance track; and in 2022, both
artists performed in the Super Bowl Halftime Show,
bringing dip hop to the masses.

42. Which choice makes the sentence most grammatically
acceptable?
   F. No Change
   G. hip hop, dip hop is not simply, rap songs translated
      into ASL, but musical expression
   H. hip hop—dip hop is not simply rap songs, translated into ASL but musical expression,
   J. hip hop, dip hop is not simply rap songs translated
      into ASL but—musical expression

43. Which choice is clearest and most precise in context?
   A. No Change
   B. congregate
   C. compound
   D. integrate

44. Which choice makes the sentence most grammatically
acceptable?
   F. No Change
   G. whom only sign their raps, and those whom
   H. which only sign their raps, and them that
   J. who only sign their raps, and them which

45. Which choice most effectively leads the reader from the
preceding paragraph to the information that follows in
this paragraph?
   A. No Change
   B. And this is just one of many styles of rap that have
      developed over time.
   C. And dip hop is resonating.
   D. But each artist is unique.

Southside Blooms

In Chicago's Englewood neighborhood, every
employee at Southside Blooms, a flower fulfillment
center, have embraced the motto painted on the wall:
           46
"Flowers that empower." The employees—all
neighborhood residents and most of whom are

under the age of thirty arrange peonies, hyacinths,
                 47
and tulips into bouquets that are delivered throughout
the area.

46. Which choice makes the sentence most grammatically
acceptable?
   F. No Change
   G. are embracing
   H. embraces
   J. embrace

47. Which choice makes the sentence most grammatically
acceptable?
   A. No Change
   B. thirty—
   C. thirty,
   D. thirty:

GO ON TO THE NEXT PAGE.

1 ■ ■ ■ ■ ■ ■ ■ ■ ■ **1**

Quilen and Hannah Blackwell opened Southside Blooms in 2020 to increase opportunity in their community. Besides flower arranging, the employees at Southside Blooms can learn how to employ sustainable agricultural techniques. For two years, "farm team" member Dionta White has planted and cultivated flowers on five vacant city lots, all of which are powered by solar panels and irrigated by rainwater. For White, it's

been revelatory, he's learning about eco-friendly methods that he didn't know existed.

And White isn't an outlier. In four years, over thirty Southside Blooms employees have earned stipends that study urban agriculture. Hoping to encourage more Englewood residents to earn such opportunities, Quilen Blackwell says, "It's a nice little village that we're building here, and everybody has something to contribute."

48. Which choice makes the sentence most grammatically acceptable?
   F. No Change
   G. member, Dionta White,
   H. member, Dionta White
   J. member Dionta White,

49. Which choice makes the sentence most grammatically acceptable?
   A. No Change
   B. revelatory, he has learned
   C. revelatory; he's learning
   D. revelatory; to learn

50. Which choice makes the sentence most grammatically acceptable?
   F. No Change
   G. employees who have earned stipends to
   H. employees, having earned stipends, to
   J. employees have earned stipends to

END OF TEST 1

STOP! DO NOT TURN THE PAGE UNTIL TOLD TO DO SO.

2 △ △ △ △ △ △ △ △ △ 2

MATHEMATICS TEST
50 Minutes—45 Questions

DIRECTIONS: Solve each problem, choose the correct answer, and then fill in the corresponding oval on your answer document.

Do not linger over problems that take too much time. Solve as many as you can; then return to the others in the time you have left for this test.

You are permitted to use a calculator on this test. You may use your calculator for any problems you choose, but some of the problems may best be done without using a calculator.

Note: Unless otherwise stated, all of the following should be assumed.

1. Illustrative figures are **not** necessarily drawn to scale.
2. Geometric figures lie in a plane.
3. The word "line" indicates a straight line.
4. The word "average" indicates arithmetic mean.

---

1. What is the solution of the equation $\sqrt{x} - 9 = 8$?
   A. 1
   B. 25
   C. 34
   D. 289

2. $\left(\frac{1}{64}\right)^{-\frac{1}{2}} = ?$

   F. $-\frac{1}{8}$

   G. $-\frac{1}{128}$

   H. 8

   J. 128

3. For which of the following fractions does the decimal expansion require 1 repeating nonzero digit?

   A. $\frac{1}{4}$

   B. $\frac{3}{5}$

   C. $\frac{5}{8}$

   D. $\frac{2}{3}$

4. When a fair coin is flipped a large number of times, the number of heads should be approximately equal to the number of tails. Assume that the fairness of a particular coin is being investigated. Which of the following results provides the **strongest** evidence that the coin is **not** fair?

   F. 2 out of 3 flips were heads.
   G. 3 out of 4 flips were heads.
   H. 4 out of 5 flips were heads.
   J. 5 out of 6 flips were heads.

DO YOUR FIGURING HERE.

GO ON TO THE NEXT PAGE.

2 △ △ △ △ △ △ △ △ △ **2**

DO YOUR FIGURING HERE.

5. Ana plans to save \$200 for a summer skate park pass. She already has \$45 and plans to save \$15 per week. At this rate of savings, what is the minimum number of weeks after which Ana will have enough money for the skate park pass?

   A. 10
   B. 11
   C. 13
   D. 14

6. Similar triangles **must** have the same:

   F. angle measures.
   G. area.
   H. perimeter.
   J. side lengths.

7. What is the greatest common factor of 45, 50, and 84?

   A. 0
   B. 1
   C. 2
   D. 3

8. Which of the following expressions is equivalent to $(3x - 9)^2$?

   F. $6x - 18$
   G. $6x^2 + 81$
   H. $9x^2 - 54x + 81$
   J. $9x^2 - 27x + 18$

9. Next year, there will be 3,432 high school students in a certain district. Each of these students will attend either East High School or West High School but **not** both. Because of the facilities, the ratio of the number of East High School students to the number of West High School students must be 11 to 13. How many of these students will attend East High School?

   A. 143
   B. 1,573
   C. 2,904
   D. 4,056

GO ON TO THE NEXT PAGE.

2 △ △ △ △ △ △ △ △ △ **2**

10. A worker earns a standard hourly wage of $20.10 per hour for the first 40 hours he works in 1 week. For each hour over 40 hours he works in 1 week, he earns $1\frac{1}{2}$ times his standard hourly wage. Which of the following gives the amount, in dollars, this worker earns for working 54 hours in 1 week?

F. $54\left(20.10 + \frac{1}{2}(20.10)\right)$

G. $54\left(20.10 + \left(1\frac{1}{2}\right)(20.10)\right)$

H. $40(20.10) + 14\left(\frac{1}{2}\right)(20.10)$

J. $40(20.10) + 14\left(1\frac{1}{2}\right)(20.10)$

11. For the complex variable z, one of the following is a solution of $z^2 = -9$. Which one?

A. -3
B. 3
C. $3i$
D. $9i$

12. A student modeled a set of paired data with the equation $y = 0.25x + 25$. The student's model and a scatterplot of the paired data are graphed in the standard (x,y) coordinate plane. Among the following possible changes to the student's equation, which one will most improve the fit to the paired data?

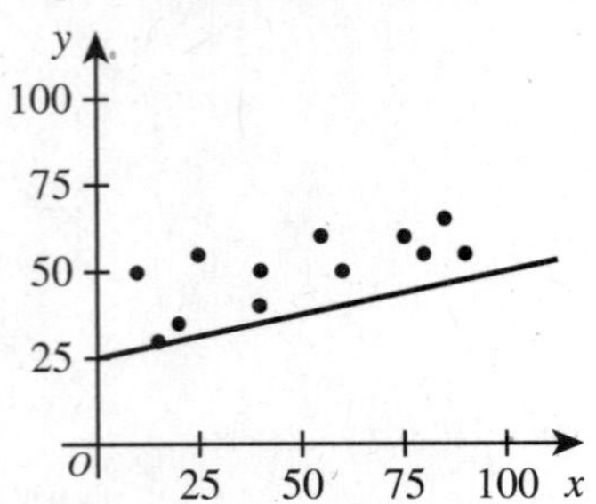

F. Increase the slope by 0.75
G. Decrease the slope by 0.25
H. Increase the y-intercept by 12.5
J. Decrease the y-intercept by 12.5

GO ON TO THE NEXT PAGE.

2 △ △ △ △ △ △ △ △ △ **2**

13. A certain committee is composed of 11 juniors and 79 seniors. Two different members of the committee will be randomly selected, each for a different leadership role. Given that the 1st member selected is a junior, what is the probability that the 2nd member selected will be a senior?

- **A.** $\frac{10}{79}$
- **B.** $\frac{10}{89}$
- **C.** $\frac{79}{89}$
- **D.** $\frac{79}{90}$

DO YOUR FIGURING HERE.

14. This table lists the engine size, x liters, and the weight, w kilograms, of each of 5 vehicles. A linear model for the data in the table is $\hat{w} = 375x + 370$. The actual weight of the vehicle with the smallest engine size differs from the linear model's predicted weight of this vehicle by how many kilograms?

Engine size (L)	Weight (kg)
2.0	1,041
4.3	2,021
3.4	1,670
2.8	1,547
4.0	1,754

- **F.** 79
- **G.** 296
- **H.** 370
- **J.** 671

15. Let d be a function of t. The given graph of the function models the distance, d meters, left to hike on a trail t minutes since beginning the hike. It took a total of 13 minutes to hike the 860-meter trail. One of the following intervals is the domain of the function. Which one?

- **A.** $[0, 13]$
- **B.** $\left[0, 66\frac{2}{13}\right]$
- **C.** $\left[0, 436\frac{1}{2}\right]$
- **D.** $[0, 860]$

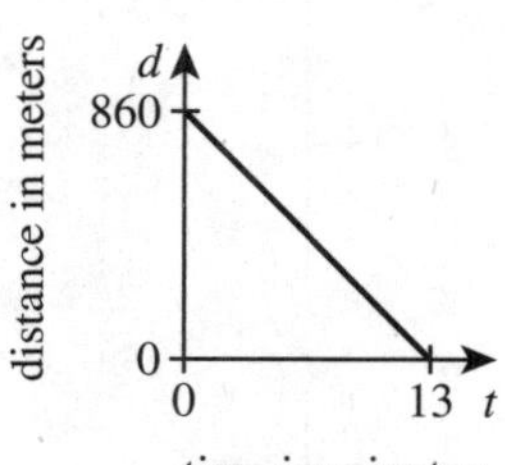

GO ON TO THE NEXT PAGE.

2 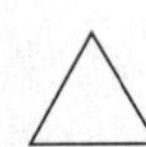        **2**

DO YOUR FIGURING HERE.

16. In the standard (x,y) coordinate plane, what is the midpoint of the line segment that has endpoints $(-5,8)$ and $(3,-1)$?

   F. $(-2,-9)$

   G. $\left(-1,\frac{7}{2}\right)$

   H. $\left(4,-\frac{9}{2}\right)$

   J. $(8,-9)$

17. Which of the following numbers is equal to $\dfrac{10i+2}{2i}$?

(Note: $i^2 = -1$)

   A. $5-i$
   B. 6
   C. $9i$
   D. $11i$

18. What is the value of x in the solution to the given system of linear equations?

$$8x + y = 6$$
$$9x - 6y = 11$$

   F. $\dfrac{25}{39}$

   G. $\dfrac{47}{57}$

   H. $\dfrac{57}{47}$

   J. $\dfrac{39}{25}$

19. The function $y = 2\sin(6\pi x)$ is graphed in the standard (x,y) coordinate plane for x radians in the interval $0 \le x \le 1$. What are the period and amplitude of the function?

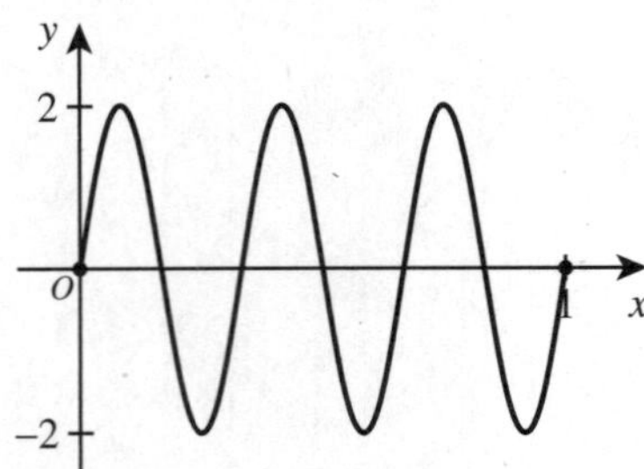

   A. Period: $\frac{1}{3}$
      Amplitude: 2

   B. Period: $\frac{1}{3}$
      Amplitude: 4

   C. Period: 3
      Amplitude: 2

   D. Period: 3
      Amplitude: 4

GO ON TO THE NEXT PAGE.

2 △ △ △ △ △ △ △ △ △ **2**

DO YOUR FIGURING HERE.

20. Let c, h, and q be distinct nonzero real numbers, and let x be a variable. Which of the following gives the solution to $c(x - h) = q$?

F. $\frac{q}{c} - h$

G. $\frac{q}{c} + h$

H. $\frac{q}{c} + \frac{h}{c}$

J. $\frac{q}{h} + \frac{c}{h}$

21. Given $\triangle RST$ with $RS = 18$ cm, $ST = 12$ cm, and $RT = 27$ cm, which of the following statements is true about the angles of this triangle?

A. The measure of $\angle R$ is the least.
B. The measure of $\angle S$ is the least.
C. The measure of $\angle R$ is the greatest.
D. The measure of $\angle T$ is the greatest.

22. Given $f(x) = 2x - 5$, what is the inverse, $f^{-1}(x)$?

F. $\frac{x - 5}{2}$

G. $\frac{x + 5}{2}$

H. $\frac{x + 2}{5}$

J. $\frac{1}{2}x + 5$

23. In the figure shown, a square is circumscribed about a circle with an 8-inch radius. Diameter $\overline{AB}$ is parallel to 2 sides of the square, and $\overline{CD}$ is a diagonal of the square. Some regions, bounded by the square, the circle, $\overline{AB}$, and $\overline{CD}$, are shaded. Which of the following is closest to the total area, in square inches, of the shaded regions?

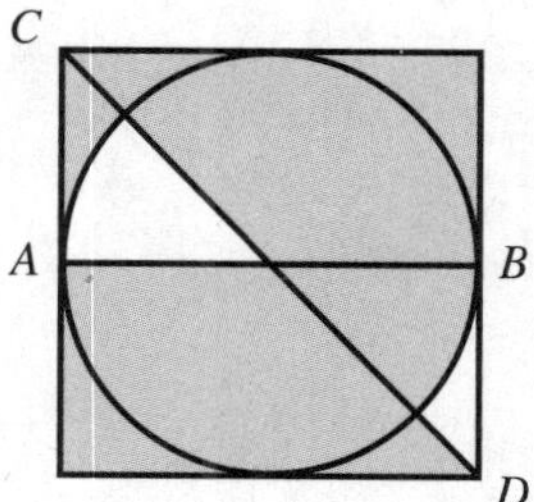

A. 64
B. 176
C. 224
D. 256

GO ON TO THE NEXT PAGE.

Your First Practice Test

2 △ △ △ △ △ △ △ △ △ **2**

24. In the standard (x,y) coordinate plane, a certain dilation maps the point $(0,0)$ to itself and maps the point $(4,-16)$ to the point $(1,-4)$. This dilation maps the point $(12,-24)$ to the point:

F. $(3,-6)$
G. $(9,-36)$
H. $(15,-36)$
J. $(16,-20)$

25. A cleaning company sends out advertisements to potential customers. The table lists the probability of an advertisement leading to a certain amount of revenue. To the nearest cent, what is the expected value of the revenue generated from an advertisement sent to a potential customer?

Revenue	Probability
$400	0.02
$100	0.02
$60	0.04
$0	0.92

A. $12.40
B. $13.32
C. $35.00
D. $80.00

26. A normal distribution for random variable X is given. Each percentage shown is the percentage of the area under that portion of the curve.

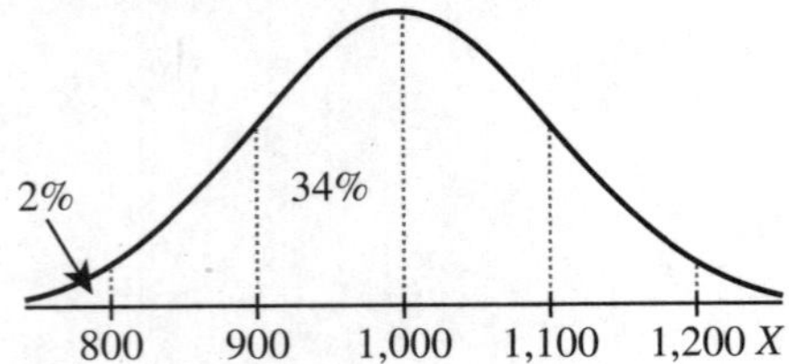

One of the following values is the value of $P(1,100 < X < 1,200)$ to the nearest 1%. Which one?

F. 14%
G. 17%
H. 18%
J. 30%

27. Consider the repeating decimal $0.\overline{7412}$ in expanded form. What is the 323rd digit to the right of the decimal point?

A. 1
B. 2
C. 4
D. 7

GO ON TO THE NEXT PAGE.

2 △ △ △ △ △ △ △ △ △ **2**

DO YOUR FIGURING HERE.

28. Jabari is walking along a straight sidewalk when he sees a tree directly ahead of him. He estimates that the angle of elevation from his feet to the top of the tree is 25°. As he continues walking, he finds that he was about 45 feet from the base of the tree when he estimated the angle of elevation. Based on Jabari's estimates, which of the following expressions represents the height, in feet, of the tree?

  F. 45 sin 25°
  G. 45 cos 25°
  H. 45 tan 25°
  J. 45 cot 25°

29. A small hole was torn in the bottom corner of an unopened 1.5-pound bag of granulated sugar. By the time the hole was plugged, the leaked sugar had formed a pile in the shape of a cone with a radius of 3 inches and a height of 2 inches. Given that granulated sugar weighs 0.025 pounds per cubic inch, which of the following values is closest to the amount of sugar, in pounds, that was left in the bag after the leak was fixed?

(Note: The volume of a cone with radius r and height h is given by $V = \frac{\pi}{3}r^2h$.)

  A. 0.086
  B. 1.029
  C. 1.350
  D. 1.475

30. Roger is pouring concrete to make a sidewalk with the dimensions, in feet, shown in the figure. He pours the concrete to a depth of 4 **inches**. One bag of concrete mix makes 0.6 cubic feet of concrete. What is the least whole number of bags of concrete mix that Roger needs in order to make the sidewalk?

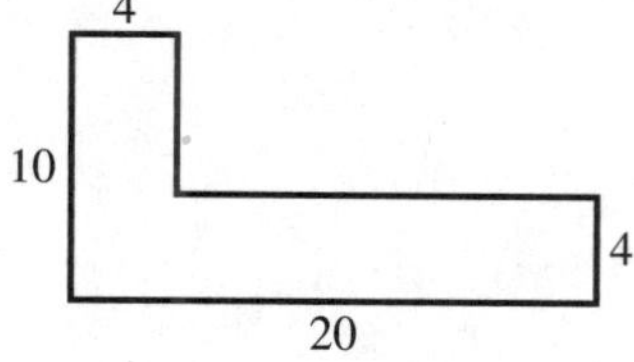

  F. 44
  G. 50
  H. 58
  J. 67

GO ON TO THE NEXT PAGE.

2 △ △ △ △ △ △ △ △ △ **2**

DO YOUR FIGURING HERE.

31. The expression $(x + by)^n$ will be expanded and like terms will be combined. The resulting terms will be arranged in descending powers of x. After these steps are done, the 2nd term will be $8x^3y$. What will be the total number of terms?

A. 5
B. 8
C. 11
D. 12

32. The concentration of a certain medication decreases each hour such that at $t = 0$ hours, the concentration is approximately equal to 850 mg/L; at $t = 6$ hours, the concentration is approximately equal to 151 mg/L; and at $t = 12$ hours, the concentration is approximately equal to 27 mg/L. One of the following identifies the best type of functional model for the data representing this 12-hour interval and gives a valid reason why that model is best. Which one?

F. Linear, because over equal time intervals, the concentration decreases by equal factors.
G. Linear, because over equal time intervals, the concentration decreases by equal differences.
H. Exponential, because over equal time intervals, the concentration decreases by equal factors.
J. Exponential, because over equal time intervals, the concentration decreases by equal differences.

33. Given that n is a rational number, which of the following statements about the number $\dfrac{-4\sqrt{14} - n}{2}$ must be true?

A. $\dfrac{-4\sqrt{14} - n}{2}$ is positive.

B. $\dfrac{-4\sqrt{14} - n}{2}$ is negative.

C. $\dfrac{-4\sqrt{14} - n}{2}$ is an irrational number.

D. $\dfrac{-4\sqrt{14} - n}{2}$ is a rational number.

34. The graph of $\dfrac{x^2}{9} - \dfrac{y^2}{49} = 1$ in the standard (x,y) coordinate plane has an x-intercept at which of the following points?

F. (0,0)
G. (3,0)
H. (7,0)
J. (9,0)

GO ON TO THE NEXT PAGE.

2 △ △ △ △ △ △ △ △ △ **2**

35. One of the following is the equation of this graph in the standard (x,y) coordinate plane. Which one?

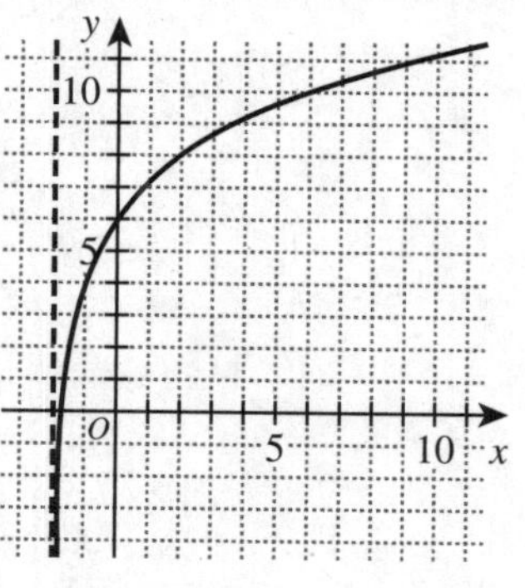

A. $y = 4(4)^{x-4} - 2$
B. $y = 4(4)^{x+2} + 4$
C. $y = 4 \log_4(x - 4) - 2$
D. $y = 4 \log_4(x + 2) + 4$

36. Event W consists of 14 simple events. Event X consists of 11 simple events, none of which are in event W. Event Y is the intersection of events W and X, and event Z is the union of events W and X. Which of the following statements is true?

(Note: Given that event E consists of n simple events, $|E| = n$.)

F. $|X| < |W| < |Y| < |Z|$
G. $|X| < |W| < |Z| < |Y|$
H. $|Y| < |X| < |W| < |Z|$
J. $|Y| < |Z| < |X| < |W|$

37. An isosceles triangle, $\triangle ABC$, with $\overline{AB} \cong \overline{CB}$ is shown. Points D, E, and H are the midpoints of $\overline{AB}$, $\overline{CB}$, and $\overline{AC}$, respectively. Points F and G are the midpoints of $\overline{DH}$ and $\overline{EH}$, respectively. What is the ratio of the area of $\triangle ABC$ to the area of $\triangle FGH$?

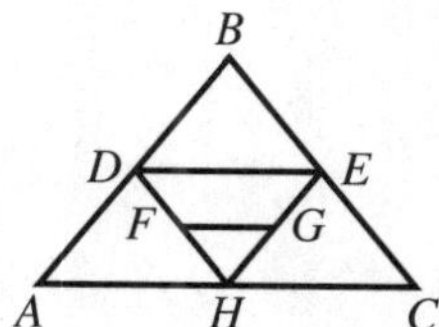

A. 4:1
B. 8:1
C. 16:1
D. 64:1

GO ON TO THE NEXT PAGE.

2 △ △ △ △ △ △ △ △ △ **2**

38. The average of 10 test scores is x. When the highest score and lowest score are removed from the 10 scores, the average is y. Which of the following is an expression for the average of the highest score and lowest score?

F. $10x - 8y$

G. $\dfrac{x+y}{2}$

H. $\dfrac{10x + 8y}{2}$

J. $\dfrac{10x - 8y}{2}$

39. Two perpendicular lines in the standard (x,y) coordinate plane each have nonzero slopes. What is the product of their slopes?

A. -2
B. -1
C. 1
D. 2

40. For integers m and n such that $-3 \le m \le 4$ and $-10 \le n \le 9$, what is the greatest possible value of $|m - n|$?

F. 5
G. 7
H. 12
J. 14

41. A factor of $2.5x^2 - 30x + c$ is $x + 4$. What is the value of c?

A. -160
B. -26
C. 80
D. 110

42. A company designed a questionnaire to be completed by its employees. The questionnaire has 5 questions with the answer choices of only "yes" or "no." Given that every question must be answered and an employee can only choose 1 answer to each question, in how many ways can an employee answer all 5 questions on the questionnaire?

F. 7
G. 25
H. 32
J. 64

GO ON TO THE NEXT PAGE.

2 △ △ △ △ △ △ △ △ △ **2**

43. Consider quantities a, b, and m. Given that 40% of m is equal to a and that $b = \frac{7a}{10}$, which of the following expressions gives 112% of m in terms of b?

   A. $4b$
   B. $12b$
   C. $40b$
   D. $84b$

44. The sum of the first 15 positive integers is 120. Which of the following values is the sum of the first 75 positive integers?

   F. 600
   G. 1,140
   H. 2,775
   J. 2,850

45. What are the equations of all the asymptotes in the standard (x,y) coordinate plane for the function $y = f(x) = \frac{3x^2}{x^2 - 9}$?

   A. $x = -3$ and $y = 3$
   B. $x = 3$ and $y = 0$
   C. $x = -3$, $x = 3$, and $y = 0$
   D. $x = -3$, $x = 3$, and $y = 3$

DO YOUR FIGURING HERE.

Your First Practice Test

END OF TEST 2
STOP! DO NOT TURN THE PAGE UNTIL TOLD TO DO SO.
DO NOT RETURN TO THE PREVIOUS TEST.

3 3

READING TEST

40 Minutes—36 Questions

DIRECTIONS: There are several passages in this test. Each passage is accompanied by several questions. After reading a passage, choose the best answer to each question and fill in the corresponding oval on your answer document. You may refer to the passages as often as necessary.

Passage I

INFORMATIONAL: This passage is from the essay "Producing and Collecting Portraits of Artists" by Anna Reynolds and Lucy Peter.

One practical consideration with painted self-portraits, which is easy to forget today, was the availability of mirrors. Flat glass mirrors were invented in Venice in around 1500. Before this date, mirrors were
5 small and convex, and therefore a potential deterrent to artists. However, attributing the development of self-portraiture purely to the development of mirrors is an oversimplification. While flat mirrors were available from *c*.1500, they were also prohibitively expensive: it
10 was not until the 1700s, when the French started producing mirrors of the same size and quality as the Venetians, that the market opened up and mirrors became more affordable. This is not to say that practical advancements in the production of mirrors had no
15 impact on the development of self-portraiture. The ability to see yourself more clearly and more frequently, around the turn of the sixteenth century, must have had a considerable social impact, encouraging greater physical self-awareness and helping to fuel the vanity of the
20 Renaissance self-portraitist.

Before the invention of flat glass in the late fifteenth century, mirrors were either made of polished stone, metal or convex glass. The latter were created from balls of blown glass filled with molten metal (typ-
25 ically lead, mercury or silver); and once cool, sections of the ball were cut to form individual pieces. The first-known representation of a self-portrait being painted with the use of a mirror is in Giovanni Boccaccio's *Concerning Famous Women* (Bibliotèque nationale de
30 France, *c*.1404): the Ancient Roman artist Iaia of Cyzicus (also known as Marcia) is shown working from a small convex glass mirror held in her hand. From the fifteenth century convex mirrors also frequently appeared in a range of narrative paintings to demon-
35 strate the skill of the artist. Even after the invention of flat mirrors, many artists continued to allude to convex mirrors in their work; indeed, it was to become an attribute of the artist, often shown hanging in the workshop of St Luke, the patron saint of artists.

40 In the early sixteenth century Parmigianino painted one of the most iconic images in the history of self-portraiture, *Self-Portrait in a Convex Mirror*. The painting itself was created on a specially prepared convex panel of wood designed to imitate the curve of
45 the convex glass. The foreground is dominated by the artist's right hand, exaggerated by the curve of the mirror, while a gold C-shaped curve on the far right probably indicates the frame of the actual mirror from which the artist was working.

50 The first flat glass mirrors were produced in Venice in the late fifteenth century thanks to two major technical developments: the discovery of a new type of glass known as 'cristallo', so clear it was compared to rock crystal, and an improved silvering technique
55 achieved through the combination of mercury and tin. By the early sixteenth century flat glass mirrors were available to artists across Europe, although they remained expensive. *A Man in Armour* after Girolamo Savoldo (*c*.1480–1548) shows the sitter, possibly the
60 artist himself, reflected in two flat glass mirrors. In Dutch paintings of the seventeenth century such mirrors often feature as part of a domestic interior, as in Vermeer's *Lady at the Virginals with a Gentleman*, which shows a half-length mirror on the wall above the
65 instrument.

Full-length mirrors did not come into use until *c*.1700, which may account for the limited number of full-length self-portraits prior to this date. It was not until the nineteenth century, with the discovery of a
70 cheaper technique for silvering glass, that mirrors of a standard thickness and quality were finally available to the mass market.

When working on a flat table or drawing board the artist could sit in front of the mirror, producing an
75 accordingly frontal pose. Use of an easel, however, meant repositioning the mirror so that it could be seen: Jean Alphonse Roehn (1799–1864), for example, shows a mirror propped on a chair to the artist's left, at right angles to her easel. In this painting the window beyond
80 the mirror has been partially covered so that the light falls onto the artist from the upper left; her painting hand is furthest from the mirror, neither casting a shadow on her canvas nor blocking her view of her body. This practical set-up resulted in the most common
85 and enduring pose in self-portraiture: the artist, in three-quarter length view, turns (usually) over the right shoulder fixing the viewer with a steady outward gaze.

Published by Royal Collection Trust / © Her Majesty Queen Elizabeth II 2016

GO ON TO THE NEXT PAGE.

3
3

1. The main purpose of the passage is to:

  A. provide an overview of famous self-portraits created using flat glass mirrors.
  B. explore trends in the art world that led to the development of self-portraiture.
  C. describe the relationship and significance of mirrors to the development of self-portraits.
  D. explain the history of and manufacturing methods involved in the development of mirrors.

2. The main point of the first paragraph (lines 1–20) is that:

  F. while mirrors were not wholly responsible for the development of self-portraiture, they likely played an important role.
  G. mirrors enabled people to see themselves, which likely had a great social impact.
  H. flat glass mirrors were invented in Venice around the year 1500.
  J. before flat mirrors were invented, convex mirrors were the norm and not particularly helpful to most self-portraitists.

3. Based on the passage, one similarity shared by *A Man in Armour* and *Lady at the Virginals with a Gentleman* is:

  A. the featuring of a convex mirror in the paintings.
  B. the inclusion of flat glass mirrors in the paintings.
  C. a focus on domestic interiors.
  D. the biographical backgrounds of the artists.

4. In the context of the passage, the author uses the phrase "fuel the vanity" (line 19) mainly to:

  F. question Renaissance artists' commitment to the genre of the self-portrait.
  G. suggest one reason why the availability of mirrors might have resulted in more self-portraits.
  H. dispute the idea that mirrors were a significant cause of vanity during the Renaissance.
  J. explain why the availability of mirrors affected some artists more than others.

5. Which of the following statements most effectively captures the process by which convex mirrors were produced?

  A. A ball of molten metal was formed, covered with glass, allowed to cool, and then cut into individual pieces.
  B. A ball of molten metal was formed, allowed to cool, cut into individual pieces, and then covered with glass.
  C. A ball of blown glass was formed, cut into individual pieces, filled with molten metal, and then allowed to cool.
  D. A ball of blown glass was formed, filled with molten metal, allowed to cool, and then cut into individual pieces.

6. Based on the passage, which of the following statements best summarizes the role of convex mirrors after flat mirrors came into use for artists?

  F. Although flat mirrors had obvious advantages for self-portraitists, many artists refused to use them, opting instead to use the older, more traditional convex mirrors.
  G. Although the convex mirror became a less popular tool for artists after flat mirrors became available, it nonetheless remained a well-known symbol of the artist.
  H. Some artists who began using flat mirrors chose to return to using convex mirrors for particular types of works, especially narrative paintings.
  J. Once convex mirrors were used less often than flat mirrors for self-portraits, the convex mirror became a symbol of outdated, unfashionable artistic practices.

7. According to the passage, one development that allowed for the invention of flat mirrors was a new kind of glass that was particularly:

  A. hard.
  B. sturdy.
  C. lightweight.
  D. clear.

8. According to the passage, mirrors became widely available in the nineteenth century primarily because of:

  F. the discovery of a new type of glass.
  G. the development of mercury and tin as silvering agents.
  H. a more economical silvering technique.
  J. consumers finally expressing a need for mirrors.

9. As it is used in line 87, the word *fixing* most nearly means:

  A. focusing on.
  B. adhering to.
  C. stabilizing.
  D. correcting.

GO ON TO THE NEXT PAGE.

3   3

Passage II

LITERARY NARRATIVE: Passage A is adapted from the short story "All the Flowers in the Air" by Aarti Monteiro (©2021 by Kweli Journal, Inc.). Passage B is adapted from the novel *Central Places* by Delia Cai (©2023 by Delia Cai).

Passage A by Aarti Monteiro

With one more day in Bombay, Rani decided to visit her old neighborhood. She followed the route to the train station Siya had laid out and bought a ticket. She snaked her way through the crowded platform and
5 stopped at a group of women. The long train staggered into view and the crowd pushed to the edge of the platform. Rani felt her heart pulse, anxious about being left behind. Before the train stopped completely, the women hoisted themselves up and pushed Rani along with
10 them.

The train didn't have doors so she gripped the sticky railing as tightly as she could. Warm air blew through the car as it crept forward. She watched the homes and trees as they passed. She'd always found
15 comfort in the anonymity of cities, how no one noticed you nor cared whether or not you belonged. In this way Bombay reminded her of New York—it wouldn't welcome you but it didn't mind that you were there.

Rani had barely seen the Lower Parel sign before
20 the current of people pushed her off. She stepped into a narrow vegetable market beneath the tracks. She knew she looked like a tourist but snapped photos anyway: a pile of drying chilies, plump green peppers, flowers strung together. The sellers called after her but she
25 couldn't understand what they said and kept walking.

She glanced at her phone to see the directions to the building. She walked up a hill, each curve a current moving her closer to her home until she finally stopped at her old street corner. A high-rise stood in place of the
30 small building where they'd lived. Scaffolding blew in the hot wind and the gate was covered in dust. Rani could feel something tangle inside her like weeds. She used to play foursquare in the parking lot with the neighborhood kids, walk to the small corner shop with
35 her brother—in matching blue and white school uniforms—to buy candy. She waited, as if the building would turn back into the home she remembered if she was just there long enough. She took a photograph of the grey scaffolding against the bright sky. A passerby
40 looked at where her camera pointed and mumbled something Rani couldn't understand.

She quickly moved the camera back into her bag, the sun beating down on her. When she was a child, she belonged to the city in a way she never had to think
45 about. The disappointment of returning home is the burden of anyone who leaves.

Passage B by Delia Cai

The narrator has just arrived with her fiancé, Ben, to visit her parents, and they've stopped at a grocery store on the way home.

Inside the H Mart, the instant confrontation with ninety thousand square feet of food laid out under a battery of flashing screens and fluorescent bulbs and
50 plastic holly makes me want to stop and massage my temples a little. Ben snaps a few pictures. My dad observes Ben with a bemused expression. "He's very good," my dad remarks to me, as if he can tell just by the way that Ben glides through the produce aisle, even
55 though I am sure that Ben is the first photographer, and journalist, and photojournalist, that my dad has ever met in his entire life. I take the shopping cart from my dad and follow him around as he gradually loses interest in watching Ben and then revs into grocery mode,
60 picking out crates of Asian pears and fat persimmons and twelve whole cartons of the soft tofu on sale for ninety-nine cents each. Ben takes a few pictures of a bin overflowing with bok choy before putting his camera away, which I'm relieved about.

65 "It's a lot," I apologize as my dad bobs ahead of us in the produce aisles. I think about what else I should preemptively say that I'm sorry for, amid the strangeness of trailing after my dad in this random Chicago suburb H Mart, but Ben squeezes my hand and tells me
70 to stop.

"You're *so* stressed out." He chuckles, and ordinarily this would be all it takes to make me roll my eyes and nod along, but I'm watching my dad closely so we don't lose him in the soy sauce aisle. "Breathe," Ben
75 reminds me. "Everything is going great, okay?"

He takes the cart from me and gestures for me to climb onto the end. I want to humor him, so I do, and he steers the cart past rows of Spam and cellophane noodles, his eyes softening with satisfaction as I try to
80 tell him to slow down but start laughing instead. Maybe this *was* a good idea, bringing my chronically starry-eyed fiancé home. If anyone could handle this trip, it was going to be Ben, Mr. Up for Whatever, and as long as I had him with me, that made me the soon-to-be
85 Mrs. Up for Whatever. And that meant I was truly coming back to this place as a different person than the one who left. How stupid it was to worry about Ben on this trip when being slightly out of place, I realize, has always been his natural element.

GO ON TO THE NEXT PAGE.

3   **3**

10. It can reasonably be inferred that the author of Passage A uses the metaphors "current of people" (line 20) and "each curve a current" (line 27) primarily to:

    F. suggest that Rani is to some degree being compelled onward by external forces.

    G. emphasize the number of people in the crowds traveling alongside Rani.

    H. indicate that Rani is trying to remind herself to stay present and aware in the moment.

    J. underscore that the thought of returning home is deeply exciting to Rani.

11. As it is used in Passage A, the phrase "laid out" (line 3) most nearly means:

    A. outlined.

    B. invented.

    C. projected.

    D. interpreted.

12. In Passage B, compared to the narrator, the narrator's father is characterized as being more focused on:

    F. chatting about the narrator's family.

    G. selecting various grocery items to buy.

    H. observing Ben's interactions with store patrons.

    J. helping Ben learn how to pick out the best produce.

13. In Passage B, the narrator's thoughts in response to her father's remark about Ben's photography most nearly suggest that the narrator is:

    A. skeptical that her father has any true understanding of photojournalism.

    B. overjoyed that her father already seems to value Ben's professional skills.

    C. proud of being the one to introduce her father to the world of photojournalism.

    D. bewildered that her father doesn't ask Ben any questions about photography.

14. As it is used in Passage B, the phrase "chronically starry-eyed" (lines 81–82) most nearly means that Ben:

    F. can often dazzle people with his charm.

    G. is regularly found daydreaming instead of working.

    H. has a consistently optimistic outlook on life.

    J. is frequently perceived by others as aloof and shy.

15. The passages are structurally similar in that both mainly:

    A. relate events that take place within a single day.

    B. recount characters' feelings and thoughts about moments from their past.

    C. describe a particular event and its long-term effects.

    D. alternate between relating characters' memories of the past and events occurring in the present.

16. Which of the following statements best captures a difference in the way the passages explore the themes of home and belonging?

    F. Passage A focuses on how Rani regrets leaving home; Passage B discusses the narrator's new-found desire to return home.

    G. Passage A considers how the place that was once home for Rani has changed; Passage B discusses how the narrator realizes that she herself is different.

    H. Passage A examines the lasting impact on Rani of leaving home as a child; Passage B considers the impact that returning home has on the narrator's relationship with her parents.

    J. Passage A focuses on how Rani feels that the people she once knew are different; Passage B examines how the narrator's hometown has changed.

17. It can most reasonably be inferred from the passages that compared to the narrator of Passage B, Rani in Passage A would be more likely to describe her experience of visiting her former home as:

    A. amusing.

    B. pleasant.

    C. stimulating.

    D. disappointing.

18. Which of the following statements best describes how the tone of the last paragraph of Passage A (lines 42–46) compares to the tone of the last paragraph of Passage B (lines 76–89)?

    F. The tones are similar in that both reflect the contentment the characters feel with their circumstances.

    G. The tones are similar in that both reflect the hesitancy and indecision the characters feel about what to do next.

    H. The tones are different in that Passage A ends with a tone of wistfulness, whereas Passage B ends on a hopeful note.

    J. The tones are different in that Passage A ends with a tone of acceptance, whereas Passage B ends on a defiant note.

GO ON TO THE NEXT PAGE.

3 · 3

Passage III

INFORMATIONAL: This passage is adapted from the article "Look Up and See!" by Robert O. Paxton.

New York is a particularly "birdy" city (to use the birder's term). Someone who makes a serious effort to find birds in the city almost every day—there are such people—can find upward of three hundred species in
5 one year without ever leaving the city limits, using only public transportation. The cumulative bird list of Central Park alone includes over 280 species, some of which, to be sure, appear only occasionally. Like Boston or San Francisco, New York has rich bird life
10 because it has extensive parkland, because it is close to the sea (which adds marsh and beach to the mix of habitats), and because the city now protects certain places where birds congregate, like tern colonies and heronries, even at some inconvenience to humans.

15 Bird life is constantly changing in New York City. We may assume that the marshy island that the first European settlers encountered in the early seventeenth century thronged with ducks, geese, herons, and other conspicuous water birds that were soon consumed or
20 chased off as the city arose. But change did not stop when the city became fully built. New York City's bird life has been altered in interesting ways in just the past fifty years.

More different kinds of birds nest in New York
25 City now than did fifty years ago, although those that just pass through may not be as numerous. The breeding bird population of New York City does not simply replicate that of the nearby countryside, however. Some birds survive very well in the city, while others stay
30 away. Ecologists classify natural species according to their response to urban environments: as exploiters, adapters, or avoiders.

Exploiters positively thrive in the thick of the city. Untroubled by human presence, they roost on our roofs,
35 nest in our eaves, and eat our trash. The exploiting birds that are most conspicuous in New York City—European starlings, house sparrows, rock pigeons (the proper name of the common street pigeon), mallard ducks, and Canada geese—are also abundant in many
40 other cities across the world. Quick to colonize any denatured landscape, they are "tramps easily dispersing across our world," writes the ecologist John Marzluff. "If they were plants, we could call them weeds." They point toward a homogenized future in which one will
45 see the same tough, streetwise birds in any city in the world.

All of these species, along with mute swans, were spread by human introduction. Two more recent introductions may produce new exploiters. A bird importer
50 about to be charged with illegal trade in native birds released some house finches, a small, wine-colored bird native to California, at Idlewild Airport (now JFK) in 1940. They bred, flourished, and are now ubiquitous,

not only in New York City but throughout eastern
55 North America. House finch numbers have recently been reduced by an eye disease, reminding us that epidemics are one of the risks faced by exploiters.

Parrots are another new exploiter group. Escaped or released pet parrots are common in cities worldwide,
60 but only monk parakeets, native to temperate Argentina and capable of surviving a northern winter, have established permanent populations in New York City. These bright green parrots with gray monks' hoods have become a nuisance to Con Edison by choosing trans-
65 formers for their enormous collective nests.

Fortunately for New Yorkers who enjoy variety in bird life, a number of adapter species, to continue with the ecologists' categories, have recently moved to the city. Even some birds usually wary of humans have
70 learned that life is possible, even advantageous, here. In 1992, a red-tailed hawk, soon to be famous as "Pale Male," established his bulky stick nest on the façade of an apartment building on Fifth Avenue. He seems to have been the first of his species to set up housekeeping
75 on a building instead of a cliff or tree. By 2007, thirty-two pairs of red-tailed hawks were established in the five boroughs.

From The New York Review of Books Copyright © 2016 by Robert O. Paxton

Bird species present in New York State* as of 2021

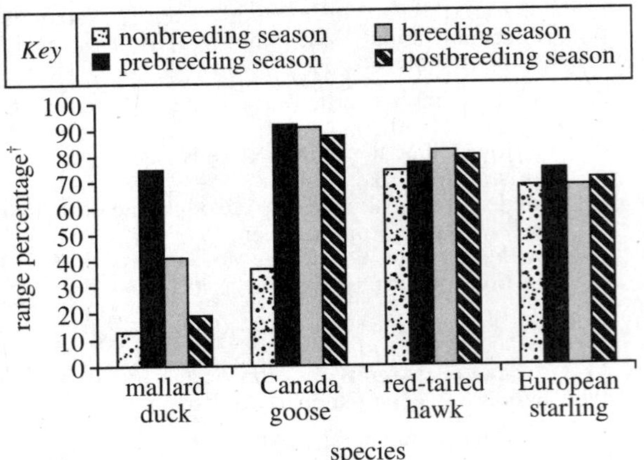

*New York state includes New York City.

†Range percentage refers to the percentage of the state in which a bird species is present.

Graphic adapted from "eBird Status and Trends, Data Version" by Daniel Fink et al. (©2022 by Cornell Lab of Ornithology).

GO ON TO THE NEXT PAGE.

3 — **3**

19. The main function of the first paragraph (lines 1–14) is to:

A. introduce New York City's Central Park and describe the types of birds that flock there.
B. persuade people who are interested in birds to come visit New York City and to explain why birders would like it there.
C. establish that New York City has rich birdlife and explain the reasons for it.
D. describe the mix of habitats present in New York City and indicate the number of bird species found in each.

20. The passage indicates that humans introduced which of the following species of birds to New York City?

F. The mute swan and the red-tailed hawk
G. The house finch and the red-tailed hawk
H. The rock pigeon and the monk parakeet
J. The rock pigeon and the mourning dove

21. What is the main point of the second paragraph (lines 15–23)?

A. New York City's birdlife has continued to change even though the city has long been established.
B. Water birds such as ducks, geese, and herons relocated as New York City expanded.
C. The same bird species that bred in New York City in the seventeenth century still breed in the city today.
D. The marshy island settled by Europeans in the seventeenth century is still home to most of New York City's water birds.

22. In the passage, the word *thronged* (line 18) most nearly emphasizes the:

F. city's overcrowded neighborhoods.
G. birds' aggressive behavior toward settlers.
H. settlers' frantic building attempts.
J. area's multitude of birds.

23. In the context of the passage, the statement "They roost on our roofs, nest in our eaves, and eat our trash" (lines 34–35) most nearly supports which of the following claims?

A. Some birds survive very well in the city.
B. Some bird species pass through the city but do not nest there.
C. The breeding bird population in the city is not the same as that in the countryside.
D. Many bird species abundant in New York City are also abundant in other large cities.

24. In the context of the passage, the statement in lines 75–77 can best be described as a:

F. fact used to cite a similarity between the red-tailed hawk and the monk parakeet populations in New York City.
G. fact used to demonstrate that red-tailed hawks succeeded in establishing themselves in New York City.
H. reasoned judgment that helps explain how red-tailed hawks have become the most prevalent bird species in New York City.
J. reasoned judgment that contradicts the author's earlier claim about when red-tailed hawks established themselves in New York City.

25. As it relates to the passage, the graph primarily functions to:

A. show a comparison of bird species present in New York City and those present throughout New York State.
B. compare bird species present in New York City to those present in Boston and San Francisco.
C. provide information about bird species in New York City's Central Park throughout different seasons.
D. elaborate on the discussion of bird species in New York City by depicting seasonal changes in their presence throughout New York State.

26. Based on the graph, which of the following statements is true for each species represented?

F. The range percentages during the prebreeding and breeding seasons are nearly equal.
G. The range percentage during the postbreeding season is lower than that during the prebreeding season.
H. The range percentage during the postbreeding season is higher than that during the nonbreeding season.
J. The range percentages during the prebreeding and breeding seasons are higher than those during the nonbreeding and postbreeding seasons.

27. Based on the graph, which two species are most similar in terms of range percentage across all seasons?

A. The Canada goose and the European starling
B. The Canada goose and the red-tailed hawk
C. The red-tailed hawk and the mallard duck
D. The red-tailed hawk and the European starling

GO ON TO THE NEXT PAGE.

3

Passage IV

INFORMATIONAL: This passage is from the article "Life Springs" by Martin J. Van Kranendonk, David Deamer, and Tara Djokic (©2017 by Scientific American).

The researchers, who are also the authors of the passage, are hiking back to their truck after spending the day at the Dresser Formation.

Heading up the side of the creek embankment, Djokic suddenly stumbles back downhill. Has she lost her balance? To stop her from falling, Van Kranendonk reaches out to stop her and pushes her back uphill,
5 which prompts a screech, something unintelligible, and finally a sputtered cry: "Sp- ... p- ... p- ... pppider!" Djokic has not stumbled at all. She is in flight mode, in fear for her life as she tries to swat away the thick spider web enveloping her. Spiders have a deservedly
10 bad reputation in Australia. In the dark, it is not a good idea to assume that you have found the odd benign species.

The reason we are feeling our way around the Pilbara at night is because we had spent the day enthralled
15 by a new discovery Djokic had made in 3.48-billion-year-old sedimentary rocks called the Dresser Formation. Some of the rocks are wrinkled orange and white layers, called geyserite, which were created by a volcanic geyser on Earth's surface. They revealed bubbles
20 formed when gas was trapped in a sticky film, most likely produced by a thin layer of bacterialike microorganisms. The surface rocks and indications of biofilms support a new idea about one of the oldest mysteries on the planet: how and where life got started. The evidence
25 pointed to volcanic hot springs and pools, on land, about 3.5 billion years ago.

This is a far different picture of life's origins from the one scientists have been sketching since 1977. That was the year the research submarine *Alvin* discovered
30 hydrothermal vents at the bottom of the Pacific Ocean pumping out minerals containing iron and sulfur and gases such as methane and hydrogen sulfide, surrounded by primitive bacteria and large worms. It was a thriving ecosystem. Biologists have since theorized that
35 such vents, protected from the cataclysms wracking Earth's surface about four billion years ago, could have provided the energy, nutrients and a safe haven for life to begin. But the theory has problems. The big one is that the ocean has a lot of water, and in it the needed
40 molecules might spread out too quickly to interact and form cell membranes and primitive metabolisms.

Now we and others believe land pools that repeatedly dry out and then get wet again could be much better places. The pools have heat to catalyze reactions,
45 dry spells in which complex molecules called polymers can be formed from simpler units, wet spells that float these polymers around, and further drying periods that maroon them in tiny cavities where they can interact and even become concentrated in compartments of fatty
50 acids—the prototypes of cell membranes.

What Djokic found was strong geologic evidence that the Dresser, now a dry, hot and barren outback environment, had once been like the steaming pools and erupting geysers of Yellowstone National Park in the
55 U.S., an active geothermal field. And everywhere in the Dresser there are fossilized signs of life intimately associated with the old hot spring system. Although the Dresser was not the actual site where the most primitive life began half a billion years earlier, it was showing us
60 that hydrothermal environments on land were present very early in Earth's history. Charles Darwin had suggested, back in 1871, that microbial life originated in "some warm little pond." A number of scientists from different fields now think that the author of *On the
65 Origin of Species* had intuitively hit on something important. And the implications of these ideas stretch beyond our own planet: in our search for alien life elsewhere in the solar system, a land-based theory about origins would guide us to different places and planets
70 than would an ocean-based theory.

Ten years before Djokic's run-in with the spider web, another of us (Deamer) had shown that volcanic pools could foster the assembly of compartments made of membranes, essential boundaries of all cellular life.

28. The primary purpose of the passage is to:

   F. relate the story of how researchers studying the Dresser Formation found indications of biofilms in geyserite.

   G. explain how evidence from the Dresser Formation supports a new idea about where life on Earth began.

   H. discuss the strengths and weaknesses of theories about where life on Earth began.

   J. provide a chronology of the prevailing beliefs about when and where life on Earth began.

29. Which of the following events mentioned in the passage occurred **last** chronologically?

   A. Van Kranendonk reached out to push Djokic back uphill.

   B. Djokic discovered indications of biofilms in the Dresser Formation.

   C. Djokic encountered the spiderweb.

   D. The researchers began hiking through the Pilbara at night.

GO ON TO THE NEXT PAGE.

3   **3**

30. Based on lines 13–26 and 71–74, what can reasonably be inferred about the relationship between Djokic's and Deamer's discoveries?

   F. Djokic found geologic evidence to support what Deamer had shown was possible.
   G. Deamer found the same geologic evidence in the Dresser a decade earlier than Djokic did.
   H. Deamer's research later proved that Djokic had found evidence of early life on Earth.
   J. Djokic's discovery undermined Deamer's research from ten years earlier.

31. Which of the following details from the passage most directly challenges the claim that life originated in the ocean?

   A. Primitive bacteria weren't found on ocean-based hydrothermal vents until 1977.
   B. In vast amounts of water, molecules may spread out too quickly to interact.
   C. Cataclysms wracked the Earth about four billion years ago.
   D. Hydrothermal vents emit gases such as hydrogen sulfide.

32. Which of the following statements best summarizes the passage's description of polymers in land pools?

   F. Polymers form during a heated dry spell, and then they float around and interact with each other during wet spells.
   G. Polymers form and interact in the pools during wet spells, then float around and become fatty acids during dry spells.
   H. Polymers form during a dry spell, float around during a wet spell, and interact with each other when the pools dry out again.
   J. Polymers repeatedly dry out and get wet again, which allows them to interact with each other.

33. As it is used in line 11, the word *odd* most nearly means:

   A. unorthodox.
   B. eccentric.
   C. miscellaneous.
   D. unlikely.

34. In the passage, what evidence mentioned by the authors best supports the claim "it was a thriving ecosystem" (lines 33–34)?

   F. Biologists' theories about hydrothermal vents after the 1977 *Alvin* discovery
   G. The minerals, gases, and organisms that the *Alvin* detected around hydrothermal vents
   H. The similarities between the ecosystems of hydrothermal vents and volcanic pools
   J. How primitive bacteria use iron and sulfur to form cell membranes

35. The passage authors include the details about Yellowstone National Park primarily to:

   A. provide an example of where fossilized signs of life have been found.
   B. acknowledge where life on Earth likely began.
   C. portray what the Dresser once looked like.
   D. emphasize how similar the Dresser's current climate is to Yellowstone's.

36. According to the passage, establishing a land-based theory for life's origins will likely influence future research pertaining to:

   F. prototypes of cell membranes.
   G. sedimentary rocks in the Pilbara.
   H. how hydrothermal vents function.
   J. the search for alien life.

Your First Practice Test

END OF TEST 3

STOP! DO NOT TURN THE PAGE UNTIL TOLD TO DO SO.

DO NOT RETURN TO A PREVIOUS TEST.

4 ○ ○ ○ ○ ○ ○ ○ ○ ○ 4

SCIENCE TEST

40 Minutes — 40 Questions

DIRECTIONS: There are several passages in this test. Each passage is followed by several questions. After reading a passage, choose the best answer to each question and fill in the corresponding oval on your answer document. You may refer to the passages as often as necessary.

You are **not** permitted to use a calculator on this test.

Passage I

When the base of a beaker is tapped, sound waves are produced. A scientist performed 2 experiments to study the frequency of the sound waves produced in a beaker containing a solution of water and salt.

Experiment 1

A scientist clamped a 1,000 mL beaker to a stand and placed a microphone attached to a signal analyzer near the base of the stand. Then, the scientist poured water at a temperature of 85°C into the beaker until the height of the water was 10 cm. Next, the scientist added 10 g of salt and stirred the solution with a lab spoon until the salt completely dissolved before beginning to tap the base of the beaker. See Figure 1.

Figure 1

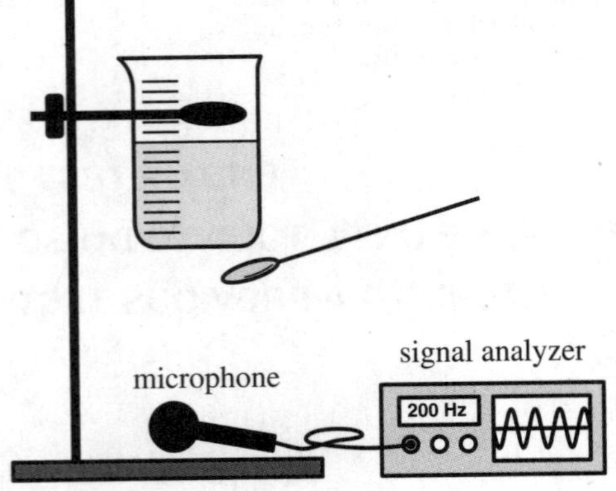

The scientist tapped the base of the beaker for 2 minutes at a constant rate. Immediately following the first tap (at 0 s), and every 10 s thereafter, the frequency, in hertz (Hz), displayed by the signal analyzer was recorded. The results are shown in Figure 2.

Figure 2

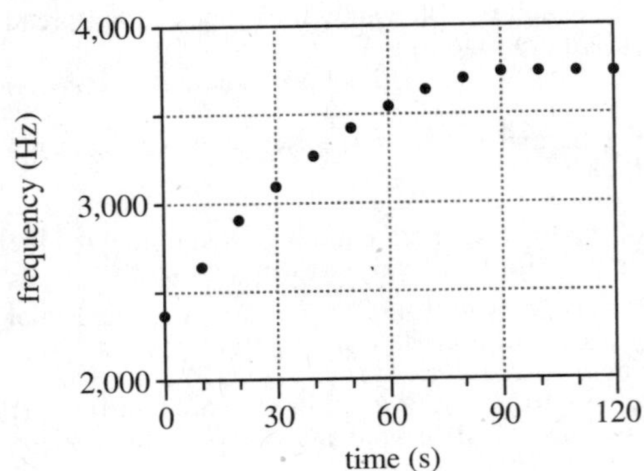

Experiment 2

The scientist repeated the procedures of Experiment 1 three times except that the scientist varied the height of the water. Table 1 shows, for each height, the frequency recorded at each of 4 times.

Table 1				
Height of water (cm)	Frequency (Hz) at time:			
	0 s	30 s	60 s	90 s
12	1,978	2,580	2,918	3,131
14	1,692	2,209	2,503	2,680
16	1,480	1,938	2,188	2,344

GO ON TO THE NEXT PAGE.

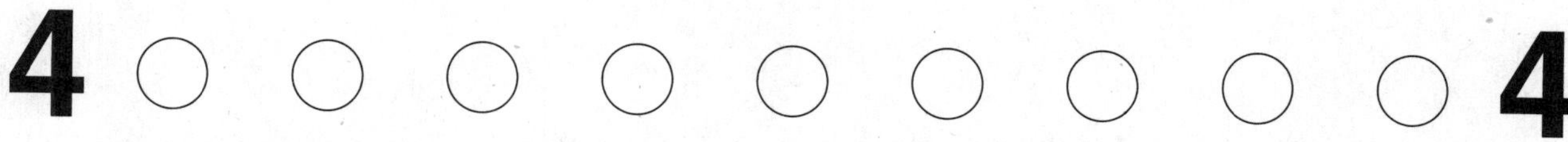

4

1. The speed of sound is directly proportional to the frequency of the sound wave. Based on the results of Experiment 1, how did the speed of sound vary, if at all, between 0 s and 120 s? The speed of sound:

   A. increased and then decreased.
   B. increased and then remained constant.
   C. decreased and then remained constant.
   D. did not vary.

2. The musical note A6 has a frequency of 1,760 Hz. How many of the frequencies listed in Table 1 are higher than the note A6?

   F. 5
   G. 6
   H. 10
   J. 12

3. Based on the results of Experiments 1 and 2, if the procedures of Experiment 1 had been repeated and the frequency of the sound wave at 60 s had been 2,300 Hz, the height of water in the beaker would most likely have been:

   A. less than 10 cm.
   B. between 12 cm and 14 cm.
   C. between 14 cm and 16 cm.
   D. greater than 16 cm.

4. In Experiment 1, during which of the following time intervals was the average rate of change in frequency least?

   F. From 0 s to 10 s
   G. From 20 s to 30 s
   H. From 40 s to 50 s
   J. From 60 s to 70 s

5. In which of the experiments, if either, did the scientist vary the rate of tapping the base of the beaker?

   A. Experiment 1 only
   B. Experiment 2 only
   C. Both Experiment 1 and Experiment 2
   D. Neither Experiment 1 nor Experiment 2

6. Based on the procedures of Experiment 1 and Experiment 2, what was the height of the water when the water had the least concentration of salt?

   F. 10 cm
   G. 12 cm
   H. 14 cm
   J. 16 cm

GO ON TO THE NEXT PAGE.

4 ◯ ◯ ◯ ◯ ◯ ◯ ◯ ◯ 4

Passage II

Lightning is an electrical discharge during which 2 oppositely charged regions, each either in the atmosphere or on the ground, temporarily equalize themselves, causing an instantaneous release of energy. Over 1 summer, observations of lightning discharges were collected during 10 thunderstorms (Storms 1–10). See Table 1.

	Table 1		
Storm	Storm duration (min)	Total number of discharges	Maximum flash rate (discharges/min)
1	35	16	1
2	130	673	11
3	130	71	1
4	40	30	2
5	85	49	1
6	75	515	20
7	130	673	10
8	111	355	9
9	84	335	8
10	265	1,212	16

Figure 1 shows the distribution of discharges (number of discharges per 5 min) over the duration of Storm 6.

Figure 1

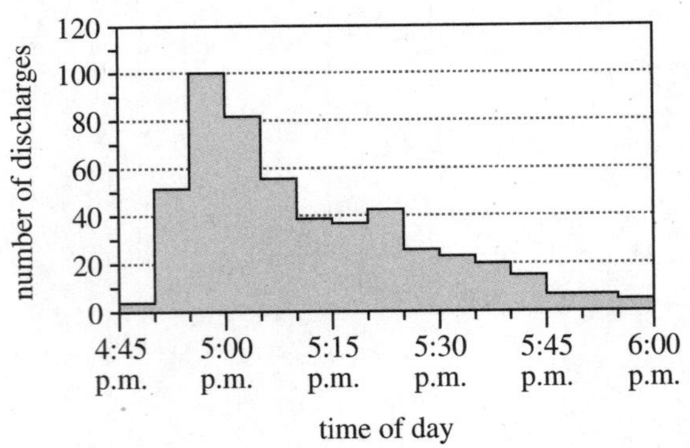

During Storm 6, the negative charge (in coulombs, C) on the ground prior to each of 70 lightning discharges was measured. Figure 2 shows, for each 5 C range, the number of discharges associated with a charge in that range.

Figure 2

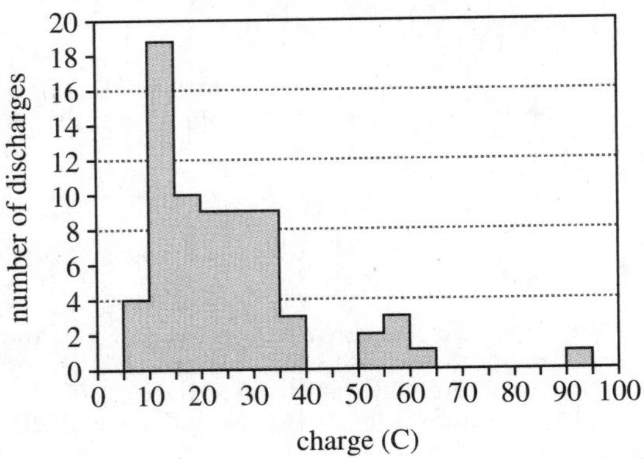

Table and figures adapted from the article "Electrostatic Field Changes Produced by Florida Lightning" by Elizabeth A. Jacobson and E. Philip Krider. (©1976 by American Meteorological Society).

7. Based on Figure 1, the greatest number of lightning discharges occurred during which time period, and approximately how many lightning discharges were observed during that time period?

   A. Time period: 4:55 p.m. to 5:00 p.m.
      Number of discharges: 85

   B. Time period: 4:55 p.m. to 5:00 p.m.
      Number of discharges: 100

   C. Time period: 5:00 p.m. to 5:05 p.m.
      Number of discharges: 85

   D. Time period: 5:00 p.m. to 5:05 p.m.
      Number of discharges: 100

8. Which of the following lists Storm 2, Storm 4, Storm 6, and Storm 8 in order from the storm with the highest maximum flash rate to the storm with the lowest maximum flash rate?

   F. Storm 4, Storm 2, Storm 8, Storm 6
   G. Storm 4, Storm 8, Storm 2, Storm 6
   H. Storm 6, Storm 2, Storm 8, Storm 4
   J. Storm 6, Storm 8, Storm 2, Storm 4

GO ON TO THE NEXT PAGE.

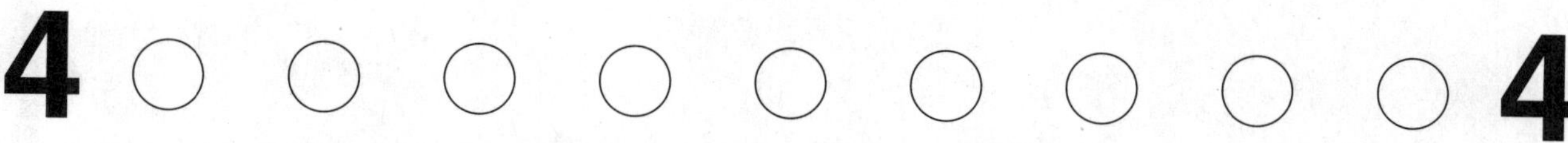

4 ○ ○ ○ ○ ○ ○ ○ ○ ○ **4**

9. For Storm 7, what was the approximate average number of discharges per minute (average flash rate), and what was the approximate difference between the maximum flash rate and the average flash rate?

A. Average flash rate: 3
Difference: 5

B. Average flash rate: 3
Difference: 15

C. Average flash rate: 5
Difference: 5

D. Average flash rate: 5
Difference: 15

10. Based on Figure 2, exactly 9 lightning discharges were detected for which range(s) of charge?

F. 15–20 C only
G. 15–20 C and 25–30 C only
H. 20–25 C and 30–35 C only
J. 20–25 C, 25–30 C, and 30–35 C only

11. Based on Figure 1, what was the approximate average flash rate per minute for the 5 min time period starting at 5:25 p.m.?

A. 5 discharges/min
B. 9 discharges/min
C. 11 discharges/min
D. 16 discharges/min

12. Based on Table 1 and the description of Figure 2, how many lightning discharges from Storm 6 are **not** represented in Figure 2?

F. 70
G. 75
H. 445
J. 515

GO ON TO THE NEXT PAGE.

4 ◯ ◯ ◯ ◯ ◯ ◯ ◯ ◯ ◯ 4

Passage III

The octane number of a fuel is a measure of how smoothly the fuel burns in a gasoline engine. Lower octane fuels knock (explode) when burned, which lowers fuel efficiency and can cause engine damage. Heptane knocks considerably when burned and is given an octane number of 0. Isooctane knocks very little and is given an octane number of 100.

Different proportions of heptane and isooctane were mixed to obtain mixtures with octane numbers between 0 and 100 (see Table 1).

Table 1

Volume of heptane (mL)	Volume of isooctane (mL)	Octane number
0	100	100
10	90	90
25	75	75
50	50	50
90	10	10
100	0	0

Experiment 1

A sample of each fuel mixture listed in Table 1 was burned in a test engine at an engine speed of 600 revolutions per minute (rpm). The number of knocks per minute was determined for each mixture. This was done so that an octane number could be assigned to any fuel by measuring its knock rate.

Experiment 2

Adding tetraethyllead (TEL) to a fuel changes its octane number. Different amounts of TEL were added to 1,000 mL samples of isooctane. Each fuel mixture was tested under the same conditions used in Experiment 1, and the measured knock rate was used to determine the octane number (see Figure 1).

Figure 1

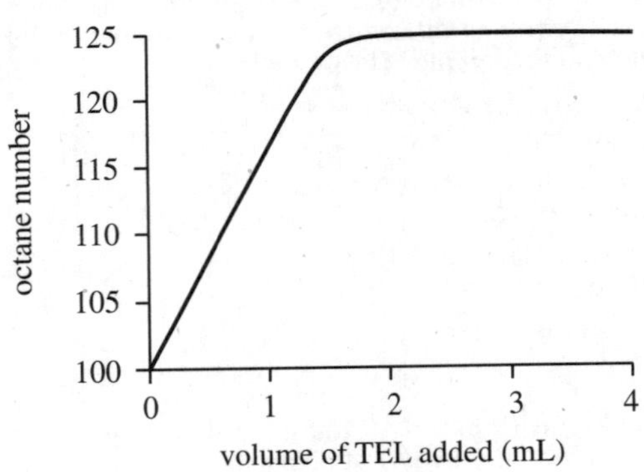

Experiment 3

The engine octane requirement (EOR) is the minimum octane number of a fuel required for an engine to operate without becoming damaged. Fuels A and B were burned separately in an engine at different speeds. Table 2 shows the octane number determined for each fuel at each engine speed and the known EOR of the engine at each speed.

Table 2

Engine speed (rpm)	EOR	Octane number in engine of:	
		Fuel A	Fuel B
1,500	97.4	98.4	96.7
2,000	95.3	96.6	96.1
2,500	93.5	95.0	95.4
3,000	91.9	92.3	93.8
3,500	90.6	90.9	92.5

13. Based on Experiment 3, as engine speed increases, the minimum octane number of fuel required for an engine to operate without becoming damaged:

   A. increases only.
   B. decreases only.
   C. increases and then decreases.
   D. decreases and then increases.

GO ON TO THE NEXT PAGE.

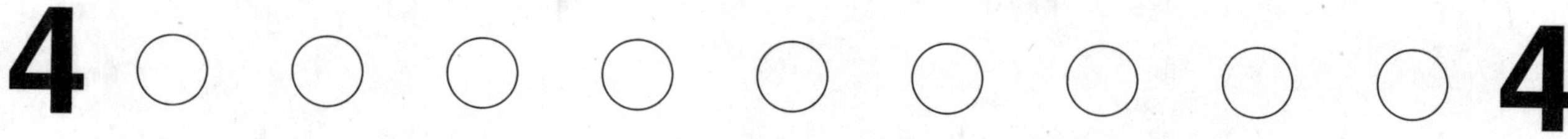

4 ○ ○ ○ ○ ○ ○ ○ ○ **4**

14. Suppose a trial had been performed in Experiment 3 at an engine speed of 2,200 rpm. At this engine speed, which of the following sets of octane numbers would most likely have been determined for Fuel A and Fuel B?

F. Fuel A: 95.0
Fuel B: 95.4

G. Fuel A: 96.1
Fuel B: 95.8

H. Fuel A: 96.6
Fuel B: 96.1

J. Fuel A: 97.6
Fuel B: 96.4

15. Which of the following expressions is equal to the octane number of each fuel mixture listed in Table 1?

A. $\dfrac{\text{volume of isooctane}}{\text{volume of heptane}} \times 100$

B. $\dfrac{\text{volume of heptane}}{\text{volume of isooctane}} \times 100$

C. $\dfrac{\text{volume of isooctane}}{(\text{volume of heptane} + \text{volume of isooctane})} \times 100$

D. $\dfrac{\text{volume of heptane}}{(\text{volume of heptane} + \text{volume of isooctane})} \times 100$

16. Based on Table 1 and Experiment 2, if 3 mL of TEL were added to a mixture of 100 mL of heptane and 900 mL of isooctane, the octane number of the resulting fuel would most likely be:

F. less than 55.
G. between 55 and 90.
H. between 90 and 125.
J. greater than 125.

17. Which of the 2 fuels from Experiment 3 would be better to use in an engine that will run at all engine speeds between 1,500 rpm and 3,500 rpm?

A. Fuel A, because its octane number was lower than the EOR at each of the engine speeds tested.
B. Fuel A, because its octane number was higher than the EOR at each of the engine speeds tested.
C. Fuel B, because its octane number was lower than the EOR at each of the engine speeds tested.
D. Fuel B, because its octane number was higher than the EOR at each of the engine speeds tested.

18. Based on Table 1, if 2 mL of heptane were mixed with 8 mL of isooctane, the octane number of this mixture would be:

F. 2.
G. 8.
H. 20.
J. 80.

Your First Practice Test

GO ON TO THE NEXT PAGE.

4 ○ ○ ○ ○ ○ ○ ○ ○ ○ 4

Passage IV

Introduction

The pancreas is an organ in mammals that contains clusters of endocrine cells. Each cluster contains 3 cell types—alpha (α), beta (β), and delta (δ). Each cluster also releases 3 hormones (chemical messengers)—insulin, glucagon, and somatostatin. These 3 hormones are involved in the regulation of blood glucose (BG) concentration.

Figure 1 shows the relationship between the amount of each hormone released and the BG concentration in millimoles per liter (mmol/L).

Figure 1

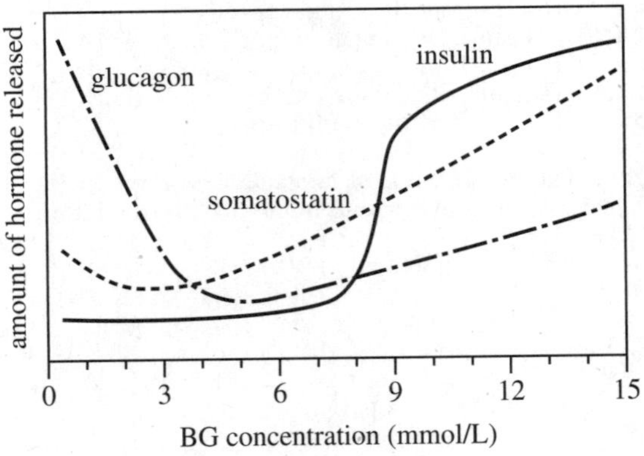

Four students discussed the release of each hormone, the BG set point (concentration range over which BG is at homeostasis), and the role of somatostatin.

Student 1

In the pancreas, α-cells release insulin, β-cells release glucagon, and δ-cells release somatostatin. The BG set point is 1–3 mmol/L. BG concentrations greater than 8 mmol/L are not recommended. The greatest amounts of insulin and glucagon are released at BG concentrations greater than the set point. Somatostatin inhibits the release of insulin and glucagon.

Student 2

In the pancreas, α-cells release glucagon, β-cells release insulin, and δ-cells release somatostatin. The BG set point is 4–6 mmol/L. BG concentrations less than 3 mmol/L and greater than 11 mmol/L are not recommended. The greatest amount of insulin is released at a BG concentration greater than the set point. The greatest amount of glucagon is released at a BG concentration less than the set point. Somatostatin inhibits the release of insulin and glucagon.

Student 3

Student 2 is correct except the BG set point is 7–9 mmol/L, and somatostatin promotes the release of insulin but does not affect the release of glucagon.

Student 4

In the pancreas, α-cells release glucagon and somatostatin, β-cells release insulin, and δ-cells release no hormone. The BG set point is 7–9 mmol/L. BG concentrations greater than 7 mmol/L are not recommended. The greatest amount of insulin is released at a BG concentration greater than the set point. The greatest amount of glucagon is released at a BG concentration less than the set point. Somatostatin inhibits the release of insulin only.

Figure adapted from the article "The Difference δ-Cells Make in Glucose Control" by Mark O. Huising et al. (©2018 by Int. Union Physiol. Sci./Am. Physiol. Soc).

19. Based on the Introduction, which of the following statements best describes the pancreas? The pancreas is:

A. a cell, the smallest functional unit of a living organism.

B. a cell, a group of tissues that perform a specific function.

C. an organ, the smallest functional unit of a living organism.

D. an organ, a group of tissues that perform a specific function.

GO ON TO THE NEXT PAGE.

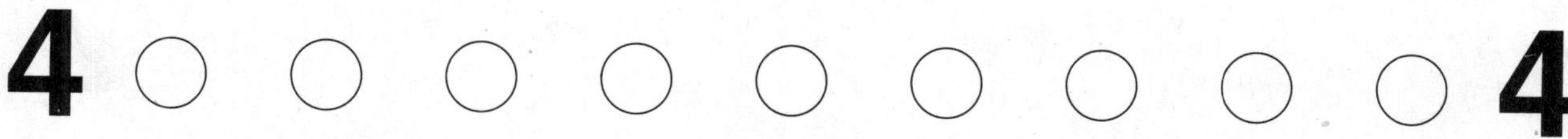

4 ◯ ◯ ◯ ◯ ◯ ◯ ◯ ◯ **4**

20. Based on the explanation given by Student 3, if the release of somatostatin increased, would the release of insulin most likely increase or decrease, and would the release of glucagon most likely decrease or stay approximately the same?

- **F.** Insulin: increase
  Glucagon: decrease
- **G.** Insulin: increase
  Glucagon: stay approximately the same
- **H.** Insulin: decrease
  Glucagon: decrease
- **J.** Insulin: decrease
  Glucagon: stay approximately the same

21. Which of Students 1, 2, and 3 would agree that a BG concentration of 2 mmol/L is not recommended?

- **A.** Student 2 only
- **B.** Students 1 and 3 only
- **C.** Students 2 and 3 only
- **D.** Students 1, 2, and 3

22. All 4 student explanations are consistent with which of the following statements about somatostatin? Somatostatin is:

- **F.** an endocrine cell that can regulate hormone release.
- **G.** an endocrine cell that cannot regulate hormone release.
- **H.** a chemical messenger that can regulate hormone release.
- **J.** a chemical messenger that cannot regulate hormone release.

23. In Figure 1, consider the BG concentration that results in the greatest amount of glucagon released. Are these data consistent with Student 1's explanation?

- **A.** Yes; Student 1 indicated that the greatest amount of glucagon is released when BG concentrations are within the set point.
- **B.** Yes; Student 1 indicated that the greatest amount of glucagon is released when BG concentrations are greater than the set point.
- **C.** No; Student 1 indicated that the greatest amount of glucagon is released when BG concentrations are within the set point.
- **D.** No; Student 1 indicated that the greatest amount of glucagon is released when BG concentrations are greater than the set point.

24. Is the explanation given by Student 4 consistent with the definition of the BG set point in the Introduction?

- **F.** No; Student 4 indicated that the BG set point was **not** recommended, but based on the Introduction, the BG set point results in optimal body functioning.
- **G.** No; Student 4 indicated that the BG set point was recommended, but based on the Introduction, the BG set point results in poor body functioning.
- **H.** Yes; Student 4 indicated that the BG set point was **not** recommended, and based on the Introduction, the BG set point results in poor body functioning.
- **J.** Yes; Student 4 indicated that the BG set point was recommended, and based on the Introduction, the BG set point results in optimal body functioning.

GO ON TO THE NEXT PAGE.

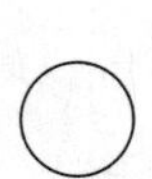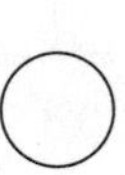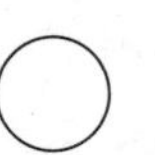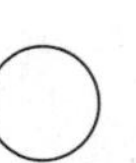

Passage V

Phenol is a toxic material often found in wastewater. Phenol reacts with hydrogen peroxide (H_2O_2) to give non-toxic products. Scientists performed 3 studies to examine the removal of phenol from wastewater with H_2O_2.

An aqueous phenol solution with a concentration of 10.0 mg of phenol per liter of solution was prepared for use in the studies. The pH of the solution was measured and found to be 6.6. In each trial of the studies, Steps 1–6 were performed.

1. A 200.0 mL volume of the phenol solution was placed in a clean flask.

2. The pH of the solution was adjusted to some particular value by addition of either concentrated sodium hydroxide (NaOH, a base) or concentrated hydrochloric acid (HCl).

3. A certain volume of 30% aqueous H_2O_2 was added to the flask.

4. The reaction was allowed to proceed for a specific amount of time at 25°C.

5. The concentration of phenol remaining was determined.

6. The percentage of phenol removed was calculated.

Study 1

Each of Trials 1–9 was conducted at a different pH, with 1.0 mL of H_2O_2 added to the phenol solution and the reaction allowed to proceed for 5.0 hr. See Figure 1.

Figure 1

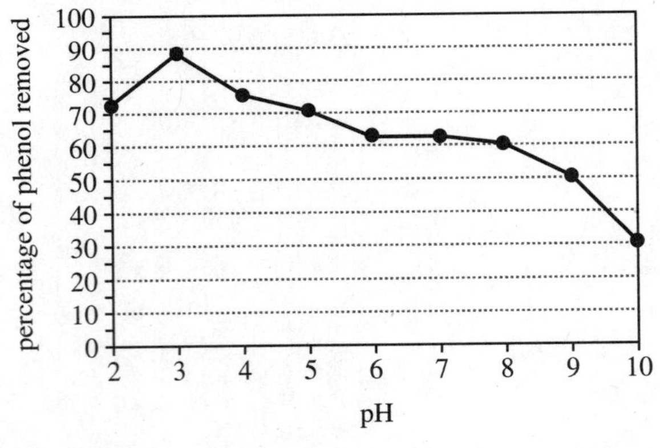

Study 2

Each of Trials 10–14 was conducted at pH = 7.0, with a different volume of H_2O_2 added to the phenol solution and the reaction allowed to proceed for 1.0 hr. See Figure 2.

Figure 2

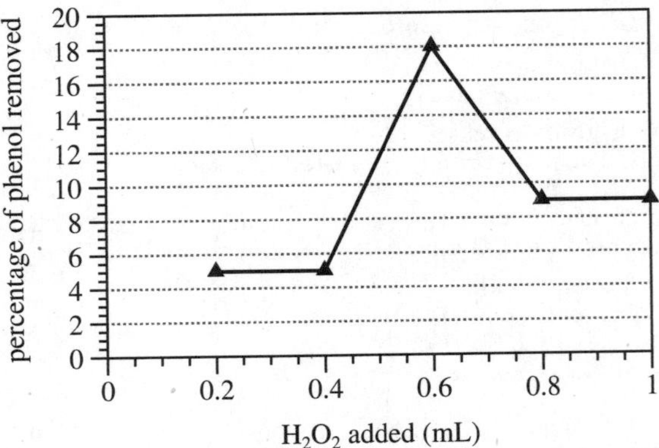

Study 3

Each of Trials 15–19 was conducted at pH = 7.0, with a different volume of H_2O_2 added to the phenol solution and the reaction allowed to proceed for 2.0 hr. See Figure 3.

Figure 3

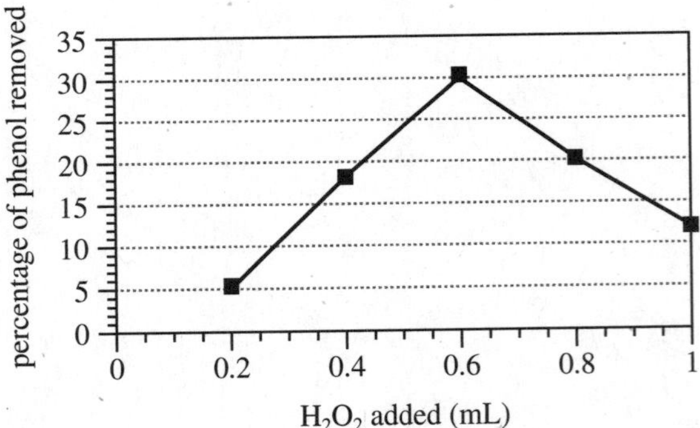

Figures adapted from the article "Study of Degradation of Phenol in Waste Water Sample via Advanced Oxidation Technology" by J. Wu et al. (©2015 by the authors through Atlantis Press).

GO ON TO THE NEXT PAGE.

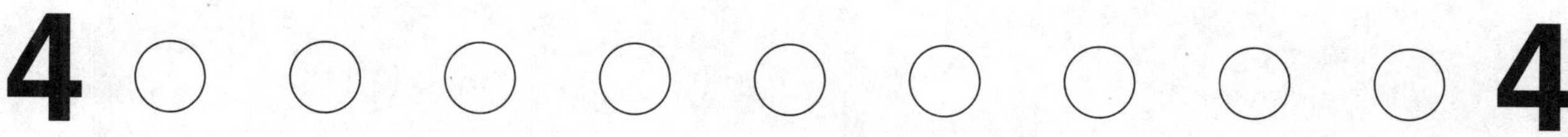

4

25. Suppose that in Study 3 a trial had been run in which 0.9 mL of H_2O_2 had been added. The percentage of phenol removed would most likely have been:

A. less than 5%.
B. between 5% and 12%.
C. between 12% and 20%.
D. greater than 20%.

26. The lowest percentage of phenol removed in Study 1 was approximately how many times as great as the lowest percentage of phenol removed in Study 3?

F. $\frac{1}{6}$

G. $\frac{1}{4}$

H. 4
J. 6

27. Less than 10% of the phenol was removed in a total of how many trials from Study 2?

A. 1 trial
B. 2 trials
C. 3 trials
D. 4 trials

28. Which of the following was an independent variable in Study 2?

F. pH
G. H_2O_2 added
H. Phenol concentration
J. Temperature

29. Suppose it were found that a typical sample of waste-water had a phenol concentration of 30 mg/L and a pH of 9. Assume that the percentage of phenol removed from a wastewater sample would be the same as for the phenol samples used in the studies. Based on the results of Study 1, after treatment with H_2O_2 under the same conditions as those used in the study, the concentration of phenol in the wastewater would most likely be closest to:

A. 10 mg/L.
B. 15 mg/L.
C. 25 mg/L.
D. 30 mg/L.

30. Consider the trial in Study 1 in which the percentage of phenol removed was closest to 60.0%. In Step 2 of that trial, is it more likely that NaOH or HCl was added to the phenol solution?

F. NaOH; the solution tested in that trial was more basic than the starting phenol solution.
G. NaOH; the solution tested in that trial was more acidic than the starting phenol solution.
H. HCl; the solution tested in that trial was more basic than the starting phenol solution.
J. HCl; the solution tested in that trial was more acidic than the starting phenol solution.

GO ON TO THE NEXT PAGE.

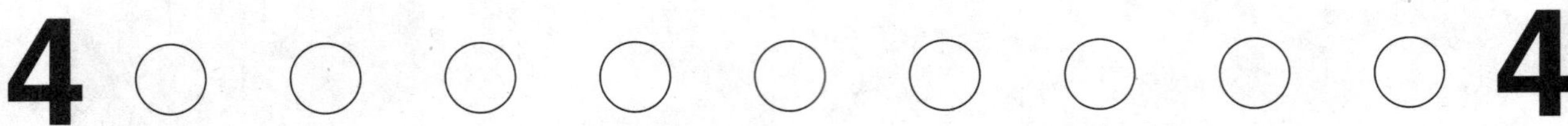

Passage VI

A mass spectrometer (MS) is a device for measuring the ratio of an ion's electric charge, Q, to the ion's mass, M. Students participated in the design of an MS (see Diagram).

Diagram

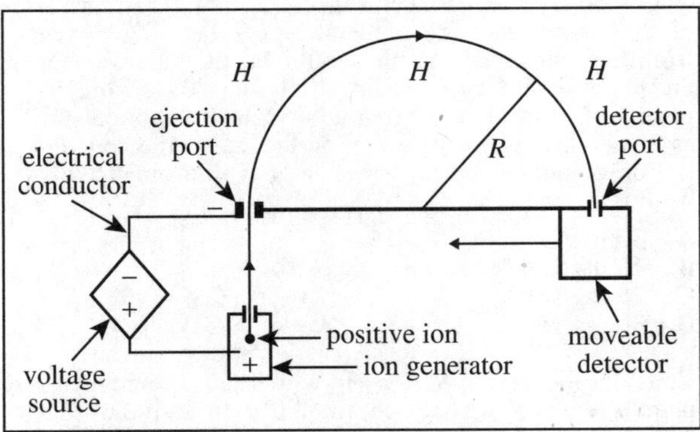

An ion generator produced a single ion at a time of either isotopically pure lithium-7 (Li^+), beryllium-9 (Be^{2+}), or boron-11 (B^{3+}). A variable voltage source accelerated the ion to a maximum speed, V, and directed the ion through the ejection port into a magnetic field of variable intensity, H. Once inside the magnetic field, the ion followed a semicircular orbit at speed V to the input port of a detector. The radius, R, of the orbit was half the distance between the ejection port and the detector port; R had to have a minimum value of 0.0150 m and a maximum value of 0.0250 m. Students were asked to determine the H required for each ion's orbit to have the minimum or maximum R value.

(Note: the ratio Q/M is equal to 1.375×10^7 coulombs per kilogram (C/kg) for Li^+, 2.14×10^7 C/kg for Be^{2+}, and 2.629×10^7 C/kg for B^{3+}.)

Study 1

For each ion, V was 1.00×10^3 meters/sec (m/s), and H (in tesla, T) was varied such that R was 0.0150 m. (See Table 1.)

		Table 1
Trial	Ion	H ($\times 10^{-3}$ T)
1	Li^+	4.85
2	Be^{2+}	3.12
3	B^{3+}	2.54

Study 2

The procedure from Study 1 was repeated, except H was varied such that R was 0.0250 m. (See Table 2.)

		Table 2
Trial	Ion	H ($\times 10^{-3}$ T)
4	Li^+	2.91
5	Be^{2+}	1.87
6	B^{3+}	1.52

Study 3

The procedure from Study 1 was repeated, except that V was 1.00×10^4 m/s. (See Table 3.)

		Table 3
Trial	Ion	H ($\times 10^{-3}$ T)
7	Li^+	48.5
8	Be^{2+}	31.2
9	B^{3+}	25.4

Study 4

The procedure from Study 2 was repeated, except that V was 1.00×10^4 m/s. (See Table 4.)

		Table 4
Trial	Ion	H ($\times 10^{-3}$ T)
10	Li^+	29.1
11	Be^{2+}	18.7
12	B^{3+}	15.2

GO ON TO THE NEXT PAGE.

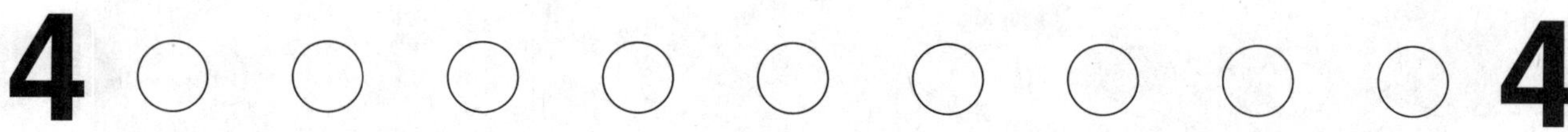

4 ○ ○ ○ ○ ○ ○ ○ ○ ○ **4**

31. The value of H was greatest in which of the following trials?

A. Trial 1
B. Trial 4
C. Trial 7
D. Trial 10

32. A difference between Study 1 and Study 3 is best described by which of the following statements?

F. The V tested in Study 1 was greater than that tested in Study 3.
G. The V tested in Study 1 was less than that tested in Study 3.
H. The R tested in Study 1 was greater than that tested in Study 3.
J. The R tested in Study 1 was less than that tested in Study 3.

33. In Study 2, what was the value of V for Li^+?

A. 1.00×10^3 m/s
B. 2.00×10^3 m/s
C. 1.00×10^4 m/s
D. 2.00×10^4 m/s

34. One millitesla (mT) equals 10^{-3} tesla (T). In Trial 8, what was H in mT?

F. 31.2×10^{-3} mT
G. 31.2 mT
H. 31.2×10^3 mT
J. 48.0×10^3 mT

35. The mass of an Li^+ ion is 1.1×10^{-26} kg and the mass of a sodium ion, Na^+, is 3.8×10^{-26} kg. Suppose the Li^+ were traveling at the maximum speed tested in Study 1 and the Na^+ were traveling at the maximum speed tested in Study 2. Compared to the kinetic energy of the Na^+, the kinetic energy of the Li^+ ion would be:

A. greater.
B. the same.
C. less.
D. sometimes greater and sometimes less.

GO ON TO THE NEXT PAGE.

4 ○ ○ ○ ○ ○ ○ ○ ○ ○ 4

Passage VII

Hippocampus kuda is a species of seahorse (see Figure 1).

Figure 1

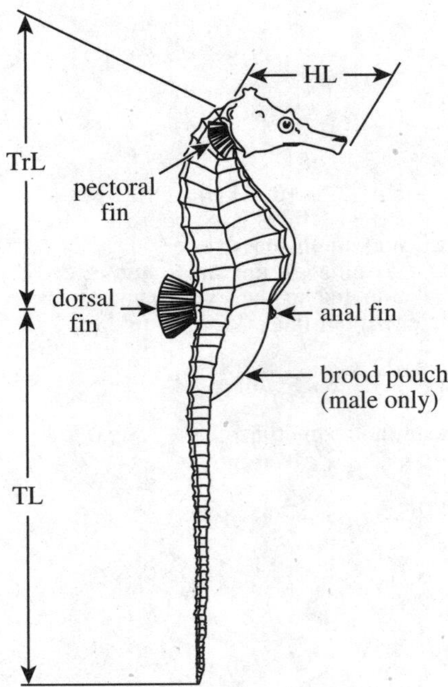

Note: Standard length = tail length (TL) + trunk length (TrL) + head length (HL)

Figure 2 shows, for a captive group of *H. kuda* (Group 1), the average standard length (SL) measured every 7 days (starting at 14 days post-hatch) during the nursery stage (0 days to 42 days post-hatch) and every 14 days during the grow-out stage (42 days to 98 days post-hatch). Figure 2 also shows the average wet mass (WM) measured every 14 days during the grow-out stage only.

Figure 2

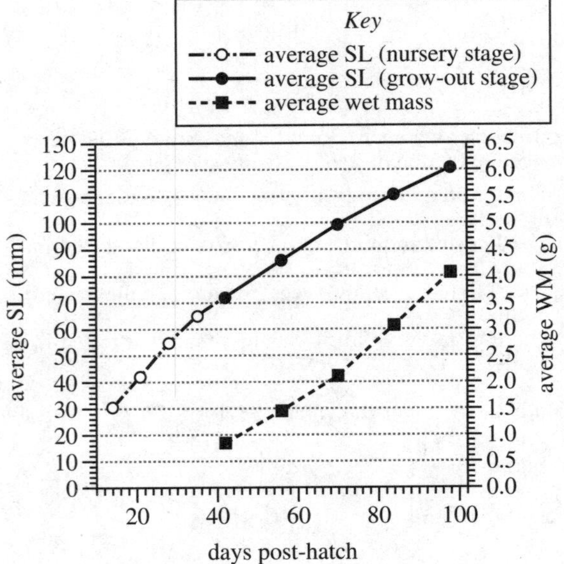

The average percent survival over a 98-day period for 3 additional groups of *H. kuda* (Groups 2–4) fed a diet of *Artemia* sp. (a type of crustacean) with 1 of 3 enrichments (see Table 1) is also shown (see Figure 3).

Table 1	
Group	Enrichment
2	blended fish only
3	*Acetes* sp.* only
4	1:1 mixture of blended fish and *Acetes* sp.
*Another type of crustacean	

GO ON TO THE NEXT PAGE.

4 ○ ○ ○ ○ ○ ○ ○ ○ ○ **4**

Your First Practice Test

Figure 3

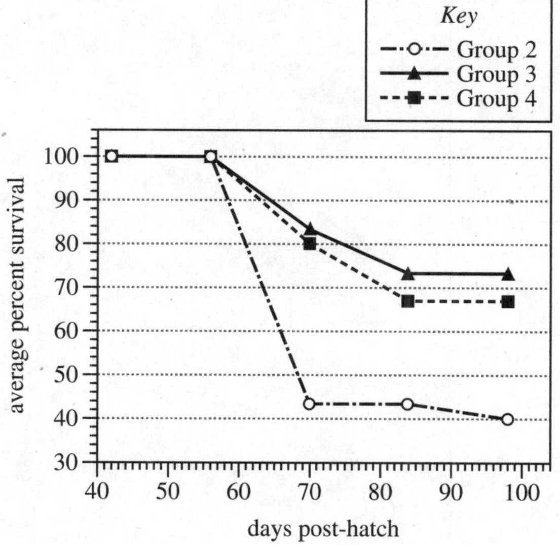

Figures 2 and 3 adapted from the article "Culturing the Oceanic Seahorse, *Hippocampus kuda*" by S.D. Job et al. (©2002 by Elsevier Science B.V.).

36. Seahorses carry their fertilized eggs in a brood pouch while the embryos fully develop. Based on Figure 1, which of male or female seahorses carry the fertilized eggs?

F. Males; females deposit the sperm into the male's brood pouch where the male deposits its eggs.

G. Males; females deposit the eggs into the male's brood pouch where the eggs are fertilized by the male's sperm.

H. Females; males deposit the sperm into the female's brood pouch where the female deposits its eggs.

J. Females; males deposit the eggs into the female's brood pouch where the eggs are fertilized by the female's sperm.

37. Which of Group 3 and Group 4, if either, experienced no mortality prior to 56 days post-hatch?

A. Group 3 only
B. Group 4 only
C. Both Group 3 and Group 4
D. Neither Group 3 nor Group 4

38. Wet mass was measured during which of the grow-out stage and the nursery stage, if either?

F. Grow-out stage only
G. Nursery stage only
H. Both the grow-out stage and the nursery stage
J. Neither the grow-out stage nor the nursery stage

39. Consider the statement "By 98 days post-hatch, seahorses fed a diet of both blended fish and *Acetes* sp. had a greater average percent survival than did seahorses fed blended fish only." Is this statement consistent with the data shown in Figure 3?

A. No; Group 2 seahorses had an average percent survival just over 30 percentage points less than that of Group 4.

B. No; Group 2 seahorses had an average percent survival just under 30 percentage points less than that of Group 4.

C. Yes; Group 2 seahorses had an average percent survival just over 30 percentage points less than that of Group 4.

D. Yes; Group 2 seahorses had an average percent survival just under 30 percentage points less than that of Group 4.

40. Based on the data available in Figure 2, was the overall rate of change in average SL greater over the course of the nursery stage or over the course of the grow-out stage?

F. Nursery stage; the overall rate of change during the nursery stage was greater than 1.0 mm/day, whereas the overall rate of change during the grow-out stage was less than 1.0 mm/day.

G. Nursery stage; the overall rate of change during the nursery stage was greater than 0.5 mm/day, whereas the overall rate of change during the grow-out stage was less than 0.5 mm/day.

H. Grow-out stage; the overall rate of change during the grow-out stage was greater than 1.0 mm/day, whereas the overall rate of change during the nursery stage was less than 1.0 mm/day.

J. Grow-out stage; the overall rate of change during the grow-out stage was greater than 0.5 mm/day, whereas the overall rate of change during the nursery stage was less than 0.5 mm/day.

END OF TEST 4

STOP! DO NOT RETURN TO ANY OTHER TEST.

You may wish to photocopy these sample answer document pages to respond to the practice ACT Writing Test.

Please enter the information at the right before beginning the writing test.

Use a No. 2 pencil only. Do NOT use a mechanical pencil, ink, ballpoint, or felt-tip pen.

WRITING TEST BOOKLET NUMBER

Print your 9-digit **Booklet Number** in the boxes at the right.

WRITING TEST FORM

Print your 5-character **Test Form** in the boxes at the right <u>and</u> fill in the corresponding ovals.

Begin WRITING TEST here.

If you need more space, please continue on the next page.

Your First Practice Test

WRITING TEST

If you need more space, please continue on the back of this page.

The ONLY Official Prep Guide from the Makers of the ACT

WRITING TEST

If you need more space, please continue on the next page.

WRITING TEST

STOP here with the writing test.

The ONLY Official Prep Guide from the Makers of the ACT

Practice Writing Test Prompt 1

Your Signature: ____
(Do not print.)

Print Your Name Here: _______________________________________

Your Date of Birth:

<table>
<tr><td>□□</td><td>–</td><td>□□</td><td>–</td><td>□□□□</td></tr>
<tr><td>Month</td><td></td><td>Day</td><td></td><td>Year</td></tr>
</table>

Form 26WT2

The **ACT**® WRITING TEST BOOKLET

Directions

This is a test of your writing skills. You will have **forty** (40) minutes to read the prompt, plan your response, and write an essay in English. Before you begin working, read all material in this test booklet carefully to understand exactly what you are being asked to do.

You will write your essay on the lined pages in the **answer document** provided. Your writing on those pages will be scored. You may use the unlined pages in this test booklet to plan your essay. Your work on these pages will not be scored.

Your essay will be evaluated based on the evidence it provides of your ability to:

- clearly state your own perspective on a complex issue and analyze the relationship between your perspective and at least one other perspective
- develop and support your ideas with reasoning and examples
- organize your ideas clearly and logically
- communicate your ideas effectively in standard written English

Lay your pencil down immediately when time is called.

DO NOT OPEN THIS BOOKLET UNTIL TOLD TO DO SO.

PO Box 168
Iowa City, IA 52243-0168

The ONLY Official Prep Guide from the Makers of the ACT

Children and Entertainment

Our society uses several methods to prevent children from consuming entertainment involving violence, profanity, and other mature themes. Rating systems prohibit children from attending certain movies or purchasing certain video games, while parental controls allow adults to regulate TV content at home. But entertainment of this nature may also possess a high degree of artistic value. For example, several influential films involve violent themes, and many important songs contain profane lyrics. Is it always wise, then, to prevent children from consuming mature entertainment?

Read and carefully consider these perspectives. Each suggests a particular way of thinking about the question above.

Perspective One	**Perspective Two**	**Perspective Three**
Mature themes are not meant for children. The harm done to children by exposure to violence, profanity, and other adult content outweighs any artistic merit.	Artists address mature themes because they are a fact of life. Sheltering children prevents them not only from experiencing significant works of art but also from developing a full sense of the real world.	Entertainment does not require mature themes to be meaningful and important. Plenty of movies, music, and even video games have artistic value while also being appropriate for children.

Essay Task

Write a unified, coherent essay in which you address the question of whether it is always wise to prevent children from consuming entertainment involving mature themes. In your essay, be sure to:

- clearly state your own perspective and analyze the relationship between your perspective and at least one other perspective
- develop and support your ideas with reasoning and examples
- organize your ideas clearly and logically
- communicate your ideas effectively in standard written English

Your perspective may be in full agreement with any of those given, in partial agreement, or completely different.

Planning Your Essay

Your work on these prewriting pages will not be scored.

Use the space below and on the back cover to generate ideas and plan your essay. You may wish to consider the following as you think critically about the task:

Strengths and weaknesses of different perspectives on the issue
- What insights do they offer, and what do they fail to consider?
- Why might they be persuasive to others, or why might they fail to persuade?

Your own knowledge, experience, and values
- What is your perspective on this issue, and what are its strengths and weaknesses?
- How will you support your perspective in your essay?

If you need more space to plan, please continue on the back of this page.

The ONLY Official Prep Guide from the Makers of the ACT

Planning Your Essay

Use this page to continue planning your essay. Your work on this page will not be scored.

Scoring Your Practice Test

After taking your first ACT practice test, you are ready to score the test to see how you did overall. In this chapter, you learn how to determine your raw score, convert raw scores to scale scores, compute your Composite score, determine your estimated percentile ranks for each of your scale scores, and score your practice writing test.

When scoring each practice test and reviewing your scores, remember that your scores on the practice tests are only estimates of the scores that you will obtain on the ACT. If your score isn't as high as you expected, it could mean a number of things. Maybe you need to review important content and skills. Maybe you should work a little faster when taking the test. Perhaps you simply weren't doing your best work on the test. Or maybe you need to take more challenging courses to be better prepared. Keep in mind that a test score is just one indicator of your level of academic knowledge and skills. You know your own strengths and weaknesses better than anyone else, so keep them in mind as you evaluate your performance.

On each of the four multiple-choice tests (English, mathematics, reading, and science), the number of questions you answer correctly is called a *raw score*. To figure out your raw scores for the practice tests in this book, count all your correct answers for each test using the scoring keys provided in the next section, "Scoring Your Multiple-Choice Practice Tests." Then you can convert your raw scores into *scale* scores.

A raw score is converted to a scale score to enhance score interpretation and allow comparability across different forms. Scale scores are the scores that ACT reports to students, high schools, colleges, and scholarship agencies. One of the reasons ACT uses scale scores is to adjust for small differences among different forms of the ACT. After you've converted your raw scores for the practice tests to scale scores, you'll want to convert your scale scores to percentile ranks. Percentile ranks, which are explained in the following pages, are useful for interpreting your scores relative to the scores of others who have taken the ACT.

If you took the optional practice writing test, the later section "Scoring Your Practice Writing Test Essay" includes an analytic rubric for evaluating your essay and estimating your writing test score. Although it is difficult to be objective about one's own work, it is to your advantage to read your own writing critically. Becoming your own editor helps you grow as a writer and as a reader, so it makes sense for you to evaluate your own practice essay. However, it likely will be helpful for you to give your practice essay to another reader to get another perspective: perhaps that of a classmate, a parent, or an English teacher, for example. To rate your essay, you and your reader should read the analytic rubric on pages 107–108 and the examples on pages 277–302, and then assign your practice essay a score of 1 (low) through 6 (high) in each of the four writing domains (Ideas and Analysis, Development and Support, Organization, and Language Use and Conventions).

Your writing test domain scores are based on the analytic rubric used to score the essays, whereas the overall score is calculated from the four domain scores.

Finally, convert your writing test score to percentile ranks using the procedures described. Percentile ranks enable you to compare your writing test score to those of others who have taken the writing test.

Scoring Your Multiple-Choice Practice Tests

Remember that each section of the test includes embedded field-test questions that do not contribute to your score and that the placement of these items varies across different test forms. To score your multiple-choice practice tests, follow these eight steps:

STEP 1. Mark a "1" in the blank for each question you answered correctly and add up the total number correct for each test. Do not count correct answers for gray cells, as those are for the field-test items not included in converting raw scores to scale scores. An example is provided in the box below:

	Key		Your answer was
1.	A		Incorrect
2.	J	1	Correct
3.	B	1	Correct
4.	G		Incorrect

English ■ Scoring Key ■ Practice Test 1

	Key			Key			Key	
1.	B		18.	H		35.	B	
2.	F		19.	A		36.	J	
3.	A		20.	G		37.	A	
4.	J		21.	B		38.	F	
5.	B		22.	F		39.	B	
6.	J		23.	C		40.	F	
7.	D		24.	H		41.	D	
8.	H		25.	A		42.	F	
9.	C		26.	J		43.	D	
10.	H		27.	B		44.	F	
11.	D		28.	H		45.	C	
12.	H		29.	A		46.	H	
13.	A		30.	G		47.	B	
14.	H		31.	A		48.	F	
15.	D		32.	G		49.	C	
16.	G		33.	C		50.	J	
17.	A		34.	J				

STEP 2. Compute your total number correct for the English test by adding the numbers you entered in Step 1. Write this total in the blank in the shaded box below. This is your raw score.

Number Correct (Raw Score) for:
Total Number Correct for English Test (40 questions) __________

STEP 3. Repeat Steps 1 and 2 for the ACT mathematics, reading, and science tests using the scoring keys on this page and the following page.

Mathematics ■ Scoring Key ■ Practice Test 1

	Key				Key					Key	
1.	D	_____		16.	G			31.	A	_____
2.	H	_____		17.	A	_____		32.	H	_____
3.	D	_____		18.	G	_____		33.	C	_____
4.	J	_____		19.	A	_____		34.	G	_____
5.	B	_____		20.	G	_____		35.	D	_____
6.	F	_____		21.	A	_____		36.	H	_____
7.	B			22.	G	_____		37.	C	_____
8.	H	_____		23.	C	_____		38.	J	
9.	B	_____		24.	F	_____		39.	B	_____
10.	J	_____		25.	A	_____		40.	J	_____
11.	C	_____		26.	F	_____		41.	A	_____
12.	H	_____		27.	A	_____		42.	H	_____
13.	C	_____		28.	H	_____		43.	A	_____
14.	F	_____		29.	B	_____		44.	J	_____
15.	A	_____		30.	H			45.	D	_____

Number Correct (Raw Score) for:
Total Number Correct for Math Test (41 questions) __________

Reading ■ Scoring Key ■ Practice Test 1

	Key			Key			Key
1.	C		13.	A		25.	D
2.	F		14.	H		26.	H
3.	B		15.	A		27.	D
4.	G		16.	G		28.	G
5.	D		17.	D		29.	A
6.	G		18.	H		30.	F
7.	D		19.	C		31.	B
8.	H		20.	H		32.	H
9.	A		21.	A		33.	D
10.	F		22.	J		34.	G
11.	A		23.	A		35.	C
12.	G		24.	G		36.	J

Number Correct (Raw Score) for:

Total Number Correct for Reading Test (27 questions) ______________

Science ■ Scoring Key ■ Practice Test 1

	Key			Key			Key
1.	B		15.	C		29.	B
2.	H		16.	H		30.	F
3.	C		17.	B		31.	C
4.	J		18.	J		32.	G
5.	D		19.	D		33.	A
6.	J		20.	G		34.	G
7.	B		21.	C		35.	C
8.	H		22.	H		36.	G
9.	C		23.	D		37.	C
10.	J		24.	F		38.	F
11.	A		25.	C		39.	D
12.	H		26.	J		40.	F
13.	B		27.	D			
14.	G		28.	G			

Number Correct (Raw Score) for:

Total Number Correct for Science Test (34 questions) ______________

STEP 4. On each of the four tests, the total number of correct responses yields a raw score. Use the conversion table on the following page to convert your raw scores to scale scores. For each of the four tests, locate and circle your raw score or the range of raw scores that includes it in the conversion table. Then, read across to either outside column of the table and circle the scale score that corresponds to that raw score. As you determine your scale scores, enter them in the blanks provided below. The highest possible scale score for each test is 36. The lowest possible scale score for any of the four tests is 1.

	Your Scale Scores
English	______________
Mathematics	______________
Reading	______________
Science	______________
Sum of Scores	______________

STEP 5. Compute your Composite score by averaging the four scale scores. To do this, add your four scale scores and divide the sum by 4. If the resulting number ends in a fraction, round it off to the nearest whole number. (Round down any fraction less than one-half; round up any fraction that is one-half or more.) Enter this number in the appropriate blank below. This is your Composite score. The highest possible Composite score is 36. The lowest possible Composite score is 1.

	Your Scale Scores
English	______________
Mathematics	______________
Reading	______________
Science	______________
Sum of Scores	______________
Composite Score (sum ÷ 4)	______________

Scale Score Conversion Table:
Practice Test 1

Scale Score	Raw Score Test 1: English	Raw Score Test 2: Mathematics	Raw Score Test 3: Reading	Raw Score Test 4: Science
36	40	41	26–27	33–34
35	37–39	39–40	25	32
34	36	37–38	24	31
33	35	36	23	30
32	34	35	22	29
31	—	33–34	—	28
30	33	32	21	—
29	32	31	20	27
28	31	29–30	19	26
27	30	28	—	25
26	29	26–27	18	24
25	27–28	25	17	22–23
24	26	23–24	16	21
23	24–25	22	15	19–20
22	23	21	14	18
21	21–22	20	—	17
20	19–20	19	13	16
19	18	18	12	15
18	17	16–17	—	14
17	—	14–15	11	13
16	16	12–13	10	11–12
15	14–15	10–11	—	10
14	13	8–9	9	9
13	12	7	8	8
12	11	6	7	6–7
11	9–10	5	6	5
10	7–8	4	5	4
9	6	3	4	—
8	5	—	—	3
7	4	2	3	—
6	—	—	—	2
5	3	—	2	—
4	2	1	—	1
3	—	—	1	—
2	1	—	—	—
1	0	0	0	0

STEP 6. Use the table on the following page to determine your estimated percentile ranks (percent at or below) for each of your scale scores. In the far left column of the table, circle your scale score for the English test (from the preceding page). Then read across to the percentile rank column for that test; circle or put a checkmark beside the corresponding percentile rank. Use the same procedure for the other three tests (from the preceding page). Using the right-hand column of scale scores for your science test and Composite scores may be easier. As you mark your percentile ranks, enter them in the blanks provided. You may also find it helpful to compare your performance with the national mean (average) score for each of the four tests and the Composite as shown at the bottom of the table.

National Norms for ACT Test Scores
Reported During the 2025–2026 Reporting Year

Score	ACT Score National Ranks						Score
	English	Math	Reading	Science	Composite	STEM	
36	100	100	100	100	100	100	36
35	99	99	98	99	99	99	35
34	97	99	97	99	99	99	34
33	96	98	95	98	98	98	33
32	95	98	93	97	97	98	32
31	94	97	91	96	96	97	31
30	93	96	89	95	94	95	30
29	91	94	87	93	92	94	29
28	90	93	85	92	91	92	28
27	88	91	83	91	88	90	27
26	86	88	80	89	86	88	26
25	84	85	78	86	83	85	25
24	81	81	75	82	80	81	24
23	77	77	71	76	76	77	23
22	73	74	66	70	72	73	22
21	69	71	60	65	68	68	21
20	63	68	55	59	63	63	20
19	58	64	50	53	57	58	19
18	53	60	46	47	52	51	18
17	49	53	41	40	46	44	17
16	46	45	37	33	40	35	16
15	40	32	32	26	34	26	15
14	33	20	27	19	27	17	14
13	27	10	21	14	20	10	13
12	22	5	16	10	12	4	12
11	17	3	9	6	5	2	11
10	11	1	4	3	2	1	10
9	6	1	2	2	1	1	9
8	3	1	1	1	1	1	8
7	2	1	1	1	1	1	7
6	1	1	1	1	1	1	6
5	1	1	1	1	1	1	5
4	1	1	1	1	1	1	4
3	1	1	1	1	1	1	3
2	1	1	1	1	1	1	2
1	1	1	1	1	1	1	1
Mean	18.6	19.0	20.1	19.6	19.2	19.5	
SD	7.0	5.6	7.1	5.8	6.1	5.4	

Note: These ranks are reported as "US Rank" on ACT score reports during the 2025–2026 reporting year (September 2025 through August 2026). The ranks are based on ACT-tested high school graduates of 2023, 2024, and 2025.

Your First Practice Test

Scoring Your Practice Writing Test Essay

To score your practice writing test essay, follow these steps:

STEP 1. Use the analytic rubric on the following two pages to score your essay. Because many essays do not fit the exact description at each score point, read each description and try to determine which paragraph in the rubric best describes most of the characteristics of your essay.

Critiquing your own writing can be difficult. If possible, ask a trusted source to help you use the rubric and determine your score. If you must evaluate your essay on your own, try to be as objective as you can and remember that any reader of your essay would understand only what you wrote, not what you meant to write. In either case, you may find it useful to consult chapters 4 and 9 for additional information regarding the rubric and sample essays to which you can compare your own.

The ACT Writing Test Analytic Rubric

	Ideas and Analysis	Development and Support	Organization	Language Use and Conventions
Score 6: **Responses at this scorepoint demonstrate effective skill in writing an argumentative essay.**	The writer generates an argument that critically engages with multiple perspectives on the given issue. The argument's thesis reflects nuance and precision in thought and purpose. The argument establishes and employs an insightful context for analysis of the issue and its perspectives. The analysis examines implications, complexities and tensions, and/or underlying values and assumptions.	Development of ideas and support for claims deepen insight and broaden context. An integrated line of skillful reasoning and illustration effectively conveys the significance of the argument. Qualifications and complications enrich and bolster ideas and analysis.	The response exhibits a skillful organizational strategy. The response is unified by a controlling idea or purpose, and a logical progression of ideas increases the effectiveness of the writer's argument. Transitions between and within paragraphs strengthen the relationships among ideas.	The use of language enhances the argument. Word choice is skillful and precise. Sentence structures are consistently varied and clear. Stylistic and register choices, including voice and tone, are strategic and effective. While a few minor errors in grammar, usage, and mechanics may be present, they do not impede understanding.
Score 5: **Responses at this scorepoint demonstrate well-developed skill in writing an argumentative essay.**	The writer generates an argument that productively engages with multiple perspectives on the given issue. The argument's thesis reflects precision in thought and purpose. The argument establishes and employs a thoughtful context for analysis of the issue and its perspectives. The analysis addresses implications, complexities and tensions, and/or underlying values and assumptions.	Development of ideas and support for claims deepen understanding. A mostly integrated line of purposeful reasoning and illustration capably conveys the significance of the argument. Qualifications and complications enrich ideas and analysis.	The response exhibits a productive organizational strategy. The response is mostly unified by a controlling idea or purpose, and a logical sequencing of ideas contributes to the effectiveness of the argument. Transitions between and within paragraphs consistently clarify the relationships among ideas.	The use of language works in service of the argument. Word choice is precise. Sentence structures are clear and varied often. Stylistic and register choices, including voice and tone, are purposeful and productive. While minor errors in grammar, usage, and mechanics may be present, they do not impede understanding.
Score 4: **Responses at this scorepoint demonstrate adequate skill in writing an argumentative essay.**	The writer generates an argument that engages with multiple perspectives on the given issue. The argument's thesis reflects clarity in thought and purpose. The argument establishes and employs a relevant context for analysis of the issue and its perspectives. The analysis recognizes implications, complexities and tensions, and/or underlying values and assumptions.	Development of ideas and support for claims clarify meaning and purpose. Lines of clear reasoning and illustration adequately convey the significance of the argument. Qualifications and complications extend ideas and analysis.	The response exhibits a clear organizational strategy. The overall shape of the response reflects an emergent controlling idea or purpose. Ideas are logically grouped and sequenced. Transitions between and within paragraphs clarify the relationships among ideas.	The use of language conveys the argument with clarity. Word choice is adequate and sometimes precise. Sentence structures are clear and demonstrate some variety. Stylistic and register choices, including voice and tone, are appropriate for the rhetorical purpose. While errors in grammar, usage, and mechanics are present, they rarely impede understanding.
Score 3: **Responses at this scorepoint demonstrate some developing skill in writing an argumentative essay.**	The writer generates an argument that responds to multiple perspectives on the given issue. The argument's thesis reflects some clarity in thought and purpose. The argument establishes a limited or tangential context for analysis of the issue and its perspectives. Analysis is simplistic or somewhat unclear.	Development of ideas and support for claims are mostly relevant but are overly general or simplistic. Reasoning and illustration largely clarify the argument but may be somewhat repetitive or imprecise.	The response exhibits a basic organizational structure. The response largely coheres, with most ideas logically grouped. Transitions between and within paragraphs sometimes clarify the relationships among ideas.	The use of language is basic and only somewhat clear. Word choice is general and occasionally imprecise. Sentence structures are usually clear but show little variety. Stylistic and register choices, including voice and tone, are not always appropriate for the rhetorical purpose. Distracting errors in grammar, usage, and mechanics may be present, but they generally do not impede understanding.

(continued)

The ACT Writing Test Analytic Rubric

	Ideas and Analysis	Development and Support	Organization	Language Use and Conventions
Score 2: **Responses at this scorepoint demonstrate weak or inconsistent skill in writing an argumentative essay.**	The writer generates an argument that weakly responds to multiple perspectives on the given issue. The argument's thesis, if evident, reflects little clarity in thought and purpose. Attempts at analysis are incomplete, largely irrelevant, or consist primarily of restatement of the issue and its perspectives.	Development of ideas and support for claims are weak, confused, or disjointed. Reasoning and illustration are inadequate, illogical, or circular, and fail to fully clarify the argument.	The response exhibits a rudimentary organizational structure. Grouping of ideas is inconsistent and often unclear. Transitions between and within paragraphs are misleading or poorly formed.	The use of language is inconsistent and often unclear. Word choice is rudimentary and frequently imprecise. Sentence structures are sometimes unclear. Stylistic and register choices, including voice and tone, are inconsistent and are not always appropriate for the rhetorical purpose. Distracting errors in grammar, usage, and mechanics are present, and they sometimes impede understanding.
Score 1: **Responses at this scorepoint demonstrate little or no skill in writing an argumentative essay.**	The writer fails to generate an argument that responds intelligibly to the task. The writer's intentions are difficult to discern. Attempts at analysis are unclear or irrelevant.	Ideas lack development, and claims lack support. Reasoning and illustration are unclear, incoherent, or largely absent.	The response does not exhibit an organizational structure. There is little grouping of ideas. When present, transitional devices fail to connect ideas.	The use of language fails to demonstrate skill in responding to the task. Word choice is imprecise and often difficult to comprehend. Sentence structures are often unclear. Stylistic and register choices are difficult to identify. Errors in grammar, usage, and mechanics are pervasive and often impede understanding.

STEP 2. Because your writing test domain scores are the sum of two readers' ratings of your essay, multiply your own 1–6 rating from step 1 by 2. Or, have both you and someone else read and score your practice essay, add those ratings together, and record the total in the Domain Score column in step 3.

STEP 3. Enter your writing test domain scores in the following box.

		Domain Score
Ideas and Analysis	__________ × 2 =	__________
Development and Support	__________ × 2 =	__________
Organization	__________ × 2 =	__________
Language Use and Conventions	__________ × 2 =	__________

STEP 4. Enter the sum of the second-column scores here _______.

STEP 5. Divide sum by 4[†] (range 2–12). This is your writing test score.

[†]Round value to the nearest whole number. Round down any fraction less than one-half; round up any fraction that is one-half or more.

STEP 6. Use the table on the following page to determine your estimated percentile rank (percent at or below) for your writing test score.

National Norms for ACT Writing Scores Reported During the 2025–2026 Reporting Year

Score	ACT Score National Ranks	
	ELA	Writing
36	100	
35	99	
34	99	
33	99	
32	99	
31	99	
30	98	
29	97	
28	96	
27	94	
26	92	
25	90	
24	87	
23	84	
22	80	
21	76	
20	71	
19	65	
18	59	
17	53	
16	47	
15	40	
14	34	
13	27	
12	21	100
11	15	99
10	10	99
9	7	97
8	4	93
7	2	74
6	1	61
5	1	34
4	1	21
3	1	9
2	1	4
1	1	
Mean	17.5	6.1
SD	5.7	1.8

Note: These ranks are reported as "US Rank" on ACT score reports during the 2025–2026 reporting year (September 2025 through August 2026). The ranks are based on ACT-tested high school graduates of 2023, 2024, and 2025 who took the ACT Writing test.

Reviewing Explanatory Answers

After scoring your test, review the questions and answers to gain a better understanding of why each correct answer is correct and why the other choices for each question are wrong. We encourage you to review the explanatory answers for all questions, not just those you missed. As you read through the explanations, note any subject matter or concepts you don't fully understand, such as subject-verb agreement on the English test or how to calculate the volume of three-dimensional objects on the mathematics test.

The following sections give the correct answers for each question along with an explanation of why each correct answer is correct, why each of the other choices is wrong, and (in some cases) insight into why certain wrong answers may have been tempting choices. For more guidance on how to identify subject areas or skills you may need to work on, turn to chapter 4.

Passage I

Question 1. The best answer is B because "in the nineteenth" is an essential element of the sentence and therefore should not be set off by commas.

The best answer is NOT:

A because "in the nineteenth" is an essential element of the sentence and therefore should not be set off by commas.

C because the comma after "nineteenth" incorrectly interrupts the prepositional phrase "in the nineteenth and twentieth centuries."

D because "in the nineteenth and twentieth centuries" is an essential element of the sentence and therefore should not be set off by commas.

Question 2. The best answer is F because it maintains the overall style and tone of the essay.

The best answer is NOT:

G because "curtail the predicaments referenced" and "may want to contemplate" introduce an elevated, formal tone that is not consistent with the rest of the essay.

H because *fix* and *just* introduce an informal tone that is not consistent with the rest of the essay, as well as clash with the too-formal "monetary assets."

J because *surefire* and *mess* introduce an informal tone that is not consistent with the rest of the essay.

Question 3. The best answer is A because this option clearly indicates what would be lost if the sentence were deleted. The sentence expresses that one advantage of removing impermeable barriers between waterways and the soil is that more rainwater can be absorbed where the rain falls.

The best answer is NOT:

B because this sentence does not provide any data about the effects of removing barriers between waterways and the soil.

C because this sentence does not describe how soil absorbs rainwater.

D because this sentence does not explain how rainwater affects daylight projects.

Question 4. The best answer is **J** because it is the only option that creates correct sentence structure. It creates a complete sentence with a main subject and main verb.

The best answer is NOT:

F because it adds a comma and *which* before the main verb, resulting in a sentence fragment.

G because it adds a comma and *these* before the main verb, resulting in a sentence fragment.

H because it adds *that* before the main verb, resulting in a sentence fragment.

Question 5. The best answer is **B** because the information about how water treatment costs are reduced as a result of keeping stormwater out of sewer systems provides a clear and relevant example that supports the claim that daylighting saves more money than it costs.

The best answer is NOT:

A because the information about how daylighting projects lessen flooding in US cities is not relevant to the discussion of how daylighting saves more money than it costs.

C because the information about how natural streambeds help clean the water that flows over them is not relevant to the discussion of how daylighting saves more money than it costs.

D because the information about how accessible waterways provide habitats for fish and other wildlife is not relevant to the discussion of how daylighting saves more money than it costs.

Question 6. The best answer is **J** because it correctly identifies a counterclaim that a daylighting opponent might reasonably assert: that its downside is the possible loss of some usable structures.

The best answer is NOT:

F because the fact that early attempts at culverting required innovative construction techniques is not a counterclaim; it's simply a statement about the history of culverting.

G because it incorrectly identifies a reasonable counterclaim based on the essay; the issue concerns buildings that are usable, not buildings that have been abandoned.

H because the fact that citizens have lived and worked above their cities' streams is not a counterclaim; it's simply a statement about an effect of culverting.

Question 7. **The best answer is D** because it uses the correct pronoun case, *who*, as well as the contextually correct word *affected*.

The best answer is NOT:

A because *whom* is an object pronoun, and this sentence requires the subject pronoun *who*; in addition, *effected* is not the correct word in this context.

B because *whom* is an object pronoun, and this sentence requires the subject pronoun *who*.

C because *effected* is not the correct word in this context.

Question 8. **The best answer is H** because *enriches* is the most precise word in the context of the essay; it means "to make richer," and the essay is conveying that daylighting can make the quality of life richer for a community.

The best answer is NOT:

F because *embellishes* does not fit the context; it means "to make something more attractive," which does not precisely describe how daylighting can affect a community's quality of life.

G because *refurbishes* does not fit the context; it means "to renovate or redecorate," which does not precisely describe how daylighting can affect a community's quality of life.

J because *fortifies* does not fit the context; it means "to make strong," which does not precisely describe how daylighting can affect a community's quality of life.

Question 9. **The best answer is C** because it is the best conclusion in the context of this essay's argument for daylighting waterways. It summarizes the writer's overall argument that daylighting not only exposes long-buried waterways but also brings life to a city's center.

The best answer is NOT:

A because it's not an effective conclusion to this essay, which is arguing that communities should invest in daylighting, not that citizens should oppose future culverting initiatives.

B because it's not an effective conclusion to this essay, which is arguing that communities should invest in daylighting going forward, not that communities have considered it over the years.

D because it's not an effective conclusion to this essay, which is arguing that communities should invest in daylighting, not that daylighting is doable if those communities work together.

Question 10. **The best answer is H** because Point C in Paragraph 3 is the only logical place to add information that refers to historical costs of flood damage that could have been mitigated if daylighting had occurred before the flood.

The best answer is NOT:

F because the proposed sentence refers to the monetary cost of historical flood damage, and no specific costs related to flood damage are introduced until Paragraph 3.

G because the proposed sentence refers to the monetary cost of historical flood damage, and no specific costs related to flood damage are introduced until the subsequent sentence.

J because the proposed sentence would be illogical at this point and would interrupt the flow of the argument in Paragraph 4.

Passage II

Question 11. **The best answer is D** because it provides the clearest, most concise wording.

The best answer is NOT:

A because *annoyingly* and *irritating* are redundant, and "to want" and "felt the urge" earlier in the sentence are redundant.

B because "make me long to" is too similar in meaning to "felt the urge" earlier in the sentence, and "throw my phone" and "hurl my phone" later in the sentence are redundant.

C because "on the phone" and *calls* are redundant.

Question 12. **The best answer is H** because *conceived* is the most precise word in the context of the essay; it means "to develop an idea," and the essay is conveying that the competition was developed as an idea to remind Finns to dispose of their phones responsibly.

The best answer is NOT:

F because *ascertained* does not fit the context; it means "to make sure of something," which does not precisely convey the development of an idea.

G because *speculated* does not fit the context; it means "to meditate on or ponder a subject," "to review something idly or casually," "to assume a business risk in hope of gain," "to take to be true on the basis of insufficient evidence," or "to be curious or doubtful about," none of which precisely convey the development of an idea.

J because *supposed* does not fit the context; it means "to think that something is likely to be true" or "to expect and need or believe," which do not precisely convey the development of an idea.

Question 13. **The best answer is A** because it maintains the overall style and tone of the essay.

The best answer is NOT:

B because it introduces an elevated, formal tone that is not consistent with the rest of the essay.

C because the first part of the clause introduces a formal tone and the latter introduces a flowery tone, neither of which is consistent with the rest of the essay.

D because it introduces an informal tone that is not consistent with the rest of the essay.

Question 14. **The best answer is H** because a "festive, cordial" atmosphere provides the clearest contrast with a *fierce* rivalry.

The best answer is NOT:

F because while the word *lively* clearly contrasts with *fierce*, the word *agitated* does not.

G because "dignified, focused" does not contrast as sharply with *fierce* as **H** does.

J because "tense, wary" does not contrast as sharply with *fierce* as **H** does.

Question 15. **The best answer is D** because "In fact" creates the most logical transition; what follows the transition emphasizes the idea in the preceding sentence that most of the athletes were not dressed in a way that made them obvious competitors.

The best answer is NOT:

A because *However* suggests that what follows will present a contrast to what came before, which is not the case here.

B because *Eventually* suggests that what follows occurs at an unspecified later time, which is not the case here.

C because *Besides* suggests that what follows will introduce something in addition to the point in the preceding sentence, which is not the case here.

Question 16. The best answer is G because this option clearly indicates what would be lost if the detail were deleted. While riding a unicycle in a circle requires talent, riding it for forty-five seconds is particularly noteworthy.

The best answer is NOT:

F because, while this unicyclist may have been the most impressive contestant, the simple fact that she rode a unicycle for forty-five seconds does not clarify that.

H because the detail indicates the amount of time the woman rode the unicycle, not that forty-five seconds was the minimum length of all the event's performances.

J because the detail indicates the amount of time the woman rode the unicycle, not why the woman chose to ride the unicycle.

Question 17. The best answer is A because the word *more* is the only option that completes the comparison: The event is being judged *more* on creativity *than* on distance.

The best answer is NOT:

B because "at least as much" does not correctly complete the comparison, and it creates an illogical sentence.

C because *primarily* does not correctly complete the comparison, and it creates an illogical sentence.

D because deleting *more* does not correctly complete the comparison, and it creates an illogical sentence.

Question 18. The best answer is H because it would place Sentence 3, the most effective topic sentence, at the beginning of the paragraph and because it would not disrupt the flow of ideas between Sentences 1 and 2.

The best answer is NOT:

F because it would use Sentence 1 (a more specific detail about the topic that does not directly connect to the preceding paragraph) as the topic sentence.

G because it would place Sentence 3 between Sentences 1 and 2. As noted above, Sentence 3 would be the best choice for a topic sentence. In addition, Sentence 3 would interrupt the flow of ideas between Sentences 1 and 2. Sentence 2 begins by referring to Sentence 1 using the pronoun *that*. Inserting Sentence 3 between Sentences 1 and 2 would create an ambiguous reference at the beginning of Sentence 2.

J because it would create an ambiguous reference in the second sentence of the paragraph (it would not be clear what the pronoun *that* was referring to).

Question 19. The best answer is A because it is the only option that creates correct sentence structure: two independent clauses separated by a semicolon.

The best answer is NOT:

B because it separates two independent clauses with a comma, creating a comma splice.

C because it separates two independent clauses with a comma, creating a comma splice.

D because it creates an error in subordination, which creates an unclear, illogical sentence.

Question 20. The best answer is G because it best expresses the idea specified in the stem. That the narrator has "linked arms with Anneli and stepped further into the crowd" most effectively suggests that the narrator has begun to connect with others in person instead of engaging with the phone.

The best answer is NOT:

F because it fails to express the idea specified in the stem. Noting that many memorable pictures and videos have been taken indicates the narrator is still engaged with the phone and has not begun to connect with others in person.

H because it is a less effective choice for expressing the idea specified in the stem. While hoping to return to the festival in the future could indicate a desire to connect with people in person instead of engaging with the phone, we do not know if that is the motivation behind the narrator's desire to return.

J because it fails to express the idea specified in the stem. That the narrator can feel the phone and mostly ignores it does not indicate that the narrator has begun to connect with others in person rather than engaging with the phone.

Passage III

Question 21. The best answer is B because it is the only option that creates correct sentence structure: two independent clauses separated by a comma and the conjunction *and*.

The best answer is NOT:

A because it uses no punctuation to separate two independent clauses, creating a run-on sentence.

C because it uses no punctuation to separate two independent clauses, creating a run-on sentence.

D because it uses a comma to separate two independent clauses, creating a comma splice.

Question 22. **The best answer is F** because this option clearly indicates what would be lost if the phrase were deleted. The fact that Torres started and completed the portraits during the same lunar phase in which the residents of his village farm clearly indicates how his *Sun Light* series was influenced by his connection to his own past and culture.

The best answer is NOT:

G because this phrase does not provide an example that clarifies how Torres depicted moonlight in his *Sun Light* series.

H because, while it may be true that Torres's connections with friends and family inspire his art, there is nothing in this particular phrase to indicate that.

J because, while this phrase does reference a cultural tradition that influenced Torres, there is no reference to Torres's upbringing.

Question 23. **The best answer is C** because it does not include any unnecessary punctuation.

The best answer is NOT:

A because it has an unnecessary dash after *portraits* and an unnecessary comma after *signature*.

B because it sets off the phrase "in his signature" with two unnecessary commas.

D because it has an unnecessary comma after *portraits*.

Question 24. **The best answer is H** because the phrase "precisely interlaced to" provides the most specific description of the strands to help readers visualize the faces in Torres's portraits.

The best answer is NOT:

F because "assembled to" is too vague and does not help the reader visualize the strands.

G because "combined in such a way" is too vague and does not help the reader visualize the strands.

J because "artistically used to" is too vague and does not help the reader visualize the strands.

Question 25. The best answer is **A** because it is the only option that creates correct sentence structure.

The best answer is NOT:

B because it makes *photographs* the subject that is drawing the renderings, which is illogical.

C because it makes *photographs* the subject that is drawing the renderings, which is illogical.

D because it makes *photographs* the subject that is drawing the renderings, which is illogical.

Question 26. The best answer is **J** because *Then* creates the most logical transition. What follows the transition is the step that occurs after the step in the preceding sentence: After Torres draws his subjects on canvases, he applies dabs of paint to the canvases.

The best answer is NOT:

F because "For instance" suggests that what follows will be an example of the preceding information, which is not the case here.

G because *Consequently* suggests that what follows occurs as a result of the preceding information, which is not the case here.

H because *Again* suggests that what follows will reiterate or emphasize a point made previously in the essay, which is not the case here.

Question 27. The best answer is **B** because it correctly sets off the nonessential element ("mostly whites, grays, and blacks") from the rest of the sentence.

The best answer is NOT:

A because *mostly* is part of the nonessential element and therefore should be included inside the dashes. In addition, there should not be a comma after *paint*.

C because the nonessential element should not be set off by both parentheses and commas; the nonessential element could be set off by parentheses *or* commas, but not both.

D because the nonessential element should be set off by two dashes *or* two commas, not one dash and one comma.

Question 28. **The best answer is H** because it provides the most logical conjunction to connect the ideas presented in this sentence. Torres chose unique textures for his painting *Sun Light—Mario*: He used a checkered texture *and* a sharp and wiry texture for the features of an older man's face.

The best answer is NOT:

F because *so* is not logical in context; in the painting, the older man's skin texture isn't checkered because the hairs of his moustache appear sharp and wiry.

G because *since* is not logical in context; in the painting, the older man's skin texture isn't checkered because the hairs of his moustache appear sharp and wiry.

J because *for* is not logical in context; in the painting, the older man's skin texture isn't checkered in order that the hairs of his moustache appear sharp and wiry.

Question 29. **The best answer is A** because it provides the most effective conclusion to the sentence and the essay; Torres's quotation summarizes how his artistic process is similar to how his family has cultivated and harvested crops; his works are like planting an idea that will eventually become realized.

The best answer is NOT:

B because Torres's quotation that creating his works is effortless because of the joy they bring him does not effectively expand on the statement in the first part of the sentence that Torres's artistic process is similar to cultivating and harvesting crops.

C because Torres's quotation about how most of the Cuban population farms does not effectively expand on the statement in the first part of the sentence that Torres's artistic process is similar to cultivating and harvesting crops.

D because Torres's quotation that he has created works out of natural elements does not effectively expand on the statement in the first part of the sentence that Torres's artistic process is similar to cultivating and harvesting crops.

Question 30. **The best answer is G** because the essay focuses on how Torres's *Sun Light* series reflects his philosophy about the interconnectedness of everything and everyone, which is a key theme in his artwork.

The best answer is NOT:

F because, while Torres's childhood relationships had a significant influence on his work, there is no indication in the essay that Torres believes childhood relationships have the most profound influence on all artists.

H because the essay does focus on some of Torres's particular artworks: his *Sun Light* series.

J because the essay does discuss the thematic elements in Torres's *Sun Light* series.

Passage IV

Question 31. The best answer is A because it clearly and succinctly indicates that the young woman arrived at the same location where the narrator was waiting.

The best answer is NOT:

B because it unnecessarily repeats the first part of the sentence, explaining again that the narrator is waiting in a veterinarian's office.

C because it unnecessarily repeats that the narrator is waiting in the office. This information has already been established in the first part of the sentence: "I was waiting in the veterinarian's office."

D because it unnecessarily repeats that the narrator is there in the office. This information is already established in the first part of the sentence: "I was waiting in the veterinarian's office."

Question 32. The best answer is G because the verb *scuttling* provides a vivid description of the iguana's movement. This choice also provides a description of the iguana's rain forest environment, "dank undergrowth."

The best answer is NOT:

F because "walking on the ground" does not satisfy the requirement in the question that the choice be a vivid description. "Walking on the ground" indicates what the iguana does but is not a vivid description of the iguana's action or environment.

H because "living underneath the treetops" states an obvious point about iguanas and nearly restates the next part of the sentence, "resting high in the trees." No vivid modifiers or verbs are used.

J because the words "down low" are repetitive and the expression "moving about down low" is vague and imprecise.

Question 33. **The best answer is C** because the comma after *trees* indicates that the iguanas, not the canopy itself, are hidden in the trees.

The best answer is NOT:

A because it is nonsensical given the context of the sentence. The comma after *trees* followed by "which are hidden in the canopy" indicates that the trees themselves are hidden in the canopy.

B because it creates a comma splice. "They're . . . trees" is an independent clause. "They are hidden in the canopy" is another independent clause. Two independent clauses cannot be joined using only a comma.

D because the semicolon is incorrectly placed between an independent clause and an explanatory phrase in a simple sentence. Semicolons are used to join two independent clauses.

Question 34. **The best answer is J** because the *rows* specified in the response indicate the pattern of spikes that appear on the reptile. The word *lined* also indicates the position and pattern of the spikes.

The best answer is NOT:

F because "a spine with tiny spikes" indicates the size of the spikes but not the pattern of the spikes.

G because "just beginning to develop" indicates the potential size of the spikes and their development but not the arrangement or pattern of the spikes as stipulated in the question.

H because "small spikes on its armored back" indicates the size of the spikes and provides a visual description of the appearance and texture of the reptile's back but does not indicate the pattern of the spikes.

Question 35. The best answer is **B** because it creates a clear, logical, and parallel sentence (the verbs *caressed* and *watched* are parallel in form). The pronoun *it* later in the sentence also has a clear and logical antecedent, *pet*.

The best answer is NOT:

A because it is overly wordy and does not fit with the rest of the sentence. The underlined text is not parallel with the phrase "and watched it" later in the sentence, and the pronoun *it* has no clear antecedent.

C because it tries to link the participle *caressing* with the finite verb *watched* later in the sentence. This creates a confusing sequence of time when part of the action is an ongoing present action, *caressing*, and part of the action occurred in the past, *watched*.

D because it results in an illogical and ungrammatical transition to the rest of the sentence. The pronoun *it* has no clear antecedent.

Question 36. The best answer is **J** because no comma is needed to separate the prepositional phrase from the modifiers describing the iguana's eyes and how they shone.

The best answer is NOT:

F because there is an unnecessary comma between the modifiers ("large and bright") and the prepositional phrase ("from its scaly face").

G because there is an unnecessary comma between the preposition (*from*) and its object ("its scaly face").

H because there is an unnecessary comma between the modifiers joined by the conjunction *and*. No comma is needed here because *and* is joining two adjectives, not two independent clauses.

Question 37. The best answer is **A** because it clearly indicates that the narrator is comparing the iguana's actions to those of a judge delivering a verdict.

The best answer is NOT:

B because the phrase "having a delivery of a verdict" is awkward and wordy, and it does not make sense in the given context.

C because the phrase "in deliverance with a verdict" does not make sense in this context. The intended meaning of this action is unclear, especially when likened to the actions of the iguana.

D because the plural verb form *deliver* does not agree with the singular noun *judge*.

Question 38. The best answer is F because the word *looking* offers a concise and effective choice to compare the appearance of the iguana and the appearance of a kitten.

The best answer is NOT:

G because the phrase "like as if it was" offers a wordy and repetitive description of the iguana. This repetition is distracting and unnecessary. It is also overly informal given the style and tone of the rest of the essay.

H because the phrase "appearing something like" is wordy and vague. The phrase also does a poor job of setting up the comparison in the sentence: "appearing something like as content as a kitten, and close its eyes again." The meaning here is unclear.

J because the phrase "sort of like it was" is wordy and vague, which makes the comparison in the sentence less clear. The phrase is also overly informal for the style and tone of the essay.

Question 39. The best answer is B because placing the sentence at Point B further explains the young woman's statement that the iguana liked being held. The sentence is a logical extension of the preceding sentence.

The best answer is NOT:

A because neither the woman nor her pet iguana has entered the office yet, so placing the sentence at Point A is incorrect. The pronoun *she* in the added sentence would have no antecedent, so it would be unclear who is speaking.

C because placing the sentence at Point C interrupts the logical flow between the narrator's statement that she dislikes iguanas and her reasons for disliking the creatures.

D because placing the sentence at Point D interrupts the narrative flow between the iguana opening its eyes and the iguana staring at the narrator.

Question 40. The best answer is F because the essay focuses on the narrator's surprise that the iguana is pampered and loved by its owner. The iguana is lovingly caressed by its owner, which the narrator finds both amazing and unsettling.

The best answer is NOT:

G because there is no indication in the essay that the narrator believes the woman is impolite. The woman politely asks the narrator if she can let the reptile out of its carrier, and the narrator gives her approval. The narrator's guarded response comes from her awe at the relationship between owner and pet, not from annoyance.

H because the essay makes it clear that the narrator does not like iguanas, but it does not tell the story of why the narrator dislikes the creatures. The essay is primarily about the narrator's observation of a bond between an iguana and its owner on a particular day at a veterinary clinic.

J because the essay focuses on the narrator's observations of one iguana in a veterinary clinic. Only a brief mention is given to where iguanas live. Any physical descriptions in the essay focus on one pet iguana, not iguanas in general or as a species.

Passage V

Question 41. The best answer is D because it is the only option that creates correct subject-verb agreement. The singular subject "dip hop" must have singular verbs.

The best answer is NOT:

A because *challenge* and *help* are plural verbs, and the subject of the sentence is singular.

B because "are challenging" and "have helped" are plural verbs, and the subject of the sentence is singular.

C because *challenge* and "are helping" are plural verbs, and the subject of the sentence is singular.

Question 42. The best answer is F because it does not include any unnecessary punctuation.

The best answer is NOT:

G because it has unnecessary commas after the words *simply* and *ASL*.

H because it has an unnecessary dash after *hop* and unnecessary commas after *songs* and *expression*.

J because it has an unnecessary dash after *but*.

Question 43. The best answer is J because *integrate* is the most precise word in the context of the essay; it means "to blend into a functioning or unified whole," and the essay is conveying that dip hop artists blend different visual elements to enhance the sound vibrations of music.

The best answer is NOT:

F because *induct* does not fit the context; it means "to put in formal possession" or "to admit as a member," which does not logically convey blending visual elements to enhance sound vibrations.

G because *congregate* does not fit the context; it means "to collect into a group or crowd," which does not logically convey blending visual elements to enhance sound vibrations.

H because *compound* does not fit the context; it means "to form by combining parts," "to settle amicably," "to become joined in a compound," or "to come to terms of an agreement," none of which precisely convey blending visual elements to enhance sound vibrations.

Question 44. The best answer is F because the subjective pronoun *who* is appropriate in both instances. The first *who* agrees with its antecedent, *artists*, and the second *who* agrees with its antecedent, *those*. In addition, the pronoun *those* is appropriate because it agrees with its antecedent, *artists*, earlier in the sentence.

The best answer is NOT:

G because *whom* is in the objective case, and the subjective case is required in both instances here.

H because the pronouns *which* and *that* should be used for things, but in this sentence the pronouns refer to people. In addition, *them* is in the objective case, but the demonstrative pronoun *those* is required here in the subjective case.

J because the pronoun *which* should be used for things, but in this sentence the pronouns refer to people. In addition, *them* is in the objective case, but the demonstrative pronoun *those* is required here in the subjective case.

Question 45. The best answer is **C** because "Dip hop is resonating" most effectively leads the reader from the preceding paragraph about dip hop artists enhancing their style and music to be accessible to all audiences to the information in this paragraph about how that music has, as a result, increased in popularity.

The best answer is NOT:

A because the idea that many people have yet to encounter dip hop does not effectively lead the reader from the idea that dip hop music is increasingly accessible to all audiences to the idea that dip hop is increasing in popularity.

B because the idea that dip hop is just one style of rap does not effectively lead the reader from the idea that dip hop music is increasingly accessible to all audiences to the idea that dip hop is increasing in popularity.

D because the idea that each dip hop artist is unique does not effectively lead the reader from the idea that dip hop music is increasingly accessible to all audiences to the idea that dip hop is increasing in popularity.

Question 46. The best answer is **H** because it is the only option that creates correct subject-verb agreement. The singular subject *employee* must have a singular verb.

The best answer is NOT:

F because "have embraced" is a plural verb, and the subject of the sentence is singular.

G because "are embracing" is a plural verb, and the subject of the sentence is singular.

J because *embrace* is a plural verb, and the subject of the sentence is singular.

Question 47. The best answer is **B** because it correctly sets off the nonessential element ("all neighborhood residents and most of whom are under the age of thirty") from the rest of the sentence.

The best answer is NOT:

A because *thirty* is part of the nonessential element and therefore should be followed by a dash to match the punctuation that precedes the first part of the element ("all neighborhood").

C because *thirty* is part of the nonessential element and therefore should be followed by a dash instead of a comma to match the punctuation that precedes the first part of the element ("all neighborhood").

D because *thirty* is part of the nonessential element and therefore should be followed by a dash instead of a colon to match the punctuation that precedes the first part of the element ("all neighborhood").

Question 48. **The best answer is F** because "Dionta White" is an essential element of the sentence and therefore should not be set off by commas.

The best answer is NOT:

G because "Dionta White" is an essential element of the sentence and should not be set off by commas.

H because the comma after *member* incorrectly separates "farm team member" from its appositive, "Dionta White."

J because the comma after *White* incorrectly separates the subject from the predicate.

Question 49. **The best answer is C** because it is the only option that creates correct sentence structure: two independent clauses separated by a semicolon.

The best answer is NOT:

A because it uses a comma to separate two independent clauses, creating a comma splice.

B because it uses a comma to separate two independent clauses, creating a comma splice.

D because it uses a semicolon to separate an independent clause from a dependent clause, creating a sentence fragment.

Question 50. **The best answer is J** because it is the only option that creates correct sentence structure. It creates a complete sentence with a main subject and main verb.

The best answer is NOT:

F because it adds *that* after *stipends*, resulting in a sentence fragment.

G because it adds *who* after *employees*, resulting in a sentence fragment.

H because the sentence features three consecutive dependent clauses, which creates a sentence fragment.

Question 1. The correct answer is D. To calculate the value of x, first isolate the radical by adding 9 to both sides: $\sqrt{x} = 8 + 9 = 17$. Then, to calculate the value of x, square both sides to eliminate the square root: $(\sqrt{x})^2 = 17^2 \rightarrow x = 289$. If you chose **A**, you may have isolated the radical before squaring both sides but subtracted 9 instead of adding 9: $x = (8 - 9)^2 = (-1)^2 = 1$. If you chose **B**, you may have multiplied by 2 to try to eliminate the square root and then isolated the variable by adding 9: $x = 2(8) + 9 = 25$. If you chose **C**, you may have isolated the radical but then multiplied by 2 to try to eliminate the square root: $2(\sqrt{x}) = 2(8 + 9) = 2(17) = 34$.

Question 2. The correct answer is H. According to exponent rules, $\left(\frac{1}{a}\right)^{-b} = \left(\frac{a}{1}\right)^b$ for all nonzero real values of a. According to this rule, $\left(\frac{1}{64}\right)^{-\frac{1}{2}} = \left(\frac{64}{1}\right)^{\frac{1}{2}} = 64^{\frac{1}{2}}$. The fraction $\frac{1}{2}$ in the exponent indicates that you should take the square root of the term, so $64^{\frac{1}{2}} = \sqrt{64} = 8$. If you chose **F**, you may have taken the square root of $\frac{1}{64}$, resulting in $\frac{1}{8}$, then used the negative exponent to change the sign of positive $\frac{1}{8}$ to $-\frac{1}{8}$. If you chose **G**, you may have multiplied the two fractions: $\left(\frac{1}{64}\right)\left(-\frac{1}{2}\right) = -\frac{1}{128}$. If you chose **J**, you may have multiplied the two fractions and then taken the reciprocal: $\left(\frac{1}{64} \cdot \frac{1}{2}\right)^{-1} = \left(\frac{1}{128}\right)^{-1} = \frac{128}{1} = 128$.

Question 3. The correct answer is D. To calculate the decimal expansion of a fraction, divide the numerator by the denominator: $2 \div 3 = 0.\overline{6}$. This decimal expansion has only one repeating nonzero digit, namely 6. If you chose **A** or **C**, you may have divided the numerator by the denominator to calculate the decimal expansion and focused on the "nonzero" part of the requirement, ignoring the "one repeating digit" part of the requirement. If you chose **B**, you may have divided the numerator by the denominator to get 0.6, a one-decimal nonzero digit, ignoring the "repeating" requirement.

Question 4. The correct answer is J. For a fair coin, the expected proportion of heads is 0.5. A significant difference between 0.5 and the observed proportion is evidence a coin is not fair. The greater this difference, and the greater the sample size, the more evidence there is that the coin is not fair. Choice **J** represents the result with the greatest sample size, 6, and the greatest difference between the observed proportion and 0.5. That is, $\frac{5}{6} \approx 0.83 > 0.5$. Therefore, it provides the strongest evidence that the coin is not fair. If you chose **F, G,** or **H,** you may not have compared the sample size and the proportion of all the options.

Question 5. The correct answer is B. Let w represent the number of weeks after which Ana will have enough money. The inequality that models the situation is $15w + 45 > 200$. Solve for w by first subtracting 45: $15w > 200 - 45 \rightarrow 15w > 155$. Second, divide by 15: $w > \frac{155}{15}$. The result for w is $w > 10.3$. The minimum number of whole weeks after which Ana will have enough money has to be the next integer after 10.3, which is 11 weeks. If you chose **A**, you may have rounded 10.3 down to the closest integer, 10. If you chose **C**, you may have not added the money Ana already has saved to the inequality and instead solved $15w > 200$, which results in $w > \frac{200}{15} \rightarrow w > 13.3$. Then, you may have rounded 13.3 down to the closest integer, 13. If you chose **D**, you may have not added the money Ana already has saved to the inequality and instead solved $15w > 200$, which results in $w > \frac{200}{15} \rightarrow w > 13.3$. Then, you may have rounded up to the next integer, 14.

Question 6. The correct answer is F. One property of similar triangles is that corresponding angles of similar triangles are congruent. This means any two similar triangles will have the same angle measures. If you chose **G**, **H**, or **J**, you may have applied the properties of congruent triangles to similar triangles. While similar triangles can be congruent, they do not have to be (and often are not) congruent. As a counterexample to choices **G**, **H**, and **J**, consider ΔPQR and ΔXYZ, shown in the figure.

According to the Side-Side-Side Similarity Theorem (SSS~), $\Delta PQR \sim \Delta XYZ$ because each of the sides of ΔXYZ is twice as long as the corresponding side in ΔPQR; the sides are proportional, but the side lengths are not equal. Therefore, the side lengths of similar triangles do not have to be the same. The perimeter of $\Delta PQR = 5 + 12 + 13 = 30$ centimeters, and the perimeter of $\Delta XYZ = 10 + 24 + 26 = 60$ centimeters; therefore, the perimeters of similar triangles do not have to be the same. The area of $\Delta PQR = \frac{1}{2}(12)(5) = 30$ square centimeters, and the area of $\Delta XYZ = \frac{1}{2}(24)(10) = 120$ square centimeters; therefore, the areas of similar triangles do not have to be the same.

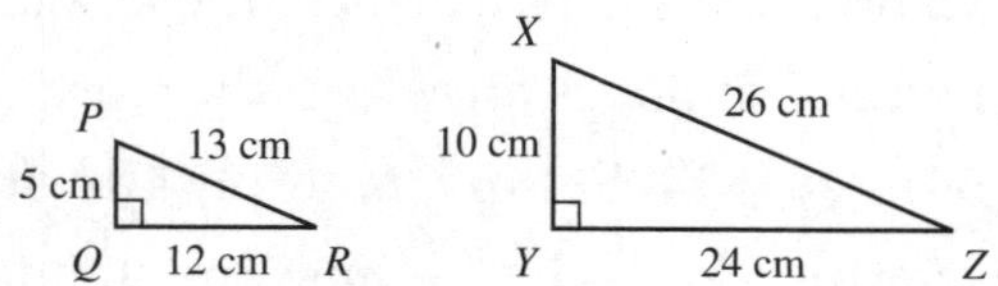

Question 7. The correct answer is B. Because $45 = 3^2 \cdot 5$, the factors of 45 are 1, 3, 5, 9, 15, and 45. Because $50 = 2 \cdot 5^2$, the factors of 50 are 1, 2, 5, 10, 25, and 50. Because $84 = 2^2 \cdot 3 \cdot 7$, the factors of 84 are 1, 2, 3, 4, 6, 7, 12, 14, 21, 28, 42, and 84. Note that 45, 50, and 84 share only the common factor 1. This means the greatest common factor of 45, 50, and 84 is 1. If you chose **A**, you may have thought that 45, 50, and 84 share no common factor. If you chose **C**, you may have considered the greatest common factor of only 50 and 84. If you chose **D**, you may have considered the greatest common factor of only 45 and 84.

Question 8. The correct answer is H. To square a binomial, multiply the binomial by itself and use the distributive property: $(3x - 9)(3x - 9) = (3x)(3x) + (3x)(-9) + (-9)(3x) + (-9)(-9)$. Alternatively, use the formula $(a - b)^2 = a^2 - 2ab + b^2$: $(3x - 9)^2 = (3x)^2 - 2(3x)(9) + 9^2 = 9x^2 - 54x + 81$. If you chose **F**, you may have distributed the exponent to each term of the binomial, multiplying each by 2 instead of squaring: $(3x - 9)^2 \rightarrow 2(3x) - 2(9) = 6x - 18$. If you chose **G**, you may have distributed the exponent to each term of the binomial but then multiplied the coefficient of the first term by 2 instead of squaring: $(3x - 9)^2 \rightarrow (3x)^2 + (-9)^2 \rightarrow (3 \cdot 2)x^2 + 81 = 6x^2 + 81$. If you chose **J**, you may have forgotten to multiply the middle term by 2 and multiplied the last term by 2 instead of squaring: $(3x - 9)^2 \rightarrow (3x)^2 - (3x)(9) + (9)^2 \rightarrow 9x^2 - 27x + (9 \cdot 2) = 9x^2 - 27x + 18$.

Question 9. The correct answer is B. Let n represent the number of East High School students in the proportion $\frac{11}{11 + 13} = \frac{n}{3{,}432}$. Solve by cross-multiplying and dividing: $(11)(3{,}432) = (11 + 13)n$, $\frac{(11)(3{,}432)}{(24)} = n$, $n = 1{,}573$. If you chose **A**, you may have let x represent the number of students and set up the equation $11x + 13x = 3{,}432$. The solution is $x = 143$; however, you would need to calculate the value of $11x$ to answer the given question. If you chose **C**, you may have set up a proportion but put 13 in the denominator instead of 24: $\frac{11}{13} = \frac{n}{3{,}432}$. If you chose **D**, you may have set up a proportion but put 13 in the denominator instead of 24 and flipped the second ratio: $\frac{11}{13} = \frac{3{,}432}{n}$.

Question 10. The correct answer is J. To calculate the amount the worker earned for 54 hours, first calculate the number of hours for which the worker earns $1\frac{1}{2}$ times the standard hourly wage (overtime): $54 - 40 = 14$. Second, multiply 40 hours by the standard hourly wage, $40(20.10)$, and the overtime hours by $1\frac{1}{2}$ times the standard hourly wage, $14\left(1\frac{1}{2}\right)(20.10)$. Lastly, calculate the sum of the two numeric expressions. If you chose **F**, you may have multiplied the total hours worked by $1\frac{1}{2}$ times the standard hourly wage. If you chose **G**, you may have multiplied the total hours worked by $2\frac{1}{2}$ times the standard hourly wage. If you chose **H**, you may have calculated the number of hours for which the worker earns overtime and multiplied the standard hourly wage by 40 hours, but then you multiplied overtime hours by $\frac{1}{2}$ instead of $1\frac{1}{2}$.

Question 11. The correct answer is C. First, isolate the variable z in the equation $z^2 = -9$ by taking the square root of each side: $\sqrt{z^2} = \pm\sqrt{-9} \rightarrow z = \pm\sqrt{-9}$. Second, evaluate the square root, recognizing that since $-9 = (9)(-1)$, each factor should be evaluated: $\pm\sqrt{-9} = \pm(\sqrt{9})(\sqrt{-1}) = \pm 3i$. Note that only the positive root is listed in answer choice **C**. If you chose **A**, you may have taken the square root of each side to isolate z but then moved the negative sign from under the radical to outside the radical: $\sqrt{-9} \rightarrow -\sqrt{9} = -3$. If you chose **B**, you may have taken the square root of each side to isolate z but then removed the negative sign from under the radical: $\sqrt{-9} \rightarrow \sqrt{9} = 3$. If you chose **D**, you may have taken the square root of each side to isolate z but then applied the radical only to -1 when evaluating the square root: $\sqrt{-9} \rightarrow 9\sqrt{-1} = 9i$.

Question 12. The correct answer is H. The line is positioned below the points, and its slope aligns with the paired data, indicating that it needs to be translated upward, thus increasing the y-intercept. Choice H is the only one that increases the y-intercept. Increasing the y-intercept by 12.5 would translate the line upward so that about half the points would be below and half would be above the line. If you chose **F**, you may have thought that the slope was 1 because the numbers on the axes are the same. The coefficient of x in the given equation indicates a slope of 0.25. Increasing the slope by 0.75 would result in a slope of 1. If you chose **G**, you may have thought that the slope should be 0 (the line should be horizontal). Decreasing the slope by 0.25 would result in a slope of 0. If you chose **J**, you may have correctly noticed that the line is below the points and that the slope aligns to the paired data, but you thought the translation was negative and so chose a decrease of the y-intercept instead of an increase.

Question 13. The correct answer is C. To calculate the probability that the second selected member will be a senior, divide the number of available seniors by the total number of available committee members (sum of 11 juniors and 79 seniors minus 1 selected junior): $\frac{79}{(11 + 79) - 1} = \frac{79}{89}$. If you chose **A**, you may have divided the number of available juniors (instead of seniors) by the number of seniors (instead of total number available): $\frac{11 - 1}{79} = \frac{10}{79}$. If you chose **B**, you may have divided the number of available juniors (instead of seniors) by the total number of available committee members: $\frac{11 - 1}{(11 + 79) - 1} = \frac{10}{89}$. If you chose **D**, you may have divided the number of seniors by the total number in the committee without subtracting 1 to represent the selected junior: $\frac{79}{11 + 79} = \frac{79}{90}$.

Question 14. **The correct answer is F.** First, identify that the smallest engine size in the table is 2 L and that it is paired with a weight of 1,041 kg. Next, calculate the **predicted** weight of a vehicle with an engine size of 2 L by evaluating the linear model at $x = 2$: $\hat{w} = 375(2) + 370 = 1,120$. Finally, find the difference between the predicted weight you just calculated and the actual weight given in the table: $1,120 - 1,041 = 79$. If you chose **G**, you may have subtracted the sum of the coefficient and constant term of the model from the actual weight of the lightest vehicle: $1,041 - (375 + 370) = 296$. If you chose **H**, you may have thought that the constant term of the model, 370, is the difference between the actual and predicted weights. If you chose **J**, you may have thought that the difference in weight is the actual weight minus the constant term of the model: $1,041 - 370 = 671$.

Question 15. **The correct answer is A.** Domain is the set of input values. Because d is a function of t, the input values are represented by all the t-values of the points on the graph. The graph is an uninterrupted line segment. The t-values of the endpoints of the graph are 0 and 13. Therefore, the domain is the set $[0, 13]$. If you chose **B**, you may have thought that the domain starts at 0 and ends at the quotient of the maximum distance and time: $\left[0, \frac{860}{13}\right] \Rightarrow \left[0, 66\frac{2}{13}\right]$. If you chose **C**, you may have thought that the domain starts at 0 and ends at the average of the maximum distance and time: $\left[0, \frac{860 + 13}{2}\right] \Rightarrow \left[0, 436\frac{1}{2}\right]$. If you chose **D**, you may have confused the domain with the range, which is the set of all d-values of the points on the graph: $[0, 860]$.

Question 16. **The correct answer is G.** The midpoint of a line segment that has endpoints at (x_1, y_1) and (x_2, y_2) is $\left(\frac{x_1 + x_2}{2}, \frac{y_1 + y_2}{2}\right)$. The midpoint of this segment is thus $\left(\frac{-5 + 3}{2}, \frac{8 + (-1)}{2}\right) = \left(-1, \frac{7}{2}\right)$. If you chose **F**, you may have added the x_1-value and subtracted the y_1-value, and you may have forgotten to divide by 2: $(-5 + 3, -1 - 8) = (-2, -9)$. If you chose **H**, you may have subtracted the x_1- and y_1-values instead of adding: $\left(\frac{3 - (-5)}{2}, \frac{-1 - 8}{2}\right) = \left(4, -\frac{9}{2}\right)$. If you chose **J**, you may have subtracted the x_1- and y_1-values instead of adding, and you may have forgotten to divide by 2: $(3 - (-5), -1 - 8) = (8, -9)$.

Question 17. **The correct answer is A.** Divide both terms of the numerator by the denominator, reduce each quotient, and rationalize: $\frac{10i}{2i} + \frac{2}{2i} \Rightarrow 5 + \frac{1}{i} \Rightarrow 5 + \frac{1(i)}{i(i)} \Rightarrow 5 + \frac{i}{i^2} \Rightarrow 5 + \frac{i}{-1} \Rightarrow 5 - i$. If you chose **B**, you may have crossed out the i's in the original expression and then evaluated what remained: $\frac{10i + 2}{2i} = \frac{12}{2} = 6$. If you chose **C**, you may have divided only the second term and then combined it with the first term: $10i + \frac{2}{2i} \Rightarrow 10i + \frac{1}{i} \Rightarrow 10i - i \Rightarrow 9i$. If you chose **D**, you may have divided only the second term and got the sign wrong before combining that with the first term: $10i + \frac{2}{2i} \Rightarrow 10i + \frac{1}{i} \Rightarrow 10i + i \Rightarrow 11i$.

Question 18. The correct answer is G. Observe that the coefficient of y in the bottom equation is an integer multiple of the coefficient of y in the top equation. Multiply the top equation by 6 so the y-terms are opposite: $\begin{cases} 6(8x + y = 6) \\ 9x - 6y = 11 \end{cases} \Rightarrow \begin{cases} 48x + 6y = 36 \\ 9x - 6y = 11 \end{cases}$. Then combine the equations (add corresponding terms) to get $57x = 47$, and finally divide both sides to solve: $x = \frac{47}{57}$. If you chose **F**, you may have multiplied the top equation by 6, but subtracted the x-terms and constant terms instead of adding: $39x = 25 \Rightarrow x = \frac{25}{39}$. If you chose **H**, you may have done everything correctly until the last step and divided in the wrong order: $x = \frac{57}{47}$. If you chose **J**, you may have multiplied the top equation by 6, subtracted instead of adding to get $39x = 25$, and then divided in the wrong order: $x = \frac{39}{25}$.

Question 19. The correct answer is A. Any function of the form $y = A \sin(Bx)$ has an amplitude of $|A|$ and a period of $\frac{2\pi}{B}$. For the given function $y = 2\sin(6\pi x)$, the value of A is 2, and the value of B is 6π. Therefore, the amplitude is $|2| = 2$ and the period is $\frac{2\pi}{6\pi} = \frac{1}{3}$. If you chose **B**, you may have thought that the amplitude was $2A$, or $2(2) = 4$. If you chose **C**, you may have thought that the period was $\frac{B}{2\pi}$, or $\frac{6\pi}{2\pi} = 3$. If you chose **D**, you may have thought that the amplitude was $2A$, or $2(2) = 4$, and the period was $\frac{B}{2\pi}$, or $\frac{6\pi}{2\pi} = 3$.

Question 20. The correct answer is G. The solution is obtained by dividing both sides by c and then adding h to both sides: $\frac{c(x - h)}{c} = \frac{q}{c} \Rightarrow x - h = \frac{q}{c}; x - h + h = \frac{q}{c} + h \Rightarrow x = \frac{q}{c} + h$. If you chose **F**, you may have subtracted h instead of adding: $x = \frac{q}{c} - h$. If you chose **H**, you may have added h to both sides and canceled the h terms on the left side before dividing by c: $c(x - h) + h = q + h \Rightarrow cx = q + h; \frac{cx}{c} = \frac{q + h}{c} \Rightarrow x = \frac{q + h}{c} = \frac{q}{c} + \frac{h}{c}$. If you chose **J**, you may have added c to the right (instead of dividing) and divided the result by h (instead of adding): $x = \frac{q + c}{h} = \frac{q}{h} + \frac{c}{h}$.

Question 21. The correct answer is A. The angle opposite the shortest side has the least measure. Segment $\overline{ST}$ is the shortest side. The angle opposite $\overline{ST}$ is $\angle R$. Therefore, the measure of $\angle R$ is the least. If you chose **B**, you may have thought that $\angle S$ has the least measure because it is opposite the longest side, $\overline{RT}$. If you chose **C**, you may have thought that $\angle R$ has the greatest measure because it is opposite the shortest side, $\overline{ST}$. If you chose **D**, you may have thought that $\angle T$ had the greatest measure because the longest side, $\overline{RT}$, ends in T.

Your First Practice Test

Question 22. The correct answer is G. The inverse is obtained by replacing $f(x)$ with y in the equation ($y = 2x - 5$), switching the variables x and y in the equation ($x = 2y - 5$), and solving the resulting equation for y by adding 5 and then dividing by 2: $x + 5 = 2y - 5 + 5 \Rightarrow$ $x + 5 = 2y$; $\frac{x+5}{2} = \frac{2y}{2} \Rightarrow \frac{x+5}{2} = y = f^{-1}(x)$. If you chose **F**, you may have subtracted 5 instead of adding before dividing by 2: $y = \frac{x-5}{2}$. If you chose **H**, you may have added 2 and divided by 5 instead of adding 5 and dividing by 2: $y = \frac{x+2}{5}$. If you chose **J**, you may have divided the variable terms only by 2 before adding 5 to both sides: $x = 2y - 5 \Rightarrow \frac{x}{2} = \frac{2y-5}{2} \Rightarrow \frac{x}{2} = y - 5$; $\frac{x}{2} + 5 = y - 5 + 5 \Rightarrow \frac{1}{2}x + 5 = y$.

Question 23. The correct answer is C. Notice that the unshaded region in the bottom right of the figure is the same size as the shaded region inside the triangle formed at the top left of the figure by point A, point C, and the center of the circle. Therefore, the area of all the shaded regions can be calculated by subtracting the area of the triangle in the top left of the figure from the area of the square. The side length, s, of the square is twice the radius: $s = 2 \times 8 = 16$ inches. The area of the square, in square inches, is the side length squared: $A_{square} = s^2 = 16^2 = 256$ square inches. The area of the triangle is $A_{triangle} = \frac{1}{2}bh$, where b is the length of the base and h is the height of the triangle. Both b and h are 8 inches: $A_{triangle} = \frac{1}{2}(8)(8) = 32$ square inches. Now, subtract the areas: $256 - 32 = 224$ square inches. If you chose **A**, you may have thought the radius was the side length of the square and calculated $8^2 = 64$. If you chose **B**, you may have used the equation for the area of a circle but known that the area is $\frac{7}{8}$ of the total area: $\frac{7}{8}\pi r^2 = \frac{7}{8}\pi(8^2) \approx 176$. If you chose **D**, you may have calculated the area of the square and forgotten to subtract the area of the unshaded regions: $16^2 = 256$.

Question 24. The correct answer is F. In order to map the point $(4, -16)$ to the point $(1, -4)$, you must multiply the x and y coordinates by a scale factor. Find the scale factor, s, by setting up the equation for either the x or the y coordinate: $4s = 1$ or $-16s = -4$. Solve either equation for s: $4s = 1 \rightarrow \frac{4s}{4} = \frac{1}{4} \rightarrow s = \frac{1}{4}$ or $-16s = -4 \rightarrow \frac{-16s}{-16} = \frac{-4}{-16} \rightarrow s = \frac{1}{4}$. Now, multiply the x and y coordinates of the point $(12, -24)$ by that scale factor: $\left(\frac{1}{4} \cdot 12, \frac{1}{4} \cdot -24\right) = (3, -6)$. Therefore, the dilation maps the given point to $(3, -6)$. If you chose **G**, you may have calculated the translation instead of the dilation: $(4, -16) + (-3, -12) = (1, -4)$. The translation of the given point is $(12 - 3, -24 - 12) = (9, -36)$. If you chose **H**, you may have confused dilation with translation and confused image with pre-image. You may have noticed that $(4, -16) = (1, -4) + (3, -12)$. Then, you may have calculated $(12 + 3, -24 - 12) = (15, -36)$. If you chose **J**, you may have thought the scale factor was 4, instead of $\frac{1}{4}$, and calculated $(12 + 4, -24 + 4) = (16, -20)$.

Question 25. The correct answer is A. The expected value is the total sum of each outcome times the chance of that outcome occurring. Multiply each revenue in the table times the corresponding probability and add those results: $400(0.02) + $100(0.02) + $60(0.04) + $0(0.92) = $8 + $2 + $2.40 + $0 = $12.40. If you chose **B**, you may have forgotten to multiply 0 times 0.92 and calculated $400(0.02) + $100(0.02) + $60(0.04) + (0.92) = $13.32. If you chose **C**, you may have calculated the average revenue and multiplied that by the average probability: $\left(\frac{\$400 + \$100 + \$60 + 0}{4} \right)\left(\frac{0.02 + 0.02 + 0.04 + 0.92}{4} \right) = (\$140)(0.25) = \$35$. If you chose **D**, you may have calculated the median of the revenue amounts. The median is half the sum of the middle two values: $\frac{\$100 + \$60}{2} = \$80$.

Question 26. The correct answer is F. In a normal distribution, the values are distributed so that half (50%) of the random variable X values are below the mean and half of the values are above the mean. The maximum of the curve is the mean, or $X = 1,000$. Notice that two of the percentages for regions below the mean are given and one is missing. The missing percentage, $P(800 < X < 900)$, is calculated by subtracting the given percentages below the mean from 50%, since that is half the X values: $50\% - 34\% - 2\% = 14\%$. The curve is symmetrical, so the missing percentages above the mean are 34%, 14%, and 2%. The area under the curve for $P(800 < X < 900) = P(1,100 < X < 1,200)$. Therefore, $P(1,100 < X < 1,200) = 14\%$. If you chose **G**, you may have thought the distribution was half of what is between 1,000 and 1,100 and calculated $\frac{34\%}{2} = 17\%$. If you chose **H**, you may have calculated half the sum of the two given percentages: $\frac{2\% + 34\%}{2} = 18\%$. If you chose **J**, you may have estimated the distribution to be slightly less than 34% since the region between 1,100 and 1,200 is smaller than the region between 900 and 1,000.

Question 27. The correct answer is A. There are four repeating decimals in the expanded form. Calculate the 323rd digit by dividing 4 into 323 to find the remainder. If the remainder is 1, then the digit will be the first repeating decimal, or 7. If the remainder is 2, then the digit will be the second repeating decimal, or 4. If the remainder is 3, then the digit will be the third repeating decimal, or 1. If the remainder is 0, then the digit will be the fourth repeating decimal, or 2. The remainder is 3, so the 323rd digit is 1.

$$
\begin{array}{r}
80\ \text{R3} \\
4\overline{)323} \\
-32 \\
\hline
03 \\
-0 \\
\hline
3
\end{array}
$$

If you chose **B, C,** or **D**, then you may have made a mistake calculating the remainder or counting digits.

Question 28. **The correct answer is H.** Drawing a picture to represent the situation is helpful. A right triangle can be drawn incorporating the angle of elevation, the distance walked, and the height of the tree. Let h represent the height of the tree in feet.

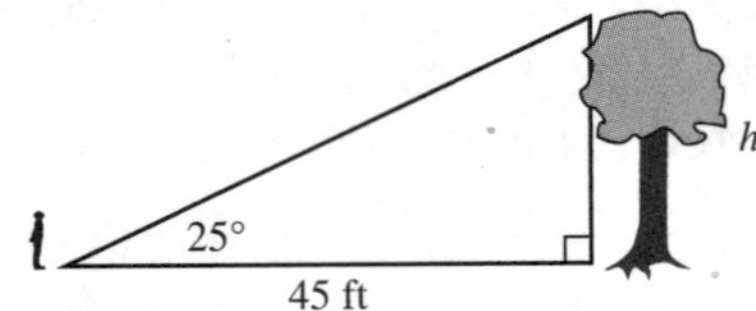

The tangent of the angle of elevation is equal to the ratio of the length of the opposite side to the length of the adjacent side: $\tan \theta = \frac{\text{opposite}}{\text{adjacent}} \rightarrow \tan 25° = \frac{h}{45}$. Solve the equation for h by multiplying both sides by 45. Therefore, $h = 45 \tan 25°$. If you chose **F**, you may have confused the ratio for sine with that for tangent: $\sin \theta = \frac{\text{opposite}}{\text{hypotenuse}}$. If you chose **G**, you may have confused the ratio for cosine with that for tangent: $\cos \theta = \frac{\text{adjacent}}{\text{hypotenuse}}$. If you chose **J**, you may have confused the ratio for cotangent with that for tangent: $\cot \theta = \frac{\text{adjacent}}{\text{opposite}}$.

Question 29. **The correct answer is B.** First, calculate the volume, V, of the cone-shaped sugar that leaked out of the bag using $V = \frac{\pi}{3}r^2h$, where r is the radius and h is the height. The volume is $\left(\frac{\pi}{3}\right)(3^2)(2) = 6\pi$ cubic inches. Next, convert cubic inches to pounds by multiplying the volume and the given conversion factor: $(6\pi \text{ in}^3)\left(\frac{0.025 \text{ lbs}}{\text{in}^3}\right) \approx 0.471$ lbs. Finally, subtract the leaked sugar volume from the volume of the bag: 1.5 lbs − 0.471 lbs = 1.029 lbs. If you chose **A**, you may have calculated the difference between the weights of the sugar bag and the leaked sugar but dropped the $\frac{1}{3}$ from the formula: $1.5 - (\pi)(3^2)(2)(0.025)$. If you chose **C**, you may have calculated the difference between the weights, but in order to calculate the cone volume, you may have multiplied only the dimensions: $1.5 - (3)(2)(0.025)$. If you chose **D**, you may have calculated the difference between the weights but used only the conversion factor for the leaked sugar volume: $1.5 - 0.025$.

Question 30. The correct answer is H. The area of the sidewalk will be $20(10) - 6(16) = 200 - 96 = 104$ square feet. The volume of concrete needed to make the sidewalk is $104 \cdot \left(4 \text{ in} \cdot \frac{1 \text{ ft}}{12 \text{ in}}\right) = \frac{104}{3}$ cubic feet. The number of bags of concrete needed to make the sidewalk is $\frac{104}{3} \div 0.6 = \frac{104}{1.8} \approx 57.8$, or 58 whole bags. If you chose **F**, you may have calculated the volume of the sidewalk as $104 \div 4 = 26$ square feet and the number of bags as $26 \div 0.6 \approx 43.3$, or 44 whole bags. If you chose **G**, you may have calculated the area of the sidewalk as $4(10) + 4(20) = 40 + 80 = 120$ square feet, the volume as $120 \cdot \left(\frac{1 \text{ ft}}{4 \text{ in}}\right) = 30$ cubic feet, and the number of bags as $30 \div 0.6 = 50$ whole bags. If you chose **J**, you may have calculated the area of the sidewalk as 120 square feet as in **G**, the volume as $120 \cdot \left(4 \text{ in} \cdot \frac{1 \text{ ft}}{12 \text{ in}}\right) = 40$ cubic feet, and the number of bags as $40 \div 0.6 \approx 66.7$, or 67 whole bags.

Question 31. The correct answer is A. In a simplified binomial expansion, the sum of the variables' exponents in a term is equal to the power of the expression, which is n. In the term $8x^3y$, the sum of the variables' exponents is $3 + 1$, or 4. Thus, $n = 4$. The number of terms in a simplified binomial expansion is one greater than the power: $4 + 1 = 5$. Therefore, the total number of terms is 5. If you chose **B**, you may have thought that the number of terms was equal to the coefficient of the second term, 8. If you chose **C**, you may have added the coefficient and the exponent of x: $8 + 3$. If you chose **D**, you may have added the coefficient and both exponents: $8 + 3 + 1$.

Question 32. The correct answer is H. There are three coordinate values given for time t and concentration $C(t)$: (0, 850), (6, 151), and (12, 27). For a function to be linear, it must have a constant rate of change, which means the slope between the points is the same. Calculate the slopes, $m = \frac{y_2 - y_1}{x_2 - x_1}$, between the points: $\frac{151 - 850}{6 - 0} = -116.5$ and $\frac{27 - 151}{12 - 6} \approx -20.667$. The function is not linear because the slopes are not the same. For a function to be exponential, it must change by equal factors over equal intervals. Exponential functions have the form $f(x) = ab^x$, where a is the initial value such that $a \neq 0$ and b is the growth or decay factor. The concentration is decreasing, so $0 < b < 1$, and exponential decay may have occurred. At $t = 0$, the concentration is 850 mg/L, so $a = 850$, and the equation is $C(t) = 850b^t$. If substituting both (6, 151) and (12, 27) into the equation results in the same value for b, then an exponential function models the situation. Calculate b for both ordered pairs by substituting, then dividing by 850, and finally canceling the power: $151 = 850b^6 \rightarrow b = \sqrt[6]{\frac{151}{850}} \approx 0.750$ and $27 = 850b^{12} \rightarrow b = \sqrt[12]{\frac{27}{850}} \approx 0.750$. Therefore, the function is exponential because over equal time intervals, the concentration decreases by equal factors. If you chose **F**, you may have confused linear and exponential functions but realized that over equal time intervals, the concentration decreased by equal factors. If you chose **G**, you may have realized the concentrations were decreasing but not known how, and you may have confused the term *linear* with *exponential*. If you chose **J**, you may have known the right model but not that the decrease in concentration was by equal factors over equal time intervals.

Question 33. The correct answer is C. A rational number can be written as an integer or a quotient of integers; examples include 7 and $\frac{1}{3}$. An irrational number cannot be written as an integer or a quotient of integers; examples include π and $\sqrt{3}$. Subtracting a rational number from an irrational number results in an irrational number. Since $-4\sqrt{14}$ is an irrational number and n is a rational number, the result of $-4\sqrt{14} - n$ must be an irrational number. Dividing that irrational number by 2 still results in an irrational number. If you chose **A**, you may have substituted a value such as $n = -20$ into the expression and gotten a positive number: $\frac{-4\sqrt{14} - -20}{2} = -2\sqrt{14} + 10 \approx 2.517$. However, a positive result is not always the outcome. For example, substituting $n = 10$ into the expression generates a negative number: $\frac{-4\sqrt{14} - 10}{2} = -2\sqrt{14} - 5 \approx -12.483$. If you chose **B**, you may have substituted a value such as $n = 10$ into the expression and gotten a negative number: -12.483. However, a negative result is not always the outcome. For example, substituting $n = -20$ generates a positive number: 2.517. If you chose **D**, you may have thought that $-4\sqrt{14}$ was a rational number and known that a rational number minus a rational number is a rational number.

Question 34. The correct answer is G. In order to determine the x-intercepts of a function, substitute $y = 0$ into the equation for the function and solve for x. Here, $\frac{x^2}{9} - \frac{y^2}{49} = 1 \rightarrow$ $\frac{x^2}{9} - \frac{0^2}{49} = 1 \leftrightarrow \frac{x^2}{9} = 1 \leftrightarrow x^2 = 9$. Take the square root of both sides: $\sqrt{x^2} = \sqrt{9} \leftrightarrow x = \pm 3$. Therefore, the two x-intercepts of the function are the points $(3, 0)$ and $(-3, 0)$. Choose the intercept that is listed in the answer choices: $(3, 0)$. If you chose **F**, you may have thought the center of the hyperbola, $(0, 0)$, was a point on the graph of the hyperbola. If you chose **H**, you may have substituted $x = 0$ instead of $y = 0$: $\frac{x^2}{9} - \frac{y^2}{49} = 1 \rightarrow \frac{0^2}{9} - \frac{y^2}{49} = 1$. Then, you may have made a sign error by dropping the negative: $\frac{y^2}{49} = 1 \leftrightarrow y^2 = 49 \leftrightarrow y = \pm 7$. If you chose **J**, you may have calculated $x^2 = 9$ but not taken the square root of both sides.

Question 35. The correct answer is D. The graph shown is a transformation of the graph of a basic logarithmic equation, $y = \log_a(x)$. This limits the possible answer choices to **C** and **D**. Because **C** and **D** are transformations of the graph of $y = \log_4(x)$, it is safe to assume $a = 4$. The graph of $y = \log_4(x)$ has a vertical asymptote at $x = 0$ and a point at $(1, 0)$. The vertical asymptote for the given graph is at $x = -2$, which means it is the result of a translation of the parent function, $y = \log_4(x)$, 2 units to the left: $y = \log_4(x + 2)$. This is enough to determine that the correct answer is **D**, but you can also verify **D** is correct by testing a point. Translating the point $(1, 0)$ to the left 2 units results in an x-coordinate of -1. Substitute -1 for x in answer choice **D** to calculate the y-coordinate: $y = 4\log_4(-1 + 2) + 4 = 4\log_4(1) + 4 = 4(0) + 4 = 4$, which means that the point $(-1, 4)$ is on the transformed graph. The given graph is shown to include this point, so the correct answer is **D**. If you chose **A** or **B**, you may have thought the given graph was a transformation of the graph of an exponential function, $y = 4^x$. If you chose **C**, you may have switched the vertical and horizontal transformations. That is, you may have thought the graph was translated right 4 units and down 2 units instead of left 2 units and up 4 units.

Question 36. The correct answer is H. Event W consists of 14 simple events, so $|W| = 14$. Similarly, $|X| = 11$. None of the simple events in event X are in event W, so the intersection of events W and X (event Y) is empty. This means $|Y| = 0$. None of the simple events in event X and event W are the same, so the union of these two events (event Z) will include all 14 simple events in W and all 11 simple events in X. This means $|Z| = 14 + 11 = 25$. Since $0 < 11 < 14 < 25$, the correct order is $|Y| < |X| < |W| < |Z|$. If you chose **F**, you may have thought that the intersection of two events would always have more simple events than the events themselves but fewer simple events than the union of the events. If you chose **G**, you may have thought that the intersection of two events would always have the most simple events. If you chose **J**, you may have thought that the events themselves would always have more simple events than either the intersection or the union of the events.

Question 37. The correct answer is C. Because $\triangle DEH$ is formed by connecting the midpoints of the sides of $\triangle ABC$, $\triangle DEH$ is similar to $\triangle ABC$, and the ratio of the side lengths of $\triangle ABC$ to the corresponding side lengths of $\triangle DEH$ is 2:1. Because F and G are midpoints of $\overline{DH}$ and $\overline{EH}$, $\overline{FG}$ is a midsegment of $\triangle DEH$. Therefore, $\triangle DEH$ and $\triangle FGH$ are similar triangles with corresponding side lengths in the ratio 2:1. This must mean that $\triangle ABC$ and $\triangle FGH$ are similar triangles with corresponding side lengths in the ratio 4:1. The ratio of the areas of similar triangles is the square of the ratio of their corresponding side lengths. Therefore, the ratio of the area of $\triangle ABC$ to the area of $\triangle FGH$ is 16:1. If you chose **A**, you may have calculated the ratio of the area of $\triangle ABC$ to the area of $\triangle DEH$. If you chose **B**, you may have thought squaring a value multiplies it by 2: $4(2) = 8$ instead of $4^2 = 16$. If you chose **D**, you may have calculated the cube of the ratio of corresponding sides rather than the square of the ratio: $4^3 : 1^3 = 64:1$.

Question 38. The correct answer is J. The average of the 10 test scores is x, so the total sum of the scores is $10x$. Let H be the highest score and L be the lowest score. Then $y = \frac{10x - (H + L)}{8} \rightarrow 8y = 10x - (H + L)$, or $H + L = 10x - 8y$. Therefore, the average of the highest and lowest scores is $\frac{H + L}{2} = \frac{10x - 8y}{2}$. If you chose **F**, you may have correctly calculated the sum of the highest and lowest values, but you forgot to average the two. If you chose **G**, you may have calculated the average of the two given averages, x and y. If you chose H, you may have incorrectly changed a sign when solving for the sum of the highest and lowest values: $y = \frac{10x - (H + L)}{8} \rightarrow H + L = 10x + 8y$.

Question 39. The correct answer is B. Let the slope of one of the lines be m, where $m \neq 0$. Any two perpendicular lines have slopes that are negative reciprocals of one another, so the slope of the other line must be $-\frac{1}{m}$. The product of the two slopes is therefore $m\left(-\frac{1}{m}\right) = -\frac{m}{m} = -1$. If you chose **A**, you might have calculated the difference rather than the product of the slopes and made a mistake when canceling the m: $\left(-\frac{1}{m}\right) - m \rightarrow -\frac{1}{m} - m \rightarrow -1 - 1 = -2$. If you chose **C**, you may have thought the slopes were only reciprocals of one another, not negative reciprocals, so their product would be $m\left(\frac{1}{m}\right) = \frac{m}{m} = 1$. If you chose **D**, you might have calculated the difference rather than the product of the slopes and made a mistake when canceling the m: $m - \left(-\frac{1}{m}\right) \leftrightarrow m + \frac{1}{m} \rightarrow m + \frac{1}{m} \rightarrow 1 + 1 = 2$.

Question 40. The correct answer is J. There are two cases to consider.

Case 1: The value of m is positive. If m is positive, then subtracting a positive value of n will decrease the absolute value of $m - n$, so n needs to be negative in order for $|m - n|$ to be as large as possible. The greatest possible value of m that fits the given constraints is $m = 4$, and the least possible value of n that fits the given constraints is $n = -10$. Therefore, $|m - n| = |4 - (-10)| = |14| = 14$.

Case 2: The value of m is negative. If m is negative, then subtracting a positive value of n will increase the absolute value of $m - n$. Therefore, in order for $|m - n|$ to be as large as possible, choose the least possible value of m that fits the given constraints, $m = -3$, and the greatest possible value of n that fits the given constraints, $n = 9$. The result is $|m - n| = |-3 - 9| = |-12| = 12$.

Since $12 < 14$, case 1 yields the greatest possible value of $|m - n|$, which is 14. If you chose **F**, you may have selected the largest possible values for both m and n that fit the given constraints: $|4 - 9| = |-5| = 5$. If you chose **G**, you may have selected the least possible values for both m and n that fit the given constraints: $|-3 - (-10)| = |7| = 7$. If you chose **H**, you may have thought case 2 resulted in the larger value.

Question 41. The correct answer is A. The remainder theorem states that $(x - a)$ is a factor of a polynomial $p(x)$ if and only if $p(a) = 0$. Here, $x + 4 = x - (-4)$ is a factor of $p(x)$, so it must be true that $p(-4) = 0$. Substitute $x = -4$ into the expression for $p(x)$, set the expression equal to 0, and solve for c: $2.5(-4)^2 - 30(-4) + c = 0 \leftrightarrow 40 + 120 + c = 0 \leftrightarrow c = -160$. If you chose **B**, you may have thought the question was asking for the value that, when summed with the root, -4, would result in the coefficient of the middle term, -30. If you chose **C**, you may have substituted $x = 4$ instead of $x = -4$: $2.5(4)^2 - 30(4) + c = 0 \leftrightarrow c = 80$. If you chose **D**, you may have forgotten the exponent on the first term and substituted $x = 4$ instead of $x = -4$: $2.5(4) - 30(4) + c = 0 \leftrightarrow c = 110$.

Question 42. The correct answer is H. The total number of ways an employee can answer all 5 questions on the questionnaire is the product of the number of ways an employee can answer each question on the questionnaire. There are two options for each question, so there are $2 \times 2 \times 2 \times 2 \times 2 = 2^5 = 32$ ways an employee can answer all 5 questions. If you chose **F**, you may have thought the total number of ways was the sum of the number of questions and the number of choices for each question, $5 + 2 = 7$. If you chose **G**, you may have calculated $5^2 = 25$ instead of 2^5. If you chose **J**, you may have thought there were 6 questions on the questionnaire and calculated $2^6 = 64$.

Question 43. The correct answer is A. The phrase "40% of m is equal to a" can be written mathematically as $\frac{40}{100}m = a$, or $m = \frac{100}{40}a$, which simplifies to $m = \frac{5}{2}a$. The equation $b = \frac{7a}{10}$ can be written as $\frac{10}{7}b = a$. The phrase "112% of m" can be written mathematically as $\frac{112}{100}m = \frac{28}{25}m$. Substituting the relationships between m and a and then b and a results in $\frac{28}{25}m = \frac{28}{25}\left(\frac{5}{2}a\right) = \frac{28}{25}\left(\frac{5}{2}\left(\frac{10}{7}b\right)\right) = \frac{1,400}{350}b = 4b$. If you chose **B**, you may have chosen $12b$ because 12 and b both appear in "112% of m in terms of b." If you chose **C**, you may have chosen the option with $40b$ because 40 was the first percentage presented in the problem. If you chose **D**, you may have correctly substituted $b = \frac{7}{10}a = \frac{7}{10}\left(\frac{4}{10}m\right) = \frac{28}{100}m$, so $b = 28\%m$. Then, you may have tried adding 84 to each side to get $84b = (28 + 84)\%m = 112\%m$.

Question 44. The correct answer is J. The first 75 positive integers form a finite arithmetic sequence with first term $a_1 = 1$ and last term $a_{75} = 75$. The sum of any finite arithmetic sequence with n terms is $S_n = \frac{n(a_n + a_1)}{2}$, where a_n is the nth term of the sequence. Based on this formula, the sum of the first 75 positive integers is $S_{75} = \frac{75(a_{75} + a_1)}{2} = \frac{75(75 + 1)}{2} = 2,850$. If you chose **F**, you may have thought that the relationship between the number of terms and the sum was proportional and solved the proportion $\frac{15}{120} = \frac{75}{x}$. If you chose **G**, you may have thought that the equation for the sum was $S_n = \frac{n(a_n + a_1)}{5}$, so $S_{75} = \frac{75(76)}{5} = 1,140$. If you chose **H**, you may have thought that the equation for the sum was $S_n = \frac{n(a_n - a_1)}{2}$, so $S_{75} = \frac{75(74)}{2} = 2,775$.

Question 45. The correct answer is D. Start by factoring the denominator of the given function: $f(x) = \frac{3x^2}{(x + 3)(x - 3)}$. For any rational function, a vertical asymptote will occur at each value of x that makes the denominator (and not the numerator) 0. Because the degrees of the given numerator and denominator are the same, the horizontal asymptote will occur at the ratio of the leading coefficients. Therefore, there will be asymptotes at $x + 3 = 0 \rightarrow x = -3$, $x - 3 = 0 \rightarrow x = 3$, and $y = \frac{3}{1} \rightarrow y = 3$. If you chose **A**, you may have considered only one of the values that causes the denominator to be 0. If you chose **B**, you may have considered only one of the values that causes the denominator to be 0 and used the value that makes the numerator 0. If you chose **C**, you may have used the value that makes the numerator 0.

Passage I

Question 1. The best answer is C because the passage describes how access to different types of mirrors enabled specific kinds of self-portraits. The passage begins by explaining that, although flat mirrors were not widely available until the 1700s (lines 9–13), they likely influenced sixteenth-century Renaissance self-portraitists during the early 1500s (lines 15–20). The passage provides examples of self-portraits painted with the aid of a convex mirror (lines 26–32 and lines 40–49) and notes that only a "limited number of full-length self-portraits" (lines 67–68) were produced before full-length mirrors became widely available in the nineteenth century (lines 68–72). The passage concludes by providing a detailed description of "the most common and enduring pose in self-portraiture" (lines 84–85), in which an artist paints a self-portrait using a flat glass mirror positioned on an easel (lines 75–76).

The best answer is NOT:

A because the passage primarily explores how the art of self-portraiture developed relative to artists' access to convex mirrors (lines 26–45) and flat glass mirrors (lines 56–65 and lines 73–87). Although the passage offers specific examples of self-portraits made with flat glass mirrors (lines 56–65), the passage does not claim that these self-portraits were famous.

B because the passage does not explore how trends in the art world influenced the development of self-portraiture. The passage instead provides specific examples of self-portraits made with the use of a mirror, starting with a 1404 painting by Boccaccio (lines 26–30) and concluding with a nineteenth-century self-portrait by Roehn (lines 75–79).

D because while the passage does provide specific information about methods used to manufacture convex mirrors (lines 21–26) and flat glass mirrors (lines 50–55 and lines 68–70), these details serve to provide context for the passage's description of the role of mirrors in self-portraiture.

Question 2. The best answer is F because the paragraph states that it would be an "oversimplification" (line 8) to attribute the development of self-portraiture solely to the development of mirrors (lines 6–8) and then subsequently acknowledge that practical advancements in mirror production likely did have an impact on self-portraitists (lines 13–20).

The best answer is NOT:

G because although the paragraph acknowledges the capacity of mirrors to influence Renaissance self-portraitists (lines 15–20), it does not make a claim about the broader social impact of mirrors.

H because although the paragraph mentions that flat glass mirrors were invented in Venice around the year 1500 (lines 3–4), this is a supporting detail rather than the main point.

J because while the paragraph mentions that the convex mirrors available were small and inconvenient for artists to use (lines 4–6), this detail provides context for the paragraph's main point that while the influence of mirrors shouldn't be overstated (lines 6–8), mirrors likely still played a role in the development of self-portraiture (lines 13–15).

Question 3. The best answer is **B** because the passage states that the painting *A Man in Armour* features the image of a person "reflected in two flat glass mirrors" (line 60) and that the painting *Lady at the Virginals with a Gentleman* "shows a half-length mirror" (line 64).

The best answer is NOT:

A because the passage does not state that either painting features an image of a convex mirror.

C because although the passage cites *Lady at the Virginals with a Gentleman* as an example of a painting that depicts a domestic interior (lines 60–63), no such information is provided about *A Man in Armour*.

D because the passage does not provide biographical information about either of the paintings' artists.

Question 4. The best answer is **G** because, in the context of lines 15–20, the phrase "fuel the vanity" suggests that Renaissance artists would enjoy seeing themselves reflected in a mirror, which would in turn motivate them to paint a self-portrait.

The best answer is NOT:

F because the passage does not explore whether Renaissance artists were committed to the genre of the self-portrait.

H because the passage does not indicate that mirrors were thought to be a significant source of vanity during the Renaissance; it instead speculates on the specific effect mirrors may have had on Renaissance artists (lines 15–20).

J because the passage does not specify that some artists were more greatly influenced by the availability of mirrors than others.

Question 5. The best answer is **D** because, as the passage states, mirrors of convex glass were "created from balls of blown glass filled with molten metal" (lines 23–24) that, once cooled, "were cut to form individual pieces" (line 26).

The best answer is NOT:

A because the mirrors were not formed from balls of molten metal. Instead, as the passage describes in lines 23–26, the mirrors were made from balls of blown glass filled with molten metal.

B because the mirrors were not formed from balls of molten metal. Instead, as the passage describes in lines 23–26, the mirrors were made from balls of blown glass filled with molten metal.

C because, as the passage specifies in lines 23–26, after a ball of blown glass was filled with molten metal, it was first allowed to cool before it was cut into individual pieces.

Question 6. The best answer is G because, as the passage explains in lines 35–39, many artists continued to refer to convex mirrors in their paintings after flat mirrors were invented. The passage additionally relates that some of these artists' paintings featured images of convex mirrors that served as symbols of "the artist" (line 38).

The best answer is NOT:

F because the passage does not state that many artists refused to use flat mirrors. Instead, the passage states that Dutch paintings of the seventeenth century "often feature" (line 62) flat mirrors. Furthermore, once mass-market full-length flat mirrors became widely available in the nineteenth century, their use was frequent enough that artists used them in "the most common and enduring pose in self-portraiture" (lines 84–85).

H because the passage does not specifically state that artists returned to using convex mirrors to make narrative paintings after flat mirrors became available. Instead, the passage states that, prior to the availability of flat mirrors to artists, convex mirrors "appeared in a range of narrative paintings" (line 34).

J because the passage doesn't state that convex mirrors were eventually regarded as a symbol of an unfashionable artistic practice. The passage instead indicates in lines 34–39 that, even after the invention of flat mirrors, artists incorporated convex mirrors into their work as a positive symbol of "the artist" (line 38).

Question 7. The best answer is D because the passage identifies the discovery of a new type of very clear glass (lines 51–54) as one technical development that enabled the production of the first flat glass mirrors.

The best answer is NOT:

A because the passage does not provide information about glass's relative hardness.

B because the passage does not mention whether the glass involved was sturdy.

C because the passage does not mention the weight of the glass.

Question 8. The best answer is H because the passage states that mirrors became widely available in the nineteenth century following "the discovery of a cheaper technique for silvering glass" (lines 69–70).

The best answer is NOT:

F because the passage does not attribute mass market availability of mirrors in the nineteenth century to the discovery of a new type of glass. The passage instead states that the discovery of a new type of glass made it possible to produce the first flat glass mirrors in the late fifteenth century (lines 50–53).

G because the passage does not attribute the mass market availability of mirrors in the nineteenth century to the development of silvering agents. The passage instead states that the development of mercury and tin as silvering agents made it possible to produce the first flat glass mirrors in the late fifteenth century (lines 50–60).

J because the passage does not indicate that consumer demand was a factor that influenced the wide availability of mirrors in the nineteenth century.

Question 9. The best answer is A because "focusing on" is a synonym for *fixing* in the context of the artist "fixing the viewer with a steady outward gaze" (line 87). In this usage, *fixing* can mean "to hold or direct steadily." The passage describes how the artist steadily directs their focus in an outward-facing gaze.

The best answer is NOT:

B because "adhering to" primarily describes a process of holding fast and physically sticking to another object. In the context of the sentence, it would be illogical to state that the artist's gaze was physically sticking to the viewer.

C because *stabilizing* primarily describes a process of increasing something's stability. In the context of the sentence, it would be illogical to state that the artist's gaze was increasing the viewer's stability.

D because *correcting* primarily describes a process of altering or counteracting a negative outcome. In the context of the sentence, it would be illogical to state that the artist's gaze was counteracting a negative aspect of the viewer.

Passage II

Question 10. The best answer is F because the metaphor of a current suggests a swiftly flowing force of movement that is similar to the flow of water in streams and rivers. In line 20, this metaphor relates that the fluid motion of the surrounding crowd pushed Rani forward. In lines 27–28, the active phrasing of "each curve a current moving her closer" suggests that Rani's surroundings are actively causing her to move forward.

The best answer is NOT:

G because although the passage mentions that the train platform was crowded (line 4), the metaphor of the current primarily connotes a force of movement rather than a crowd of a particular size or density.

H because the passage does not indicate that Rani is actively reminding herself to stay present and aware.

J because the passage does not indicate that Rani looked forward to her return home with excitement. Although Rani "felt her heart pulse" (line 7) at the start of the excursion, this was due to her anxiety about boarding the train (lines 7–8). As lines 45–46 indicate, Rani's visit home concluded with a feeling of disappointment rather than excitement.

Question 11. The best answer is A because *outlined* can be used as a synonym for "laid out" in the context of lines 2–3. In this usage, "laid out" means "to plan in detail." *Outlined* would maintain the meaning of the original sentence, stating that Siya created a detailed plan for Rani, outlining the route that she should travel.

The best answer is NOT:

B because *invented* primarily describes a process of using innovative and creative thinking to create something new. *Invented* is a contextually inappropriate synonym in this context, because it would suggest that Siya used her imagination to create an entirely new route for Rani to follow.

C because *projected* primarily means "to make estimates about a future outcome." *Projected* is a contextually inappropriate synonym because it can be inferred that Siya was knowledgeable about the route she planned. Therefore, there was no need for Siya to estimate whether the route would prove accurate.

D because *interpreted* primarily describes a process of making a complex concept easier to understand. The passage does not indicate whether the route was complicated or whether Siya had to simplify the route to make it understandable to Rani.

Question 12. The best answer is G because the passage relates that, after first observing Ben, the narrator's father "revs into grocery mode" (line 59), selecting grocery items that include produce and tofu (lines 60–62), ultimately proceeding ahead to further produce aisles (lines 65–66) and the soy sauce aisle (line 74). In contrast, the narrator does not consider any grocery items to select and buy.

The best answer is NOT:

F because neither the narrator nor her father mentions the narrator's family.

H because Ben does not interact with any of the store's patrons.

J because neither the narrator nor her father instructs Ben on how to pick out the best produce.

Question 13. The best answer is A because it can be inferred that the narrator's thought that "Ben is the first photographer, and journalist, and photojournalist, that my dad has ever met" (lines 55–57) reflects the narrator's belief that her father has little familiarity with the field of photojournalism.

The best answer is NOT:

B because there's no evidence in the passage that the narrator feels joyful after her father's remark. Instead, her thoughts in lines 55–57 suggest that she is doubtful of her father's compliment.

C because there's no evidence in the passage that the narrator feels proud in response to her father's remark. Rather than the narrator feeling proud of Ben's photography, it can be inferred that the narrator feels tension, since she is "relieved" (line 64) when Ben puts his camera away.

D because there's no evidence in the passage that the narrator expected her father to ask Ben questions about photography.

Question 14. **The best answer is H** because the narrator characterizes Ben as someone who "could handle this trip" (line 82) because he was "Mr. Up for Whatever" (line 83). In combination with Ben's cheerful demeanor throughout the passage, this characterization can be inferred to mean that Ben has a positive and optimistic outlook. Additionally, Ben's upbeat assessment that everything with their visit is "going great" (line 75) provides further evidence of Ben's optimistic nature.

The best answer is NOT:

F because the passage does not provide information about how people typically respond to Ben.

G because there's no evidence in the passage that Ben daydreams when he should be working.

J because the passage does not provide information about how people typically perceive Ben's personality. Furthermore, throughout the passage, Ben is presented as seeming relaxed and easygoing, rather than aloof and shy. He "glides through the produce aisle" (line 54) and playfully invites the narrator to climb onto the front of the grocery cart (lines 76–80).

Question 15. **The best answer is A** because Passage A focuses solely on describing Rani's visit to her old neighborhood on the last day of her visit to Bombay (lines 1–2), and Passage B recounts a single scene in which the narrator visits a grocery store with her father and fiancé. Passage A begins with Rani's train travel (lines 2–18), proceeds to her disembarking at the station for Lower Parel and navigating the neighborhood (lines 19–29), and concludes with her impressions of visiting the site of her former home (lines 29–46). Passage B begins with the narrator's arrival at the store (lines 47–51), proceeds to relate her experiences and impressions (lines 51–80), and concludes while she is still inside the store (lines 76–84).

The best answer is NOT:

B because neither passage relates the thoughts and feelings of multiple characters; the passages instead both focus on the perspective of an individual character. Passage A primarily focuses on describing the sights and impressions surrounding Rani's visit to her old neighborhood. Passage B primarily focuses on describing the thoughts and feelings of the narrator.

C because while each passage primarily provides an in-depth description of a single event, neither passage describes the event's long-term effects.

D because neither passage alternates between relating past memories and describing the present narrative action. Each passage primarily focuses on relating the present action of the scene recounted.

Question 16. **The best answer is G** because, in Passage A, Rani observes that "a high-rise stood in place of the small building where they'd lived" (lines 29–30). Scaffolding, wind, and dust suggest a harsh atmosphere in the neighborhood where "she used to play foursquare" (lines 32–33) and "walk to the small corner shop with her brother" (lines 34–35). In Passage B, as the narrator contemplates her visit home, she concludes that she is "coming back to this place as a different person than the one who left" (lines 86–87).

The best answer is NOT:

F because, although Rani's visit to her old neighborhood causes her to feel emotion (lines 31–32), Passage A does not indicate whether she feels regret about leaving home. Passage B does not indicate that the narrator had felt a new desire to return home. Instead, it relates that she had previously felt "worry" (line 87) about her visit home with Ben.

H because although Passage A relates that Rani feels "disappointment" (line 45) during her visit to her old neighborhood, it does not specify how leaving home has had a long-term impact on Rani. While Passage B features a brief dialogue between the narrator and her father (lines 53–54), it does not provide information about whether the narrator's relationship with her parents has changed.

J because Passage A does not provide any information to suggest that the people Rani knew in the past have changed. Passage B does not provide information about the narrator's hometown aside from mentioning that the grocery store is located in a "random Chicago suburb" (lines 68–69).

Question 17. **The best answer is D** because, as Rani reflects on her visit in Passage A, she concludes that leaving home means having to feel "the disappointment of returning" (line 45). In contrast, over the course of Passage B, the narrator comes to believe that it had in fact been "a good idea" (line 81) to visit home with Ben.

The best answer is NOT:

A because there's no indication in Passage A that Rani found any aspect of her visit home amusing. The narrator of Passage B would instead be more likely to characterize her experience as amusing, since she laughed while riding the grocery cart in lines 77–80.

B because there's no evidence in Passage A to suggest that Rani found her visit home pleasurable. During her trip there, she felt "anxious" (line 7) and concludes that her visit caused her to feel "disappointment" (line 45). The narrator of Passage B would instead be more likely to characterize her experience as pleasurable, since she laughed while riding the grocery cart in lines 77–80 and came to a positive conclusion about her visit home (lines 80–84).

C because while both Rani in Passage A and the narrator of Passage B are active participants and observers during their visits home, neither passage indicates that they feel stimulated by these experiences in an unusual way.

Question 18. The best answer is H because the last paragraph of Passage A (lines 42–46) expresses Rani's yearning and sadness that she no longer "belonged to the city" (line 44) that was once home. The last paragraph of Passage B (lines 76–89) concludes with the narrator's upbeat realization that it had been stupid to worry (line 87) about this trip when in fact she could be hopeful that having Ben with her would make the trip go well (lines 82–84).

The best answer is NOT:

F because neither passage primarily reflects contentedness in its last paragraph. The last paragraph of Passage A reflects Rani's disappointment, while the last paragraph of Passage B reflects the narrator's newfound optimism that the trip will go well.

G because neither passage indicates that its characters are feeling indecision about what to do next.

J because while Rani does seem to accept disappointment as a condition of having left in the last paragraph of Passage A, there is no evidence that the last paragraph of Passage B reflects a defiant tone. Instead, the narrator of Passage B concludes hopefully that having Ben with her will make the trip go well (lines 82–84).

Passage III

Question 19. The best answer is C because the paragraph begins by characterizing New York as a " 'birdy' city" (line 1), using a birder's term to suggest that New York City "has rich bird life" (line 9). The paragraph establishes that there are up to three hundred different species of birds in the city (lines 2–8) and attributes the city's bird diversity to its extensive parkland (line 10), its location close to the sea (lines 10–12), and its bird conservation efforts (lines 12–14).

The best answer is NOT:

A because the mention of the Central Park bird list (lines 6–7) supports the paragraph's primary function of giving an overview of the city's rich bird life. Additionally, the paragraph does not describe specific types of birds that flock in the park.

B because the paragraph does not discuss whether people should visit New York City to observe birds.

D because although the paragraph does provide a short list of habitats (lines 10–14), as well as an estimate of the number of bird species (lines 4–7), these details mainly serve to illustrate that New York City "has rich bird life" (line 9).

Question 20. The best answer is H because the passage states that all the exploiter species listed in lines 36–39, including the rock pigeon, "were spread by human introduction" (lines 47–48), and the passage also notes that monk parakeets were introduced by humans. Native to Argentina, monk parakeets were imported to New York City as pets that later escaped or were released into the environment, establishing permanent populations in New York City (lines 58–62).

The best answer is NOT:

F because although the passage states that mute swans were spread by human introduction (lines 47–48), the passage does not state that red-tailed hawks were spread by human introduction.

G because even though the passage describes how the house finch was spread by human introduction (lines 48–55), the passage does not state that red-tailed hawks were spread by human introduction.

J because although the passage states that the rock pigeon was "spread by human introduction" (line 48), the passage does not make any reference to mourning doves.

Question 21. The best answer is A because the paragraph begins by establishing that "bird life is constantly changing in New York City" (line 15). After speculating on how seventeenth-century settlement affected the city's bird life, the passage cites how "New York City's bird life has been altered . . . in just the past fifty years" (lines 21–23) to relate that bird life has continued to change over time.

The best answer is NOT:

B because the paragraph does not state that water birds relocated as New York City expanded. Instead, it states that water birds "were soon consumed or chased off" (lines 19–20) as the city was established.

C because the paragraph does not state that the same bird species have continued to breed in New York City since the seventeenth century. Instead, the paragraph emphasizes that "bird life is constantly changing in New York City" (line 15).

D because the paragraph instead states that the water birds that inhabited the marshy island in the seventeenth century "were soon consumed or chased off" (lines 19–20).

Question 22. The best answer is J because the verb *throng* in this context means "to be crowded and busy." Stating that the island was crowded with water birds (lines 16–19) serves to emphasize that there were many birds.

The best answer is NOT:

F because the passage does not describe the city's neighborhoods as overcrowded.

G because the passage does not indicate that birds behaved aggressively toward settlers.

H because the passage does not indicate that the settlers' attempts at building were frantic or rushed.

Question 23. The best answer is A because the statement follows the claim that exploiter bird species "thrive in the thick of the city" (line 33), and it describes some of the strategies these "tough, streetwise birds" (line 45) use to live in an urban environment.

The best answer is NOT:

B because although the passage mentions that some birds pass through without nesting (lines 25–26), this acknowledgment is unrelated to the description of the exploiter birds' nesting and feeding strategies in lines 34–35.

C because although the passage states that New York City's breeding bird population is different from that of the countryside (lines 26–28), this detail is unrelated to the description of the exploiter birds' nesting and feeding strategies in lines 34–35.

D because although the passage states that certain exploiter birds are "also abundant in many other cities across the world" (lines 39–40), this detail serves to further illustrate the claim that exploiter birds manage to "positively thrive" (line 33) in urban environments.

Question 24. **The best answer is G** because the number of established red-tailed hawk pairs is a verifiable fact that serves to demonstrate the species' success in adapting to New York's urban environment. As the passage states, the first red-tailed hawk established a nest in 1992 (lines 70–73), and by 2007, thirty-two red-tailed hawk pairs had followed suit (lines 75–77), which shows that the species succeeded, over time, in establishing a presence.

The best answer is NOT:

F because the passage does not cite a similarity between New York City's red-tailed hawk and monk parakeet populations. The passage instead establishes their difference, describing the monk parakeet as a "new exploiter group" (line 58) and the red-tailed hawk as an "adapter species" (line 67).

H because the passage does not claim that red-tailed hawks have become the most prevalent bird species in New York City.

J because the statement does not contradict the claim that a red-tailed hawk established a nest in New York City in 1992 (lines 70–73). Rather, the statement provides information about how New York City's red-tailed hawk population continued to grow in the years that followed.

Question 25. **The best answer is D** because the graph provides information about the seasonal range areas of four bird species discussed in the passage. The passage distinguishes between the bird populations of New York City and those of the nearby countryside (lines 26–28), and the graph offers further context by showing seasonal variations in the mallard duck, Canada goose, red-tailed hawk, and European starling populations across the entire state.

The best answer is NOT:

A because the information in the graph represents the seasonal bird population changes for all of New York state, which includes New York City. The graph does not distinguish between the bird populations of New York City and those of the entire state, and so a comparison is not possible.

B because the information in the graph represents the seasonal bird population changes for New York state only. The graph does not provide information about the bird species of Boston or San Francisco, which are not located in New York state.

C because the information in the graph represents the seasonal bird population changes for all of New York state. The graph does not provide information about seasonal bird species variations in New York City's Central Park.

Question 26. **The best answer is H** because the graph shows that the range percentage for the Canada goose is significantly higher in the postbreeding season than in the prebreeding season. The range percentages for the mallard duck, red-tailed hawk, and European starling are slightly higher in the postbreeding season than in the prebreeding season.

The best answer is NOT:

F because while the range percentage for the mallard duck's prebreeding season is significantly higher than that for its breeding season, the prebreeding range percentages for the Canada goose and the European starling are both slightly higher than their breeding range percentages.

G because while the range percentage for the Canada goose's postbreeding season is significantly higher than that for its nonbreeding season, the postbreeding range percentages for the mallard duck, red-tailed hawk, and European starling are all slightly higher than their prebreeding range percentages.

J because while the range percentages during the prebreeding and breeding seasons are higher for the mallard duck and Canada goose, the red-tailed hawk's postbreeding range percentage is higher than its prebreeding range percentage. Furthermore, the European starling's postbreeding range percentage is higher than its breeding range percentage.

Question 27. **The best answer is D** because the range percentages for both the red-tailed hawk and the European starling remain relatively stable, hovering between 70 and 80 percent through all four seasons.

The best answer is NOT:

A because the range percentages for the Canada goose vary greatly between the nonbreeding and prebreeding seasons, rising from a low of approximately 35 to a high of approximately 90. In contrast, the European starling's range percentages vary slightly between the nonbreeding and prebreeding seasons, remaining between approximately 65 and 75.

B because the range percentages for the Canada goose vary greatly between the nonbreeding and prebreeding seasons, rising from a low of approximately 35 to a high of approximately 90. In contrast, the red-tailed hawk's range percentages vary slightly between the nonbreeding and prebreeding seasons, remaining between approximately 75 and 80.

C because while the range percentages for the red-tailed hawk remain very stable, with percentages of approximately 75 to 80 through all four seasons, the range percentages for the mallard duck are much lower in the nonbreeding and postbreeding seasons than in the prebreeding and breeding seasons. The mallard duck's range percentage falls to within approximately 10 and 20 during the nonbreeding and postbreeding seasons and rises to approximately 75 in the prebreeding season.

Passage IV

Question 28. The best answer is G because the passage describes how Djokic's discovery in the Dresser Formation supports "a new idea about one of the oldest mysteries on the planet: how and where life got started" (lines 23–24). The passage explains that Djokic's evidence of land-based volcanic hot springs and pools from 3.5 billion years ago presents "a far different picture" (line 27) of life's origins than a prevailing theory that underwater hydrothermal vents fostered the planet's earliest life (lines 28–38). The many "fossilized signs of life" (line 56) that Djokic found in the Dresser Formation support the theory that land-based volcanic pools could have fostered the planet's earliest forms of cellular life (line 71–74).

The best answer is NOT:

F because while the passage does state that the researchers found evidence of biofilms in the Dresser Formation geyserite (lines 17–22), this supporting detail helps explain the significance of Djokic's discovery in the Dresser Formation.

H because while the passage does relate that the theory of the role of hydrothermal vents in the origins of life "has problems" (line 38), this acknowledgment helps explain why Djokic's Dresser Formation discovery provides persuasive evidence of the alternate "land-based theory" (line 68) of the origins of life.

J because the passage does not present a chronology of beliefs but instead focuses on explaining how a recent discovery made in the Dresser Formation presents "a far different picture" (line 27) from the one that "scientists have been sketching since 1977" (line 28).

Question 29. The best answer is A because, as lines 1–6 describe, after Djokic reacts fearfully to a spider, she stumbles downhill, and then Van Kranendonk pushes her back uphill to keep her from falling. This takes place after the researchers began hiking through the Pilbara after they "had spent the day enthralled" (line 14) by Djokic's discovery of biofilms in the Dresser Formation.

The best answer is NOT:

B because Djokic discovered indications of biofilms in the Dresser Formation before the researchers began their return hike through the Pilbara at night (lines 13–17).

C because Djokic encountered the spider web before Van Kranendonk pushed her back uphill. Her reaction to the spider web had caused her to fall backward downhill (lines 1–4).

D because Djokic's encounter with the spider and Van Kranendonk's response took place while the researchers' nighttime hike through the Pilbara was already underway (lines 1–17).

Question 30. The best answer is F because, as the passage explains in lines 71–74, Deamer's earlier work showed that volcanic pools could provide an environment conducive to the formation of cellular life. Djokic discovered 3.5-billion-year-old evidence of "volcanic hot springs and pools" (line 25) and fossil markings "most likely produced by a thin layer of bacteria-like microorganisms" (lines 20–22). Therefore, the discovery of "fossilized signs of life" (line 56) that originated in "the steaming pools . . . of an active geothermal field" (lines 53–55) would support Deamer's theory.

The best answer is NOT:

G because the passage does not indicate that Deamer found the same geologic evidence in the Dresser Formation a decade prior to Djokic's discovery. Instead, the passage makes clear that Djokic discovered the evidence in the Dresser Formation ten years after Deamer's earlier work (lines 71–74).

H because the passage does not provide information about Deamer's later research, nor does it claim that Djokic found evidence of early life on Earth. Instead, the passage states that "the Dresser was not the actual site where the most primitive life began half a billion years earlier" (lines 57–59).

J because the passage does not claim that Djokic's discovery undermined Deamer's research from ten years earlier. The passage instead suggests that Djokic's evidence that volcanic pools at the Dresser Formation fostered cellular life supports Deamer's theory.

Question 31. The best answer is B because the passage states that, in the ocean environment, the energy and nutrients needed for cellular life "might spread out too quickly to interact and form cell membranes" (lines 40–41). This detail most directly challenges the claim that life originated in an ocean environment.

The best answer is NOT:

A because, as the passage states, the 1977 discovery of hydrothermal vents and primitive bacteria in the Pacific Ocean (lines 28–33) supported biologists' later theory that the ocean could have provided "a safe haven for life to begin" (lines 37–38). This evidence would therefore not challenge the claim that life originated in the ocean.

C because while the passage acknowledges that cataclysms wracked the Earth's surface about four billion years ago (lines 35–36), it clarifies that biologists theorized that the hydrothermal vents would have been "protected from the cataclysms" (line 35), which, in turn, would have made them more conducive to cellular life. This evidence would therefore not challenge the claim that life originated in the ocean.

D because the passage mentions hydrogen sulfide as a key element of the "thriving ecosystem" (line 34) found at the hydrothermal vents, so this detail would therefore not detract from a claim that life originated in the ocean.

Question 32. **The best answer is H** because, as the passage states, in the environment of a land pool, dry spells enable "complex molecules called polymers" (line 45) to form. Wet spells "float these polymers around" (lines 46–47), and "further drying periods" (line 47) in the pools can send the polymers to small cavities where they can interact (lines 47–48).

The best answer is NOT:

F because the summary is inaccurate. Although the polymers do float around during wet spells (lines 46–47), the passage states that they interact with each other during subsequent drying periods (lines 47–48).

G because the summary is inaccurate. As the passage states, polymers interact during drying periods (lines 47–48). Moreover, they do not become fatty acids. Instead, during drying periods, polymers can collect in the compartments of fatty acids (lines 47–50).

J because the summary is incomplete. The passage describes a specific sequence of dryness and wetness that causes polymers to form and interact: They form in dry spells (line 45), disperse in wet spells (lines 45–46), and then interact in further drying periods (lines 47–48).

Question 33. **The best answer is D** because, in the context of lines 11–12, both *unlikely* and *odd* suggest that the chances of encountering a benign spider species are low. The paragraph explains that "spiders have a deservedly bad reputation in Australia" (lines 9–10), which implies that dangerous spiders would be more common than harmless ones. In this context, *odd* most nearly means "unexpected," and therefore *unlikely* would serve as a contextually appropriate synonym.

The best answer is NOT:

A because *unorthodox* would suggest that the spider species encountered had rare or unconventional features or attributes. In lines 11–12, however, *odd* is used to instead imply that, in Australia, dangerous spider species generally outnumber benign spider species.

B because *eccentric* would suggest that the spider species was known for being especially strange or peculiar, which is not consistent with the meaning of the original sentence.

C because *miscellaneous* usually means "consisting of many things of different sorts," which would not be a contextually appropriate way to describe the spider species referred to in lines 11–12.

Question 34. The best answer is **G** because it can be inferred from the passage that the minerals and gases supported the bacteria and worm populations that grew around the hydrothermal vents. The passage states that the bacteria and large worms "surrounded" (lines 32–33) the hydrothermal vents, which suggests both that their populations were thriving and that they were directly sustained by the molecules found in the minerals and gasses.

The best answer is NOT:

F because although the passage suggests that the biologists' later theory was inspired by the 1977 discovery (lines 34–38), this theory is a result of the discovery rather than proof of a thriving ecosystem.

H because although the passage mentions that cellular life could thrive both in volcanic hot springs and pools (lines 24–26) and around hydrothermal vents (lines 29–33), it does not directly emphasize similarities between the ecosystems of hydrothermal vents and volcanic pools.

J because while the passage indicates that iron and sulfur were present at the hydrothermal vents discovered by the researchers on the *Alvin* (line 31), it does not explain how primitive bacteria might use iron and sulfur to form cell membranes.

Question 35. The best answer is **C** because the passage states that though now hot and dry (line 52), the Dresser Formation "had once been like the steaming pools and erupting geysers of Yellowstone National Park" (lines 53–54). This reference helps portray what an active geothermal field would look like.

The best answer is NOT:

A because while the passage does relate that fossilized signs of life were found at the Dresser Formation (line 56), it does not state that fossilized signs of life were found in the pools and geysers of Yellowstone National Park.

B because the passage does not acknowledge the specific place where life on Earth likely began. The passage instead directly states that "the Dresser was not the actual site" (lines 57–58) where life began.

D because the passage does not emphasize any similarities between the Dresser Formation's current climate and the climate of Yellowstone National Park.

Question 36. The best answer is **J** because the passage states that the implications of a land-based theory of the origins of life would "stretch beyond our own planet" (lines 66–67) and influence the search for alien life "elsewhere in the solar system" (lines 67–68).

The best answer is NOT:

F because the passage does not suggest that the land-based theory will have any impact on future research efforts involving prototypes of cell membranes.

G because although the passage relates that research concerning sedimentary rocks in the Pilbara has contributed to the land-based theory's development (lines 13–26), it does not indicate that the land-based theory will directly influence sedimentary rock research in the future.

H because hydrothermal vents are primarily relevant to the ocean-based theory described in lines 34–38. The passage does not indicate that establishing a land-based theory would directly influence hydrothermal vent research in the future.

Passage I

Question 1. The best answer is B. According to Figure 2, the frequency of the sound waves increased from approximately 2,300 Hz at 0 s to about 3,800 Hz at 90 s and then remained constant from 90 s to 120 s. Thus, the speed of sound, which is directly proportional to frequency, also increased and then remained constant over this time. Therefore, **B** is correct. **A** and **C** are incorrect because the frequency did not decrease at any time between 0 s and 120 s. **D** is incorrect because the frequency increased from 0 s to 90 s.

Question 2. The best answer is H. The question indicates that the musical note A6 has a frequency of 1,760 Hz. There are 10 frequencies listed in Table 1 that are higher than 1,760 Hz. Therefore, **H** is correct. **F, G,** and **J** are incorrect; there are 10 frequencies listed in Table 1 that are higher than 1,760 Hz.

Question 3. The best answer is C. Based on the results of Experiments 1 and 2, the frequency at 60 s decreases from about 3,550 Hz at 10 cm to 2,188 Hz at 16 cm. A frequency of 2,300 Hz falls between the recorded values of 2,503 Hz at 14 cm and 2,188 Hz at 16 cm. Therefore, the height of water in the beaker would most likely have been between 14 cm and 16 cm. Thus, **C** is correct. **A** is incorrect; at a height less than 10 cm, the frequency at 60 s would be higher than 3,550 Hz. **B** is incorrect; at a height between 12 cm and 14 cm, the frequency at 60 s would be between 2,503 Hz and 2,918 Hz. **D** is incorrect; at a height greater than 16 cm, the frequency at 60 s would be lower than 2,188 Hz.

Question 4. The best answer is J. According to Figure 2, the frequency increased during all the intervals listed, but the rate of increase lessened as time increased from 0 s through 90 s. Therefore, of the intervals listed, the interval from 60 s to 70 s had the least average rate of change. Thus, **J** is correct. **F, G,** and **H** are incorrect because they all have greater average rates of change.

Question 5. The best answer is D. The scientist did not vary the rate of tapping the base of the beaker in either Experiment 1 or Experiment 2. Therefore, **D** is correct. **A, B,** and **C** are incorrect because the tapping rate was not varied in either experiment.

Question 6. The best answer is J. The same amount of salt was added to the beaker in each experiment, and in Experiment 2, water was added to increase the height of the water in the beaker. Thus, the concentration of salt in the water decreased as more water was added. Therefore, **J** is correct. **F, G,** and **H** are incorrect because they each represent heights that correspond to higher concentrations of salt.

Passage II

Question 7. The best answer is B. According to Figure 1, the greatest number of lightning discharges occurred from 4:55 p.m. to 5:00 p.m., and there were approximately 100 discharges during this time period. Therefore, **B** is correct. **A**, **C**, and **D** are incorrect; they each state an incorrect time period and/or number of discharges.

Question 8. The best answer is H. According to Table 1, the maximum flash rates for Storms 2, 4, 6, and 8 are 11 discharges/min, 2 discharges/min, 20 discharges/min, and 9 discharges/min, respectively. The order from highest to lowest is Storm 6, Storm 2, Storm 8, Storm 4. Therefore, **H** is correct. **F**, **G**, and **J** are incorrect because they do not list the storms in the correct order.

Question 9. The best answer is C. According to Table 1, the total number of discharges for Storm 7 was 673 and the duration was 130 min; 673 discharges divided by 130 min is approximately 5 discharges/min. The maximum flash rate for Storm 7 was 10 discharges/min, resulting in a difference between the maximum and average flash rates of 5 discharges/min. Therefore, **C** is correct. **A** and **B** are incorrect because they both give an incorrect average flash rate. **D** correctly identifies the average flash rate but gives an incorrect difference in flash rates.

Question 10. The best answer is J. According to Figure 2, the ranges with exactly 9 discharges are 20–25 C, 25–30 C, and 30–35 C. Therefore, **J** is correct. **F** and **G** are incorrect because they both include the range 15–20 C, which has 10 discharges, not 9. **H** is incorrect because it does not include the 25–30 C range.

Question 11. The best answer is A. According to Figure 1, there were about 25 discharges recorded from 5:25 p.m. to 5:30 p.m. The average flash rate per minute for this 5-minute time period is 25 discharges divided by 5 min, which equals 5 discharges/min. Therefore, **A** is correct. **B**, **C**, and **D** are incorrect because they each provide an incorrect average discharge rate for the specified time period.

Question 12. The best answer is H. According to Table 1, the total number of discharges for Storm 6 was 515. The description of Figure 2 states that 70 lightning discharges were measured. The number of lightning discharges from Storm 6 that are not represented in Figure 2 is 515 minus 70, which equals 445. Therefore, **H** is correct. **F**, **G**, and **J** are incorrect because they do not give the correct difference between the total number of discharges for Storm 6 and the number of discharges represented in Figure 2.

Passage III

Question 13. The best answer is B. The description of Experiment 3 indicates that the engine octane requirement (EOR) is the minimum octane number required for an engine to operate without becoming damaged. According to Table 2, as engine speed increases, EOR decreases only from 97.4 at 1,500 rpm to 90.6 at 3,500 rpm. Therefore, **B** is correct. **A, C,** and **D** are incorrect because the EOR does not increase at any point.

Question 14. The best answer is G. According to Table 2, at an engine speed of 2,000 rpm, Fuel A has an octane number of 96.6, and Fuel B has an octane number of 96.1. At an engine speed of 2,500 rpm, Fuel A has an octane number of 95.0, and Fuel B has an octane number of 95.4. If an engine speed of 2,200 rpm had been tested, the octane number for Fuel A would most likely have been between 95.0 and 96.6, and the octane number for Fuel B would most likely have been between 95.4 and 96.1. Therefore, **G** is correct. **F, H,** and **J** are incorrect; the octane numbers are outside the expected range for an engine speed of 2,200 rpm.

Question 15. The best answer is C. The data shown in Table 1 lead to the conclusion that, for mixtures containing only heptane and isooctane, the octane number is equal to the percent by volume of isooctane in the mixture. Therefore, **C** is correct. **A** and **B** are both incorrect because they are ratios of one component of the mixture to the other component, not percent by volume. **D** is incorrect because it calculates the percent by volume of heptane, not isooctane, in the mixture.

Question 16. The best answer is H. According to Table 1, a mixture of 100 mL of heptane and 900 mL of isooctane would have an octane number of 90. The results of Experiment 2 indicate that adding 3 mL of TEL will increase the octane number by about 25, assuming that TEL acts the same way in this mixture that it did with pure isooctane. Therefore, **H** is correct. **F** and **G** are incorrect because they are less than the octane number of the initial mixture. **J** is incorrect; while TEL increases the octane number, the results of Experiment 2 indicate that 3 mL of TEL will most likely add about 25 to the initial octane number, not increase the initial octane number by more than 35.

Question 17. The best answer is B. According to Table 2, the octane number for Fuel A is higher than the EOR at all tested engine speeds, indicating that Fuel A will not cause engine damage at any engine speed between 1,500 rpm and 3,500 rpm. Therefore, **B** is correct. **A** is incorrect because an octane number lower than the EOR would indicate that engine damage is likely to occur. **C** and **D** are incorrect because they state that Fuel B is the better fuel, but Fuel B's octane number is less than the EOR at 1,500 rpm.

Question 18. The best answer is J. The data shown in Table 1 suggest that the octane number of a mixture of heptane and isooctane is equal to the percent by volume of isooctane in the mixture. Thus, a mixture that contains 2 mL of heptane and 8 mL of isooctane would have an octane number of 80. Therefore, **J** is correct. **F, G,** and **H** are incorrect; they do not accurately reflect the percentage of isooctane in this mixture.

Passage IV

Question 19. The best answer is D. According to the Introduction, the pancreas is an organ that contains clusters of endocrine cells. To answer this question, the examinee must know that an organ is a group of tissues that perform a specific function. Therefore, **D** is correct. **A** and **B** are incorrect; they inaccurately describe the pancreas as a cell rather than an organ. **C** is incorrect because it refers to the pancreas as the smallest functional unit, not a group of tissues.

Question 20. The best answer is G. According to Student 3, somatostatin promotes the release of insulin and does not affect glucagon release. Therefore, if somatostatin release increased, insulin would most likely increase, while glucagon would most likely stay approximately the same, so **G** is correct. **F, H,** and **J** are incorrect because they each say that either or both of insulin and glucagon decrease.

Question 21. The best answer is C. Student 2 states that BG concentrations less than 3 mmol/L are not recommended, and Student 3 agrees with this statement. Therefore, **C** is correct. **A** is incorrect because it includes only Student 2. **B** is incorrect because it excludes Student 2. **D** is incorrect because it includes Student 1, who said that BG concentrations greater than 8 mmol/L are not recommended.

Question 22. The best answer is H. The Introduction indicates that somatostatin is a hormone (chemical messenger) involved in the regulation of BG concentration. All four students indicate that somatostatin either promotes or prevents the release of at least one hormone. Therefore, **H** is correct. **F** and **G** are incorrect because they describe somatostatin as a cell, not a messenger. **J** is incorrect because it says that somatostatin does not regulate hormone release.

Question 23. **The best answer is D.** Based on Figure 1, the greatest amount of glucagon is released when BG concentrations are less than 1 mmol/L. Student 1 indicated that the greatest amount of glucagon is released when BG concentrations are greater than the set point; Student 1 also indicated that the set point was 1 to 3 mmol/L. Therefore, **D** is correct. **A** and **B** are incorrect because they each conclude that the data are consistent with Student 1's explanation. **C** is incorrect because Student 1 said that the greatest amount of glucagon is released when BG concentration is greater than, not within, the set point.

Question 24. **The best answer is F.** Student 4 indicated that the BG set point was 7–9 mmol/L and that BG concentrations greater than 7 mmol/L are not recommended. Furthermore, the Introduction indicates that the set point is the concentration range over which BG is at homeostasis. To answer this question, the examinee must understand that homeostasis results in optimal body function. Therefore, **F** is correct. **G** is incorrect because Student 4 indicated that the set point was not recommended. **H** and **J** are incorrect because they both incorrectly conclude that Student 4's explanation is consistent with the definition of BG set point.

Passage V

Question 25. **The best answer is C.** According to Figure 3, if a trial had been run with 0.9 mL of H_2O_2 added, the percentage of phenol removed would most likely have been between 12% (the percentage removed for an H_2O_2 volume added of 1.0 mL) and 20% (the percentage removed for an H_2O_2 volume added of 0.8 mL). Therefore, **C** is correct. **A**, **B**, and **D** are incorrect; the percentage removed at 0.9 mL would most likely have been between 12% and 20%.

Question 26. **The best answer is J.** According to Figure 1, the lowest percentage of phenol removed in Study 1 was approximately 30% at pH 10. According to Figure 3, the lowest percentage of phenol removed in Study 3 was approximately 5% at 0.2 mL of H_2O_2. A value of 30% is 6 times as great as a value of 5. Therefore, **J** is correct. **F**, **G**, and **H** are incorrect; 30% is 6 times as great as 5%.

Question 27. **The best answer is D.** According to Figure 2, there were four trials in Study 2 in which less than 10% of the phenol was removed: 0.2 mL, 0.4 mL, 0.8 mL, and 1.0 mL of H_2O_2. Therefore, **D** is correct. **A**, **B**, and **C** are incorrect; there were four trials in Study 2 in which the percentage of phenol removed was less than 10%.

Question 28. The best answer is **G**. In Study 2, the independent variable was the amount of H_2O_2 added, because it was the factor that was manipulated so the scientists could observe its effect on the percentage of phenol removed. Therefore, **G** is correct. **F, H,** and **J** are incorrect; pH, phenol concentration, and temperature were each held constant in Study 2.

Question 29. The best answer is **B**. According to Figure 1, at pH 9, approximately 50% of phenol was removed. Starting with a phenol concentration of 30 mg/L, removing 50% would result in a concentration of 15 mg/L remaining after treatment. Therefore, **B** is correct. **A, C,** and **D** are incorrect; treatment would remove about 50% of the phenol, leaving about 15 mg/L of phenol in the wastewater.

Question 30. The best answer is **F**. According to Figure 1, the trial with the percentage of phenol removed that was closest to 60.0% was at a pH of 8. The passage states that the pH of the initial phenol solution was 6.6. A pH of 8 is more basic than a pH of 6.6, so it would require the addition of NaOH (a base) to increase the pH from 6.6 to 8. To answer this question, the examinee must know that a pH of 8 is more basic than a pH of 6.6 and that adding a base will increase the pH of the solution. Therefore, **F** is correct. **G** is incorrect because a pH of 8 is more basic than a pH of 6.6. **H** and **J** are incorrect because adding HCl would lower the pH of the solution.

Passage VI

Question 31. The best answer is **C**. According to the tables, the values of H for Trials 1, 4, 7, and 10, respectively, are 4.85×10^{-3} T, 2.91×10^{-3} T, 48.5×10^{-3} T, and 29.1×10^{-3} T. Of these values, 48.5×10^{-3} T is the greatest. Therefore, **C** is correct. **A, B,** and **D** are incorrect because they all have lower values of H than does Trial 7.

Question 32. The best answer is **G**. The passage states that in Study 1, V was 1.00×10^3 m/s, while in Study 3, V was 1.00×10^4 m/s. Therefore, **G** is correct. **F** is incorrect because V was less in Study 1 than in Study 3. **H** and **J** are incorrect because R was the same (0.0150 m) in Study 1 and in Study 3.

Question 33. The best answer is **A**. According to the passage, Study 2 repeated the procedure from Study 1, which stated that V for each ion was 1.00×10^3 m/s. Therefore, **A** is correct. **B, C,** and **D** are incorrect; in Study 2, V was 1.00×10^3 m/s for each ion.

Question 34. The best answer is **G**. According to Table 3, for Trial 8, the value of H was 31.2×10^{-3} T. Based on the conversion given in the question, 31.2×10^{-3} T is equal to 31.2 mT. Therefore, **G** is correct. **F, H,** and **J** are incorrect; the value of H for Trial 8 is 31.2 mT.

Question 35. **The best answer is C.** To answer this question, the examinee must know that, for two objects with the same speed, kinetic energy is proportional to mass. The passage indicates that the speed tested in Study 2 was the same as the speed tested in Study 1, and the question indicates that the Na^+ ion has a greater mass. Therefore, the kinetic energy of the Na^+ ion in Study 2 is greater than the kinetic energy of the Li^+ ion in Study 1. Thus, **C** is correct. **A**, **B**, and **D** are incorrect; the Na^+ ion in Study 2 has a greater kinetic energy than does the Li^+ ion in Study 1.

Passage VII

Question 36. **The best answer is G.** To answer this question, the examinee must know that eggs come from females and sperm come from males. According to Figure 1, only male *H. kuda* have a brood pouch, and the question states that fertilized eggs are carried in the brood pouch. Thus, males carry the fertilized eggs and provide sperm. Therefore, **G** is correct. **F** is incorrect; it states that males deposit eggs. **H** and **J** are incorrect; they both incorrectly assign the role of carrying fertilized eggs to females.

Question 37. **The best answer is C.** According to Figure 3, both Group 3 and Group 4 had 100% survival at 42 days post-hatch and at 56 days post-hatch. Therefore, **C** is correct. **A**, **B**, and **D** are incorrect; both Group 3 and Group 4 experienced no mortality prior to 56 days post-hatch.

Question 38. **The best answer is F.** According to the passage and Figure 2, wet mass (WM) was measured only during the grow-out stage, starting at 42 days post-hatch. Therefore, **F** is correct. **G** and **H** are incorrect because wet mass was not measured during the nursery stage. **J** is incorrect because wet mass was measured during the grow-out stage.

Question 39. **The best answer is D.** According to Table 1, Group 2 had a diet of blended fish only, and Group 4 had a diet of a 1:1 mixture of blended fish and *Acetes* sp. Furthermore, Figure 3 indicates that at Day 98, the average percent survival for Group 2 was about 40%, and the average percent survival for Group 4 was about 67%, a difference of about 27%. Therefore, the statement given in the question is consistent with the data shown in Figure 3. Thus, **D** is correct. **A** and **B** are incorrect because they both conclude that the statement is not consistent with the data. **C** is incorrect because the average percent survival for Group 2 was a little under 30 percentage points less than the average percent survival for Group 4.

Question 40. The best answer is F. According to Figure 2, during the nursery stage, the average SL increased from 30 mm at Day 7 to 70 mm at Day 42, resulting in a change of 40 mm over a duration of 35 days, which gives a rate of change of approximately 1.14 mm/day. During the grow-out stage, the average SL increased from 70 mm at Day 42 to 120 mm at Day 98, resulting in a change of 50 mm over 56 days, yielding a rate of change of approximately 0.89 mm/day. Therefore, the overall rate of change in average standard length (SL) during the nursery stage exceeded 1.0 mm/day, while during the grow-out stage, it was less than 1.0 mm/day. Thus, **F** is correct. **G** is incorrect because the rates of change are misstated. **H** and **J** are incorrect because they conclude that the grow-out stage had the greater rate of change.

Chapter 4: Identifying Areas for Improvement

Your practice test scores alone provide very little insight into what you need to do to improve your score. For example, you may have missed a certain math question because you haven't yet taken trigonometry or because you misread the question or the answer choices or because you were anxious about finishing the test on time.

When evaluating your performance on any of the practice tests in this book or elsewhere, examine not only *whether* you answered a question correctly or incorrectly but also *why* you answered it correctly or incorrectly. Recognizing why you chose the correct or incorrect answer sheds light on what you need to do to improve your score on future practice tests and on the ACT. Perhaps you need to review certain subjects, take a particular course, develop a better sense of how much time to spend on each question, or read questions and answer choices more carefully.

In this chapter, we offer guidance on how to evaluate your performance on ACT Practice Test 1 in order to identify subject areas and test-taking strategies and skills that you may need to work on. Take a similar approach to evaluate your performance on subsequent practice tests.

Reviewing Your Overall Performance

After you have determined your scores, consider the following questions as you evaluate how you did on the practice tests. Keep in mind that many of these questions require you to make judgment calls based on what you were thinking or the steps you took to decide on the answer choice you selected. The answer explanations in chapter 4 may help you make these determinations, but ultimately you are the only one who can determine why or how you chose the correct or incorrect answer.

Did you run out of time before you completed a test?

If so, read the sections in this book on pacing yourself. See chapter 2 for general advice that applies to all tests, and see chapters 5 through 9 for advice specific to each test. Perhaps you need to adjust the way you use your time in responding to the questions. Remember, there is no penalty for guessing, so try to answer all questions, even if you have to make an educated guess.

Did you spend too much time trying to understand the directions to the tests?

Make sure you understand them now, so you won't have to spend too much time reading them when you take the test.

Did you rush through the test and make mistakes?

People tend to make mistakes when they are in a hurry. If you had plenty of time remaining at the end of the test but made mistakes, you probably hurried through the test and made errors such as these:

- Misreading a passage
- Misreading a question
- Not reading or considering all answer choices
- Selecting a response that was an incomplete answer
- Selecting an answer that did not directly respond to the question

Did a particular type of question confuse you?

Use the explanatory answers following each practice test to help you identify any mistakes you may have made regarding certain question types or answer choices. The explanatory answers can help you understand why you may have chosen the incorrect answer and avoid making that same mistake again. Look at your percentage correct in each reporting category of the test. This will provide you with either clusters of skills and strengths or areas for improvement.

Highlighting Strengths and Areas for Improvement on the English Test

The process of scoring your English practice test and reviewing the answer explanations should reveal the reason you chose the correct or incorrect answer for each question. If you struggled to answer questions on the test because you have not yet acquired certain English language knowledge and skills, review the questions and your answers closely to determine more specifically what you need to work on.

The English test requires knowledge and skills in several areas. The best way to raise your score is to improve your English language skills, which you can accomplish in the following ways:

- Take an English composition course. Such a course will help you write more clearly, logically, and concisely while developing a better understanding of English punctuation, grammar, and usage conventions.

- Practice your writing skills in other courses. In most courses, including English literature, social science, speech, and perhaps even science, you have opportunities to practice your writing skills and receive feedback.

- Read well-written publications in the form of books, magazine articles, and online content from reputable sources—material that has been professionally edited. As you read, pay attention to punctuation, grammar, usage, sentence structure, writing strategy, organization, and style to see how a variety of writers express themselves while adhering to the same conventions.

- Practice writing and having your writing edited by an English teacher or someone else who is qualified to provide feedback.

Test-Taking Errors

A low test score does not necessarily mean that you lack the English language knowledge and skills required to do well on the test. It may indicate that you rushed through the test and made mistakes, spent too much time on certain questions that you didn't finish, or committed some other test-taking error(s). As you evaluate your answers to determine *why* you missed certain questions, consider your test-taking strategies and skills. Place a checkmark next to each of the following common test-taking errors you think you need to work on eliminating:

Worked too slowly: You may need to improve your reading speed and comprehension or try answering the easy questions first and then returning to the harder questions if time remains.

Rushed through the test: If you finished with plenty of time remaining but made mistakes, you may need to spend more time reading and understanding the passages, reading the questions, or carefully considering all of the answer choices.

Misread passages: If you missed questions because of misreading or misinterpreting passages, work on your reading comprehension. Try reading more carefully and rereading when you do not fully understand a passage.

Misread questions: Every question points to the correct answer, so read questions carefully and make sure you understand what a question is asking before you choose your answer.

Did not consider all answer choices: If you tend to select the first answer choice that seems to be correct, try considering all answer choices before making your final selection. A good way to double-check an answer is to find reasons to eliminate the other three choices.

Did not consider the writing style: The entire passage conveys the author's overall writing style, which you may need to consider when answering certain style-related questions.

Did not consider a question's context: Writing strategy and organization questions often require consideration of surrounding text. You may need to skim the passage first before answering these questions or read one or two sentences before or after the sentence in question.

Did not account for a word's connotations: Many words have a *denotation* (a literal meaning or dictionary definition) and a *connotation* (a thought or emotion that the word evokes from the reader or listener). To answer some usage questions, you must consider what the word means in the context in which it is used.

Did not connect an underlined portion of text with its corresponding question: The underlined portion of the text and the corresponding question work together to point to the correct answer choice, so be sure to consider them both when selecting your answer.

Overlooked differences in the answer choices: Answer choices may differ so subtly that you overlook the differences, so be sure to recognize what's different about each choice before selecting your answer.

Chose an answer that introduced a new error: Some answer choices correct the error in the underlined text but introduce a new error. Do not choose an answer that creates a new error.

Did not choose the best answer: Two or more answers may be correct, but the English test requires that you choose the *best* answer. Again, consider all answer choices before selecting an answer.

Did not reread the sentence using the selected answer: A great way to double-check an answer is to insert it in place of the underlined text and then reread the sentence to make sure it makes sense.

Missed a two-part question: With a two-part question, each of the answer choices typically starts with "yes" or "no" followed by a reason, so you must determine first whether the answer is yes or no and then why. Carefully compare and consider the reasons before making your selection.

Did not consider interrelated questions: A question may be easier to answer after you have answered the next question, so consider skipping back to a question if you feel that answering the current question has given you new insight.

See chapter 5 for in-depth coverage of test-taking strategies and skills that may help to raise your English test score.

Highlighting Strengths and Areas for Improvement on the Mathematics Test

The process of scoring your mathematics practice test and reviewing the answer explanations should reveal your strengths and any areas for improvement. You may discover that you are a whiz at algebra and geometry but are in dire need of a refresher course in trigonometry. Or, you may find that your math knowledge and skills are sound in all areas but you need to work on test-taking strategies to ensure that your test results accurately reflect your knowledge and skills.

Use the checklists in the following sections to flag subject areas and test-taking skills you may need to focus on.

Math Subject Areas

If you struggled to answer questions on the test because you have not yet acquired the requisite math language knowledge and skills, review the questions and your answers closely to determine more specifically what you need to work on.

Your performance on the ACT mathematics test may be affected by your ability to handle certain types of questions. For example, you may breeze through straightforward, basic math questions but get tripped up by word problems. As you evaluate your performance on mathematics in Practice Test 1, try to identify the types of questions you struggle with most:

Basic math: These questions are straightforward with very little text. You just need to do the math.

Basic math in settings: These are word problems that challenge your ability to translate the problem into one or more mathematical equations and then solve those equations.

Very challenging math problems: These can be basic math or basic math in settings questions that challenge your ability to reason mathematically and perhaps draw from your knowledge of more than one math subject area to solve them. In addition to the differences in how math problems are presented, you may encounter *question sets*—two or more sequential math problems related to the same information.

Test-Taking Errors

Incorrect or unanswered questions on the practice test may be less of a reflection of your math knowledge and skills and more a reflection of your test-taking strategies and skills. As you review your scores and answers, try to determine whether you committed any of the following common test-taking errors:

Worked too slowly: If you answered questions correctly but your score suffered from unanswered questions because you ran out of time, you may simply need more practice to improve your speed.

Rushed through the test: If you finished with plenty of time remaining but made mistakes, you may need to spend more time reading and understanding the questions and doing the math before selecting an answer.

Got stuck on a very challenging question: Answering the easy questions first and then returning to the harder questions later may help you address this issue.

Misread the question: The question contains all information you need to answer it. Misreading the question may cause you to extract and use the wrong information in your calculations or calculate an answer for something other than what the question directed.

Overlooked information in the answer choices: Answer choices often provide clues as to what form the answer is in. A glance at the answer choices can often clarify what the question is asking for.

Overlooked or misinterpreted information in an image: Many math questions include an image, table, or graph that provides key information. Misreading an image will lead you to select the wrong answer choice.

Did not use logic to solve a problem: Math questions, especially the very challenging ones, often test your ability to reason through problems.

Not doing the math: Although you are not required to show your work on the test, consider writing out your calculations to double-check your reasoning and avoid mental errors. Also, when a question includes an image, consider writing any dimensions provided in the question on to the image so that the image contains all of the measurements you have to work with.

Not double-checking your answers: For many questions, you can insert the answer you think is correct into the equation provided and do the math to double-check the answer choice. Take the opportunity to double-check answers when given the opportunity.

For math test strategies and tips, turn to chapter 6.

Highlighting Strengths and Areas for Improvement on the Reading Test

The process of scoring the reading practice test and reviewing the answer explanations should reveal the reason you chose the correct or incorrect answer for each question. Reasons for choosing wrong answers or struggling with certain questions can be classified in three categories:

Subject matter

The type of passage—literary narrative or informational—may affect your ability to read and comprehend the passage and answer questions about it. For example, you may have no trouble answering questions about fact-based passages in social science and natural science but struggle reading and understanding literary narratives.

Reading skills

The reading test is designed to evaluate numerous skills, including the ability to identify details in the text, draw generalizations about those details, and understand the meaning of a word or phrase based on how it is used in a sentence. In addition, each passage challenges you to read quickly and with understanding.

Test-taking strategies and skills

Not reading the entire passage, misreading the question or answer choices, and not verifying an answer choice with the passage can all lead to careless mistakes.

Use the checklists in the following sections to flag the types of reading passages, reading skills, and test-taking strategies and skills you may need to focus on.

Types of Reading Passages

Your ability to comprehend reading passages and answer questions about them may vary based on the type of passage. For example, if you are accustomed to reading science books and articles, you are probably familiar with many of the concepts and vocabulary in the science passages on the test; therefore, you might expect to have no trouble reading, comprehending, and answering questions about such passages. However, if you have read very little fiction, you may find it challenging to identify the plot (sequence of events), draw conclusions about characters, or sense the mood that a passage is intended to evoke. In short, you may struggle more with certain types of reading passages than with others.

As you score your reading test and review the answer explanations, use the following checklist to flag any types of reading passages you found particularly challenging:

Literary narrative: Passages from short stories, novels, and memoirs

Social science: Informational passages that cover topics such as anthropology, archaeology, biography, business, economics, education, geography, history, political science, psychology, and sociology

Humanities: Informational passages about topics including architecture, art, dance, ethics, film, language, literary criticism, music, philosophy, radio, television, and theater

Natural science: Informational passages related to subjects such as anatomy, astronomy, biology, botany, chemistry, ecology, geology, medicine, meteorology, microbiology, natural history, physiology, physics, technology, and zoology

Reading Skills Tested

The ability to read, comprehend, and answer questions about passages involves numerous skills. Questions on the test are written specifically to evaluate these skills. As you review the answer explanations, place a checkmark next to any of the following skills you think you need to develop more fully:

Identify and interpret details: Nearly all questions require an ability to identify and interpret details from the passage that support whichever answer choice you select.

Many questions specifically state, "According to the passage …" This skill is essential for performing well on the reading test.

Determine the main idea of a paragraph(s) or passage: A few questions may require an ability to recognize the general meaning or point of one or more paragraphs.

Understand comparative relationships (comparison and contrast): Questions may ask about comparisons and contrasts made in the passage.

Understand cause-effect relationships: Some reading passages explore cause-effect relationships. Others are accompanied by questions that more subtly test your ability to identify cause-effect relationships.

Make generalizations: To answer many reading questions, you must be able to draw conclusions from or make generalizations about details provided in the passage.

Determine the meaning of words or phrases from context: You are likely to encounter several questions on the ACT reading test that challenge you to determine the meaning of a word or phrase based on the context in which it is used.

Understand sequences of events: A few reading test questions may require an ability to read and comprehend a series of events.

Draw conclusions about the author's purpose and method: You may be asked to get into the mind of the author and figure out what their attitude, purpose, or method is.

Understand arguments: Some items may ask you to identify an argument being made in a passage or to examine support for an argument.

Synthesize information from multiple texts or different formats: You may be asked to put together information from multiple texts or put together information from a text and a graphic element (e.g., chart, table, diagram).

For more about reading skills tested, including examples of the types of questions used to evaluate these skills, turn to chapter 7.

Test-Taking Errors

Even if your reading speed and comprehension are solid, you may miss questions by committing one or more of the following common test-taking errors. Place a checkmark next to each error you think you may be susceptible to making:

Read too slowly or too quickly: By reading too slowly, you may not have sufficient time to read all passages and answer all questions. However, reading too quickly may result in errors or having to return to a passage several times to locate the evidence needed to decide which answer choice is correct.

Did not read the entire passage: Skim-reading a passage is useful for understanding what a passage is about, but it often results in overlooking the details required to answer specific questions. Read the entire passage word for word.

Misread the question: Questions, especially those that contain the word *NOT*, can be tricky. Make sure you understand what a question is asking as you evaluate the various answer choices.

Misread or overlooked an answer choice: Misreading an answer choice or not considering all answer choices can result in mistakes. Consider all answer choices and read them carefully.

Did not verify an answer choice with the passage: If time allows, try to verify every answer choice by locating details in the passage that support it. Use the same technique to rule out other answer choices when necessary.

For additional reading test strategies and tips, turn to chapter 7.

Highlighting Strengths and Areas for Improvement on the Science Test

The process of scoring the science practice test and reviewing the answer explanations should reveal the reason you chose the correct or incorrect answer for each question. Reasons for choosing wrong answers or struggling with certain questions can be classified into three categories:

Subject matter

The science test does not require in-depth knowledge of biology, chemistry, earth science, space science, or physics. Nor does it require you to memorize formulas or solve complex math problems. However, questions are presented in the context of these subject areas, and you may need some knowledge of scientific terms or concepts to answer some of the questions.

Passage type

Science passages are presented in three different formats: Data Representation (graphs, tables, illustrations); Research Summaries (from experiments); and Conflicting Viewpoints (alternative theories and hypotheses). You may struggle more with the items presented in one type of passage than in the others.

Test-taking strategies and skills

The science test evaluates your ability to extract and use information presented in a variety of formats to solve problems and answer questions. Even if you are highly skilled and knowledgeable in all science subject areas, your score will suffer if you make careless mistakes or are so careful that you run out of time before answering all of the questions.

Use the checklists in the following sections to flag the subject areas, passage types, and test-taking strategies and skills you may need to focus on.

Science Subject Areas

You may benefit from identifying subject areas in which you struggle. Use the following checklist to flag subject matter you may need to review:

Biology: Cell biology, botany, zoology, microbiology, ecology, biochemistry, genetics, and evolution

Chemistry: Properties of matter, acids and bases, kinetics and equilibria, thermo-chemistry, organic chemistry, and nuclear chemistry

Earth and Space sciences: Geology, meteorology, oceanography, environmental science, stars, planets, galaxies, and the universe.

Physics: Mechanics, gravitation, thermodynamics, electromagnetism, fluids, solids, and optics

Types of Science Passages

As you review answer explanations and evaluate your performance on the science test, check to see whether you had more trouble with items in certain types of science passages than others. Place a checkmark next to any passage types that you found particularly challenging:

Data Representation passages focus primarily on assessing your ability to understand, evaluate, and interpret information presented in graphs, tables, and illustrations.

Research Summary passages focus primarily on assessing your ability to understand, analyze, and evaluate the design, execution, and results of one or more experiments.

Conflicting Viewpoints passages focus primarily on assessing your ability to compare and evaluate alternative theories, hypotheses, or viewpoints on a specific observable phenomenon.

For more about these different passage types and guidance on how to approach the items in them effectively, turn to chapter 8.

Test-Taking Errors

As mentioned previously, the science test does not require in-depth scientific knowledge. It relies more on your ability to understand and identify detailed information presented in a variety of formats—text, graphs, tables, and diagrams. If your science test score is lower than you had hoped, you may have committed one or more test-taking errors. Place a checkmark next to each of the following test-taking errors that you think you need to work on avoiding:

Worked too slowly: If time expired before you had a chance to answer all 40 questions, you need to practice guessing and moving to the next question if an item is taking too much time.

Worked too quickly: If you finished with plenty of time remaining but made mistakes, you need to practice slowing down and reading the science passages, questions, and answer choices more carefully.

Misread or misinterpreted text: If you missed questions because you misread a passage, question, or answer choice, check this box.

Misread or misinterpreted a graph or table: Graphs, tables, and images contain much of the information required to answer the science test questions.

Misread or misinterpreted a research summary: You may need to develop a better understanding of the scientific method for designing and conducting experiments.

Did not use reason effectively to find the answer: Most of the questions on the science test challenge your ability to think and reason. If you struggled to understand questions, check this box. You may be able to improve your score by adopting a problem-solving strategy that steps you through the question, as discussed in chapter 8.

For science test-taking strategies that will help you avoid these common mistakes and others, turn to chapter 8.

Highlighting Strengths and Areas for Improvement on the Writing Test

The optional writing test is designed to evaluate your ability to write at a level expected of students entering first-year college English composition courses. A solid essay demonstrates your ability to clearly state your perspective on a complex issue and analyze the relationship between your perspective and at least one other perspective, develop and support your ideas with reasoning and examples, organize your ideas clearly and logically, and communicate your ideas effectively in standard written English.

As noted in chapter 3, we strongly recommend consulting others to help you evaluate your writing practice test. Self-assessment is an invaluable skill, but others often see what we cannot. If you must work independently, read your essay with the most critical eye you can, asking yourself whether a reader who came to it with no knowledge of the prompt or what you meant to say would understand your argument. After scoring your writing practice test, use the checklists in the following sections (organized by domain) to highlight writing skills you may need to develop more fully and to avoid errors related to writing strategy and process.

Writing Skills Tested

As you evaluate your writing practice test, consider which skills contributed to your scores. In chapter 9, a full set of sample essays is included. Though the prompt there is different than the one in chapter 3, the quality of writing in each of the essays is similar to that of essays for any topic. Comparing your own work to those samples will help you evaluate the skill displayed in your practice test. You may be able to improve your scores significantly by more fully developing only one or two of the following skills. Place a checkmark next to each skill you think you need to work on:

Clearly state your own perspective on a complex issue and analyze the relationship between your perspective and at least one other perspective: If another reader cannot easily identify a clear perspective, practice formulating thesis statements. Whenever you write an essay, practice stating your thesis in the first few sentences of the essay. By presenting your perspective in the introduction, you not only state your main idea clearly but also give your essay a focal point.

If you had trouble analyzing the relationship between your perspective and at least one other perspective, practice writing counterarguments. Pick a debatable issue and choose a stance. Now, imagine what someone who disagrees with you might say, and practice writing paragraphs that first present the other person's side of the issue. Then offer your response. Next, imagine a perspective that is in general agreement with yours but differs in some important ways. How do you respond to this perspective? As you think and write, ask yourself: What accounts for the similarities and differences among your perspective and others you can imagine? Where are the strengths and weaknesses in these other perspectives, and where are the strengths and weaknesses in your own? Most importantly, ask yourself how engaging with another view—whether it generally agrees or disagrees with your own—can help you advance an argument. Considering these questions as you practice can help you learn to analyze and engage with different perspectives.

Develop and support your ideas with reasoning and examples: Failure to support your assertions can result in a lower score. Remember that every claim you make should be backed up with good supporting evidence. Ask yourself whether the reasoning or evidence you provided sufficiently explains your thinking, or whether another sentence or two would help clarify your meaning. As you explain the reasoning behind your argument, remember that logical fallacies, including overgeneralization and moral equivalence (associating minor offenses with moral atrocities), can weaken your ideas. Additionally, the assumption that a reader shares or inherently understands your viewpoint can lead to underdevelopment of ideas.

Organize your ideas clearly and logically: An essay should flow directly from point A to point B and not repeat itself or wander off track. Consider the extent to which the ideas in the body paragraphs are focused on arguing the thesis: are there ideas present that are not obviously connected to your main point? Are the ideas clearly related to one another? How might transitions be improved? Similarly, think about the order in which your ideas are presented: does the arrangement add meaning (e.g., opening with a metaphor that describes the issue in the prompt, refuting counterarguments before building your own, or concluding with an example that illustrates the argument) or are the ideas essentially listed? Do the ideas build upon one another or do they function in isolation? Thinking about questions such as these can help you learn to write a more cohesive essay. (Prewriting, discussed in the next section, can help ensure that your essay is well organized.)

Communicate your ideas effectively in standard written English: If your essay contains several errors in grammar, usage, and mechanics, it would be beneficial to review rules and practice a variety of exercises associated with those. Equally important, however, are word choice, sentence structure, and style. If your essay does not include much variety of either vocabulary or sentence type, you might practice constructing the same sentences in different ways, experimenting with synonyms and fluctuating between simple and complex sentences. Pay close attention to the voice and tone: how might a reader interpret your attitude about the issue? How much personality belongs in the argument, and how can it be conveyed through word choice? Answering these sorts of questions can help you with evaluating your writing and improving your use of language to reach an audience.

You can develop all of these skills in high school English classes and other classes that require you to write essays and where you receive feedback that targets these skills. For more about improving your writing test score, along with sample essays that demonstrate the differences between high-scoring and lower-scoring essays, turn to chapter 9.

Writing Strategy or Process Errors

When scoring an essay, the focus is on the product, but the score may be a reflection of the process used to produce that essay. For example, prewriting (planning) can help you think of good ideas, ensure that your ideas are presented logically, and remind you to provide evidence to support your ideas. After scoring your practice essay, think back on your process, including planning, and how it impacted your essay and place a checkmark next to any of these writing strategy or process errors you may have committed:

Poor pacing: Composing too quickly may result in careless errors, whereas working too slowly may result in an incomplete essay or insufficient time to review and correct errors.

Insufficient prewriting (planning): It is difficult to write an effective essay, especially in timed conditions, if you have not spent time thinking about how to approach the task, considering what you might want to say and how to say it most constructively. If you had trouble generating and developing ideas or engaging with multiple perspectives, consider using the guided prewriting section found in the test booklet. The questions presented in this section are intended to help you produce a perspective and analyze its relationships with other points of view. They are also useful as you think about how you will support your ideas. Because it can be difficult to organize your ideas as you write, you may want to consider using the prewriting space to write an outline or draw a diagram. You do not need a detailed outline, but starting with a thesis and mapping a structure to support it can help you define the logic of your argument before you begin to write it. This can be particularly helpful when writing in timed conditions.

Not reviewing or editing: If you completed your essay with time to spare, did not review or edit it, and your essay has errors related to grammar, usage, sentence structure, or style, check this box. Practice with reading and editing while you write, even just with sentences and paragraphs, will help you get better at this.

Insufficient practice: Producing well-written essays requires practice and feedback, which you often receive only in a formal English composition course. The practice writing tests in this book provide additional opportunities, but we strongly recommend that you have your practice writing tests evaluated by a qualified third party—perhaps an English teacher or a fellow student who is a strong writer.

For additional tips on improving your writing test score, turn to chapter 9.

Part Three: Improving Your Score

In This Part

This part features various ways to improve your scores on the English, mathematics, reading, and optional science and writing tests. Here, you get a preview of the types of questions you can expect on each test, along with test-taking strategies and skills that apply specifically to each test:

English: Find out more about test content, look at sample questions, and develop strategies for choosing the best answer.

Mathematics: Learn about the subject areas covered on the test, the types of math problems you will encounter, and strategies for improving your speed and accuracy in answering questions.

Reading: Discover the types of reading passages you will encounter on the test, the types of questions you will need to answer, and strategies for improving your reading speed and comprehension.

Science: Identify the areas of science covered on the test, the types of questions you will encounter, and test-taking strategies and skills for extracting information from passages and using it to reason your way to the correct answers.

Writing: Check out a sample writing prompt, find out what the people scoring your essay will be looking for, read sample scored essays from poor to excellent, and pick up a few strategies that may help to raise your writing score.

Chapter 5: Improving Your English Score

On the ACT English test, you have 35 minutes to read six to seven passages, or essays, and answer 50 multiple-choice questions about them. Essays will vary in length, and you may see four longer essays and two short essays, or three longer essays and four short essays. Longer essays will have 10 items each and shorter essays will have 5 items each, so each test will have the same number of total items, though the number of essays varies. On each test, 40 of the items will be scored; those items will be attached to either one longer essay or two short essays.

The essays on the English test cover a variety of subjects; the sample passages that follow this discussion range from a personal essay about the different ways of figuring one's age to an informative essay about the legal history of school dress codes.

Content of the ACT English Test

The ACT English test is designed to measure your ability to make the wide variety of decisions involved in revising and editing a given piece of writing. The test measures your understanding of the Conventions of Standard English (punctuation, usage, and sentence structure); Production of Writing (topic development, organization, unity, and cohesion); and Knowledge of Language (word choice, style, and tone). Although you may use more informal or conversational language in your own writing, the test emphasizes the standard written English that is taught in schools around the country.

Different passage types are used to provide a variety of rhetorical situations. Passages are chosen not only for their appropriateness in assessing writing skills but also to reflect students' interests and experiences.

Questions on the English test fall into three categories:

- **Production of Writing** (topic development, organization, unity, and cohesion)
- **Knowledge of Language** (precision and concision in word choice, consistency in style and tone)
- **Conventions of Standard English** (sentence structure and formation, punctuation, and usage)

You will receive four scores for the ACT English test: a total test score based on 40 questions and three reporting category scores based on specific knowledge and skills in the categories previously described. If you choose to take the writing test, you will also receive an English Language Arts (ELA) score based on an average of your English, reading, and writing test scores.

You will **not** be tested on spelling, vocabulary, or rote recall of the rules of grammar. Grammar and usage are tested only within the context of the essay, not by questions such as "Must an appositive always be set off by commas?" Likewise, you won't be tested directly on your vocabulary, although the better your vocabulary is, the better equipped you'll be to comprehend the reading passages and answer questions that involve choosing the most appropriate word.

The English test doesn't require you to memorize what you read. The questions and essays are side-by-side for easy reference. This is **not** a memorization test.

The questions discussed on the following pages are taken from the sample passages and questions that follow on pages 203–209. If you prefer, you can work through the sample passages and questions before you read the rest of this discussion. However, to better understand the English test, you may want to first read the discussion, then work through the sample passages and questions.

Types of Questions on the ACT English Test

Many questions refer to an underlined portion of the essay. (As noted in Chapter 1, items taken online will be marked by highlighting instead of underlining. In the examples that follow, which show items as they would appear on paper, we'll stick to underlining.) You must decide on the best alternative for that underlined portion. Usually, your options include **No Change**, which means that the essay is best as it's written. Sometimes, you'll also have the option of deleting the underlined portion. For example, the following question (from Sample Passage II on pages 205–207) offers you the option of removing the word *to* from the sentence.

Otherwise, this difference points
21
to significant underlying cultural values.
22

22. Which choice is clearest and most grammatically acceptable in context?
  F. **No Change**
  G. on
  H. at
  J. **Delete** the underlined portion.

In this example, the best answer is not to delete the underlined portion but to leave it as it is (**F**).

Other questions on the English test may ask about a section of the essay or an aspect of the essay as a whole. For example, in the following question (from Sample Passage I on pages 203–205), you're given a sentence to be added to the essay, and then you're asked to decide the most logical place in the essay to add that sentence.

15. The writer wants to add the following accurate sentence to the essay:

> Those same German influences helped spawn a similar musical form in northern Mexico known as *norteño*.

The sentence would most logically be placed at:

A. Point A in Paragraph 1.
B. Point B in Paragraph 2.
C. Point C in Paragraph 3.
D. Point D in Paragraph 4.

In this example, the best answer is **C**, because Paragraph 3 focuses on the European musical influences on the O'odham people of Arizona, and the last sentence of the paragraph specifically refers to the musical influences of German immigrants.

Let's look at some additional examples of the kinds of questions you're likely to find on the ACT English test. If you want to know what an individual question looks like in the context of the passage in which it appears, turn to the pages indicated. You can also use those sample passages and questions for practice, either before or after reading this discussion.

Conventions of Standard English

Conventions of Standard English questions focus on the conventions of punctuation, grammar and usage, and sentence structure and formation.

Punctuation questions involve identifying and correcting the following misplaced, missing, or unnecessary punctuation marks:

- Commas

- Apostrophes

- Colons, semicolons, and dashes

- Periods, question marks, and exclamation points

These questions address not only the rules of punctuation but also the use of punctuation to express ideas clearly. For example, you should be prepared to show how punctuation can be used to indicate possession or to set off a parenthetical element.

In many punctuation questions, the words in every choice will be identical, but the commas or other punctuation marks will vary. It's important to read the choices carefully in order to notice the presence or absence of commas, semicolons, colons, periods, and other punctuation. The following example of a punctuation question comes from Sample Passage I on pages 203–205.

Around this time the polka music and button

accordion played by German immigrant rail-

road <u>workers; left</u> their mark on waila.
      <u>14</u>

14. Which choice makes the sentence most grammatically acceptable?
- **F.** **No Change**
- **G.** workers
- **H.** workers:
- **J.** workers,

It may help you to read through this sentence without paying attention to the punctuation so you can identify its grammatical construction. The subject of this sentence is "the polka music and button accordion." What follows that subject might seem like the predicate verb of the sentence, but it's not. The phrase "played by German immigrant railroad workers" is a participial phrase (a phrase formed with the past participle "played"). This participial phrase functions as an adjective because it modifies the nouns it follows ("the polka music and button accordion").

After the participial phrase is the predicate verb of the main clause, "left." Then comes a phrase that explains what was left (the direct object "their mark") and a prepositional phrase that explains where it was left ("on waila").

Now we can deal with the question about what kind of punctuation should follow that participial phrase. Sometimes, these phrases are set off from the main clause with commas to indicate that the phrase is parenthetical or provides information not essential to the meaning of the sentence. That's not the case here for two reasons. First, there's no comma at the beginning of the participial phrase. Second, the phrase is essential to the sentence; the sentence is not referring to just any polka music and button accordion but to the music and accordion played by those German immigrant railroad workers (presumably, not while they were working on the railroad).

Ignoring the participial phrase for a minute, we need to ask ourselves what kind of punctuation we would usually place between the subject "the polka music and button accordion" and the verb "left." Our answer should be no punctuation at all, making **G** the best answer. Of course, you could answer this question without this rather tedious analysis of the parts of the sentence. You might simply decide that because the sentence contains no other punctuation, you would never insert a single punctuation mark between the subject and the predicate of the main clause. Or you might just plug in each of the four punctuation choices—semicolon, no punctuation, colon, comma—and choose the one that looks or sounds best to you.

Grammar and usage questions involve choosing the best word or words in a sentence based on grammar and usage conventions. Some examples of poor and better phrases are given in the following.

- Grammatical agreement

  (Subject and verb)

  "The owner of the bicycles *are* going to sell them."
  should be:
  "The owner of the bicycles *is* going to sell them."

  (Pronoun and antecedent)

  "Susan and Mary left *her* briefcases in the office."
  should be:
  "Susan and Mary left *their* briefcases in the office."

- Pronoun forms and cases

  "Seymour and Svetlana annoyed *there* parents all the time."
  should be:
  "Seymour and Svetlana annoyed *their* parents all the time."

Questions dealing with pronouns often have to do with using the proper form and case of the pronoun. Sometimes they address a pronoun's agreement with its antecedent, or referent. In such cases, consider the entire sentence, and sometimes the preceding sentence, to make sure you know what the antecedent is. Consider the following question (from Sample Passage I on pages 203–205).

<table>
<tr><td>

As the dancers step to

the music, they <u>were also stepping</u> in time to a
8

sound that embodies <u>their</u> unique history and
9

suggests the influence of outside cultures on

their music.

</td><td>

9. Which choice makes the sentence most grammatically acceptable?

   A. No Change
   B. they're
   C. it's
   D. its'

</td></tr>
</table>

Here, the possessive pronoun in question refers back to the subject of the main clause ("they"), which in turn refers back to the subject of the introductory subordinate clause ("the dancers"). Thus, the best answer is the third-person plural possessive pronoun ("their" **A**). Choice **B** might seem like a possibility because *they're* sounds like *their* (that is, they're homonyms). However, *they're* is a contraction for *they are*. We can rule out **C** and **D** because of the pronoun-antecedent agreement problem and also because *it's* is not a possessive pronoun but a contraction for *it is*, and *its'* is not even a word.

Sentence structure questions involve the effective formation of sentences, including dealing with relationships between and among clauses, placement of modifiers, and shifts in construction. Following are some examples:

- Subordinate or dependent clauses and participial phrases

    "These hamsters are excellent pets *because providing* hours of cheap entertainment."

    This sentence could be rewritten as:

    "These hamsters are excellent pets, providing hours of cheap entertainment." (participial phrase)

    It could also be revised as:

    "These hamsters are excellent pets because they provide hours of cheap entertainment." (subordinate/dependent clause)

- Run-on or fused sentences

    "We discovered that all of our friends had already seen the *movie they* thought it was terrible.

    This sentence should actually be two:

    "We discovered that all of our friends had already seen the *movie. They* thought it was terrible.

- Comma splices

"The anteaters had terrible *manners, they* just ate and ran."

This sentence could be rewritten as:

"The anteaters had terrible *manners. They* just ate and ran."

Because a semicolon can serve as a "soft" period, the sentence could also be rewritten as:

"The anteaters had terrible *manners; they* just ate and ran."

- Sentence fragments

"*When he* burned his lunch."

This needs a subject to let us know who "he" is and what he did:

"*Julio didn't lose his temper when he* burned his lunch."

- Misplaced modifiers

"*Snarling and snapping, Juanita* attempted to control her pet turtle."

Unless Juanita was doing the snarling and snapping, the sentence should be rewritten:

"*Snarling and snapping, the pet turtle* resisted Juanita's attempt to control it." It could also be rewritten this way:

"Juanita attempted to control her *pet turtle, which snarled and snapped.*"

- Shifts in pronoun person or number

"Hamsters should work at the most efficient pace that *one* can."

This should be rewritten as:

"Hamsters should work at the most efficient pace that *they* can."

Many questions about sentence structure and formation will ask you about how clauses and phrases are linked. This means that you may have to consider punctuation or the lack of punctuation, which can create problems such as comma splices, run-on sentences, or sentence fragments. You also may have to consider various words that can be used to link clauses and phrases: conjunctions such as *and, but, because,* and *when,* and pronouns such as *who, whose, which,* and *that.* The following question (from Sample Passage I on pages 203–205) is a good example of a sentence structure question.

> It is a social
>
> music that performed at weddings, birthday
> ————
>   4
> parties, and feasts.

4. Which choice makes the sentence most grammatically acceptable?
- **F.** **No Change**
- **G.** music in which it is performed
- **H.** music, performing
- **J.** music, performed

What would be the best way to link the clause "It is a social music" and the phrase "performed [or performing] at weddings, birthday parties, and feasts"? Relative pronouns such as *that* and *which* stand in for the noun that the relative clause modifies. (They relate the clause to the noun.) One way to try out choices such as **F** and **G** is to replace the relative pronoun with the noun and then decide if the resulting statement makes sense:

> Social music performed at weddings, birthday parties, and feasts. (**F**)

This does not make sense. Musicians perform, but the music itself does not. Music *is* performed.

> In social music it is performed at weddings, birthday parties, and feasts. (**G**)

This also seems nonsensical. What does *it* refer to—social music?

The other two choices offer a different approach to connecting information in a sentence. The phrases "performing at weddings, birthday parties, and feasts" (**H**) and "performed at weddings, birthday parties, and feasts" (**J**) are participial phrases. Similar to adjective clauses, these phrases modify a noun. We can rule out **H** for the same reason that we rejected **F**: it doesn't make sense to think of "social music" as "performing." However, it sounds fine to refer to "social music" as "performed" (**J**).

Production of Writing

Production of Writing questions focus on writing strategy and organization.

Topic development questions focus on the choices made and strategies used by a writer in the act of composing or revising an essay. These questions may ask you to make decisions concerning the appropriateness of a sentence or essay in relation to purpose, audience, unity, or focus, or the effect of adding, revising, or deleting supporting material.

The following question (from Sample Passage I on pages 203–205) is a fairly typical example of the kinds of writing decisions that strategy questions ask you to make.

In the early 1900s the O'odham became acquainted with marching bands and wood-wind instruments <u>(which explains the presence of saxophones in waila)</u>.
<u>13</u>

13. Given that all of the choices are accurate, which one provides the most relevant information at this point in the essay?

   A. **No Change**
   B. (although fiddles were once widely used in waila bands).
   C. (even though they're now often constructed of metal).
   D. (which are frequently found in jazz bands also).

It's important to read these questions carefully and, sometimes, to reread the essay or parts of the essay. This question is fairly clear-cut, but it does suggest that you need a pretty good sense of what Paragraph 3 is about. A quick review of the paragraph indicates that it is focused on how the O'odham and their music were influenced by other musical styles and instrumentation they encountered.

Which of these parenthetical statements is most relevant to that focus? Choice **D**, which states that woodwind instruments are frequently found in jazz bands, is not. Likewise, choice **C**, which indicates that woodwind instruments are now often constructed of metal, strays from the paragraph's topic. Choice **B**, which points out that fiddles were once widely used in waila bands, is getting closer, but this too seems a diversion, unconnected to the other information in this paragraph. Guitars, woodwinds, and button accordions are mentioned but not fiddles or violins.

Choice **A**, however, provides an appropriate and relevant elaboration. It draws the connection between the O'odhams' introduction to marching bands and woodwinds in the early 1900s and the eventual inclusion of saxophones in a typical waila band.

Organization questions deal with the order and coherence of ideas in an essay and the effective choice of opening, transitional, and closing statements. For example, you may be asked about the organization of ideas (the most logical order for sentences within a paragraph or paragraphs within an essay) or about the most logical transitional phrase or statement.

The following question (from Sample Passage II on pages 205–207) is a good example of the kind of organization question you might encounter.

> Today, after many birthdays and New Year's Days, I now find meaningful the difference I once found confusing. <u>Otherwise,</u>
> 21
> this difference points <u>to significant underlying</u>
> 22
> cultural values.

21. Which transition word or phrase is most logical in context?
- **A. No Change**
- **B.** Though,
- **C.** In fact,
- **D.** Then,

The choices in this question are sometimes referred to as conjunctive adverbs or transitional words or phrases because their main job is to connect or link the statement in one sentence with the statement in a preceding sentence. These are often little words—*so, thus, soon, yet, also*—that do a lot of work to make an essay logical.

In order to answer such questions correctly, it helps to think about the logical relationship between the sentences, as well as the logical relationships expressed by the choices. The main statement of the opening sentence of this paragraph is "I now find meaningful the difference [in computing one's age] I once found confusing." The second sentence states, "This difference points to significant underlying cultural values." The writer then goes on to explain those cultural values.

Which of these four choices enables readers to move most easily from the opening sentence into the rest of this paragraph? Choice **A** suggests that the second statement contrasts with the first statement. A typical dictionary definition for *otherwise* is "in different circumstances." Similarly, choice **B**, *though,* suggests that the statement to follow is contrary to or in opposition to the preceding statement. Neither of those adverbs works well here. Nor does *then* (choice **D**), which usually expresses a time relationship—meaning "next" or "soon after in time."

The best choice here is **C**. The phrase *in fact* is often used to introduce a statement that builds on the preceding statement. We can pare down these opening sentences to their bare essentials to show that the phrase works well here: "I now find the difference in computing one's age meaningful. In fact, the difference points to important cultural values about life experience and longevity."

Knowledge of Language

These questions involve effective word choices in terms of writing style, tone, clarity, and economy. Sometimes, a phrase or sentence that isn't technically ungrammatical is nevertheless confusing because it's poorly written. Sometimes, a word or phrase clashes with the tone of the essay. Good writing also involves eliminating excessively wordy or redundant material and vague or awkward expressions.

Similar to most writing strategy and organization questions, style questions require a general understanding of the essay as a whole. The following style question (from Sample Passage III on pages 207–209) focuses on the issues of economy and consistency of tone.

<table>
<tr><td>

The school board members
believed that wearing "play clothes" to school
made the students <u>inefficient toward</u> their
32
school work, while more formal attire estab-
lished a positive educational climate.

</td><td>

32. Which choice most effectively maintains the essay's tone?

  F. **No Change**
  G. lazy and bored to tears with
  H. blow off
  J. lax and indifferent toward

</td></tr>
</table>

You will be better able to recognize the appropriateness of choice **J** if you know that *lax* means "lacking necessary strictness, severity, or precision" and *indifferent* means "lacking interest, enthusiasm, or concern." These terms touch on two related but distinct concerns—academic laziness and apathy. One could imagine school board members using these very words in their meetings. And the words are consistent with the overall style and tone of this straightforward, informative essay about a legal case.

Choices **G** and **H** are fairly easy to rule out if you think about the generally formal tone of the essay. It's not that one should never use slang phrases such as "bored to tears" or "blow off" in one's writing; it's just that this particular essay is not the place to use them. When we consider that this statement is describing the school board members' belief, these phrases are even more inappropriate.

It seems more in character for school board members to be concerned about student inefficiency, but **F** is a weak choice because the phrase "inefficient toward their school work" sounds odd or awkward. Perhaps it's the preposition that trips us up. The word *toward* works fine in **J** when describing attitudes ("lax," "indifferent") toward school work, but the word *inefficient* is describing an ability or skill.

* * *

The questions provided here are a small sample of the kinds of questions that might be on the test. The previous question, for example, is only one kind of style question; it doesn't cover all the elements of style that might be addressed on the test. The sample passages and questions at the end of this section have all the examples referred to in this chapter as they would appear in a test. These sample passages and questions and the later practice tests will provide you with a thorough understanding of the ACT English test.

Strategies for Taking the ACT English Test

Pace Yourself

The ACT English test contains 50 questions to be completed in 35 minutes, which works out to exactly 42 seconds per question. Spending $1\frac{1}{2}$ minutes skimming through each long essay and roughly half that for each short essay leaves you about 30 seconds to respond to each question. If you spend less time than that on each question, you can use the remaining time allowed for this test to review

Improving Your Score

your work and to return to the questions that were most difficult for you. Another way to think of it is that you have 35 minutes to read and answer the questions for all of the essays, giving you approximately 7 minutes for each long essay and its questions and 3.5 minutes for each short essay and its questions.

Be Aware of the Writing Style Used in the Essay

The essays cover a variety of topics and are written in a variety of styles. It's important that you take into account the writing style used in each essay as you respond to the questions.

Some of the essays will be anecdotes or narratives written from an informal, first-person point of view. Others will be more formal essays, scholarly or informative in nature, often written in the third person. Some essays will be argumentative and are designed to persuade an audience. Some questions will ask you to choose the best answer based not on its grammatical correctness but on its consistency with the style and tone of the essay as a whole. For example, an expression that's too breezy for an essay on the life of President Herbert Hoover might be just right for a personal narrative about a writer's attempt at learning to skateboard.

Consider a Question's Context before Choosing an Answer

Some people find it helpful to skim an essay before trying to answer the associated questions. Having a general sense of the essay in mind before you begin to answer questions involving writing strategy or style can help. If you encounter questions about the order of sentences within a paragraph, or where to add a sentence in an essay, you may want to answer those questions first to make sure that the major elements of the essay are arranged logically. Understanding the order of the passage may make it easier for you to answer some of the other questions.

As you're answering each question, be sure to read at least a sentence or two beyond the sentence containing the portion being questioned. You may need to read even more than that to understand what the writer is trying to say.

Be Aware of the Connotations of Words

Vocabulary isn't tested in an isolated way on the ACT English test. Nevertheless, a good vocabulary and an awareness of not only the dictionary definitions of words but also the connotations (feelings and associations) suggested by those words will help you do well on the test.

The following question (from Sample Passage II on pages 205–207) asks you to think about how certain words and their connotations can function in terms of the rest of the essay.

Many people might be surprised to learn that the American way of computing a person's age differs from the traditional Korean way. In Korean tradition, a person is considered to be already one year old at the time of his or her birth.

As a child growing up in two cultures, I found this <u>contest</u> a bit confusing.
16

16. Which choice is clearest and most precise in context?

F. No Change
G. change
H. dispute
J. difference

Which word best captures or summarizes what has been described in the preceding paragraph? The word *contest* (**F**) doesn't seem right because it suggests a competition between opposing sides or teams. In a similar vein, the word *dispute* (**H**) doesn't fit here because it generally refers to a verbal debate or argument. The word *change* (**G**) is a little off because it expresses the idea of transformation, making something or someone different, which doesn't accurately summarize that opening paragraph. The word *difference* (**J**), however, seems just right. It echoes the verb in the first sentence of the preceding paragraph, but more importantly, it accurately reflects the writer's perspective up to this point in the essay that the American way and the Korean way of computing a person's age are not competing or arguing with each other. They are simply unlike each other (and because of that mismatch, a bit confusing).

In questions such as this one, you have to focus on what the words mean and what associations the words have for the typical reader.

Look at the Stated Question

Before responding to a question identified by an underlined portion, read the stated question preceding the options. This question will provide you with some guidelines for deciding on the best choice. Some questions will ask you to choose the alternative to the underlined portion that is **not** or **least** acceptable. Here's an example from Sample Passage I on pages 203–205.

The music is

mainly instrumental—the bands generally con-
                          3

sist of guitar, bass guitar, saxophones, accor-

dion, and drums.

3. Which of the following alternatives to the underlined portion would **not** be acceptable?
- **A.** instrumental; in general, the bands
- **B.** instrumental, the bands generally
- **C.** instrumental. The bands generally
- **D.** instrumental; the bands generally

For these types of questions, look closely at the underlined portion, because the question has told you that it *is* acceptable. Likewise, three of the alternative choices are acceptable. The best answer, in this case, is the one that is *not* acceptable. In the underlined portion, a dash is used between two independent clauses: "The music is mainly instrumental" and "the bands generally consist of guitar, bass guitar, saxophones, accordion, and drums." The dash is sometimes thought of as a less formal type of punctuation, but it can work quite well to provide emphasis or to signal that an explanation will follow.

Placing a period (**C**) or a semicolon (**D**) between these two independent clauses would also be acceptable. Likewise, choice **A** is acceptable because it too places a semicolon between the two clauses, using the phrase "in general" rather than the adverb "generally." Choice **B** is not acceptable and is, therefore, the best answer. A comma is not usually a strong enough punctuation mark between two independent clauses not joined by a conjunction. Notice that this sentence has other commas, used to distinguish nouns in a series. How would a reader know that the comma between the clauses is a much stronger break than those other commas?

No matter what the stated question is, you should carefully examine what is underlined in the essay. Consider the features of writing that are included in the underlined portion. The options for each question will contain changes in one or more aspects of writing.

Note the Differences in the Answer Choices

Many of the questions will involve more than one aspect of writing. Examine each choice and note how it differs from the others. Consider all the features of writing that are included in each option.

Avoid Making New Mistakes

Beware of correcting mistakes in the essay and, in your haste, picking a response that creates a new mistake. Be observant, especially in questions where the responses have similar wording. One comma or apostrophe can make all the difference, as the following question (from Sample Passage III on pages 207–209) illustrates.

His challenge

initiated a <u>review, of students' rights and admin-</u> | **43.** Which choice makes the sentence
istrative <u>responsibility in public education.</u> | most grammatically acceptable?

43

44

43. Which choice makes the sentence most grammatically acceptable?
A. **No Change**
B. review, of students' rights,
C. review of students' rights
D. review of students' rights,

Perhaps you took only a moment to reject choice **A** because of the unnecessary comma between the noun *review* and the prepositional phrase "of students' rights." And if you were able to make that call, you may have ruled out choice **B** for the same reason. It is probably more difficult to recognize that the comma between the noun *rights* and the conjunction *and* (**D**) is unnecessary and misleading. Because you were thinking about how the underlined portion should be punctuated, you may also have wondered about the plural apostrophe in the word *students'* but then realize that the apostrophe is in the same place in all four choices. (The best answer is **C**.)

Determine the Best Answer

There are at least two approaches you can take to determine the best answer to a question about an underlined portion. One approach is to reread the sentence or sentences containing this portion, substitute each of the answer choices in turn, and decide which is best. Another approach is to decide how the underlined portion might best be phrased and then look for your phrasing among the choices offered. If the underlined portion is correct as it is, select the **No Change** option.

If you can't decide which option is best, you may want to mark the question in your test booklet so you can return to it later. Remember: you're not penalized for guessing, so after you've eliminated as many options as you can, take your best guess.

Reread the Sentence Using Your Selected Answer

After you have selected the answer you feel is best, reread the corresponding sentence or sentences in the essay, substituting the answer you've selected for the underlined portion or for the boxed numeral. Sometimes an answer that sounds fine out of context doesn't fit within the sentence or essay. Be sure to keep in mind both the punctuation marks and words in each possible response; sometimes just the omission of a comma can make an important difference.

Watch for Questions about the Entire Essay or a Section of the Essay

Some questions ask about a section of the essay. They are identified by a question number in a box at the appropriate point in the essay, rather than by an underlined portion. (If you're taking the test online, you will see highlighted asterisks in brackets instead of numbers in boxes.) Here's an example from Sample Passage II on pages 205–207.

Perhaps the celebration of New

Year's Day in Korean culture is <u>heightened</u>
19

because it is thought of as everyone's birthday

party.   20

20. If the writer were to delete the preceding sentence, the paragraph would primarily lose:

   F. a comment on the added significance of the Korean New Year celebration.

   G. a repetitive reminder of what happens every birthday.

   H. a defense of the case for celebrating every birthday.

   J. an illustration of the Korean counting system.

This question asks you to think about the role this sentence plays in terms of the paragraph as a whole. If the sentence were deleted, the paragraph would lose the elaboration on the point that Korean tradition indicates that everyone becomes a year older on New Year's Day, regardless of when they were actually born. Without the sentence, the point about the "added significance of the Korean New Year celebration" (**F**) would have been unstated.

Some other questions ask about an aspect of the essay as a whole. If you are taking the test on paper, these questions are placed at the end of the essay, following boxed instructions like these:

Question 15 asks about the
preceding passage as a whole.

If you are testing online, similar instructions will appear above the individual items at the end of the item set. You may want to read any questions that ask about the essay as a whole first so you can keep them in mind while you're reading through the essay. For questions about a section of the essay or the essay as a whole, you must decide the best answer on the basis of the particular writing or revision problem presented in the question.

Be Careful with Two-Part Questions

Some questions require extra thought because you must decide not only which option is best but also which supporting reason for an option is most appropriate or convincing. The following question occurs at the end of Sample Passage III on pages 207–209. Each option begins with either a yes or no response, followed by a supporting reason for that response.

> **Question 45 asks about the preceding passage as a whole.**

45. Suppose the writer's primary purpose had been to write a persuasive essay urging students to exercise their constitutional rights. Would this essay accomplish that purpose?

- **A.** Yes, because the essay focuses on how Kevin encouraged other students to exercise their constitutional rights.
- **B.** Yes, because the essay focuses on various types of clothing historically worn by students as a freedom of expression.
- **C.** No, because the essay suggests that the right to wear blue jeans was not a substantial constitutional right in the 1970s.
- **D.** No, because the essay objectively reports on one case of a student exercising a particular constitutional right.

Once you decide whether the essay would or would not fulfill the writer's goal, as described in the question, you need to decide which reason or explanation provides the most appropriate support for the answer and is most accurate in terms of the essay. Sometimes, the supporting reason does not accurately reflect the essay (the explanations in **B** and **C**, for example). Sometimes, the reason accurately reflects the essay but doesn't logically support the answer to the question. And sometimes, the reason might logically support the question (that is, the writer's goal) but that reason overstates the focus of the essay. It may be fair to say that Kevin Bannister's case led to a review of student rights, but this essay does not at any point describe Kevin encouraging other students to exercise their rights, as **A** states. The best answer is **D**; this essay is more an objective reporting on a legal case about student rights (and that case's historical significance) than it is a persuasive argument or call to students to exercise those rights.

Watch for Interrelated Questions

As pointed out previously, you'll sometimes find that the best way to answer questions about a passage is not necessarily in their numbered order. Occasionally, answering a question after you've answered the one that follows it is easier. Or you might find two questions about different elements of the same sentence, in which case considering them both together may be helpful.

In the following example (from Sample Passage III on pages 207–209), considering questions 40 and 41 together may be helpful, because they're contained in the same sentence. First, answer the question that seems easier to you. Once you've solved that problem in the sentence, turn to the other question.

<table>
<tr><td>

The court remained unconvinced, <u>therefore,</u> that

                                40

<u>when wearing jeans</u> would actually impair the

    41

learning process of Kevin or of his fellow class-

mates.

</td><td>

40. Which transition word is most logical in context?
- **F.   No Change**
- **G.   thus,**
- **H.   moreover,**
- **J.   however,**

41. Which choice makes the sentence most grammatically acceptable?
- **A.   No Change**
- **B.   by wearing**
- **C.   wearing**
- **D.   having worn**

</td></tr>
</table>

Questions 40 and 41 deal with different kinds of writing problems. Question 40 is about choosing the most logical transitional word, and question 41 is about the correct use in this sentence of the gerund (a verb form with an *-ing* ending that's used as a noun). You might find that answering question 41 helps you to figure out the answer to question 40. The best answer to question 41 is **C**—the noun phrase "wearing jeans" works as the subject of the dependent clause "that wearing jeans would actually impair the learning process of Kevin or of his fellow classmates." Try penciling in your answer choice for 41 (that is, edit the essay) so that you can more easily read the sentence while responding to question 40. Does this approach make it easier for you to decide that the most logical answer to question 40 is **J** ("however")?

* * *

Remember that this section is only an overview of the English test. Directly or indirectly, a question may test you in more than one of the areas mentioned, so do not become overly concerned with categorizing a question before you answer it. And, although awareness of the types of questions can help you be a more critical and strategic test-taker, just remember: the type of question you're answering isn't important. Most importantly, focus on what the question asks and do your best to pick the best answer based on evidence provided in the passage.

The sample passages below contain more items than you will actually see per passage on a test. This is simply to offer a wide variety of samples. The practice tests in this book will provide experiences that more closely mirror the testing experience.

Sample Passage I

The Music of the O'odham

[1]

For some people, traditional American Indian music is <u>associated and connected</u> with high penetrating vocals
₁
accompanied by a steady drumbeat. In tribal communities in the southwestern United States, however, one is likely to hear something similar to the polka-influenced dance music of northern Mexico. The music is called "waila." Among the O'odham tribes of Arizona, waila has been <u>popular for</u> more than a century. The music is mainly
₂

<u>instrumental—the bands generally</u> consist of guitar, bass
₃
guitar, saxophones, accordion, and drums. [A]

[2]

Unlike some traditional tribal music, waila does not serve a religious or spiritual purpose. It is a social <u>music that performed</u> at weddings, birthday parties,
₄

and feasts. The <u>word itself</u> comes from the Spanish
₅

word for dance, *baile*. <u>Check to cheek, the dance is</u>
₆
<u>performed to the relaxed two-step tempo,</u> and the bands
₆

1. Which choice is least redundant in context?
   A. No Change
   B. connected by some of them
   C. linked by association
   D. associated

2. Which choice is least redundant in context?
   F. No Change
   G. popular, one might say, for
   H. really quite popular for
   J. popular for the duration of

3. Which of the following alternatives to the underlined portion would **not** be acceptable?
   A. instrumental; in general, the bands
   B. instrumental, the bands generally
   C. instrumental. The bands generally
   D. instrumental; the bands generally

4. Which choice makes the sentence most grammatically acceptable?
   F. No Change
   G. music in which it is performed
   H. music, performing
   J. music, performed

5. Which choice makes the sentence most grammatically acceptable?
   A. No Change
   B. word, itself,
   C. word, itself
   D. word itself.

6. Which choice makes the sentence most grammatically acceptable?
   F. No Change
   G. Couples dance cheek to cheek to the relaxed two-step tempo,
   H. A relaxed two-step tempo, the couples dance cheek to cheek,
   J. Cheek to cheek, the two-step tempo relaxes dancing couples,

Improving Your Score

often <u>play long past</u> midnight. As the dancers step to the
₇

music, they <u>were also stepping</u> in time to a sound that
₈

embodies <u>their</u> unique history and suggests the influence
₉

of outside cultures on their music. [10] [B]

[3]

The O'odham <u>in the 1700s</u> first encountered the
₁₁
guitars of Spanish missionaries. In the 1850s the O'odham

<u>have borrowed</u> from the waltzes and mazurkas of
₁₂
people of European descent on their way to California.

In the early 1900s the O'odham became acquainted

with marching bands and woodwind instruments

<u>(which explains the presence of saxophones in waila).</u>
₁₃
Around this time the polka music and button accordion

played by German immigrant railroad <u>workers; left</u> their
₁₄

mark on waila. [C]

7. Which choice makes the sentence most grammatically
   acceptable?

   A. No Change
   B. play long, past,
   C. play, long past,
   D. play, long past

8. Which choice makes the sentence most grammatically
   acceptable?

   F. No Change
   G. are also stepping
   H. have also stepped
   J. will also step

9. Which choice makes the sentence most grammatically
   acceptable?

   A. No Change
   B. they're
   C. it's
   D. its'

10. At this point, the writer is considering adding the fol-
    lowing true statement:

    > The agricultural practices of the O'odham are
    > similar to those of the Maya.

    Should the writer make this addition here?

    F. Yes, because the sentence establishes that the
       O'odham often borrowed ideas from other groups.
    G. Yes, because the sentence provides important
       information about the O'odham people.
    H. No, because the sentence is not supported by evidence
       of a connection between the O'odham and the Maya.
    J. No, because the sentence distracts from the para-
       graph's focus on waila's uses and influences.

11. All of the following would be acceptable placements
    for the underlined portion **except**:

    A. where it is now.
    B. at the beginning of the sentence (revising the capi-
       talization accordingly).
    C. after the word *guitars.*
    D. after the word *missionaries* (ending the sentence
       with a period).

12. Which choice makes the sentence most grammatically
    acceptable?

    F. No Change
    G. have been borrowing
    H. were borrowed
    J. borrowed

13. Given that all of the choices are accurate, which one provides
    the most relevant information at this point in the essay?

    A. No Change
    B. (although fiddles were once widely used in waila bands).
    C. (even though they're now often constructed of metal).
    D. (which are frequently found in jazz bands also).

14. Which choice makes the sentence most grammatically
    acceptable?

    F. No Change
    G. workers
    H. workers:
    J. workers,

[4]

It should be no surprise that musicians these days are adding touches of rock, country, and reggae to waila. Some listeners fear that an American musical form may soon be lost. But the O'odham are playing waila with as much energy and devotion as ever. A unique blend of traditions, waila will probably continue changing for as long as the O'odham use it to express their own sense of harmony and tempo. [D]

Question 15 asks about the preceding passage as a whole.

15. The writer wants to add the following accurate sentence to the essay:

> Those same German influences helped spawn a similar musical form in northern Mexico known as *norteño*.

This sentence would most logically be placed at:

   A. Point A in Paragraph 1.
   B. Point B in Paragraph 2.
   C. Point C in Paragraph 3.
   D. Point D in Paragraph 4.

Sample Passage II

How Old Am I?

Many people might be surprised to learn that the American way of computing a person's age differs from the traditional Korean way. In Korean tradition, a person is considered to be already one year old at the time of his or her birth.

As a child growing up in two cultures, I found this <u>contest</u> a bit confusing. When I was in the fifth
₁₆
grade, was I ten or eleven years old? To add to the confusion, every New Year's Day a <u>person</u> according
₁₇
to this Korean counting system, becomes a year older, regardless of his or her actual birthday. <u>Birthdays are important throughout the world</u>. A person
₁₈
who is sixteen years old on his or her birthday in March would become seventeen years old on the following New Year's Day, even though he or she isn't expected to turn seventeen (in "American" years) until that next birthday in March. Perhaps the celebration of New Year's Day in Korean culture is <u>heightened</u> because it is thought of as
₁₉

16. Which choice is clearest and most precise in context?
   F. **No Change**
   G. change
   H. dispute
   J. difference

17. Which choice makes the sentence most grammatically acceptable?
   A. **No Change**
   B. person,
   C. person;
   D. person who,

18. Which choice provides the most relevant information at this point in the essay?
   F. **No Change**
   G. Most cultures celebrate birthdays.
   H. Birthdays focus attention on a culture's youth.
   J. **Delete** the underlined portion.

19. Which choice is clearest and most precise in context?
   A. **No Change**
   B. raised
   C. lifted
   D. lighted

everyone's birthday party. 20

Today, after many birthdays and New Year's
Days, I now find meaningful the difference I once
found confusing. <u>Otherwise,</u> this difference points
                  21

<u>to</u> significant underlying cultural values. The practice of
22

advancing a <u>person's age</u> seems to me to reflect the value a
             23

society places on life experience and longevity. <u>Their</u> idea
                                                   24

was demonstrated often <u>when</u> my elderly relatives, who
                        25
took pride in reminding younger folk of their "Korean

age." <u>With great enthusiasm,</u> they added on a year every
       26
New Year's Day. By contrast American society has often

been described as one <u>that</u> values the vibrant energy of
                      27

youth over the wisdom and experience gained with age. 28

After a certain age, many Americans I know would

<u>balk, refuse, and hesitate</u> at the idea of adding a year or
      29
two to what they regard as their actual age.

20. If the writer were to delete the preceding sentence, the paragraph would primarily lose:
    F. a comment on the added significance of the Korean New Year celebration.
    G. a repetitive reminder of what happens every birth-day.
    H. a defense of the case for celebrating every birth-day.
    J. an illustration of the Korean counting system.

21. Which transition word or phrase is most logical in context?
    A. **No Change**
    B. Though,
    C. In fact,
    D. Then,

22. Which choice is clearest and most grammatically acceptable in context?
    F. **No Change**
    G. on
    H. at
    J. **Delete** the underlined portion.

23. Which choice makes the sentence most grammatically acceptable?
    A. **No Change**
    B. persons' age
    C. persons age
    D. person's age,

24. Which choice is clearest and most grammatically acceptable in context?
    F. **No Change**
    G. One's
    H. Its
    J. This

25. Which choice is clearest and most precise in context?
    A. **No Change**
    B. by
    C. while
    D. as if

26. Which choice would most clearly communicate the elderly relatives' positive attitude toward this practice?
    F. **No Change**
    G. Duplicating an accepted practice,
    H. Living with two birthdays themselves,
    J. Obligingly,

27. Which choice makes the sentence most grammatically acceptable?
    A. **No Change**
    B. whose
    C. this
    D. whom

28. If the writer were to delete the phrases "the vibrant energy of" and "the wisdom and experience gained with" from the preceding sentence, the sentence would primarily lose:
    F. its personal and reflective tone.
    G. an element of humor.
    H. details that illustrate the contrast.
    J. the preference expressed by the writer.

29. Which choice is least redundant in context?
    A. **No Change**
    B. balk and hesitate
    C. refuse and balk
    D. balk

Even something as visibly simple or natural as
<u>30</u>
computing a person's age can prove to be not so clear-cut.
Traditions like celebrating birthdays reveal how deeply we
are affected by the culture we live in.

30. Which choice is clearest and most
logical in context?

F. No Change
G. apparently
H. entirely
J. fully

Sample Passage III

Wearing Jeans in School

In 1970, the school board in Pittsfield,
New Hampshire, approved a dress code that
prohibited students from wearing certain types
of <u>clothing.</u> The school board members believed that
<u>31</u>
wearing "play clothes" to school made the students

31. Given that all the choices are accurate, which one would best
illustrate the term *dress code* as it is used in this sentence?

A. No Change
B. clothing that was inappropriate.
C. clothing, including sandals, bell-bottom pants, and
"dungarees" (blue jeans).
D. clothing that is permitted in some schools today.

<u>inefficient toward</u> their school work, while more formal
<u>32</u>
attire established a positive educational climate. When
twelve-year-old Kevin Bannister wore a pair of blue jeans
to school, he was sent home for violating the dress code.

32. Which choice most effectively maintains the essay's tone?

F. No Change
G. lazy and bored to tears with
H. blow off
J. lax and indifferent toward

<u>Kevin and his parents believed that his constitutional</u>
<u>33</u>
<u>rights had been violated.</u> The United States District
<u>33</u>

33. Given that all the choices are accurate, which one would most
effectively introduce the main idea of this paragraph?

A. No Change
B. The principal said dungarees and blue jeans were
the same thing, so Kevin should have known
better.
C. If Kevin's jeans had been dirty and torn, the principal might have been justified in expelling him.
D. These events occurred in a time of social unrest,
and emotions were running high.

<u>Court of New Hampshire;</u> agreed to hear Kevin's case.
<u>34</u>
His claim was based on the notion of personal liberty—the
right of every individual to the control of his or her own

34. Which choice makes the sentence most grammatically
acceptable?

F. No Change
G. Court, of New Hampshire
H. Court of New Hampshire
J. Court of New Hampshire,

person—protected by the Constitution's Fourteenth Amendment. The court agreed with Kevin that a person's right <u>for wearing</u> clothing of his or her own choosing is, in fact, protected by the Fourteenth Amendment.

The <u>court noted, however</u> that restrictions may be justified in some circumstances, such as in the school setting.

So did Kevin have a right to wear blue jeans to school? The court determined that the school board had failed to show that wearing jeans actually inhibited the educational <u>process, which is guided by authority figures.</u>

Furthermore, the board offered no evidence to back up <u>it's</u>

claim <u>that</u> such clothing created a negative educational environment. Certainly the school board would be justified in prohibiting students from wearing clothing that was unsanitary, revealing, or obscene. The court remained unconvinced, <u>therefore,</u> that

<u>when wearing</u> jeans would actually impair the learning process of Kevin or of his fellow classmates.

<u>Kevin Bannister's case was significant in that it was the first in the United States to address clothing prohibitions of a school dress code.</u> His challenge

35. Which choice makes the sentence most grammatically acceptable?

   A. No Change
   B. of wearing
   C. to wear
   D. wearing

36. Which choice makes the sentence most grammatically acceptable?

   F. No Change
   G. court noted, however,
   H. court, noted however,
   J. court noted however,

37. Which choice best avoids wordiness and redundancy in context?

   A. No Change
   B. process, which has undergone changes since the 1970s.
   C. process, a process we all know well.
   D. process.

38. Which choice makes the sentence most grammatically acceptable?

   F. No Change
   G. they're
   H. its
   J. ones

39. Which choice makes the sentence most grammatically acceptable?

   A. No Change
   B. where
   C. which
   D. in which

40. Which transition word is most logical in context?

   F. No Change
   G. thus,
   H. moreover,
   J. however,

41. Which choice makes the sentence most grammatically acceptable?

   A. No Change
   B. by wearing
   C. wearing
   D. having worn

42. Which choice would most effectively begin this paragraph and convey the importance of this case?

   F. No Change
   G. Therefore, Kevin's case reminds us that you should stand up for your rights, no matter how old you are.
   H. The case for personal liberty means the right to speak up must be taken seriously by the courts.
   J. All in all, clothing is an important part of our identity.

initiated a <u>review, of students' rights</u> and administrative
                              43

<u>responsibility in public education.</u>
                    44

43. Which choice makes the sentence most grammatically acceptable?

   A. **No Change**
   B. review, of students' rights,
   C. review of students' rights
   D. review of students' rights,

44. Which choice is clearest and most precise in context?

   F. **No Change**
   G. on
   H. with
   J. about

Question 45 asks about the preceding passage as a whole.

---

45. Suppose the writer's primary purpose had been to write a persuasive essay urging students to exercise their constitutional rights. Would this essay accomplish that purpose?

   A. Yes, because the essay focuses on how Kevin encouraged other students to exercise their constitutional rights.
   B. Yes, because the essay focuses on various types of clothing historically worn by students as a freedom of expression.
   C. No, because the essay suggests that the right to wear blue jeans was not a substantial constitutional right in the 1970s.
   D. No, because the essay objectively reports on one case of a student exercising a particular constitutional right.

Answer Key for English Test Sample Questions

1.	D	16.	J	31.	C
2.	F	17.	B	32.	J
3.	B	18.	J	33.	A
4.	J	19.	A	34.	H
5.	A	20.	F	35.	C
6.	G	21.	C	36.	G
7.	A	22.	F	37.	D
8.	G	23.	A	38.	H
9.	A	24.	J	39.	A
10.	J	25.	B	40.	J
11.	C	26.	F	41.	C
12.	J	27.	A	42.	F
13.	A	28.	H	43.	C
14.	G	29.	D	44.	F
15.	C	30.	G	45.	D

Prep Online!

Want even more ways to prep? Go to https://study.learning.wiley.com/ to access our online platform and take practice tests. To get started, go to https://study.learning.wiley.com/, select your title, answer the redemption question, and start studying!

Chapter 6: Improving Your Math Score

The ACT mathematics test asks you to answer 45 multiple-choice questions (41 of which will count toward your score) in 50 minutes. The questions are designed to measure your mathematical achievement—the knowledge, skills, and reasoning techniques that are taught in mathematics courses through the beginning of grade 12 and that are prerequisites for college mathematics courses. Therefore, the questions cover a wide variety of concepts, techniques, and procedures. Naturally, some questions will require computation, but you are allowed to use a calculator on the mathematics test. You'll need to understand basic mathematical terminology and to recall some basic mathematical principles and formulas. However, the questions on the test are designed to emphasize your ability to reason mathematically, not to focus on your computation ability or your ability to recall definitions, theorems, or formulas.

Content of the ACT Mathematics Test

The ACT mathematics test emphasizes the major content areas that are prerequisites to successful performance in entry-level courses in college mathematics.

Nine scores are reported for the ACT mathematics test: a total test score based on all 41 scored questions and eight reporting category scores based on specific mathematical knowledge and skills. The reporting categories are Preparing for Higher Mathematics (which includes separate scores for Number and Quantity, Algebra, Functions, Geometry, and Statistics and Probability); Integrating Essential Skills; and Modeling. Descriptions follow.

Preparing for Higher Math

This category captures the more recent mathematics that students are learning, starting when they begin using algebra as a general way of expressing and solving equations. This category is divided into the following five subcategories:

- **Number and Quantity:** Demonstrate knowledge of real and complex number systems. You will understand and reason with numerical quantities in many forms, including integer and rational exponents, and vectors and matrices.

- **Algebra:** Solve, graph, and model multiple types of expressions. You will employ many different kinds of equations, including but not limited to linear, polynomial, radical, and exponential relationships. You will find solutions to systems of equations, even when represented by simple matrices, and apply your knowledge to applications.

- **Functions:** The questions in this category test knowledge of function definition, notation, representation, and application. Questions may include, but are not limited to, linear, radical, piecewise, polynomial, and logarithmic functions. You will manipulate and translate functions, as well as find and apply important features of graphs.

- **Geometry:** Define and apply knowledge of shapes and solids, such as congruence and similarity relationships or surface area and volume measurements. Understand composition of objects and solve for missing values in triangles, circles, and other figures, including using trigonometric ratios and equations of conic sections.

- **Statistics and Probability:** Describe center and spread of distributions, apply and analyze data collection methods, understand and model relationships in bivariate data, and calculate probabilities, including the related sample spaces.

Integrating Essential Skills

These questions address concepts typically learned before grade 9, such as rates and percentages; proportional relationships; area, surface area, and volume; average and median; and expressing numbers in different ways. You will solve problems of increasing complexity, combine skills in longer chains of steps, apply skills in more varied contexts, understand more connections, and become more fluent.

Modeling

This category represents all questions that involve producing, interpreting, understanding, evaluating, and improving models. Each question is also counted in the other previously identified appropriate reporting categories. This category is an overall measure of how well you use modeling skills across mathematical topics. This is always an additional content code beyond the reporting category, so these items count towards a reporting category and to the modeling score.

Types of Questions on the ACT Mathematics Test

The questions on the ACT mathematics test differ in terms of content and complexity. The rest of this section gives you examples of questions—of various types and complexities from all content areas. All of the questions used in the examples are from actual ACT mathematics tests that have been taken by students from across the country. A solution strategy is given for each question. As you read and work through each example, please keep in mind that the strategy given is just one way to solve the problem. Other strategies may work even better for you. These example items have five answer options. Future ACT math items will have four answer options.

Basic Math Problems

The type of question you're probably the most familiar with (and probably find the easiest) is the stripped-down, bare-bones, basic math problem. Problems of this type are simple and straightforward. They test readily identifiable skills in the content areas, usually have very few words and no extra information, ask the very question you'd expect them to ask, and usually have a numeric answer.

Question 1 is a good example of a basic math problem.

1. What is 4% of 1,100?

   A.   4
   B.   4.4
   C. 40
   D. 44
   E. 440

This problem has very few words, asks a direct question, and has a numeric answer. The solution is simple: Convert 4% to a decimal and multiply by 1,100 to get $(0.04)(1,100) = 44$, choice **D**. You probably wouldn't need your calculator on this problem, but remember that you may use it if you wish. If you chose answer **B** or **E**, you may have used rules about moving decimal points and moved the wrong number of places.

Question 2 is a basic algebra problem.

> **2.** For all x, $(x + 4)(x - 5) = ?$
>
>   **F.** $x^2 - 20$
>
>   **G.** $x^2 - x - 20$
>
>   **H.** $2x - 1$
>
>   **J.** $2x^2 - 1$
>
>   **K.** $2x^2 - x + 20$

You should know what to do to answer the question the instant you read the problem—
use the distributive property (FOIL—first, outside, inside, last) and get
$x(x - 5) + 4(x - 5) = x^2 - 5x + 4x + 4(-5) = x^2 - x - 20$, choice **G**. On this problem, you probably
wouldn't use your calculator. If you chose **F**, you probably just multiplied the first terms and the
last terms. Check your answer by substituting a number (try 6) into the original expression and
into your answer. If the results are not equal, then the expressions cannot be equivalent.

Question 3 is an example of a basic problem from algebra.

> **3.** If $x + y = 1$, and $x - y = 1$, then $y = ?$
>
>   **A.** -1
>
>   **B.** 0
>
>   **C.** $\dfrac{1}{2}$
>
>   **D.** 1
>
>   **E.** 2

This problem gives you a system of linear equations with unknowns x and y and asks for the
value of y. You might be able to solve this problem intuitively—the only number that can be
added to and subtracted from another number and give the same result for the problem
($x + y$ and $x - y$ both give 1) is 0, so y must be 0, choice **B**. Or, you could use algebra and reason
that, because $x + y$ and $x - y$ both equal 1, they equal each other, and $x + y = x - y$ gives $2y = 0$, so
$y = 0$. Although some calculators have graphing or matrix functions for solving problems of this
type, using a calculator on this problem would probably take most students longer than solving
it with one of the strategies given here. If you chose answer **D**, you probably found the value of x
rather than the value of y.

Question 4 is an example of a basic problem in geometry.

> **4.** What is the slope of the line containing the points $(-2, 7)$ and $(3, -3)$?
>
> F. 4
>
> G. $\dfrac{1}{4}$
>
> H. 0
>
> J. $-\dfrac{1}{2}$
>
> K. -2

This problem has a few more words than some of the other examples of basic problems you've seen so far, but the most important word is *slope*. Seeing that you are given two points, you would probably think of the formula that defines the slope of a line through two points:

$$\frac{y_1 - y_2}{x_1 - x_2}.$$

Applying the formula gives $\dfrac{7 - (-3)}{-2 - 3} = \dfrac{10}{-5} = -2$, choice **K**. If you chose answer **J**, you probably got the expression for slope upside down. The change in y goes on top.

Here is another basic geometry problem from the ACT mathematics test.

> **5.** If the measure of an angle is $37\frac{1}{2}°$, what is the measure of its supplement, shown in the figure below?
>
> 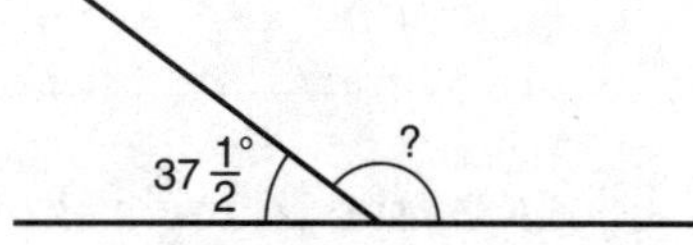
>
>
> A. $52\frac{1}{2}°$
>
> B. $62\frac{1}{2}°$
>
> C. $127\frac{1}{2}°$
>
> D. $142\frac{1}{2}°$
>
> E. Cannot be determined from the given information

Improving Your Score

Similar to many geometry problems, this problem has a figure. The figure tells you what you are given (an angle of $37\frac{1}{2}°$) and what you're asked to find (its supplement, marked by "?"). You need not mark anything on the figure, because all the important information is already there. If you know that the sum of the measure of an angle and the measure of its supplement equals 180°, a simple subtraction gives the correct answer ($180° - 37\frac{1}{2}° = 142\frac{1}{2}°$), choice **D**. If you chose **A,** you found the complement, not the supplement.

A word of caution is in order here. You probably noticed that "Cannot be determined from the given information" is one of the options for question 5. Statistics gathered over the years for the ACT mathematics test show that many students choose "Cannot be determined from the given information" even when the answer can be determined. You should not think that whenever "Cannot be determined from the given information" is an option, it is automatically the correct answer. It isn't, as question 5 demonstrates. Later in this section is a question for which the correct answer is "Cannot be determined from the given information." Be sure to think carefully about problems with this answer choice.

You'll also find basic geometry problems, such as question 6, on the ACT mathematics test.

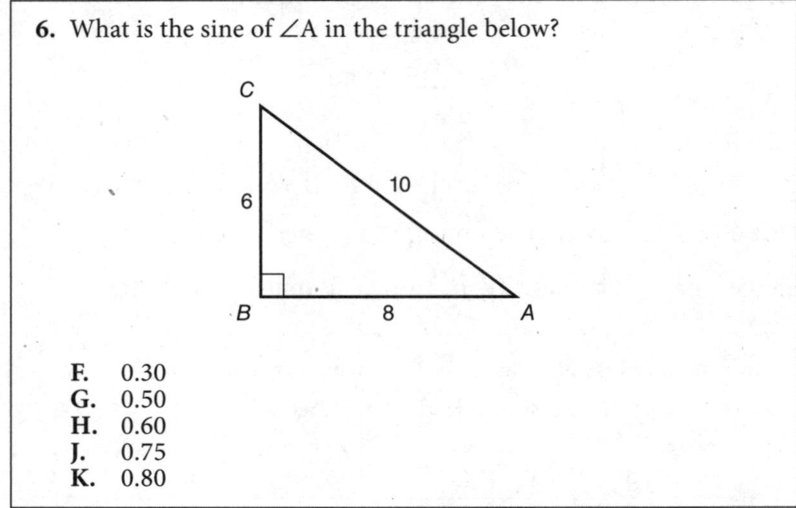

This question asks you to find the sine of ∠A in the triangle shown in the figure. If you have studied trigonometry, you've seen questions similar to this before. The lengths of all three sides of the triangle are given on the figure, even though only two are actually needed for finding sin ∠A. The extra information is there not to confuse you but rather to test your ability to sort out the information you need from the information you are given. Picking 6 (the length of the side opposite ∠A) and 10 (the length of the hypotenuse) and forming the ratio gives the correct answer, 0.60, choice **H**. The cosine and the tangent of ∠A are also present in the answer choices. In order to do well on problems such as this one, you need to be able to tell which trigonometric function is which.

Basic Math Problems in Settings

Basic math problems in settings are what people often call *word problems* or *story problems.* They typically describe situations from everyday life in which you need to apply mathematics in order to answer a real-life question. The major difference between this type of problem and the basic math problems that you've seen in the examples so far is that the problem isn't set up for you— you have to set it up yourself. Most people find this to be the most difficult part of word problems. The key steps are reading the problem carefully, deciding what you're trying to find, sorting out what you really need from what's given, and then devising a strategy for finding the answer. Once the problem is set up, finding the answer is not much different from solving a basic math problem.

You can find basic math problems in settings in all of the content areas. Question 7 is an example.

---

7. What is the total cost of 2.5 pounds of bananas at $0.34 per pound and 2.5 pounds of tomatoes at $0.66 per pound?

   A. $1.00
   B. $2.40
   C. $2.50
   D. $3.50
   E. $5.00

Here, you're asked to find the total cost of some bananas and tomatoes. The important information is that the total cost includes 2.5 pounds of bananas at $0.34 per pound and 2.5 pounds of tomatoes at $0.66 per pound. A straightforward solution strategy would be to multiply to find the cost of the bananas and the cost of the tomatoes and then add to find the total cost. Now, the problem you're left with is very basic—calculating $2.5(0.34) + 2.5(0.66)$. Using your calculator might save time and avoid computation errors, but if you see that $2.5(0.34) + 2.5(0.66) = 2.5(0.34 + 0.66) = 2.5(1.00) = 2.50$, answer **C**, you might be able to do the computation more quickly in your head.

Basic algebra problems also can be in settings. Question 8 is an example.

---

8. The relationship between temperature expressed in degrees Fahrenheit (*F*) and degrees Celsius (*C*) is given by the formula

$$F = \frac{9}{5}C + 32$$

   If the temperature is 14 degrees Fahrenheit, what is it in degrees Celsius?

   F. $-10°$
   G. $-12°$
   H. $-14°$
   J. $-16°$
   K. $-18°$

In this problem, you're given a relationship (in the form of an equation) between temperatures expressed in degrees Fahrenheit (F) and degrees Celsius (C). You're also given a temperature of 14 degrees Fahrenheit and asked what the corresponding temperature would be in degrees Celsius. Your strategy would probably be to substitute 14 into the equation in place of the variable F. This leaves you with a basic algebra problem—solving the equation $14 = \frac{9}{5}C + 32$ for C. Before going on to the next problem, checking your answer would probably be a good idea. If you chose $-10°$ (answer choice **F**), substitute -10 for C, multiply by $\frac{9}{5}$, and add 32 to see if the result is $14°F$ and confirm that your answer choice was indeed correct. Checking doesn't take long, and you might catch an error.

Question 9 is an example of an algebra problem in a setting.

9. Amy drove the 200 miles to New Orleans at an average speed 10 miles per hour faster than her usual average speed. If she completed the trip in 1 hour less than usual, what is her usual driving speed, in miles per hour?

   A. 20
   B. 30
   C. 40
   D. 50
   E. 60

After reading the problem, you know that it is about travel and that the basic formula "distance equals the rate multiplied by the time" ($D = rt$) or one of its variations $\left(r = \frac{D}{t} \text{ or } t = \frac{D}{r}\right)$ will probably be useful. For travel problems, a table is often an efficient way to organize the information. Because the problem asks for Amy's usual speed (rate), it would probably be wise to let the variable r represent her usual speed in miles per hour (mph). You might organize your table like this:

	Distance (miles)	Rate (mph)	Time (hours)
Usual trip	200	r	$\dfrac{200}{r}$
This trip	200	$r + 10$	$\dfrac{200}{(r+10)}$

Then, because the time for this trip $\left(\frac{200}{(r+10)}\right)$ is 1 hour less than the time for the usual trip $\left(\frac{200}{r}\right)$, solving $\frac{200}{(r+10)} = \frac{200}{r} - 1$ will give the answer. Solving this equation is a matter of using routine algebra skills and procedures. The solution, $r = 40$, choice **C,** answers the question, "What is her usual driving speed?" A quick check shows that driving 200 miles at 40 mph takes 5 hours and that driving 200 miles at 50 mph (which is 10 mph faster) takes 4 hours (which is 1 hour less). This quick check should convince you that your answer is correct.

Geometry problems can be in settings, too. Question 10 is an example.

> **10.** A map is laid out in the standard (x,y) coordinate plane. How long, in units, is an airplane's path on the map as the airplane flies along a straight line from City A located at (20,14) to City B located at (5,10)?
>
> F. $\sqrt{1,201}$
> G. $\sqrt{241}$
> H. $\sqrt{209}$
> J. 7
> K. $\sqrt{19}$

In this problem, you're told that you will be working with the standard (x,y) coordinate plane and that you will need to find a distance. The distance formula should immediately come to mind. All you need is two points, and those are given. The problem now becomes a basic math problem—applying the distance formula:

$$\sqrt{(x_1-x_2)^2+(y_1-y_2)^2} = \sqrt{(20-5)^2+(14-10)^2} = \sqrt{241}\,(\mathbf{G}).$$

Your calculator might be useful in finding $(20 - 5)^2 + (14 - 10)^2$, but you should not press the square root key because most of the answer choices are in radical form.

A geometry problem in a setting is illustrated by question 11.

> **11.** A person 2 meters tall casts a shadow 3 meters long. At the same time, a telephone pole casts a shadow 12 meters long. How many meters tall is the pole?
>
> A. 4
> B. 6
> C. 8
> D. 11
> E. 18

Question 11 has no figure, which is sometimes the case with geometry problems. It might be wise to draw your own figure and label it with the appropriate numbers from the problem. "A person 2 meters tall casts a shadow 3 meters long" is a pretty good clue that you should draw a right triangle with the vertical leg labeled 2 and the horizontal leg labeled 3. And, "a telephone pole casts a shadow 12 meters long" suggests that you should draw another right triangle with the horizontal leg labeled 12. Finding the height of the pole amounts to finding the length of the other leg of your second triangle, which you would label with a variable, say h. Your figure would be similar to this:

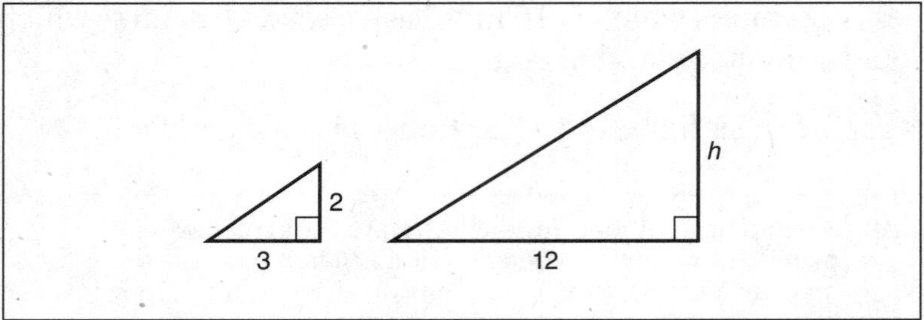

The triangles are similar (they're both right triangles and the angle that the sun's rays make with the ground is the same for both because the shadows were measured at the same time), so finding the height of the pole amounts to setting up and solving a proportion between corresponding sides of the triangles—a basic math problem. Your proportion might be $\frac{3}{12}=\frac{2}{h}$. Cross multiply—that is, multiply the numerator of each (or one) side by the denominator of the other side—to get $3(h) = 12(2)$, or $3h = 24$, and solve to get $h = 8$, choice **C**. Because the numbers are quite simple to work with, you probably wouldn't use your calculator on this problem.

Last (but not least) of the basic math questions, question 12 shows an example of a trigonometry problem in a setting.

12. The hiking path to the top of a mountain makes, at the steepest place, an angle of 20° with the horizontal, and it maintains this constant slope for 500 meters, as illustrated below. Which of the following is the closest approximation to the change in elevation, in meters, over this 500-meter section?

(Note: You may use the following values, which are correct to 2 decimal places:
cos 20° ≈ 0.94; sin 20° ≈ 0.34; tan 20° ≈ 0.36)

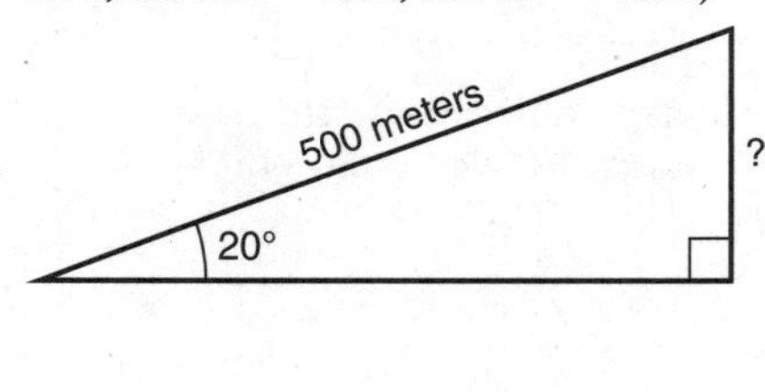

F.   20
G.   170
H.   180
J.   250
K.   470

This problem has a figure, and the figure is labeled with all the necessary information, including a question mark to tell you what you need to find. To set up the problem, you need to decide which of the trigonometric ratios involves the hypotenuse and the side opposite the given angle of a right triangle. Once you decide that the sine ratio is appropriate, you have only a basic trigonometry problem to solve: $\sin 20° = \frac{h}{500}$, or $500 \sin 20° = h$. Then, using the approximation for sin 20° given in the note, calculate $h \approx 500(0.34) = 170$, choice **G**. You may want to use your calculator to avoid computation errors. If you chose **K**, then you probably used the value for cosine rather than sine. Answer **H** comes from using tangent rather than sine.

Very Challenging Problems

The ACT mathematics test emphasizes reasoning ability, so it naturally has problems that can be very challenging. Because these problems are designed to test your understanding of mathematical concepts and your ability to pull together what you have learned in your math classes, they will probably be unlike problems you usually see. Some will be in settings, and some won't. Some will have figures, and some won't. Some will have extra information that you should ignore, and some won't have enough information, so the correct answer will be "Cannot be determined from the given information." Some will have numeric answers, some will have answers that are expressions or equations that you have to set up, and some will have answers that are statements for you to interpret and judge. On some questions your calculator will be helpful, and on others it will be better not to use it. All of the questions will share one important characteristic, however—they will challenge you to think hard and plan a strategy before you start to solve them.

Question 13 is a challenging problem.

> **13.** If 537^{102} were calculated, it would have 279 digits. What would the digit farthest to the right be (the ones digit)?
>
> **A.** 1
> **B.** 3
> **C.** 4
> **D.** 7
> **E.** 9

You certainly wouldn't want to calculate 537^{102} by hand, and your calculator doesn't display enough digits for you to be able to read off the ones digit for this very large number, so you have to figure out another way to see the ones digit. A good place to start might be to look at the ones digit for powers of 7 because 7 is the ones digit of 537. Maybe there will be a pattern: $7^0 = 1$, $7^1 = 7$, $7^2 = 49$, $7^3 = 343$, $7^4 = 2{,}401$, $7^5 = 16{,}807$, $7^6 = 117{,}649$, $7^7 = 823{,}543$. It looks like the pattern of the ones digits is 1, 7, 9, 3, 1, 7, 9, 3, . . ., with the sequence of these 4 digits repeating over and over. Now, if you can decide where in this pattern the ones digit of 537^{102} falls, you'll have the problem solved. You might organize a chart like this:

Ones digit	1	7	9	3
Power of 7	0	1	2	3
	4	5	6	7

The next row would read "8 9 10 11" to show that the ones digits of 7^8, 7^9, 7^{10}, and 7^{11}, respectively, are 1, 7, 9, and 3. You could continue the chart row after row until you got up to 102, but that would take a lot of time. Instead, think about where 102 would fall. The numbers in the first column are the multiples of 4, so 100 would fall there because it is a multiple of 4. Then 101 would be in the second column, and 102 would fall in the third column. Therefore, the ones digit of 537^{102} is 9, choice **E**.

Question 14 is an algebra problem designed to challenge your ability to think mathematically and use what you've learned.

14. If $a < -1$, which of the following best describes a general relationship between a^3 and a^2?

F. $a^3 > a^2$

G. $a^3 < a^2$

H. $a^3 = a^2$

J. $a^3 = -a^2$

K. $a^3 = \dfrac{1}{a^2}$

Here you are told that $a < -1$. Then you are asked for the relationship between a^3 and a^2. By stopping to think for a moment before trying to manipulate the given inequality or experimenting with numbers plugged into the answer choices, you might realize that if $a < -1$, then a is a negative number, so its cube is a negative number. Squaring a negative number, however, gives a positive number. Every negative number is less than every positive number, so the correct relationship between a^3 and a^2 is $a^3 < a^2$, choice **G**. Of course, there are other ways to approach the problem.

For another very challenging algebra problem, look at question 15.

15. If $\left(\dfrac{4}{5}\right)^n = \sqrt{\left(\dfrac{5}{4}\right)^3}$, then $n = ?$

A. $-\dfrac{3}{2}$

B. -1

C. $-\dfrac{2}{3}$

D. $\dfrac{2}{3}$

E. $\dfrac{3}{2}$

In this problem, you're asked to find the value of a variable, but the variable is in the exponent. After some thought you might decide to try to rewrite $\sqrt{\left(\frac{5}{4}\right)^3}$ so that it is $\frac{5}{4}$ raised to a power.

You should remember that the square root is the same as the $\frac{1}{2}$ power, so, after using some properties of exponents, $\sqrt{\left(\sqrt{\frac{5}{4}}\right)^3} = \left(\left(\sqrt{\frac{5}{4}}\right)^3\right)^{\frac{1}{2}} = \left(\frac{5}{4}\right)^{\frac{3}{2}}$. Now at least the left side and the right side of the equation have the same form, but the bases of the two expressions aren't the same—they're reciprocals. In thinking about the connection between reciprocals and exponents, it is good to realize that taking the opposite of the exponent (that is, making it have the opposite sign) will flip the base, because $a^{-k} = \frac{1}{a^k}$. That means $\left(\frac{5}{4}\right)^{\frac{3}{2}} = \left(\frac{4}{5}\right)^{-\frac{3}{2}}$. So now, with $\left(\frac{4}{5}\right)^n = \left(\frac{4}{5}\right)^{-\frac{3}{2}}$, $n = -\frac{3}{2}$, choice **A**.

Geometry problems can also be very challenging. Question 16 is an example.

> **16.** In the standard (x,y) coordinate plane, the triangle with vertices at $(0,0)$, $(0,k)$, and $(2,m)$, where m is constant, changes shape as k changes. What happens to the triangle's area, expressed in square coordinate units, as k increases starting from 2?
>
> **F.** The area increases as k increases.
> **G.** The area decreases as k increases.
> **H.** The area always equals 2.
> **J.** The area always equals m.
> **K.** The area always equals $2m$.

This problem might seem confusing at first because it contains two different variables and no figure to clarify. You're told that m is a constant but k changes. So, to get started, you could pick a value for m, say $m = 1$. Then, at least you can start sketching a figure. The point $(0,k)$ is on the y-axis and k increases starting with 2, so you could start by drawing a figure similar to this:

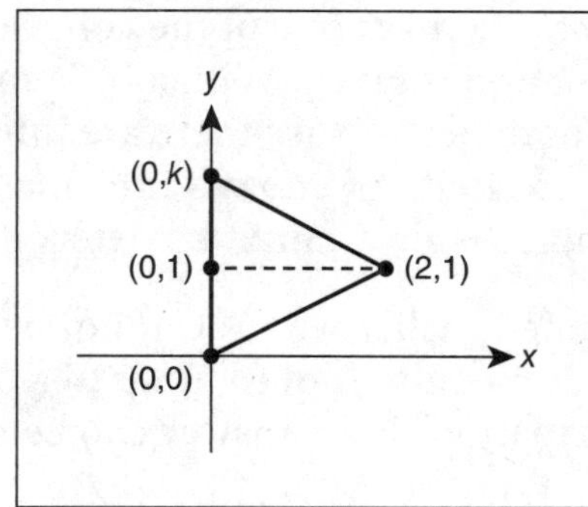

You can see the triangle that the problem mentions. If you think of the line segment from $(0,0)$ to $(0,k)$ as the base and the line segment from $(2,1)$ to $(0,1)$ as the height, you can see that as k increases, the base of the triangle gets longer but the height remains the same. From geometry, you know that the area of a triangle is given by $\frac{1}{2}$(base)(height). Therefore, the area will increase as the base gets longer. So, the area will increase as k increases, choice **F**. You should be able to reason that for any value of *m*, the result would have been the same, and you can feel confident that the correct answer is the first answer choice.

Question 17 is an example of a very challenging geometry problem.

17. In the figure below, $\overline{AB} \cong \overline{AC}$ and $\overline{BC}$ is 10 units long. What is the area, in square inches, of $\triangle ABC$?

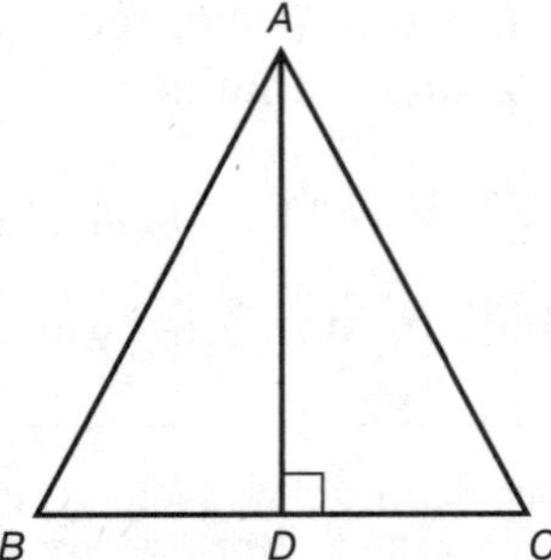

A. 12.5

B. 25

C. $25\sqrt{2}$

D. 50

E. Cannot be determined from the given information

This problem has a figure, but none of the information given is marked on the figure. A wise move is to mark the figure yourself to indicate which sides are congruent and which side is 10 units long. You need to find the area of $\triangle ABC$, and you know that the base $\overline{BC}$ is 10 units long. You need the measure of the height $\overline{AD}$ before you can apply the formula for the area of a triangle. You might ask yourself, "Is there any way to get the height?" If you were given the measure of one of the angles or the measure of one of the congruent sides, you might be able to find the height, but no other information is given. With a little more thought, you should realize that the height can be any positive number because there are infinitely many isosceles triangles with bases 10 units long. You conclude that not enough information is given to solve this problem, and the correct answer choice is **E**: "Cannot be determined from the given information."

This is the example that was mentioned earlier when "Cannot be determined from the given information" is the correct answer. Remember not to jump to a hasty conclusion when "Cannot be determined from the given information" is an answer choice. Sometimes it is the right answer, but sometimes it isn't.

Very challenging problems can be in settings, too. Question 18 is an example.

18. A bag of pennies could be divided among 6 children, or 7 children, or 8 children, with each getting the same number, and with 1 penny left over in each case. What is the smallest number of pennies that could be in the bag?

   F. 22
   G. 43
   H. 57
   J. 169
   K. 337

In this problem, whenever the pennies in the bag (which contains an unknown number of pennies) are divided evenly among 6 children, 7 children, or 8 children, 1 penny is always left over. This means that if you take the extra penny out of the bag, then the number of pennies left in the bag will be divisible (with no remainder) by 6, 7, and 8. You should ask yourself, "What is the smallest number that is divisible by 6, 7, and 8?" In mathematical terminology, you're looking for the least common multiple of 6, 7, and 8. One way to find the least common multiple is to use the prime factorizations of the three numbers and to find the product of the highest power of each prime that occurs in one or more of the three numbers. This process will yield $2^3 \cdot 3 \cdot 7 = 168$. (As a check: $168 \div 6 = 28$, $168 \div 7 = 24$, and $168 \div 8 = 21$.) But wait! You're not quite finished. Remember to add back in the penny that you took out of the bag originally to make the divisions come out even. Thus, your answer is 169, choice **J**.

Question 19 is an example of an algebra word problem that is very challenging.

19. There are n students in a class. If, among those students, p% play at least 1 musical instrument, which of the following general expressions represents the number of students who play NO musical instrument?

   A. np

   B. $.01np$

   C. $\dfrac{(100 - p)n}{100}$

   D. $\dfrac{(1 - p)n}{.01}$

   E. $100(1 - p)n$

This is an example of a problem that has a mathematical expression as its answer. Finding an expression to answer a question usually makes you think more than finding a numerical answer because the variables require you to think abstractly. In this problem, you are told that out of a class of n students, p% play 1 or more musical instruments. Finding the percent of students who play no musical instrument is simple: $(100 - p)$%. To find the number of students who play no musical instrument, you'd probably want to convert $(100 - p)$% to a decimal and multiply by n. If $100 - p$ were a number you'd automatically move the decimal point two places to the left. But,

Improving Your Score

because there's no decimal point to move in $100 - p$, you have to think about what you need to do to convert $(100 - p)\%$ to a decimal. Moving the decimal point two places to the left is the same as dividing by 100, so $(100 - p)\%$ as a decimal is $\dfrac{100 - p}{100}$, and the number of students who play no musical instrument is $\dfrac{(100 - p)n}{100}$, choice **C**.

Question 20 is an example of a very challenging geometry problem in a setting.

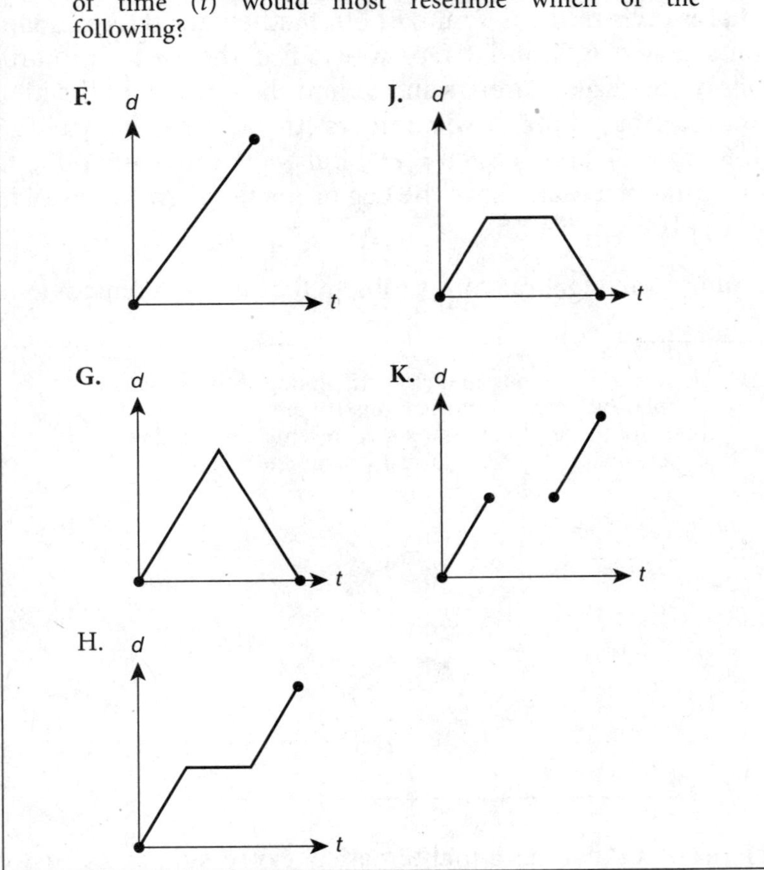

This problem is different from any of the problems you've seen so far because its answer is a graph. And, instead of giving you an equation and asking you to identify the equation's graph, this problem describes a situation and asks you to decide which graph represents the situation. You need to think about what the description of each of Ramona's activities says in terms of distance as a function of time and what each activity would translate into graphically. For example, at first, Ramona walked at a constant rate down the sidewalk. Therefore, she moved farther away from her doorstep as time elapsed, and her distance from her doorstep increased at a constant rate as time increased. So, the first part of the graph should be a line segment with a positive slope. Unfortunately, all five graphs start out this way, so none of the options can be eliminated at this point. The next thing Ramona did was stop for 4 seconds. If she stood still, her distance from her doorstep would not change even though time was still elapsing. This part of the graph should then reflect a constant value for d as time increases. It should be a horizontal line segment. This information allows you to eliminate options **F**, **G**, and **K**, because they do not have a horizontal line segment. Ramona's next activity helps you decide between **H** and **J**. Ramona walked back home at the same rate along the same route as before. On her way back home, her distance from her doorstep decreased at a constant rate as elapsed time increased. This would be graphed as a line segment with a negative slope, and therefore **J** is the correct graph.

Another word problem that challenges you to think mathematically is question 21.

> **21.** An object detected on radar is 5 miles to the east, 4 miles to the north, and 1 mile above the tracking station. Among the following, which is the closest approximation to the distance, in miles, that the object is from the tracking station?
>
> **A.** 6.5
> **B.** 7.2
> **C.** 8.3
> **D.** 9.0
> **E.** 10.0

This problem is about computing a distance, but it's a distance in three-dimensional space without a picture to help you. For this problem, drawing a sketch of the situation might help. Your sketch might be a "box" such as this:

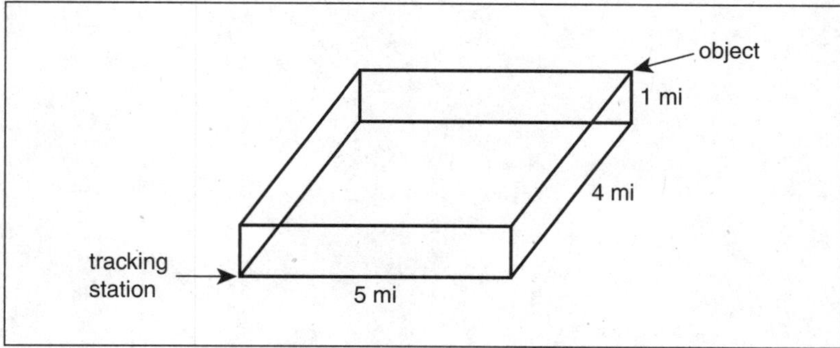

Improving Your Score

You need to find the length of the diagonal from the lower left corner of the front of the box to the top right corner of the back of the box. This is the hypotenuse of a right triangle ($\triangle OBT$ on the following redrawn figure) that has its right angle at B. One leg of this triangle has length 1, but the other leg is $\overline{BT}$, and you don't know the length of $\overline{BT}$.

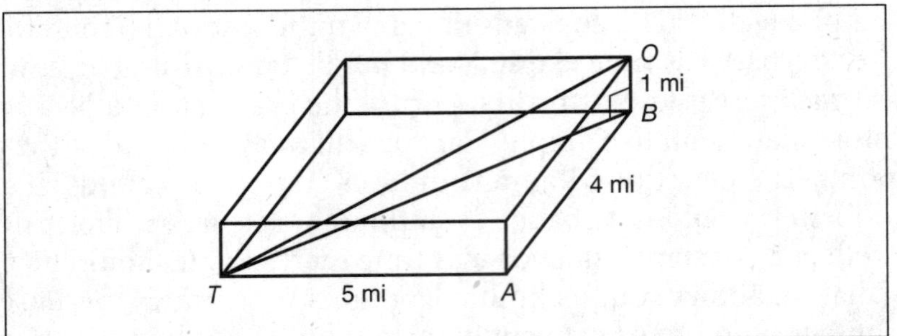

A closer look shows that $\overline{BT}$ is the hypotenuse of $\triangle TAB$, which has its right angle at A and legs that measure 5 and 4. Using the Pythagorean theorem gives $BT = \sqrt{5^2 + 4^2} = \sqrt{41}$.

Now you can use the Pythagorean theorem again to get $OT = \sqrt{BT^2 + OB^2} = \sqrt{\left(\sqrt{41}\right)^2 + 1^2} = \sqrt{42}$ which is about 6.5, choice **A**.

As you have seen in the sample questions in this section, the mathematics test includes many types of questions. Some will be easy for you, and some will be hard. They all will require you to demonstrate as much as possible about what you know and can do in mathematics.

Answer Key for Mathematics Test Sample Questions

1.	D	8.	F	15.	A
2.	G	9.	C	16.	F
3.	B	10.	G	17.	E
4.	K	11.	C	18.	J
5.	D	12.	G	19.	C
6.	H	13.	E	20.	J
7.	C	14.	G	21.	A

Strategies for Taking the ACT Mathematics Test

Pace Yourself

You have 50 minutes to answer 45 questions, which gives you an average of approximately 66 seconds per problem. Some problems will take you less than 1 minute, and some will take you more. Don't spend too much time on any one question. You should keep a close eye on your watch to make sure you work at a pace that will enable you to finish the test in the 50 minutes allotted. When determining your pace, be aware that the questions are arranged approximately in order of difficulty: easier questions first and hardest last.

Answer All Questions

Answer all questions even if you have no idea how to solve some of them. If you're stumped and have time, eliminate as many of the options as you can and then guess from among the remaining choices. If time is running out and you don't have time to eliminate any of the options, guess anyway. Even a wild guess has a 25% chance of being correct, but a blank has no chance of being correct. Remember, your score is based solely on the number of questions you answer correctly—there is no penalty for guessing and no penalty for wrong answers. Scores are most comparable if everyone answers every question.

Answer All the Easy Questions First, Then Go Back to Answer the Hard Ones

Easy and *hard* are relative terms. What might be easy for one student might be hard for another. You know which math topics are easy for you and which are hard. Answer all the questions that are easy for you and then go back to the hard ones. Remember that you don't get more points for answering hard questions. All questions, no matter how easy or hard, count equally toward your mathematics total score. If you don't see a way to solve a problem, or if the method you're using seems to be taking a lot of time, take your best guess (as explained in the previous section) or skip the question and move on to questions that you can answer more easily. If you skip the question, don't forget to mark in the test booklet (never on the answer document) or flag on the computer all those questions that you skip so that you can easily return to them later.

Read Each Problem Carefully

Read carefully enough so you know what you're trying to find before you start looking for it and so you know what you have to work with to help you find it. Remember that questions may contain extraneous details you will need to ignore or insufficient information to solve the problem. Think twice before choosing "Cannot be determined from the given information," because test-takers often choose this option when the answer, in fact, can be determined from the information given. Make sure you are not overlooking a key piece of information provided or an alternate strategy for solving the problem.

Look for Information in the Answer Choices

Sometimes looking at the answer choices provides valuable information about the form of the answer. For example, you might be able to judge whether your answer should be left in radical form or converted to a decimal approximation, whether your polynomial answer should be left in factored form or multiplied out, or whether you should spend time reducing a probability to lowest terms. For some problems, you have to analyze the options as part of your solution strategy. For example, when a question asks, "Which of the following statements is true?" and the statements are the four options, you probably need to examine each option in turn. Sometimes, using the options gives you an alternate way to solve a problem. For example, suppose you're trying to solve a quadratic equation and you can't get the quadratic expression to factor and can't remember the quadratic formula. You might be able to get the correct answer by substituting the options, in turn, into the equation until one works. This strategy should be used very sparingly, however, because it can be more time-consuming than other strategies.

Use Illustrations Wisely and Whenever You Can

The old saying "A picture is worth a thousand words" holds true on the mathematics test:

- Refer to illustrations whenever they are provided.

- If no illustration is provided and one might be useful, draw your own illustration in the test booklet or on your scratch paper for computer testing. This can be especially helpful in solving word problems.

- Transfer information from the question to the illustration, if you think it might be helpful. For example, you might write dimensions on the figure that are given in the question but aren't shown on the figure or that you calculate in the process of solving the problem, or you might add marks to show congruences or draw auxiliary lines such as perpendiculars and diagonals.

Note: If you are testing on computer, you'll be given scratch paper to use.

Use Your Calculator Wisely

Each problem on the mathematics test can be solved in a reasonable amount of time without a calculator. A calculator is most helpful if you are very familiar with the one you bring to the test and you use it wisely during the test. Experimenting with the capabilities of a new calculator during the testing session or using a calculator in situations when a non-calculator approach would be better can cost you precious time. Bring the calculator that you are most familiar with—the one you use in your math classes or at home—but make sure it is an ACT-permitted calculator (visit https://www.act.org/content/act/en/products-and-services/the-act/test-day/calculator-policy.html for details). Don't worry that other students have more sophisticated calculators than yours; the type of calculator that students use should not make a difference in their scores. Use your calculator wisely; remember that a non-calculator strategy is often better than a calculator strategy. And don't believe everything your calculator tells you. Make sure the numbers it gives you are reasonable and make sense.

Think!

Your head is by far a more powerful and efficient problem-solving tool than a pencil or a calculator. Think before you plunge in and begin working on a problem. Don't panic if you suddenly can't remember a formula or all of the steps of a procedure you've been taught. You can often find another way to do a problem that will work just as well. For example, you don't have to write and solve an equation for every algebra word problem. You might be able to reason through such a problem and get the correct answer without an equation. Sometimes the best option is to let your common sense about numbers take over.

Show Your Work

You have certainly heard this before—probably in every math class you've ever taken. Of course, you're not going to have time during the test to write down every step for every problem the way you might on a homework assignment, but writing down at least some of what you are thinking and doing as you solve a problem will be worth the time it takes. If you're using a calculator, you can write down the numbers that you plug into it and the intermediate results it gives you, to keep a running record of what you did. If you don't write anything down and your answer for a problem doesn't match any of the answer choices, your only alternative is to start over. But, if you have at least something written down, you may be able to go back over your work and find your mistake. Also, if you have time at the end of the test to go back and check your answers, having something written down will enable you to check your work more quickly.

Check Your Answers

Before you leave a question, make sure your answer makes sense. Don't believe everything your calculator tells you; make sure that the answer your calculator displays makes sense to you and that your answer actually answers the question. For example, if a problem about oranges and apples asks for the number of apples, make sure your answer doesn't give the number of oranges, or if a problem asks for the altitude of a triangle, make sure your answer isn't the hypotenuse. Remember, if you have time remaining after answering all of the questions, use it wisely and go back and check your work. That's a skill that will help you in college and career, too.

Prep Online!

Want even more ways to prep? Go to https://study.learning.wiley.com/ to access our online platform and take practice tests. To get started, go to https://study.learning.wiley.com/, select your title, answer the redemption question, and start studying!

Chapter 7: Improving Your Reading Score

Designed to measure your reading comprehension, the ACT reading test comprises four sections, three of which will count toward your score. These sections may contain either one long prose passage or two shorter prose passages. One of the sections may include a mixed-information format—visual and quantitative elements (like graphs, diagrams, and tables) that accompany the passage and contain information relevant to the passage topic. Each passage or passage set is followed by 9 multiple-choice questions, for a total of 36 questions, 27 of which will be scored. You are given 40 minutes to complete the test. The passages on the reading test come from published materials, such as books and magazines, written at a level that a first-year college student can expect to read for a class.

Content of the ACT Reading Test

The ACT reading test contains a mix of passages from the following categories:

- **Literary narrative** (literary passages from short stories, novels, and memoirs)

- **Humanities** (informational passages on architecture, art, dance, ethics, film, language, literary criticism, music, philosophy, radio, television, and theater)

- **Social science** (informational passages on anthropology, archaeology, biography, business, economics, education, environmentalism, geography, history, political science, psychology, and sociology)

- **Natural science** (informational passages on anatomy, astronomy, biology, botany, chemistry, ecology, geology, medicine, meteorology, microbiology, natural history, physiology, physics, technology, and zoology)

Each passage is preceded by a heading that identifies what type of passage it is ("Informational" or "Literary Narrative"), names the author, and may include a brief note that helps in understanding the passage. Each section contains a set of multiple-choice test questions. These questions do not test the rote recall of facts from outside the passage, isolated vocabulary terms, or rules of formal logic. In sections that contain two short passages, some of the questions involve both of the passages in the section. In sections that contain an element like a graph, figure, or table, some of the questions will involve the graphic or quantitative element.

You will receive four scores for the ACT reading test: a total test score based on all 27 scored questions and three reporting category scores based on the following specific knowledge and skills.

Key Ideas and Details

Read texts closely to determine central ideas and themes. Summarize information and ideas accurately. Read closely to understand relationships and draw logical inferences and conclusions including understanding sequential, comparative, and cause-effect relationships.

Craft and Structure

Determine word and phrase meanings, analyze an author's word choice, analyze text structure, understand authorial purpose and perspective, and analyze characters' points of view. You will interpret authorial decisions and differentiate between various perspectives and sources of information.

Integration of Knowledge and Ideas

Understand authors' claims, differentiate between facts and opinions, and make connections between different texts. Some questions will require you to analyze how authors construct arguments, evaluating reasoning and evidence from various sources; others will require you to piece together information from multiple texts or from different formats (e.g., graphs, diagrams, or tables).

If you choose to take the writing test, you will also receive an English Language Arts (ELA) score based on an average of your English, reading, and writing test scores.

Types of Questions on the ACT Reading Test

On the reading test, the questions fall into one of the three reporting categories previously described. You shouldn't worry about these categories while you're taking the reading test. It's most important that you focus on the questions themselves and on what they ask you about a given passage. Because each passage is different, the kinds of questions will vary from passage to passage. Still, there are some general types of questions you're likely to encounter. Most questions will ask you to do one of the following:

- Identify and interpret details.

- Determine the main idea of a paragraph, paragraphs, or a passage.

- Understand comparative relationships (comparisons and contrasts).

- Understand cause-effect relationships.

- Make generalizations.

- Determine the meaning of words from context.

- Understand sequences of events.

- Analyze the author's purpose and method.

- Understand and analyze arguments.

- Understand information across multiple texts.

Sometimes the reading test contains other types of questions, but don't worry. Just make sure you read each passage and its questions carefully. You'll find that the information you need to determine the best answer for a question is always available in the passage. Questions that illustrate some common types of questions on the reading test follow.

Representative ACT Reading Test Questions

Details. Some test questions ask you to locate or understand a key detail from a passage. A detail can be something as seemingly simple as a characteristic of a person, place, or thing, or a particular date. Other questions of this type require you to do a bit more interpreting of minor or subtly stated details. The question below was taken from a literary narrative about a violin lesson, which is found on page 247.

---

1.   Allegra states that Mr. Kaplan will know she hasn't practiced the concerto if:

   A.   she isn't ready for the shift on the second page.
   B.   the dynamics in her playing are unacceptable.
   C.   she has trouble playing the first movement's cadenza fast enough.
   D.   her tape doesn't sound good enough.

You'll have to look around the passage for the information you need—not unusual for this kind of question. Choice **A** is the best answer. In the fifth paragraph (lines 17–27), Allegra is getting ready to play for Mr. Kaplan. She notes that "he was going to know the instant I got to the top of the second page that I hadn't been practicing the Mozart. At that spot there's a fast shift from first finger to fourth finger on the G string, and you have to get ready for it. You can't let a shift like that take you by surprise" (lines 22–27). It is clear from these lines that Allegra thinks Mr. Kaplan will know she hasn't practiced if she isn't ready for this shift. Mr. Kaplan mentions the dynamics of Allegra's playing, but this is after she has played the piece for him **(B)**. Likewise, the cadenza and Allegra's tape are mentioned in the passage, but neither is mentioned in relation to Mr. Kaplan knowing that Allegra hasn't practiced. In the sixth paragraph (lines 28–33), Allegra notes that there are three cadenzas in the concerto, but she doesn't state that she's worried about playing the first movement's fast enough **(C)**. In lines 59–62, it's clear that the tape was made before this particular lesson **(D)**.

Main Ideas. To answer this kind of question, you need to be able to determine the focus of a passage or of a paragraph or paragraphs in a passage. You shouldn't count on finding this information summed up in the first paragraph of a passage or in the first sentence of a paragraph. You may have been advised to make the first sentence of each paragraph the topic sentence in your own writing, but not every writer does that. You'll need to figure out what the author's main point is in one or more paragraphs or in an entire passage by reading the paragraph(s) or passage carefully.

Main idea questions can be fairly straightforward. The following question, based on a social science passage about the development of perceptual abilities (page 250), is pretty direct:

> 2. The main point of the passage is that:
>
>   F. during the first four to seven months of life, babies learn at an accelerated pace.
>   G. organisms deprived of critical life experiences may or may not develop normal sensory performance.
>   H. the development of perceptual abilities is the result of the interaction between nature and experience.
>   J. research concerned with physical skills and abilities adds little to our knowledge of the growth of the mind.

The idea that the interaction between nature and experience shapes the development of perceptual abilities **(H)** is the clear focus of the entire passage. In the first paragraph, the author states that "the ancient central question of psychology" is "how much is due to nature and how much to nurture (or, in developmental terms, to maturation and to learning)" (lines 5–8). The second through eighth paragraphs (lines 9–85) describe research designed to help answer this question as it relates to the development of perceptual abilities in children. The last paragraph sums up the passage by saying that this research helps us "catch the first glimpse of how mind is constructed out of matter by experience" (lines 88–89). Though in lines 50–53 the author describes the rapid development of infants between four and seven months old, this is only a minor part of the passage, so **F** is incorrect. The seventh paragraph (lines 61–73) does mention that organisms can be permanently harmed if they miss critical life experiences, but this, also, isn't the main point of the passage, making **G** incorrect. Choice **J** is just plain wrong: the whole passage deals with how research on physical skills and abilities has added to our knowledge of the growth of the mind.

As that example shows, you may have to rule out answer choices that either are supporting (rather than main) ideas or simply misstate what the passage says. Both types of wrong answers appear in this next example, based on the natural science passage about lightning and fire (page 252):

---

3. One of the main points of the third paragraph (lines 41–61) is that:

    A. Arizona researchers record tree mortality by volume.
    B. tree mortality rates fail to capture the true extent of lightning-inflicted damage.
    C. ponderosa pine trees are resistant to secondary diseases.
    D. pine tree forests draw fewer lightning strikes than many other habitat types in Arizona.

Choice **B** is the best answer here. Tree mortality rates "describe only direct injury" to trees (line 56), but lightning can also kill trees indirectly by making them vulnerable to insects, wind, and mistletoe and by causing fires. Although **A** is true, according to lines 54–56, the fact that Arizona researchers record tree mortality by volume is a minor point. The paragraph never claims that ponderosa pine trees are resistant to secondary diseases or that pine tree forests draw fewer lightning strikes than do many other habitat types in Arizona, so both **C** and **D** are incorrect.

Some questions for literary narrative passages will use phrases such as *main conflict* or *main theme* instead of *main idea*, but you should approach the questions in the same way as you would other main idea questions. Here's an example based on a literary narrative passage about a young woman, Cally Roy (page 248):

---

4. The main conflict in this passage could best be described as the:

    F. tension between the narrator's mother and Frank.
    G. hostility expressed between the narrator and her mother.
    H. narrator's efforts to break her ties to her mother and grandmothers.
    J. narrator's internal struggle to connect with her past and find her future.

You have to read the whole passage carefully to sort out what the main conflict is because there's at least some truth to all of the answer choices. Choice **J** turns out to be the best of the four choices because the main conflict is within the narrator herself. She journeys away from home and "into the city's bloody heart" (lines 18–19), she wonders "about the meaning of [her] spirit name" (line 22), she feels out of place in her "Frankenstein body" (line 76), and she ends the passage torn between her "city corner" and her life "back home" (lines 82–83). The narrator says her mother loves Frank "too much to live with" him (lines 36–37) and also that Frank "can't drag himself away from the magnetic field of mother's voice" (lines 68–69), but the tension between the narrator's mother and Frank isn't the main conflict of the passage, making **F** wrong. There could be some hostility between the narrator and her mother because the narrator doesn't seem to want to go to the tribal college like her mother wants her to (see lines 79–82), but the narrator also wants to "curl next to her and be a small girl again" (lines 74–75), so mother-daughter hostility isn't the main conflict, either, ruling out **G**. Choice **H** misses the mark because although

Improving Your Score

the narrator has left her home and her mother, her grandmothers are only briefly talked about in the passage (see lines 24–33), so the main conflict can't revolve around them.

Comparative Relationships. You're likely to find questions asking you to make comparisons and contrasts in passages that contain a lot of information or that feature multiple characters or points of view. This kind of test question can make you process a lot of information—you may be asked to weigh one concept against another and identify a significant difference between the two. But comparison and contrast questions aren't always overly complicated. In the following example, based on a humanities passage about the artist Pieter Saenredam (page 251), the comparison is directly made in a few lines in the passage:

---

5.   According to the passage, Saenredam and Vermeer were similar in their:

    A.   weak draftsmanship despite their careful observation of subjects.
    B.   principles of design and spatial dimension.
    C.   use of shadow and religious subjects.
    D.   limited production and their desire for perfection.

Lines 16–17 state, "Like Vermeer, Saenredam was a perfectionist and his output was fairly small." Thus, **D** is the best answer. It speaks to both parts of the similarity—their output being fairly small and the idea that they were both perfectionists. The passage states that Saenredam was an "outstanding draftsman" (lines 17–18), so **A** cannot be true. The passage does not give us information about Vermeer's principles of design and spatial dimension (**B**), nor does it indicate that Vermeer used shadows and religious subjects in a way similar to Saenredam (**C**).

Cause-Effect Relationships. Cause-effect questions can arise in passages when it is important to understand the cause or result of specific actions, events, or ideas. In a literary narrative passage, perhaps one character's actions caused another character to act a certain way. In an informational passage, it might be important to understand the consequences of a specific decision or policy. Sometimes the answer to a cause-effect question is stated in the passage; sometimes you have to piece together the information you've read and work out the answer on your own.

Here's an example of a fairly direct cause-effect question, based on the literary narrative passage about Cally Roy (page 248):

---

6.   The narrator implies that losing her indis has caused her to:

    F.   cling to her family.
    G.   leave her home.
    H.   remember its every detail.
    J.   fight with her family.

The information needed to answer this question is in the first paragraph: once the narrator lost her indis, she says, she "began to wander from home, first in my thoughts, then my feet took after" (lines 11–13). Choice **G** is therefore the best answer. Choice **F** is pretty much the opposite of the truth, in the sense that the narrator decided to leave home. Although the narrator claims she "remember[s] every detail" of her indis (line 5), this isn't because she lost it but because "the turtle hung near my crib, then off my belt, and was my very first play toy" (lines 5–7). So **H** can't be the best answer. Choice **J** is incorrect because the narrator never really implies that losing her indis has caused her to fight with her family. Although her mother was "in a panic" (line 27) over the narrator's decision to leave, this seems more out of concern for the narrator than the result of a fight.

Following is an example of a somewhat more complex cause-effect question, this time based on the natural science passage on lightning and fire (page 252):

---

7.   The third paragraph (lines 41–61) suggests that if lightning did not fix atmospheric nitrogen, then:

   A.   rain could not fall to Earth, leaving nitrogen in the atmosphere.
   B.   less nitrogen would be found on Earth.
   C.   electrical current could not be conducted by air.
   D.   lightning bolts would strike the earth with less frequency.

Although the question lets you know to look in the third paragraph, the wording of that paragraph is subtle and requires close reading. The relevant information is in lines 45–46: "Lightning helps to fix atmospheric nitrogen into a form that rain can bring to Earth." This matches nicely with **B**, which says that less nitrogen would be found on Earth. Although nitrogen would remain in the atmosphere if lightning didn't fix it, the paragraph never suggests that rain wouldn't fall to Earth, making **A** tempting but wrong. The paragraph doesn't suggest that if lightning didn't fix atmospheric nitrogen, electrical current couldn't be conducted by air or that lightning bolts would strike the earth with less frequency, making **C** and **D** incorrect.

Generalizations. This type of question usually asks you to take a lot of information—sometimes the whole passage—and boil it down into a more concise form. A generalization question may involve interpreting mood, tone, or character, or it may ask you to make some kind of general observation or draw a conclusion about the nature of an argument the author is making. The following example, based on the literary narrative about Allegra's violin lesson (page 247), focuses on personality or character:

---

8.   Based on the passage, Allegra's attitude toward Mr. Kaplan is best described as one of:

   F.   low-key ridicule.
   G.   good-natured respect.
   H.   resentful obedience.
   J.   close friendship.

This question requires you to sum up Allegra's attitude toward Mr. Kaplan based on the passage as a whole. The best answer is **G**. Though there is no one specific moment that establishes this good-natured respect, their interactions and conversation most strongly suggest Allegra's attitude toward her teacher. Allegra clearly wants to perform well for Mr. Kaplan, which shows her respect for him. We can see this in the way Allegra practices the shift without making any noise (lines 46–47) and in the fact that she had worked so hard on her tape for the Bloch Competition. And there are lighthearted moments throughout that speak to this respect being good-natured. Allegra loves her lessons ("In the summer I get to have morning lessons twice a week, and I love it" [lines 14–15]); she notes with affection the way Mr. Kaplan looks (lines 41–42); and she and Mr. Kaplan smile or laugh at moments during practice (lines 76, 88, 90). There is no indication in the passage that Allegra views Mr. Kaplan with an attitude of ridicule (**F**). There are moments that could be misread as ridicule, like when Allegra notes that Mr. Kaplan's "ears stick out in a funny way" (line 41), but it's important to read those moments in the larger context of the passage. Allegra goes on to say, "I love the way he looks" (lines 41–42), which speaks to her fondness for Mr. Kaplan. There's also nothing in the passage to point to a general attitude of resentful obedience (**H**). Allegra takes direction from Mr. Kaplan, but she doesn't display any resentment. And while Allegra and Mr. Kaplan are comfortable with each other, it goes too far to say that Allegra's attitude toward Mr. Kaplan is one of close friendship (**J**). They have a good working relationship, but there's nothing in the passage to suggest that Allegra considers Mr. Kaplan a close friend. At one point Allegra compares Mr. Kaplan to her softball coach when she says, "My softball coach and my violin teacher were overlapping each other" (5–6). This suggests that Allegra views Mr. Kaplan as another adult in a role of authority rather than a close friend.

Meanings of Words. Questions about meanings of words ask you to determine from context what a particular word, phrase, or statement most nearly means. In some cases, the word or words will probably be unfamiliar to you, but even when familiar words are tested, you'll have to look at the context in which they appear to determine the closest synonym or paraphrase. Sometimes looking at a single sentence of the passage is enough to figure this out, but other times you'll have to look at sentences before or after the given word, phrase, or statement in order to determine the closest meaning.

Many meanings-of-words questions will focus on a single word or a short phrase. The answer choices will include synonyms for the word or phrase that you might find in a dictionary or thesaurus, but only one of the choices will truly reflect how the word or phrase is used in this particular case. Look at the following example, based on the humanities passage about Pieter Saenredam (page 251):

---

9. As it is used in line 71, the word *fixes* most nearly means:

    A. establishes.
    B. corrects.
    C. repairs.
    D. hardens.

All of the answer choices could be synonyms for *fixes* depending on context. Only Choice **A**, though, makes sense here. The passage tells us that certain drawings contain such detailed information that we can place the artist at a specific time and place. Thus, the ink-wash shadow in this drawing establishes (fixes) a time. It would not make sense to say that the shadow corrects (**B**), repairs (**C**), or hardens (**D**) the time.

Sequence of Events. In some passages, the order, or sequence, in which events happen is important. Sequence-of-events questions may ask you to determine when, for example, a character in a literary narrative passage did something or to figure out the order in which the researchers described in an informational passage performed certain steps in a biology experiment.

Sequence questions will often require you to take in information from the whole passage or from large sections of the passage in order to determine a correct order of events. This is true of the question below, based on a natural science passage about the small-comet theory (page 253):

---

10. Which of the following events mentioned in the passage occurred first chronologically?

   F. Frank and Sigwarth presented new evidence that leaves little doubt Earth is being bombarded by something.
   G. Frank and Sigwarth first put forth the small-comet theory.
   H. Frank and Sigwarth analyzed photos of the electrical phenomena that accompany sunspots.
   J. Frank and Sigwarth had difficulty getting the scientific community to accept their ideas.

The passage details how Frank and Sigwarth came up with the small-comet theory, the scientific community's reaction to the theory, and new developments since the theory was first presented. Because the timeline skips around in the passage, it's important to read carefully to understand the sequence of events. The best answer is **H**. In the sixth paragraph (lines 41–50), we're told that the small-comet theory first started to take shape when Sigwarth was Frank's graduate student. As they analyzed photos, they noticed dark specks appearing in images from a NASA satellite. Lines 59–62 state: "Based on their images, the Iowa scientists estimated 20 comets an hour . . . were bombarding the Earth." Thus, the analysis of the images eventually led to the small-comet theory. Choice **F** cannot be correct because this new evidence was presented after the small-comet theory had been put forth (lines 15–19). This choice may be tempting because it appears in the passage before Choice **H**. The same is true of Choice **G**. But since the photo analysis eventually led to the small-comet theory, it would be incorrect to state that the theory was put forth first (**G**). The passage also makes clear that Frank and Sigwarth's theory was not well received by the scientific community when it was first put forth, so Choice **J** has to come after Choices **G** and **H**.

Author's Purpose and Method. Questions about the author's purpose or method focus on the craft of writing—the main purpose of a passage, what role parts of a passage (such as a paragraph) play in the whole work, and so on.

An example should help clear up what this category is about. Taken from a social science passage on the Erie Canal (page 249), this question asks you to consider the function of a paragraph in the passage:

> **11.** In the context of the passage, the sixth paragraph (lines 39–52) primarily functions to:
>
>   **A.** outline the obstacles Clinton faced in getting public approval for the Erie Canal.
>   **B.** explain how Clinton's plan won over a reluctant state legislature when the federal government refused to help.
>   **C.** detail how the Erie Canal gamble paid off in the economic advancement of New York.
>   **D.** describe the vast logistical and financial concerns of the Erie Canal project.

In the fifth paragraph, we're told that the idea of a canal connecting the Hudson with the Great Lakes "had been around for many years but always dismissed as hopelessly impracticable" (lines 28–29). The sixth paragraph builds on this by describing the major issues involved in the construction of the Erie Canal. Therefore, the best answer is Choice **D**. The first sentence of this paragraph states, "One can understand the reluctance, for the project was huge by the standards of the day" (lines 39–40). The paragraph then details what made the project so daunting: the canal would be the longest in the world, it would require moving 11.4 million cubic yards of earth and rock, and its expense was equal to 1 percent of the entire country's gross domestic product. Choice **A** is incorrect because these are not obstacles Clinton himself had to face to gain public support; in fact, the passage notes only that Clinton built public support (line 37) and doesn't indicate that there were obstacles to this at all. Choice **B** is incorrect because there's no information in the paragraph about how the plan won over the reluctant state legislature. Choice **C** is incorrect because although the paragraph notes that the Erie Canal "put the Empire in the Empire State" (lines 51–52), it doesn't *detail how*; this is explored in the rest of the passage.

Arguments. Some questions deal with the arguments and claims made in passages. These questions may ask you to identify an argument or to examine support for a statement made in the passage. They may also ask you to identify the difference between fact and opinion, or to understand how an author might try to persuade readers. The examples below will help you understand what kinds of questions you might see in this category. The first is taken from the humanities passage about Pieter Saenredam (page 251) and asks you to identify a main claim from the passage:

> **12.** One of the passage's central claims is that:
>
>   **F.** Saenredam's detailed drawings provide deep insights into his paintings and his life.
>   **G.** Saenredam was an outstanding draftsman, though he produced relatively little of importance.
>   **H.** Vermeer, Rembrandt, and Saenredam all incorporated fiction into their art in some degree.
>   **J.** taken together, the work of Vermeer, Rembrandt, and Saenredam represents the Golden Age of Dutch art.

Choice **F** is the correct answer because it identifies one of the passage's central claims. In the second paragraph of the passage, we're told that many of Saenredam's drawings survive, and that "they offer intimate insights into his art and life" (line 20). The passage author then spends a significant portion of the passage exploring what those insights are. We can see this in lines 39–80, which detail the different aspects of Saenredam's life and art that can be gleaned from his drawings. Since so much of the passage is spent exploring this idea, we can call this a central claim of the passage. Choice **G** might be tempting because we're told that Saenredam was an outstanding draftsman and that "his output was fairly small" (line 17). But Choice **G** goes a step beyond this in asserting that Saenredam produced little of importance. While we know that he doesn't enjoy the same level of fame as Vermeer or Rembrandt, the passage does not assert that his work is of little importance; rather, the author notes that many connoisseurs consider Saenredam an equal of these more famous artists and that Saenredam produced works "among the supreme masterpieces of Dutch art" (lines 51–52). Choice **H** is incorrect because it is a detail in the last paragraph of the passage (lines 81–89) rather than a central claim. Choice **J** is incorrect because this is not a statement made in the passage. In the first line of the passage we're told that "thanks to Vermeer and Rembrandt, art of the 17th-century Dutch Golden Age is box-office magic" (lines 1–2), but this is not further explored or explained in the passage.

The next example is from the social science passage about the Erie Canal (page 249). It focuses on a specific statement in the passage and asks you to determine how the author supports that statement:

13. What evidence does the author provide to support the claim that "New York became the greatest boomtown the world has ever known" (lines 70–72)?

   A. A quotation from Holmes regarding New York's status after the Eric Canal opened
   B. The percentage of American exports passing through the port of New York in 1800
   C. Statistics that show New York's population from 1790 to 1860
   D. Details about other projects undertaken in New York after the Erie Canal was completed

The answer to this question can be found in the ninth paragraph (lines 70–78), right after the claim in lines 70–72. Questions that ask for supporting evidence will not always be this straightforward and will often require that you look at the wider passage to find the answer, but in this case the answer can be found in the same paragraph as the claim. The best answer is **C** because this paragraph follows up the claim by providing statistics to show how the population of New York increased after the Erie Canal opened. Earlier in the passage we're told that the Erie Canal was finished in 1825. According to population statistics provided in the ninth paragraph, the population of New York had been increasing at a rate of roughly 30,000 every decade before the Erie Canal opened. After the canal's opening, the population increased at a much faster pace: by more than 100,000 from 1830 to 1840, more than 200,000 from 1840 to 1850, and almost 300,000 from 1850 to 1860. Choice **A** is incorrect because the quotation from Holmes in lines 66–67 mainly helps show how much produce flowed eastward after the canal opened; it points to prosperity but doesn't provide specific support for the claim. Choice **B** is incorrect because the canal had not been finished in 1800. The 9 percent of American exports passing through New York in 1800 is low; in 1860, after the canal had been open for several decades, that percentage was much higher. Choice **D** is incorrect because the passage doesn't describe other projects undertaken in New York after the canal was completed. "Megaprojects" are mentioned in lines 90–92, but they are not specific to New York, and they are provided as examples to show how the success of the Erie Canal encouraged big thinking.

Answer Key for Reading Test Sample Questions

1.	A	6.	G	11.	D
2.	H	7.	B	12.	F
3.	B	8.	G	13.	C
4.	J	9.	A		
5.	D	10.	H		

Strategies for Taking the ACT Reading Test

Performance on the ACT reading test relies not only on reading speed and comprehension but also on test-taking strategies and skills. The following sections describe strategies and skills specifically for improving your ACT reading test score.

Pace Yourself

Before you read the first passage of the reading test, you may want to take a quick look through the entire reading test. If you choose to do this, flip through the pages and look at each of the passages and their questions. (Note that the passages begin on the pages to your left, and the questions follow.) You don't need to memorize anything—you can look at any of the reading test passages and questions during the time allotted for that test.

Some readers find that looking quickly at the questions first gives them a better idea of what to look for as they're reading the passage. It you're a slow reader, though, this may not be a good strategy. If you do decide to preview the questions, don't spend too much time on them—just scan for a few key words or ideas that you can watch for when you read the passage. To see what approach works best for you, you might want to try alternating between previewing the questions and not previewing the questions as you work through the practice tests in this book. Remember that when you take the ACT for real, a clock will be running. Plan your approach for the reading test before you take the actual ACT.

Use the Time Allotted

You have 40 minutes to read four passages and answer 36 questions. You'll want to pace yourself so you don't spend too much time on any one passage or question. If you take 2 to 3 minutes to read each passage or passage set, you'll have around 50 seconds to answer each question associated with the passage. Some of the questions will take less time, which will allow you more time for the more challenging ones.

Because time is limited, you should be very careful in deciding whether to skip more difficult questions. If you skip the difficult questions from the first passage until you work through the entire reading test, for example, you may find that you've forgotten so much of the first passage that you have to reread it before you can answer the questions that puzzled you the first time through. It may work better for you to think of the test as four separate units, giving yourself time to finish every passage and item set (approximately 10 minutes each). Then you can try to complete all the questions for a passage within its allotted time. Answer all the questions; you're not penalized for guessing.

Think of an Overall Strategy That Works for You

Are you the kind of person who likes to get the big picture first, then carefully go over your work? Do you like to answer the questions you're sure of right away and then go back and puzzle out the tougher ones? Or are you something of a perfectionist? (Do you find it hard to concentrate on a question until you know you got the one before it right?) There isn't any right way or wrong way to approach the reading test—just make sure the way you choose is the way that works best for you.

Keep the Passage as a Whole in Mind

Your initial look at the whole reading test should give you some ideas about how to approach each passage. Notice the subject heading and short paragraph before each passage. These "advance organizers" tell you whether the passage is literary narrative or informational, where the passage comes from, who wrote it, and sometimes a little information about the passage. Occasionally an advance organizer will define a difficult word, explain a concept, or provide background information. Reading the advance organizers carefully should help you be more prepared as you approach each passage.

Always remember that the reading test asks you to refer to and reason on the basis of the passage. You may know a lot about the subject of some of the passages you read, but try not to let what you already know influence the way you answer the questions, because the author's perspective may differ from yours. There's a reason why many questions begin with "According to the passage" or "It can reasonably be inferred from the passage." If you read and understand the passage well, your reasoning ability will help you to figure out the correct answer. During the reading test, you can refer back to the passages as often as you like.

Find a Strategy for Approaching Each Question

First, read each question carefully so you know what it asks. Look for the best answer, but read and consider all the options, even though you may feel you've identified the best one. Ask yourself whether you can justify your choice as the best answer.

Some people find it useful to answer the easy questions first and skip the difficult ones (being careful, of course, to mark the answer document correctly and to mark in the test booklet or

Improving Your Score

flag on the computer the questions they skipped). Then they go back and consider the difficult questions. When you're working on a test question and aren't certain about the answer, try to eliminate choices you're sure are incorrect. You can cross them off on paper or use the eliminator tool on the computer to mark eliminated answers. This may save you time if you come back to a difficult question. If you can rule out a couple of choices, you'll improve your chances of selecting the correct answer. Keep referring back to the passage for information.

Reading Strategies Summary

The sample passages used as examples in this section can be found on the following pages. They come from ACT tests that thousands of students have already taken. Remember, the passages and items in this section don't represent every type you're likely to see. For a more complete picture of what the ACT reading test will look like, four complete reading tests are included in the four practice ACT tests in chapters 3 and 10. And remember that the best way to do well on the ACT reading test is to have a solid understanding of each passage—so read quickly but carefully.

Prep Online!

Want even more ways to prep? Go to https://study.learning.wiley.com/ to access our online platform and take practice tests. To get started, go to https://study.learning.wiley.com/, select your title, answer the redemption question, and start studying!

Sample Passage I

LITERARY NARRATIVE: This passage is adapted from the novel *The Mozart Season* by Virginia Euwer Wolff (©1991 by Virginia Euwer Wolff).

The hair on a violin bow is the part of the bow, traditionally made of horsehair, that makes contact with the strings when the violin is played.

"Now that you're warmed up, let's revisit Mr. Mozart," said Mr. Kaplan.

It was a gorgeous June morning and in my mind I heard another voice: "Now that you're warmed up, let's
5 demolish those Vikings." My softball coach and my violin teacher were overlapping each other.

With my softball coach, it was stairsteps and laps and endless batting practice. With Mr. Kaplan it was eight repetitions of very fast B-major scales and five
10 minutes of octaves. Two weeks after being the shortstop on the team that had lost in the second round of the district play-offs, I was at my lesson, looking for the Mozart concerto.

In the summer I get to have morning lessons twice
15 a week, and I love it. I work best in the mornings. Things haven't had time to get so cluttered yet.

I put the music on the stand and got ready. With Mr. Kaplan you don't whine or mutter. It doesn't help. "We want right notes, not excuses" is what all music
20 teachers say, I guess. He doesn't have to say it very many times; you learn it fast. Mr. Kaplan and I'd been together for seven years, and he was going to know the instant I got to the top of the second page that I hadn't been practicing the Mozart. At that spot there's a fast
25 shift from first finger to fourth finger on the G string, and you have to get ready for it. You can't let a shift like that take you by surprise.

"Straight through. Right, Allegra? Including cadenzas." A cadenza is the part where the violin plays
30 alone; it's harder than the rest of the piece, and it gets the audience all excited when you do it in a concert. There are three cadenzas in this concerto, one in each movement.

"Right."

35 The introduction is forty-one measures long. This time, instead of playing just the last two measures of it on the piano, Mr. Kaplan played the whole thing. He wears half-glasses, and he has a balding head with some blondish-gray hair on the back, and a mostly gray
40 short beard, and he's a little bit slumped over when he sits at the piano. His ears stick out in a funny way. I love the way he looks. The introduction to the first movement, the part the orchestra would play, mostly announces what the solo violin will play when it
45 begins. That way you get to listen to it twice.

While he was doing it, I practiced the G-string shift without making any noise, sliding my hand up and down the fingerboard.

I love this concerto. Mozart only wrote five of
50 them for the violin. The year before, Mr. Kaplan had let me choose which one to learn, the third one or this one, and I'd taken them both home and spun my bow the way you spin a tennis racquet. If it landed with the hair toward me, I'd learn the third, in G; and if it landed
55 with the hair away from me, I'd learn this one. When Mr. Kaplan and my parents found out I'd treated my bow With Such Astonishing Disrespect, they got very alarmed about it.

I'd worked very hard on it for several months, and
60 in February, we'd made a tape of it to send to a contest. I'd worried and fretted and trembled, but we'd gotten the tape made. After that, I'd sort of neglected it. In softball season I'd practically stopped being a violinist.

Mr. Kaplan, who was having fun playing the intro-
65 duction, got to the BUM-*pum-pa-pum* part that comes right before the violin begins. I was ready. It starts on a high D and goes on up from there.

I got through the first movement all right, and I made some genuine messes of the beautiful double-
70 stops near the end of the second-movement cadenza. Double-stops are two notes at once, on separate strings. And I was sure the last-movement cadenza was making it Abundantly Clear to Mr. Kaplan that I hadn't even seen it for a long time. But the end was fine. The *Blip-
75 te-de-bip-bip-bip* came out very, very soft and nice.

Mr. Kaplan leaned back, smiling and saying a kind of "ah." Then he turned sideways on the bench. "Isn't this a beautiful song, Allegra?"

"Yep." It is. Mr. Kaplan calls overtures and
80 symphonies and concertos "songs" sometimes. I waited for him to say the rest.

He leaned forward and flipped the pages. "Hmmm. I'm concerned about the articulation in spots, and some of the dynamics aren't at all what they should be
85 and . . . Hmmm." Then he turned sideways on the bench again, straddling it. "Are you willing to play this concerto a thousand times by September?"

I laughed. That would be more times than I'd brush my teeth by then. He watched me thinking. He
90 started to smile, then he got up and walked across the studio, away from me. Then he turned around. "Your tape was accepted," he said. "For the Bloch Competition. The finals are on Labor Day."

Sample Passage II

LITERARY NARRATIVE: This passage is adapted from *The Antelope Wife* by Louise Erdrich (©1998 by Louise Erdrich).

My mother sewed my birth cord, with dry sage and sweet grass, into a turtle holder of soft white buckskin. She beaded that little turtle using precious old cobalts and yellows and Cheyenne pinks and greens in a careful
5 design. I remember every detail of it, me, because the turtle hung near my crib, then off my belt, and was my very first play toy. I was supposed to have it on me all my life, bury it with me on reservation land, but one day I came in from playing and my indis was gone.
10 I thought nothing of it, at first and for many years, but slowly over time the absence . . . it will tell. I began to wander from home, first in my thoughts, then my feet took after, so at last at the age of eighteen, I walked the road that led from the front of our place to the wider
15 spaces and then the country beyond that, where that one road widened into two lanes, then four, then six, past the farms and service islands, into the dead wall of the suburbs and still past that, finally, into the city's bloody heart.

20 My name is Cally Roy. Ozhawashkwamashko-deykway is what the spirits call me. All my life so far I've wondered about the meaning of my spirit name but nobody's told it, seen it, got ahold of my history flying past. Mama has asked, she has offered tobacco, even
25 blankets, but my grandmas Mrs. Zosie Roy and Mary Shawano only nod at her, holding their tongues as they let their eyes wander. In a panic, once she knew I was setting out, not staying home, Mama tried to call up my grandmas and ask if I could live at their apartment in
30 the city. But once they get down to the city, it turns out they never stop moving. They are out, and out again. Impossible to track down. It's true, they are extremely busy women.

So my mom sends me to Frank.

35 Frank Shawano. Famous Indian bakery chef. My Mama's eternal darling, the man she loves too much to live with.

I'm weary and dirty and sore when I get to Frank's bakery shop, but right away, walking in and the bell
40 dinging with a cheerful alertness, I smell those good bakery smells of yeasty bread and airy sugar. Behind the counter, lemony light falls on Frank. He is big, strong, pale brown like a loaf of light rye left to rise underneath a towel. His voice is muffled and weak, like
45 it is squeezed out of the clogged end of a pastry tube. He greets me with gentle pleasure.

"Just as I'm closing." His smile is very quiet. He cleans his hands on a towel and beckons me into the back of the bakery shop, between swinging steel doors.
50 I remember him as a funny man, teasing and playing games and rolling his eyes at us, making his pink sugar-cookie dogs bark and elephants trumpet. But now he is serious, and frowns slightly as I follow him up the back

stairs and into the big top-floor apartment with the
55 creaky floors, the groaning pipes, odd windows that view the yard. My little back room, no bigger than a closet, overlooks this space.

I'm so beat, though, I just want to crawl into my corner and sleep.

60 "Not too small, this place?" He sounds anxious.

I shake my head. The room seems okay, the mattress on the floor, the blankets, and the shelves for my things.

"Call your mom?" Frank gives orders in the form
65 of a question. He acts all purposeful, as though he is going back downstairs to close up the store, but as I dial the number on the kitchen wall phone he lingers. He can't drag himself away from the magnetic field of my mother's voice, muffled, far off, but on the other
70 end of the receiver. He stands in the doorway with that same towel he brought from downstairs, folding and refolding it in his hands.

"Mama," I say, and her voice on the phone suddenly hurts. I want to curl next to her and be a small
75 girl again. My body feels too big, electric, like a Frankenstein body enclosing a tiny child's soul.

We laugh at some corny joke and Frank darts a glance at me, then stares at his feet and frowns. Reading between my Mama's pauses on the phone, I
80 know she is hoping I'll miss the real land, and her, come back and resume my brilliant future at the tribal college. In spite of how I want to curl up in my city corner, I picture everything back home. On the wall of my room up north, there hang a bundle of sage and
85 Grandma Roy's singing drum. On the opposite wall, I taped up posters and photos. Ever since I was little, I slept with a worn bear and a new brown dog. And my real dog, too, curled at my feet sometimes, if Mama didn't catch us. I never liked dolls. I made good scores
90 in math. I get to missing my room and my dog and I lose track of Mama's voice.

Sample Passage III

INFORMATIONAL: This passage is adapted from the article "10 Moments that Made American Business" by John Steele Gordon (©2007 by American Heritage Publishing).

The cost of overland transportation had been a limiting factor in the world economy since time immemorial. Any material with a low value-to-weight ratio, such as foodstuffs, that couldn't be transported to [5] distant markets by water couldn't be sold in those markets at a price anyone would pay. This meant that national economies were fragmented into an infinity of local ones.

Until the Industrial Revolution, there was only one [10] way to reduce these transportation costs: build artificial rivers. By the end of the eighteenth century England was well laced with canals, greatly facilitating industrialization as factories could sell their goods profitably throughout the entire country.

[15] But the new United States was 10 times the size of England and far less developed. And a considerable mountain range divided the more developed eastern seaboard from the fertile, resource-rich, and rapidly growing West. Settlers west of the Appalachians had no [20] choice but to send their crops down the Mississippi to market.

Along the whole great chain of mountains that stretched from Maine to Alabama, there was only a single gap—where the Mohawk River tumbles into the [25] Hudson near Albany—at which a canal was even theoretically possible.

The idea of building a canal to connect the Hudson with the Great Lakes there had been around for many years but always dismissed as hopelessly impracticable. [30] Even Thomas Jefferson thought the idea "little short of madness." DeWitt Clinton, however, did not. Born into a prominent New York family (his uncle had been governor of New York and then Vice President under James Madison), Clinton would be the mayor of New York [35] City and governor of the state for most of the first quarter of the nineteenth century. A shrewd politician, he built public support for the canal and pushed it through a reluctant state legislature.

One can understand the reluctance, for the project [40] was huge by the standards of the day. At 363 miles the Erie would be by far the longest canal in the world. It would require moving, largely by hand, 11.4 million cubic yards of earth and rock—well over three times the volume of the Great Pyramid of Egypt—and build- [45] ing 83 locks in what was still a semiwilderness. The budget, seven million dollars, was about equal to one percent of the gross domestic product of the entire country. Nonetheless, when the federal government refused to help, New York decided to go it alone. It was [50] a gigantic roll of the economic dice, but one that paid off beyond even Clinton's dreams. The Erie Canal put the Empire in the Empire State.

The canal was a success even before it fully opened, as traffic burgeoned on the completed parts, [55] helping fund continuing construction. When it was finished in 1825, ahead of schedule and under budget, traffic was tremendous from the start. It is not hard to understand why. Before, it had taken three weeks and cost $120 to ship a ton of flour from Buffalo to New [60] York City. With the canal, it took eight days and cost $6.

Produce that had gone down the Mississippi to New Orleans now began to flow eastward. In a few years the Boston poet and physician Oliver Wendell [65] Holmes (father of the Supreme Court justice) described New York as "that tongue that is licking up the cream of commerce and finance of a continent." In 1800 about 9 percent of American exports passed through the port of New York. By 1860 it was 62 percent.

[70] With the opening of the Erie Canal, New York became the greatest boomtown the world has ever known. The population of New York had been increasing by about 30,000 every decade since 1790, with 123,000 inhabitants in 1820. By 1830, however, New [75] York's population had reached 202,000; by 1840, 313,000. It was 516,000 in 1850 and 814,000 in 1860. Development roared up Manhattan Island, at the astonishing rate of about two blocks a year.

Thanks to the Erie Canal, by the 1840s New [80] York's financial market was the largest in the country. In that decade the telegraph began to spread quickly, allowing more and more people to trade in the New York market, which has dominated American financial activity ever since.

[85] Even so, perhaps the greatest consequence of the Erie Canal was that its success made the country far more receptive to other projects of unprecedented scale and scope and encouraged its entrepreneurs and politicians to think big. The result was a still-continuing [90] string of megaprojects—the Atlantic cable, the Brooklyn Bridge, the Panama Canal, Hoover Dam, the interstate highway system, the Apollo missions—that have marked the economic history of the United States and shaped the national character.

Sample Passage IV

INFORMATIONAL: This passage is adapted from Morton Hunt's *The Story of Psychology* (© 1993 by Morton Hunt).

In the passage, the term *maturation* refers to the process of growth and development, and the term *perceptual ability* refers to the capacity to recognize something through the senses (sight, smell, touch, etc.).

Much maturation research is concerned with physical skills and physical attributes, and adds little to our knowledge of the growth of the mind. But research on the development of perceptual abilities begins to provide solid factual answers to the ancient central question of psychology: How much is due to nature and how much to nurture (or, in developmental terms, to maturation and to learning)?

The work has been focused on early infancy, when perceptual abilities evolve rapidly; its aim is to discover when each new ability first appears, the assumption being that at its first appearance, the new ability arises not from learning but from maturation of the optic nervous structures and especially of that part of the brain cortex where visual signals are received and interpreted.

Much has been learned by simply watching infants. What, exactly, do very young infants see? Since we cannot ask them what they see, how can we find out?

In 1961, the psychologist Robert Fantz devised an ingenious method of doing so. He designed a stand in which, on the bottom level, the baby lies on her back, looking up. A few feet above is a display area where the experimenter puts two large cards, each containing a design—a white circle, a yellow circle, a bull's-eye, a simple sketch of a face. The researcher, peering down through a tiny peephole, can watch the movement of the baby's eyes and time how long they are directed at one or the other of each pair of patterns. Fantz found that at two months babies looked twice as long at a bull's-eye as at a circle of solid color, and twice as long at a sketch of a face as at a bull's-eye. Evidently, even a two-month-old can distinguish major differences and direct her gaze toward what she finds more interesting.

Using this technique, developmental psychologists have learned a great deal about what infants see and when they begin to see it. In the first week infants distinguish light and dark patterns; during the first month they begin to track slowly moving objects; by the second month they begin to have depth perception, coordinate the movement of the eyes, and differentiate among hues and levels of brightness; by three months they can glance from one object to another, and can distinguish among family members; by four months they focus at varying distances, make increasingly fine distinctions, and begin to recognize the meaning of what they see (they look longer at a normal sketch of a face than at one in which the features have been scrambled); and from four to seven months they achieve stereopsis, recognize that a shape held at different angles is still the same shape, and gain near-adult ability to focus at varying distances.

Exactly how maturation and experience interact in the brain tissues to produce such developmental changes is becoming clear from neuroscience research. Microscopic examination of the brains of infants shows that as the brain triples in size during the first two years of life, a profusion of dendrites (branches) grow from its neurons and make contact with one another.

By the time a human is twelve, the brain has an estimated hundred trillion synapses (connections between nerve cells). Those connections are the wiring plan that establishes the brain's capabilities. Some of the synaptic connections are made automatically by chemical guidance, but others are made by the stimulus of experience during the period of rapid dendrite growth. Lacking such stimulus, the dendrites wither away without forming the needed synapses. Mice reared in the dark develop fewer dendritic spines and synaptic connections in the visual cortex than mice reared in the light, and even when exposed to light never attain normal vision.

Why should nature have done that? Why should perceptual development be possible only at a critical period and not later? It does not make evolutionary sense for the organism to be permanently impaired in sensory performance just because it fails to have the proper experiences at specific times in its development. But some brain researchers say that there is an offsetting advantage: the essential experiences are almost always available at the right time, and they fine-tune the brain structure so as to provide far more specific perceptual powers than could result from genetic control of synapse formation.

With that, the vague old terms nature and nurture take on precise new meaning. Now, after so many centuries of speculation, we catch the first glimpse of how mind is constructed out of matter by experience.

Sample Passage V

INFORMATIONAL: This passage is adapted from the article "Sublime Architecture: Sacred Interiors Aglow" by Holland Cotter (©2002 by The New York Times Company).

Thanks to Vermeer and Rembrandt, art of the 17th-century Dutch Golden Age is box-office magic. One reason is obvious: both artists are charismatic stylists and humane thinkers. The same is true of Pieter
5 Saenredam (1597–1665), their contemporary and, in the view of many connoisseurs, their equal, but who doesn't enjoy their popular fame. While they painted people, he painted buildings: church interiors in which the human figure was insignificant or absent. In fact,
10 Saenredam is often referred to as an architectural portraitist, whose exacting eye for measurement, light and detail gives his pictures the accuracy of scientific photographs. But are they really so true to life? Or are they, like photographs, a mix of fact, error and wishful
15 illusion?

Like Vermeer, Saenredam was a perfectionist and his output was fairly small. He was also an outstanding draftsman and—this is not true of Vermeer—many of his drawings survive. All directly related to the paint-
20 ings, they offer intimate insights into his art and life.

About that life we know both a little and a lot. He was born in Assendelft. After his father died when he was 10, the family moved to Haarlem, where Saenredam stayed for the rest of his life. He studied art
25 but, being financially independent, never had to make a living from it. At 30 he decided to devote himself to architectural subjects, or perspectives, as they were called. When he died he was buried in the Church of St. Bavo, which he had often painted.

30 Saenredam's fascination with Dutch churches was real, and intense enough to take him on occasional trips away from Haarlem. The longest was to Utrecht, where he stayed from June to October 1636. His long stay in Utrecht may have been forced by a plague outbreak that
35 hit Haarlem soon after he left. In any event, his time in Utrecht was the most fruitful of his career, when he produced some of his greatest images and a visual record of his activities.

Through his drawings we can trace his where-
40 abouts. We learn that he worked in seven different churches, five of which still exist. A soaring Gothic cathedral, called the Dom, was leveled in 1674; his drawings and paintings are the only documentation of its original appearance. The smaller, older Mariakerk—
45 *kerk* is Dutch for church—was derelict when he visited and was pulled down in the 19th century. He spent six weeks there, more time than anywhere else, and in his many views of its interior and exterior, he captured its beauties and eccentricities, as if he were portraying a
50 friend, newly met but instantly beloved. It inspired three paintings of its exterior, which are among the supreme masterpieces of Dutch art.

His work routine was the same for each church. First, he made highly detailed on-the-spot sketches of a
55 building, including close-ups of specific features. Later, in the studio, he converted these studies into more polished drawings, adjusting perspective and scale. Still later—in some cases a quarter century later—he turned these drawings into paintings.

60 Few buildings, at least before photography, were observed with more passionate care. In his on-site drawings, Saenredam seems intent on getting every last little thing down, with epic results. Whole architectural histories can be read in the structural particulars he
65 drew, civic histories in tomb inscriptions he transcribed, histories of religion and fashion in the ornaments he rendered.

Personal and professional stories also come across. Through certain drawings, we can place the artist at a
70 particular church on a particular day, say June 30, 1636. An ink-wash shadow fixes the time: 8 a.m. Another shadow to the left has a different angle: 9 a.m. So we see him moving systematically across the page. Over weeks, we see him succeeding and failing, making bril-
75 liant decisions or botching a job. Some on-site drawings are awesomely exact; others wildly misjudge spatial dimensions or cram surreal amounts of data into a single image. Certain errors of judgment can be corrected later; others are disastrous, resulting in paintings
80 that are architectural fictions.

But fiction is built into this art, just as it is into the portraits of Rembrandt and Vermeer. Reality is deliberately adjusted, edited, dramatized, simplified. A church interior cluttered with the unruly stuff of life—benches,
85 gravestones, water-stained stones—is jotted down on paper, then refined into a network of lines and grids, finally into a painted solid, a container of light, golden-brown or dove gray: a utopian vision with one foot on earth and one foot beyond.

Sample Passage VI

INFORMATIONAL: This passage is adapted from *Fire in America: A Cultural History of Wildland and Rural Fire* by Stephen J. Pyne (©1982 by Princeton University Press).

Lightning affects electrical equilibrium on the earth. Air is a poor conductor, but some electricity constantly leaks to the atmosphere, creating an electrical potential. Electricity moves back according to the gra-
5 dient [change in potential with distance]. During a thunderstorm, the gradient becomes very steep, and the electrical potential discharges as lightning. The discharge may move between any oppositely charged regions—from cloud to earth, from earth to cloud, or
10 from cloud to cloud. It was calculated as early as 1887 that the earth would lose almost all its charge in less than an hour unless the supply were replenished; that is, on a global scale, lightning will discharge to the earth every hour a quantity of electricity equal to the earth's
15 entire charge. Thunderstorms are thus an electromagnetic as well as a thermodynamic necessity. It has been reckoned that the earth experiences some 1,800 storms per hour, or 44,000 per day. Collectively, these storms produce 100 cloud-to-ground discharges per second, or
20 better than 8 million per day globally. And these estimates are probably low. The total energy in lightning bolts varies greatly, but about 250 kilowatt hours of electricity are packed into each stroke. Almost 75 percent of this total energy is lost to heat during discharge.

25 Two types of discharge patterns are commonly identified: the cold stroke, whose main return [ground-to-cloud] stroke is of intense current but of short duration, and the hot stroke, involving lesser currents of longer duration. Cold lightning, with its high voltage,
30 generally has mechanical or explosive effects; hot lightning is more apt to start fires. Studies in the Northern Rockies suggest that about one stroke in 25 has the electrical characteristics needed to start a fire. Whether it does or not depends strongly on the object it
35 strikes, the fuel properties of the object, and the local weather. Ignition requires both heat and kindling. Lightning supplies the one with its current and occasionally finds the other among the fine fuels of rotten wood, needles, grass, or dustlike debris blown from a
40 tree by the explosive shock of the bolt itself.

The consequences of lightning are complex. Any natural force of this magnitude will influence the biological no less than the geophysical environment, and the secondary effects of lightning are significant to life.
45 Lightning helps to fix atmospheric nitrogen into a form that rain can bring to earth. In areas of heavy thunderstorm activity, lightning can function as a major predator on trees, either through direct injury or by physiological damage. In the ponderosa pine forests of
50 Arizona, for example, one forester has estimated that lightning mortality runs between 0.7 and 1.0 percent per year. Other researchers have placed mortality as high as 25—33 percent. For southern pines, the figure may be even steeper. A study in Arkansas calculated
55 that 70 percent of mortality, by volume, was due to

lightning. These figures describe only direct injury, primarily the mechanical destruction of branches and bole; the other major causes of mortality—insects, wind, and mistletoe—are likely secondary effects brought about
60 in trees weakened by lightning. All of these effects, in turn, may be camouflaged by fire induced by lightning.

The process of "electrocution" is increasingly recognized. Lightning scorch areas of between 0.25 and 25 acres have been identified. Nor is the process lim-
65 ited to trees: it has been documented for grasses, tomatoes, potatoes, cabbages, tea, and other crops. Long attributed to inscrutable "die-offs" or to infestation by insects or diseases (often a secondary effect), such sites are now recognized worldwide as a product of physio-
70 logical trauma caused by lightning.

The most spectacular product of lightning is fire. Except in tropical rain forests and on ice-mantled land masses, lightning fire has occurred in every terrestrial environment on the globe, contributing to a natural
75 mosaic of vegetation types. Even in tropical landscapes lightning bombardment by itself may frequently be severe enough to produce a mosaic pattern similar to that resulting from lightning fire. Lightning fires have ignited desert grasslands, tundra, chaparral, swamp-
80 lands, marshes, grasslands, and, of course, forests. Though the intensity and frequency of these fires vary by region, their existence is undeniable.

Sample Passage VII

INFORMATIONAL: This passage is adapted from "Publish and Punish: Science's Snowball Effect" by Jon Van (©1997 by The Chicago Tribune Company).

It's a scientific finding so fundamental that it certainly will make the history books and maybe snag a Nobel Prize if it pans out, but the notion that cosmic snowballs are constantly pelting Earth is something
5 Louis Frank just as soon would have ducked.

Frank is the University of Iowa physicist whose research led him to declare more than a decade ago that Earth is being bombarded by hundreds of house-sized comets day after day that rain water on our planet and
10 are the reason we have oceans. That weather report caused the widely respected scientist to acquire a certain reputation among his colleagues as a bit unstable, an otherwise estimable fellow whose hard work may have pushed him over the edge.

15 Frank and his associate, John Sigwarth, probably went a way toward salvaging their reputations when they presented new evidence that leaves little doubt Earth is indeed being bombarded by *something* in a manner consistent with Frank's small-comet theory.
20 Rather than gloating or anticipating glory, Frank seemed relieved that part of a long ordeal was ending. "I knew we'd be in for it when we first put forth the small-comet theory," Frank conceded, "but I was naive about just how bad it would be. We were outvoted by
25 about 10,000 to 1 by our colleagues. I thought it would have been more like 1,000 to 1."

To the non-scientist this may seem a bit strange. After all, the point of science is to discover information and insights about how nature works. Shouldn't every
30 scientist be eager to overturn existing ideas and replace them with his or her own? In theory, that is the case, but in practice, scientists are almost as loath to embrace radically new ideas as the rest of us.

"Being a scientist puts you into a constant schizo-
35 phrenic existence," contends Richard Zare, chairman of the National Science Board. "You have to believe and yet question beliefs at the same time. If you are a complete cynic and believe nothing, you do nothing and get nowhere, but if you believe too much, you fool your-
40 self."

It was in the early 1980s when the small-comet theory started to haunt Frank and Sigwarth, who was Frank's graduate student studying charged particles called plasmas, which erupt from the sun and cause the
45 aurora borealis (northern lights). As they analyzed photos of the electrical phenomena that accompany sunspots, they noted dark specks appearing in several images from NASA's Dynamics Explorer 1 satellite. They assumed these were caused by static in the trans-
50 mission.

After a while their curiosity about the dark spots grew into a preoccupation, then bordered on obsession.

Try as they did, the scientists couldn't find any plausible explanation of the pattern of dark spots that
55 appeared on their images. The notion that the equipment was picking up small amounts of water entering Earth's upper atmosphere kept presenting itself as the most likely answer.

Based on their images, the Iowa scientists esti-
60 mated 20 comets an hour—each about 30 feet or so across and carrying 100 tons of water—were bombarding the Earth. At that rate, they would produce water vapor that would add about an inch of water to the planet every 10,000 years, Frank concluded. That may
65 not seem like much, but when talking about a planet billions of years old, it adds up.

Such intimate interaction between Earth and space suggests a fundamentally different picture of human evolution—which depends on water—than is com-
70 monly presented by scientists. Frank had great difficulty getting his ideas into a physics journal 11 years ago and was almost hooted from the room when he presented his theory at scientific meetings. Despite the derision, colleagues continued to respect Frank's main-
75 stream work on electrically charged particles in space and the imaging cameras he designed that were taken aboard recent NASA spacecraft to explore Earth's polar regions.

Unbeknown to most, in addition to gathering
80 information on the northern lights, Frank and Sigwarth designed the equipment to be able to snatch better views of any small comets the spacecraft might happen upon. It was those images from the latest flights that caused even harsh critics of the small-comet theory to
85 concede that some water-bearing objects appear to be entering Earth's atmosphere with regularity.

To be sure, it has not been proved that they are comets, let alone that they have anything to do with the oceans. But Frank's evidence opens the matter up to
90 study. Had he been a researcher of lesser standing, his theory probably would have died long ago.

Chapter 8:
Improving Your Science Score

The ACT science test asks you to answer 40 multiple-choice questions (34 scored) in 40 minutes. The questions measure the interpretation, analysis, evaluation, and problem-solving skills associated with science. The science test is made up of several passages, each of which is followed by multiple-choice questions.

Content of the ACT Science Test

The content areas of the ACT science test parallel the content of courses commonly taught in grades 7 through 12 and in entry-level college courses. Passages on the test represent the following content areas (examples of subjects included in each content area are given in parentheses):

- **Biology** (cell biology, botany, zoology, microbiology, ecology, biochemistry, genetics, and evolution)

- **Chemistry** (properties of matter, acids and bases, kinetics and equilibria, thermo-chemistry, organic chemistry, and nuclear chemistry)

- **Earth and Space sciences** (geology, meteorology, oceanography, environmental science, stars, planets, galaxies, and the universe)

- **Physics** (mechanics, gravitation, thermodynamics, electromagnetism, fluids, solids, and optics)

Advanced knowledge in these areas is not required, but background knowledge acquired in general, introductory science courses may be needed to correctly respond to some of the items. Some passages will have a secondary content code of Engineering and Design Thinking as the science content is applied to investigating and solving real-world problems.

The science test stresses science skills and practices over recall of scientific content, complex mathematics skills, and reading ability. The science skills and practices fall into three reporting categories. A brief description of each reporting category is as follows.

- **Interpretation of Data:** Manipulate and analyze scientific data presented in tables, graphs, and diagrams (e.g., recognize trends in data, translate tabular data into graphs, interpolate and extrapolate, and reason mathematically).

- **Scientific Investigation:** Understand experimental tools, procedures, and design (e.g., identify variables and controls) and compare, extend, and modify experiments (e.g., predict the results of additional trials).

- **Evaluation of Models, Inferences, and Experimental Results:** Judge the validity of scientific information and formulate conclusions and predictions based on that information (e.g., determine which explanation for a scientific phenomenon is supported by new findings).

The use of calculators is not permitted on the science test but should also not be needed.

Format of the ACT Science Test

The scientific information presented in each passage of the ACT science test is conveyed in one of three different formats:

- The **Data Representation** format requires you to understand, evaluate, and interpret information presented in graphic or tabular form.

- The **Research Summaries** format requires you to understand, evaluate, analyze, and interpret the design, execution, and results of one or more experiments.

- The **Conflicting Viewpoints** format requires you to evaluate several alternative theories, hypotheses, or viewpoints on a specific observable phenomenon.

You'll find examples of the kinds of passages that you're likely to find in each of the formats in the pages that follow.

The sample ACT science test passages and questions in this section are representative of those you'll encounter in the actual ACT. The following chart illustrates the content area, format, and topic covered by each sample passage given in the remainder of this section:

Passage	Content area	Format	Topic of passage
I	Chemistry	Data Representation	Calorimetry
II	Physics	Research Summaries	Illuminance
III	Biology	Conflicting Viewpoints	Conjugation

Data Representation Format

This type of passage presents scientific information in charts, tables, graphs, and diagrams similar to those found in science journals and texts. Examples of tables used in an actual Data Representation passage administered to students are found in Sample Passage I that follows.

The questions you'll find in the Data Representation format ask you to interpret charts and tables, read graphs, evaluate scatterplots, and analyze information presented in diagrams. There are five sample questions presented with the sample Data Representation passage.

Sample Passage I

A *bomb calorimeter* is used to determine the amount of heat released when a substance is burned in oxygen (Figure 1). The heat, measured in kilojoules (kJ), is calculated from the change in temperature of the water in the bomb calorimeter. Table 1 shows the amounts of heat released when different foods were burned in a bomb calorimeter. Table 2 shows the amounts of heat released when different amounts of sucrose (table sugar) were burned. Table 3 shows the amounts of heat released when various chemical compounds were burned.

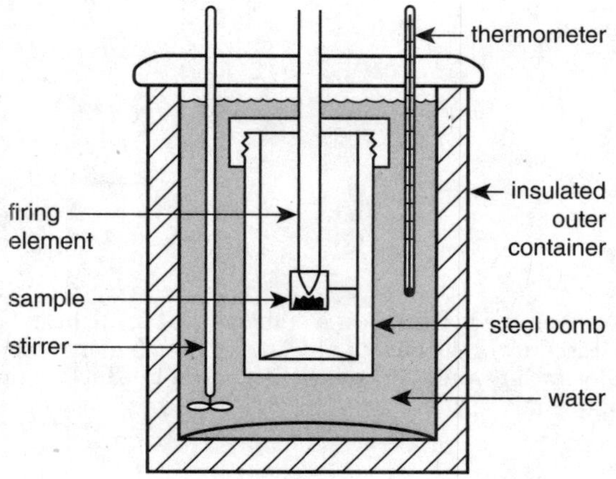

thermometer

firing element

sample

stirrer

insulated outer container

steel bomb

water

Figure 1

Figure 1 adapted from Antony C. Wilbraham, Dennis D. Staley, and Michael S. Matta, *Chemistry.* ©1995 by Addison-Wesley Publishing Company, Inc.

Table 2	
Amount of sucrose (g)	Heat released (kJ)
0.1	1.6
0.5	8.0
1.0	16.0
2.0	32.1
4.0	64.0

Table 3			
Chemical compound	Molecular formula	Mass (g)	Heat released (kJ)
Methanol	CH_3OH	0.5	11.4
Ethanol	C_2H_5OH	0.5	14.9
Benzene	C_6H_6	0.5	21.0
Octane	C_8H_{18}	0.5	23.9

Table 1			
Food	Mass (g)	Change in water temperature (°C)	Heat released (kJ)
Bread	1.0	8.3	10.0
Cheese	1.0	14.1	17.0
Egg	1.0	5.6	6.7
Potato	1.0	2.7	3.2

Table 1 adapted from American Chemical Society, *ChemCom: Chemistry in the Community.* ©1993 by American Chemical Society.

1. According to Tables 1 and 2, as the mass of successive sucrose samples increased, the change in the water temperature produced when the sample was burned most likely:

    A. increased only.
    B. decreased only.
    C. increased, then decreased.
    D. remained the same.

2. Which of the following graphs best illustrates the relationship between the heat released by the foods listed in Table 1 and the change in water temperature?

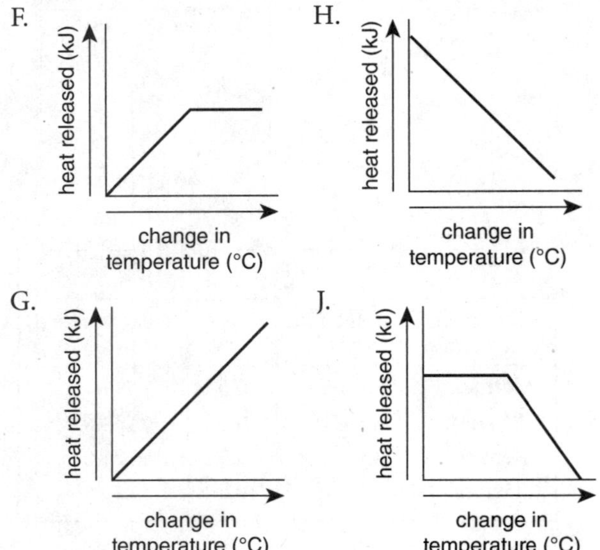

4. Which of the following lists the foods from Tables 1 and 2 in increasing order of the amount of heat released per gram of food?
    F. Potato, egg, bread, sucrose, cheese
    G. Sucrose, cheese, bread, egg, potato
    H. Bread, cheese, egg, potato, sucrose
    J. Sucrose, potato, egg, bread, cheese

3. Based on the data in Table 2, one can conclude that when the mass of sucrose is decreased by one-half, the amount of heat released when it is burned in a bomb calorimeter will:
    A. increase by one-half.
    B. decrease by one-half.
    C. increase by one-fourth.
    D. decrease by one-fourth.

5. Based on the information in Tables 1 and 2, the heat released from the burning of 5.0 g of potato in a bomb calorimeter would most likely be closest to which of the following?
    A.   5 kJ
    B. 10 kJ
    C. 15 kJ
    D. 20 kJ

Discussion of Sample Passage I (Data Representation)

According to this Data Representation passage, the amount of heat generated when a material is burned in oxygen can be determined using a *bomb calorimeter*. The bomb calorimeter has an outer shell made of an insulating material. Inside this shell is a *bomb* (steel casing) immersed in a fixed amount of water. When a material is burned inside the bomb, the water absorbs heat generated by the combustion, causing the temperature of the water to increase. The amount of the increase in water temperature depends on the amount of heat absorbed by the water. So, if we measure the increase in water temperature, we can calculate the amount of heat released when a material is burned inside the bomb.

Note that the passage contains three tables. Table 1 lists the temperature change of the water and the amount of heat generated when 1 g of each of four foods is burned in the calorimeter. Table 2 lists the amounts of heat released when various quantities of the sugar sucrose are burned. Table 3 lists several chemical compounds and their chemical formulas, as well as the amount of heat released for each compound when 0.5 g of the compound is burned in the calorimeter.

> **1.** According to Tables 1 and 2, as the mass of successive sucrose samples increased, the change in the water temperature produced when the sample was burned most likely:
>
> **A.** increased only.
> **B.** decreased only.
> **C.** increased, then decreased.
> **D.** remained the same.

Question 1 asks you to determine how the change in water temperature varied as the amount of sucrose burned increased, based on the data in Tables 1 and 2. Notice that the change in water temperature and the amount of heat released are listed in Table 1 for each material burned. In Table 2, the amount of sucrose burned and the amount of heat released are listed, but the change in water temperature is not listed. Let us assume that the relationship between the amount of heat released and the change in water temperature for sucrose is the same as the relationship between the amount of heat released and the change in water temperature for the materials listed in Table 1. According to Table 2, as the amount of sucrose burned increased, the amount of heat released steadily increased. According to Table 1, as the amount of heat released increased, the magnitude of the change in water temperature steadily increased. Therefore, as the amount of sucrose burned increased, the magnitude of the change in the water temperature steadily increased. The best answer is **A**.

> **2.** Which of the following graphs best illustrates the relationship between the heat released by the foods listed in Table 1 and the change in water temperature?

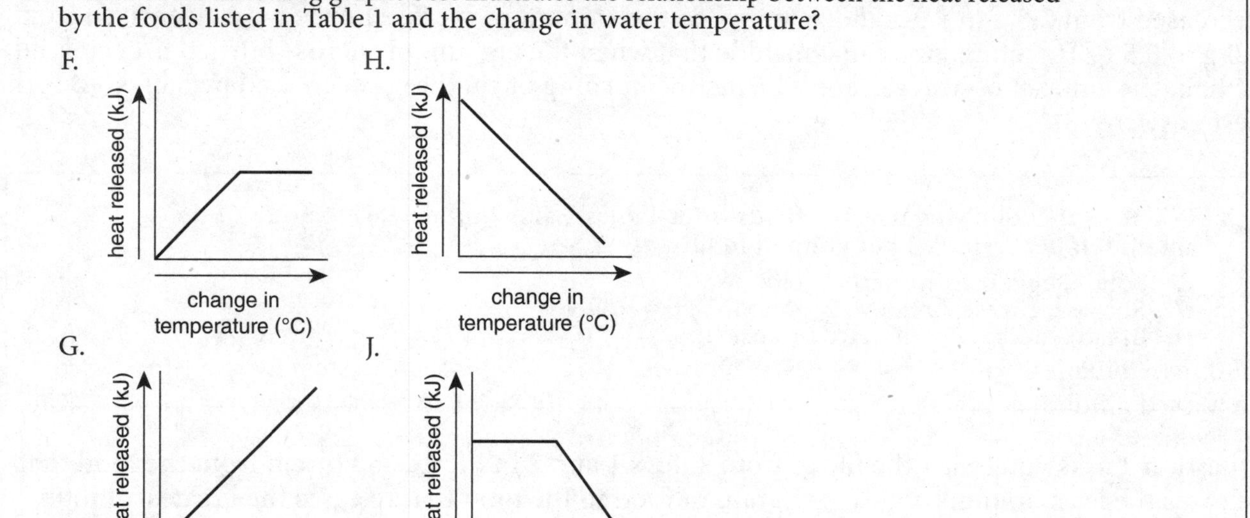

Question 2 asks you to choose a graph that best illustrates the relationship between the amount of heat released and the change in water temperature for the four substances listed in Table 1. According to the data in Table 1, as the change in water temperature increased, the amount of heat released steadily increased. No data in Table 1 supports the conclusion that as the change in water temperature increased the amount of heat released decreased or remained constant. Therefore, **G** is the best answer.

---

3. Based on the data in Table 2, one can conclude that when the mass of sucrose is decreased by one-half, the amount of heat released when it is burned in a bomb calorimeter will:

  A. increase by one-half.
  B. decrease by one-half.
  C. increase by one-fourth.
  D. decrease by one-fourth.

Question 3 asks you to predict, based on the data in Table 2, the fractional change in the amount of heat released by sucrose when the amount of sucrose burned is decreased by half. An examination of the data in Table 2 shows that when the amount of sucrose burned was decreased by half, the amount of heat released decreased by half. For example, when the amount of sucrose burned was decreased from 4.0 g to 2.0 g, the amount of heat released decreased from 64.0 kJ to 32.1 kJ; that is, the amount of heat released also decreased by half. (The amount of heat released actually decreased by 31.9 kJ, which is not exactly half of 64.0 kJ, but the 0.1 kJ difference between 31.9 kJ and 32.0 kJ can be attributed to limitations in the precision of the measurements [the amount of heat released is rounded off to the nearest 0.1 kJ] and can be ignored.) The amount of heat released was also decreased by half when the amount of sucrose burned was decreased from 2.0 g to 1.0 g and again when the amount of sucrose burned was decreased from 1.0 g to 0.5 g. Therefore, one can conclude that when the amount of sucrose burned is decreased by half, the amount of heat released during the burning of sucrose is decreased by half, so **B** is the best answer.

---

4. Which of the following lists the foods from Tables 1 and 2 in increasing order of the amount of heat released per gram of food?

  F. Potato, egg, bread, sucrose, cheese
  G. Sucrose, cheese, bread, egg, potato
  H. Bread, cheese, egg, potato, sucrose
  J. Sucrose, potato, egg, bread, cheese

Question 4 asks you to list the foods from Tables 1 and 2 in increasing order, from the food that releases the least amount of heat per gram of food to the food that releases the greatest amount of heat per gram of food. According to Table 1, the amount of heat released was determined for 1 g samples of each of the foods listed. Therefore, the amount of heat listed in Table 1 for each food item is the amount of heat released per gram of food. In Table 2, the amount of heat released is given for various masses of sucrose. To get the amount of heat released per gram of sucrose we can divide the amount of heat released by the mass of sucrose that was burned. However, an easier method is to notice that a trial was conducted using 1.0 g of sucrose, and during that trial, the amount of heat released was 16.0 kJ. Therefore, the amount of heat released per g of sucrose was 16.0 kJ/g. An inspection of the heat released by the combustion of the foods in Table 1 shows that the potato sample released the least amount of heat (3.2 kJ/g), followed by the egg sample (6.7 kJ/g), the bread sample (10.0 kJ/g), and the cheese sample (17.0 kJ/g). The amount of heat per g released by sucrose, 16.0 kJ/g, places sucrose between the cheese sample and the bread sample. Therefore, the correct order is potato, egg, bread, sucrose, cheese. The best answer is **F**.

---

5. Based on the information in Tables 1 and 2, the heat released from the burning of 5.0 g of potato in a bomb calorimeter would be closest to which of the following?

   A.   5 kJ
   B.   10 kJ
   C.   15 kJ
   D.   20 kJ

Question 5 asks you to use Tables 1 and 2 to estimate the amount of heat released when 5.0 g of potato is burned. Notice that Table 1 provides you with the amount of heat released (3.2 kJ) when 1.0 g of potato is burned. You might guess that burning 5.0 g of potato in the calorimeter would cause the release of five times the amount of heat released when 1.0 g of potato is burned. Do you have any evidence to support this guess? Table 1 only lists the amount of heat released when 1.0 g of potato is burned. Table 2 provides the amount of heat released from various amounts of sucrose, but not potatoes. In the absence of information to the contrary, you can assume that the relationship between the amount of potato burned and the amount of heat released is similar to the relationship between the amount of sucrose burned and the amount of heat released. According to Table 2, the heat released in kJ equals 16 times the mass of sucrose burned in grams. Note that this relationship holds whether 0.1 g of sucrose is burned or 4.0 g of sucrose is burned. For example, if 0.1 g of sucrose is burned, 0.1 g × 16 kJ released per g of sucrose = 1.6 kJ of heat released. If 4.0 g of sucrose is burned, 4.0 g × 16 kJ released per g of sucrose = 64 kJ of heat released. This relationship is a linear relationship. If the relationship between the amount of potato burned and the amount of heat released is also linear, then burning five times the amount of potato will release five times the amount of heat. Because 3.2 kJ of heat was released when 1.0 g of potato was burned, 5 × 3.2 kJ = 16 kJ will be released when 5.0 g of potato is burned. The answer closest to 16 kJ is 15 kJ, choice **C**.

Research Summaries Format

This type of passage provides descriptions of one or more related experiments or studies similar to those conducted by researchers or science students. The descriptions typically include the design, procedures, and results of the experiments or studies. The results are often depicted in graphs or tables. Sample Passage II provides an example of the Research Summaries format that shows the results of two different experiments with light bulbs. The questions you'll find in the Research Summaries format ask you to understand, evaluate, and interpret the design and procedures of the experiments or studies and to analyze the results. There are five sample questions presented with this sample Research Summaries passage.

Sample Passage II

A student studied illumination using the following equipment:

- 6 identical light bulbs (Bulbs A–F)
- Fixture 1, light fixture for Bulbs A–E
- Fixture 2, light fixture for Bulb F
- 2 identical paraffin blocks
- A sheet of aluminum foil having the same length and width as a paraffin block
- A meterstick

Light could pass through each paraffin block, and each block glowed when light passed through it. The aluminum foil was placed between the 2 blocks. The light fixtures, light bulbs, blocks, foil, and the meterstick were arranged as shown in Figure 1.

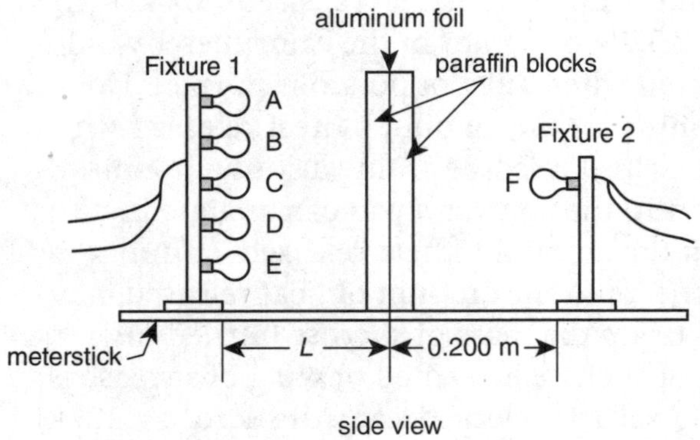

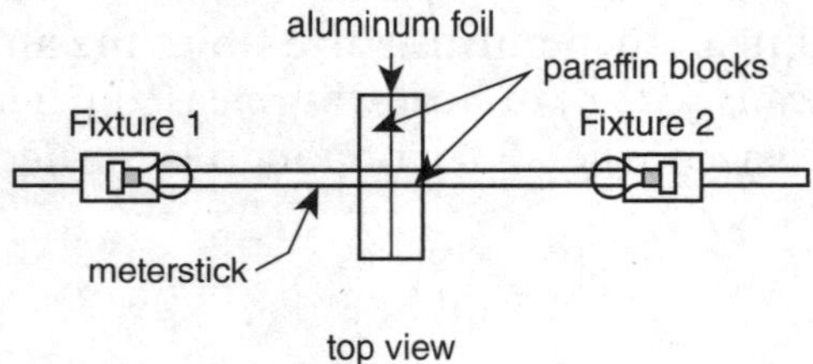

Figure 1

In the following experiments, the base of Fixture 2 was always 0.200 m from the aluminum foil, and L was the distance from the base of Fixture 1 to the aluminum foil. The distance between adjacent bulbs in Fixture 1 was the same for all of the bulbs.

Bulb F was always lit.

Experiment 1

The student turned the room lights off, lit Bulb A, and varied L until the 2 blocks looked equally bright. This process was repeated using Bulbs B–E. The results are shown in Table 1.

Table 1	
Bulb lit (in addition to Bulb F)	L (m) when the blocks looked equally bright
A	0.198
B	0.203
C	0.205
D	0.195
E	0.199

Experiment 2

The procedure from Experiment 1 was repeated using various combinations of Bulbs A–E. The results are shown in Table 2.

Table 2	
Bulb lit (in addition to Bulb F)	L (m) when the blocks looked equally bright
A and B	0.281
A, B, and C	0.347
A, B, C, and D	0.400
A, B, C, D, and E	0.446

6. Which of the following best explains why the student turned off the room lights?
   - F. To ensure that only the light from Bulbs A–F illuminated the 2 paraffin blocks
   - G. To ensure that light from outside the room illuminated the 2 paraffin blocks unequally
   - H. To keep the 2 paraffin blocks from casting shadows, because shadows would make the meterstick harder to read
   - J. To keep the 2 light fixtures from casting shadows, because shadows would make the meterstick harder to read

7. During Experiment 2, suppose the student replaced Fixture 1 with a new fixture. The new fixture held 6 light bulbs, each bulb identical to Bulb F. When all 6 bulbs in the new fixture were lit and the paraffin blocks looked equally bright, L would probably have been closest to:
   - A. 0.262 m.
   - B. 0.331 m.
   - C. 0.415 m.
   - D. 0.490 m.

8. The main purpose of Experiment 1 was to:
   F. calibrate the meterstick.
   G. determine the relationship between L and the number of lit bulbs.
   H. determine if L depended on a lit bulb's position in Fixture 1.
   J. find the brightness of Bulb F.

9. Suppose that all of the light bulbs in Fixture 1 were replaced with a single bulb. Based on Experiments 1 and 2, if the 2 paraffin blocks looked equally bright when Fixture 2 was 0.200 m from the aluminum foil and $L = 0.446$ m, the brightness of the new light bulb was most likely:
   A. $\frac{1}{6}$ the brightness of one of the original bulbs.
   B. $\frac{1}{5}$ the brightness of one of the original bulbs.
   C. 5 times the brightness of one of the original bulbs.
   D. 6 times the brightness of one of the original bulbs.

10. In Experiment 2, suppose the student had replaced Bulb F with a much brighter light bulb, Bulb G. Compared to L when Bulb F was used, L when Bulb G was used would have been:
    F. greater for every combination of lit bulbs.
    G. smaller for every combination of lit bulbs.
    H. smaller when Bulbs A–E were simultaneously lit and greater when other combinations of light bulbs were lit.
    J. greater when both Bulbs A and B were simultaneously lit and smaller when other combinations of light bulbs were lit.

Discussion of Sample Passage II (Research Summaries)

This Research Summaries passage describes two experiments in which a student uses two identical paraffin blocks to compare the brightness of the light from one source (Fixture 1) with the brightness of the light from another source (Fixture 2). Fixture 1 contains five light bulbs, Bulbs A through E, and Fixture 2 contains only one light bulb, Bulb F (see Figure 1 in the passage). The two paraffin blocks are set between the fixtures. The two blocks are separated by a sheet of aluminum foil, so that the block on the left is illuminated only by bulbs in Fixture 1, and the block on the right is illuminated only by Bulb F in Fixture 2. The distance, L, between Fixture 1 and the aluminum foil can be varied, but the distance between Fixture 2 and the foil, 0.200 m, is fixed. This passage would have a secondary coding for engineering as it examines how to arrange lights to meet illumination needs, which could be applied to real-world problems like lighting a field, a parking lot, or a street.

In Experiment 1, one bulb at a time is lit in Fixture 1, and Bulb F is lit in Fixture 2. For each combination of lit bulbs, L is varied until the two blocks glow equally brightly. This value of L is recorded in Table 1 along with the combination of lit bulbs used to obtain this value of L. In Experiment 2, two or more bulbs at a time are lit in Fixture 1, and Bulb F is lit in Fixture 2. For each combination of lit bulbs, L is varied until the two blocks glow equally brightly. This value of L is recorded in Table 2 along with the combination of lit bulbs.

6. Which of the following best explains why the student turned off the room lights?
   F. To ensure that only the light from Bulbs A–F illuminated the 2 paraffin blocks
   G. To ensure that light from outside the room illuminated the 2 paraffin blocks unequally
   H. To keep the 2 paraffin blocks from casting shadows, because shadows would make the meterstick harder to read
   J. To keep the 2 light fixtures from casting shadows, because shadows would make the meterstick harder to read

Question 6 asks you why the student turned off the room lights before measuring L. Recall that the student was to compare the brightness of the light produced by Fixture 1 to the brightness of the light produced by Fixture 2 under a variety of conditions. The presence of light sources other than Fixtures 1 and 2 could have introduced error into the measurements of L by making one fixture or the other seem brighter than it really was. The overhead lights were turned off so that all of the light on the blocks came from the light bulbs in Fixtures 1 and 2. Thus, **F** is the best answer.

---

7. During Experiment 2, suppose the student replaced Fixture 1 with a new fixture. The new fixture held 6 light bulbs, each bulb identical to Bulb F. When all 6 bulbs in the new fixture were lit and the paraffin blocks looked equally bright, L would probably have been closest to:

    A. 0.262 m.
    B. 0.331 m.
    C. 0.415 m.
    D. 0.490 m.

Question 7 proposes that Fixture 1 be replaced by a different fixture holding six light bulbs instead of five. Each of the light bulbs in the new fixture is identical to Bulb F. The question asks you to estimate L for the case that all six light bulbs in the new fixture, as well as Bulb F, are lit. According to Table 2, as the number of lit bulbs in Fixture 1 increased from two to five, L increased. So if the new fixture is used, increasing the number of lit bulbs from five to six, one would expect L to be greater than the value of L given in Table 2 for five lit bulbs in Fixture 1, 0.446 m. Only **D** contains a value for L exceeding 0.446 m, so **D** is the best answer.

---

8. The main purpose of Experiment 1 was to:

    F. calibrate the meterstick.
    G. determine the relationship between L and the number of lit bulbs.
    H. determine if L depended on a lit bulb's position in Fixture 1.
    J. find the brightness of Bulb F.

Question 8 asks you to determine the main purpose of Experiment 1. In Experiment 1, one bulb at a time was lit in Fixture 1, but the location of the lit bulb in Fixture 1 was varied. Thus, the main purpose of Experiment 1 must have been to determine the effect, if any, that the location of the lit bulb had on the value of L. Only **H** states that the purpose of Experiment 1 was to determine if the position of the lit bulb within Fixture 1 affected L, so **H** must be the best answer.

---

9. Suppose that all of the light bulbs in Fixture 1 were replaced with a single bulb. Based on Experiments 1 and 2, if the 2 paraffin blocks looked equally bright when Fixture 2 was 0.200 m from the aluminum foil and $L = 0.446$ m, the brightness of the new light bulb was most likely:

    A. $\frac{1}{6}$ the brightness of one of the original bulbs.

    B. $\frac{1}{5}$ the brightness of one of the original bulbs.

    C. 5 times the brightness of one of the original bulbs.

    D. 6 times the brightness of one of the original bulbs.

Question 9 proposes that the five light bulbs in Fixture 1 be replaced with a single light bulb, and that when the new bulb and Bulb F are lit, for the two blocks to glow equally brightly, L must equal 0.446 m. You are asked to compare the brightness of the new bulb to the brightness of one of the original bulbs in Fixture 1. According to Table 2, the two paraffin blocks glowed equally brightly when all five bulbs in Fixture 1 were lit and L was 0.446 m, the same as the L obtained with the new bulb. Thus, the brightness of the new bulb would have to equal the sum of the brightness of the five original bulbs. Because each of the five original bulbs had the same brightness, the new bulb would have to be five times as bright as one of the original bulbs. Only **C** is consistent with this conclusion, so the best answer is **C**.

---

10. In Experiment 2, suppose the student had replaced Bulb F with a much brighter light bulb, Bulb G. Compared to L when Bulb F was used, L when Bulb G was used would have been:

   F. greater for every combination of lit bulbs.
   G. smaller for every combination of lit bulbs.
   H. smaller when Bulbs A–E were simultaneously lit and greater when other combinations of light bulbs were lit.
   J. greater when both Bulbs A and B were simultaneously lit and smaller when other combinations of light bulbs were lit.

Question 10 proposes that in Experiment 2, Bulb F be replaced by a much brighter bulb, Bulb G. For each combination of lit bulbs in Fixture 1 and Bulb G lit in Fixture 2, when the two paraffin blocks are equally bright, how would the value of L compare to that obtained when Bulb F was used in Fixture 2? Because Bulb G is brighter than Bulb F and would be the same distance (0.200 m) away from the aluminum foil as Bulb F, the paraffin block closer to Bulb G would glow more brightly than it glowed when Bulb F was used. Thus, for each combination of lit bulbs in Fixture 1, to make the two blocks glow with equal brightness, Fixture 1 would have to be closer to the blocks than when Bulb F was used. That is, when Bulb G was used, L for each combination of lit bulbs in Fixture 1 would have to be less than when Bulb F was used for the two blocks to glow with equal brightness. Only choice **G** is consistent with this conclusion. The best answer is **G**.

Conflicting Viewpoints Format

This type of passage provides several alternative theories, hypotheses, or viewpoints on a specific observable phenomenon. These conflicting viewpoints are based on differing premises or on incomplete data and are inconsistent with one another. Sample Passage III, a biology passage on gene replication, is an example of the Conflicting Viewpoints format. Notice that this passage presents the theories of four different students.

The questions you'll find in Conflicting Viewpoints passages ask you to understand, analyze, evaluate, and compare several competing theories, hypotheses, or viewpoints. Five sample questions are presented with this sample Conflicting Viewpoints passage.

Sample Passage III

Many bacteria contain *plasmids* (small, circular DNA molecules). Plasmids can be transferred from 1 bacterium to another. For this to occur, the plasmid *replicates* (produces a linear copy of itself). The relative position of the genes is the same on the original plasmid and on the linear copy, except that the 2 ends of the linear copy do not immediately connect.

While replication is occurring, 1 end of the linear copy leaves the donor bacterium and enters the recipient bacterium. Thus, the order in which the genes are repli- cated is the same as the order in which they are transferred. Unless this process is interrupted, the entire plasmid is transferred, and its 2 ends connect in the recipient bac-terium.

Four students studied the way in which 6 genes (F, X, R, S, A, and G) on a specific plasmid were donated by a type of bacterium (see the figure). The students determined that the entire plasmid is transferred in 90 min and that the rate of transfer is constant. They also determined that the genes are evenly spaced around the plasmid, so 1 gene is transferred every 15 min. They disagreed, however, about the order in which the genes are replicated and thus transferred. Four models are presented.

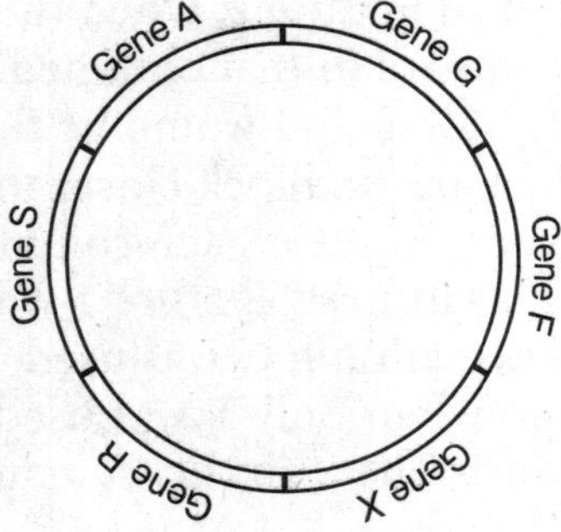

Student 1

Replication always begins between Gene F and Gene X. Gene X is replicated first and Gene F is replicated last.

Student 2

Replication always begins between Gene F and Gene X. However, the direction of replication varies. If Gene F is replicated first, Gene X is replicated last. Conversely, if Gene X is replicated first, Gene F is replicated last.

Student 3

Replication can begin between any 2 genes. Replication then proceeds around the plasmid in a clockwise direction (with respect to the figure). Thus, if Gene S is replicated first, Gene A is replicated second, and Gene R is replicated last.

Student 4

Replication can begin between any 2 genes. Likewise, replication can proceed in either direction. So the order of replication varies.

11. Based on the information presented, if the transfer of the linear copy was interrupted 50 min after transfer began, how many complete genes would have been transferred to the recipient bacterium?

    A. 2
    B. 3
    C. 4
    D. 5

12. Based on the model presented by Student 3, if all 6 genes are replicated and the first gene replicated is Gene G, the third gene replicated would be:

    F. Gene F.
    G. Gene A.
    H. Gene S.
    J. Gene X.

13. Which students believe that any of the 6 genes on the plasmid can be the first gene transferred to a recipient bacterium?

    A. Students 2 and 3
    B. Students 2 and 4
    C. Students 3 and 4
    D. Students 2, 3, and 4.

14. Suppose that Student 2's model is correct and that the transfer of genes between 2 bacteria was interrupted after 30 min. Under these conditions, which of the following genes would definitely NOT be transferred from the donor bacterium to the recipient bacterium?

    F. Gene A
    G. Gene R
    H. Gene G
    J. Gene X

15. Suppose that the transfer of genes between 2 bacteria was interrupted, that the last gene transferred was Gene A, and that no incomplete copies of a gene were transferred. Based on this information, Student 1 would say that transfer was most likely interrupted how many minutes after the transfer began?

    A. 15
    B. 30
    C. 45
    D. 60

Discussion of Sample Passage III (Conflicting Viewpoints)

According to this Conflicting Viewpoints passage, plasmids (small DNA molecules, each molecule consisting of genes arranged in a circle) are found in bacteria. While a plasmid is replicating (producing an identical copy of itself) in one bacterium, the gene copies are being transferred to a second bacterium, the recipient bacterium, eventually forming a complete copy of the plasmid in the recipient bacterium.

Notice the diagram of a plasmid in the passage. The plasmid in the diagram contains six genes. The passage tells us that when the plasmid replicates, it produces a linear copy of itself; that is, the six genes in the copy are arranged in the same order as in the original plasmid, but the genes in the copy are first arranged in a row rather than in a circle. The plasmid copies one gene at a time, and, according to the passage, the gene copies are transferred to the recipient bacterium one at a time in the order in which the copies are produced. For example, if the plasmid copies Gene F, followed by Gene X, Gene F will be transferred to the recipient bacterium first, followed by Gene X. Once all of the genes of the original plasmid have been copied and transferred to a recipient bacterium, the two ends of the linear plasmid copy connect to each other, forming a circle just like the one in the passage.

Four students agree that the rate of gene transfer between bacteria is constant and occurs at the rate of one gene every 15 minutes, so a complete plasmid is transferred between the bacteria in $6 \times 15 = 90$ minutes. However, the identity of the first gene to be replicated and the direction (clockwise or counterclockwise around the circle) in which replication proceeds are subjects of disagreement among the four students.

- According to Student 1, Gene X is always replicated and transferred first, and Gene F is always replicated and transferred last. That is, replication always starts with Gene X and proceeds in a clockwise direction around the plasmid.

- According to Student 2, replication always begins with either Gene F or Gene X. If Gene F is first, then Gene X is last; that is, if replication begins with Gene F, then replication proceeds in a counterclockwise direction around the plasmid. If Gene X is first, then Gene F is last; that is, if replication begins with Gene X, then replication proceeds in a clockwise direction around the plasmid.

- According to Student 3, replication can start with any gene but always proceeds in a clockwise direction around the plasmid.

- According to Student 4, replication can start with any gene and can proceed in either direction around the plasmid.

---

11. Based on the information presented, if the transfer of the linear copy was interrupted 50 min after transfer began, how many complete genes would have been transferred to the recipient bacterium?

    A. 2
    B. 3
    C. 4
    D. 5

Question 11 asks you to predict how many complete genes would have been transferred to the recipient bacterium if gene transfer had been interrupted 50 minutes after transfer had begun. According to the passage, one gene was transferred every 15 minutes. Therefore, three genes would have been transferred in $3 \times 15 = 45$ minutes. A partial gene transfer would have occurred in the remaining 5 minutes, but the question asks about complete gene transfers, so you can ignore the partial gene transfer. The answer is three genes. Therefore, the best choice is **B**.

---

12. Based on the model presented by Student 3, if all 6 genes are replicated and the first gene replicated is Gene G, the third gene replicated would be:

    F. Gene F.
    G. Gene A.
    H. Gene S.
    J. Gene X.

Question 12 asks you to suppose that all six genes in a plasmid are replicated and that Gene G is the first gene replicated. You are asked to predict the third gene replicated, assuming that Student 3's model is correct. According to Student 3's model, replication can start with any gene but always proceeds around the plasmid in a clockwise direction. Therefore, starting with Gene G and proceeding in a clockwise direction, Gene F would be the second gene replicated and Gene X would be the third gene replicated. The best answer is **J**.

---

13. Which students believe that any of the 6 genes on the plasmid can be the first gene transferred to a recipient bacterium?

    A. Students 2 and 3
    B. Students 2 and 4
    C. Students 3 and 4
    D. Students 2, 3, and 4

Question 13 asks which students believe that any of the six genes on the plasmid can be the first gene transferred to a recipient bacterium. According to the passage, the order in which genes are transferred is the same as the order in which genes are replicated. Student 1 asserts that replication always begins with Gene X, so Student 1 would *disagree* with the statement that any of the six genes on the plasmid can be the first gene transferred. Student 2 asserts that replication always begins with either Gene X or Gene F, so Student 2 would *disagree* with the statement that any of the six genes on the plasmid can be the first gene transferred.

According to Students 3 and 4, replication can begin between any two genes on the plasmid, so they *agree* that any of the six genes on the plasmid can be the first gene transferred to a recipient bacterium. Because only Students 3 and 4 agree that any gene on the plasmid can be the first gene transferred, the best answer is **C**.

---

14. Suppose that Student 2's model is correct and that the transfer of genes between 2 bacteria was interrupted after 30 min. Under these conditions, which of the following genes would definitely NOT be transferred from the donor bacterium to the recipient bacterium?

    F. Gene A
    G. Gene R
    H. Gene G
    J. Gene X

Question 14 asks you to suppose that the transfer of genes between two bacteria was interrupted 30 minutes after the transfer began. You are asked to select from among a list of genes (A, R, G, and X) the gene that could NOT have been transferred to the recipient bacterium within the allotted 30 minutes, assuming that Student 2's model is correct. According to the passage, one complete gene transfer occurs every 15 minutes. Therefore, two complete gene transfers would have occurred after $2 \times 15 = 30$ minutes. Based on Student 2's model, gene transfer can start with Gene X and proceed around the plasmid in a clockwise direction, or transfer can start with Gene F and proceed around the plasmid in a counterclockwise direction. If transfer had started with Gene X, Gene R would have been the second gene transferred. If transfer had started with Gene F, Gene G would have been the second gene transferred. Therefore, we conclude Genes X, R, F, and G could have been transferred. The only gene in the list that could not have been transferred is Gene A. Based on Student 2's model, if Gene X had been the first gene transferred, then $4 \times 15 = 60$ minutes would have been required for Gene A to be transferred, because Gene A is the fourth gene in the clockwise direction from Gene X. If Gene F had been the first gene transferred, $3 \times 15 = 45$ minutes would have been required for Gene A to be transferred, because Gene A is the third gene in the counterclockwise direction from Gene F. The best answer is **F**.

---

15. Suppose that the transfer of genes between 2 bacteria was interrupted, that the last gene transferred was Gene A, and that no incomplete copies of a gene were transferred. Based on this information, Student 1 would say that transfer was most likely interrupted how many minutes after the transfer began?

    A. 15
    B. 30
    C. 45
    D. 60

Question 15 asks you to suppose that the transfer of genes between two bacteria was interrupted after the transfer of Gene A had been completed, and that no incomplete transfer of a gene occurred after the transfer of Gene A. You are asked to determine the number of minutes between the time that gene transfer began and the time at which gene transfer was interrupted, assuming that Student 1's model is correct. According to Student 1, Gene X is always transferred first, and Gene F is always transferred last. That is, transfer always starts with Gene X and proceeds in a clockwise direction around the plasmid. If we count genes in the clockwise direction, starting with Gene X, we find that Gene A is the fourth gene, so Gene A would have been the fourth gene transferred. According to the passage, each complete transfer of a gene requires 15 minutes. Thus, the number of minutes between the time at which the transfer of Gene X began and the time at which the transfer of Gene A was completed would have been $4 \times 15 = 60$ minutes. The best answer is **D**.

Answer Key for Science Test Sample Questions

1.	A	6.	F	11.	B
2.	G	7.	D	12.	J
3.	B	8.	H	13.	C
4.	F	9.	C	14.	F
5.	C	10.	G	15.	D

Strategies for Taking the ACT Science Test

Performance on the ACT science test relies mainly on the ability to understand and process scientific information presented in various formats but can also be affected by problem-solving strategies and skills. The following sections describe strategies and skills specifically for improving your ACT science score.

Develop a Problem-Solving Method

Because you have only a limited time in which to take the science test, you may find it helpful to work out a general problem-solving method that you can use for all or most of the questions. The method described here is certainly not the only way to solve the problems, but it is one that works for most science problems. Whether you see a way to adapt this method, or you work out your own approach, use the method that works best for you.

One approach to solving problems is to break the process into a series of smaller steps, such as these:

1. Restate the problem in your own words.

2. Decide what information is needed to solve the problem.

3. Extract the needed information from the passage. Information may include data, concepts, or even conclusions you've been able to draw from the information provided.

4.   Consider any additional scientific knowledge (terms or concepts) you may have.

5.   Organize the information and use reason to arrive at the answer.

6.   Compare your answer to the answer choices and choose the option you think is correct.

Take Notes

As you read a question, take notes in the test booklet or, when taking the test on computer, on scratch paper to record what the question is asking and what information you have at your disposal to answer the question. Sometimes, the process of writing down or reviewing notes reveals the answer or helps you develop an effective approach to finding the answer. You can also take brief notes when you read, identifying important aspects of a viewpoint or the independent and dependent variable of an investigation.

Pace Yourself

Remember, you have 40 minutes to read several passages and their accompanying questions (40 questions altogether). That's about 5.7 minutes for each of the seven passages and the accompanying questions. You can think of it as 40 questions in 40 minutes, or a minute per question. If you're like most people, you'll find some of the passages more familiar and probably easier than some of the others, so it's a good idea to try to work fast enough to allow yourself time to come back to any questions you have trouble answering the first time.

Practice Interpreting Graphs, Tables, and Diagrams

Much of the information you need to answer the science test questions is presented graphically in the form of graphs, tables, and diagrams. Practice interpreting tables and different types of graphs, including pie charts, line charts, bar or column charts, and scatter charts, especially those included in science articles. Examine graphs and tables closely until you understand the data and can pick out specific pieces of data.

Tip: Pay attention to any and all text in graphs, tables, or diagrams, because any of this text is likely present to serve as instruction for how to interpret the data:

Graphs

Read the axis labels and the labels for any lines (curves) present. Typically, the y-axis indicates what is being measured (the dependent variable) and the x-axis most often indicates what is being manipulated (the independent variable). Some graphs may have a legend (labeled *Key*) that identifies line styles and the quantities they represent. Graphs may also have notes at the bottom of the graph to supply additional information.

Tables

Look at the column and row headings, which will identify quantities and their units of measure. Often (but not always) manipulated variables (independent variables) will be on the left side of the table and the measured quantity (the dependent variable) will be to the right of the table. Some tables will have notes at the bottom that provide vital information for interpreting the data.

Diagrams

Diagrams often contain labeled parts and could represent everything from a food web to a laboratory setup or show the cross-section of an object, such as the layers of Earth or of Earth's atmosphere. Diagrams generally contain more text than numbers. Look for a title (above the diagram) or a caption (below the diagram) and for labels on the diagram itself. The diagram may not have a title, but parts of it may be labeled, as in a diagram of a laboratory setup that sheds light on how an experiment works.

Give yourself some time to figure out what the graph, table, or diagram is showing you in general. You can always look at these graphic representations more closely when answering questions, but having a general idea of what they show may shed light on what the questions are asking.

Make the Most of the Information in Graphs

Graphs illustrate data in ways that can be very useful if you follow a few rules. First, it's important to identify what is being displayed in the graph (e.g., mass, volume, velocity). What unit or units of measurement is (are) used (e.g., grams, liters, kilometers per hour)? Graphs usually have axis labels that provide this information and some will have a key or legend or other short explanation of the information presented. Many graphs consist of two axes (horizontal and vertical), both of which will be labeled, and some may have dual axes with more than one curve. Remember, the first thing to find out about any graph is exactly what the numbers represent.

Once you've identified what is being presented in a graph, you can begin to look for trends in the data. The main reason for using a graph is to show how one characteristic of the data tends to influence other characteristics.

For a coordinate graph, notice how a change on the horizontal axis (or x-axis) relates to the position of the variable on the vertical axis (or y-axis). If the curve shows angles upward from lower left to upper right (as in Figure 1a), then, as the variable shown on the x-axis increases, so does the variable on the y-axis (a *direct relationship*). An example of a direct relationship is that a person's weight increases as his or her height increases. If the curve goes from the upper left to the lower right (as in Figure 1b), then, as the variable on the x-axis increases, the variable on the y-axis decreases (an *inverse relationship*). An example of an inverse relationship is that the more players there are on a soccer team, the less time each of them gets to play (assuming everyone gets equal playing time). If the graph shows a vertical or horizontal line (as in Figure 1c), the variables are probably unrelated.

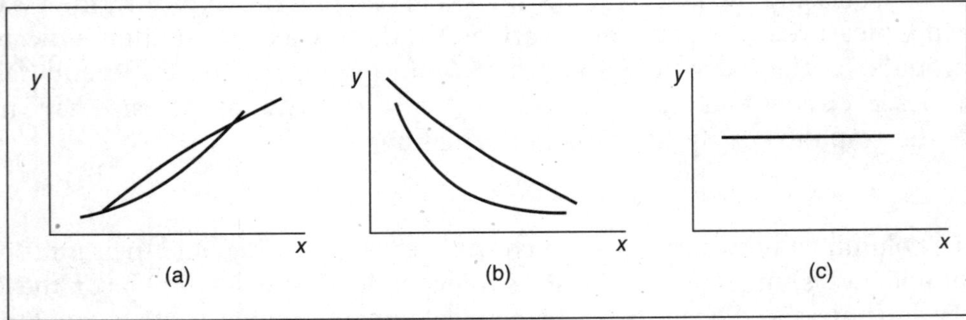

Figure 1

Sometimes, a question will ask you to estimate a value for one characteristic based on a given value of another characteristic that is beyond the limits of the curve shown on the graph. In this case, the solution will require you to *extrapolate,* or extend, the graph. If the curve is a relatively straight line, just use your pencil to extend that line far enough for the value called for to be included. If the graphed line is a curve, use your best judgment to extend the line to follow the apparent pattern. Figure 2 shows how to extend both types of graphs.

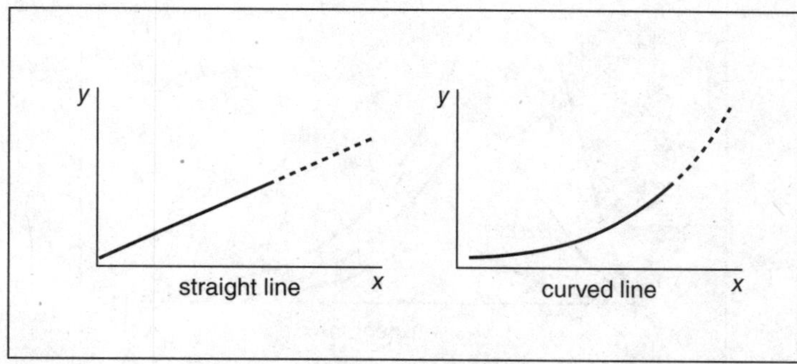

Figure 2

Another type of graph problem asks you to estimate a value that falls between two known values on a curve. This process is called *interpolation*. If the curve is shown, it amounts to finding a point on the curve that corresponds to a given value for one characteristic and reading the value for the other characteristic. (For example, "For a given x, find y.") If only scattered points are shown on the graph, draw a "best-fit line," a line that comes close to all of the points. Use this line to estimate the middle value. Figure 3 shows a best-fit line.

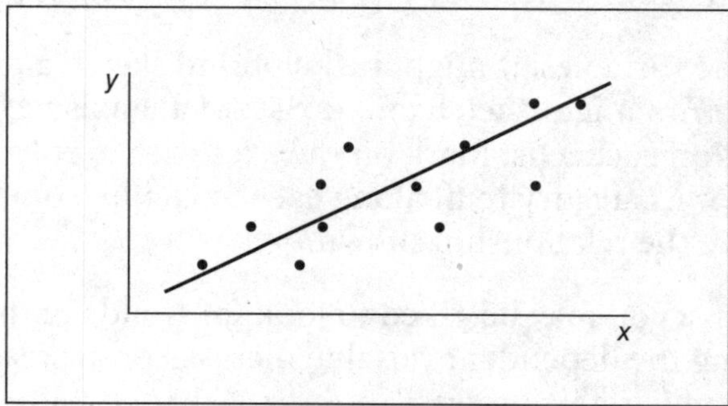

Figure 3

Improving Your Score

One very useful kind of graph shows more than one curve on the same pair of axes. Such a graph might be used when the results of a number of experiments are compared or when an experiment involves more than two variables. Analysis of this sort of graph requires that you determine the relationship shown by each curve and then determine how the curves are related to one another. Figure 4 shows a graph with multiple curves.

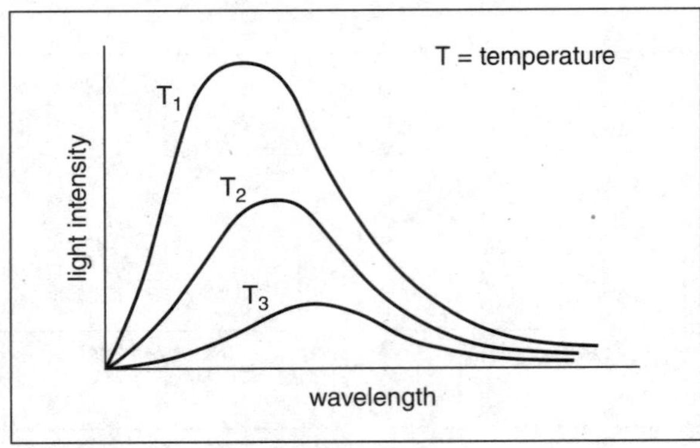

Figure 4

Make the Most of the Information in Tables

To understand what a table is showing you, you need to identify the information or data presented. You need to know two things about the information or data: the purpose it serves in the experiment and the unit (or units) of measurement used to quantify it. Generally, experiments intentionally vary one characteristic (the independent variable) to see how it affects another (the dependent variable). Tables may report results for either or both.

Once you have identified the variables, it might be helpful to sketch a graph to illustrate the relationship between them. You might sketch an x-axis and a y-axis next to the table and decide which variable to represent on each axis. Mark off the axes with evenly spaced intervals that enable all of the numbers for a category to fit along each axis. Plot some points. Again, draw a best-fit line and characterize the relationship shown.

As with graphs and diagrams, you may be asked to look for trends in the data. For example, do the numbers representing the dependent variable increase or decrease as the numbers representing the independent variable increase or decrease? If no pattern is clear, you may want to sketch a rough graph as discussed above. You may also need to make predictions about values of quantities between the data points shown (interpolation) or beyond the limits of those shown on the table (extrapolation). Another type of problem may require you to compare data from multiple columns of a table or between two or more graphs or tables. A simple examination of the numbers may be enough to see a relationship, but you may find it helpful to sketch a graph containing a curve for each category. The curves may be compared as described previously in "Make the Most of the Information in Graphs."

Develop an Understanding of Scientific Investigations

When working with a Research Summaries passage, you should be able to understand scientific processes. This includes identifying the designs of experiments, identifying assumptions and hypotheses underlying the experiments, identifying controls and variables, determining the effects of altering the experiments, identifying similarities and differences between the experiments, identifying the strengths and weaknesses of the experiments, developing other experiments that will test the same hypothesis, making hypotheses or predictions from research results, and creating models from research results.

Carefully Analyze Conflicting Viewpoints

When reading a Conflicting Viewpoints passage, first read the introductory information. This describes the phenomena about which the viewpoints will differ. It may also present a graph, table, or diagram, as well as discuss aspects that all of the viewpoints share. Then, read each viewpoint closely and note what is the same and different in each. Note each viewpoint's strengths and weaknesses. Use your own scientific knowledge and common sense to draw conclusions about each viewpoint. Which viewpoint sounds most credible? Which has the most evidence to back it up? With an understanding of and opinion about each viewpoint, you are better equipped to understand and answer questions about them.

Prep Online!

Want even more ways to prep? Go to https://study.learning.wiley.com/ to access our online platform and take practice tests. To get started, go to https://study.learning.wiley.com/, select your title, answer the redemption question, and start studying!

Chapter 9: Improving Your Score on the Optional Writing Test

On the ACT writing test, you have 40 minutes to read a prompt and to plan and write an essay in response to it. The prompts on the writing test cover a variety of subjects intended to reflect engaging conversations about contemporary issues, and they are designed to be appropriate for response in a 40-minute timed test.

The writing test is an optional test on the ACT. Should you decide to take the writing test, it will be administered after the multiple-choice tests. Taking the writing test will not affect your scores on any of the multiple-choice tests or the Composite score. Rather, *in addition* to your scores from the multiple-choice tests and your Composite score, you will receive a writing score and may receive an English Language Arts (ELA) score.

You will have a short break between the end of the last multiple-choice test and the beginning of the writing test.

Content of the ACT Writing Test

The test consists of one writing prompt that describes a complex issue and provides three different perspectives on the issue. You are asked to read the prompt and write an essay in which you develop your own perspective on the issue. Your essay must analyze the relationship between your perspective and one or more perspectives. You may adopt one of the perspectives given in the prompt as your own, or you may introduce one that is completely different from those given. The test offers guidance and structure for planning and prewriting, but planning and prewriting are optional and do not count toward the score. Your score will also not be affected by the perspective you take on the issue. Your essay will be evaluated based on the evidence that it provides of your ability to do the following:

- Clearly state your own perspective on a complex issue and analyze the relationship between your perspective and at least one other perspective.

- Develop and support your ideas with reasoning and examples.

- Organize your ideas clearly and logically.

- Communicate your ideas effectively in standard written English.

How Your Essay Will Be Scored

Your essay will be scored analytically using a rubric with four domains that correspond to different writing skills (turn to chapter 3 for a copy of the actual analytic rubric for the ACT writing test). Two trained readers will separately score your essay, giving it a rating from 1 (low) to 6 (high) in each of the following four domains: Ideas and Analysis, Development and Support, Organization, and Language Use and Conventions. Each domain score represents the sum of the two readers' scores using the ACT Writing Test Analytic Rubric in chapter 3. If the readers' ratings differ by more than one point, a third reader will evaluate the essay and resolve the discrepancy. Your writing score is calculated from your domain scores and is reported on a scale of 2 to 12.

The readers take into account that you had merely 40 minutes to compose and write your essay. Within that time limit, polish your essay as best as you can. Make sure that all words are legible; handwriting is not scored, but readers must be able to decipher the essay. With careful planning, you should have time to briefly review and edit your essay after you have finished writing it. Keep in mind that you probably will not have time to rewrite or even recopy your essay. Instead, you should take a few minutes to think through your essay and jot preliminary notes on the planning pages in the scoring booklet before you begin to write. Prewriting (planning) helps you organize your ideas, manage your time, and keep you on track as you compose your essay.

Sample Prompt and Essays

In preparation for the ACT writing test, examine the sample writing prompt, essays, and scoring explanations in the following sections. The sample prompt shows what you can expect to encounter on test day; the sample essays serve as models of low-, medium-, and high-scoring essays; and the scoring explanations provide insight into the criteria the readers will use to score your essay.

Sample ACT Writing Test Prompt

Writing test prompts are similar to the following example. The standard directions in the Essay Task section are a part of all prompts used in the writing test. You might want to practice by planning for and writing in response to this prompt for 40 minutes before you look ahead to the sample responses from other writers. If you took the practice test in chapter 3 and choose not to respond to this sample prompt, you may want to compare your essay to the sample essays that follow. Although the topics are different, evaluating the quality of the writing is a similar process.

Online Instruction

Traditional classroom instruction has a number of benefits. Teachers and students often build better relationships when education happens in a face-to-face environment, which can promote personalized instruction and deeper learning. But recent years have seen the rise of online education, where instruction is carried out through videos, web streams, and discussion boards. Learners are increasingly turning to these options for everything from high school and college coursework to technical training and workforce certification. Given the benefits of classroom instructions, how beneficial is this trend toward online education?

Read and carefully consider these perspectives. Each suggests a particular way of thinking about the question above.

Perspective One

Traditional education has never served all learners well. Online options ensure that more people have access to an education that meets their needs.

Perspective Two

The purpose of education is to learn as much as you can, and the best way to learn is in a classroom with the teacher. The trend toward online education offers little benefit for people who wish to be truly educated.

Perspective Three

The most important factor in education is the quality of instruction. Learners can benefit more from a great teacher online than a poor one in the classroom.

Essay Task

Write a unified, coherent essay in which you address the question of whether the trend of online instruction is beneficial. In your essay, be sure to:

- clearly state your own perspective and analyze the relationship between your perspective and at least one other perspective
- develop and support your ideas with reasoning and examples
- organize your ideas clearly and logically
- communicate your ideas effectively in standard written English

Your perspective may be in full agreement with any of those given, in partial agreement, or completely different.

Planning Your Essay

Your work on these prewriting pages will not be scored.

Use the space below to generate ideas and plan your essay. You may wish to consider the following as you think critically about the task:

Strengths and weaknesses of different perspectives on the issue

- What insights do they offer, and what do they fail to consider?
- Why might they be persuasive to others, or why might they fail to persuade?

Your own knowledge, experience, and values

- What is your perspective on this issue, and what are its strengths and weaknesses?
- How will you support your perspective in your essay?

Sample Essay Responses

The essays that follow are sample essays produced in response to the given writing prompt. The essays and the accompanying scoring explanations illustrate how writing at different levels is evaluated and scored for the ACT writing test. The essays in no way represent a full range of ideas, approaches, or styles that could be used. Although we all can learn from reading other people's writing, you are encouraged to bring your own distinct voice and writing skills to the test. You want to produce your own best essay for the writing test—not an imitation of someone else's essay writing.

The following essays have been evaluated using the analytic rubric for the ACT writing test (see chapter 3). This same rubric will be used to score the response that you write for the ACT writing test. Each essay is followed by a scoring explanation that comments on the essay.

Sample Essay 1

From my perspective I agree with the first perspective because even though traditional learning has served learners well dont mean that everyone that was taught had gotten caught on to everything. Also I agree to where online education has the access to meet others needs because sometimes traditional education isn't meant for some people, others my like to learn in other ways and that may be not in a class room with a teacher.

Sample Essay 1 (Score: 1111)

Score Explanation

The attempt to take a position by agreeing with one of the perspectives does not demonstrate skill in writing an argumentative essay.

Ideas and Analysis (1): Limited evaluation of the issue is confusing. Though the writer claims agreement with a position, the analysis results in a contradiction ("even though traditional learning has served learners well [that doesn't] mean that . . . [everyone understood] everything"). A thesis is absent, and the writer's intentions are difficult to discern.

Development and Support (1): An attempt to relay ideas provided in the prompt's first perspective is present, but the effort lacks development and support. Reasoning is largely absent, as it consists of a single, unsupported assertion ("others [may] like to learn in other ways and that may not be in a class room with a teacher"), and no illustration is provided.

Organization (1): This response does not exhibit an organizational structure, in part because there are very few ideas to organize. There is little evidence of grouped ideas, and a lone transition word ("also") is misused, failing to connect one sentence to the other ("caught on to everything. Also I agree . . .").

Language Use and Conventions (1): The response indicates little ability to use language to support an argument. Word choice is imprecise and often difficult to comprehend, even when words from the prompt are incorporated. Sentence structures are unclear, stylistic and register choices are difficult to identify, and errors in grammar, usage, and mechanics are pervasive ("I agree to where online education has the access to meet others needs").

Sample Essay 2

Online instruction

Online Instruction. Could be good for certain people. People that just wanna know whats going on. And only want a grade. I disagree with perspective #1 because only a teacher that is face to face with the student can answer their questions. In an online course students who may have question probably won't be able to be answered and left with questions because it's only a video. Which could lead to bad grades. Either the student won't do the work or get the answers wrong without reason. Online work is so boxed in and the world isn't boxed in. It's better for students to go to class with other students. You'll need help one day and your parents won't be able to help so you'll use family and friends. Same with school. If your teacher can't help your classmate will. Online schools are all one on one without help. I think online Instruction is bad for people.

And it should be made differently. But some
people do better alone which is why
I don't think it should be tooken away.

Sample Essay 2 (Score: 2222)

Score Explanation

The writer acknowledges that there are multiple perspectives but limits an imprecise discussion to only one.

Ideas and Analysis (2): There is some confusion around the thesis—the response recognizes that online instruction is good for some students and bad for others ("Online Instruction could be good for certain people."), but focuses an incomplete discussion on the idea that online instruction is not beneficial ("In an online course . . . [questions cannot be answered]," "Online work is so boxed in," "I think Online Instruction is bad for people"). The argument consists primarily of the repeated claim that the traditional classroom environment is better for students' educational experiences; attempts to consider a different perspective are presented without any discussion ("I think Online Instruction is bad for people, And it should be made differently"), making them seem irrelevant to the argument.

Development and Support (2): The response neglects exploration of how online instruction may be beneficial. Insubstantial discussion of the detriments of online instruction leads to weak development. The idea that students would be left with questions is based on an unconsidered assumption that online instruction is limited to videos and that there would be no avenue for students to seek clarification (such as a discussion board or message to the instructor). Additionally, the idea that students need peers for help essentially repeats that assumption. While the response has the appearance of moving toward additional support, the repetition fails to push the argument forward.

Organization (2): The response does attempt to organize an argument, but it exhibits a rudimentary organizational structure. Introductory and concluding statements are included but weakly frame the writer's argument; as noted above, inattention to a second perspective (benefits of online instruction) and repetition in support inhibit coherence around a central idea. Transitions throughout the single paragraph are largely absent and relationships among ideas are not clear ("get the answers wrong without reason. Online work is so boxed in . . .").

Language Use and Conventions (2): Like the other domains, the use of language to convey an argument is dominated by imprecision. For example, what exactly does it mean that students might "just wanna know what's going on" or "only want a grade"? Similarly, "parents" and "family" are used as if they are distinct from one another. Errors in sentence construction and punctuation influence meaning and stylistic choices, including the casual tone, are not appropriate for the rhetorical purpose. In combination, these issues weaken the argument.

Sample Essay 3

In recent years more citizens have been using online classes instead of entering a classroom with teachers by your side. While a teacher right by your side could be nice, would it be better to learn by teachers in videos?

When learning pupils normally want to feel like they are in a safe environment or even be comfortable. Learning online gives the oppertunity to learn in your own home or somewhere that makes you feel relaxed and safe. Most pupils will say they learn better in an environment that they enjoy, with online they can have the best environment they desire. While being in a classroom with others might keep learners company, it could also be a distraction. Learning while other pupils are talking or horseplaying makes it extreamly difficurt.

Nobody likes taking classes that they wont use with their major, with online classes there is a wide variety of classes to take that will boost the learners knowlage and assist them with their work life. Also with normally schooling a decent teacher isn't always provided. Imagine being in a class that won't provide any knowlage for your job and the teacher doesnt teach well; so you're in a class getting horendous grades for a class you may never use again.

In some asspects being face to face with a teach would be nice theres also reasons why it wouldnt. With videos you can rewind if you dont understand, teachers on the other hand would be getting annoyed if they were requested to repeat the samething till you understood the concept. Also with online classes the program normally doesnt go on till you understand the concept, so you can go at your own pace.

In recent year online learning has became an option for learners. While having a teacher face to face may be helpful they wouldnt always stop and wait for you to understand. In upcoming years online schooling may be the new form of education.

Sample Essay 3 (Score: 3333)

Score Explanation

The writer generates an argument that recognizes multiple perspectives, but is simplistic in its analysis.

Ideas and Analysis (3): The response offers a clear position that online instruction is more beneficial than the traditional classroom method, but the analysis does not explore the issue with any depth. The idea that "using online classes" is on the rise allows the writer to contextualize the issue (suggesting we should consider the issue because the phenomenon is common), but the discussion remains superficial and repetitious. An alternative perspective (that traditional classroom instruction "could be nice") is shared at several points, but in what ways this may be true is never addressed.

Development and Support (3): The argument offers more in the way of claims than support for those claims. The points made to support the main idea that online instruction is more beneficial than traditional instruction are repetitious or left to speak for themselves (rather than clarifying for the reader why the point is worth considering). For example, the first body paragraph offers support for the idea that students need a safe environment, but feeling "relaxed and safe" and having "the best environment they desire" repeat rather than elaborate the point. An attempt to introduce complexity (that students are distracted by peers) receives the same superficial treatment. The second body paragraph follows a similar pattern and the third body paragraph introduces two new ideas that go largely unattended.

Organization (3): A basic organizational structure allows for most ideas to be logically grouped (e.g., the first body paragraph discusses the learning environment, while the second discusses availability and utility of classes). In this way, the response largely coheres around evaluation of the benefits of online learning. Transitions between and within paragraphs sometimes clarify the relationships among ideas ("When learning," "While being in a classroom with others might," "Also with normally schooling," "With videos you can"), though an occasional misstep forces the reader to make assumptions. For instance, the transition to the third body paragraph, "In some asspects being face to face with a teach would be nice," suggests these positive aspects will be discussed, but the reader must use the entire paragraph to determine that its topic is pace.

Language Use and Conventions (3): The use of language is basic. Word choice is general and occasionally imprecise ("more citizens," "have the best environment they desire," "classes that they wont use with their major," "would be nice"). Sentence structures are usually clear but show little variety. The writer's ability to make appropriate stylistic and register choices is hindered at times by general language and errors, even as the errors generally do not impede understanding ("In some asspects being face to face with a teach would be nice theres also reasons why it wouldnt," "learn by teachers in videos," "the learners knowlage," "Also with normally schooling").

Sample Essay 4

The growing trend of online education is both beneficial and unbeneficial to learning students. Students need to have face-to-face interactions with other students and instructors in order to get the most out of their learning experience, yet online classes offer courses that certain schools might not offer. Online education provides a disadvantage to students in social relations, doesn't allow for deeper understanding achieved in the classroom setting, yet does provide opportunity for advanced courses.

If students were to attend online schooling alone, without face-to-face interactions, the student may lack in social situations. The traditional classroom settings allow students to practice public speaking skills and daily social interactions. When entering the workforce this is extremely important. for example; Someone hoping to be hired as a doctor will 'll likely be a better candidate if they have strong social relationship skills, because communication is a major part of the job.

The traditional classroom setting also allows opportunity for students to ask insightful questions and engage in meaningful discussions. These interactions are the basis from which deeper understanding grows. A deeper understanding is very important in learning. Memorization of information and answers is a good skill, but does not test critical thinking or real-life scenarios. Having a deeper understanding and knowledge will better your problem solving skills. In real-life situations, knowing the facts will get you nowhere unless you know how to apply them.

Online education has many drawbacks, but also has some benefits. Many small schools do not offer particular classes. If students wish to take that class, online opportunities will allow that. Students will have opportunities to expand their knowledge and take advanced courses with the option of online education.

My perspective is much different than the perspectives provided. I believe that

Improving Your Score

online education can be beneficial in particular situations and to a certain extent, but the traditional classroom setting will offer critical-life-skills that an online education cannot provide. Finding a balance between traditional and online education can be beneficial. Taking online classes to expand knowledge while still participating in traditional learning settings to better social relationships can be the perfect combination to maximize your learning experience.

Sample Essay 4 (Score: 4444)

Score Explanation

Despite the limited extent to which it conveys the significance of the issue, the argument engages with multiple perspectives, comparing the benefits of traditional and online education.

Ideas and Analysis (4): This argument recognizes the complexity of the issue: the question under examination does not have a simple answer and because there are benefits to both methods of instruction, the best opportunities for students to maximize their learning will come from a balance between the two. The response maintains clear focus on this purpose throughout, making it easy for the reader to follow the analysis. The societal value of education is not explicitly stated, but the discussion of benefits and drawbacks implies that education is a priority. The writer understands that there are merits to more than one side of this issue—recognizing them contributes to analysis and developing them contributes to supporting that analysis.

Development and Support (4): The clear focus of this response contributes to its development. For each point intended to support the thesis, ideas are extended through elaboration rather than repetition, occasionally pointing toward implications (that "public speaking skills and daily social interactions" will be relevant when joining the workforce supports the claim that face-to-face interactions are important). Though it continues to illustrate adequately, the second body paragraph lacks some clarity around why students cannot ask meaningful questions in an online environment and neglects to explain why online instruction is limited to "memorization of information." Importantly, acknowledging that online education can offer more advanced courses and help students expand their knowledge complicates an argument that is otherwise focused on the positive implications of traditional education. Considering qualifications and complications is one key distinction between the upper and lower halves of the rubric.

Organization (4): The response exhibits a clear, common organizational strategy. The structure provides clarity in grouped ideas, though it does not support synthesis of ideas. Although somewhat abrupt from paragraph to paragraph, clear transitions help move the reader from one idea to the next and understand the relationships among ideas ("If students were to attend online schooling alone . . .," "The traditional classroom setting also allows . . ."). Within paragraphs, movement from one idea to another is solid ("meaningful discussions. These interactions . . . deeper understanding. A deeper understanding . . ."). The overall shape of the response reflects an emergent controlling purpose: exploring each of the three supporting points to build support for the thesis, which is fully expressed in the conclusion. The ideas flow logically from a statement that a balanced approach is most appropriate to evaluation of the strongest method to consideration of benefits of the alternative to a concluding statement that emphasizes the thesis.

Language Use and Conventions (4): The use of language in this response conveys the argument with clarity. Despite some instances of awkward phrasing ("provides a disadvantage to students in social relations," "the student may lack in social situations") and some repetition (e.g., interactions), overall word choice is adequate and sometimes precise ("likely be a better candidate," "insightful questions," "engage in meaningful discussions"). Varied sentence structures ("If students were to attend . . .," "The traditional classroom settings allow . . .," "for example; someone hoping . . .") contribute to clarity in organization and analysis, serving as transitions and development of the argument. Stylistic and register choices, including a practical and contemplative tone, are appropriate for an argument that advocates for a balance of both types of learning methods. Errors in grammar, usage, and mechanics are present, but they rarely impede understanding.

Sample Essay 5

When it comes to choosing between traditional classroom instruction and online learning, people are gradually giving up the former and adopting the latter for the reason that it provides convenience; but as far as I am concerned, traditional classroom teaching can be more beneficial and has more advantages. In fact, there are certainly many more benefits to interacting with your teacher directly.

First of all, when people learn from others face-to-face, the most critical advantage is the ability to communicate if there are some problems or confusion. Teachers will give answers to clarify confusing topics and offer help to find solutions when there are issues. What the student needs can be taken into consideration and result in an answer tailored to those needs, which improves efficiency in learning and comprehension. Perspective one claims that traditional education doesn't provide a good fit for everybody, but online options ensure that people will meet their needs due to the various options available on the internet. If one doesn't want to learn deeply about a topic, the online platform may be sufficient.

However, people who want to learn about a specific topic in depth may need a teacher fact-to-face to truly absorb the material and come to a competent understanding of it. For example, I once studied a math topic that was very difficult to comprehend. I first looked on the Internet for online courses. I was happy to find a lot of study materials, but as I got further through them, I became confused on certain points that I didn't get from the courses. I felt that the online instructors talked too fast and weren't always easy to follow. But I could not stop a video to ask questions, so my mom got me a tutor to help with the ideas that I was struggling with. That was really a better experience compared to learning online on my own. When I didn't understand things, I called on my tutor to help me, and I talked to him about my thought process, from which he could assess where I went astray. Learning what I did wrong at first helped me when I moved to more difficult levels of the math subject later on. It would be very difficult to learn a complicated subject, where you have to build an understanding step by step, if you couldn't address confusion as it comes up.

If people want to get further on what they learn, the best way is to listen to teachers directly. Scientists work together fact-to-face so that they can collaborate on projects by communicating. If they were working apart, only communicating through the Internet, they wouldn't quickly understand each other, if at all. So when ideas and processes rise to a certain level of complexity, the ability to interact in person is crucial to comprehending what one wants to learn.

From what has been mentioned above there are many benefits that people gain from classroom learning, for the reason that it provides a more efficient, high quality education and results a greater understanding between learners and instructors. Therefore, students should choose to learn with a teacher in the classroom because it will have a greater outcome for them.

Sample Essay 5 (Score: 5555)

Score Explanation

The writer uses a detailed personal example to analyze multiple perspectives on the issue, addressing implications and critiquing underlying values.

Ideas and Analysis (5): The argument productively engages with multiple perspectives. The detailed example allows the writer to elaborate on and support Perspective Two while evaluating the limitations of Perspective One. The thesis—face-to-face communication is more beneficial because "it provides a more efficient, high quality education and results [in] a greater understanding between learners and instructors"—addresses the idea that there are layers to the educational experience, which reflects precision in thought and purpose. Analysis involves consideration of underlying values (e.g., efficiency, quality) and challenges the assumption that online instruction could provide a student with complete understanding, even when concepts rise to a certain level of complexity ("If one doesn't want to learn deeply about a topic, the online platform may be sufficient."). Analysis also addresses complexities of online communication by discussing that not all online instruction is equal in its ability to instruct ("It would be very difficult to learn a complicated subject, where you have to build an understanding step by step, if you couldn't address confusion as it comes up."; "If they were working apart, only communicating through the internet, they wouldn't quickly understand each other, if at all.").

Development and Support (5): Development of ideas and support deepen the reader's understanding of the argument. The writer recognizes that online instruction may be sufficient in some circumstances, but not if one hopes to achieve a higher level of understanding; this qualification enriches the thesis that traditional classroom instruction is more advantageous to a student's educational experience. While the example of collaboration among scientists is underdeveloped, the brief discussion illustrates the importance of communication when working with complex problems—reasoning that supports the thesis. The detailed example exhibits purposeful reasoning and illustration and is well integrated—the focus is entirely on elaborating the point that interacting with teachers face-to-face is most beneficial for learning deeply. The account capably conveys the significance of the argument.

Organization (5): The chronological order of the personal example contributes to a productive organizational strategy. The response is focused on the thesis throughout, reflecting an argument that maintains a controlling idea. A logical sequencing of ideas contributes to the effectiveness of the argument as it first establishes that direct interaction with teachers has more benefits than online instruction, then complicates the assumption that online instruction can meet all needs of all students, before exploring drawbacks of online education, and ultimately leads to a conclusion that reaffirms the thesis. Though the transition to scientists is not smooth or effective, most of the movement from idea to idea throughout the response consistently clarifies relationships ("If one doesn't want to learn deeply about a topic, the online platform may be sufficient. However, people who want to learn about a specific topic in depth may need a teacher . . .").

Language Use and Conventions (5): Advanced sentence structures ("It would be very difficult to learn a complicated subject, where you have to build an understanding step by step, if you couldn't address confusion as it comes up.") contribute to clarity and convey ideas with precision, while the stylistic choice to describe a personal experience particularly suited to discussing the issue is purposeful and productive. Though vocabulary choices are not elevated, word choices are specific and suit the purpose of explaining the argument ("critical advantage," "confused on certain points," "greater understanding between learners and instructors"). Due to the precision and clarity throughout the essay, occasional imprecision is largely unnoticeable.

Sample Essay 6

The contemporary classroom is the result of several improvements made by each subsequent generation in order to achieve the highest quality and efficiency of teaching possible. Of these changes in more recent times, online support and even entirely internet based courses have been adopted to further improve the modern learning environment. However, the question of whether or not these drastic changes truly have a beneficial impact has been raised. While both physical and online institutions present harms and benefits, I believe the use of both in tandem accomplishes the shared goal of education: to equip students with the tools to succeed in their futures.

To begin, the traditional classroom has its perks over the sole use of online instruction. A hands on education bestows on students so much more than information about particular subjects. For example, open-ended discussion and other group activities encourage and develop cooperation, collaboration, and overall social skills. It would be exceedingly difficult to synthesize these critical skills within a digital platform. Additionally, classroom instruction benefits students through organization and regimentation that online courses can only hope to achieve. Deadlines embody this juxtaposition, because while most online courses allow students to put off their work to an end-of-course deadline, in a traditional classroom a teacher guides students through their workload by requiring proof of progress day-to-day. Students can further benefit from teamwork and guidance as they further develop in-person relationships with instructors and peers, especially if they choose tak an active role in their education by reaching out to teachers and classmates when help is needed.

This, however, does not mean that the traditional classroom is superior in all aspects. In every physical classroom there exists a "back row," often populated by less engaged students who are less encouraged to participate. While social skills may be better learned in person, engagment is necessary to learn at all. Online courses usually require participation in discussion forums that provide a platform in which to consider all contributions equally. Engagement is also better promoted in online instruction through a broad range of subjets, offering greater access to courses that interest an individual student. Beyond more subjects, online instruction may also provide a richer context for understanding. Traditional instruction can be limited in scope of subject matter, as well as restricted to the knowledge and opinions of the school— or even classroom— and then further restricted to the knowledge and opinions of those ready to speak up. This is evidenced across many university campuses where one dominant political or social view tends to dictate the discussions and even sentiments of a student body. While a tradional classroo may be a better environment to equip students with social skills, an online environment may allow for greater diversity of thought.

The thing is, developing the skills to socially interact with a narrow segment of the population is about as useful as developing the ability to consider many perspectives in forming your own opinion, but not the skills to contribute to a larger discussion: not at all. After weighing both sides, it is difficult to decide that one is superior to the other. That is why I advocate for compromise. A system that utilizes the strengths of both education platforms will eradicate the weaknesses of both as well. If it is truly the quality and efficiency of education that we most value, then students should be offered the best, most engaging instruction regardless of platform.

Sample Essay 6 (Score: 6666)

Score Explanation

This argument critically examines each instructional method, ultimately framing the issue as a matter of individual contribution to larger conversations.

Ideas and Analysis (6): The precise thesis acknowledges the nuances of traditional and online education. Analysis of the value of each method on its own and in comparison to the other concludes that compromise is a necessity and not just a way to appease everyone ("A system that utilizes the strengths of both education platforms will eradicate the weaknesses of both as well."). An examination of the complexities of student engagement leads to an exploration of how online instruction can serve those students who remain unengaged by traditional instruction. The factors that keep each method from fully serving all students are situated in the context of educational trends across time, always with the goals to "achieve the highest quality and efficiency of teaching" and "to equip students with the tools to succeed in their future."

Development and Support (6): Having established the historical context of continuous efforts to improve education, the writer develops an argument that the "contemporary classroom" has the power to provide the highest quality of education by integrating traditional and online methods. Critical evaluation emerges in the comparisons between the two methods, and qualifications and complications enrich and bolster ideas and analysis. For example, the truism that traditional classrooms provide socialization is complicated by such observations as students develop only limited social skills in the physical classroom ("skills to socially interact with a narrow segment of the population") and "an online environment may allow for greater diversity of thought." This bolsters the analysis that, in both social skills and subject matter, a combination of traditional and online instruction provides the education students need to prepare for the future.

Organization (6): The response exhibits a skillful organizational strategy which is unified by the controlling idea that using physical and online instruction in tandem eliminates the limitations and increases the benefits of both. The precise thesis brings unity and cohesion to this argument. The thesis guides a logical progression of ideas: The piece begins by introducing the main idea but uses the development of supporting ideas to build toward the clarity of that main idea ("the use of both in tandem accomplishes the shared goal of education"), and then restates the thesis more forcefully in the conclusion ("A system that utilizes the strengths of both education platforms will eradicate the weaknesses of both as well."). Transitions between and within paragraphs are extremely effective at unifying the essay. The clarity with which the writer moves back and forth between instructional methods and advantages and disadvantages strengthens relationships among ideas ("open-ended discussion and other group activities encourage and develop cooperation, collaboration, and overall social skills. It would be exceedingly difficult to synthesize these critical skills within a digital platform.").

Language Use and Conventions (6): The use of language enhances the argument. Skillful and precise word choice creates distinctions which add depth to ideas ("In every physical classroom there exists a 'back row,' often populated by less engaged students who are less encouraged to participate."). Sentence structures are consistently varied and clear, and help convey complex relationships among ideas ("If it is truly the quality and efficiency of education that we most value, then students should be offered the best, most engaging instruction regardless of platform."). Stylistic and register choices, including notes of caution that convey the high stakes of the argument, are strategic and effective in advocating for a compromise to best equip students for their futures ("one dominant . . . view tends to dictate . . . discussions and even sentiments"). A few minor errors in grammar, usage, and mechanics have no impact on the clarity of the argument.

Strategies for Taking the ACT Writing Test

Although your writing score reflects the quality of the product (the essay) you write, the writing process you follow can have a major impact on your score. For example, if you do not spend a few minutes prewriting (planning) before you start writing, you could "paint yourself into a corner" by following a line of logic that leads to an illogical conclusion and have no time left to start over.

The following sections present a few writing, prewriting, and postwriting strategies to improve the process you follow when writing your essay. Of course, no writing process can make up for a lack of knowledge and skill, which take years of study and practice to develop. If you need to sharpen your writing skills, we recommend that you take a course in English composition and practice writing and studying others' writing frequently.

Prewrite

Some writers like to plunge right in, but this is seldom a good way to do well on a timed essay. Prewriting gets you acquainted with the issue, suggests patterns for presenting your thoughts, and gives you a little breathing room to come up with interesting ideas for introducing and concluding your essay. Before writing, then, carefully consider the prompt and make sure you understand it—reread it if you aren't sure. Decide how you want to answer the question in the prompt. Then jot down your ideas on the topic: identify your own position and list reasons and/or examples that you will use to explain your point of view on the issue. Write down what you think someone might say in opposition to your point of view, and think about how you would refute their argument. Consider the broader context: what economic, social, historical, cultural, political, etc. circumstances surround it, and how do the specifics of your argument connect to that bigger picture? Try creating an outline or drawing a diagram to help you determine how best to organize the ideas in your essay. You should do your prewriting on the pages provided in your writing test booklet. You can refer back to these notes as you write the essay itself on the lined pages in your answer document.

Write

When you're ready to write your essay, proceed with the confidence that you have prepared well and that you will have attentive and receptive readers who are interested in your ideas. At the beginning of your essay, make sure readers will see that you understand the issue. Explain your point of view in a clear and logical way. If possible, discuss the issue in a broader context and evaluate the implications or complications of the issue. Address other perspectives presented in the prompt. Also consider what others might say to refute your point of view and present a counterargument to those potential objections. Employ logical reasoning and use specific examples to explain and illustrate what you're saying. Vary the structure of your sentences, and choose varied and precise words. Make logical relationships clear by using transitional words and phrases. Don't wander off the topic. End with a strong conclusion that summarizes or reinforces your position.

Is it advisable to organize the essay by using a formula, such as the five-paragraph essay? Points are neither awarded nor deducted for following familiar formulas, so feel free to use one or not as best suits your preference. Some writers find formulas stifling, other writers find them a solid basis on which to build a strong argument, and still other writers just keep them handy to use when needed. The exact numbers of words and paragraphs in your essay are less important than the clarity and development of your ideas. Writers who have something to say usually find that their ideas have a way of sorting themselves out at reasonable length and in an appropriate number of paragraphs.

Review Your Essay

Aim to allow for a few minutes at the end of the testing session to read over your essay. Correct any mistakes in grammar, usage, punctuation, and spelling. If you find any words that are hard to read, recopy them so your readers can read them easily. Make any corrections and revisions neatly, between the lines (but not in the margins). Your readers take into account that you had merely 40 minutes to compose and write your essay. Within that time limit, try to make your essay as polished as you can.

Practice

There are many ways to prepare for the ACT writing test. You may be surprised that these include reading newspapers and magazines, listening to news analysis on television or radio, and participating in discussions and debates about issues and problems. These activities help you become more familiar with current issues, with different perspectives on those issues, and with strategies that skilled writers and speakers use to present their points of view and respond to a range of viewpoints.

Of course, one of the best ways to prepare for the ACT writing test is to practice writing. Practice writing different kinds of texts, for different purposes, with different audiences in mind. The writing you do in your English classes will help you, as will independent practice in writing essays, stories, poems, plays, editorials, reports, letters to the editor, a personal journal, or other kinds of writing that you do on your own. Strive to consider the quality of your writing from someone else's perspective: would a reader see it as well developed and well organized, and having precise, clear, and concise language? Because the ACT writing test asks you to explain your perspective on an issue in a convincing way, engaging in exercises related to persuasive and argumentative writing (such as editorials or essays discussing controversial issues) is especially helpful. However, since many writing skills are transferable from one genre to another, practicing a variety of different kinds of writing will help make you a versatile writer able to adjust to different writing occasions and assignments. Additionally, analyzing others' writing will help you strengthen and evaluate your own. Practice writing critiques of arguments in which you assess clarity of thought, logical reasoning and evidence used to support the thesis, organization of ideas, and the effects of language choices.

Share your writing with others and get feedback. Feedback helps you anticipate how readers might interpret your writing and what types of questions they might have. It will also help you identify your strengths and weaknesses as a writer. Also, keep in mind what the ACT readers will be looking for as they score your essay by examining the analytic rubric for the ACT writing test (in chapter 3). Consult with others (teachers, peers, etc.) to make sure your writing meets the criteria described for the high-scoring essays.

You should also get some practice writing within a time limit. This will help build skills that are important in college and career. Taking the practice ACT writing tests in this book will give you a good idea of what timed writing is like and how much additional practice you may need.

Part Four:
Taking Additional Practice Tests

In This Part

This part features three additional practice tests. Here, you take and score the tests and look at your scores from a number of different perspectives, so you can use the results more effectively in your educational and career planning. Specifically, this part gives you the opportunity to do the following:

Take three additional practice tests.

Score your practice tests to determine your raw score, scaled scores (similar to the scores the ACT reports), and your estimated percentage rank (how well you did compared to other students who took the tests).

Evaluate your ACT scores from different perspectives to gain insight into what your scores mean in terms of college and career planning.

Chapter 10: Taking Additional Practice Tests

In this chapter, you'll find three additional practice ACT tests, copies of real answer documents for recording your answers, and explanatory answers for the questions on all of the multiple-choice tests. Each section of the test includes embedded field-test questions that do not contribute to the test taker's score. Please note: the placement of embedded field-test questions varies across different test forms, and will NOT remain in the same test item slots each test administration.

Each practice test features the contents of the tests in the same order as they will be on the ACT: the English test, the mathematics test, the reading test, the optional science test, and the optional writing test. Following each complete practice test, you will find the explanatory answers for the multiple-choice questions on that test in the same pattern as the individual tests (English, mathematics, reading, and science).

Prep Online!

Want even more ways to prep? Go to https://study.learning.wiley.com to access our online platform. Access all practice tests and track your progress.

Two copies of the answer documents that you can tear out and use to record your answers for the multiple-choice tests precede each practice test. (Two copies of these answer documents have been provided in case you make errors or if you would like to retake a practice test. When you take the actual ACT test, however, only one answer document will be provided.) One copy of the writing test answer document, which you can tear out (or photocopy) and use to write your essay, is provided for each practice writing test.

Simulating Testing Conditions

We recommend that you take all practice tests under conditions similar to those you will experience on test day. See chapter 3 for instructions.

The ACT® *Sample Answer Document*

EXAMINEE STATEMENTS, CERTIFICATION, AND SIGNATURE

1. **Statements**: I understand that by registering for, launching, starting, or submitting answer documents for an ACT® test, I am agreeing to comply with and be bound by the *Terms and Conditions: Testing Rules and Policies for the ACT® Test* ("Terms").

I UNDERSTAND AND AGREE THAT THE TERMS PERMIT ACT TO CANCEL MY SCORES IN CERTAIN CIRCUMSTANCES. THE TERMS ALSO LIMIT DAMAGES AVAILABLE TO ME AND REQUIRE ARBITRATION OF CERTAIN DISPUTES. BY AGREEING TO ARBITRATION, ACT AND I BOTH WAIVE THE RIGHT TO HAVE THOSE DISPUTES HEARD BY A JUDGE OR JURY.

I understand that ACT owns the test questions and responses, and I will not share them with anyone by any form of communication before, during, or after the test administration. I understand that taking the test for someone else may violate the law and subject me to legal penalties. I consent to the collection and processing of personally identifying information I provide, and its subsequent use and disclosure, as described in the ACT Privacy Policy (www.act.org/privacy.html). If I am taking the test outside of the United States, I also permit ACT to transfer my personally identifying information to the United States, to ACT, or to a third-party service provider, where it will be subject to use and disclosure under the laws of the United States, including being accessible to law enforcement or national security authorities.

2. **Certification**: Copy the italicized certification below, then sign and date in the spaces provided.

*I agree to the **Statements** above and certify that I am the person whose information appears on this form.*

____

____

Your Signature   Today's Date

Do NOT mark in this shaded area.

USE A NO. 2 PENCIL ONLY.
(Do NOT use a mechanical pencil, ink, ballpoint, correction fluid, or felt-tip pen.)

A — NAME, MAILING ADDRESS, AND TELEPHONE
(Please print.)

Last Name   First Name   MI (Middle Initial)

House Number & Street (Apt. No.); or PO Box & No.; or RR & No.

City   State/Province   ZIP/Postal Code

Area Code   Number   Country

ACT, Inc.—Confidential Restricted when data present

ALL examinees must complete block A – please print.

Blocks B, C, and D are required for all examinees. Find the MATCHING INFORMATION on your ticket. Enter it EXACTLY the same way, even if any of the information is missing or incorrect. Fill in the corresponding ovals. If you do not complete these blocks to match your previous information EXACTLY, your scores will be **delayed up to 8 weeks**.

ACT®

PO BOX 168, IOWA CITY, IA 52243-0168

B — MATCH NAME
(First 5 letters of last name)

Columns of ovals: A B C D E F G H I J K L M N O P Q R S T U V W X Y Z (five columns)

C — MATCH NUMBER

Columns of ovals: 1 2 3 4 5 6 7 8 9 0

D — DATE OF BIRTH

Month	Day	Year
○ January		
○ February		
○ March	1 1	1 1
○ April	2 2	2 2
○ May	3 3	3 3
○ June	4	4
○ July	5	5 5
○ August	6	6 6
○ September	7	7 7
○ October	8	8 8
○ November	9	9 9
○ December	0	0 0

          01121525W   (A)204361-001:654321   ISD39683   Printed in the US.

The ONLY Official Prep Guide from the Makers of the ACT

PAGE 2

Marking Directions: Mark only **one** oval for each question. Fill in response completely. Erase errors cleanly without smudging.

Correct mark: ○ ● ○ ○

Do NOT use these *incorrect* or *bad* marks.

Incorrect marks: ○ ○ ○ ○
Overlapping mark: ○ ○ ○ ○
Cross-out mark: ○ ○ ○ ○
Smudged erasure: ○ ○ ○ ○
Mark is too light: ○ ○ ○ ○

BOOKLET NUMBER

FORM

Print your 5-character **Test Form** in the boxes at the right <u>and</u> fill in the corresponding ovals.

TEST 1: ENGLISH

1 Ⓐ Ⓑ Ⓒ Ⓓ	14 Ⓕ Ⓖ Ⓗ Ⓙ	27 Ⓐ Ⓑ Ⓒ Ⓓ	40 Ⓕ Ⓖ Ⓗ Ⓙ	53 Ⓐ Ⓑ Ⓒ Ⓓ	66 Ⓕ Ⓖ Ⓗ Ⓙ
2 Ⓕ Ⓖ Ⓗ Ⓙ	15 Ⓐ Ⓑ Ⓒ Ⓓ	28 Ⓕ Ⓖ Ⓗ Ⓙ	41 Ⓐ Ⓑ Ⓒ Ⓓ	54 Ⓕ Ⓖ Ⓗ Ⓙ	67 Ⓐ Ⓑ Ⓒ Ⓓ
3 Ⓐ Ⓑ Ⓒ Ⓓ	16 Ⓕ Ⓖ Ⓗ Ⓙ	29 Ⓐ Ⓑ Ⓒ Ⓓ	42 Ⓐ Ⓑ Ⓒ Ⓓ	55 Ⓐ Ⓑ Ⓒ Ⓓ	68 Ⓕ Ⓖ Ⓗ Ⓙ
4 Ⓕ Ⓖ Ⓗ Ⓙ	17 Ⓐ Ⓑ Ⓒ Ⓓ	30 Ⓕ Ⓖ Ⓗ Ⓙ	43 Ⓐ Ⓑ Ⓒ Ⓓ	56 Ⓕ Ⓖ Ⓗ Ⓙ	69 Ⓐ Ⓑ Ⓒ Ⓓ
5 Ⓐ Ⓑ Ⓒ Ⓓ	18 Ⓕ Ⓖ Ⓗ Ⓙ	31 Ⓐ Ⓑ Ⓒ Ⓓ	44 Ⓕ Ⓖ Ⓗ Ⓙ	57 Ⓐ Ⓑ Ⓒ Ⓓ	70 Ⓕ Ⓖ Ⓗ Ⓙ
6 Ⓕ Ⓖ Ⓗ Ⓙ	19 Ⓐ Ⓑ Ⓒ Ⓓ	32 Ⓕ Ⓖ Ⓗ Ⓙ	45 Ⓐ Ⓑ Ⓒ Ⓓ	58 Ⓕ Ⓖ Ⓗ Ⓙ	71 Ⓐ Ⓑ Ⓒ Ⓓ
7 Ⓐ Ⓑ Ⓒ Ⓓ	20 Ⓕ Ⓖ Ⓗ Ⓙ	33 Ⓐ Ⓑ Ⓒ Ⓓ	46 Ⓕ Ⓖ Ⓗ Ⓙ	59 Ⓐ Ⓑ Ⓒ Ⓓ	72 Ⓕ Ⓖ Ⓗ Ⓙ
8 Ⓕ Ⓖ Ⓗ Ⓙ	21 Ⓐ Ⓑ Ⓒ Ⓓ	34 Ⓕ Ⓖ Ⓗ Ⓙ	47 Ⓐ Ⓑ Ⓒ Ⓓ	60 Ⓕ Ⓖ Ⓗ Ⓙ	73 Ⓐ Ⓑ Ⓒ Ⓓ
9 Ⓐ Ⓑ Ⓒ Ⓓ	22 Ⓕ Ⓖ Ⓗ Ⓙ	35 Ⓐ Ⓑ Ⓒ Ⓓ	48 Ⓕ Ⓖ Ⓗ Ⓙ	61 Ⓐ Ⓑ Ⓒ Ⓓ	74 Ⓕ Ⓖ Ⓗ Ⓙ
10 Ⓕ Ⓖ Ⓗ Ⓙ	23 Ⓐ Ⓑ Ⓒ Ⓓ	36 Ⓕ Ⓖ Ⓗ Ⓙ	49 Ⓐ Ⓑ Ⓒ Ⓓ	62 Ⓕ Ⓖ Ⓗ Ⓙ	75 Ⓐ Ⓑ Ⓒ Ⓓ
11 Ⓐ Ⓑ Ⓒ Ⓓ	24 Ⓕ Ⓖ Ⓗ Ⓙ	37 Ⓐ Ⓑ Ⓒ Ⓓ	50 Ⓕ Ⓖ Ⓗ Ⓙ	63 Ⓐ Ⓑ Ⓒ Ⓓ	
12 Ⓕ Ⓖ Ⓗ Ⓙ	25 Ⓐ Ⓑ Ⓒ Ⓓ	38 Ⓕ Ⓖ Ⓗ Ⓙ	51 Ⓐ Ⓑ Ⓒ Ⓓ	64 Ⓕ Ⓖ Ⓗ Ⓙ	
13 Ⓐ Ⓑ Ⓒ Ⓓ	26 Ⓕ Ⓖ Ⓗ Ⓙ	39 Ⓐ Ⓑ Ⓒ Ⓓ	52 Ⓕ Ⓖ Ⓗ Ⓙ	65 Ⓐ Ⓑ Ⓒ Ⓓ	

TEST 2: MATHEMATICS

1 Ⓐ Ⓑ Ⓒ Ⓓ Ⓔ	11 Ⓐ Ⓑ Ⓒ Ⓓ Ⓔ	21 Ⓐ Ⓑ Ⓒ Ⓓ Ⓔ	31 Ⓐ Ⓑ Ⓒ Ⓓ Ⓔ	41 Ⓐ Ⓑ Ⓒ Ⓓ Ⓔ	51 Ⓐ Ⓑ Ⓒ Ⓓ Ⓔ
2 Ⓕ Ⓖ Ⓗ Ⓙ Ⓚ	12 Ⓕ Ⓖ Ⓗ Ⓙ Ⓚ	22 Ⓕ Ⓖ Ⓗ Ⓙ Ⓚ	32 Ⓕ Ⓖ Ⓗ Ⓙ Ⓚ	42 Ⓕ Ⓖ Ⓗ Ⓙ Ⓚ	52 Ⓕ Ⓖ Ⓗ Ⓙ Ⓚ
3 Ⓐ Ⓑ Ⓒ Ⓓ Ⓔ	13 Ⓐ Ⓑ Ⓒ Ⓓ Ⓔ	23 Ⓐ Ⓑ Ⓒ Ⓓ Ⓔ	33 Ⓐ Ⓑ Ⓒ Ⓓ Ⓔ	43 Ⓐ Ⓑ Ⓒ Ⓓ Ⓔ	53 Ⓐ Ⓑ Ⓒ Ⓓ Ⓔ
4 Ⓕ Ⓖ Ⓗ Ⓙ Ⓚ	14 Ⓕ Ⓖ Ⓗ Ⓙ Ⓚ	24 Ⓕ Ⓖ Ⓗ Ⓙ Ⓚ	34 Ⓕ Ⓖ Ⓗ Ⓙ Ⓚ	44 Ⓕ Ⓖ Ⓗ Ⓙ Ⓚ	54 Ⓕ Ⓖ Ⓗ Ⓙ Ⓚ
5 Ⓐ Ⓑ Ⓒ Ⓓ Ⓔ	15 Ⓐ Ⓑ Ⓒ Ⓓ Ⓔ	25 Ⓐ Ⓑ Ⓒ Ⓓ Ⓔ	35 Ⓐ Ⓑ Ⓒ Ⓓ Ⓔ	45 Ⓐ Ⓑ Ⓒ Ⓓ Ⓔ	55 Ⓐ Ⓑ Ⓒ Ⓓ Ⓔ
6 Ⓕ Ⓖ Ⓗ Ⓙ Ⓚ	16 Ⓕ Ⓖ Ⓗ Ⓙ Ⓚ	26 Ⓕ Ⓖ Ⓗ Ⓙ Ⓚ	36 Ⓕ Ⓖ Ⓗ Ⓙ Ⓚ	46 Ⓕ Ⓖ Ⓗ Ⓙ Ⓚ	56 Ⓕ Ⓖ Ⓗ Ⓙ Ⓚ
7 Ⓐ Ⓑ Ⓒ Ⓓ Ⓔ	17 Ⓐ Ⓑ Ⓒ Ⓓ Ⓔ	27 Ⓐ Ⓑ Ⓒ Ⓓ Ⓔ	37 Ⓐ Ⓑ Ⓒ Ⓓ Ⓔ	47 Ⓐ Ⓑ Ⓒ Ⓓ Ⓔ	57 Ⓐ Ⓑ Ⓒ Ⓓ Ⓔ
8 Ⓕ Ⓖ Ⓗ Ⓙ Ⓚ	18 Ⓕ Ⓖ Ⓗ Ⓙ Ⓚ	28 Ⓕ Ⓖ Ⓗ Ⓙ Ⓚ	38 Ⓕ Ⓖ Ⓗ Ⓙ Ⓚ	48 Ⓕ Ⓖ Ⓗ Ⓙ Ⓚ	58 Ⓕ Ⓖ Ⓗ Ⓙ Ⓚ
9 Ⓐ Ⓑ Ⓒ Ⓓ Ⓔ	19 Ⓐ Ⓑ Ⓒ Ⓓ Ⓔ	29 Ⓐ Ⓑ Ⓒ Ⓓ Ⓔ	39 Ⓐ Ⓑ Ⓒ Ⓓ Ⓔ	49 Ⓐ Ⓑ Ⓒ Ⓓ Ⓔ	59 Ⓐ Ⓑ Ⓒ Ⓓ Ⓔ
10 Ⓕ Ⓖ Ⓗ Ⓙ Ⓚ	20 Ⓕ Ⓖ Ⓗ Ⓙ Ⓚ	30 Ⓕ Ⓖ Ⓗ Ⓙ Ⓚ	40 Ⓕ Ⓖ Ⓗ Ⓙ Ⓚ	50 Ⓕ Ⓖ Ⓗ Ⓙ Ⓚ	60 Ⓕ Ⓖ Ⓗ Ⓙ Ⓚ

TEST 3: READING

1 Ⓐ Ⓑ Ⓒ Ⓓ	8 Ⓕ Ⓖ Ⓗ Ⓙ	15 Ⓐ Ⓑ Ⓒ Ⓓ	22 Ⓕ Ⓖ Ⓗ Ⓙ	29 Ⓐ Ⓑ Ⓒ Ⓓ	36 Ⓕ Ⓖ Ⓗ Ⓙ
2 Ⓕ Ⓖ Ⓗ Ⓙ	9 Ⓐ Ⓑ Ⓒ Ⓓ	16 Ⓕ Ⓖ Ⓗ Ⓙ	23 Ⓐ Ⓑ Ⓒ Ⓓ	30 Ⓕ Ⓖ Ⓗ Ⓙ	37 Ⓐ Ⓑ Ⓒ Ⓓ
3 Ⓐ Ⓑ Ⓒ Ⓓ	10 Ⓕ Ⓖ Ⓗ Ⓙ	17 Ⓐ Ⓑ Ⓒ Ⓓ	24 Ⓕ Ⓖ Ⓗ Ⓙ	31 Ⓐ Ⓑ Ⓒ Ⓓ	38 Ⓕ Ⓖ Ⓗ Ⓙ
4 Ⓕ Ⓖ Ⓗ Ⓙ	11 Ⓐ Ⓑ Ⓒ Ⓓ	18 Ⓕ Ⓖ Ⓗ Ⓙ	25 Ⓐ Ⓑ Ⓒ Ⓓ	32 Ⓕ Ⓖ Ⓗ Ⓙ	39 Ⓐ Ⓑ Ⓒ Ⓓ
5 Ⓐ Ⓑ Ⓒ Ⓓ	12 Ⓕ Ⓖ Ⓗ Ⓙ	19 Ⓐ Ⓑ Ⓒ Ⓓ	26 Ⓕ Ⓖ Ⓗ Ⓙ	33 Ⓐ Ⓑ Ⓒ Ⓓ	40 Ⓕ Ⓖ Ⓗ Ⓙ
6 Ⓕ Ⓖ Ⓗ Ⓙ	13 Ⓐ Ⓑ Ⓒ Ⓓ	20 Ⓕ Ⓖ Ⓗ Ⓙ	27 Ⓐ Ⓑ Ⓒ Ⓓ	34 Ⓕ Ⓖ Ⓗ Ⓙ	
7 Ⓐ Ⓑ Ⓒ Ⓓ	14 Ⓕ Ⓖ Ⓗ Ⓙ	21 Ⓐ Ⓑ Ⓒ Ⓓ	28 Ⓕ Ⓖ Ⓗ Ⓙ	35 Ⓐ Ⓑ Ⓒ Ⓓ	

TEST 4: SCIENCE

1 Ⓐ Ⓑ Ⓒ Ⓓ	8 Ⓕ Ⓖ Ⓗ Ⓙ	15 Ⓐ Ⓑ Ⓒ Ⓓ	22 Ⓕ Ⓖ Ⓗ Ⓙ	29 Ⓐ Ⓑ Ⓒ Ⓓ	36 Ⓕ Ⓖ Ⓗ Ⓙ
2 Ⓕ Ⓖ Ⓗ Ⓙ	9 Ⓐ Ⓑ Ⓒ Ⓓ	16 Ⓕ Ⓖ Ⓗ Ⓙ	23 Ⓐ Ⓑ Ⓒ Ⓓ	30 Ⓕ Ⓖ Ⓗ Ⓙ	37 Ⓐ Ⓑ Ⓒ Ⓓ
3 Ⓐ Ⓑ Ⓒ Ⓓ	10 Ⓕ Ⓖ Ⓗ Ⓙ	17 Ⓐ Ⓑ Ⓒ Ⓓ	24 Ⓕ Ⓖ Ⓗ Ⓙ	31 Ⓐ Ⓑ Ⓒ Ⓓ	38 Ⓕ Ⓖ Ⓗ Ⓙ
4 Ⓕ Ⓖ Ⓗ Ⓙ	11 Ⓐ Ⓑ Ⓒ Ⓓ	18 Ⓕ Ⓖ Ⓗ Ⓙ	25 Ⓐ Ⓑ Ⓒ Ⓓ	32 Ⓕ Ⓖ Ⓗ Ⓙ	39 Ⓐ Ⓑ Ⓒ Ⓓ
5 Ⓐ Ⓑ Ⓒ Ⓓ	12 Ⓕ Ⓖ Ⓗ Ⓙ	19 Ⓐ Ⓑ Ⓒ Ⓓ	26 Ⓕ Ⓖ Ⓗ Ⓙ	33 Ⓐ Ⓑ Ⓒ Ⓓ	40 Ⓕ Ⓖ Ⓗ Ⓙ
6 Ⓕ Ⓖ Ⓗ Ⓙ	13 Ⓐ Ⓑ Ⓒ Ⓓ	20 Ⓕ Ⓖ Ⓗ Ⓙ	27 Ⓐ Ⓑ Ⓒ Ⓓ	34 Ⓕ Ⓖ Ⓗ Ⓙ	
7 Ⓐ Ⓑ Ⓒ Ⓓ	14 Ⓕ Ⓖ Ⓗ Ⓙ	21 Ⓐ Ⓑ Ⓒ Ⓓ	28 Ⓕ Ⓖ Ⓗ Ⓙ	35 Ⓐ Ⓑ Ⓒ Ⓓ	

The ACT® *Sample Answer Document*

EXAMINEE STATEMENTS, CERTIFICATION, AND SIGNATURE

1. **Statements**: I understand that by registering for, launching, starting, or submitting answer documents for an ACT® test, I am agreeing to comply with and be bound by the *Terms and Conditions: Testing Rules and Policies for the ACT® Test* ("Terms").

I UNDERSTAND AND AGREE THAT THE TERMS PERMIT ACT TO CANCEL MY SCORES IN CERTAIN CIRCUMSTANCES. THE TERMS ALSO LIMIT DAMAGES AVAILABLE TO ME AND REQUIRE ARBITRATION OF CERTAIN DISPUTES. BY AGREEING TO ARBITRATION, ACT AND I BOTH WAIVE THE RIGHT TO HAVE THOSE DISPUTES HEARD BY A JUDGE OR JURY.

I understand that ACT owns the test questions and responses, and I will not share them with anyone by any form of communication before, during, or after the test administration. I understand that taking the test for someone else may violate the law and subject me to legal penalties. I consent to the collection and processing of personally identifying information I provide, and its subsequent use and disclosure, as described in the ACT Privacy Policy (www.act.org/privacy.html). If I am taking the test outside of the United States, I also permit ACT to transfer my personally identifying information to the United States, to ACT, or to a third-party service provider, where it will be subject to use and disclosure under the laws of the United States, including being accessible to law enforcement or national security authorities.

2. **Certification**: Copy the italicized certification below, then sign and date in the spaces provided.

*I agree to the **Statements** above and certify that I am the person whose information appears on this form.*

____

____

____   ___________________

Your Signature   Today's Date

Do NOT mark in this shaded area.

USE A NO. 2 PENCIL ONLY.
(Do NOT use a mechanical pencil, ink, ballpoint, correction fluid, or felt-tip pen.)

A   **NAME, MAILING ADDRESS, AND TELEPHONE**
(Please print.)

Last Name   First Name   MI (Middle Initial)

House Number & Street (Apt. No.); or PO Box & No.; or RR & No.

City   State/Province   ZIP/Postal Code

Area Code   Number   Country

ACT, Inc.—Confidential Restricted when data present

ALL examinees must complete block A – please print.

Blocks B, C, and D are required for all examinees. Find the MATCHING INFORMATION on your ticket. Enter it EXACTLY the same way, even if any of the information is missing or incorrect. Fill in the corresponding ovals. If you do not complete these blocks to match your previous information EXACTLY, your scores will be **delayed up to 8 weeks**.

ACT
PO BOX 168, IOWA CITY, IA 52243-0168

B MATCH NAME
(First 5 letters of last name)

C MATCH NUMBER

D DATE OF BIRTH

Month	Day	Year
January		
February		
March	① ① ① ①	
April	② ② ② ②	
May	③ ③ ③ ③	
June	④ ④ ④	
July	⑤ ⑤ ⑤	
August	⑥ ⑥ ⑥	
September	⑦ ⑦ ⑦	
October	⑧ ⑧ ⑧	
November	⑨ ⑨ ⑨	
December	⓪ ⓪ ⓪	

The ONLY Official Prep Guide from the Makers of the ACT

PAGE 2

Marking Directions: Mark only **one** oval for each question. Fill in response completely. Erase errors cleanly without smudging.

Correct mark: ○ ● ○ ○

Do NOT use these *incorrect* **or** *bad* **marks.**

Incorrect marks: ⊘ ⊗ ⊖ ⊙
Overlapping mark: ○ ○ ● ●
Cross-out mark: ○ ⊘ ○ ●
Smudged erasure: ○ ○ ◐ ○
Mark is too light: ◐ ○ ○ ○

BOOKLET NUMBER

FORM

Print your 5-character **Test Form** in the boxes at the right <u>and</u> fill in the corresponding ovals.

TEST 1: ENGLISH

1 Ⓐ Ⓑ Ⓒ Ⓓ	14 Ⓕ Ⓖ Ⓗ Ⓙ	27 Ⓐ Ⓑ Ⓒ Ⓓ	40 Ⓕ Ⓖ Ⓗ Ⓙ	53 Ⓐ Ⓑ Ⓒ Ⓓ	66 Ⓕ Ⓖ Ⓗ Ⓙ
2 Ⓕ Ⓖ Ⓗ Ⓙ	15 Ⓐ Ⓑ Ⓒ Ⓓ	28 Ⓕ Ⓖ Ⓗ Ⓙ	41 Ⓐ Ⓑ Ⓒ Ⓓ	54 Ⓕ Ⓖ Ⓗ Ⓙ	67 Ⓐ Ⓑ Ⓒ Ⓓ
3 Ⓐ Ⓑ Ⓒ Ⓓ	16 Ⓕ Ⓖ Ⓗ Ⓙ	29 Ⓐ Ⓑ Ⓒ Ⓓ	42 Ⓕ Ⓖ Ⓗ Ⓙ	55 Ⓐ Ⓑ Ⓒ Ⓓ	68 Ⓕ Ⓖ Ⓗ Ⓙ
4 Ⓕ Ⓖ Ⓗ Ⓙ	17 Ⓐ Ⓑ Ⓒ Ⓓ	30 Ⓕ Ⓖ Ⓗ Ⓙ	43 Ⓐ Ⓑ Ⓒ Ⓓ	56 Ⓕ Ⓖ Ⓗ Ⓙ	69 Ⓐ Ⓑ Ⓒ Ⓓ
5 Ⓐ Ⓑ Ⓒ Ⓓ	18 Ⓕ Ⓖ Ⓗ Ⓙ	31 Ⓐ Ⓑ Ⓒ Ⓓ	44 Ⓕ Ⓖ Ⓗ Ⓙ	57 Ⓐ Ⓑ Ⓒ Ⓓ	70 Ⓕ Ⓖ Ⓗ Ⓙ
6 Ⓕ Ⓖ Ⓗ Ⓙ	19 Ⓐ Ⓑ Ⓒ Ⓓ	32 Ⓕ Ⓖ Ⓗ Ⓙ	45 Ⓐ Ⓑ Ⓒ Ⓓ	58 Ⓕ Ⓖ Ⓗ Ⓙ	71 Ⓐ Ⓑ Ⓒ Ⓓ
7 Ⓐ Ⓑ Ⓒ Ⓓ	20 Ⓕ Ⓖ Ⓗ Ⓙ	33 Ⓐ Ⓑ Ⓒ Ⓓ	46 Ⓕ Ⓖ Ⓗ Ⓙ	59 Ⓐ Ⓑ Ⓒ Ⓓ	72 Ⓕ Ⓖ Ⓗ Ⓙ
8 Ⓕ Ⓖ Ⓗ Ⓙ	21 Ⓐ Ⓑ Ⓒ Ⓓ	34 Ⓕ Ⓖ Ⓗ Ⓙ	47 Ⓐ Ⓑ Ⓒ Ⓓ	60 Ⓕ Ⓖ Ⓗ Ⓙ	73 Ⓐ Ⓑ Ⓒ Ⓓ
9 Ⓐ Ⓑ Ⓒ Ⓓ	22 Ⓕ Ⓖ Ⓗ Ⓙ	35 Ⓐ Ⓑ Ⓒ Ⓓ	48 Ⓕ Ⓖ Ⓗ Ⓙ	61 Ⓐ Ⓑ Ⓒ Ⓓ	74 Ⓕ Ⓖ Ⓗ Ⓙ
10 Ⓕ Ⓖ Ⓗ Ⓙ	23 Ⓐ Ⓑ Ⓒ Ⓓ	36 Ⓕ Ⓖ Ⓗ Ⓙ	49 Ⓐ Ⓑ Ⓒ Ⓓ	62 Ⓕ Ⓖ Ⓗ Ⓙ	75 Ⓐ Ⓑ Ⓒ Ⓓ
11 Ⓐ Ⓑ Ⓒ Ⓓ	24 Ⓕ Ⓖ Ⓗ Ⓙ	37 Ⓐ Ⓑ Ⓒ Ⓓ	50 Ⓕ Ⓖ Ⓗ Ⓙ	63 Ⓐ Ⓑ Ⓒ Ⓓ	
12 Ⓕ Ⓖ Ⓗ Ⓙ	25 Ⓐ Ⓑ Ⓒ Ⓓ	38 Ⓕ Ⓖ Ⓗ Ⓙ	51 Ⓐ Ⓑ Ⓒ Ⓓ	64 Ⓕ Ⓖ Ⓗ Ⓙ	
13 Ⓐ Ⓑ Ⓒ Ⓓ	26 Ⓕ Ⓖ Ⓗ Ⓙ	39 Ⓐ Ⓑ Ⓒ Ⓓ	52 Ⓕ Ⓖ Ⓗ Ⓙ	65 Ⓐ Ⓑ Ⓒ Ⓓ	

TEST 2: MATHEMATICS

1 Ⓐ Ⓑ Ⓒ Ⓓ Ⓔ	11 Ⓐ Ⓑ Ⓒ Ⓓ Ⓔ	21 Ⓐ Ⓑ Ⓒ Ⓓ Ⓔ	31 Ⓐ Ⓑ Ⓒ Ⓓ Ⓔ	41 Ⓐ Ⓑ Ⓒ Ⓓ Ⓔ	51 Ⓐ Ⓑ Ⓒ Ⓓ Ⓔ
2 Ⓕ Ⓖ Ⓗ Ⓙ Ⓚ	12 Ⓕ Ⓖ Ⓗ Ⓙ Ⓚ	22 Ⓕ Ⓖ Ⓗ Ⓙ Ⓚ	32 Ⓕ Ⓖ Ⓗ Ⓙ Ⓚ	42 Ⓕ Ⓖ Ⓗ Ⓙ Ⓚ	52 Ⓕ Ⓖ Ⓗ Ⓙ Ⓚ
3 Ⓐ Ⓑ Ⓒ Ⓓ Ⓔ	13 Ⓐ Ⓑ Ⓒ Ⓓ Ⓔ	23 Ⓐ Ⓑ Ⓒ Ⓓ Ⓔ	33 Ⓐ Ⓑ Ⓒ Ⓓ Ⓔ	43 Ⓐ Ⓑ Ⓒ Ⓓ Ⓔ	53 Ⓐ Ⓑ Ⓒ Ⓓ Ⓔ
4 Ⓕ Ⓖ Ⓗ Ⓙ Ⓚ	14 Ⓕ Ⓖ Ⓗ Ⓙ Ⓚ	24 Ⓕ Ⓖ Ⓗ Ⓙ Ⓚ	34 Ⓕ Ⓖ Ⓗ Ⓙ Ⓚ	44 Ⓕ Ⓖ Ⓗ Ⓙ Ⓚ	54 Ⓕ Ⓖ Ⓗ Ⓙ Ⓚ
5 Ⓐ Ⓑ Ⓒ Ⓓ Ⓔ	15 Ⓐ Ⓑ Ⓒ Ⓓ Ⓔ	25 Ⓐ Ⓑ Ⓒ Ⓓ Ⓔ	35 Ⓐ Ⓑ Ⓒ Ⓓ Ⓔ	45 Ⓐ Ⓑ Ⓒ Ⓓ Ⓔ	55 Ⓐ Ⓑ Ⓒ Ⓓ Ⓔ
6 Ⓕ Ⓖ Ⓗ Ⓙ Ⓚ	16 Ⓕ Ⓖ Ⓗ Ⓙ Ⓚ	26 Ⓕ Ⓖ Ⓗ Ⓙ Ⓚ	36 Ⓕ Ⓖ Ⓗ Ⓙ Ⓚ	46 Ⓕ Ⓖ Ⓗ Ⓙ Ⓚ	56 Ⓕ Ⓖ Ⓗ Ⓙ Ⓚ
7 Ⓐ Ⓑ Ⓒ Ⓓ Ⓔ	17 Ⓐ Ⓑ Ⓒ Ⓓ Ⓔ	27 Ⓐ Ⓑ Ⓒ Ⓓ Ⓔ	37 Ⓐ Ⓑ Ⓒ Ⓓ Ⓔ	47 Ⓐ Ⓑ Ⓒ Ⓓ Ⓔ	57 Ⓐ Ⓑ Ⓒ Ⓓ Ⓔ
8 Ⓕ Ⓖ Ⓗ Ⓙ Ⓚ	18 Ⓕ Ⓖ Ⓗ Ⓙ Ⓚ	28 Ⓕ Ⓖ Ⓗ Ⓙ Ⓚ	38 Ⓕ Ⓖ Ⓗ Ⓙ Ⓚ	48 Ⓕ Ⓖ Ⓗ Ⓙ Ⓚ	58 Ⓕ Ⓖ Ⓗ Ⓙ Ⓚ
9 Ⓐ Ⓑ Ⓒ Ⓓ Ⓔ	19 Ⓐ Ⓑ Ⓒ Ⓓ Ⓔ	29 Ⓐ Ⓑ Ⓒ Ⓓ Ⓔ	39 Ⓐ Ⓑ Ⓒ Ⓓ Ⓔ	49 Ⓐ Ⓑ Ⓒ Ⓓ Ⓔ	59 Ⓐ Ⓑ Ⓒ Ⓓ Ⓔ
10 Ⓕ Ⓖ Ⓗ Ⓙ Ⓚ	20 Ⓕ Ⓖ Ⓗ Ⓙ Ⓚ	30 Ⓕ Ⓖ Ⓗ Ⓙ Ⓚ	40 Ⓕ Ⓖ Ⓗ Ⓙ Ⓚ	50 Ⓕ Ⓖ Ⓗ Ⓙ Ⓚ	60 Ⓕ Ⓖ Ⓗ Ⓙ Ⓚ

TEST 3: READING

1 Ⓐ Ⓑ Ⓒ Ⓓ	8 Ⓕ Ⓖ Ⓗ Ⓙ	15 Ⓐ Ⓑ Ⓒ Ⓓ	22 Ⓕ Ⓖ Ⓗ Ⓙ	29 Ⓐ Ⓑ Ⓒ Ⓓ	36 Ⓕ Ⓖ Ⓗ Ⓙ
2 Ⓕ Ⓖ Ⓗ Ⓙ	9 Ⓐ Ⓑ Ⓒ Ⓓ	16 Ⓕ Ⓖ Ⓗ Ⓙ	23 Ⓐ Ⓑ Ⓒ Ⓓ	30 Ⓕ Ⓖ Ⓗ Ⓙ	37 Ⓐ Ⓑ Ⓒ Ⓓ
3 Ⓐ Ⓑ Ⓒ Ⓓ	10 Ⓕ Ⓖ Ⓗ Ⓙ	17 Ⓐ Ⓑ Ⓒ Ⓓ	24 Ⓕ Ⓖ Ⓗ Ⓙ	31 Ⓐ Ⓑ Ⓒ Ⓓ	38 Ⓕ Ⓖ Ⓗ Ⓙ
4 Ⓕ Ⓖ Ⓗ Ⓙ	11 Ⓐ Ⓑ Ⓒ Ⓓ	18 Ⓕ Ⓖ Ⓗ Ⓙ	25 Ⓐ Ⓑ Ⓒ Ⓓ	32 Ⓕ Ⓖ Ⓗ Ⓙ	39 Ⓐ Ⓑ Ⓒ Ⓓ
5 Ⓐ Ⓑ Ⓒ Ⓓ	12 Ⓕ Ⓖ Ⓗ Ⓙ	19 Ⓐ Ⓑ Ⓒ Ⓓ	26 Ⓕ Ⓖ Ⓗ Ⓙ	33 Ⓐ Ⓑ Ⓒ Ⓓ	40 Ⓕ Ⓖ Ⓗ Ⓙ
6 Ⓕ Ⓖ Ⓗ Ⓙ	13 Ⓐ Ⓑ Ⓒ Ⓓ	20 Ⓕ Ⓖ Ⓗ Ⓙ	27 Ⓐ Ⓑ Ⓒ Ⓓ	34 Ⓕ Ⓖ Ⓗ Ⓙ	
7 Ⓐ Ⓑ Ⓒ Ⓓ	14 Ⓕ Ⓖ Ⓗ Ⓙ	21 Ⓐ Ⓑ Ⓒ Ⓓ	28 Ⓕ Ⓖ Ⓗ Ⓙ	35 Ⓐ Ⓑ Ⓒ Ⓓ	

TEST 4: SCIENCE

1 Ⓐ Ⓑ Ⓒ Ⓓ	8 Ⓕ Ⓖ Ⓗ Ⓙ	15 Ⓐ Ⓑ Ⓒ Ⓓ	22 Ⓕ Ⓖ Ⓗ Ⓙ	29 Ⓐ Ⓑ Ⓒ Ⓓ	36 Ⓕ Ⓖ Ⓗ Ⓙ
2 Ⓕ Ⓖ Ⓗ Ⓙ	9 Ⓐ Ⓑ Ⓒ Ⓓ	16 Ⓕ Ⓖ Ⓗ Ⓙ	23 Ⓐ Ⓑ Ⓒ Ⓓ	30 Ⓕ Ⓖ Ⓗ Ⓙ	37 Ⓐ Ⓑ Ⓒ Ⓓ
3 Ⓐ Ⓑ Ⓒ Ⓓ	10 Ⓕ Ⓖ Ⓗ Ⓙ	17 Ⓐ Ⓑ Ⓒ Ⓓ	24 Ⓕ Ⓖ Ⓗ Ⓙ	31 Ⓐ Ⓑ Ⓒ Ⓓ	38 Ⓕ Ⓖ Ⓗ Ⓙ
4 Ⓕ Ⓖ Ⓗ Ⓙ	11 Ⓐ Ⓑ Ⓒ Ⓓ	18 Ⓕ Ⓖ Ⓗ Ⓙ	25 Ⓐ Ⓑ Ⓒ Ⓓ	32 Ⓕ Ⓖ Ⓗ Ⓙ	39 Ⓐ Ⓑ Ⓒ Ⓓ
5 Ⓐ Ⓑ Ⓒ Ⓓ	12 Ⓕ Ⓖ Ⓗ Ⓙ	19 Ⓐ Ⓑ Ⓒ Ⓓ	26 Ⓕ Ⓖ Ⓗ Ⓙ	33 Ⓐ Ⓑ Ⓒ Ⓓ	40 Ⓕ Ⓖ Ⓗ Ⓙ
6 Ⓕ Ⓖ Ⓗ Ⓙ	13 Ⓐ Ⓑ Ⓒ Ⓓ	20 Ⓕ Ⓖ Ⓗ Ⓙ	27 Ⓐ Ⓑ Ⓒ Ⓓ	34 Ⓕ Ⓖ Ⓗ Ⓙ	
7 Ⓐ Ⓑ Ⓒ Ⓓ	14 Ⓕ Ⓖ Ⓗ Ⓙ	21 Ⓐ Ⓑ Ⓒ Ⓓ	28 Ⓕ Ⓖ Ⓗ Ⓙ	35 Ⓐ Ⓑ Ⓒ Ⓓ	

Practice Test 2

EXAMINEE STATEMENTS, CERTIFICATION, AND SIGNATURE

1. **Statements:** I understand that by registering for, launching, starting, or submitting answer documents for an ACT® test, I am agreeing to comply with and be bound by the *Terms and Conditions: Testing Rules and Policies for the ACT® Test* ("Terms").

   I UNDERSTAND AND AGREE THAT THE TERMS PERMIT ACT TO CANCEL MY SCORES IN CERTAIN CIRCUMSTANCES. THE TERMS ALSO LIMIT DAMAGES AVAILABLE TO ME AND REQUIRE ARBITRATION OF CERTAIN DISPUTES. BY AGREEING TO ARBITRATION, ACT AND I BOTH WAIVE THE RIGHT TO HAVE THOSE DISPUTES HEARD BY A JUDGE OR JURY.

   I understand that ACT owns the test questions and responses, and I will not share them with anyone by any form of communication before, during, or after the test administration. I understand that taking the test for someone else may violate the law and subject me to legal penalties.

   I consent to the collection and processing of personally identifying information I provide, and its subsequent use and disclosure, as described in the ACT Privacy Policy (www.act.org/privacy.html). If I am taking the test outside of the United States, I also permit ACT to transfer my personally identifying information to the United States, to ACT, or to a third-party service provider, where it will be subject to use and disclosure under the laws of the United States, including being accessible to law enforcement or national security authorities.

2. **Certification:** Copy the italicized certification below, then sign, date, and print your name in the spaces provided.

   *I agree to the **Statements** above and certify that I am the person whose information appears on this form.*

____

____

Your Signature   Today's Date   Print Your Name

The **ACT**®   **Form 25MC2**
2026 | 2027

Directions

This booklet contains tests in English, mathematics, reading, and science. These tests measure skills and abilities highly related to high school course work and success in college. **Calculators may be used on the mathematics test only.**

The questions in each test are numbered, and the suggested answers for each question are lettered. On the answer document, the rows of ovals are numbered to match the questions, and the ovals in each row are lettered to correspond to the suggested answers.

For each question, first decide which answer is best. Next, locate on the answer document the row of ovals numbered the same as the question. Then, locate the oval in that row lettered the same as your answer. Finally, fill in the oval completely. Use a soft lead pencil and make your marks heavy and black. **Do not use ink or a mechanical pencil.**

Mark only one answer to each question. If you change your mind about an answer, erase your first mark thoroughly before marking your new answer. For each question, make certain that you mark in the row of ovals with the same number as the question.

Only responses marked on your answer document will be scored. Your score on each test will be based only on the number of questions you answer correctly during the time allowed for that test. You will **not** be penalized for guessing. **It is to your advantage to answer every question even if you must guess.**

You may work on each test **only** when the testing staff tells you to do so. If you finish a test before time is called for that test, you should use the time remaining to reconsider questions you are uncertain about in that test. You may **not** look back to a test on which time has already been called, and you may **not** go ahead to another test. To do so will disqualify you from the examination.

Lay your pencil down immediately when time is called at the end of each test. You may **not** for any reason fill in or alter ovals for a test after time is called for that test. To do so will disqualify you from the examination.

Do not fold or tear the pages of your test booklet.

**DO NOT OPEN THIS BOOKLET
UNTIL TOLD TO DO SO.**

The ONLY Official Prep Guide from the Makers of the ACT

1 ▪ ▪ ▪ ▪ ▪ ▪ ▪ ▪ ▪ 1

ENGLISH TEST

35 Minutes—50 Questions

DIRECTIONS: In the passages that follow, certain words and phrases are underlined and numbered. In the right-hand column, you will find alternatives for the underlined part. You are to choose the best answer to each question. If you think the original version is best, choose "**No Change.**"

You will also find questions about a section of the passage, or about the passage as a whole. These questions do not refer to an underlined portion of the passage, but rather are identified by a number or numbers in a box.

For each question, choose the alternative you consider best and fill in the corresponding oval on your answer document. Read each passage through once before you begin to answer the questions that accompany it. For many of the questions, you must read several sentences beyond the question to determine the answer. Be sure that you have read far enough ahead each time you choose an alternative.

PASSAGE I

NASA's Inaugural Artist in Residence

[1]

For over forty years, Laurie Anderson has appropriated electronics, video, and sound, to create
art that defies categorization. In 1972, Anderson ignited her career by conducting a symphony using only car horns. [A] Five years later, she invented a violin that clones as an audiotape player. Anderson went on to stage technology-enhanced performance art, direct music videos, and invent tools to manipulate sound. [B] In 2002, Anderson's fascination with technology contributed to her being named the first artist in residence at NASA, where she was given free rein to explore the facilities in search of inspiration. [C]

1. Which choice makes the sentence most grammatically acceptable?
   A. **No Change**
   B. sound, to create,
   C. sound to create,
   D. sound to create

2. Which choice is clearest and most precise in context?
   F. **No Change**
   G. duplicates
   H. doubles
   J. copies

3. Which choice makes the sentence most grammatically acceptable?
   A. **No Change**
   B. the invention of
   C. inventing
   D. to invent

GO ON TO THE NEXT PAGE.

1 ■ ■ ■ ■ ■ ■ ■ ■ ■ 1

[2]

She found her inspiration in how technology has developed over time. When Anderson was growing up in the 1950s, space travel and artificial intelligence existed only in science fiction stories. A half century later, at NASA, Anderson witnessed the realization of both.
4
During a visit to a virtual airport control center,

Anderson viewed panoramic images of the red
5
planet, courtesy of a video feed provided by the Mars Global Surveyor satellite. At the Jet Propulsion Laboratory in Pasadena, California, she was introduced to robots that function autonomously through control-and-sensor-processing software. [D]

[3]

Drawing on her NASA experiences, Anderson wrote and produced a ninety-minute performance art piece titled *The End of the Moon*. The performance features Anderson on a candlelit stage, standing in front of an image of the moon's surface. 6 Anderson begins the show by referencing the technology to which she was privy at NASA. Anderson then complements these references by subtly demonstrating technology's impact on music.

4. Which choice provides the most effective transition from the first two sentences of the paragraph to the rest of the paragraph?

F. No Change
G. In fact, science fiction masters like Ray Bradbury and Isaac Asimov received much acclaim for their work at this time.
H. Anderson, who grew up in Chicago, studied classical violin as a child.
J. NASA has grown considerably since it was established in 1958.

5. Which choice most effectively maintains the essay's tone?

A. No Change
B. eyeballed all-encompassing snapshots
C. beheld wide-ranging pictorial images
D. ogled comprehensive photographs

6. At this point, the writer is considering adding the following true sentence:

> Neil Armstrong was the first man to be photographed walking on the moon's surface.

Should the writer make this addition?

F. Yes, because the sentence contributes to the paragraph's discussion of how Anderson uses photography in her performance art.
G. Yes, because the sentence contributes to the paragraph's discussion of how and why *The End of the Moon* is a reimagining of NASA's first moon landing.
H. No, because the sentence is not relevant to the paragraph's description and interpretation of *The End of the Moon*.
J. No, because the sentence is not relevant to the paragraph's critique of Anderson's struggle to make performance art commercially viable.

GO ON TO THE NEXT PAGE.

1 ▪ ▪ ▪ ▪ ▪ ▪ ▪ ▪ ▪ 1

While <u>sweeping the bow over the strings of a viola,</u>
₇
Anderson manipulates the music via a laptop computer.

The string <u>music that transforms</u> into electronic sounds,
₈
which then reverberate into futuristic, otherworldly music.

The result is surreal and <u>stimulating exactly</u> what you
₉
might expect from NASA's inaugural artist in residence.

7. Which choice provides the most vivid description of Anderson's action?
   A. **No Change**
   B. moving a bow over a stringed instrument,
   C. producing music by playing a viola,
   D. rubbing an instrument with a bow,

8. Which choice makes the sentence most grammatically acceptable?
   F. **No Change**
   G. music is transformed
   H. music, transforming
   J. music transforming

9. Which choice makes the sentence most grammatically acceptable?
   A. **No Change**
   B. stimulating: and
   C. stimulating—
   D. stimulating;

> Question 10 asks about the preceding passage as a whole.

10. The writer is considering adding the following sentence to the essay:

    > Her "talking stick," for instance, was a six-foot-long baton that could record and replicate sounds.

    If the writer were to add this sentence, it would most logically be placed at:

    F. Point A in Paragraph 1.
    G. Point B in Paragraph 1.
    H. Point C in Paragraph 1.
    J. Point D in Paragraph 2.

GO ON TO THE NEXT PAGE.

PASSAGE II

Zebra ID: Biological Bar Codes

To help biologists monitoring zebras in the wild, scientists at the University of Illinois and Princeton University developed a software program called StripeSpotter, which catalogs and identifies zebras. StripeSpotter translates the pattern of stripes on a zebra's <u>side, into an identifier,</u> similar to a bar
₁₁
code, that can be compared to other zebra stripe-pattern identifiers that have been stored in a database. ☐12

The process begins when a researcher uploads a still photograph of a zebra to StripeSpotter. The researcher then crops a rectangular section of the photograph, making sure to <u>capture</u> the stripes on the zebra's
₁₃
side. StripeSpotter converts that section into <u>a stark</u>
₁₄
<u>black-and-white image composed of parallel, vertical lines.</u>
₁₄

11. Which choice makes the sentence most grammatically acceptable?

  A. **No Change**
  B. side into an identifier,
  C. side, into an identifier
  D. side into an identifier

12. At this point, the writer is considering adding the following true sentence:

> Some researchers believe that the stripes on zebras help the animals identify one another in a herd.

Should the writer make this addition here?

  F. Yes, because it makes clear that zebras have always been able to do what StripeSpotter can do.
  G. Yes, because it shifts the essay back to its main topic, interpreting the stripes on zebras.
  H. No, because it isn't relevant to the explanation of what StripeSpotter is and how it works.
  J. No, because it doesn't specify why it is important that zebras are able to identify one another.

13. Which choice is clearest and most precise in context?

  A. **No Change**
  B. apprehend
  C. acquire
  D. take

14. The writer is considering revising the underlined portion to the following:

> an image of even, black-and-white lines.

Given that the information is accurate, should the writer make this revision?

  F. Yes, because the revision reveals that StripeSpotter can be used to make line art based on a zebra's stripes.
  G. Yes, because unlike the original wording, the revision highlights that a zebra identification code is made up of parallel lines.
  H. No, because the revision lacks the clarity and specificity of the description in the original wording.
  J. No, because the revision suggests that the means through which StripeSpotter creates images are largely unscientific.

GO ON TO THE NEXT PAGE.

1 ▪ ▪ ▪ ▪ ▪ ▪ ▪ ▪ 1

The widths of the lines <u>correspond</u> perfectly to the
                            15
widths of the zebra's stripes. This is the zebra's
"StripeCode," unique to each animal in much the
same way a fingerprint is unique to each person. The
StripeCode is logged in the database, where a researcher
uploading a new photograph of a zebra can scan the
stored codes to find a potential match.

15. Which choice makes the sentence most grammatically
acceptable?
  A. No Change
  B. has corresponded
  C. is corresponding
  D. corresponds

PASSAGE III

Celadon Remnants

[1] At the Broadway Station of the Long Island
Rail Road in Flushing, Queens, commuters ponder a mural
spanning over three hundred square feet on the station's
south wall. [2] But as they come closer, commuters notice
the silhouettes are also mosaics, constructed entirely of
ceramic shards. [3] From afar, the mural appears as a
series of aquamarine, vase-shaped silhouettes against
a white tile background. ☐16

The mural, titled *Celadon Remnants*, is
artist Jean Shin's homage to the Korean American
community in Flushing. When she was commissioned
by the Metropolitan Transportation Authority of
New York City to <u>spawn</u> a site-specific artwork,
                    17

<u>visually representing her dual identity was a means</u>
                            18
<u>sought by Shin</u> as an American and a Korean. She chose
      18
to use traditional celadon pottery, albeit in a new way.

16. Which sequence of sentences makes this paragraph most
logical?
  F. No Change
  G. 1, 3, 2
  H. 2, 1, 3
  J. 3, 1, 2

17. Which choice is clearest and most precise in context?
  A. No Change
  B. accomplish
  C. perform
  D. produce

18. Which choice makes the sentence most grammatically
acceptable?
  F. No Change
  G. sought by Shin was a means of visually representing her dual identity
  H. a means of visually representing her dual identity
was sought by Shin
  J. Shin sought a means of visually representing her
dual identity

GO ON TO THE NEXT PAGE.

1 ■ ■ ■ ■ ■ ■ ■ ■ ■ 1

Celadon is a ceramic ware named for its'
aquamarine glaze. Originally from China, celadon was
further developed in the tenth and eleventh centuries in
Korea, where inlaid designs and decorative elements
were added. Over the centuries, celadon became a
cultural treasure in Korea. Today, South Korean
ceramicists will accept nothing less than perfection
in creating their art. In fact, if the ceramicist deems a
piece imperfect, he or she will often scrap it entirely.

Shin decided that these scraps, or shards,
would be an ideal medium for her mural. In 2008, she
contacted ceramicists in the South Korean city of Icheon
for celadon shards and arranged to be shipped to Queens.
The ceramicists sent Shin over six thousand shards.

Using the shards—many of whose are adorned with

alphabetic symbols and assorted patterns—Shin
constructed her mural.

For Shin, the shards themselves took on
significance: they represented her feeling of being
broken off or "fractured" from her birthplace of

Seoul, South Korea. In Queens, Shin's use of the
fragments to construct an artwork that celebrated a
Korean tradition. The result is sublime. The silhouettes
merge Shin's past and present, creating an exquisite
meditation on Korean American identity.

19. Which choice makes the sentence most grammatically
acceptable?
A. **No Change**
B. it is
C. it's
D. its

20. Given that all the choices are true, which one most
effectively leads the reader from the first two sentences of the paragraph to the rest of the paragraph?
F. **No Change**
G. The celadon's color is a result of iron oxide's
transformation from ferric to ferrous iron during
the firing process.
H. It has been theorized that the name "celadon"
derives from the Sanskrit words for *green* and
stone.
J. Shin Sang-ho, one of Korea's most celebrated
modern ceramicists, began his career re-creating
traditional celadon.

21. The best placement for the underlined portion would be:
A. where it is now.
B. after the word *ceramicists.*
C. after the word *city.*
D. after the word *arranged.*

22. Which choice makes the sentence most grammatically
acceptable?
F. **No Change**
G. which
H. whom
J. that

23. Which choice provides the most specific description of
the adornments on the shards of celadon?
A. **No Change**
B. Korean characters and labyrinthine patterns—
C. different letters and a plethora of patterns—
D. numerous symbols and various designs—

24. Which choice makes the sentence most grammatically
acceptable?
F. **No Change**
G. significance: and
H. significance,
J. significance

25. Which choice makes the sentence most grammatically
acceptable?
A. **No Change**
B. Shin used
C. using
D. **Delete** the underlined portion.

GO ON TO THE NEXT PAGE.

1 ▪ ▪ ▪ ▪ ▪ ▪ ▪ ▪ ▪ 1

Captain Charles Young's Road to the Giant Sequoias

Able to grow as tall as a twenty-six-story building and as wide as a city street, giant sequoia trees are the largest living things on Earth. Sequoia National Park in California's Sierra Nevada mountain range contains 275 known caves. [26] Yet until 1903, few visitors could gain access to the trees in the park's Giant Forest: there was no completed road.

The US Army—which from 1891 to 1913 was responsible for improving national parks during the summer months—had managed to complete only about six miles of the road to the Giant Forest. Army Captain Charles Young, however, was not deterred. The first Black superintendent of a national park and a revered leader of the army's all-Black 9th and 10th Cavalries, Young had [27] the experience needed to direct the completion of the project.

In June 1903, under Young's command, the soldiers began work on the road. Soon the eleven-mile route was complete. By the middle of August, vehicles could enter the park. Young and his troops had succeeded where no one else had; they enabled visitors to get to the giant sequoias more easily.

Because he had his troops [28]

send most of their efforts into the road, Young [29] was just as concerned with maintaining the park's natural features. His troops guarded the grounds against illegal grazing, poaching, and logging.

26. Given that all the choices are accurate, which one provides the most effective transition between the first sentence of this paragraph and the last sentence of this paragraph?

F. **No Change**
G. harbors endangered species like the bighorn sheep and the California condor.
H. boasts the greatest concentration of giant sequoia groves in the world.
J. is approximately 84% wilderness.

27. Which choice makes the sentence or sentences most grammatically acceptable?

A. **No Change**
B. Cavalries, Young having
C. Cavalries; Young had
D. Cavalries. Young had

28. Which choice is clearest and most precise in context?

F. **No Change**
G. Although
H. Unless
J. If

29. Which choice is clearest and most precise in context?

A. **No Change**
B. channel
C. convey
D. shape

GO ON TO THE NEXT PAGE.

Nevertheless, since tourist foot traffic tended to damage
<u>30</u>
some of the giant sequoias, Young had his soldiers place
fences around the most damaged trees to protect them

from <u>future bad stuff.</u>
<u>31</u>

Over one hundred years later, the contributions
Young made possible <u>has been</u> counted among the most
<u>32</u>

significant in the park's history. $\boxed{33}$ In 2003, the National
Park Service decided to formally recognize the efforts of
Captain Young (who had been promoted to lieutenant
colonel in 1916). Today, those who visit the park use

Young's road to reach the Giant Forest, <u>which is home</u>
<u>34</u>
<u>to General Sherman, the world's largest tree.</u>
<u>34</u>

30. Which transition word is most logical in context?

- **F. No Change**
- **G.** Additionally,
- **H.** Thus,
- **J.** Still,

31. Which choice most effectively maintains the essay's tone?

- **A. No Change**
- **B.** further harm in the future.
- **C.** further harm.
- **D.** bad stuff.

32. Which choice makes the sentence most grammatically acceptable?

- **F. No Change**
- **G.** was
- **H.** are
- **J.** is

33. At this point, the writer is considering adding the following true statement:

> Park enthusiast George Palmer was the one who petitioned the National Park Service to recognize Young's contributions.

Should the writer make this addition here?

- **A.** Yes, because it explains why it took so long for the National Park Service to formally recognize Young's accomplishments.
- **B.** Yes, because it provides information about how Palmer inspired Young's actions at the park.
- **C.** No, because it suggests that other people besides Palmer had already petitioned the National Park Service on Young's behalf.
- **D.** No, because it provides information that is only loosely related to the main subject of the essay.

34. Which of the following choices best concludes the sentence and the essay?

- **F. No Change**
- **G.** where, among the trees dedicated to and named for US generals and presidents, the Colonel Young Tree also stands.
- **H.** where, even beneath the cover of nightfall, people can enjoy park-sponsored activities such as lantern tours.
- **J.** which is a popular place to visit.

Taking Additional Practice Tests

GO ON TO THE NEXT PAGE.

1 ■ ■ ■ ■ ■ ■ ■ ■ 1

> Question 35 asks about the preceding passage as a whole.

35. Suppose the writer's primary purpose had been to provide an overview of the history of Sequoia National Park. Would this essay accomplish that purpose?

   A. Yes, because it explains how the construction of roads through the park has led to broadscale changes from the park's establishment to today.

   B. Yes, because it describes how Young's contributions led to a historic surge in annual visits to the park.

   C. No, because it focuses on Young's military career rather than on the history of the park.

   D. No, because it instead chronicles one significant part of the park's history.

The Curious Case of *Turritopsis dohrnii*

In 1988, marine biology student Christian Sommer
<u>   36   </u>
observed *Turritopsis dohrnii*, a diminutive jellyfish,

doing something astonishing: reverting from mature

jellyfish to hydroid colonies, an earlier life stage.

In a sense, they grew younger.
<u>   37   </u>

T. dohrnii has <u>no brain or heart. After</u>
             38

fertilization, a *T. dohrnii* egg develops into a free-

swimming, ovoid larva. In time, the larva settles on

the ocean floor and transforms into a mound of cells—a

hydroid colony. Buds grow on the colony and develop

into young jellyfish with the familiar bell-like shape and

tentacles. These jellyfish then detach from the colony

and drift away, reaching maturity in a few weeks.

36. Which choice makes the sentence most grammatically acceptable?

   F. **No Change**
   G. marine, biology student, Christian Sommer,
   H. marine biology student, Christian Sommer,
   J. marine biology student Christian Sommer,

37. If the writer were to delete the underlined sentence, the paragraph would primarily lose:

   A. information explaining that *T. dohrnii* had been observed reverting from maturity to an earlier life stage.

   B. a statement that helps clarify the previous details about *T. dohrnii*'s reversion to hydroid colonies.

   C. an alternate perspective that contradicts Sommer's conclusions about *T. dohrnii*.

   D. evidence that Sommer continued to observe *T. dohrnii* over time.

38. Given that all the choices are accurate, which one best helps the sentence introduce the main focus of the paragraph?

   F. **No Change**
   G. been found primarily in the Mediterranean Sea and in waters near Japan.
   H. only eight tentacles as a young jellyfish but over eighty as an adult.
   J. a multistage life cycle.

GO ON TO THE NEXT PAGE.

After Sommer's discovery, studies confirmed that *T. dohrnii*'s life cycle is not a one-way street. An adult *T. dohrnii, if stressed*—by injury, disease, or even just old age, has the ability to revert to a hydroid colony. That colony can then create new jellyfish, which in turn can also revert to hydroid colonies. There's no apparent limit to these perpetual cycles of metamorphic transformation.

In the 1990s, journalists nicknamed *T. dohrnii* the "immortal jellyfish."

39. Which choice makes the sentence most grammatically acceptable?
- **A. No Change**
- **B.** *T. dohrnii, if stressed*
- **C.** *T. dohrnii if stressed,*
- **D.** *T. dohrnii if stressed*

40. Which choice is least redundant in context?
- **F. No Change**
- **G.** endlessly recurring cycles of transformation.
- **H.** transformative cycles of metamorphosis.
- **J.** cycles of transformation.

Ukulele Life

My older sister was a guitar buff *and my idol* when I was growing up. She would teach me songs on her acoustic guitar now and then after school and on long family road trips to the beach. In those moments, my sister and I were the closest we've ever been. And my guitar itself felt like, well, family.

When my sister left Chicago for college in California, I began carting my guitar around everywhere: to school, to work, to *friends houses*. Years later, my guitar accompanied me on business trips. No matter where I was, playing it made me feel a little bit closer to home.

41. If the writer were to delete the underlined portion, the paragraph would primarily lose:
- **A.** an indication of why the narrator became interested in playing the guitar.
- **B.** an indication that the narrator learned to play guitar at a relatively young age.
- **C.** a detail that specifies how much older the sister is compared to the narrator.
- **D.** a detail that reveals the amount of musical talent the narrator's sister had.

42. Which choice makes the sentence most grammatically acceptable?
- **F. No Change**
- **G.** friend's house's.
- **H.** friends' houses.
- **J.** friend's houses.

GO ON TO THE NEXT PAGE.

1 ◼ ◼ ◼ ◼ ◼ ◼ ◼ ◼ **1**

But one day, after landing in Honolulu, Hawai'i, for an extended trip, I couldn't locate my guitar on the luggage carousel. Panicked, I assailed[43] airport personnel, who assured myself[44] that they would try to recover my beloved instrument. At that moment of my extended trip,[45] continuing the trip without it seemed impossible.

My worries began to dissipate, though, as I walked out of the airport and into the balmy Hawaiian air. In front of me, a man was playing what looked like a miniature guitar. Warm, mellow tones accrued from[46] the instrument, complementing the lyrical rhythm of the Hawaiian words he sang. It was a ukulele.

As soon as I could, I bought a ukulele of my own. I began to linger on[47] the beach, where several native Hawaiians often played. I watched them for hours, my ukulele in my hands, and practiced. Unlike the guitar, which has six strings, my ukulele had four; to make the same chords with the uke, I had to learn completely different finger positions. I also had trouble with dexterity at first because the neck of the uke is much narrower then that of a guitar.[48] I had to retrain my fingers to make smaller movements in order to shape the chords.

43. Which choice best illustrates the fervor with which the narrator communicated with the airport personnel?
  A. **No Change**
  B. approached
  C. questioned
  D. contacted

44. Which choice makes the sentence most grammatically acceptable?
  F. **No Change**
  G. whom assured myself
  H. whom assured me
  J. who assured me

45. Which choice is least redundant in context?
  A. **No Change**
  B. moment, due to the fact that I was on an extended trip,
  C. very moment during my time in Honolulu,
  D. moment,

46. Which choice is clearest and most precise in context?
  F. **No Change**
  G. distributed
  H. appeared
  J. issued

47. Which choice makes the sentence most grammatically acceptable?
  A. **No Change**
  B. Beginning to linger on
  C. Lingering on
  D. On

48. Which choice makes the sentence most grammatically acceptable?
  F. **No Change**
  G. than that of a guitar.
  H. than it.
  J. then it.

GO ON TO THE NEXT PAGE.

When I wasn't working, I was on the beach,

losing myself in the bright notes of the uke. Eventually,

I began playing <u>music</u> like "He'eia" with the locals.
       49

<u>And the sound of the ukulele is synonymous with</u>
                        50
<u>the romance and beauty of Hawai'i's beaches.</u>
                        50

49. Which choice best specifies the type of songs the narrator played on the ukulele?

   A. **No Change**
   B. Hawaiian classics
   C. tropical tunes
   D. things

50. Which choice best concludes the essay by emphasizing the central point made in the first and second paragraphs?

   F. **No Change**
   G. And I couldn't think of a better way to spend my guitarless time in Honolulu.
   H. And although I was guitarless and far from family, I felt like I was home.
   J. And even though I was on a business trip, I didn't want to leave.

END OF TEST 1

STOP! DO NOT TURN THE PAGE UNTIL TOLD TO DO SO.

2   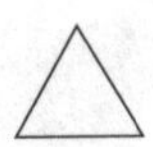 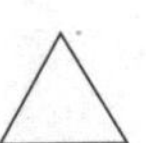       2

MATHEMATICS TEST
50 Minutes—45 Questions

DIRECTIONS: Solve each problem, choose the correct answer, and then fill in the corresponding oval on your answer document.

Do not linger over problems that take too much time. Solve as many as you can; then return to the others in the time you have left for this test.

You are permitted to use a calculator on this test. You may use your calculator for any problems you choose, but some of the problems may best be done without using a calculator.

Note: Unless otherwise stated, all of the following should be assumed.

1. Illustrative figures are **not** necessarily drawn to scale.
2. Geometric figures lie in a plane.
3. The word "line" indicates a straight line.
4. The word "average" indicates arithmetic mean.

---

1. For all nonzero values of x and y, which of the following expressions is equivalent to $-\dfrac{35x^5y^4}{5xy}$?

    A. $-7x^4y^3$
    B. $-7x^5y^4$
    C. $-7x^6y^5$
    D. $-40x^4y^3$

2. The degree measures of the 3 angles of the triangle shown are expressed in terms of x. What is the value of x?

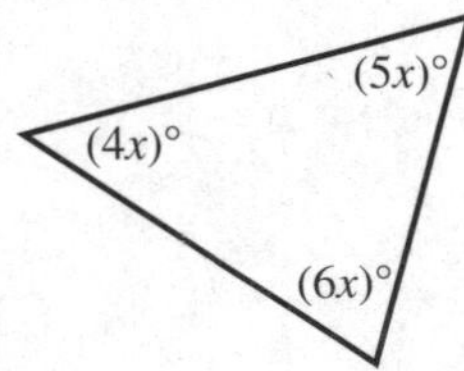

    F. 10
    G. 12
    H. 24
    J. 30

3. A 48.5-ounce batch of cologne will be used to fill empty bottles. Each full bottle will contain 0.35 ounces of cologne. This batch of cologne will fill at most how many bottles full of cologne?

    A. 13
    B. 14
    C. 138
    D. 139

DO YOUR FIGURING HERE.

GO ON TO THE NEXT PAGE.

2          **2**

DO YOUR FIGURING HERE.

4. Of the 200 parking spaces in a parking lot, 6% of the spaces are reserved for accessible parking. Of those parking spaces **not** reserved for accessible parking, 20 are suitable for compact cars only. How many spaces that are **not** reserved for accessible parking are suitable for noncompact cars?

   F. 160
   G. 168
   H. 180
   J. 188

5. Ricardo started a savings account for his daughter Ruth by depositing \$500 into the account for her 1st birthday. For each successive birthday, Ricardo deposits \$200 more than the amount deposited for the previous birthday. This is the only money deposited into the account. What is the total amount of money Ricardo will have deposited into the account for Ruth up to and including her 6th birthday?

   A. \$4,000
   B. \$4,200
   C. \$4,700
   D. \$6,000

6. Which of the following matrices is equal to
$$\begin{bmatrix} 9 & 2 \\ -4 & 1 \end{bmatrix} + \begin{bmatrix} -6 & 8 \\ 7 & 6 \end{bmatrix}?$$

   F. $\begin{bmatrix} -40 & 84 \\ 31 & -26 \end{bmatrix}$

   G. $\begin{bmatrix} 3 & 10 \\ 3 & 7 \end{bmatrix}$

   H. $\begin{bmatrix} 3 & 10 \\ 11 & 7 \end{bmatrix}$

   J. $\begin{bmatrix} 11 & 2 \\ -3 & 13 \end{bmatrix}$

7. Lyle and Ming are painting an art room. They started with 4 gallons of paint. On the first day, Lyle used $\frac{1}{2}$ gallon of paint and Ming used $1\frac{1}{4}$ gallons of paint. How many gallons of paint were left when they completed their first day of painting?

   A. $1\frac{3}{4}$

   B. $2\frac{1}{4}$

   C. $2\frac{3}{4}$

   D. $3\frac{1}{2}$

GO ON TO THE NEXT PAGE.

2 △ △ △ △ △ △ △ △ △ **2**

DO YOUR FIGURING HERE.

8. In the standard (x,y) coordinate plane, what is the slope of the line through $(-3,1)$ and $(5,6)$?

F. $-\dfrac{5}{2}$

G. $-\dfrac{5}{8}$

H. $\dfrac{5}{8}$

J. $\dfrac{5}{2}$

9. The lengths of corresponding sides of 2 similar right triangles are in the ratio 4:5. The hypotenuse of the smaller triangle is 24 inches long. How many inches long is the hypotenuse of the larger triangle?

A. 1.25
B. 20
C. 25
D. 30

10. The lengths of the 3 sides of right triangle $\triangle ABC$ shown are given in meters. What is $\sin A$?

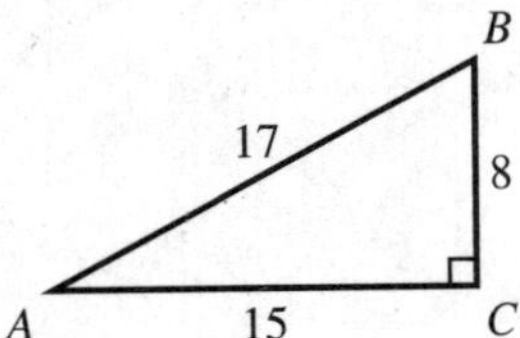

F. $\dfrac{8}{17}$

G. $\dfrac{15}{17}$

H. $\dfrac{17}{15}$

J. $\dfrac{17}{8}$

11. In the figure shown, C is on the segment with endpoints A and D. The distance between A and B is 2,000 km, between A and C is 1,600 km, between A and D is 2,500 km, and between B and C is 1,200 km. What is the distance, in kilometers, between B and D?

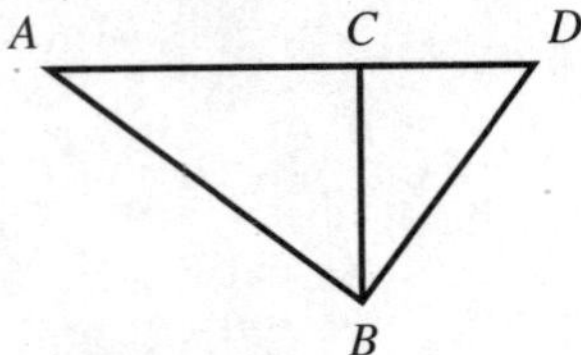

A. $300\sqrt{7}$
B. 900
C. 1,200
D. 1,500

GO ON TO THE NEXT PAGE.

2 △ △ △ △ △ △ △ △ △ **2**

DO YOUR FIGURING HERE.

12. What is the sum of the 2 solutions of the equation $x^2 - 4x - 45 = 0$?

  F. -45
  G. -5
  H. 0
  J. 4

13. Quadrant I of the standard (x,y) coordinate plane is shown on a large computer screen. A blinking dot is positioned at $(2,3)$. The dot makes exactly 2 moves: first, horizontally in the positive x direction for 4 seconds at a speed of 0.5 coordinate units per second; then, vertically in the positive y direction for 2 seconds at the same speed. At what point is the dot located after these 2 moves?

  A. $(2,6)$
  B. $(3,5)$
  C. $(4,4)$
  D. $(5,3)$

14. What value of x makes the equation $-\dfrac{1}{81} = -3^x$ true?

  F. -4
  G. 4
  H. 27
  J. $\dfrac{1}{243}$

15. The equation $R = \dfrac{P}{I^2}$ gives the resistance, R, in terms of the power, P, and the current, I, of an electrical system. Which of the following expressions gives I in terms of P and R?

  A. $\sqrt{\dfrac{R}{P}}$
  B. $\sqrt{\dfrac{P}{R}}$
  C. $\dfrac{P}{R}$
  D. $\dfrac{R}{P}$

16. One welcome sign flashes every 8 seconds, and another welcome sign flashes every 12 seconds. At a certain instant, the 2 signs flash at the same time. How many seconds elapse until the 2 signs next flash at the same time?

  F. 4
  G. 20
  H. 24
  J. 96

GO ON TO THE NEXT PAGE.

2 △ △ △ △ △ △ △ △ △ **2**

DO YOUR FIGURING HERE.

17. The area of a certain square is 900 square inches. What is the perimeter of this square in inches?

A. 30
B. 60
C. 120
D. 225

18. The Department of Natural Resources (DNR) is estimating the deer population in Twin Pines County. Several months ago, DNR rangers captured, tagged, and then released 108 deer. Recently, DNR rangers captured 54 deer and found that 36 of them had been tagged in the earlier capture. The DNR estimates the county's deer population using the proportion shown. What is the DNR's estimate of the deer population in the county?

$$\frac{\text{tagged deer in capture 1}}{\text{deer population}} = \frac{\text{tagged deer in capture 2}}{\text{deer in capture 2}}$$

F. 108
G. 126
H. 144
J. 162

19. In an arithmetic sequence, the 10th term (a_{10}) is 30, and the common difference is 2. What is the 1st term (a_1)?

A. 6
B. 11
C. 12
D. 15

20. A pedometer records the number of steps a person takes as he or she walks. When a pedometer records 3,898 steps taken by a person who covers a distance of 2.25 feet per step, how much distance, to the nearest 0.1 miles, did the person cover?

(Note: 1 mile = 5,280 feet)

F. 0.3
G. 0.6
H. 1.7
J. 3.0

GO ON TO THE NEXT PAGE.

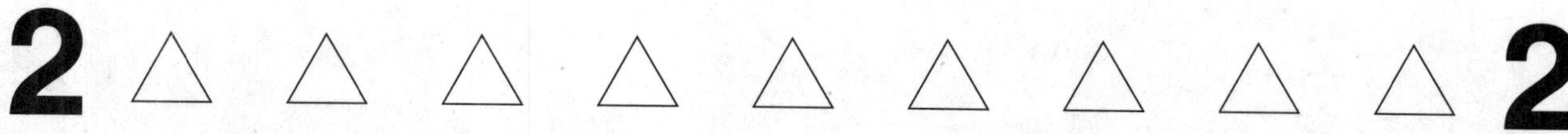

2 △ △ △ △ △ △ △ △ △ **2**

DO YOUR FIGURING HERE.

21. Among a group of 20 students, 13 are members of the Math Club, 11 are members of the Drama Club, and 9 are members of both clubs. How many of the 20 students are **not** members of either club?

A. 4
B. 5
C. 11
D. 13

22. For the mean of 7 numbers to increase by 4, by how much would the sum of the 7 numbers have to increase?

F. 4
G. 7
H. 11
J. 28

23. Which of the following is an equation of the circle in the standard (x,y) coordinate plane whose center is at $(4,-3)$ and whose radius is 5 coordinate units long?

A. $(x-4)^2 + (y+3)^2 = 25$
B. $(x-3)^2 + (y+4)^2 = 25$
C. $(x+3)^2 + (y-4)^2 = 5$
D. $(x+4)^2 + (y-3)^2 = 25$

24. All 25 students in a chemistry class took a test. Each student earned a test score that was an integer number of points, and no 2 students earned the same test score. The median test score was 80 points. How many students earned a test score that was greater than 80 points?

F. 12
G. 13
H. 14
J. 20

GO ON TO THE NEXT PAGE.

The ONLY Official Prep Guide from the Makers of the ACT

2     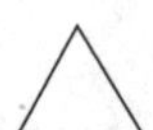   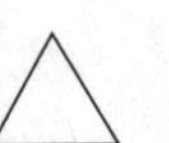  **2**

DO YOUR FIGURING HERE.

25. Shefali goes to a farmers' market every Saturday. Two Saturdays ago, Shefali purchased 3 apples and 4 oranges for a total of \$3.47. Last Saturday, she purchased 12 oranges but no apples and spent \$6.36. Today, she has only one \$10 bill. Given that none of the prices have changed over the last 3 weeks, what is the maximum number of apples she can purchase today?

(Note: No sales tax is charged at this farmers' market.)

A. 19
B. 21
C. 22
D. 23

26. In $\triangle DEF$, shown in the figure, $\overline{EG}$ is an altitude, $\angle DEF$ is a right angle, $EF = 20$ centimeters, and the measure of $\angle EDF$ is 30°. What is EG in centimeters?

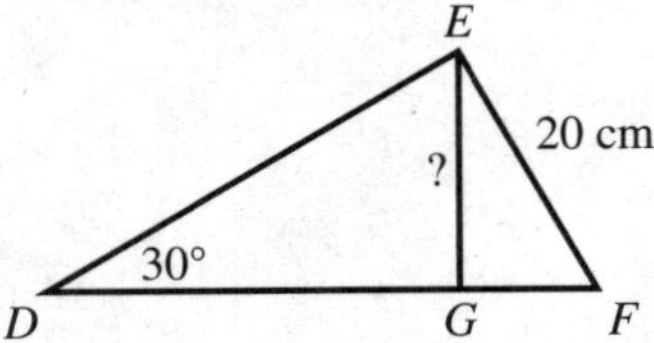

F. 10
G. $10\sqrt{3}$
H. 20
J. $20\sqrt{3}$

27. Let the polynomial functions f and g be defined as $f(x) = x^2 + 7x - 3$ and $g(x) = x^2 - 4x + 5$. Let $h(x) = f(x) - g(x)$. What is $h(2)$?

A. 8
B. 14
C. 22
D. 24

28. For real numbers x and y such that $0 \le x \le 5$ and $y \ge 9$, the expression $\frac{x+y}{y}$ can have which of the following values?

F. 6

G. $\frac{14}{5}$

H. $\frac{10}{9}$

J. 0

GO ON TO THE NEXT PAGE.

2 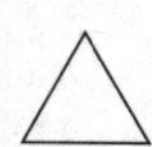 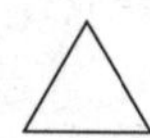     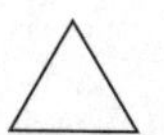  **2**

29. Given the functions $f(x) = x^2 + 1$ and $g(x) = x - 3$, which of the following expressions is $f(g(x))$?

A. $x^2 - 8$

B. $x^2 - 6x + 10$

C. $x^2 + x - 2$

D. $x^3 - 3x^2 + x - 3$

DO YOUR FIGURING HERE.

30. Given that the equation $\dfrac{4x - y}{x + y} = \dfrac{5}{2}$ is true, what is the value of $\frac{x}{y}$?

F. $\dfrac{2}{3}$

G. $\dfrac{5}{2}$

H. $\dfrac{7}{3}$

J. $\dfrac{7}{5}$

31. Juro traveled to 3 locations during a workday. Juro remained at each location a whole number of hours. The graph shows the relationship between the time, in hours, in his workday and total distance, in kilometers, traveled. Which of the following values is closest to the average speed, in kilometers per hour, when Juro was traveling?

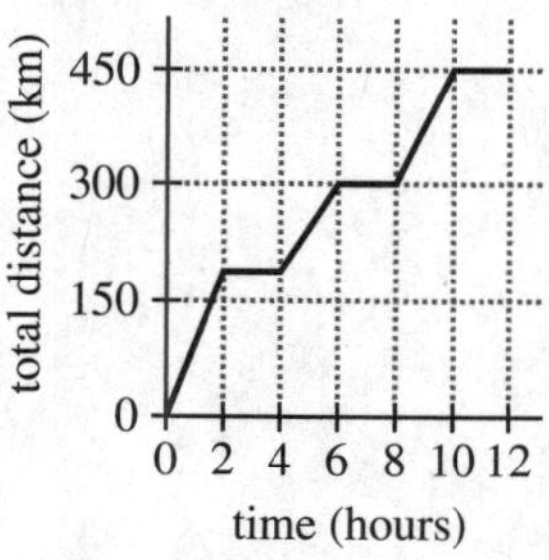

A. 45
B. 57
C. 60
D. 75

32. What is the amplitude of the function $y = 3 \sin x$?

F. $\dfrac{1}{3}$

G. 1

H. 3

J. 6

GO ON TO THE NEXT PAGE.

2 △ △ △ △ △ △ △ △ △ **2**

33. For all nonzero values of w, which of the following expressions is equivalent to $\frac{4}{w} + \frac{2}{w^2}$?

A. $\dfrac{2w+1}{w^2}$

B. $\dfrac{4w+2}{w^2}$

C. $\dfrac{6}{w+w^2}$

D. $\dfrac{6}{w^2}$

34. A number line graph includes the points at real numbers a and b, as shown. Which of the following inequalities expresses an interval that must include the product ab?

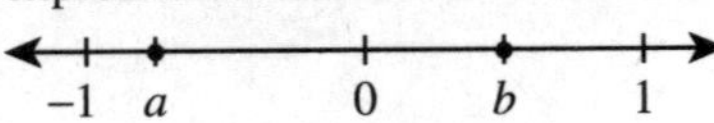

F. $-1 < ab < a$
G. $a < ab < 0$
H. $0 < ab < b$
J. $b < ab < 1$

35. Sani's course grade in his chemistry class is based on 3 tests and 1 final exam. Each of the 3 test scores is weighted as 20% of the course grade, and the final exam score is weighted as 40% of the course grade. Sani's 3 test scores are 78, 86, and 82. What is the minimum score that Sani will have to earn on the final exam to receive a course grade of at least 86?

A. 84
B. 90
C. 92
D. 98

GO ON TO THE NEXT PAGE.

2 △ △ △ △ △ △ △ △ △ 2

36. The shown triangle has vertices $A(-1,-2)$, $B(2,2)$, and $C(-1,4)$. What is the area of $\triangle ABC$ in square coordinate units?

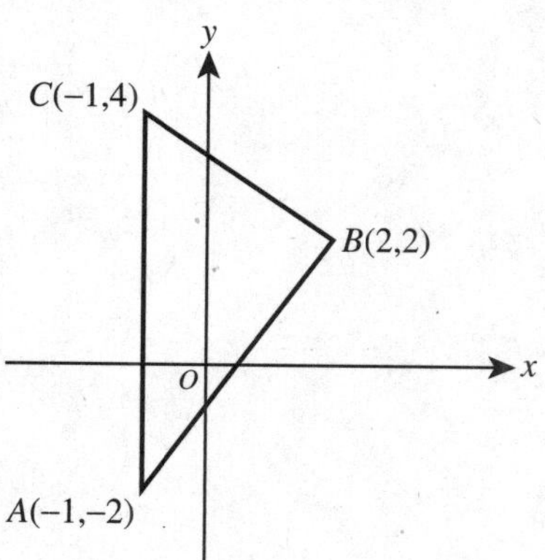

F. 9
G. 15
H. 18
J. $3\sqrt{13}$

37. For some real number x, $\sqrt{x^2} \neq x$. Therefore, x is:
A. greater than π.
B. irrational.
C. negative.
D. undefined.

38. In the standard (x,y) coordinate plane shown, point A has coordinates $(2,-4)$, and point $B(8,-1)$ divides $\overline{AC}$ so that the ratio $AB:BC$ is 1:3. What are the coordinates of point C?

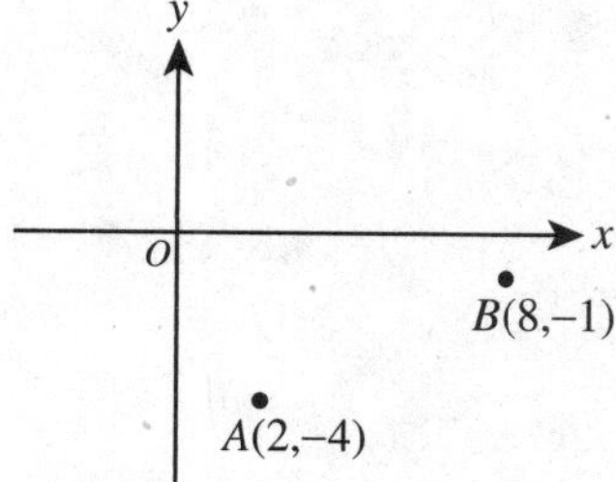

F. (32,11)
G. (26,8)
H. (14,2)
J. (10,0)

GO ON TO THE NEXT PAGE.

The ONLY Official Prep Guide from the Makers of the ACT

2 △ △ △ △ △ △ △ △ △ **2**

DO YOUR FIGURING HERE.

39. A wire binds 4 identical posts together as shown. Each post has a 3-inch radius. What is the length, to the nearest inch, of the shortest wire that will go around the 4 posts without overlap?

   A. 31
   B. 33
   C. 43
   D. 52

40. Given that b is rational and $i = \sqrt{-1}$, the product of the expression $(3 + bi)$ and which of the following expressions must be a rational number?

   F. bi
   G. $3bi$
   H. $3 + bi$
   J. $3 - bi$

41. For positive integers x and y where $x < 8$, $\log_x 8 = y$. What is the value of y?

   A. 1
   B. 2
   C. 3
   D. 4

42. For all positive integers x, which of the following expressions is equivalent to $x^{\frac{1}{4}} \cdot x^{\frac{1}{6}}$?

   F. $\sqrt[5]{x}$
   G. $\sqrt[5]{x^{12}}$
   H. $\sqrt[12]{x^5}$
   J. $\sqrt[24]{x}$

GO ON TO THE NEXT PAGE.

2 △ △ △ △ △ △ △ △ △ 2

43. The sides of an acute triangle measure 17 cm, 16 cm, and 15 cm. The measure of the smallest angle of the triangle is a solution for A to which of the following equations?

A. $17^2 = 15^2 + 16^2 - 2(15)(16)\sin A$

B. $17^2 = 15^2 + 16^2 - 2(15)(16)\cos A$

C. $15^2 = 16^2 + 17^2 - 2(16)(17)\sin A$

D. $15^2 = 16^2 + 17^2 - 2(16)(17)\cos A$

44. Set A and set B each consist of 5 distinct numbers. The 2 sets contain identical numbers with the exception of the number with the least value in each set. The number with the least value in set B is greater than the number with the least value in set A. The value(s) of which of the following measures **must** be greater for set B than for set A?

F. Mean only
G. Median only
H. Range only
J. Mean and range only

45. Of the 16 cars on a rental-car lot, 6 are minivans, 7 are sedans, and 3 are hatchbacks. Thalia will rent 3 of these cars, chosen at random, for business associates. What is the probability that Thalia will rent 1 of each of the 3 types of cars?

A. $\dfrac{1}{3}$

B. $\dfrac{3}{16}$

C. $\dfrac{9}{40}$

D. $\dfrac{9}{80}$

DO YOUR FIGURING HERE.

END OF TEST 2

STOP! DO NOT TURN THE PAGE UNTIL TOLD TO DO SO.

DO NOT RETURN TO THE PREVIOUS TEST.

3   3

READING TEST
40 Minutes—36 Questions

DIRECTIONS: There are several passages in this test. Each passage is accompanied by several questions. After reading a passage, choose the best answer to each question and fill in the corresponding oval on your answer document. You may refer to the passages as often as necessary.

Passage I

LITERARY NARRATIVE: Passage A is adapted from the autobiography *A Peculiar Treasure* by Edna Ferber (©1960 by Morris L. Ernst, et al., Trustees). Passage B is adapted from the memoir *Pull Me Up: A Memoir* by Dan Barry (©2004 by Dan Barry).

Passage A by Edna Ferber

The printing shop and pressroom were separated from the front office only by a doorway, and the door never was closed. There were the type forms and tables, the linotype machine (a new and fearsome invention to
5 me), the small press, the big newspaper press, the boiler plate, the trays of type, all the paraphernalia that goes to make up the heart of a small-town newspaper. The front room is its head, but without the back room it could not function or even live. The linotype and the
10 small press went all day, for there the advertising was set up and printed, as well as handbills, programs, all the odds and ends classified as job printing. Mac, who ruled this domain, was the perfect example of the fictional printer. He had come in years before, his brown
15 hair curled over a mild brow, his limp shirt seemed perennial. But his eye was infallible, and few if any shrdlus and etaoins marred the fair sequence of Mac's copy. His voice was soft, gentle, drawling, but he was boss of the print shop from the cat to the linotype oper-
20 ator. Mac seldom talked but sometimes—rarely—he appeared in the front office, a drooping figure, with a piece of news by which he had come in some devious way. Standing at the side of the city editor's desk he would deliver himself of this information, looking mild
25 and limply romantic. It always proved to be a bombshell.

Such was the make-up of the Appleton, Wisconsin, Daily Crescent office.

In the past thirty years all sorts of ex-newspaper
30 men from Richard Harding Davis to Vincent Sheean and John Gunther have written about the lure of the reporter's life, the smell of printer's ink, the adventure of reporting. It all sounds slightly sentimental and silly, but it's true—or it was, at least, in my newspaper expe-
35 rience. To this day I can't smell the scent of white paper, wet ink, oil, hot lead, mucilage and cats that goes to make up the peculiar odor of any newspaper plant, be it Appleton, Wisconsin, or Cairo, Egypt, that I don't get a pang of nostalgia for the old reporting days.
40 "I was once a newspaper man myself" has come to be a fun phrase. But practically everyone seems to have been, or to have wanted to be, a newspaper reporter.

Passage B by Dan Barry

Ink. The building smelled of ink, spilled and bled. It was a tart and chemical smell, the kind that weaves
45 into the fabric of your clothes and then under your skin, the kind that comes home with you, sits with you at the dinner table, tells you constantly what it is you do. Car mechanics know their smell, as do fishermen and hair stylists, nurses and short-order cooks. You are a man
50 who chases halibut, a woman who perms hair. You smell of it.

I waded into that invisible veil of ink, inhaled it deeply, allowed it to wash over me. It smelled of words and phrases, rants and ideas, sports scores and felony
55 arrests, announcements of marriage and notices of death. Maybe the chemical-like aroma was inducing hallucination, but I doubted it. In a squat concrete building, no different from all the others in a drab Connecticut industrial park, I was experiencing a moment
60 of revelation—an epiphany, really, at the age of twenty-five.

This is what I do.

Pinned like a manifesto to a bulletin board in the center of this ink-perfumed building was a typewritten
65 note from my new employer, announcing that on this day, October 17, 1983, I would begin working as a reporter for a daily newspaper. The note formalized my calling in life with a splash of perspective that would stay with me forever:

70   *Dan is a former intern at the* Daily News *in New York and a graduate assistant for the journalism department at New York University. His writing has appeared in the* Daily News, *the* New York Times *and the* Rocky Mountain News. *Soon it will appear in*
75 *trashcans throughout north-central Connecticut. Please make him feel relevant.*

Reading the note, I thought, I'm home.

GO ON TO THE NEXT PAGE.

3   3

Finding my way had not been easy. The internship
at the *Daily News* had ended, the graduate degree from
80 NYU had been shoved in a drawer, and I had returned
to living beside the sump pump in my parents' basement. I spent my days splitting sod for a lawn and
sprinkling company alongside Eddie, who had taken to
calling me "Professor," and my nights typing out pro-
85 fessional love letters to the *New London Day*, the
Asbury Park Press, the *Poughkeepsie Journal*, the
Stamford Advocate, the *Anywhere Clarion-Bugle-
Star-Record-Sentinel*, and every other Northeastern
newspaper that I had never read.

1. It can reasonably be inferred that Passage A is narrated
   from the point of view of someone who:

   A. once worked in the newspaper business.
   B. recently started a career in the newspaper business.
   C. is outside the newspaper business and is evaluat-
      ing the inner workings of various news offices.
   D. is outside the newspaper business and longs to be a
      reporter.

2. Based on Passage A, the narrator believes that, compared to what goes on in the front office, what goes on
   in the printing shop and pressroom is:

   F. more tedious.
   G. equally critical.
   H. equally chaotic.
   J. less regulated.

3. According to the narrator of Passage A, Mac would
   occasionally appear in the front office in order to:

   A. set up and print the advertising.
   B. supervise the linotype operator.
   C. chastise the reporters for having too many errors
      in their copy.
   D. share newsworthy information with the city editor.

4. What is the epiphany the narrator of Passage B experienced at the age of twenty-five?

   F. He couldn't live in his parents' basement forever.
   G. His dream of being a reporter had finally been
      realized.
   H. He would rather write news stories than work for a
      lawn company.
   J. His success as a reporter would depend on his
      work ethic.

5. Based on Passage B, the note that the narrator's
   employer wrote can best be described as:

   A. mildly sarcastic.
   B. overtly solemn.
   C. blatantly apologetic.
   D. particularly optimistic.

6. The last sentence of Passage B mainly serves to indicate
   that the narrator:

   F. had disdain for most northeastern newspapers.
   G. was familiar with the newspapers published around
      the area.
   H. was desperate to find a newswriting job.
   J. had extensive newswriting experience.

7. Compared to the description of the newspaper office
   mentioned in Passage A, the description of the newspaper office mentioned in Passage B provides less
   information about the:

   A. types of machines used to print the newspaper.
   B. outside appearance of the office building.
   C. number of people who work in the office.
   D. types of stories being written and printed for the
      newspaper.

8. Compared to Passage A, the style of Passage B is more
   strongly characterized by its use of:

   F. technical jargon.
   G. dialogue.
   H. formal diction.
   J. figurative language.

9. Based on the passages, who would be most likely to
   associate the smell of ink with pleasant memories?

   A. The narrator of Passage A only
   B. The narrator of Passage B only
   C. Both narrators
   D. Neither narrator

GO ON TO THE NEXT PAGE.

3 � **3**

Passage II

INFORMATIONAL: This passage is adapted from the book *Lost Discoveries: The Ancient Roots of Modern Science—from the Babylonians to the Maya* by Dick Teresi (©2002 by Dick Teresi).

"In the history of culture," wrote mathematician Tobias Dantzig in 1930, "the discovery of zero will always stand out as one of the greatest single achieve-ments of the human race." Zero, he said, marked a
5 "turning point" in math, science, and industry. He also noted that the zero was invented not in the West but by the Indians in the early centuries after Christ. Negative numbers followed soon thereafter. The Maya invented zero in the New World at approximately the same time.
10 Europe, says Dantzig, did not accept zero as a number until the twelfth or thirteenth century.

There are many "biographies of zero," and Dantzig's concise and spirited account of the birth of a number is adequate for most of us. He sees zero's
15 invention appearing on an Indian's counting board in, say, the first or second century A.D. The Indian count-ing board had columns for the ones, tens, hundreds, thousands, and so on. To "write" 302, for instance, a mathematician would put a 2 in the first (right) column
20 and a 3 in the third, leaving the second column empty. On one fateful day, as Dantzig sees it, an unknown Indian drew an oval in the second column. He called it *sunya*, for "empty" or "blank." *Sunyata*, an important concept in Buddhism, is often translated as "emptiness"
25 or "void."

The Arabs turned *sunya* into *sifr* ("empty" in Arabic), which became *zephirum* in Italy, and eventu-ally zero. In Germany and elsewhere, *sifr* became *cifra*, and then, in English, *cipher*. In other words, it took
30 over a thousand years for Western civilization to accept a number for "nothing." Dantzig blames the Greeks. "The concrete mind of the ancient Greeks could not conceive the void as a number, let alone endow the void with a symbol."

35 Zero lay rustling in the weeds for many centuries before that Indian drew it on a counting board. It was an unnamed, unwritten force. It took many more centu-ries after the Indians and the Maya dared speak its name before zero was promoted to a full-fledged number.

40 The Babylonians had no zero, but they knew something was wrong. If they numbered the first year of each king's reign as year 1, then added up the number of years of each separate reign, they'd end up with too many years unless each king died just before
45 midnight on New Year's Eve and his successor took the throne after midnight. Thus, the Babylonians called a king's first year the *accession year*. The following year was year 1. The accession year was a kind of year 0. The Babylonians, so far as we know, never articulated
50 zero, but seemed aware that there was a missing number in their system.

The contemporary mathematician who has con-ducted the most rigorous research on nothing is Robert Kaplan, the author of *The Nothing That Is: A Natural*
55 *History of Zero*. Zero turns up throughout history in different cultures as a series of dots and circles, and Kaplan writes of following "the swarm of dots we find in writings from a host of languages, across great spans of time, and on topics mathematical and otherwise."

60 Kaplan traces the roots of zero to Sumer and Bab-ylonia. The Sumerians counted by tens and sixties, a system adopted by the Babylonians, who eclipsed them in Mesopotamia. The Babylonians, far ahead of the Romans and Greeks to come, imposed a positional
65 notation on the old Sumerian sexagesimal system. Writ-ing their numbers on clay, the Babylonians needed a symbol to put in the "empty" columns, just as we today use zero to differentiate between 302 and 32.

Somewhere between the sixth and third centuries
70 B.C., the Babylonians began using two slanted tacklike symbols to insert in the empty columns. They used their "zero" only in the middle of numbers, never at the end.

Kaplan argues that when Alexander invaded the Babylonian empire in 331 B.C., he hauled off zero
75 along with the gold. Shortly thereafter we find the symbol 0 for zero in the papyri of Greek astronomers, but the mathematicians never pursued the concept.

10. According to the passage, the Babylonian and Indian civilizations were similar in that they both:

   F. wrote zero using tacklike symbols.
   G. referred to their rulers' first year in power as the *accession year*.
   H. derived their names for zero from their respective religions.
   J. used a symbol for zero in the middle of numbers.

11. As it is presented in the second paragraph (lines 12–25), the story of an unknown person drawing an oval on a counting board is best described as:

   A. a factual account from a document Dantzig discovered.
   B. a factual account from ancient Indian writings.
   C. Dantzig's theory of how a historic invention occurred.
   D. Kaplan's theory of how a historic invention occurred.

12. According to the passage, the Maya invented zero at about the same time as:

   F. the Indians invented zero.
   G. the Sumerians invented zero.
   H. Alexander invaded Babylonia.
   J. Europe accepted zero as a number.

GO ON TO THE NEXT PAGE.

3   3

13. As it is used in line 21, the phrase *fateful day* most nearly refers to a day that was:

    A. unfortunate.
    B. momentous.
    C. ominous.
    D. foretold.

14. According to the passage, in Germany, the word for "zero" became:

    F. *sunya.*
    G. *zephirum.*
    H. *sifr.*
    J. *cifra.*

15. In the passage, Dantzig criticizes the ancient Greeks because he thinks they:

    A. lacked the abstract thinking necessary to think of the void as a number.
    B. attempted to use zero in their mathematics before they understood it fully.
    C. were unwilling to share their knowledge of zero with other European countries.
    D. focused so much on negative numbers that they couldn't imagine a number for the void.

16. The passage author most clearly indicates that he thinks his readers wouldn't be interested in hearing:

    F. the story of how the Maya conceived of zero.
    G. what Dantzig contributed to mathematics.
    H. the long version of the story of zero.
    J. who drew the oval on the counting board in India.

17. The statement "Zero lay rustling in the weeds for many centuries" (line 35) most nearly means that the concept of zero:

    A. had far-reaching effects on mathematics.
    B. existed long before it was articulated.
    C. had been developed and then forgotten.
    D. was initially rejected by mathematicians.

18. The passage author most clearly indicates that compared to other contemporary mathematicians' research on zero, Kaplan's research is more:

    F. interesting.
    G. speculative.
    H. thorough.
    J. admired.

GO ON TO THE NEXT PAGE.

3 ━━━━━━━━━━━━━━━━━━━━━━━━━ **3**

Passage III

INFORMATIONAL: This passage is adapted from *I'll Take You There: Mavis Staples, The Staples Singers, and the March Up Freedom's Highway* by Greg Kot (©2014 by Greg Kot).

To fans of the Staples Singers in the '60s, the relative anonymity of Mavis Staples was puzzling. With an improbably deep voice bursting out of a diminutive five-foot frame, she projected the deepest commitment
5 to whatever she was singing, losing herself in every word as though reliving a critical moment in her personal story.

And yet she still wasn't a marquee name like Aretha Franklin, Gladys Knight, Diana Ross, and Dusty
10 Springfield. Part of this was by design—Mavis enjoyed singing with her family and preferred to melt into the group. Even when her father brought her out front to sing lead after her brother Pervis's voice changed in the '50s, she did so reluctantly. "I loved singing those bari-
15 tone harmonies, I always thought that was the best job you could have," Mavis said. She also felt a certain comfort being guided by her father, who had essentially taught her how and what to sing. Little had changed in the decades since, even as it was apparent that Mavis
20 had star power. "Mavis was and is a quartet singer," says Anthony Heilbut. "From a very early age she grew up singing harmony or singing lead in a group with four voices and her father's guitar. She was trained to sing with the guitar, whereas Aretha sang with the piano.
25 It's a very different approach."

Not only that, Pops's idiosyncratic guitar style made it difficult for Mavis to easily adapt to a different context. So, too, was the unspoken communication between Mavis and her siblings, the way they harmo-
30 nized with her, even the way they clapped hands together, a high-speed ripple that approximated an entire percussion section by itself. "I've been singing a long time," Mavis says, "and I could never find anyone to clap like Pervis and Cleedi."

35 But Al Bell never forgot the day in Arkansas when the teenage Mavis's voice bowled him over and left him in tears in what was essentially a solo performance of "On My Way to Heaven" during a Staples Singers show.

40 "In signing the Staples Singers, I thought of it as signing three acts in one," Bell says. "I wanted to record Pops and Mavis as solo artists. I knew it would add more to them from a personal appearance stand-point, bring them a broader, more diverse audience. I
45 would hear Pops sitting around and just playing his guitar at Stax Records and I thought, 'I've got to get this man down on tape.' His singing, I knew there was a lot more songs that could have been done with Pops as a vocalist, because he was so distinctive. With Mavis I
50 saw no boundaries at all—I saw her walking past all of them."

Steve Cropper had already won the Staples family's trust while recording *Soul Folk in Action*, so Bell had him produce what would be Mavis's self-titled
55 debut album.

"The attitude at Stax was that she's a superstar who nobody really knows about, and we have to figure out how to get her out there," Cropper recalls. "But it wasn't easy, because she puts limits on herself. There
60 were only certain songs she would try. Her upbringing, her feeling about what songs would or wouldn't go down with Pops, gave me the impression she didn't want to go too far too fast. So I approached the whole thing with kid gloves. I didn't want to lose her trust or
65 do something damaging."

Cropper found Pops a thoughtful and willing collaborator in the studio, but there was no question his word still counted more than anyone else's in the family, even though his children were well into adult-
70 hood. "Every now and then, Mavis would reference Pops in terms of putting his foot down about dating," Cropper says. "There were lines he didn't want to cross when it came to his family's well-being, and that included what kind of songs they would sing, what
75 message they would put out."

The guitarist knew he was running a risk presenting Mavis with a set of secular songs that didn't have any of the gospel or message-oriented underpinnings favored by Pops and the Staples Singers. Whereas her
80 first attempt at cutting a solo single, a cover of "Crying in the Chapel" for Epic Records, had some tenuous religious imagery, the tracks chosen for the *Mavis Staples* solo album were the sort of pop-oriented love and relationship songs that Pops typically shunned.

85 But Mavis was hardly insulated from the pop world as a fan and listener. She swooned over Sam Cooke's "You Send Me" the first time she heard it, and her cover of it on her debut album sounds wistful, as if she were singing both to a newfound love and Cooke's
90 memory.

19. The main purpose of the passage is to:
- **A.** introduce Bell as an important figure in the career of the Staples Singers.
- **B.** compare Mavis Staples to other famous female singers like Ross and Franklin.
- **C.** present a theory that Pops Staples was the driving force behind Mavis Staples's success as a singer.
- **D.** describe Mavis Staples's transition from a quartet singer to a solo artist.

GO ON TO THE NEXT PAGE.

3 ━━━━━━━━━━━━━━━━━━━━━━━━━━━ **3**

20. It can most reasonably be inferred from the passage that Mavis Staples's relative anonymity in the '60s was puzzling to her fans mainly because she had a:

- **F.** more distinct voice than her brother, who became more famous than she did.
- **G.** greater vocal range than many other artists of the time.
- **H.** voice that reminded fans of singers whose names were on the marquee.
- **J.** powerful voice and a personal approach to her performances.

21. The main purpose of the third paragraph (lines 26–34) is to:

- **A.** clarify how each member of the Staples Singers contributed to creating the group's unique sound.
- **B.** show that change was difficult for Mavis Staples because of her musical connection with her family.
- **C.** explain that Pops Staples chose the songs his family sang during concerts.
- **D.** describe the performance style of the Staples Singers.

22. The main idea of the seventh paragraph (lines 56–65) is that:

- **F.** Cropper brought the Staples Singers success by pushing them to try genres outside of their usual repertoire.
- **G.** Cropper was careful about how he encouraged Mavis Staples to explore new opportunities with her music.
- **H.** Stax Records was innovative because they took risks by signing unknown singers.
- **J.** Mavis Staples was initially unwilling to perform without backup singers.

23. Based on the passage, regarding his family, Pops Staples's attitude can best be described as:

- **A.** tolerant.
- **B.** resentful.
- **C.** protective.
- **D.** ambivalent.

24. As it is used in line 5, the phrase *losing herself* most nearly refers to the way Mavis Staples:

- **F.** sang as if the song lyrics evoked poignant episodes from her past.
- **G.** clapped her hands along with a song.
- **H.** transitioned to a new song when she felt moved by her siblings' harmonies.
- **J.** danced on stage when her father or brother sang.

25. According to the passage, what event led directly to Mavis Staples becoming the lead singer of the Staples Singers?

- **A.** Pops Staples leaving the group
- **B.** Cleedi Staples learning the guitar
- **C.** Pervis Staples's voice changing
- **D.** Mavis Staples's voice becoming deeper

26. Based on the passage, Bell's reaction to hearing Mavis Staples's performance of "On My Way to Heaven" can most nearly be described as one of:

- **F.** utter dismay.
- **G.** reluctant acceptance.
- **H.** mild amusement.
- **J.** deep admiration.

27. The passage indicates that, compared to the songs traditionally chosen by the Staples Singers, the songs chosen for Mavis Staples's first solo album were:

- **A.** more serious; they focused on global issues.
- **B.** more pop oriented; they focused on love and relationships.
- **C.** less personal; they were not originally written for her.
- **D.** less upbeat; they were not meant to be played on a dance floor.

GO ON TO THE NEXT PAGE.

3   **3**

Passage IV

INFORMATIONAL: This passage is adapted from the book *Mycophilia: Revelations from the Weird World of Mushrooms* by Eugenia Bone (©2011 by Eugenia Bone).

There are a number of fungi that live in mutualist relationships in which a balance of interests occurs between two organisms. Lichen has a mutualistic relationship with photosynthesizing algae and bacteria.
5 And there are also commensal relationships, where the fungus may not be doing the host any good or any harm, either—the raison d'être of some yeasts in our body, for example, is unknown and may be commensal. But mycorrhizal fungi are the princes of mutualism.
10 "Fungi can't make their own food," said Gary Lincoff. "So they made a strategic choice to team up with plants."

Ninety percent of natural land plants are thought to have mycorrhizal fungi partners. It's a masterpiece
15 of evolution: Mycorrhizal fungi break down nutrients like phosphorus, carbon, water, and nitrogen into a readily assimilable form and deliver them to the plant in return for sugar produced by the plant via photosynthesis. The fungus needs sugar for energy and to launch
20 its spores, and the tree needs nutrients because (despite what I learned in school) tree roots don't do the job adequately. Tree roots primarily anchor the tree in the soil. While tree roots will absorb moisture if watered and nutrients if fertilized, it is the mycorrhizal fungus
25 *growing on and in the tree roots* that provides the tree with the lion's share of its nutrition and water. Mycorrhizal fungi significantly expand the reach of plant roots, and by extending the root system, increase the tree's nutrient and water uptake.

30 In the wild, mycorrhizal fungi are key to not just the health of single trees but to healthy forest ecosystems. A single fungal genotype or clone can colonize the roots and maintain the nutritional requirements of many trees at once. And multiple fungi can colonize the
35 roots of all or most of the trees in a forest. The hyphae, those threadlike strings of cells that are the fungus, function as pathways for shuttling nutrients, water, and organic compounds around the forest. The mycologist Paul Stamets believes that mycorrhizal fungi function
40 as a giant communications network between multiple trees in a forest—he calls it "nature's Internet." Others have described this linkage as the "architecture of the wood-wide web."

Weaker plants are able to tap into this network,
45 too, like hitchhikers on a nutritional superhighway. Young seedlings struggling to grow in the shadow of established trees tap into the larger, older tree's fungal network to improve their nutritional uptake. This network exists to benefit not only established trees and
50 seedlings of the same species but also trees from different species, and at different stages of development. So one multitasking fungus, its hyphae attached to the roots of multiple trees in the forest, can simultaneously provide a different nutritional load as needed to differ-
55 ent trees. It's a couture service.

The old trees in a forest function as hubs for these mycelial networks. "Like spokes of a wheel," said Suzanne Simard, a professor of forestry at the University of British Columbia who studies mycorrhizae. Rhi-
60 zomorphs (ropes of hyphae) connect the foundation tree with other trees—like an express stop on a subway system where lots of local trains come through—and the bigger the tree, the larger the hub. That's because the largest trees have the greatest root system, and the
65 more roots there are, the more real estate there is for the fungus to colonize. "In one forest, we found 47 trees linked by two species of fungi composed of 12 individuals," said Simard. (By individuals, she means two genetically distinct fungal entities.) "Talk about two
70 degrees of separation!" Even nonphotosynthesizing plants take advantage of "the hub." Parasites like the Indian pipe depend totally on mycorrhizal fungi for its nutritive needs. It taps into the nutrients and water provided by the mycorrhizae and connects via the mycor-
75 rhizae to a photosynthesizing plant for sugar.

Despite the fact that fungi are microscopic organisms, the functions they perform are often on an ecosystem or landscape scale. If you could take an x-ray look at the soil, you'd see that underneath the forest
80 duff there is a layer of mycorrhizal mycelium running between, on, and in the roots of plants. It's like a stratum of life between the duff and the soil that holds water and nutrients in the ground. And when that stratum is disrupted, or not present, plants suffer. In fact,
85 ecosystems with inadequate mycorrhizal fungi can experience catastrophic losses of plant biomass.

28. The main purpose of the passage is to:

F. contrast mutualist relationships with commensal relationships and contend that mycorrhizal fungi have a commensal relationship with plants.

G. describe mycorrhizal fungi's relationship with plants and explain how this relationship plays an integral role in ecosystems.

H. summarize how the internet was inspired by networks of mycorrhizal fungi and clarify how the internet and mycorrhizal networks are similar.

J. establish that mycorrhizal fungi pose a threat to forests and suggest a way of curbing their influence on ecosystems.

29. The main idea of the fourth paragraph (lines 44–55) is that:

A. networks of fungi benefit different species of trees at various levels of development.

B. young seedlings typically tap into the roots of trees that are the same species as the seedlings.

C. established trees genetically alter fungal networks to benefit different species of trees.

D. different species of trees can be identified based on their nutritional uptake.

GO ON TO THE NEXT PAGE.

3   3

30. The author uses the metaphor of an express stop in a subway system in order to:

  F. explain why parasites are harmful to larger trees.
  G. contrast two distinct mycelial networks.
  H. clarify how larger trees function in a mycelial network.
  J. illustrate how different species of fungi grow to be different sizes.

31. In the passage, the relationship between yeast and the human body is cited as an example of a:

  A. definite commensal relationship.
  B. possible commensal relationship.
  C. definite mutualist relationship.
  D. possible mutualist relationship.

32. The author most likely includes the quote from Lincoff (lines 10–12) to:

  F. suggest that mycorrhizal fungi have a commensal relationship with plants.
  G. contend that mycorrhizal fungi serve the same function as some yeasts in the human body.
  H. indicate why mycorrhizal fungi have a mutualist relationship with plants.
  J. explain why mycorrhizal fungi cannot make their own food.

33. As it is used in line 44, the phrase *tap into* most nearly means:

  A. endorse.
  B. finish.
  C. lift.
  D. use.

34. Based on the passage, young seedlings often depend on fungal networks because the seedlings are:

  F. struggling to grow in an established tree's shadow.
  G. trying to defend themselves against parasites.
  H. in need of a specific nutrient that is unused by established trees.
  J. susceptible to a wider range of diseases than established trees are.

35. Based on the passage, the author would most likely agree that Indian pipe's level of dependency on mycorrhizal fungi is:

  A. absolute.
  B. about the same as its dependence on nonphotosynthesizing plants.
  C. less than its dependence on nonphotosynthesizing plants.
  D. uncertain.

36. Which of the following statements, if true, would most **weaken** the claim made by the author in lines 83–86 of the passage?

  F. Over a three-year span, two forests with different tree types increase the amount of mycorrhizal mycelium at the same rate.
  G. Over a three-year span, two forests with the same amount of mycorrhizal mycelium both lost the majority of their plant biomass.
  H. During a given year, after the majority of mycorrhizal mycelium dies in a forest, the plants in the forests flourish.
  J. During a given year, after the majority of mycorrhizal mycelium dies in a forest, the plants in the forests suffer.

END OF TEST 3

STOP! DO NOT TURN THE PAGE UNTIL TOLD TO DO SO.

DO NOT RETURN TO A PREVIOUS TEST.

4 ○ ○ ○ ○ ○ ○ ○ ○ ○ 4

SCIENCE TEST

40 Minutes—40 Questions

DIRECTIONS: There are several passages in this test. Each passage is followed by several questions. After reading a passage, choose the best answer to each question and fill in the corresponding oval on your answer document. You may refer to the passages as often as necessary.

You are **not** permitted to use a calculator on this test.

Passage I

The freezing point of an aqueous solution (T_f), in °C, can be calculated using the equation

$$T_f = -1.86 \times m \times i$$

where m is the concentration of the solute in moles of solute per kilogram of H_2O (mol/kg H_2O) and i is the average number of particles produced by 1 formula unit of the solute when the formula unit dissolves in H_2O. The theoretical i value of a solute is the total number of particles produced when 1 formula unit of the solute dissolves in H_2O. Table 1 gives, for 4 ionic compounds, the chemical formula and the theoretical i value. Table 2 shows how the observed i value at 25°C for these compounds changes with solute concentration.

Table 1		
Name	Chemical formula	Theoretical i value
Sodium chloride	NaCl	2
Potassium chloride	KCl	2
Magnesium chloride	$MgCl_2$	3
Ammonium sulfate	$(NH_4)_2SO_4$	3

Concentration of aqueous solution (mol/kg H_2O)	Observed i value at 25°C for:			
	NaCl	KCl	$MgCl_2$	$(NH_4)_2SO_4$
0.1	1.87	1.85	2.58	2.30
0.2	1.85	1.83	2.63	2.19
0.3	1.84	1.81	2.68	2.12
0.4	1.84	1.80	2.76	2.07
0.5	1.84	1.80	2.84	2.03
0.6	1.85	1.80	2.92	2.00
0.7	1.85	1.79	3.01	1.97
0.8	1.86	1.79	3.11	1.96
0.9	1.86	1.79	3.21	1.94
1.0	1.87	1.80	3.32	1.92
2.0	1.97	1.83	4.57	1.87

Table 2 is titled "Table 2".

Table 2 adapted from B. A. Kunkel, "Comments on 'A Generalized Equation for the Solution Effect in Droplet Growth.'" ©1969 by American Meteorological Society.

GO ON TO THE NEXT PAGE.

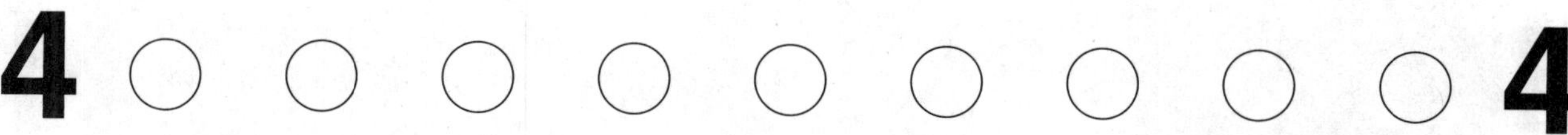

4 ◯ ◯ ◯ ◯ ◯ ◯ ◯ ◯ **4**

1. Based on Table 2, which compounds have observed i values less than 2.50 at all the concentrations listed?

   A. NaCl, KCl, and $MgCl_2$ only
   B. NaCl, KCl, and $(NH_4)_2SO_4$ only
   C. KCl, $MgCl_2$, and $(NH_4)_2SO_4$ only
   D. NaCl, KCl, $MgCl_2$, and $(NH_4)_2SO_4$

2. Based on Table 2, at which of the following concentrations is the observed i value for KCl the lowest?

   F. 0.3 mol/kg H_2O
   G. 0.6 mol/kg H_2O
   H. 0.9 mol/kg H_2O
   J. 2.0 mol/kg H_2O

3. Based on Tables 1 and 2, which ionic compound has the largest deviation from its theoretical i value at a concentration of 2.0 mol/kg H_2O?

   A. NaCl
   B. KCl
   C. $MgCl_2$
   D. $(NH_4)_2SO_4$

4. Consider the following substances: sodium chloride, potassium chloride, magnesium chloride, ammonium sulfate, and water. Which of these substances would be classified as a solvent in the solutions represented in Table 2?

   F. Ammonium sulfate only
   G. Water only
   H. Sodium chloride, potassium chloride, and magnesium chloride only
   J. Water, sodium chloride, potassium chloride, magnesium chloride, and ammonium sulfate

5. Sucrose $(C_{12}H_{22}O_{11})$ is a molecular compound and remains intact when it dissolves in water. Based on this information and the passage, would the theoretical i value for $C_{12}H_{22}O_{11}$ more likely be less than that of KCl or greater than that of KCl?

   A. Less; the theoretical i value for $C_{12}H_{22}O_{11}$ is most likely 1.
   B. Less; the theoretical i value for $C_{12}H_{22}O_{11}$ is most likely 4 or greater.
   C. Greater; the theoretical i value for $C_{12}H_{22}O_{11}$ is most likely 1.
   D. Greater; the theoretical i value for $C_{12}H_{22}O_{11}$ is most likely 4 or greater.

GO ON TO THE NEXT PAGE.

4 ○ ○ ○ ○ ○ ○ ○ ○ 4

Passage II

Some mutations in *Escherichia coli* allow the bacteria to survive exposure to an antibiotic. These antibiotic-resistant bacteria may have a different relative fitness (a measure of survival and reproductive success) than *E. coli* without mutations. Scientists conducted a study to determine the relative fitness of 5 *E. coli* strains—1 nonmutated (Strain U) and 4 mutated (Strains W, X, Y, and Z)—when the strains were exposed for 24 hr to each of 5 different concentrations of the antibiotic streptomycin (see Table 1). The effect of the mutation in each of Strains W–Z is listed in Table 2.

Table 1

Strain	Relative fitness of *E. coli* exposed for 24 hr to a streptomycin concentration (in μg/mL*) of:				
	0	2	4	6	8
U	1.0	0.5	0.0	0.0	0.0
W	1.2	0.3	0.1	0.0	0.0
X	0.9	0.8	0.5	0.2	0.0
Y	0.7	0.8	0.7	0.5	0.3
Z	1.0	0.1	0.9	0.8	1.5

*micrograms per milliliter

Note: A relative fitness of 0.0 indicates no surviving bacteria.

Table 2

Strain	Effect of mutation
W	Increased rate of cell division
X	Increased rate of streptomycin removal from the cell
Y	Decreased rate of streptomycin entry into the cell
Z	Decreased rate of DNA damage repair

Table 1 adapted from Viktória Lázár et al., "Bacterial Evolution of Antibiotic Hypersensitivity." ©2013 by EMBO and Macmillan Publishers Limited.

6. Based on Table 1, if Strain X had been exposed for 24 hr to a streptomycin concentration of 3 μg/mL, its relative fitness would most likely have been:

F. less than 0.5.
G. between 0.5 and 0.8.
H. between 0.8 and 0.9.
J. greater than 0.9.

GO ON TO THE NEXT PAGE.

4 ⭕ ⭕ ⭕ ⭕ ⭕ ⭕ ⭕ ⭕ **4**

7. Based on Table 2, which of the following statements best describes the effect of the mutation in Strain X cells? Compared to nonmutated *E. coli* cells, Strain X cells move streptomycin:

   A. into the cell at a decreased rate.
   B. into the cell at an increased rate.
   C. out of the cell at a decreased rate.
   D. out of the cell at an increased rate.

8. Suppose an equal number of Strain W cells and Strain X cells were exposed for 24 hr to a streptomycin concentration of 2 µg/mL. Based on Table 1, which of Strain W or Strain X would more likely have the greater number of cells survive and reproduce?

   F. Strain W; Strain W had a relative fitness of 0.3, and Strain X had a relative fitness of 0.8.
   G. Strain W; Strain W had a relative fitness of 1.2, and Strain X had a relative fitness of 0.9.
   H. Strain X; Strain X had a relative fitness of 0.8, and Strain W had a relative fitness of 0.3.
   J. Strain X; Strain X had a relative fitness of 0.9, and Strain W had a relative fitness of 1.2.

9. Consider the mutated strain with an increased rate of cell division. Based on Table 1, what was the relative fitness of this strain when it was exposed for 24 hr to a streptomycin concentration of 4 µg/mL?

   A. 0.0
   B. 0.1
   C. 0.5
   D. 0.7

10. In the study, the relative fitness of a nonmutated strain that was grown for 24 hr in the absence of an antibiotic was set to 1.0. Was this strain more likely Strain U or Strain Z, and was this strain grown for 24 hr at a streptomycin concentration of 0 µg/mL or at a streptomycin concentration of 8 µg/mL?

   F. Strain U; 0 µg/mL
   G. Strain U; 8 µg/mL
   H. Strain Z; 0 µg/mL
   J. Strain Z; 8 µg/mL

GO ON TO THE NEXT PAGE.

4 ◯ ◯ ◯ ◯ ◯ ◯ ◯ ◯ 4

Passage III

When waves of laser light pass through a narrow slit and onto a screen, they form a pattern of light and dark bands on the screen, as shown in Figure 1.

Figure 1

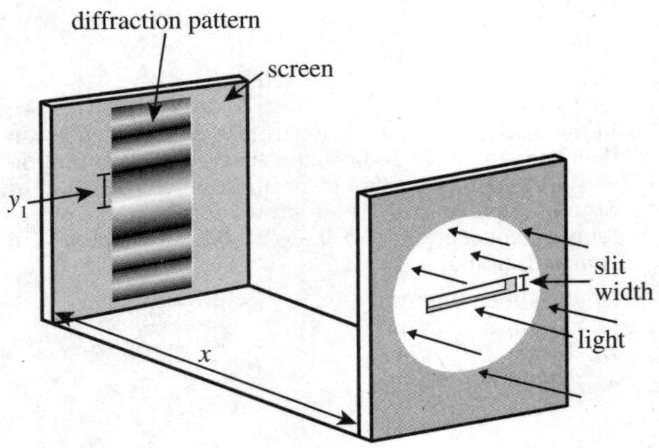

This phenomenon is called diffraction, and the pattern is called a diffraction pattern.

In each of the following studies of diffraction, students directed laser light through a slit, forming a diffraction pattern on a screen. They measured y_1, the distance from the center of the brightest band in the pattern to the center of one of the 2 adjacent dark bands. In each study, x was the distance between the slit and the screen.

Study 1

In Trials 1–4, the slit width was varied, the wavelength of the laser light was fixed, and x was 6.00 m. The results are shown in Table 1.

	Table 1	
Trial	Slit width (mm)	y_1 (mm)
1	0.12	30.0
2	0.24	15.0
3	0.36	10.0
4	0.48	7.5

Study 2

In Trials 5–8, the slit width was 0.24 mm, the wavelength (color) of the laser light was varied, and x was 6.00 m. The results are shown in Table 2.

	Table 2	
Trial	Wavelength (nm)	y_1 (mm)
5	400 (violet)	10.0
6	500 (green)	12.5
7	600 (yellow)	15.0
8	700 (red)	17.5

Study 3

In Trials 9–12, the slit width was 0.24 mm, the wavelength was the same as in Study 1, and x was varied. The results are shown in Table 3.

	Table 3	
Trial	x (m)	y_1 (mm)
9	3.00	7.5
10	6.00	15.0
11	9.00	22.5
12	12.00	30.0

Figure 1 adapted from Francis Sears and Mark Zemanski, College Physics. ©1960 by Addison Wesley Publishing Co., Inc.

11. In Study 2, y_1 would most likely have been less than 10.0 mm if the students had used a laser emitting light having which of the following wavelengths?

   A. 300 nm
   B. 500 nm
   C. 700 nm
   D. 900 nm

GO ON TO THE NEXT PAGE.

4 ○ ○ ○ ○ ○ ○ ○ ○ ○ **4**

12. For fixed values of wavelength and slit width, which of the following graphs best represents the relationship between y_1 and x?

F. 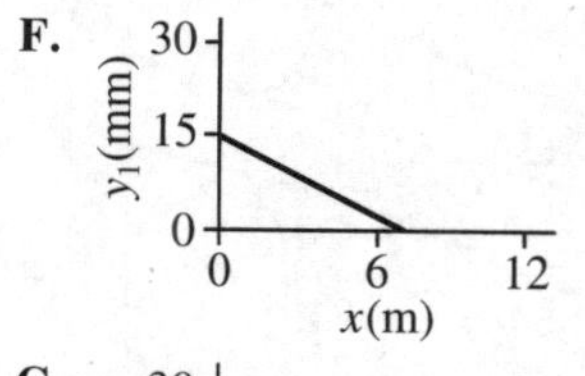

H. 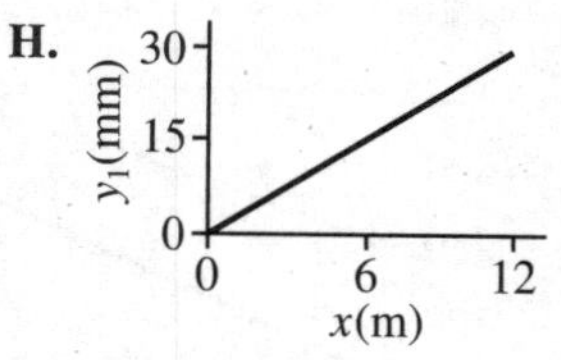

G. 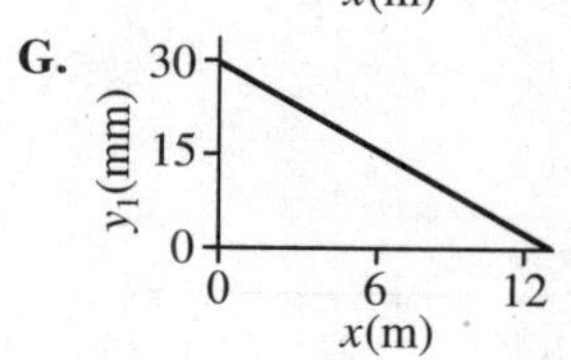

J. 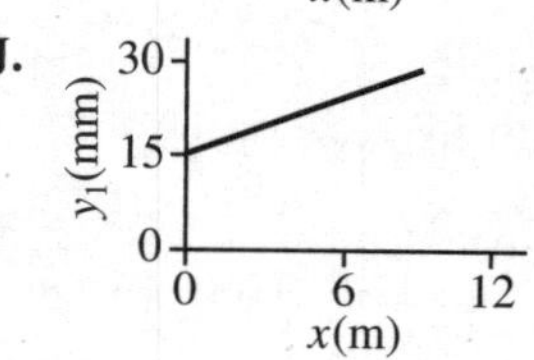

13. Suppose that the procedure performed in Trial 2 was repeated, except that x was 9.00 m. Based on the results of Studies 1 and 3, would y_1 more likely have been greater than 15.0 mm or less than 15.0 mm?

A. Greater, because y_1 increased as x increased.
B. Greater, because y_1 increased as x decreased.
C. Less, because y_1 decreased as x increased.
D. Less, because y_1 decreased as x decreased.

14. As the wavelength of light increases, the energy of a photon (particle of light) decreases. In which of the following trials of Study 2 was the energy of a photon greatest?

F. Trial 5
G. Trial 6
H. Trial 7
J. Trial 8

15. For fixed values of wavelength and x, when the slit width was doubled, the distance from the center of the brightest band in the pattern to the center of one of the 2 adjacent dark bands:

A. was doubled.
B. was halved.
C. remained unchanged.
D. varied with no general trend.

16. What is the result of Trial 7 expressed in meters (m)?

F. 0.00150 m
G. 0.0150 m
H. 0.150 m
J. 1.50 m

GO ON TO THE NEXT PAGE.

The ONLY Official Prep Guide from the Makers of the ACT

4 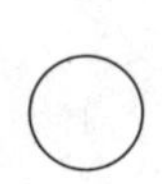 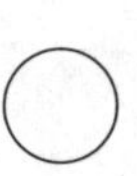      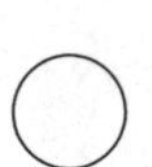 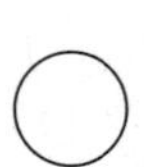 **4**

Passage IV

Antimony trioxide (Sb_2O_3) is a chemical compound that is used as a flame retardant in manufacturing plastic bottles made of polyethylene terephthalate (PET). PET bottles can retain some Sb_2O_3 after manufacturing, and small amounts of the antimony ion (Sb^{3+}) can be absorbed out of the plastic by water stored in those bottles. Two experiments were performed to study the absorption of Sb^{3+} by water stored in clear plastic bottles made of PET.

Experiment 1

The following steps were performed:

1. An unused PET bottle was filled with 2.0 L of pure water and sealed.

2. The bottle was placed into a box that was maintained at 10°C. An ultraviolet (UV) lightbulb was mounted inside the box (see diagram); only UV light was shone upon the bottle for 16 hr.

Diagram

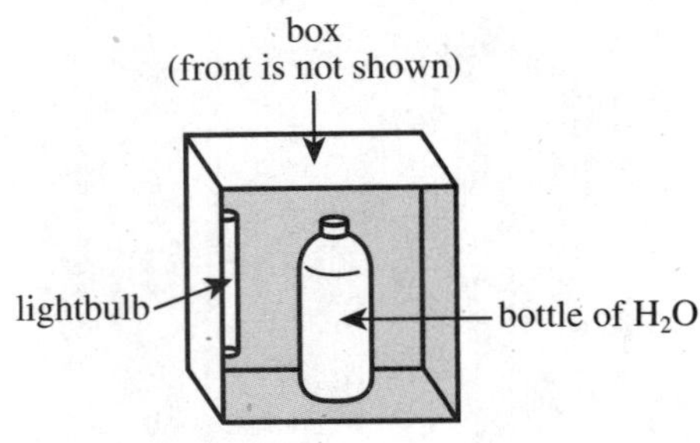

3. The bottle was then removed from the box, opened, and a 2.0 mL sample of water was removed. The concentration of Sb^{3+} in the sample of water, in nanograms per liter (ng/L; 1 ng = 10^{-9} g), was determined.

4. The bottle was emptied, cleaned, and air-dried.

5. The same bottle was then refilled with 2.0 L of pure water and sealed.

6. Steps 2–5 were repeated until the bottle had been reused 28 times at the temperature of 10°C.

Steps 1–6 were repeated 2 more times, except that the box was maintained at temperatures of 30°C and 50°C, respectively. The results for each of the 3 temperatures are shown in Figure 1.

Figure 1

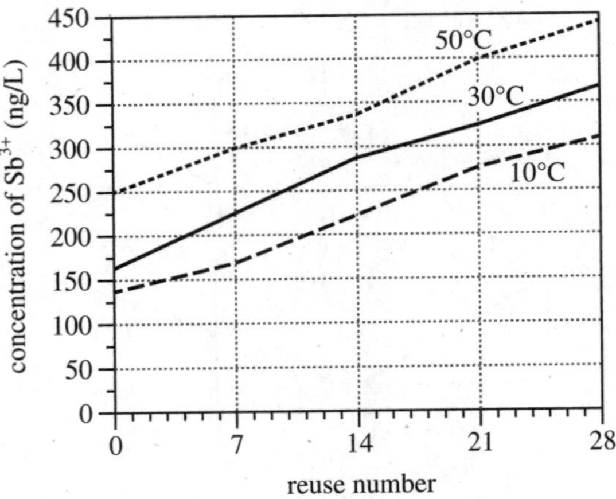

Experiment 2

The procedure in Experiment 1 was repeated, except that in Step 2, the lightbulb inside the box was one that emitted only visible light. The results for each of the 3 temperatures are shown in Figure 2.

Figure 2

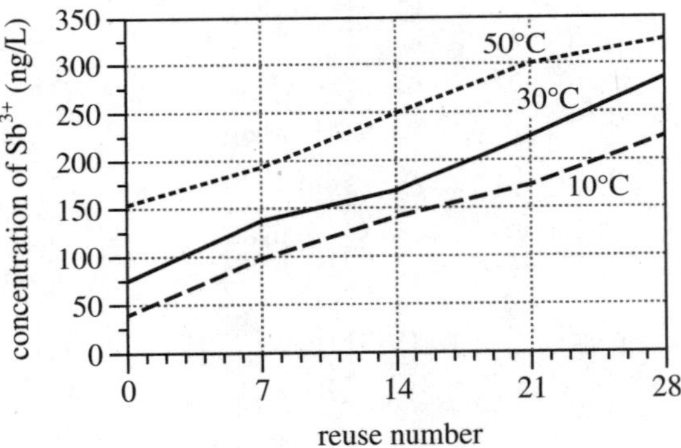

Figures adapted from S. S. Andra, K. C. Makris, and J. P. Shine, "Frequency of Use Controls Chemical Leaching from Drinking-water Containers Subject to Disinfection." ©2011 by Elsevier, B. V.

GO ON TO THE NEXT PAGE.

4 ○ ○ ○ ○ ○ ○ ○ ○ 4

17. Suppose that in Experiment 2 the bottle containing water stored at 50°C had been reused 35 times. At that reuse number, the approximate concentration of Sb^{3+} in the water would have been:

   A. less than 270 ng/L.
   B. between 270 ng/L and 300 ng/L.
   C. between 300 ng/L and 330 ng/L.
   D. greater than 330 ng/L.

18. Assume that the maximum acceptable concentration of Sb^{3+} in drinking water is 6,000 ng/L. This concentration of Sb^{3+} is how many times as great as the concentration of Sb^{3+} in water stored at 50°C in a bottle that was reused 21 times in Experiment 2?

   F. 2
   G. 3
   H. 20
   J. 30

19. Which set of experimental conditions resulted in an Sb^{3+} concentration of 140 ng/L in water stored in a bottle that had been reused 14 times?

   A. 10°C, UV light
   B. 10°C, visible light
   C. 30°C, UV light
   D. 30°C, visible light

20. The substance composing the bottles tested in the experiments is best classified as which of the following?

   F. Alloy
   G. Polymer
   H. Element
   J. Salt

21. Suppose that in Experiment 1 a temperature of 20°C had been tested. At a reuse number of 21, the Sb^{3+} concentration would most likely have been between:

   A. 125 ng/L and 175 ng/L.
   B. 175 ng/L and 225 ng/L.
   C. 225 ng/L and 275 ng/L.
   D. 275 ng/L and 325 ng/L.

22. Did Experiment 1 and Experiment 2, respectively, take more than 1 day or less than 1 day to complete?

   F. Experiment 1: more
      Experiment 2: more

   G. Experiment 1: more
      Experiment 2: less

   H. Experiment 1: less
      Experiment 2: more

   J. Experiment 1: less
      Experiment 2: less

GO ON TO THE NEXT PAGE.

4 ◯ ◯ ◯ ◯ ◯ ◯ ◯ ◯ **4**

Passage V

Introduction

During the early Earth period (the first 2 billion years after Earth formed), the Sun produced only about 70% of the light and heat that it does today. Consequently, if early Earth's atmosphere had been identical to Earth's atmosphere today, the average surface temperature would have been well below the freezing point of water. However, geologic evidence indicates that a large amount of liquid water was present on the surface. Two hypotheses were proposed to explain how 3 heat-absorbing greenhouse gases—carbon dioxide (CO_2), ammonia (NH_3), and methane (CH_4)—in early Earth's atmosphere contributed to the presence of liquid water on the surface.

Hypothesis 1

During the early Earth period, volcanic eruptions released both CO_2 and NH_3 into the atmosphere. In addition, microbes produced CH_4 by metabolizing hydrogen (H_2) gas. Compared with atmospheric greenhouse gas concentrations at present day, those on early Earth were considerably greater: the CO_2 concentration was about 100 times as great, the NH_3 concentration was about 20 times as great, and the CH_4 concentration was about 1,000 times as great. These higher-than-present atmospheric concentrations of CO_2, NH_3, and CH_4 absorbed enough heat to maintain an average surface temperature that allowed for liquid water.

Hypothesis 2

The only source of atmospheric CO_2, NH_3, and CH_4 on early Earth was volcanic eruptions. Compared with atmospheric CO_2 and NH_3 concentrations at present day, those on early Earth were somewhat greater: the CO_2 concentration was about 40 times as great and the NH_3 concentration was about 10 times as great. The CH_4 concentration was about the same as its present value. At those concentrations, the 3 gases by themselves would not have absorbed enough heat to raise the average surface temperature above freezing. However, atmospheric concentrations of both nitrogen (N_2) and H_2 were approximately twice what they are today. These higher-than-present concentrations of N_2 and H_2 greatly enhanced the heat-absorbing effects of the 3 greenhouse gases, maintaining an average surface temperature that allowed for liquid water.

23. Suppose that the current atmospheric CO_2 concentration on Earth is approximately 395 parts per million (ppm). Based on Hypothesis 2, the atmospheric CO_2 concentration on early Earth was most likely closest to which of the following values?

A. 395 ppm
B. 15,800 ppm
C. 39,500 ppm
D. 197,500 ppm

24. Which of the hypotheses, if either, indicated that 2 additional gases were necessary for CO_2, NH_3, and CH_4 to absorb enough heat for liquid water to exist on early Earth's surface?

F. Hypothesis 1 only
G. Hypothesis 2 only
H. Both Hypothesis 1 and Hypothesis 2
J. Neither Hypothesis 1 nor Hypothesis 2

25. In regard to the source of CH_4 in early Earth's atmosphere, which of the following statements describes a difference between Hypothesis 1 and Hypothesis 2? Based on Hypothesis 1, CH_4 was:

A. released from volcanic eruptions, whereas according to Hypothesis 2, CH_4 was produced by microbial metabolism.
B. released from volcanic eruptions, whereas according to Hypothesis 2, CH_4 was produced by chemical reactions between CO_2 and H_2O.
C. produced by microbial metabolism, whereas according to Hypothesis 2, CH_4 was released from volcanic eruptions.
D. produced by microbial metabolism, whereas according to Hypothesis 2, CH_4 was produced by chemical reactions between CO_2 and H_2O.

GO ON TO THE NEXT PAGE.

4 ○ ○ ○ ○ ○ ○ ○ ○ ○ **4**

26. The metabolism of the microbes referred to in Hypothesis 1 is most likely represented by which of the following balanced chemical equations?

F. $CO_2 + 4H_2 \rightarrow CH_4 + 2H_2O$
G. $CO_2 + 2H_2O \rightarrow CH_4 + 2O_2$
H. $CH_4 + 2O_2 \rightarrow CO_2 + 2H_2O$
J. $CH_4 + 2H_2O \rightarrow CO_2 + 4H_2$

27. Hypothesis 1 would be best supported by which of the following findings involving CO_2 or CH_4?

A. Evidence that 4 billion years ago the concentration of CO_2 was 20 times the present concentration
B. Evidence that 4 billion years ago the concentration of CH_4 was 20 times the present concentration
C. 3.5-billion-year-old rock samples containing evidence of CO_2 produced by microbes
D. 3.5-billion-year-old rock samples containing evidence of CH_4 produced by microbes

28. Suppose that if Earth's atmospheric N_2 concentration were increased from its present value, the atmosphere would scatter a higher percentage of incoming sunlight, resulting in cooler surface temperatures. This information would weaken which of the hypotheses, if either?

F. Hypothesis 1 only
G. Hypothesis 2 only
H. Both Hypothesis 1 and Hypothesis 2
J. Neither Hypothesis 1 nor Hypothesis 2

GO ON TO THE NEXT PAGE.

4 ◯ ◯ ◯ ◯ ◯ ◯ ◯ ◯ 4

Passage VI

Viscous fluid flow occurs when various parts of a fluid interact with each other to produce forces that inhibit flow and generate heat. Students performed 3 studies of viscous fluid flow using the experimental setup shown in Figure 1.

Figure 1

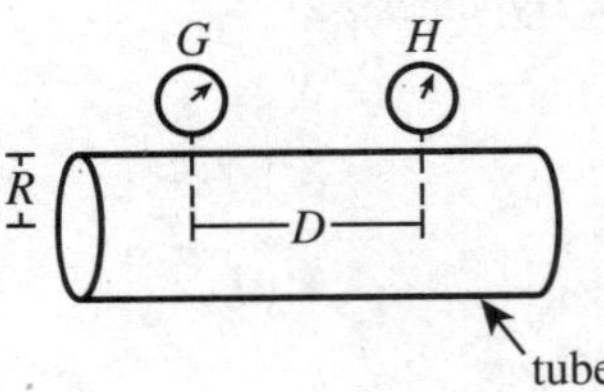

In each trial of the studies, the students sent a fluid through a tube such that the fluid completely filled the tube. The fluid had a viscosity η; the tube had a radius R and was fitted with 2 pressure gauges, Gauge G and Gauge H, that were a distance D apart. The pressure of the fluid at Gauge G minus the pressure of the fluid at Gauge H always equaled 5 kilopascals. (A kilopascal, kPa, is a unit of pressure, which is defined as force per unit area.) Using a flow meter, the students measured the fluid's flow rate through the tube, F, in milliliters per second (mL/s).

Study 1

The students measured F for various fluids, each having a different η, that flowed, one at a time, through a tube having an R of 5.00 mm and a D of 1.00 m (see Table 1).

Table 1	
η (10^{-3} Pa·s*)	F (mL/s)
1.00	1,230
2.00	615
3.00	410
4.00	307
5.00	246
*pascal second	

Study 2

The students measured F for a fluid having an η of 1.0×10^{-3} Pa·s that flowed through each of various tubes having the same D, 1.00 m, but different R (see Table 2).

Table 2	
R (mm)	F (mL/s)
1.00	1.97
2.00	31.5
3.00	159
4.00	504
5.00	1,230

Study 3

The students measured F for a fluid having an η of 1.0×10^{-3} Pa·s that flowed through each of various tubes having the same R, 5.00 mm, but different D (see Table 3).

Table 3	
D (m)	F (mL/s)
0.50	2,460
1.00	1,230
1.50	820
2.00	615
2.50	492

29. Suppose that a sixth trial had been performed in Study 1 for which the fluid's flow rate had equaled 920 mL/s. In that trial, the viscosity of the fluid would most likely have been:

   A. less than 1.00×10^{-3} Pa·s.
   B. between 1.00×10^{-3} Pa·s and 2.00×10^{-3} Pa·s.
   C. between 2.00×10^{-3} Pa·s and 3.00×10^{-3} Pa·s.
   D. greater than 3.00×10^{-3} Pa·s.

GO ON TO THE NEXT PAGE.

4 ○ ○ ○ ○ ○ ○ ○ ○ ○ **4**

30. In Study 2, which variables were held constant?

   F. R and F
   G. F and η
   H. η and D
   J. R and D

31. Based on the information given, in what direction was the fluid flowing?

   A. From Gauge G toward Gauge H, because the pressure at Gauge G was greater than the pressure at Gauge H.
   B. From Gauge G toward Gauge H, because the pressure at Gauge G was less than the pressure at Gauge H.
   C. From Gauge H toward Gauge G, because the pressure at Gauge H was greater than the pressure at Gauge G.
   D. From Gauge H toward Gauge G, because the pressure at Gauge H was less than the pressure at Gauge G.

32. The viscosity of each fluid investigated in the studies resulted from which of the following types of interaction between parts of the fluid?

   F. Friction
   G. Combustion
   H. Magnetism
   J. Gravity

33. In Study 3, when D was equal to 2.50 m, approximately what volume of fluid flowed past either gauge in 1 minute?

   A. 25,000 mL
   B. 30,000 mL
   C. 37,000 mL
   D. 49,000 mL

34. The pressure gradient between any 2 points lying on a horizontal line inside a tube equaled the absolute value of the difference in pressure between the 2 points divided by the distance between the 2 points. What was the pressure gradient between Gauges G and H during Study 1?

   F. 5 kPa/m
   G. 1 kPa/m
   H. 5 kPa/mm
   J. 1 kPa/mm

GO ON TO THE NEXT PAGE.

4 ○ ○ ○ ○ ○ ○ ○ ○ **4**

Passage VII

Wheat growth is negatively affected by higher-than-normal salt (NaCl) concentrations in the soil. Scientists investigated whether the negative effects are countered by adding to the soil either a species of bacteria (Species R) or a mixture of proteins from marine algae (PMA).

Study 1

First, 240 identical 2 L pots were each filled with 1.5 kg of a certain soil. Next, 5 wheat seeds were planted in each pot, and the pots were divided equally into 4 groups (Groups 1–4). Then, all the pots in each group received 1 of 4 treatments (see Table 1).

Table 1	
Group	Treatment
1	0.5 L of H_2O
2	0.5 L of H_2O containing 9.3 g/L of NaCl
3	0.5 L of H_2O containing Species R and 9.3 g/L of NaCl
4	0.5 L of H_2O containing PMA and 9.3 g/L of NaCl

Note: The addition of 9.3 g/L of NaCl to the pots in Groups 2–4 resulted in a higher-than-normal NaCl concentration in the soil in those pots.

After treatment, each pot was irrigated once every 3 days with either 0.5 L of H_2O only (Group 1) or 0.5 L of H_2O containing 9.3 g/L of NaCl (Groups 2–4). The average number of seeds germinated per pot was then determined for each group at 3, 5, 7, and 9 days after treatment (see Table 2).

Table 2				
Days after treatment	Average number of seeds germinated per pot			
	Group 1	Group 2	Group 3	Group 4
3	4.8	0.0	1.1	2.8
5	5.0	0.0	4.3	4.0
7	5.0	0.2	5.0	4.6
9	5.0	0.4	5.0	4.8

Study 2

An additional 240 of the 2 L pots were prepared, treated, and irrigated as in Study 1. Nine days after treatment, all but 1 seedling were removed from each of the pots that had multiple seedlings. Each pot was then irrigated as in Study 1 for an additional 75 days. The average plant height was then determined for each group (see Figure 1).

Figure 1

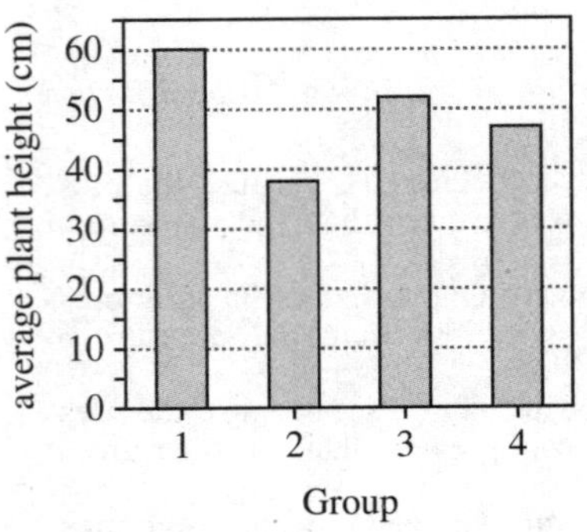

Table 2 and Figure 1 adapted from Elhafid Nabti et al., "Restoration of Growth of Durum Wheat (*Triticum durum* var. waha) Under Saline Conditions Due to Inoculation with the Rhizosphere Bacterium *Azospirillum brasilense* NH and Extracts of the Marine Alga *Ulva lactuca*." ©2010 by Springer Science and Business Media, LLC.

35. Based on the results of Study 2, how many of the groups had an average plant height greater than 1 meter?

- **A.** 0
- **B.** 1
- **C.** 3
- **D.** 4

36. The presence of more than 1 plant in a pot can negatively affect the growth of all the plants in the pot, due to competition among the plants. What action was taken in Study 2 to prevent competition among the plants?

- **F.** Only one seed was planted per pot.
- **G.** Only one seedling was planted per pot.
- **H.** After an initial period of growth, all seeds except one were removed from each pot that had multiple seeds.
- **J.** After an initial period of growth, all seedlings except one were removed from each pot that had multiple seedlings.

GO ON TO THE NEXT PAGE.

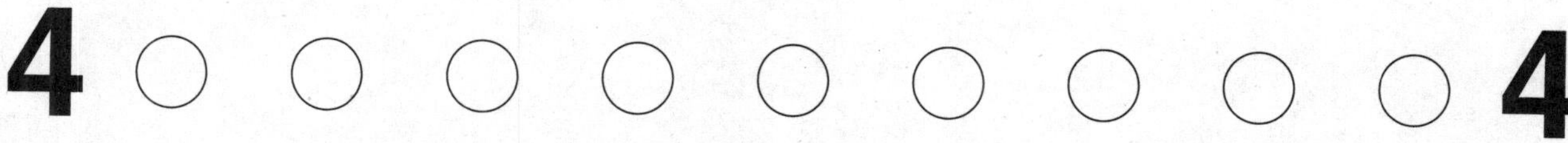

4 ○ ○ ○ ○ ○ ○ ○ ○ ○ **4**

37. Consider the claim "The average height of the plants in a group was affected by the number of days that the pots in that group were irrigated." Can this claim be evaluated on the basis of the results of Study 2?

   A. Yes, because the number of days of irrigation was the same for all the groups.

   B. Yes, because the number of days of irrigation was different for each group.

   C. No, because the number of days of irrigation was the same for all the groups.

   D. No, because the number of days of irrigation was different for each group.

38. Consider the statement "Treatment with Species R was more effective at promoting seed germination in soil with a higher-than-normal NaCl concentration than was treatment with PMA." Are the results of Study 1 for 5, 7, and 9 days after treatment consistent with this statement?

   F. Yes; on each of those days, the average number of seeds germinated per pot was greater for Group 3 than for Group 4.

   G. Yes; on each of those days, the average number of seeds germinated per pot was greater for Group 4 than for Group 3.

   H. No; on each of those days, the average number of seeds germinated per pot was greater for Group 3 than for Group 4.

   J. No; on each of those days, the average number of seeds germinated per pot was greater for Group 4 than for Group 3.

39. Let x represent the number of days after treatment until germination was first observed among the Group 2 pots in Study 1. Based on the results of Study 1, x is given by which of the following expressions?

   A. $x < 3$

   B. $3 \leq x < 5$

   C. $5 < x \leq 7$

   D. $x > 7$

40. Consider the statement "On average, plant height was greater for the plants treated with H_2O containing PMA and NaCl than it was for the plants treated with either H_2O containing NaCl only or H_2O containing Species R and NaCl." Do the results of Study 2 support this statement?

   F. Yes; the average plant height in Group 3 was greater than the average plant height in Groups 2 and 4.

   G. Yes; the average plant height in Group 4 was greater than the average plant height in Groups 2 and 3.

   H. No; the average plant height in Group 3 was greater than that in Group 2 but less than that in Group 4.

   J. No; the average plant height in Group 4 was greater than that in Group 2 but less than that in Group 3.

END OF TEST 4

STOP! DO NOT RETURN TO ANY OTHER TEST.

You may wish to photocopy these sample answer document pages to respond to the practice ACT Writing Test.

Please enter the information at the right before beginning the writing test.

Use a No. 2 pencil only. Do NOT use a mechanical pencil, ink, ballpoint, or felt-tip pen.

WRITING TEST BOOKLET NUMBER

Print your 9-digit **Booklet Number** in the boxes at the right.

WRITING TEST FORM

Print your 5-character **Test Form** in the boxes at the right <u>and</u> fill in the corresponding ovals.

Begin WRITING TEST here.

If you need more space, please continue on the next page.

WRITING TEST

If you need more space, please continue on the back of this page.

2

WRITING TEST

If you need more space, please continue on the next page.

The ONLY Official Prep Guide from the Makers of the ACT

WRITING TEST

STOP here with the writing test.

4

Practice Writing Test Prompt 2

Your Signature: _______________________________
(Do not print.)

Print Your Name Here: _______________________________

Your Date of Birth:

☐☐ –	☐☐ –	☐☐☐☐
Month	Day	Year

Form 21WT8

The **ACT®** WRITING TEST
BOOKLET

You must take the multiple-choice tests before you take the writing test.

Directions

This is a test of your writing skills. You will have **forty** (40) minutes to read the prompt, plan your response, and write an essay in English. Before you begin working, read all material in this test booklet carefully to understand exactly what you are being asked to do.

You will write your essay on the lined pages in the **answer document** provided. Your writing on those pages will be scored. You may use the unlined pages in this test booklet to plan your essay. Your work on these pages will not be scored.

Your essay will be evaluated based on the evidence it provides of your ability to:

- clearly state your own perspective on a complex issue and analyze the relationship between your perspective and at least one other perspective
- develop and support your ideas with reasoning and examples
- organize your ideas clearly and logically
- communicate your ideas effectively in standard written English

Lay your pencil down immediately when time is called.

DO NOT OPEN THIS BOOKLET UNTIL TOLD TO DO SO.

PO Box 168
Iowa City, IA 52243-0168

The ONLY Official Prep Guide from the Makers of the ACT

Digital Disconnect

Some people purposely avoid digital tools and technology because they value a "disconnected" lifestyle. These people may choose not to carry cell phones, have internet service at home, or participate in social media. But digital tools and technologies are a part of almost every aspect of modern life. Banking, shopping, schoolwork, and all forms of business communication become more dependent on digital connections each year. Is it wise, then, to avoid the digital world?

Read and carefully consider these perspectives. Each suggests a particular way of thinking about the question above.

Perspective One	Perspective Two	Perspective Three
Most digital tools and technology make life easier. Avoiding those things is foolish because it often means making a simple task harder for ourselves.	Some things can't be done digitally: experiencing nature, exercising, and spending time with other people. We should avoid the digital world more often so we don't neglect these important parts of life.	Avoiding the digital world is the same as isolating yourself from society. It is unwise and possibly even unhealthy to stay away from digital tools and technologies.

Essay Task

Write a unified, coherent essay in which you address the question of whether it is wise to avoid the digital world. In your essay, be sure to:

- clearly state your own perspective and analyze the relationship between your perspective and at least one other perspective
- develop and support your ideas with reasoning and examples
- organize your ideas clearly and logically
- communicate your ideas effectively in standard written English

Your perspective may be in full agreement with any of those given, in partial agreement, or completely different.

Planning Your Essay

Your work on these prewriting pages will not be scored.

Use the space below and on the back cover to generate ideas and plan your essay. You may wish to consider the following as you think critically about the task:

Strengths and weaknesses of different perspectives on the issue
- What insights do they offer, and what do they fail to consider?
- Why might they be persuasive to others, or why might they fail to persuade?

Your own knowledge, experience, and values
- What is your perspective on this issue, and what are its strengths and weaknesses?
- How will you support your perspective in your essay?

If you need more space to plan, please continue on the following page.

Planning Your Essay

Use this page to continue planning your essay. Your work on this page will not be scored.

Passage I

Question 1. The best answer is **D** because it does not include any unnecessary punctuation.

The best answer is NOT:

A because it has an unnecessary comma after *sound*.

B because it has two unnecessary commas that incorrectly set off "to create" from the rest of the sentence.

C because it has an unnecessary comma after *create*.

Question 2. The best answer is **H** because *doubles* is precise and appropriately conveys how the violin can be used both as a violin and as an audiotape player.

The best answer is NOT:

F because *clones* is illogical and imprecise in the context of the sentence.

G because *duplicates* is illogical and imprecise in the context of the sentence.

J because *copies* is illogical and imprecise in the context of the sentence.

Question 3. The best answer is **A** because it is structurally sound, and the verb *invent* is parallel in structure to the verbs in the surrounding phrases.

The best answer is NOT:

B because the phrase "the invention of" disrupts the parallel structure of the series of phrases and creates an ambiguous meaning.

C because the word *inventing* disrupts the parallel structure of the series of phrases and creates an ambiguous meaning.

D because the phrase "to invent" disrupts the parallel structure of the series of phrases and creates an ambiguous meaning.

Question 4. **The best answer is F** because it provides the most effective transition between Anderson's childhood interests and her witnessing of major achievements in space travel and artificial intelligence later in life.

The best answer is NOT:

G because commentary about science fiction writers Ray Bradbury and Isaac Asimov provides a weak transition in context, with little relation to the sentences that follow in the paragraph.

H because the reference to Anderson's childhood music study provides an illogical transition in context, having no relation to the other sentences in the paragraph.

J because the statement about NASA's growth provides a weak transition in context and has little relation to the other sentences in the paragraph.

Question 5. **The best answer is A** because it maintains the overall style and tone of the essay.

The best answer is NOT:

B because with *eyeballing* and *snapshots*, the phrasing introduces an informal tone that is not consistent with the rest of the essay.

C because with *beheld* and "pictorial images," the phrasing introduces an elevated, formal tone that is not consistent with the rest of the essay.

D because *ogled* introduces an informal tone that is not consistent with the rest of the essay.

Question 6. **The best answer is H** because it clearly and correctly explains why the new sentence should not be added. The suggested addition's information about Neil Armstrong is not directly relevant to the paragraph's description of Anderson's performance art piece.

The best answer is NOT:

F because the suggested addition does not contribute information that is directly relevant to the paragraph's description of Anderson's performance art piece. The paragraph does not discuss how Anderson uses photography in her performance art.

G because the suggested addition does not contribute information that is directly relevant to the paragraph's description of Anderson's performance art piece. The paragraph does not directly claim that the piece was a reimagining of the first moon landing.

J because it provides an incorrect reason for not adding the sentence. The paragraph does not relate any information about whether Anderson's art was commercially viable.

Question 7. **The best answer is A** because it provides the clearest and most vivid information about the action ("sweeping the bow over the strings") and the instrument used by Anderson ("a viola").

The best answer is NOT:

B because the phrase does not specify the instrument in use, which makes it less vivid than the description in **A**.

C because the phrase "producing music" does not vividly describe Anderson's action while playing a viola.

D because the word *rubbing* makes it unclear how or where the bow moves, and the phrase "an instrument" does not indicate what kind of instrument is involved in Anderson's action.

Question 8. **The best answer is G** because it is the only option that has correct sentence structure. It creates a complete sentence, with an independent clause that has a subject and a main verb, followed by a comma and a dependent clause.

The best answer is NOT:

F because it adds the relative pronoun *that* before the verb, creating a sentence with two dependent clauses that lack a main verb, which is a sentence fragment.

H because it creates a long dependent clause that lacks a main verb, which is a sentence fragment.

J because it creates a long dependent clause that lacks a main verb, which is a sentence fragment.

Question 9. **The best answer is C** because the dash provides the appropriate punctuation to signal a sharp break in thought and to set off the nonessential phrase that follows in the rest of the sentence.

The best answer is NOT:

A because punctuation is needed to set off the nonessential phrase that follows from the rest of the sentence.

B because a colon should not be combined with *and* when introducing a nonessential phrase.

D because a semicolon is not used to set off a nonessential phrase that lacks a subject and main verb.

Question 10. The best answer is G because Anderson's talking stick provides a clear and relevant example that supports the claim that Anderson invented tools that manipulated sound.

The best answer is NOT:

F because placing the sentence at Point A would interrupt the chronological sequence established by "in 1972" and "five years later." The reference "five years later" would be unclear with this sentence placement. Additionally, in contrast to the symphony and violin mentioned in the second and third sentences, it is unclear whether the talking stick qualifies as "art that defies categorization."

H because placing the sentence at Point C would undermine the logic of the paragraph. The sentence does not indicate whether Anderson created the talking stick while at NASA, and so it is unclear whether this sentence would provide an example relevant to the sentence that precedes Point C.

J because placing the sentence at Point D weakens the logic of the paragraph, which focuses on describing technological innovations that Anderson witnessed and was inspired by.

Passage II

Question 11. The best answer is B because it inserts a comma before the nonessential phrase "similar to a bar code," effectively setting off that phrase from the sentence.

The best answer is NOT:

A because it inserts an unnecessary comma after *side*.

C because it inserts an unnecessary comma after *side* and omits the necessary comma after *identifier* that sets that phrase off from the sentence.

D because it fails to include the necessary comma after *identifier*.

Question 12. The best answer is H because it clearly explains why the new sentence should not be added. The information about how zebras might use stripes to identify one another is not relevant to the paragraph's discussion of StripeSpotter and how it works.

The best answer is NOT:

F because the information about whether zebras can do what StripeSpotter can do isn't relevant at this point in the essay, and the sentence should not be added.

G because the essay hasn't shifted away from its focus on interpreting stripes on zebras, so this reason to add the sentence is inaccurate.

J because although the sentence should not be added, the issue of whether zebras can identify one another is not a sufficient reason to add the irrelevant sentence here.

Question 13. The best answer is **A** because *capture* is precise and appropriately conveys what the researcher is doing while cropping the photograph.

The best answer is NOT:

B because *apprehend* is illogical and imprecise in the context of the sentence.

C because *acquire* is illogical and imprecise in the context of the sentence.

D because *take* is illogical and imprecise in the context of the sentence.

Question 14. The best answer is **H** because it clearly explains why the revision should not be made. The original phrase is clearer and includes more details about the image than the proposed revision does.

The best answer is NOT:

F because the proposed revision does not indicate that StripeSpotter can be used to make line art.

G because the original wording more clearly conveys that the image is composed of parallel lines, so the statement in G is false.

J because although it correctly indicates that the revision should not be made, the proposed revision does not imply that the way StripeSpotter creates images is unscientific.

Question 15. The best answer is **A** because it is the only option with correct subject-verb agreement. The plural subject *widths* must have a plural verb.

The best answer is NOT:

B because "has corresponded" is a singular verb, and the subject of the sentence is plural.

C because "is corresponding" is a singular verb, and the subject of the sentence is plural.

D because *corresponds* is a singular verb, and the subject of the sentence is plural.

Passage III

Question 16. The best answer is G because it places the sentences and ideas in logical order. Sentence 1 introduces the idea of the mural. Sentence 3 describes what the mural looks like from afar. Sentence 2 contrasts what the mural looks like from afar with what the mural looks like up close.

The best answer is NOT:

F because it has the sentences in illogical order. The sentence that contrasts what the mural looks like up close appears before the description of what the mural looks like from afar, which doesn't make sense in context.

H because it has the sentences in illogical order. It begins the essay with a sentence that contrasts the appearance of the mosaics up close, but the essay hasn't mentioned the mosaics yet.

J because it has the sentences in illogical order. It begins the essay by describing what the mural looks like from a distance, but the essay hasn't explained which mural is being discussed yet.

Question 17. The best answer is D because *produce* is precise and appropriately explains what Shin was asked to do.

The best answer is NOT:

A because *spawn* is illogical and imprecise in the context of creating a work of art.

B because *accomplish* is imprecise because it doesn't convey what exactly Shin is doing.

C because *perform* is illogical and imprecise in the context of creating a visual work of art.

Question 18. The best answer is J because it creates a logical sentence with correctly placed modifiers. The introductory dependent clause is meant to modify *Shin*, and option D correctly places Shin's name right after the introductory clause, making the meaning of the sentence clear.

The best answer is NOT:

F because the introductory clause incorrectly modifies "visually representing," creating an illogical sentence.

G because the introductory clause incorrectly modifies *sought*, creating an illogical sentence.

H because the introductory clause incorrectly modifies "a means," creating an illogical sentence.

Question 19. The best answer is **D** because it is the only choice that uses the correct form of the possessive pronoun *its*.

The best answer is NOT:

A because *its'* is an incorrect form of the possessive pronoun *its*.

B because the phrase "it is" is ungrammatical and not the possessive pronoun needed here.

C because *it's* is a contraction for "it is," not the possessive pronoun *its*.

Question 20. The best answer is **F** because it is the only option that provides a logical transition from the first two sentences, which lay out the origins of celadon, to the next two sentences, which focus on celadon ceramicists in South Korea today.

The best answer is NOT:

G because the information about why celadon changes color is not an effective transition here.

H because the origin of the word *celadon* is not an effective transition here.

J because the information about Shin Sang-ho is not an effective transition here.

Question 21. The best answer is **D** because it creates a logical sentence with correctly placed modifiers. The phrase "for celadon shards" must be placed after *arranged*; otherwise, the sentence says that Shin arranged for herself to be shipped to Queens.

The best answer is NOT:

A because the phrase "for celadon shards" is incorrectly placed so that it appears to modify *Icheon*, creating an illogical sentence.

B because the phrase "for celadon shards" is incorrectly placed so that it appears to modify *ceramicists*, creating an illogical sentence.

C because the phrase "for celadon shards" is incorrectly placed so that it appears to modify *city*, creating an illogical sentence.

Question 22. The best answer is G because the relative pronoun *which* is appropriate in the context and agrees with its antecedent, *shards*.

The best answer is NOT:

F because the relative pronoun *whose* refers to people, not objects, such as shards.

H because the pronoun *whom* refers to people, not objects, such as shards.

J because the demonstrative pronoun *that* in the phrase "of that" refers to one thing, and the antecedent in the sentence (*shards*) is plural.

Question 23. The best answer is B because it provides the most specific information about what is on the shards, specifying that the characters on the shards are in Korean and that the designs are labyrinthine.

The best answer is NOT:

A because "alphabetic symbols and assorted patterns" is not as specific as B is.

C because "different letters and a plethora of patterns" is a vague description, not a specific one.

D because "numerous symbols and various designs" is also a vague description.

Question 24. The best answer is F because it correctly uses a colon to mark a sharp break in the sentence. By using a colon after *significance*, the writer is showing that the clause following the colon explains the shards' significance.

The best answer is NOT:

G because it incorrectly inserts the conjunction *and* before the clause that follows the colon.

H because it uses a comma to indicate a sharp break in thought, which is incorrect. Moreover, it creates a run-on sentence.

J because it fails to use punctuation to indicate a sharp break in thought, which is incorrect.

Question 25. The best answer is B because it is the only option that has correct sentence structure. It creates a grammatically correct sentence by including a subject and main verb.

The best answer is NOT:

A because the phrase "Shin's use of" lacks a main verb, which creates a sentence fragment.

C because the verb *using* lacks a subject, which creates a sentence fragment.

D because deleting the phrase results in a sentence that lacks a subject and main verb, which creates a sentence fragment.

Passage IV

Question 26. The best answer is H because it provides the most logical transition in context. To facilitate the transition from the previous sentence's general description of giant sequoia trees to the following sentence's details about the lack of road access to the Giant Forest, it is logical to focus this sentence on the giant sequoia groves in Sequoia National Park.

The best answer is NOT:

F because the number of caves in the park provides no logical transition from the description of giant sequoia trees generally to the details about the lack of road access to the Giant Forest.

G because the information about the endangered species provides no logical transition from the description of giant sequoia trees generally to the details about the lack of road access to the Giant Forest.

J because the park's percentage of wilderness provides no logical transition from the description of giant sequoia trees generally to the details about the lack of road access to the Giant Forest.

Question 27. The best answer is A because it is the only option that has correct sentence structure. It correctly supplies the sentence's subject and verb.

The best answer is NOT:

B because it is a sentence fragment. It does not provide a main verb to accompany the subject, *Young*.

C because it is a sentence fragment. The semicolon incorrectly isolates the phrases before it from the main structure of the sentence.

D because it creates a sentence fragment. What precedes the period is not an independent clause.

Question 28. **The best answer is G** because it provides the most logical conjunction to frame the ideas presented in this sentence. *Although* pairs logically with "Young was just as concerned" in the sentence.

The best answer is NOT:

F because the conjunction *because* is illogical in context.

H because the conjunction *unless* is illogical in context.

J because the conjunction *if* is also illogical in context.

Question 29. **The best answer is B** because *channel* is precise and appropriately expresses that the troops were focusing their efforts on the road.

The best answer is NOT:

A because the meaning of *send* is illogical and imprecise in the context of describing the troops' efforts.

C because the meaning of *convey* is illogical and imprecise in the context of describing the troops' efforts.

D because the meaning of *shape* is illogical and imprecise in the context of describing the troops' efforts.

Question 30. **The best answer is G** because the transition word *additionally* signals clearly and logically that this sentence is related to and building upon the previous sentence's idea of the troops guarding the park's grounds.

The best answer is NOT:

F because the adverb *nevertheless* suggests that the idea in this sentence is in opposition to the idea in the preceding sentence, which is illogical.

H because the adverb *thus* suggests a cause-and-effect relationship with the idea in the preceding sentence, which is illogical.

J because the adverb *still* suggests that the actions described in this sentence happened despite the actions described in the previous sentence, which is illogical.

Question 31. **The best answer is** C because it maintains the overall style and tone of the essay. The language here is neither overly informal nor too formal.

The best answer is NOT:

A because the wording is too informal compared to the rest of the essay.

B because although the wording maintains the overall style and tone of the essay, the wording itself is redundant. The phrase "further harm" already expresses the idea of protecting the trees in the future, making "in the future" redundant.

D because the wording is too informal compared to the rest of the essay.

Question 32. **The best answer is** H because it is the only option with correct subject-verb agreement. The plural subject *contributions* must have a plural verb.

The best answer is NOT:

F because "has been counted" is a singular verb, and the subject of the sentence is plural.

G because "was counted" is a singular verb, and the subject of the sentence is plural.

J because "is counted" is a singular verb, and the subject of the sentence is plural.

Question 33. **The best answer is** D because it clearly explains why the new sentence should not be added. The information about who petitioned for the National Park Service to recognize Captain Young is not directly relevant within the context of the paragraph and the essay.

The best answer is NOT:

A because the proposed addition does not explain why it took so long for the National Park Service to recognize Captain Young, and the sentence should not be added.

B because there is no information to indicate that Palmer inspired Young's actions, and the context would suggest that Palmer petitioned the National Park Service sometime after Young completed his work there. Also, the sentence should not be added.

C because although the sentence should not be added, the suggested addition does not suggest that other people had already petitioned the National Park Service to recognize Young.

Question 34. **The best answer is G** because the information that there is a tree named after Young alongside other trees named after prominent people is the best conclusion in the context of this paragraph's discussion of the National Park Service recognizing Young's efforts. This choice resonates with the essay's overall appreciative description of Young's work in Sequoia National Park.

The best answer is NOT:

F because the detail about the world's largest tree isn't closely related to the essay's focus on Young's work in Sequoia National Park. Therefore, it is not a fitting conclusion to the sentence and the essay.

H because the details about present-day activities in the Giant Forest isn't closely related to the essay's focus on Young's work in Sequoia National Park. Therefore, it is not a fitting conclusion to the sentence and the essay.

J because the claim that the Giant Forest is a popular spot to visit isn't closely related to the essay's focus on Young's work in Sequoia National Park. Therefore, it too is not a fitting conclusion to the sentence and the essay.

Question 35. **The best answer is D** because this option clearly indicates why the essay does not meet the writer's primary purpose. The essay focuses on the vital road project—completed under the leadership of Captain Young—that opened Sequoia National Park's Giant Forest to visitors.

The best answer is NOT:

A because the essay does not describe changes that roads have brought about from the park's establishment to present day.

B because the essay does not develop the idea that Young's actions created a surge in visitors to the park.

C because the essay does not describe Young's military career as a whole, but rather his specific role in the construction of the road to Giant Forest.

Passage V

Question 36. The best answer is F because the name "Christian Sommer" is an essential element and should not be set off by commas in the sentence. If Sommer's name were set off from the rest of the sentence, that would indicate that the identity of the marine biology student is clear without having to provide a name, which isn't the case.

The best answer is NOT:

G because the name "Christian Sommer" is an essential element and should not be set off with commas. It also adds an unnecessary comma after *marine*.

H because the name "Christian Sommer" is an essential element and should not be set off with commas.

J because the name "Christian Sommer" is an essential element and should not be set off with a comma.

Question 37. The best answer is B because this option clearly indicates what would be lost if the sentence were deleted. The sentence expresses, in plain language, that the jellyfish were essentially growing younger, an idea that clarifies information presented earlier in the paragraph.

The best answer is NOT:

A because the paragraph makes clear that the jellyfish revert to an earlier life stage in the preceding sentence, so deleting this sentence would not remove the information from the paragraph.

C because this sentence does not present a different perspective or contradict anything Sommer concluded.

D because this sentence does not suggest that Sommer continued to observe the jellyfish.

Question 38. The best answer is J because it is the only option that provides a logical introduction to the paragraph's focus on the jellyfish's life stages.

The best answer is NOT:

F because the details about the jellyfish's anatomy do not logically introduce the information in the rest of the paragraph.

G because the details about where the jellyfish lives do not logically introduce the information in the rest of the paragraph.

H because the details about the jellyfish's anatomy do not logically introduce the information in the rest of the paragraph.

Question 39. The best answer is B because it uses a comma to set off the nonessential phrase introduced by the subordinating conjunction *if*. This phrase is closed by a matching comma after *age*.

The best answer is NOT:

A because it has an unnecessary dash that interrupts the phrase introduced by *if*.

C because it lacks punctuation setting off the phrase introduced by *if* and includes an unnecessary comma after *stressed*.

D because it lacks punctuation setting off the phrase introduced by *if*.

Question 40. The best answer is J because it provides the clearest, most concise wording.

The best answer is NOT:

F because it is redundant; "no apparent limit" and "perpetual cycles" have similar meanings, and "metamorphic transformation" is itself redundant.

G because it is redundant; "no apparent limit" and "endlessly recurring" have similar meanings, and *transformative* and *metamorphosis* have essentially the same meaning.

H because it is redundant; *transformative* and *metamorphosis* have essentially the same meaning.

Passage VI

Question 41. The best answer is A because it correctly identifies the rhetorical impact of losing the phrase "and my idol." An idol is greatly admired, so it is logical to conclude that if the narrator idolized her sister—"a guitar buff"—she would want to learn to play the guitar, too.

The best answer is NOT:

B because it fails to correctly identify the rhetorical impact of the phrase "and my idol." This phrase indicates nothing about the narrator's age when she learned to play the guitar.

C because it fails to correctly identify the rhetorical impact of the phrase "and my idol." This phrase suggests nothing about the age difference between the narrator and her sister.

D because it fails to correctly identify the rhetorical impact of the phrase "and my idol." This phrase suggests nothing about degree of musical talent.

Question 42. The best answer is H because it correctly distinguishes between possessives and plurals by using an apostrophe to form the plural possessive *friends'* and no apostrophe in the plural noun *houses*.

The best answer is NOT:

F because it incorrectly provides the plural noun *friends* where the plural possessive *friends'* is needed.

G because it incorrectly provides the singular possessive *friend's* where a plural is needed and incorrectly provides the singular possessive *house's* where the plural noun *houses* is needed.

J because it incorrectly provides the singular possessive *friend's*.

Question 43. The best answer is A because it provides the most precise expression of the idea described in the stem. The word *assailed* best illustrates "the fervor with which the narrator communicated with the airport personnel" because it figuratively conveys the narrator's energy in the interaction.

The best answer is NOT:

B because it provides a word choice that fails to precisely describe the idea identified in the stem; the neutral word *approached* does not adequately illustrate fervor.

C because it provides a word choice that fails to precisely describe the idea identified in the stem; the neutral word *questioned* does not adequately illustrate fervor.

D because it provides a word choice that fails to precisely describe the idea identified in the stem; the neutral word *contacted* does not adequately illustrate fervor.

Question 44. The best answer is J because it provides the appropriate pronouns for this sentence. The subjective pronoun case *who* is needed here because the word *who* serves as the subject of the dependent clause, and the pronoun *me* is the object.

The best answer is NOT:

F because it inappropriately uses a reflexive pronoun. The object is not the same person as the subject, so the reflexive pronoun *myself* is grammatically incorrect.

G because it incorrectly provides the objective pronoun case *whom* where the subjective pronoun case is needed. In addition, the object is not the same person as the subject, so the reflexive pronoun *myself* is grammatically incorrect.

H because it incorrectly provides the objective pronoun case *whom* where the subjective pronoun case is needed.

Question 45. The best answer is D because it eliminates redundancy and unnecessary wordiness.

The best answer is NOT:

A because it fails to eliminate redundancy at the paragraph level; the idea that this is an extended trip is mentioned earlier in the paragraph.

B because it fails to eliminate wordiness and redundancy at the paragraph level; the phrase "due to the fact that I was on an extended trip" contains a redundant reference to the extended trip and lacks concision.

C because it fails to eliminate redundancy at the paragraph level; the idea that the narrator is in Hawaii is mentioned earlier in the paragraph.

Question 46. The best answer is J because it is the most precise word for the context. The word *issued* correctly and logically conveys the idea that the tones came from an instrument.

The best answer is NOT:

F because it supplies an imprecise word choice for the context; the word *accrued* conveys the idea of accumulating, which does not make sense for describing musical tones.

G because it supplies an imprecise word choice for the context; the word *distributed* conveys the idea of something being passed out or delivered, which does not make sense for describing musical tones.

H because it supplies an imprecise word choice for the context; the word *appeared* conveys the idea of something becoming visible, which does not make sense for describing musical tones.

Question 47. The best answer is A because it is a complete statement, preventing the introduction of a rhetorically ineffective fragment.

The best answer is NOT:

B because it creates a sentence fragment.

C because it creates a sentence fragment.

D because it creates a sentence fragment.

Question 48. **The best answer is G** because it uses the appropriate conjunction for indicating a comparison (the word *than*), and the phrase "that of a guitar" clearly indicates that the comparison is between the guitar and the ukulele.

The best answer is NOT:

F because it uses the adverb *then* instead of the conjunction *than*.

H because it contains the pronoun *it*, which has no clear antecedent here, making the sentence unclear in terms of what is being compared.

J because it incorrectly supplies the adverb *then* where the conjunction *than* is needed. In addition, it contains the pronoun *it*, which has no clear antecedent here, making the sentence unclear in terms of what is being compared.

Question 49. **The best answer is B** because it provides the most specific description of the music the narrator played, as defined in the stem.

The best answer is NOT:

A because it uses the general word *music*, which lacks the specificity of the term "Hawaiian classics."

C because it uses the general term "tropical tunes," which lacks the specificity of the term "Hawaiian classics."

D because it uses the general word *things*, which is too vague to have any specific meaning.

Question 50. **The best answer is H** because it best expresses the idea specified in the stem by referring to the narrator's closeness to her sister and love of playing the guitar. These are key points in the first two paragraphs.

The best answer is NOT:

F because it fails to fulfill the goal specified in the stem; neither the ukulele nor Hawaii is mentioned in the first two paragraphs.

G because it fails to fulfill the goal specified in the stem; the narrator's time in Hawaii is not discussed in the first two paragraphs.

J because it fails to fulfill the goal specified in the stem; the narrator's business trip is not the central focus of the first two paragraphs.

Question 1. The correct answer is A. First, divide the constants to simplify $-\frac{35}{5} = -7$, then apply the exponent rule for division: $x^{5-1}y^{4-1} = x^4y^3$. By combining the constant and the variable expression, the fraction is equivalent to $-7x^4y^3$. If you chose **B**, you may have correctly calculated the constant as -7 but thought the exponents in the denominator of the fraction were both 0 and applied the exponent rule for division: $x^{5-0}y^{4-0} = x^5y^4 \rightarrow -7x^5y^4$. If you chose **C**, you may have correctly calculated the constant as -7 but incorrectly applied the exponent rule for division and added exponents: $x^{5+1}y^{4+1} = x^6y^5 \rightarrow -7x^6y^5$. If you chose **D**, you may have added the constants $-(35 + 5) = -40$ and correctly applied the exponent rule for division: $x^{5-1}y^{4-1} = x^4y^3 \rightarrow -40x^4y^3$.

Question 2. The correct answer is G. The sum of the measures of the interior angles of any triangle is $180°$. To find the value of x, solve the equation $4x + 5x + 6x = 180$. Thus, $15x = 180 \Leftrightarrow x = 12$. If you chose **F**, you may have thought adjacent angles are complementary (or sum to $90°$) and solved $4x + 5x = 90$ to get $9x = 90 \Leftrightarrow x = 10$. If you chose **H**, you may have thought the sum of the measures of the interior angles was $360°$ and solved $4x + 5x + 6x = 360$ to get $15x = 360 \Leftrightarrow x = 24$. If you chose **J**, you may have thought only one of the interior angles was needed and solved $6x = 180$ to get $x = 30$.

Question 3. The correct answer is C. First, divide the total volume of the batch of cologne by the volume of cologne that will be contained in each full bottle to calculate the total number of bottles: $\frac{48.5 \text{ oz}}{0.35 \text{ oz/bottle}} \approx 138.57$ bottles. Because the approximate 0.57 represents a partially filled bottle, round down to the nearest whole number of bottles, 138. If you chose **A** or **B**, you may have computed $\frac{48.5}{3.5} \approx 13.86$ and then either rounded down to 13 or rounded up to 14. If you chose **D**, you may have divided correctly but then incorrectly rounded 138.57 up to 139.

Question 4. The correct answer is G. The number of spaces reserved for accessible parking is equal to $200(0.06) = 12$. So, there are $200 - 12 = 188$ spaces **not** reserved for accessible parking. Of these 188 spaces, 20 are suitable for compact cars only. Thus, the remaining $188 - 20 = 168$ spaces are suitable for noncompact cars. If you chose **F**, you may have subtracted 20% of the number of spaces in the parking lot from the total, $200 - 200(0.20) = 200 - 40 = 160$. If you chose **H**, you may have subtracted only the 20 spaces that are suitable for compact cars from the total, $200 - 20 = 180$. If you chose **J**, you may have subtracted only the 6% of spaces that are reserved for accessible parking from the total, $200 - 200(0.06) = 200 - 12 = 188$.

Question 5. The correct answer is D. Every year Ricardo will put in at least \$500, and on years 2, 3, 4, 5, and 6 he will put in \$200 more than the previous year. So, there will be 5 birthdays when the additional \$200 will need to be accounted for. The equation to calculate the total is \$500(6) + \$200(1 + 2 + 3 + 4 + 5), which yields a total of \$6,000. If you chose **A**, you may have forgotten to increase the amount by \$200 for each successive birthday: \$500(6) + \$200(6 − 1). If you chose **B**, you may have just added the dollar amounts and multiplied by the number of years: (\$500 + \$200)(6). If you chose **C**, you may have calculated \$500(6 + 1) + \$200(6).

Question 6. **The correct answer is G.** To add matrices, add elements in the same position to each other: $\begin{bmatrix} 9 & 2 \\ -4 & 1 \end{bmatrix} + \begin{bmatrix} -6 & 8 \\ 7 & 6 \end{bmatrix} = \begin{bmatrix} 9+(-6) & 2+8 \\ (-4)+7 & 1+6 \end{bmatrix} = \begin{bmatrix} 3 & 10 \\ 3 & 7 \end{bmatrix}$. If you chose **F**, you may have multiplied the matrices instead of adding: $\begin{bmatrix} 9 & 2 \\ -4 & 1 \end{bmatrix}\begin{bmatrix} -6 & 8 \\ 7 & 6 \end{bmatrix} = \begin{bmatrix} 9(-6)+2(7) & 9(8)+2(6) \\ -4(-6)+1(7) & -4(8)+1(6) \end{bmatrix}$.
If you chose **H**, you may have added 4 instead of −4 to 7 in the 2nd row 1st column: $\begin{bmatrix} 9+(-6) & 2+8 \\ 4+7 & 1+6 \end{bmatrix}$. If you chose **J**, you may have added elements from the same matrix to each other: $\begin{bmatrix} 9+2 & -6+8 \\ (-4)+1 & 7+6 \end{bmatrix}$.

Question 7. **The correct answer is B.** Subtract the amount that both Lyle and Ming used from the starting amount: $4 - \left(\frac{1}{2} + 1\frac{1}{4}\right) = 4 - 1\frac{3}{4} = 2\frac{1}{4}$. There were $2\frac{1}{4}$ gallons of paint left. If you chose **A**, you may have added the amounts that Lyle and Ming used: $\frac{1}{2} + 1\frac{1}{4}$. If you chose **C**, you may have only subtracted the amount that Ming used: $4 - 1\frac{1}{4}$. If you chose **D**, you may have only subtracted the amount Lyle used: $4 - \frac{1}{2}$.

Question 8. **The correct answer is H.** The formula for the slope of a line between two points (x_1, y_1) and (x_2, y_2) is $m = \frac{y_2 - y_1}{x_2 - x_1}$. Substituting the two given points into the formula yields $m = \frac{6-1}{5-(-3)} = \frac{5}{8}$. If you chose **F**, you may have switched the numerator values and made a sign error in the denominator: $\frac{1-6}{5-3}$. If you chose **G**, you may have switched the values in the denominator: $\frac{6-1}{-3-5}$. If you chose **J**, you may have made an error with the negative value in the denominator and computed $\frac{6-1}{5-3}$.

Question 9. **The correct answer is D.** Let x be the length, in inches, of the larger triangle's hypotenuse. The hypotenuse length of the smaller triangle corresponds to the hypotenuse length of the larger triangle, so the ratio of the side lengths is 24:x. Because the ratios of corresponding side lengths are equal, 24:x is equivalent to 4:5. Write each ratio as a fraction and set the ratios equal: $\frac{24}{x} = \frac{4}{5}$. Solve for x by cross-multiplying and dividing: $4x = 5 \cdot 24 \rightarrow x = \frac{5 \cdot 24}{4} = 30$. If you chose **A**, you may have thought that the length of the larger triangle's hypotenuse is equal to the ratio of the greater lengths to the shorter lengths, expressed as a decimal: $\frac{5}{4} = 1.25$. If you chose **B**, you may have thought the solution is the product of the ratio values: $4 \cdot 5$. If you chose **C**, you may have thought the solution is the difference of the ratio values added to the shorter hypotenuse length: $24 + (5 - 4)$.

Question 10. **The correct answer is F.** In a right triangle, the sine of an angle measure is equal to the ratio of the opposite side to the hypotenuse. The hypotenuse is the longest side in a right triangle. So, $\sin A = \frac{8}{17}$. If you chose **G**, you may have thought sine was the ratio of the adjacent side to the hypotenuse. If you chose **H**, you may have thought it was the ratio of the hypotenuse to the adjacent side. If you chose **J**, you may have thought it was the ratio of the hypotenuse to the opposite side.

Question 11. **The correct answer is D.** The Pythagorean theorem states that the sum of the squares of the legs (a and b) of a right triangle is equal to the square of the hypotenuse (c). The formula is $a^2 + b^2 = c^2$. Notice that $1{,}600^2 + 1{,}200^2 = 2{,}000^2$. Because $AC^2 + BC^2 = AB^2$, $\triangle ABC$ is a right triangle with hypotenuse $\overline{AB}$, and $m\angle ACB = 90°$. The measure of $\angle BCD$ is also 90° because $\angle ACB$ and $\angle BCD$ form a straight angle. This makes $\triangle BCD$ a right triangle. CD can be found by computing $AD - AC = 2{,}500 - 1{,}600 = 900$ km. Applying the Pythagorean theorem and substituting yields $BC^2 + CD^2 = BD^2 \rightarrow 1{,}200^2 + 900^2 = BD^2$. Therefore, $BD = \sqrt{1{,}200^2 + 900^2} = 1{,}500$ km. If you chose **A**, you may have mixed up BD and 1,200 in your equation: $BD^2 + 900^2 = 1{,}200^2$. If you chose **B**, you may have thought that CD and BD were equal: $2{,}500 - 1{,}600$. If you chose **C**, you may have thought that BC and BD were equal.

Question 12. **The correct answer is J.** First, factor the equation: $(x - 9)(x + 5) = 0$. Then, set each factor equal to zero: $x - 9 = 0$ and $x + 5 = 0$. Next, solve for x by adding 9 to both sides and subtracting 5 from both sides, respectively. This yields $x = 9$ and $x = -5$. Finally, add the solutions: $9 + (-5) = 4$. If you chose **F**, you may have thought that the constant term in the equation was the sum of the solutions. If you chose **G**, you may have found one of the solutions and stopped. If you chose **H**, you may have thought that since the equation is equal to zero, the sum of the solutions was zero.

Question 13. **The correct answer is C.** To find the new coordinates, you add the distance traveled to the starting coordinate values since the dot is moving in the positive direction for both x and y. The distance traveled is the speed multiplied by the time. Because the horizontal and vertical moves take different amounts of time, perform 2 separate calculations, one for the x-coordinate and one for the y-coordinate: $(2 + (0.5)(4), 3 + (0.5)(2)) \rightarrow (2 + 2, 3 + 1) \rightarrow$ (4,4). The dot's final location is at (4,4). If you chose **A**, you may have combined the times for the horizontal and vertical moves and added the distance traveled to just the y-coordinate: $(2{,}3 + (0.5)(4 + 2))$. If you chose **B**, you may have switched the times for the horizontal and vertical moves: $(2 + (0.5)(2), 3 + (0.5)(4))$. If you chose **D**, you may have combined the times for the horizontal and vertical moves and added the distance traveled to just the x-coordinate: $(2 + (0.5)(4 + 2), 3)$.

Question 14. **The correct answer is F.** The left side of the equation can be rewritten using exponents: $-\frac{1}{81} = -\frac{1}{3^4} = -3^{-4}$. Therefore, $-3^{-4} = -3^x$. Since the bases are equal, the exponents are equal. This means $x = -4$. If you chose **G**, you may have solved $-81 = -3^x$, not knowing that the exponent should be negative because 81 is in the denominator. If you chose **H**, you may have divided -81 by -3. If you chose **J**, you may have divided the left side of the equation by -3: $-\frac{1}{81} \div -3 = \frac{1}{243}$.

Question 15. **The correct answer is B.** First, multiply both sides of the equation by I^2 to get $I^2R = P$. Then, divide by R to get $I^2 = \frac{P}{R}$. Finally, cancel the exponent by taking the square root to get $I = \sqrt{\frac{P}{R}}$. If you chose **A**, you may have thought dividing both sides by P would result in $\frac{R}{P} = I^2$ instead of $\frac{R}{P} = \frac{1}{I^2}$. If you chose **C**, you may have forgotten to take the square root. If you chose **D**, you may have thought dividing both sides by P would result in $\frac{R}{P} = I^2$ and forgotten to take the square root.

Question 16. **The correct answer is H.** The time between simultaneous light flashes is the least common multiple of 8 and 12. Multiples for 8 are 8, 16, 24, 32, 40, $\cdots$. Now, list multiples for 12 until one number matches one of the multiples for 8: 12, 24, $\cdots$. Because 24 is the least number in both lists, the answer is 24 seconds. If you chose **F**, you may have calculated the difference of the times: $12 - 8 = 4$. If you chose **G**, you may have calculated the sum of the times: $8 + 12$. If you chose **J**, you may have calculated the product of the times: $8 \cdot 12 = 96$.

Question 17. **The correct answer is C.** First, take the square root of the area, A, to find the side length, s, because $A = s^2$. So, $s = \sqrt{900} = 30$ inches. Then, multiply by 4 to find the perimeter, P, because $P = 4s$. Therefore, $P = 4 \cdot 30 = 120$ inches. If you chose **A**, you may have found only the side length: $\sqrt{900} = 30$. If you chose **B**, you may have multiplied the side length by 2 instead of 4, giving half the perimeter: $2\sqrt{900} = 60$. If you chose **D**, you may have divided the area by 4: $\frac{900}{4} = 225$.

Question 18. **The correct answer is J.** Substitute the given values into the proportion and solve by cross multiplying and dividing to find x, the deer population: $\frac{108}{x} = \frac{36}{54} \rightarrow 36x = 54(108) \rightarrow x = \frac{54(108)}{36} = 162$. If you chose **F**, you may have thought the population was 108 since it is the greatest given value. If you chose **G**, you may have added and subtracted instead of multiplying and dividing: $108 + 54 - 36 = 126$. If you chose **H**, you may have added the counts of tagged deer from both captures: $108 + 36 = 144$.

Question 19. **The correct answer is C.** The formula for an arithmetic sequence is $a_n = a_1 + (n - 1)d$, where a_n is the nth term, a_1 is the first term, and d is the common difference. Substitute and solve for a_1: $30 = a_1 + (10 - 1)2 \rightarrow 30 = a_1 + 18 \rightarrow a_1 = 30 - 18 = 12$. If you chose **A**, you may have substituted correctly, but then attempted to divide both sides of the equation by 2 (incorrectly ignoring a_1): $30 = a_1 + (10 - 1)2 \rightarrow \frac{30}{2} = a_1 + 9 \rightarrow a_1 = 15 - 9 = 6$. If you chose **B**, you may have substituted correctly, but failed to distribute 2 to both the 10 and 1 inside the parentheses: $30 = a_1 + (10 - 1)2 \rightarrow 30 = a_1 + 20 - 1 \rightarrow 30 = a_1 + 19 \rightarrow a_1 = 30 - 19 = 11$. If you chose **D**, you may have divided 30, the 10th term, by 2, the common difference: $30 \div 2 = 15$.

Question 20. The correct answer is H. Convert from steps to miles using conversion fractions, making sure the units **feet** and **steps** cancel and the unit **mile** remains in the numerator: $3{,}898 \text{ steps} \cdot \frac{2.25 \text{ ft}}{1 \text{ step}} \cdot \frac{1 \text{ mile}}{5{,}280 \text{ ft}} = \frac{3{,}898 \cdot 2.25}{5{,}280}$ miles ≈ 1.7 miles. If you chose **F**, you may have divided by 2.25 instead of multiplying: $\frac{3{,}898}{5{,}280 \cdot 2.25} \approx 0.3$. If you chose **G**, you may have set up conversion fractions where the units **feet** and **steps** canceled but the unit **mile** was in the denominator, giving the reciprocal of the correct answer: $\frac{5{,}280}{2.25 \cdot 3{,}898} \approx 0.6$. If you chose **J**, you may have computed $\frac{5{,}280 \cdot 2.25}{3{,}898} \approx 3.0$.

Question 21. The correct answer is B. First, find the total number of members in the clubs. Keep in mind that 9 students are in both clubs, which means you have to subtract so you do **not** count some students twice: $13 + 11 - 9 = 15$. Then, subtract the number of members from the total number of students: $20 - 15 = 5$. Therefore, 5 students are **not** members of either club. If you chose **A**, you may have ignored the intersection of 9 and calculated $13 + 11 - 20$. If you chose **C**, you may have ignored the club counts of 13 and 11 and calculated $20 - 9$. If you chose **D**, you may have calculated $13 + 11 + 9 - 20$.

Question 22. The correct answer is J. The mean is the sum of all the values divided by the number of values. To increase the mean of 7 numbers by 4, you must increase the sum by $4(7)$, or 28, because the total sum will be divided by 7. If you chose **F**, you may have increased the sum by 4, forgetting to account for the division in the formula. If you chose **G**, you may have thought the sum needed to increase by the number of values in the group. If you chose **H**, you may have added the given numbers: $4 + 7$.

Question 23. The correct answer is A. The equation of a circle with center (h, k) and a radius length of r is $(x - h)^2 + (y - k)^2 = r^2$. Substituting the given values into the equation yields $(x - 4)^2 + (y - (-3))^2 = 5^2$, which simplifies to $(x - 4)^2 + (y + 3)^2 = 25$. If you chose **B**, you may have switched the center's (x, y) coordinates and added rather than subtracted the coordinates. If you chose **C**, you may have switched the (x, y) coordinates and forgotten to square the radius. If you chose **D**, you may have thought the coordinates should be added to x and y instead of subtracted.

Question 24. The correct answer in F. The median is the middle term in a set of terms ordered from least to greatest. The middle term in a set of 25 terms is the 13th term because $\frac{25}{2} = 12.5$. Since $25 - 13 = 12$, there are 12 students that earned a test score greater than 80 points. If you chose **G**, you may have computed $\frac{25}{2}$ and rounded up, thinking 13 students earned a score greater than 80 points. If you chose **H**, you may have computed $\frac{25}{2} + 1$ and rounded up, thinking 14 students earned a score greater than 80 points. If you chose **J**, you may have computed $0.8(25)$, which is 80% of the total number of students.

Question 25. The correct answer is C. Let x be the cost of apples and y be the cost of oranges in dollars. Next, set up the system of equations: $3x + 4y = 3.47$ and $12y = 6.36$. Solve for y in the second equation by dividing by 12: $y = \frac{6.36}{12} = 0.53$. Then, substitute the cost of oranges into the first equation and solve for the cost of apples: $3x + 4(0.53) = 3.47 \rightarrow 3x + 2.12 = 3.47 \rightarrow x = \frac{3.47 - 2.12}{3} = 0.45$. Finally, divide the \$10 by the cost of apples and round down: $\frac{10}{x} = \frac{10}{0.45} \approx 22$. Therefore, 22 apples is the maximum number Shefali can purchase. If you chose **A**, you may have calculated $\frac{10}{y} = \frac{10}{0.53} \approx 18.9$ and rounded up. If you chose **B**, you may have confused the numbers of apples and oranges: $4x + 3y = 3.47$. So, $x = \frac{3.47 - 3(0.53)}{4} = 0.47$ and $\frac{10}{0.47} \approx 21$. If you chose **D**, you may have calculated $\frac{10}{x} = \frac{10}{0.45} \approx 22.2$ and rounded up.

Question 26. The correct answer is G. Triangle $\triangle DEF$ is a right triangle, so $m\angle F = 180° - 90° - 30° = 60°$. Triangle $\triangle EFG$ is a right triangle because $\overline{EG}$ is an altitude, so $m\angle EGF = 90°$. In right triangle trigonometry, the sine of an angle measure is equal to the length of the opposite side divided by the length of the hypotenuse (SOH). Therefore, $\sin(\angle F) = \frac{EG}{EF}$. Substituting $EF = 20$ and $m\angle F = 60°$ into that equation and then solving for EG yields $\sin(60°) = \frac{EG}{20} \rightarrow EG = 20 \cdot \sin(60°) = 20 \cdot \frac{\sqrt{3}}{2} = 10\sqrt{3}$. If you chose **F**, you may have thought that $\sin(60°)$ was $\frac{1}{2}$ instead of $\frac{\sqrt{3}}{2}$. If you chose **H**, you may have thought $EF = EG$. If you chose **J**, you may have computed $20 \tan(60°)$ instead of $20 \sin(60°)$.

Question 27. The correct answer is B. First, write function h by subtracting the other functions: $h(x) = [x^2 + 7x - 3] - [x^2 - 4x + 5] = x^2 + 7x - 3 - x^2 + 4x - 5 = 11x - 8$. Then, substitute 2 for x and simplify: $h(2) = 11(2) - 8 = 22 - 8 = 14$. If you chose **A**, you may have incorrectly calculated $x^2 + 7x - 3 - x^2 - 4x + 5 = 3x + 2 \rightarrow 3(2) + 2$. If you chose **C**, you may have incorrectly calculated $x^2 + 7x - 3 + x^2 + 4x - 5 = 2x^2 + 11x - 8 \rightarrow 2(2^2) + 11(2) - 8$. If you chose **D**, you may have incorrectly calculated $x^2 + 7x - 3 - x^2 + 4x + 5 = 11x + 2 \rightarrow 11(2) + 2$.

Question 28. The correct answer is H. Substituting $x = 1$ and $y = 9$ into the expression yields $\frac{x+y}{y} = \frac{1+9}{9} = \frac{10}{9}$. If you chose **F**, you may have substituted $x = 5$ and $y = 9$ and made a simplification error: $\frac{x+y}{y} = \frac{5+9}{9} \rightarrow 5 + \frac{9}{9} = 5 + 1$. If you chose **G**, you may have switched the range of values for x and y and then substituted $x = 9$ and $y = 5$: $\frac{x+y}{y} = \frac{9+5}{5}$. If you chose **J**, you may have substituted $x = 0$ and $y = 0$ and thought the y-values could cancel as $\frac{x+y}{y} \rightarrow x$ and therefore substituted 0 for x.

Question 29. The correct answer is **B**. First, substitute function g into function f: $f(g(x)) = (x - 3)^2 + 1$. Then, simplify the exponent by multiplying the binomial times itself: $(x - 3)(x - 3) + 1 = x^2 - 3x - 3x + 9 + 1$. Finally, combine the like terms: $x^2 - 6x + 10$. If you chose **A**, you may have made a mistake with the exponent: $x^2 - 3^2 + 1$. If you chose **C**, you may have added the functions: $x^2 + 1 + x - 3$. If you chose **D**, you may have multiplied the functions: $(x^2 + 1)(x - 3)$.

Question 30. The correct answer is **H**. Rearrange the given equation by cross multiplying: $\frac{4x - y}{x + y} = \frac{5}{2} \rightarrow 2(4x - y) = 5(x + y) \rightarrow 8x - 2y = 5x + 5y$. Then, isolate the variables on opposite sides of the equal sign: $8x - 5x = 5y + 2y \rightarrow 3x = 7y$. Finally, get the constants on one side of the equal sign and the variables on the other by dividing by 3 and y: $\frac{x}{y} = \frac{7}{3}$. If you chose **F**, you may have distributed incorrectly: $24(x - y) = 5(x + y) \rightarrow 8x - y = 5x + y$. If you chose **G**, you may have thought the answer was the fraction given in the equation. If you chose **J**, you may have set the numerators and denominators equal to each other, added the equations, and solved for x: $4x - y = 5$ and $x + y = 2 \rightarrow 5x = 7 \rightarrow x = \frac{7}{5}$.

Question 31. The correct answer is **D**. Because the graph stops at a vertical height of 450, the graph shows a total distance traveled of 450 km. The horizontal axis shows 12 hours of data; however, the three flat parts (horizontal line segments) of the line represent the time when Juro was **not** traveling. Each flat part of the line represents 2 hours. Subtracting those times from the 12 hour total $(12 - (3)(2))$ yields the actual travel time of 6 hours. To find the average speed when Juro was traveling, divide the distance traveled by the travel time: $\frac{450}{6} = 75$ km per hour. If you chose **A**, you may have calculated $\frac{450}{10}$. If you chose **B**, you may have calculated $\frac{450}{10 - 2(1)}$. If you chose **C**, you may have calculated $\frac{300}{6 - 1}$.

Question 32. The correct answer is **H**. The amplitude of a sine function is half the distance between the greatest and the least values of the curve. In the equation $y = A \sin(x)$, the value of $|A|$ is the amplitude. Therefore, the amplitude of $y = 3 \sin(x)$ is 3. If you chose **F**, you may have calculated 3^{-1}. If you chose **G**, you may have calculated $\frac{3}{3}$. If you chose **J**, you may have calculated the distance between the greatest and least value of the curve: $3(2)$.

Question 33. The correct answer is **B**. Find a common denominator by multiplying the first term by $\frac{w}{w}$, which yields $\frac{4w}{w^2} + \frac{2}{w^2}$. Then, add the numerators: $\frac{4w + 2}{w^2}$. If you chose **A**, you may have incorrectly canceled a factor of 2: $\frac{4w + 2}{w^2} \rightarrow \frac{2w + 1}{w^2}$. If you chose **C**, you may have just added the numerators and denominators: $\frac{4 + 2}{w + w^2}$. If you chose **D**, you may have just added the numerators and used the denominator with the greatest power: $\frac{4}{w^2} + \frac{2}{w^2}$.

Question 34. The correct answer is G. The number line shows that a is located to the left of 0, so the value of a is negative, or $a < 0$. Similarly, b is located between 0 and 1, so $0 < b < 1$. The multiplication property of inequality states that multiplying an inequality by a negative value will change the direction of the inequality symbol. Multiplying $0 < b < 1$ by a therefore yields $0(a) > b(a) > 1(a)$, or $a < ab < 0$. If you chose **F**, you may have forgotten to change the direction of the inequality symbols when multiplying by a and then used the fact $-1 < 0$ to get $0(a) < b(a) < 1(a) \rightarrow 0 < ab < a \rightarrow -1 < ab < a$. If you chose **H**, you may not have realized that because the inequalities $a < 0$ and $b > 0$ are true, it follows that the inequality $ab < 0$ is true. Thus, the inequality $0 < ab < b$ must be false. If you chose **J**, you may not have realized that because the inequalities $ab < 0$ and $b > 0$ are true, it follows that $ab < b$ is true. Thus, the inequality $b < ab < 1$ must be false.

Question 35. The correct answer is C. Let the final exam grade be represented by f. Because Sani's test scores of 78, 86, and 82 are each worth 20% of the course grade and the final exam score is worth 40% of the course grade, Sani's course grade can be calculated as $0.2(78) + 0.2(86) + 0.2(82) + 0.4f = 49.2 + 0.4f$. For Sani's course grade to be at least 86, the final exam score, f, must satisfy the inequality $49.2 + 0.4f \geq 86$. Subtracting 49.2 from each side of the inequality and then dividing each side by 0.4 yields $f \geq 92$. Therefore, Sani will have to earn a minimum score of 92 on the final exam to receive a course grade of at least 86. If you chose **A**, you may have calculated the average of Sani's highest two test scores: $\frac{86 + 82}{2} = \frac{168}{2} = 84$.

If you chose **B**, you may have tried to minimize the score too early by rounding $86 - 49.2 = 36.8$ down to 36 on the right-hand side of the inequality and then divided by 0.4 to get $f \geq 90$. If you chose **D**, you may have weighted all the exams equally and then solved the inequality $\frac{78 + 86 + 82 + f}{4} \geq 86$ to get $246 + f \geq 86(4)$, or $f \geq 98$.

Question 36. The correct answer is F. The area of any triangle is $\frac{1}{2}bh$, where b is the length of the base of the triangle and h is the length of the height of the triangle. In this triangle, the base is the vertical line segment $\overline{AC}$. Since $A(-1, -2)$ and $C(-1, 4)$ share an x-coordinate, the length of the base $\overline{AC}$ can be found by subtracting the y-coordinates of the two points: $AC = 4 - (-2) = 4 + 2 = 6$. The base and the height must be perpendicular, so the length of the height of the triangle is the horizontal distance from point $B(2,2)$ to a new point $D(-1,2)$ (not shown) that lies on $\overline{AC}$. Because $B(2, 2)$ and $D(-1, 2)$ share a y-coordinate, this distance can be found by subtracting the x-coordinates of the two points: $BD = 2 - (-1) = 2 + 1 = 3$. Therefore, the area of $\triangle ABC$, in square coordinate units, is $\frac{1}{2}(AC)(BD) = \frac{1}{2}(6)(3) = 9$. If you chose **G**, you may have used side $\overline{AB}$ as the base of the triangle and then used the distance formula to calculate $AB = \sqrt{(2 - (-2))^2 + (2 - (-1))^2} = \sqrt{16 + 9} = 5$ so that $\frac{1}{2}(5)(6) = 15$. If you chose **H**, you may have forgotten to include the factor of $\frac{1}{2}$ in the area equation. If you chose **J**, you may have used side $\overline{BC}$ as the height of the triangle and then used the distance formula to calculate $BC = \sqrt{(2 - (-2))^2 + (2 - 4)^2} = \sqrt{9 + 4} = \sqrt{13}$ so that $\frac{1}{2}(6)(\sqrt{13}) = 3\sqrt{13}$.

Question 37. **The correct answer is C.** For all real numbers, $\sqrt{x^2} = |x|$, so the statement $\sqrt{x^2} \neq x$ is equivalent to $|x| \neq x$. This is true only if x is negative. If you chose **A**, **B**, or **D**, you may have been unable to find a counterexample. Consider $x = -2$, which is less than π, rational, and defined. In this example, $\sqrt{(-2)^2} = \sqrt{4} = 2$, but $2 \neq -2$. Thus, $\sqrt{x^2} \neq x$.

Question 38. **The correct answer is G.** The change in the x-coordinate from point A to point B is $\Delta x = 8 - 2 = 6$. The change in the y-coordinate from point A to point B is $\Delta y = -1 - (-4) = -1 + 4 = 3$. For the ratio $AB{:}BC$ to be equal to 1:3, the change in the x-coordinate from point B to point C must be $3(\Delta x) = 3(6) = 18$, and the change in the y-coordinate from point B to point C must be $3(\Delta y) = 3(3) = 9$. Therefore, point C has coordinates $(8 + 18, -1 + 9) = (26, 8)$. If you chose **F**, you may have multiplied Δx and Δy by $1 + 3 = 4$ before adding the results to the respective coordinates of point B, resulting in $(8 + 4(6), -1 + 4(3))$. If you chose **H**, you may have forgotten to multiply Δx and Δy by 3 before adding the results to the respective coordinates of point B, resulting in $(8 + 6, -1 + 3)$. If you chose **J**, you may have thought the ratio $AB{:}BC$ was 3:1 and therefore divided Δx and Δy by 3 before adding the results to the respective coordinates of point B, resulting in $\left(8 + \frac{6}{3}, -1 + \frac{3}{3}\right)$.

Question 39. **The correct answer is C.** By drawing a vertical diameter and a horizontal diameter through each post, we see that the wire will touch each of the 4 circular posts on $\frac{1}{4}$ of the post's circumference. Each circular post has a circumference of $(2\pi)(3) = 6\pi$, so the total length of wire needed to span $\frac{1}{4}$ of each post's circumference is $4\left(\frac{1}{4}\right)(6\pi) = 6\pi$ inches. The wire will also span the distance between the centers of two adjacent posts 4 times. The distance between the centers of adjacent circles is twice the radius length, or $2(3) = 6$ inches, so the total length of wire needed to span this distance four times is $4(6) = 24$ inches. Therefore, the length of the shortest wire that will go around the 4 posts without overlap is $24 + 6\pi \approx 43$ inches. If you chose **A**, you may have calculated the correct amount of wire that touches each post, but you calculated only half of the amount needed between posts: $\frac{1}{2}(24) + 6\pi \approx 31$ inches. If you chose **B**, you may have calculated the correct amount of wire needed between posts, but you calculated only half the amount of wire that touches each post: $24 + \frac{1}{2}(6\pi) = 24 + 3\pi \approx 33$ inches. If you chose **D**, you may have performed your calculations using the cross-sectional area of the circular posts instead of the circumference: $24 + (3)^2\pi = 24 + 9\pi \approx 52$ inches.

Question 40. The correct answer is J. Multiplying any imaginary number of the form $a + bi$, where a and b are rational numbers, by its conjugate, $a - bi$, will always result in a rational number. Using $i^2 = (\sqrt{-1})^2 = -1$, we have $(3 + bi)(3 - bi) = 9 + 3bi - 3bi - b^2i^2 = 9 - b^2(-1) = 9 + b^2$. Because b is a rational number, b^2 is also a rational number, so $9 + b^2$ is a rational number. If you chose **F**, you may have thought the conjugate of any complex number was its imaginary part, bi, but $(3 + bi)(bi) = 3bi + b^2i^2 = 3bi - b^2$, which is not rational because $3bi$ is imaginary. If you chose **G**, you may have thought the conjugate of any complex number was the product of its real and imaginary parts, but $(3 + bi)(3bi) = 9bi + 3b^2i^2 = 9bi - 3b^2$, which is not rational because $9bi$ is imaginary. If you chose **H**, you may have thought the square of any complex number was rational, but $(3 + bi)(3 + bi) = 9 + 3bi + 3bi + b^2i^2 = 9 + 6bi - b^2$, which is not rational because $6bi$ is imaginary.

Question 41. The correct answer is C. Start by converting the logarithmic equation $\log_x(8) = y$ to its equivalent exponential equation, $x^y = 8$. The only two ways to write 8 in the form x^y where x and y are positive integers are 8^1 and 2^3. The only one of these expressions that fits the requirement that the base (x) be strictly less than 8 is 2^3. Therefore, $y = 3$. If you chose **A**, you may have thought x could be 8. If you chose **B**, you may have thought $4^2 = 8$. If you chose **D**, you may have thought $2^4 = 8$.

Question 42. The correct answer is H. To multiply exponential expressions that have the same base, apply the product rule, $x^m \cdot x^n = x^{m+n}$. Thus, $x^{\frac{1}{4}} \cdot x^{\frac{1}{6}} = x^{\frac{1}{4}+\frac{1}{6}}$. Next, to simplify the sum in the exponent, find the least common denominator, use it to rewrite each fraction, and then add: $x^{\frac{1}{4}+\frac{1}{6}} = x^{\frac{3}{12}+\frac{2}{12}} = x^{\frac{5}{12}}$. Finally, to rewrite the expression $x^{\frac{5}{12}}$ as a radical expression, use the fractional exponent rule, $x^{\frac{m}{n}} = \sqrt[n]{x^m}$, where the numerator, m, gives the power on the base, x, and the denominator, n, gives the root in the radical symbol. Therefore, $x^{\frac{5}{12}} = \sqrt[12]{x^5}$. If you chose **F**, you may have correctly applied the product rule for exponents to get $x^{\frac{1}{4}+\frac{1}{6}}$, but then you incorrectly simplified the sum in the exponent by adding both numerators and both denominators: $x^{\frac{1}{4}+\frac{1}{6}} \Rightarrow x^{\frac{1+1}{4+6}} \Rightarrow x^{\frac{2}{10}} \Rightarrow x^{\frac{1}{5}} \Rightarrow \sqrt[5]{x}$. If you chose **G**, you may have correctly applied the product rule for exponents and simplified to get $x^{\frac{5}{12}}$, but then you incorrectly applied the fractional exponent rule and used 5 as the root and 12 as the power on x: $\sqrt[5]{x^{12}}$. If you chose **J**, you may have incorrectly multiplied the exponents instead of adding: $x^{\left(\frac{1}{4}\right)\left(\frac{1}{6}\right)} \rightarrow x^{\frac{1}{24}} \rightarrow \sqrt[24]{x}$.

Question 43. The correct answer is D. In any triangle, the shortest side is opposite the smallest interior angle. The shortest side in the given triangle, 15 cm, is opposite angle A. Let $a = 15$ cm, $b = 16$ cm, and $c = 17$ cm be the lengths of the legs of the triangle opposite angles A, B, and C, respectively. The law of cosines states that $a^2 = b^2 + c^2 - 2bc \cos A$. Substitute the values for a, b, and c into the law of cosines: $15^2 = 16^2 + 17^2 - 2(16)(17) \cos A$. If you chose **A**, you may have picked an equation with the sides incorrectly substituted and with an incorrect trigonometric function. If you chose **B**, you may have picked an equation with the sides incorrectly substituted. If you chose **C**, you may have picked an equation with the sides correctly substituted but with an incorrect trigonometric function.

Question 44. The correct answer is F. Let set A be represented by $A = \{a, w, x, y, z\}$, where $a < w < x < y < z$. Set B may be represented by $B = \{b, w, x, y, z\}$, where $a < b$. The mean of set A is equal to $\frac{a + w + x + y + z}{5}$, and the mean of set B is equal to $\frac{b + w + x + y + z}{5}$. Because $a < b$, $\frac{a + w + x + y + z}{5} < \frac{b + w + x + y + z}{5}$. If you chose **G**, you may not have noted that both sets have the same median, x, the middle value of the ordered data. If you chose **H** or **J**, you may not have noted the range of set B, $z - b$, is less than the range of set A, $z - a$. To show $z - b < z - a$, start with the inequality $a < b$. Multiply the inequality by -1 and flip the direction of the inequality: $-b < -a$. Add z to both sides: $z - b < z - a$.

Question 45. The correct answer is C. In total, there are $16 \cdot 15 \cdot 14 = 3{,}360$ different ways that 3 cars may be chosen from 16 cars: 16 choices for the first pick, 15 choices for the second pick, and 14 choices for the third pick. Let M = minivan, S = sedan, and H = hatchback. The set of possible outcomes for the random choice of 1 of each of the 3 types of cars may be represented by the set $\{MSH, MHS, SMH, SHM, HMS, HSM\}$. Each of the 6 outcomes in the set is equally likely and has a probability of $\frac{6 \cdot 7 \cdot 3}{16 \cdot 15 \cdot 14}$. Therefore, the probability that Thalia will rent 1 of each of the 3 types of cars is equal to $6 \cdot \left(\frac{6 \cdot 7 \cdot 3}{16 \cdot 15 \cdot 14}\right) = \frac{756}{3{,}360} = \frac{9}{40}$. If you chose **A**, you may have calculated the probability of choosing 1 specific car type out of the 3 available car types. If you chose **B**, you may have calculated the proportion of the 16 cars that will be chosen, $\frac{3}{16}$. If you chose **D**, you may have thought there were only 3 possible outcomes instead of 6 and computed $3 \cdot \left(\frac{6 \cdot 7 \cdot 3}{16 \cdot 15 \cdot 14}\right) = \frac{9}{80}$.

Passage I

Question 1. The best answer is A because the narrator of Passage A describes the inner workings of a newspaper office and print shop in detail in the first paragraph (lines 1–26), which suggests that she witnessed and participated in daily operations there. In the context of a discussion of "the lure of the reporter's life" (lines 31–32), the narrator directly refers to her experiences in the newspaper business: "It all sounds slightly sentimental and silly, but it's true—or it was, at least, in my newspaper experience" (lines 33–35). She also recalls the scents that cause her to feel "a pang of nostalgia for the old reporting days" (line 39).

The best answer is NOT:

B because the narrator of Passage A refers to being reminded of the newsroom "to this day" (line 35) with "a pang of nostalgia" (line 39), suggesting a former career in the newspaper business, not a recently started one.

C because the narrator of Passage A reveals that the Appleton, Wisconsin *Daily Crescent* office (lines 27–28) is the news office she describes in the first paragraph (lines 1–26), an office with which she seems very familiar; the narrator does not evaluate the inner workings of various news offices.

D because the narrator of Passage A demonstrates knowledge of the newspaper business in the first paragraph (lines 1–26) and in lines 33–39, when she refers to her past newspaper experiences. The narrator does not suggest that she longs to be a reporter; in fact, it would be more reasonable to conclude from Passage A that she used to be one.

Question 2. The best answer is G because the narrator of Passage A suggests that the back room was made up of the printing shop and pressroom, which "were separated from the front office only by a doorway, and the door never was closed" (lines 1–3). The narrator emphasizes that the front office and the back room are equally critical to the newspaper. Lines 7–9: "The front room is its head, but without the back room it could not function or even live."

The best answer is NOT:

F because the narrator of Passage A does not characterize what goes on in the printing shop and pressroom as more tedious than what goes on in the front office. In fact, the narrator describes the linotype machine in the back room as "a new and fearsome invention" (line 4), which suggests some excitement.

H because the narrator of Passage A does not suggest that what goes on in either the front office or the printing shop and pressroom is chaotic. The first paragraph (lines 1–26) suggests a robust but steady daily routine at the newspaper.

J because the printing shop and the pressroom are portrayed by the narrator of Passage A as being regulated, and no less regulated than the front office; for instance, "the linotype and the small press went all day" (lines 9–10), overseen by Mac. Without the steady operations in the back room, the newspaper "could not function or even live" (line 9).

Question 3. **The best answer is D** because the narrator of Passage A states that on the rare moments when Mac would appear in the front office, he would do so "with a piece of news" (lines 21–22), his purpose to share his newsworthy find with the city editor. Lines 23–25: "Standing at the side of the city editor's desk he would deliver himself of this information, looking mild and limply romantic."

The best answer is NOT:

A because although the narrator of Passage A states that "the linotype and the small press went all day, for there the advertising was set up and printed" (lines 9–11), the narrator does not specify that Mac would appear in the front office to set up and print the advertising.

B because although the narrator of Passage A states that Mac "was boss of the print shop from the cat to the linotype operator" (lines 18–20), the narrator does not make clear that Mac would appear in the front office to supervise the linotype operator.

C because although the narrator of Passage A states that Mac's "eye was infallible" (line 16), the narrator also points out that Mac's voice was "soft, gentle, drawling," (line 18) and that he "seldom talked" (line 20). The narrator does not indicate that Mac would appear in the front office to chastise reporters.

Question 4. **The best answer is G** because the narrator of Passage B experiences the epiphany that "this is what I do" (lines 62) at the age of twenty-five, as he "waded into that invisible veil of ink" (line 52) at his first newswriting job, realizing that he was finally living his dream of being a reporter.

The best answer is NOT:

F because the narrator of Passage B does not directly connect the epiphany he describes in lines 59–62 to how long he might continue to live in his parents' basement.

H because the narrator of Passage B already knows that he would rather write news stories than work for a lawn company, which is why he was trying to find a newswriting job (lines 82–89).

J because the narrator of Passage B does not directly discuss his work ethic or how it might relate to his success as a reporter.

Question 5. **The best answer is A** because the note written by the employer of the narrator of Passage B (lines 70–76) lists publications in which the narrator's writing has appeared, before stating that his writing soon "will appear in trashcans throughout north-central Connecticut" (lines 74–75), lightly mocking the narrator's new job as a reporter. The office bulletin board note, conveyed in a serious tone, is a workplace introduction and welcome to the narrator, and yet it ends sarcastically with the request for others in the office to "please make him feel relevant" (lines 75–76).

The best answer is NOT:

B because although the note appears to be formal and serious in tone and approach, it can't accurately be described as overtly solemn due to its sarcastic humor regarding the relevance of the writing of the narrator of Passage B.

C because the note is not obviously apologetic, even regarding the mocking suggestion that the writing of the narrator of Passage B will end up in trash cans (lines 74–75).

D because the note does not convey optimism but rather teasingly suggests that the new career of the narrator of Passage B might prove not to be impressive or influential.

Question 6. **The best answer is H** because the last sentence of Passage B (lines 82–89) describes the narrator working at a job unrelated to newswriting but, at night, "typing out professional love letters" (lines 84–85) to various northeastern newspapers that he admits he "had never read" (line 89), showing that he was desperate to find a newswriting job. The name of one newspaper listed, the seemingly fictitious *Anywhere Clarion-Bugle-Star-Record-Sentinel*, strongly conveys that the narrator was willing to work at just about any newspaper in the region.

The best answer is NOT:

F because although the sentence conveys that the narrator of Passage B had never read most northeastern newspapers, the sentence does not show that he had disdain for them.

F because although the sentence makes clear that the narrator of Passage B is familiar with the newspapers published in the area, the sentence mainly serves to portray the narrator as reaching out to any newspaper that might offer him a job.

J because the sentence does not refer to the newswriting experience of the narrator of Passage B at all; instead, the sentence conveys that the narrator is working for a lawn company as he contacts several newspapers to find a job.

Question 7. The best answer is A because Passage A includes detailed information about the types of machines used to print the newspaper (lines 3–12) as part of its description of the office, whereas Passage B does not provide such information.

The best answer is NOT:

B because Passage B provides information about the outside appearance of the office building, whereas Passage A does not. The office in Passage B is in "a squat concrete building, no different from all the others in a drab Connecticut industrial park" (lines 57–59).

C because neither Passage A nor Passage B provides information about the number of people who work in the office.

D because neither Passage A nor Passage B provides information about the stories being written and printed for the newspaper. Passage B, though, does allude to the newspaper's printed "rants and ideas, sports scores and felony arrests, announcements of marriage and notices of death" (lines 54–56).

Question 8. The best answer is J because the use of figurative language is central to the storytelling style of Passage B. The smell of ink is personified in lines 44–47. As the narrator began his new job, he "waded into that invisible veil of ink" (line 52), a metaphor. The narrator exaggerates with the statement that "maybe the chemical-like aroma was inducing hallucination" (lines 56–57), and the bulletin board note is "pinned like a manifesto" (line 63), figurative language in the form of a simile. Although Passage A uses some figurative language, its overall writing style is not as strongly characterized by figurative language as the style of Passage B is.

The best answer is NOT:

F because Passage B does not use technical jargon at length, whereas Passage A refers to technical names of machines and materials (line 3–6) and technical jargon and terms such as "shrdlus and etaoins" (line 17) and "mucilage" (line 36).

G because although Passage A and Passage B both contain quoted material, neither passage uses dialogue.

H because the style of Passage A, not Passage B, is more strongly characterized by its use of formal diction, with more straightforward descriptions and slightly elevated word choices overall, whereas Passage B is more casual in its approach to storytelling. It begins with a sentence fragment (line 43), includes second-person narration (lines 49–51), and has moments of humor, especially in lines 70–89.

Question 9. The best answer is C because the passages support that both narrators associate the smell of ink with pleasant memories. The narrator of Passage A connects other writers' reflections regarding "the smell of printer's ink" (line 32) to her own experiences: "To this day I can't smell the scent of white paper, wet ink, oil, hot lead, mucilage and cats that goes to make up the peculiar odor of any newspaper plant, be it Appleton, Wisconsin, or Cairo, Egypt, that I don't get a pang of nostalgia for the old reporting days" (lines 35–39). The narrator of Passage B recalls, "I waded into that invisible veil of ink, inhaled it deeply, allowed it to wash over me" (lines 52–53), and later describes the building in which he worked as "ink-perfumed" (line 64).

The best answer is NOT:

A because the narrator of Passage B also associates the smell of ink with pleasant memories, as conveyed in details and descriptions in lines 43–67.

B because the narrator of Passage A also associates the smell of ink with pleasant memories, as conveyed in details and descriptions in lines 29–39.

D because both narrators associate the smell of ink with pleasant memories, as conveyed in details and descriptions in lines 29–39 of Passage A and lines 43–69 of Passage B.

Passage II

Question 10. The best answer is J because the passage explains Dantzig's theory that zero was first represented as an oval on an Indian counting board. The oval, a symbol, was drawn in the empty space that served as a placeholder in a middle of columns of numbers (lines 14–25). Later, the passage states that when writing numbers in clay, "the Babylonians began using two slanted tacklike symbols to insert in the empty columns" (lines 70–71) and specifies that "they used their 'zero' only in the middle of numbers, never at the end" (lines 71–72).

The best answer is NOT:

F because the passage states that the Babylonians used tacklike symbols in the empty columns between numbers to write zero (lines 70–71), but the passage does not indicate that Indian civilizations did so.

G because the passage states that "the Babylonians called a king's first year the *accession year*" (lines 46–47), but the passage does not indicate that Indian civilizations did so.

H because although the passage connects the name *sunya* for the oval drawn on an Indian counting board to "*Sunyata*, an important concept in Buddhism" (lines 23–24), the passage does not indicate that the Babylonians had a name for zero that was derived from their religion. "The Babylonians, so far as we know, never articulated zero" (lines 49–50).

Question 11. The best answer is C because the paragraph begins with a reference to "Dantzig's concise and spirited account" (line 13) of the invention of zero and describes how Dantzig "sees zero's invention" (lines 14–15) occurring on a counting board. The story of an unknown person drawing an oval on a counting board is presented as Dantzig's theory with the phrase, "as Dantzig sees it" (line 21).

The best answer is NOT:

A because the paragraph does not provide information that suggests Dantzig discovered a document that offers a factual account of the story.

B because the paragraph does not refer to particular ancient Indian writings from which a factual account of the story has been drawn.

D because the paragraph does not connect the story to Kaplan or mention any of Kaplan's theories directly.

Question 12. The best answer is F because the passage states that, according to Dantzig, "the zero was invented not in the West but by the Indians in the early centuries after Christ" (lines 6–7). The passage then indicates that "the Maya invented zero in the New World at approximately the same time" (lines 8–9).

The best answer is NOT:

G because the passage discusses the Sumerian roots of zero (lines 61–65), not the Sumerians' invention of zero. Based on the historical context provided in the last three paragraphs of the passage (lines 60–77), the Sumerian contributions to zero occurred long before the Maya invented zero.

H because the passage states that Alexander invaded the Babylonian empire in 331 BC (lines 73–74), much earlier than when the Maya invented zero, which was around the same time the Indians did, according to Dantzig (lines 5–9). Dantzig speculates the time frame for the invention of zero as the first or second century AD (lines 14–16).

J because the passage indicates that, according to Dantzig, Europe "did not accept zero as a number until the twelfth or thirteenth century" (lines 10–11), much later than when the Maya invented zero.

Question 13. The best answer is **B** because the passage begins with Dantzig's ideas that the invention of zero "will always stand out as one of the greatest single achievements of the human race" (lines 2–4) and "marked a 'turning point' in math, science, and industry" (lines 4–5). Lines 14–25 describe Dantzig's account of zero's first appearance on a counting board as a day best characterized as "momentous," based on the context of the passage.

The best answer is NOT:

A because the passage characterizes the invention of zero as groundbreaking and transformative (lines 1–5). Therefore, to describe the day on which zero was first drawn as "unfortunate," which suggests that regrettable outcomes followed, does not make sense in the context of the passage.

C because the passage suggests that the invention of zero revolutionized math, science, and industry (lines 4–5). Therefore, to describe the day that zero was first drawn as "ominous," which suggests a threat or danger to come, does not make sense in the context of the passage.

D because the passage presents the invention of zero as occurring on a random day, naturally and unplanned, as a person worked on a counting board (lines 14–25). Therefore, to describe the day that zero was first drawn as "foretold," which suggests that the events of the day were prophesied or predicted, does not make sense in the context of the passage.

Question 14. The best answer is **J** because the passage states that "the Arabs turned *sunya* into *sifr* ('empty' in Arabic), which became *zephirum* in Italy, and eventually zero. In Germany and elsewhere, *sifr* became *cifra*" (lines 26–28).

The best answer is NOT:

F because the passage indicates that *sunya* was a word given to zero in Indian civilizations (lines 21–23), likely in the first or second century AD (lines 14–16).

G because the passage indicates that *zephirum* became the word for zero in Italy (line 27).

H because the passage indicates that "the Arabs turned *sunya* into *sifr*" (line 26).

Question 15. The best answer is **A** because the passage states that Dantzig "blames the Greeks" (line 31) for Western civilization taking over a thousand years to accept a number that represents a void. Dantzig explains, "The concrete mind of the ancient Greeks could not conceive the void as a number, let alone endow the void with a symbol" (lines 32–34).

The best answer is NOT:

B because although the last paragraph (lines 86–90) states that we find the symbol "0" for zero in the papyri of Greek astronomers shortly after 331 BC, "the mathematicians never pursued the concept" (lines 73–77).

C because the passage does not indicate that the ancient Greeks were unwilling to share their knowledge of zero with other European countries.

D because the passage does not support that a focus on negative numbers is the reason the ancient Greeks could not imagine a number for the void. The passage simply mentions that negative numbers soon followed the invention of zero (lines 7–8).

Question 16. The best answer is **H** because the passage author states that "Dantzig's concise and spirited account of the birth of a number is adequate for most of us" (lines 12-13).

The best answer is NOT:

F because the passage author does not indicate that he thinks readers wouldn't be interested in hearing the story of how the Maya conceived of zero. Instead, he provides details about the concept and use of zero by the Maya in lines 8–9 and 38–39.

G because the passage author does not indicate that he thinks readers wouldn't be interested in hearing what Dantzig contributed to mathematics, a topic that is not central to the passage.

J because the passage author does not indicate that he thinks readers wouldn't be interested in hearing about who drew the oval on the counting board. He does make clear, though, that the exact identity of the person is unknown (lines 21–22).

Question 17. The best answer is **B** because it offers an accurate, literal meaning of the figurative statement "Zero lay rustling in the weeds for many centuries" (line 35) in the context of the passage. The phrase "lay rustling in the weeds" suggests something present that has not yet been fully realized. This is reflected in part in the idea that "the Babylonians had no zero, but they knew something was wrong" (lines 40–41); their knowledge of zero was emerging but not yet fully shaped.

The best answer is NOT:

A because the far-reaching effects of the concept of zero on mathematics are long established and clearly present (lines 4–5), lacking the suggestion of something subtle and undiscovered, as the phrase "lay rustling in the weeds for many centuries" (line 35) implies in context.

C because if the concept of zero "had been developed and then forgotten," the concept could not accurately be described as "rustling in the weeds" (line 35). This figurative phrase suggests steady but nearly imperceptible activity that is difficult to draw out.

D because for the concept of zero to have been rejected, it would need to have been openly known and articulated, which would require an interpretation of the phrase "lay rustling in the weeds for centuries" (line 35) that does not make sense in context.

Question 18. The best answer is **H** because the passage author directly states that "the contemporary mathematician who has conducted the most rigorous research on nothing is Robert Kaplan, the author of *The Nothing That Is: A Natural History of Zero*" (lines 53–55).

The best answer is NOT:

F because the passage author does not directly make the point that Kaplan's research on zero is more interesting than that of other contemporary mathematicians.

G because the passage author does not offer the idea that Kaplan's research is more speculative than that of other contemporary mathematicians. In fact, by stating that Kaplan's research on zero is "the most rigorous" (line 53), the passage author suggests that it is less speculative than others' research.

J because although the passage author presents Kaplan's research as valuable, he does not directly mention that it is more admired than other contemporary mathematicians' research.

Passage III

Question 19. The best answer is D because the passage describes both Mavis Staples's experience as a quartet singer with her family as well as details about the production of her first solo album. Lines 8–25 demonstrate how Mavis Staples's identity was shaped by her early experience as a quartet singer, and the passage proceeds to relate Bell's efforts to record Mavis Staples as a solo artist (lines 41–42), and Cropper's production of "what would be Mavis's self-titled debut album" (lines 54–55).

The best answer is NOT:

A because although the fourth and fifth paragraphs (lines 35–51) describe Bell's work with Mavis Staples, this information contributes to the passage's overall focus on Mavis Staples and the trajectory of her career.

B because Franklin and Ross are only briefly mentioned in lines 8–10, and the comparison mainly serves to introduce how Mavis Staples's experience singing in the family quartet shaped her outlook as a performer.

C because although the passage author indicates that Pops Staples was an influential figure in Mavis Staples's career, he does not directly attribute her success to his influence.

Question 20. The best answer is J because the passage describes how "fans of the Staples Singers" (line 1) witnessed how Mavis Staples performed with "an improbably deep voice" (line 3) and with "the deepest commitment to whatever she was singing" (lines 4–5). Her voice and personal style of singing put her on par with talents such as Franklin, Knight, Ross, and Springfield even as she experienced "relative anonymity" (lines 1–2) as a singer. It can be inferred that the contrast between her great talent and her anonymity is what puzzled her fans.

The best answer is NOT:

F because although details in the first paragraph (lines 1–7) relate that Mavis Staples's voice was "improbably deep" (line 3), the passage does not indicate that her brother became more famous than Mavis Staples did.

G because the passage does not provide details about Mavis Staples's vocal range or how it compared to that of other artists of the time. Instead, it is stated only that she "loved singing those baritone harmonies" (lines 14–15).

H because the passage author does not directly compare Mavis Staples's voice to that of any other artists of the time. Rather, he notes a contrast between Mavis Staples's lack of celebrity and the popularity of other artists of the time (lines 8–10).

Question 21. The best answer is B because the paragraph mainly provides examples indicating what may have made it "difficult for Mavis to easily adapt to a different context" (lines 27–28). The passage author notes Pops Staples's guitar style and Mavis Staples's innate musical connection with Pervis and Cleedi (line 34) as factors that made it more challenging for Mavis Staples to move on from the quartet.

The best answer is NOT:

A because although the paragraph mentions Pops Staples's distinctive way of playing guitar, it does not describe the individual contributions of the other members of the group.

C because the paragraph does not contain a reference to Pops Staples making the song choices, nor does the paragraph focus on the songs the Staples Singers sang in concert.

D because although the paragraph makes clear that the Staples Singers' performances included guitar, harmonization, and clapping, it does not characterize a particular performance style.

Question 22. The best answer is G because the paragraph relates Cropper's perspective as he worked "to figure out how to get her out there" (lines 57–58). Mindful that "she didn't want to go too far too fast" (lines 62–63), Cropper acted carefully. As he states, "I didn't want to lose her trust or do something damaging" (lines 64–65).

The best answer is NOT:

F because the paragraph primarily focuses on Cropper's work with Mavis Staples as a solo performer. The paragraph does not include detailed information about his work with the Staples Singers.

H because the paragraph primarily focuses on Cropper's work with Mavis Staples. The paragraph does not include information about the overall strategy at Stax Records for working with unknown singers.

J because the paragraph provides no information that suggests that Mavis Staples was unwilling to perform without backup singers.

Question 23. The best answer is C because, as Cropper reflects on Pops Staples's guiding involvement with the family quartet, he states that "there were lines he didn't want to cross when it came to his family's well-being" (lines 72–73), which suggests that protecting his family was a priority for Pops Staples.

The best answer is NOT:

A because Pops Staples is characterized as someone who would put "his foot down" (line 71) about things like dating. The passage also indicates that there were certain songs that "wouldn't go down with Pops" (lines 61–62), suggesting that there were certain things he was not tolerant of when it came to his family.

B because the passage provides no characterization of Pops Staples as being resentful, and he is described as being a "thoughtful and willing contributor in the studio" (lines 66–67).

D because the passage provides no information that suggests that Pops Staples was uncertain or wavering in his decisions about his family. The description of Pops Staples "putting his foot down about dating" (line 71) suggests that his decisions were final and not negotiable.

Question 24. The best answer is F because the passage author indicates that Mavis Staples's way of "losing herself in every word" (lines 5–6) derived from her "deepest commitment to whatever she was singing" (lines 4–5). He further clarifies that Mavis Staples sang "as though reliving a critical moment in her personal history" (lines 6–7).

The best answer is NOT:

G because the passage states that Mavis Staples committed herself totally "to whatever she was singing" (line 5) and does not indicate whether clapping contributed as a factor.

H because the passage does not provide any information about how Mavis Staples may have led her siblings in a transition to a new song.

J because the passage does not provide any information that indicates whether Mavis Staples may have danced while other members of the quartet sang.

Question 25. **The best answer is C** because, as the passage states, Mavis Staples's "father brought her out front to sing lead after her brother Pervis's voice changed in the '50s" (lines 12–14).

The best answer is NOT:

A because the passage does not provide any information indicating that Pops Staples left the Staples Singers.

B because although the passage indicates that Pops Staples played the guitar (line 26), it does not provide information that indicates that Cleedi also played guitar.

D because although the passage author does describe Mavis Staples's voice as "deep" (line 3), he directly attributes Pervis's voice change as the reason for her father's decision to have her sing lead (lines 12–14).

Question 26. **The best answer is J** because the passage states that Mavis Staples's performance of "On My Way to Heaven" "bowled [Bell] over and left him in tears" (lines 36–37). It can be inferred that Bell's admiration was deep and persistent because he "never forgot the day" (line 35) when he witnessed this performance.

The best answer is NOT:

F because "dismay" connotes a negative reaction to Mavis Staples's singing while the passage clearly characterizes Bell's reaction as very positive.

G because "reluctant acceptance" indicates that Bell didn't really want to like Mavis Staples's performance while the passage makes clear that Bell responded positively to the performance without reservation.

H because there is no indication in the passage that Bell found Mavis Staples's performance amusing or humorous.

Question 27. **The best answer is B** because the passage makes clear that the songs chosen for Mavis Staples's first solo album were "secular songs" (line 77) that lacked the "gospel or message-oriented underpinnings" (line 78) that Pops Staples chose for the Staples Singers. Instead, her solo album featured "the sort of pop-oriented love and relationship songs that Pops typically shunned" (lines 83–84).

The best answer is NOT:

A because the passage indicates that the songs were primarily focused on love and relationships.

C because the passage does not specify who wrote the songs that Mavis Staples sang on her solo album or whether they were written specifically for her.

D because the passage provides no information about the upbeat tone or danceability of the music of the Staples Singers or the songs on Mavis Staples's solo album.

Passage IV

Question 28. **The best answer is G** because the passage primarily focuses on describing mycorrhizal fungi and explaining how it helps plants thrive. Describing its impact on plants, the passage author states that "mycorrhizal fungi break down nutrients like phosphorous, carbon, water, and nitrogen into a readily assimilative form and deliver them to the plant" (lines 15–17) and describes how the fungi "increase the tree's nutrient and water uptake" (lines 28–29). She goes on to explain how the fungi play a key role in ecosystems, noting that, "In the wild, mycorrhizal fungi are key to not just the health of single trees but to healthy forest ecosystems" (lines 30–32) and "the functions they perform are often on an ecosystem or landscape scale" (lines 77–78).

The best answer is NOT:

F because although the first paragraph (lines 1–12) briefly compares mutualist and commensal relationships, the passage focuses on the mutualistic relationship between mycorrhizal fungi and forest plants.

H because although the passage describes mycorrhizal fungi functioning as a "giant communications network" (line 40) that has been referred to as "nature's Internet" (line 41), the passage's purpose is to describe the mycorrhizal fungi's network and its relationship to plants, not to discuss the invention of the Internet.

J because the passage instead explores the beneficial effects of mycorrhizal fungi on plants.

Question 29. **The best answer is A** because the overall focus of the paragraph is to describe how fungal networks benefit all different types of plants, from weaker plants to young seedlings to established trees. Lines 48–51: "This network exists to benefit not only established trees and seedlings of the same species but also trees from different species, and at different stages of development."

The best answer is NOT:

B because although the paragraph mentions young seedlings tapping into the roots of trees that are of the same species (lines 46–48), the main point of the paragraph is that the fungal network benefits many different types of plants at many different stages.

C because the paragraph does not indicate that established trees or any type of plant can genetically alter fungal networks for further benefit. Rather, the paragraph makes clear that it's the network itself that benefits the trees.

D because although the paragraph mentions that nutritional uptake can differ among different trees (lines 54–55), the main point of the paragraph is not about how these trees are identified. Rather, the paragraph focuses on describing how the fungal network benefits many different types of plants at many different stages.

Question 30. The best answer is **H** because the metaphor serves to further illustrate the passage author's statement that "The old trees in a forest function as hubs for these mycelial networks" (lines 56–57). Just as express stops on a subway are connected to numerous train lines, large foundational trees host numerous connections to other trees with the help of mycelial networks.

The best answer is NOT:

F because neither the metaphor mentioned nor the surrounding text describes the Indian pipe parasite as being damaging to trees.

G because neither the metaphor mentioned nor the surrounding text discusses two distinct mycelial networks.

J because neither the metaphor mentioned nor the surrounding text suggests that different species of fungi grow to be different sizes.

Question 31. The best answer is **B** because the passage author states that the purpose of "some yeasts in our body, for example, is unknown and may be commensal" (lines 7–8). "Unknown" and "may be" indicate that it is possible, but not definite, that the relationship is commensal.

The best answer is NOT:

A because the words "unknown" and "may be" in the above lines indicate that such a relationship is possible but not definite.

C because there is no indication in the passage that the relationship between some yeasts and the human body is mutualistic. The passage only mentions the possibility of a commensal relationship.

D because there is no indication in the passage that the relationship between some yeasts and the human body is mutualistic. The passage only mentions the possibility of a commensal relationship.

Question 32. **The best answer is H** because Lincoff's quotation helps define mycorrhizal fungi's relationship with plants as mutualistic. The passage author states that mutualistic relationships are ones "in which a balance of interests occurs between two organisms" (lines 1–3). Lincoff's quotation (lines 10–12) explains how the relationship is beneficial to fungi: fungi can't make their own food but obtain food through their mutually beneficial partnership with plants.

The best answer is NOT:

F because the passage author states just before the quote from Lincoff that "mycorrhizal fungi are the princes of mutualism" (line 9). There is no indication in the passage that the fungi have a commensal relationship with plants.

G because earlier in the passage, it is made clear that some yeasts may have commensal relationships with the human body (lines 5–8), and, as the passage author states just before the quote from Lincoff, "mycorrhizal fungi are the princes of mutualism" (line 9). Based on these details, mycorrhizal fungi cannot serve the same function as do yeasts in the human body.

J because although the quote from Lincoff (lines 10–11) states that mycorrhizal fungi are unable to produce their own food, it does not provide a reason or explanation as to why this is the case.

Question 33. **The best answer is D** because the sentences that follow describe how the fungal network can benefit trees and other plants. Lines 46–48: "Young seedlings struggling to grow in the shadow of established trees tap into the larger, older tree's fungal network to improve their nutritional uptake." Using the information in this quotation as well as information in lines 44–45, it can be inferred that "tap into" means "use."

The best answer is NOT:

A because the word "endorse" would indicate that the weaker plants approve or recommend the fungi network, which does not make sense in this context. The paragraph makes clear that weaker plants use the fungal network to obtain nutrition.

B because the word "finish" would indicate that the weaker plants cause the fungal network to cease to exist, which does not make sense in this context. The paragraph makes clear that weaker plants use the fungal network to obtain nutrition.

C because the word "lift" would indicate that the weaker plants cause the fungal network to be shifted to a higher elevation, which does not make sense in this context. The paragraph makes clear that weaker plants use the fungal network to obtain nutrition.

Question 34. **The best answer is F** because the passage states that "Young seedlings struggling to grow in the shadow of established trees tap into the larger, older tree's fungal network to improve their nutritional uptake" (lines 46–48).

The best answer is NOT:

G because the passage does not indicate that young seedlings utilize an older tree's fungal network to defend themselves against parasites.

H because the passage does not indicate that young seedlings need a specific nutrient from an older tree's fungal network. Instead, it indicates that they "improve their overall nutritional uptake" (lines 46–48).

J because the passage does not indicate that young seedlings are susceptible to a wider range of diseases. Instead, the passage indicates that the fungal network supports "young seedlings struggling to grow in the shadow of established trees" (lines 46–47).

Question 35. **The best answer is A** because the passage states that "Indian pipe depend totally on mycorrhizal fungi for its nutritive needs" (lines 72–73). Total dependency is synonymous with "absolute."

The best answer is NOT:

B because the passage states that Indian pipe is a nonphotosynthesizing plant that is "totally" (line 72) dependent on mycorrhizal fungi, and it does not further indicate that Indian pipe is also dependent on other nonphotosynthesizing plants. Therefore, this comparison is inaccurate.

C because the passage states that Indian pipe is a nonphotosynthesizing plant that is "totally" (line 72) dependent on mycorrhizal fungi, and it does not further indicate that Indian pipe is also dependent on other nonphotosynthesizing plants. Therefore, this comparison is inaccurate.

D because the passage establishes that the Indian pipe depends "totally" (line 72) on mycorrhizal fungi for its needs. The relationship between the Indian pipe and the network is clear and absolute, not uncertain.

Question 36. **The best answer is H** because the statement provided claims that plants in the forests flourished after the death of most of its mycorrhizal mycelium. This directly contradicts the passage's claim that a lack of adequate mycorrhizal fungi will correlate with "catastrophic losses of plant biomass" (line 86). If the statement in H is assumed to be true, it would weaken the passage's point about the effects of low mycorrhizal fungi in an ecosystem.

The best answer is NOT:

F because the statement provided does not challenge the passage's statement in lines 83–86. It mentions an increase in the amount of mycorrhizal mycelium, but it does not mention the effects of this increase on the forest ecosystem.

G because the statement provided does not challenge the passage's statement in lines 83–86. It mentions that two forests with the same amount of mycorrhizal mycelium lost most of their plant biomass, but it doesn't mention whether the forests had an adequate amount of fungi to begin with.

J because the statement provided corroborates rather than challenges the passage's statement in lines 83–86 by stating that a loss of mycorrhizal mycelium would correlate with negative effects on the forest's plants.

Passage I

Question 1. The best answer is B. According to Table 2, the observed i values for each of NaCl, KCl, and $(NH_4)_2SO_4$ are less than 2.50 at all listed concentrations. According to Table 2, the observed i values for $MgCl_2$ are greater than 2.50 at all listed concentrations. Therefore, the compounds with observed i values less than 2.50 at all concentrations listed are NaCl, KCl, and $(NH_4)_2SO_4$ only; **B** is correct. **A** is incorrect because it both includes $MgCl_2$ and does not include $(NH_4)_2SO_4$. **C** is incorrect because it both includes $MgCl_2$ and does not include NaCl. **D** is incorrect because it includes $MgCl_2$.

Question 2. The best answer is H. According to Table 2, the lowest observed i value for KCl is 1.79, which occurs at concentrations of 0.7, 0.8, and 0.9 mol/kg H_2O. Therefore, **H** is correct. **F** is incorrect because the observed i value for KCl at a concentration of 0.3 mol/kg H_2O is 1.81, which is not the lowest observed i value. **G** is incorrect because the observed i value for KCl at a concentration of 0.6 mol/kg H_2O is 1.80, which is not the lowest observed i value. **J** is incorrect because the observed i value for KCl at a concentration of 2.0 mol/kg H_2O is 1.83, which is not the lowest observed i value.

Question 3. The best answer is C. Table 1 lists the theoretical i value for each of the 4 compounds, whereas Table 2 lists the observed i value at a concentration of 2.0 mol/kg H_2O for each of the 4 compounds. The compound's deviation from its theoretical i value is the difference between the corresponding values from each table. For NaCl, the difference is 0.03. For KCl, the difference is 0.17. For $MgCl_2$, the difference is 1.57. For $(NH_4)_2SO_4$, the difference is 1.13. The difference for $MgCl_2$ is the greatest. Therefore, $MgCl_2$ has the largest deviation from its theoretical i value at a concentration of 2.0 mol/kg H_2O; **C** is correct. **A**, **B**, and **D** are each incorrect because the difference for each compound is not the greatest.

Question 4. The best answer is G. The passage states that the solutions represented in Table 2 are all aqueous solutions. An aqueous solution is a solution in which the solvent is water. The passage also states that each of the solutes are dissolved in H_2O, which is the chemical formula for water. A solvent of a solution is the substance that is used to dissolve the solute. Therefore, water is the only solvent for all the solutions represented in Table 2; **G** is correct. **F** is incorrect because ammonium sulfate is not a solvent in the data presented. **H** is incorrect because sodium chloride, potassium chloride, and magnesium chloride are not solvents in the data presented. **J** is incorrect because sodium chloride, potassium chloride, magnesium chloride, and ammonium sulfate are not solvents in the data presented.

Question 5. The best answer is A. The passage describes the theoretical i value as the total number of particles produced when 1 formula unit of the solute dissolves in water. Because a sucrose molecule remains intact when it dissolves in water, 1 formula unit of sucrose would produce 1 particle when dissolved in water. Therefore, the theoretical i value for sucrose is most likely 1. According to Table 1, the theoretical i value for KCl is 2. Therefore, the theoretical i value for sucrose would more likely be less than that of KCl; **A** is correct. **B** is incorrect; the theoretical i value of sucrose is most likely 1. **C** is incorrect; the theoretical i value of sucrose would more likely be less than that of KCl. **D** is incorrect; the theoretical i value of sucrose would more likely be less than that of KCl, and the value is most likely 1.

Passage II

Question 6. The best answer is G. According to Table 1, as the streptomycin concentration increased, the relative fitness of Strain X decreased only. According to Table 1, at a streptomycin concentration of 2 µg/mL, the relative fitness for Strain X was 0.8, and at a streptomycin concentration of 4 µg/mL, the relative fitness of Strain X was 0.5. Therefore, at a streptomycin concentration of 3 µg/mL, the relative fitness of Strain X would most likely have been between 0.5 and 0.8, so **G** is correct. **F** is incorrect; the relative fitness would most likely have been less than 0.5 at streptomycin concentrations greater than 4 µg/mL, not at 3 µg/mL. **H** is incorrect; the relative fitness would most likely have been between 0.8 and 0.9 at streptomycin concentrations between 0 µg/mL and 2 µg/mL. **J** is incorrect; the relative fitness would most likely never have been greater than 0.9.

Question 7. The best answer is D. Table 2 states that the effect of the mutation present in Strain X is an increased rate of streptomycin removal from the cell. This implies that each Strain X cell moves streptomycin out of the cell faster than a nonmutated cell does, so **D** is correct. **A**, **B**, and **C** are each incorrect; they are each inconsistent with the effect of mutation for Strain X given in Table 1.

Question 8. The best answer is H. According to the passage, relative fitness is a measure of survival and reproductive success, and according to the note within Table 1, a relative fitness of 0.0 indicates no surviving bacteria. This implies that the greater the relative fitness, the greater the cell survival and reproductive success. According to Table 1, at a streptomycin concentration of 2 µg/mL, the relative fitness of Strain W was 0.3 and the relative fitness of Strain X was 0.8, so **H** is correct. **F** is incorrect; Strain W would not have more likely had a greater number of cells survive and reproduce. **G** is incorrect; Strain W would not have more likely had a greater number of cells survive and reproduce, and the relative fitness values of Strain W and Strain X are inconsistent with the data in Table 1. **J** is incorrect; the relative fitness values of Strain W and Strain X are inconsistent with the data in Table 1.

Question 9. The best answer is B. According to Table 2, the strain with an increased rate of cell division was Strain W. According to Table 1, at a streptomycin concentration of 4 μg/mL, the relative fitness of Strain W was 0.1, so **B** is correct. **A, C,** and **D** are each incorrect; each of the relative fitness values is for a strain other than Strain W at a streptomycin concentration of 4 μg/mL.

Question 10. The best answer is F. According to the passage, the study contained 1 nonmutated strain, Strain U. According to Table 1, Strain U had a relative fitness of 1.0 at a streptomycin concentration of 0 μg/mL and a relative fitness of 0.0 at a streptomycin concentration of 8 μg/mL. Therefore, **F** is correct. **G** is incorrect; at a streptomycin concentration of 8 μg/mL, Strain U did not survive. **H** and **J** are each incorrect; Strain Z was a mutated strain according to the passage and Table 2.

Passage III

Question 11. The best answer is A. According to the results of Study 2, as the wavelength decreased, y_1 also decreased. At a wavelength of 400 nm, $y_1 = 10.0$ mm. A value of y_1 less than 10.0 mm would most likely be obtained at a wavelength shorter than 400 nm; **A** is correct. **B** is incorrect; when the wavelength was 500 nm, $y_1 = 12.5$ mm. **C** is incorrect; when the wavelength was 700 nm, $y_1 = 17.5$ mm. **D** is incorrect; at a wavelength of 900 mm, y_1 would most likely be greater than 17.5 mm.

Question 12. The best answer is H. In Study 3, slit width and wavelength were fixed while x was varied. The results shown in Table 3 indicate that y_1 increased as x increased; therefore, C is correct. **F** and **G** are incorrect; both graphs show y_1 decreasing as x increases. **J** is incorrect; according to Table 3, when $x = 3.00$ m, $y_1 = 7.5$ mm. The graph shown in **J** does not show this data point.

Question 13. The best answer is A. According to the passage, $x = 6.00$ m in Trial 2. Table 1 shows that for Trial 2, $y_1 = 15.0$ mm. The results of Study 3 in Table 3 show that as x increased, y_1 also increased. Therefore, repeating Trial 2 with $x = 9.00$ m would likely result in a value of y_1 greater than 15.0 mm; **A** is correct. **B** is incorrect; y_1 increased as x increased. **C** and **D** are incorrect; y_1 would be greater than 15.0 mm.

Question 14. The best answer is F. According to Table 2, the wavelength was shortest in Trial 5 (400 nm), and therefore the energy of the photons was greatest in Trial 5; F is correct. **G** is incorrect; the wavelength of light used in Trial 6 was 500 nm, a longer wavelength than that used in Trial 5. **H** is incorrect; the wavelength of light used in Trial 7 was 600 nm, a longer wavelength than that used in Trial 5. **J** is incorrect; the wavelength of light used in Trial 8 was 700 nm, a longer wavelength than that used in Trial 5.

Question 15. The best answer is B. According to Table 1, when the slit width was doubled from 0.12 mm to 0.24 mm, the distance between the bands (y_1) decreased from 30.0 mm to 15.0 mm. As the slit width doubled, y_1 was halved; **B** is correct. **A** is incorrect; y_1 was cut in half. **C** is incorrect; y_1 decreased. **D** is incorrect; y_1 consistently decreased by one-half. As slit width increased further, from 0.24 mm to 0.48 mm, y_1 decreased from 15.0 mm to 7.5 mm.

Question 16. The best answer is G. To answer this item, the examinee must know that 1 m = 1,000 mm. According to Table 2, in Trial 7 y_1 = 15.0 mm. In meters this is equal to 0.015 m; **G** is correct. **F**, **H**, and **J** are incorrect; 15.0 mm is equal to 0.015 m.

Passage IV

Question 17. The best answer is D. Figure 2 indicates that, for a temperature of 50°C, as reuse number increased from 0 through 28, the concentration of Sb^{3+} increased only. Further, at reuse number 28 (the highest reuse number tested in the experiments), the Sb^{3+} concentration in the water was approximately 330 ng/L. Thus, at reuse number 35, the Sb^{3+} concentration in the water would likely have been greater than 330 ng/L. Therefore, **D** is correct. **A**, **B**, and **C** are each incorrect; the trend indicates that as reuse number increases, the Sb^{3+} concentration increases only.

Question 18. The best answer is H. Figure 2 indicates that water stored at 50°C in a bottle that was reused 21 times had a Sb^{3+} concentration of approximately 300 ng/L. A value of 6,000 ng/L is 20 times as great as 300 ng/L. Therefore, **H** is correct. **F**, **G**, and **J** are each incorrect; 6,000 ng/L divided by 300 ng/L is 20 times as great.

Question 19. The best answer is B. Figures 1 and 2 indicate that, at a reuse number of 14, the concentration of Sb^{3+} was approximately 140 ng/L for 10°C in Experiment 2. The description of Experiment 2 indicates that the lightbulb used emitted visible light only. Therefore, **B** is correct. **A** is incorrect; the lightbulb used in Experiment 2 emitted visible light only. **C** and **D** are each incorrect; at a reuse number of 14, the concentration of Sb^{3+} at 30°C was greater than 140 ng/L in both experiments.

Question 20. The best answer is G. The passage states that the bottles used in the experiments were made of plastic. Plastics are examples of materials called polymers. Therefore, **G** is correct. **F** is incorrect; plastics are not examples of alloys. **H** is incorrect; plastics are not single elements. **J** is incorrect; plastics are not examples of salts.

Question 21. The best answer is D. Figure 1 indicates that, at reuse number 21, the Sb^{3+} concentration was approximately 275 ng/L at 10°C, approximately 325 ng/L at 30°C, and approximately 400 ng/L at 50°C. Thus, it is reasonable to conclude that as temperature increases at a constant reuse number, the Sb^{3+} concentration increases only. So, if a temperature of 20°C had been tested, the resulting Sb^{3+} concentration at a reuse number of 21 would most likely have been greater than the result for 10°C and less than the result for 30°C. Therefore, **D** is correct. **A**, **B**, and **C** are each incorrect; the result at reuse number 21 and 20°C would most likely be greater than 275 ng/L and less than 325 ng/L.

Question 22. The best answer is F. The description of Experiment 1 indicates that Step 2 of the procedure required 16 hr to complete. Moreover, Step 2 was repeated multiple times for the same bottle, making it impossible to complete Experiment 1 within the span of a single day (24 hr). Since the procedure of Experiment 1 was repeated for Experiment 2 (with a different type of lightbulb), neither experiment could have been completed in a single day. Therefore, **F** is correct. **G, H,** and **J** are each incorrect; both experiments must have required more than 1 day to complete.

Passage V

Question 23. The best answer is B. According to Hypothesis 2, compared to present day, the CO_2 concentration on early Earth was about 40 times as great. If the current CO_2 concentration is 395 ppm, 40 times 395 ppm is equal to 15,800 ppm. Therefore, **B** is correct. **A, C,** and **D** are each incorrect; each is inconsistent with Hypothesis 2.

Question 24. The best answer is G. According to Hypothesis 1, on early Earth, the higher-than-present concentrations of CO_2, NH_3, and CH_4 absorbed enough heat to allow for liquid water. According to Hypothesis 2, on early Earth, the concentrations of CO_2, NH_3, and CH_4 alone would not have absorbed enough heat to allow for liquid water. However, the higher-than-present concentrations of N_2 and H_2 in the atmosphere enhanced the heat-absorbing effects of CO_2, NH_3, and CH_4 and allowed liquid water to exist. Therefore, **G** is correct. **F, H,** and **J** are each incorrect; each is inconsistent with the question asked.

Question 25. The best answer is C. According to Hypothesis 1, on early Earth, volcanoes only released CO_2 and NH_3 into the atmosphere, and microbes produced CH_4 by metabolizing H_2. In contrast, Hypothesis 2 stated that, on early Earth, the only source of atmospheric CO_2, NH_3, and CH_4 was volcanic eruptions. Therefore, **C** is correct. **A, B,** and **D** are incorrect; each is inconsistent with at least one hypothesis.

Question 26. The best answer is F. Hypothesis 1 states that microbes produced CH_4 by metabolizing H_2. Therefore, in a balanced chemical equation that represented microbial metabolism, CH_4 would be a product and H_2 would be a reactant. So, **F** is correct. **G** is incorrect; H_2 is not metabolized in the reaction. **H** and **J** are each incorrect; in each equation, H_2 is not metabolized and CH_4 is not produced as a product.

Question 27. The best answer is D. Hypothesis 1 states that on early Earth, microbes produced CH_4, so evidence of CH_4 producing microbes supports Hypothesis 1. Therefore, **D** is correct. **A** is incorrect; Hypothesis 1 states that on early Earth the CO_2 concentration was 100 times the present concentration. **B** is incorrect; Hypothesis 1 states that on early Earth the CH_4 concentration was 1,000 times the present concentration. **C** is incorrect; Hypothesis 1 states that CO_2 was produced by volcanic eruptions.

Question 28. The best answer is G. Hypothesis 1 does not mention N_2. Hypothesis 2 states that on early Earth the concentration of N_2 was approximately twice what it is today and that the higher-than-present concentration of N_2 contributed to an increase in the heat-absorbing effects of greenhouse gases, maintaining a surface temperature that allowed for liquid water. The supposition that an increase in N_2 concentration from its present value would result in cooler surface temperatures would weaken Hypothesis 2. Therefore, **G** is correct. **F**, **H**, and **J** are each incorrect; each is inconsistent with the question asked.

Passage VI

Question 29. The best answer is B. The results of Study 1 indicate that as η increased, F decreased only. Further, when η was 1.00×10^{-3} Pa·s, F was 1,230 mL/s; and when η was 2.00×10^{-3} Pa·s, F was 615 mL/s. Therefore, if F were 920 mL/s, that would most likely result from testing a viscosity greater than 1.00×10^{-3} Pa·s and less than 2.00×10^{-3} Pa·s. So, **B** is correct. **A**, **C**, and **D** are each incorrect because each is inconsistent with the data in Table 1.

Question 30. The best answer is H. The description of Study 2 indicates that each trial was performed with $\eta = 1.0 \times 10^{-3}$ Pa·s and $D = 1.00$ m. Further, Table 2 indicates that both R and F varied from trial to trial. So, **H** is correct. **F** is incorrect because neither R nor F was held constant. **G** is incorrect because F was not held constant. **J** is incorrect because R was not held constant.

Question 31. The best answer is A. To answer this item correctly, one must understand that fluids flow from regions of high pressure to regions of low pressure. The description of the apparatus shown in Figure 1 indicates that the pressure at Gauge G was always 5 kPa greater than the pressure at Gauge H. Therefore, **A** is correct. **B** is incorrect because it is contrary to the fact that fluids flow from regions of high pressure to regions of low pressure. **C** is incorrect because it is inconsistent with the description of the apparatus. **D** is incorrect because it is both inconsistent with the description of the apparatus and contrary to the fact that fluids flow from regions of high pressure to regions of low pressure.

Question 32. The best answer is F. To answer this item correctly, one must know that viscosity in a fluid is a result of frictional forces within the fluid. So, **F** is correct. **G** is incorrect because combustion is an example of a chemical reaction, and no chemical reactions were involved in the studies. **H** is incorrect because viscosity is not a magnetic phenomenon. **J** is incorrect because viscosity is not dependent upon, or affected by, gravity.

Question 33. The best answer is B. According to the results of Study 3, when D was 2.50 m, F was 492 mL/s. So, each second the fluid was flowing, 492 mL of fluid flowed past either gauge. Therefore, the volume of fluid that flowed past either gauge in 1 minute was (492 mL/s) × (60 s) = 29,250 mL, which is approximately 30,000 mL. So, **B** is correct. **A** is incorrect; 25,000 mL is too low an estimate. **C** and **D** are each incorrect; each is too high an estimate.

Question 34. The best answer is F. The description of Study 1 indicates that D was 1.00 m in each trial. Further, the description of the apparatus shown in Figure 1 indicates that the fluid pressure at Gauge G was always 5 kPa greater than the fluid pressure at Gauge H. Thus, the absolute value of the pressure difference between the gauges was 5 kPa, and the distance between them was 1 m. Therefore, the pressure gradient between the gauges during Study 1 was (5 kPa) ÷ (1 m) = 5 kPa/m. So, **F** is correct. **G** is incorrect; it mistakenly involves the value of R. **H** is incorrect; it mistakenly involves the units of measure for R. **H** is incorrect; it mistakenly involves both the value of R and the units of measure for R.

Passage VII

Question 35. The best answer is A. According to the results of Study 2, the greatest average plant height was approximately 60 cm, which is only 0.6 m. Thus, no group had an average plant height greater than 1 m. So, **A** is correct. **B**, **C**, and **D** are each incorrect; they are each inconsistent with the data in Figure 1.

Question 36. The best answer is J. The description of Study 2 indicates that the procedures of Study 1 were repeated with an additional 240 pots. However, nine days after treatment, all but 1 of the seedlings were removed from pots that had multiple seedlings. This helped to ensure that there would be only 1 seedling per pot during the 75-day growing period that followed. So, **J** is correct. **F** is incorrect; the pots in Study 2 were prepared in the same manner as in Study 1, so 5 seeds were planted in each pot. **G** is incorrect; seeds were planted not seedlings. **H** is incorrect; at no time were seeds removed from any pot.

Question 37. The best answer is C. The description of Study 2 indicates that the procedures of Study 1 were repeated for an additional 240 pots. This implies that all 240 pots in Study 2 were irrigated over a period of 9 days. The description of Study 2 goes on to indicate that after those procedures had been completed, each pot was then irrigated as in Study 1 over a period of 75 additional days. Thus, the number of irrigation days was the same for each pot, regardless of which group it was assigned to. Therefore, it is not possible to determine whether average plant height was or was not affected by the number of irrigation days. So, **C** is correct. **A**, **B**, and **D** are each incorrect because the number of irrigation days was not varied among groups, so the claim cannot be evaluated based on Study 2.

Question 38. The best answer is F. Table 1 indicates that Group 3 was treated with Species R, Group 4 was treated with PMA, and both were treated with higher-than-normal NaCl concentrations. At 5 days after treatment, the average number of germinated seeds per pot was higher for Group 3 (4.3) than for Group 4 (4.0). At 7 days after treatment, the result for Group 3 (5.0) was also higher than that for Group 4 (4.6). And the results were similar for 9 days after treatment. Therefore, the results indicate that treatment with Species R resulted in more germinated seeds on average than did treatment with PMA on each of those days. So, **F** is correct. **G** is incorrect; on those days, the average number of seeds germinated per pot was greater for Group 3 than for Group 4. **H** and **J** are each incorrect; the results of the study are consistent with the statement.

Question 39. The best answer is C. The results of Study 1 indicate that the average number of seeds germinated per pot in Group 2 was 0.0 at both 3 and 5 days after treatment, 0.2 at 7 days after treatment, and 0.4 at 9 days after treatment. This implies that the first observations of seed germination could not have occurred any earlier than 5 days after treatment and must have occurred no later than 7 days after treatment. So, **C** is correct. **A** and **B** are each incorrect; the results indicate that no seed germination was observed any earlier than 5 days after treatment. **D** is incorrect; the results indicate that seed germination must have been observed no later than 7 days after treatment.

Question 40. The best answer is J. According to Table 1, Group 2 was treated with H_2O containing NaCl only, Group 3 was treated with H_2O containing Species R and NaCl, and Group 4 was treated with H_2O containing PMA and NaCl. So, if the statement were supported, the average plant height would be greater for Group 4 than for either of Group 2 or 3. However, the results of Study 2 show that the average plant height for Group 4 was less than that for Group 3 and greater than that for Group 2. So, **J** is correct. **F** and **G** are each incorrect; the results of Study 2 do not support the statement. **H** is incorrect; the average plant height for Group 4 was less than that for Group 3.

The ACT® *Sample Answer Document*

EXAMINEE STATEMENTS, CERTIFICATION, AND SIGNATURE

1. **Statements**: I understand that by registering for, launching, starting, or submitting answer documents for an ACT® test, I am agreeing to comply with and be bound by the *Terms and Conditions: Testing Rules and Policies for the ACT® Test* ("Terms").

I UNDERSTAND AND AGREE THAT THE TERMS PERMIT ACT TO CANCEL MY SCORES IN CERTAIN CIRCUMSTANCES. THE TERMS ALSO LIMIT DAMAGES AVAILABLE TO ME AND REQUIRE ARBITRATION OF CERTAIN DISPUTES. BY AGREEING TO ARBITRATION, ACT AND I BOTH WAIVE THE RIGHT TO HAVE THOSE DISPUTES HEARD BY A JUDGE OR JURY.

I understand that ACT owns the test questions and responses, and I will not share them with anyone by any form of communication before, during, or after the test administration. I understand that taking the test for someone else may violate the law and subject me to legal penalties. I consent to the collection and processing of personally identifying information I provide, and its subsequent use and disclosure, as described in the ACT Privacy Policy (www.act.org/privacy.html). If I am taking the test outside of the United States, I also permit ACT to transfer my personally identifying information to the United States, to ACT, or to a third-party service provider, where it will be subject to use and disclosure under the laws of the United States, including being accessible to law enforcement or national security authorities.

2. **Certification**: Copy the italicized certification below, then sign and date in the spaces provided.

*I agree to the **Statements** above and certify that I am the person whose information appears on this form.*

____

____

Your Signature	Today's Date

Do NOT mark in this shaded area.

USE A NO. 2 PENCIL ONLY.
(Do NOT use a mechanical pencil, ink, ballpoint, correction fluid, or felt-tip pen.)

A — NAME, MAILING ADDRESS, AND TELEPHONE (Please print.)

Last Name   First Name   MI (Middle Initial)

House Number & Street (Apt. No.); or PO Box & No.; or RR & No.

City   State/Province   ZIP/Postal Code

Area Code   Number   Country

ACT, Inc.—Confidential Restricted when data present

ALL examinees must complete block A – please print.

Blocks B, C, and D are required for all examinees. Find the MATCHING INFORMATION on your ticket. Enter it EXACTLY the same way, even if any of the information is missing or incorrect. Fill in the corresponding ovals. If you do not complete these blocks to match your previous information EXACTLY, your scores will be **delayed up to 8 weeks**.

ACT®

PO BOX 168, IOWA CITY, IA 52243-0168

B — MATCH NAME (First 5 letters of last name)

C — MATCH NUMBER

D — DATE OF BIRTH

Month	Day	Year
January		
February		
March		
April		
May		
June		
July		
August		
September		
October		
November		
December		

     01121525W   (A)204361-001:654321   ISD39683   Printed in the US.

The ONLY Official Prep Guide from the Makers of the ACT

PAGE 2

Marking Directions: Mark only **one** oval for each question. Fill in response completely. Erase errors cleanly without smudging.

Correct mark: ○ ● ○ ○

Do NOT use these *incorrect or bad* **marks.**

Incorrect marks: ⊘ ⊗ ◑ ⊙
Overlapping mark: ○ ○ ◐◑
Cross-out mark: ○ ⊗ ○
Smudged erasure: ○ ○ ◔ ○
Mark is too light: ◔ ○ ○ ○

BOOKLET NUMBER

FORM

Print your 5-character **Test Form** in the boxes at the right <u>and</u> fill in the corresponding ovals.

TEST 1: ENGLISH

1 Ⓐ Ⓑ Ⓒ Ⓓ	14 Ⓕ Ⓖ Ⓗ Ⓙ	27 Ⓐ Ⓑ Ⓒ Ⓓ	40 Ⓕ Ⓖ Ⓗ Ⓙ	53 Ⓐ Ⓑ Ⓒ Ⓓ	66 Ⓕ Ⓖ Ⓗ Ⓙ
2 Ⓕ Ⓖ Ⓗ Ⓙ	15 Ⓐ Ⓑ Ⓒ Ⓓ	28 Ⓕ Ⓖ Ⓗ Ⓙ	41 Ⓐ Ⓑ Ⓒ Ⓓ	54 Ⓕ Ⓖ Ⓗ Ⓙ	67 Ⓐ Ⓑ Ⓒ Ⓓ
3 Ⓐ Ⓑ Ⓒ Ⓓ	16 Ⓕ Ⓖ Ⓗ Ⓙ	29 Ⓐ Ⓑ Ⓒ Ⓓ	42 Ⓕ Ⓖ Ⓗ Ⓙ	55 Ⓐ Ⓑ Ⓒ Ⓓ	68 Ⓕ Ⓖ Ⓗ Ⓙ
4 Ⓕ Ⓖ Ⓗ Ⓙ	17 Ⓐ Ⓑ Ⓒ Ⓓ	30 Ⓕ Ⓖ Ⓗ Ⓙ	43 Ⓐ Ⓑ Ⓒ Ⓓ	56 Ⓕ Ⓖ Ⓗ Ⓙ	69 Ⓐ Ⓑ Ⓒ Ⓓ
5 Ⓐ Ⓑ Ⓒ Ⓓ	18 Ⓕ Ⓖ Ⓗ Ⓙ	31 Ⓐ Ⓑ Ⓒ Ⓓ	44 Ⓕ Ⓖ Ⓗ Ⓙ	57 Ⓐ Ⓑ Ⓒ Ⓓ	70 Ⓕ Ⓖ Ⓗ Ⓙ
6 Ⓕ Ⓖ Ⓗ Ⓙ	19 Ⓐ Ⓑ Ⓒ Ⓓ	32 Ⓕ Ⓖ Ⓗ Ⓙ	45 Ⓐ Ⓑ Ⓒ Ⓓ	58 Ⓕ Ⓖ Ⓗ Ⓙ	71 Ⓐ Ⓑ Ⓒ Ⓓ
7 Ⓐ Ⓑ Ⓒ Ⓓ	20 Ⓕ Ⓖ Ⓗ Ⓙ	33 Ⓐ Ⓑ Ⓒ Ⓓ	46 Ⓕ Ⓖ Ⓗ Ⓙ	59 Ⓐ Ⓑ Ⓒ Ⓓ	72 Ⓕ Ⓖ Ⓗ Ⓙ
8 Ⓕ Ⓖ Ⓗ Ⓙ	21 Ⓐ Ⓑ Ⓒ Ⓓ	34 Ⓕ Ⓖ Ⓗ Ⓙ	47 Ⓐ Ⓑ Ⓒ Ⓓ	60 Ⓕ Ⓖ Ⓗ Ⓙ	73 Ⓐ Ⓑ Ⓒ Ⓓ
9 Ⓐ Ⓑ Ⓒ Ⓓ	22 Ⓕ Ⓖ Ⓗ Ⓙ	35 Ⓐ Ⓑ Ⓒ Ⓓ	48 Ⓕ Ⓖ Ⓗ Ⓙ	61 Ⓐ Ⓑ Ⓒ Ⓓ	74 Ⓕ Ⓖ Ⓗ Ⓙ
10 Ⓕ Ⓖ Ⓗ Ⓙ	23 Ⓐ Ⓑ Ⓒ Ⓓ	36 Ⓕ Ⓖ Ⓗ Ⓙ	49 Ⓐ Ⓑ Ⓒ Ⓓ	62 Ⓕ Ⓖ Ⓗ Ⓙ	75 Ⓐ Ⓑ Ⓒ Ⓓ
11 Ⓐ Ⓑ Ⓒ Ⓓ	24 Ⓕ Ⓖ Ⓗ Ⓙ	37 Ⓐ Ⓑ Ⓒ Ⓓ	50 Ⓕ Ⓖ Ⓗ Ⓙ	63 Ⓐ Ⓑ Ⓒ Ⓓ	
12 Ⓕ Ⓖ Ⓗ Ⓙ	25 Ⓐ Ⓑ Ⓒ Ⓓ	38 Ⓕ Ⓖ Ⓗ Ⓙ	51 Ⓐ Ⓑ Ⓒ Ⓓ	64 Ⓕ Ⓖ Ⓗ Ⓙ	
13 Ⓐ Ⓑ Ⓒ Ⓓ	26 Ⓕ Ⓖ Ⓗ Ⓙ	39 Ⓐ Ⓑ Ⓒ Ⓓ	52 Ⓕ Ⓖ Ⓗ Ⓙ	65 Ⓐ Ⓑ Ⓒ Ⓓ	

TEST 2: MATHEMATICS

1 Ⓐ Ⓑ Ⓒ Ⓓ Ⓔ	11 Ⓐ Ⓑ Ⓒ Ⓓ Ⓔ	21 Ⓐ Ⓑ Ⓒ Ⓓ Ⓔ	31 Ⓐ Ⓑ Ⓒ Ⓓ Ⓔ	41 Ⓐ Ⓑ Ⓒ Ⓓ Ⓔ	51 Ⓐ Ⓑ Ⓒ Ⓓ Ⓔ
2 Ⓕ Ⓖ Ⓗ Ⓙ Ⓚ	12 Ⓕ Ⓖ Ⓗ Ⓙ Ⓚ	22 Ⓕ Ⓖ Ⓗ Ⓙ Ⓚ	32 Ⓕ Ⓖ Ⓗ Ⓙ Ⓚ	42 Ⓕ Ⓖ Ⓗ Ⓙ Ⓚ	52 Ⓕ Ⓖ Ⓗ Ⓙ Ⓚ
3 Ⓐ Ⓑ Ⓒ Ⓓ Ⓔ	13 Ⓐ Ⓑ Ⓒ Ⓓ Ⓔ	23 Ⓐ Ⓑ Ⓒ Ⓓ Ⓔ	33 Ⓐ Ⓑ Ⓒ Ⓓ Ⓔ	43 Ⓐ Ⓑ Ⓒ Ⓓ Ⓔ	53 Ⓐ Ⓑ Ⓒ Ⓓ Ⓔ
4 Ⓕ Ⓖ Ⓗ Ⓙ Ⓚ	14 Ⓕ Ⓖ Ⓗ Ⓙ Ⓚ	24 Ⓕ Ⓖ Ⓗ Ⓙ Ⓚ	34 Ⓕ Ⓖ Ⓗ Ⓙ Ⓚ	44 Ⓕ Ⓖ Ⓗ Ⓙ Ⓚ	54 Ⓕ Ⓖ Ⓗ Ⓙ Ⓚ
5 Ⓐ Ⓑ Ⓒ Ⓓ Ⓔ	15 Ⓐ Ⓑ Ⓒ Ⓓ Ⓔ	25 Ⓐ Ⓑ Ⓒ Ⓓ Ⓔ	35 Ⓐ Ⓑ Ⓒ Ⓓ Ⓔ	45 Ⓐ Ⓑ Ⓒ Ⓓ Ⓔ	55 Ⓐ Ⓑ Ⓒ Ⓓ Ⓔ
6 Ⓕ Ⓖ Ⓗ Ⓙ Ⓚ	16 Ⓕ Ⓖ Ⓗ Ⓙ Ⓚ	26 Ⓕ Ⓖ Ⓗ Ⓙ Ⓚ	36 Ⓕ Ⓖ Ⓗ Ⓙ Ⓚ	46 Ⓕ Ⓖ Ⓗ Ⓙ Ⓚ	56 Ⓕ Ⓖ Ⓗ Ⓙ Ⓚ
7 Ⓐ Ⓑ Ⓒ Ⓓ Ⓔ	17 Ⓐ Ⓑ Ⓒ Ⓓ Ⓔ	27 Ⓐ Ⓑ Ⓒ Ⓓ Ⓔ	37 Ⓐ Ⓑ Ⓒ Ⓓ Ⓔ	47 Ⓐ Ⓑ Ⓒ Ⓓ Ⓔ	57 Ⓐ Ⓑ Ⓒ Ⓓ Ⓔ
8 Ⓕ Ⓖ Ⓗ Ⓙ Ⓚ	18 Ⓕ Ⓖ Ⓗ Ⓙ Ⓚ	28 Ⓕ Ⓖ Ⓗ Ⓙ Ⓚ	38 Ⓕ Ⓖ Ⓗ Ⓙ Ⓚ	48 Ⓕ Ⓖ Ⓗ Ⓙ Ⓚ	58 Ⓕ Ⓖ Ⓗ Ⓙ Ⓚ
9 Ⓐ Ⓑ Ⓒ Ⓓ Ⓔ	19 Ⓐ Ⓑ Ⓒ Ⓓ Ⓔ	29 Ⓐ Ⓑ Ⓒ Ⓓ Ⓔ	39 Ⓐ Ⓑ Ⓒ Ⓓ Ⓔ	49 Ⓐ Ⓑ Ⓒ Ⓓ Ⓔ	59 Ⓐ Ⓑ Ⓒ Ⓓ Ⓔ
10 Ⓕ Ⓖ Ⓗ Ⓙ Ⓚ	20 Ⓕ Ⓖ Ⓗ Ⓙ Ⓚ	30 Ⓕ Ⓖ Ⓗ Ⓙ Ⓚ	40 Ⓕ Ⓖ Ⓗ Ⓙ Ⓚ	50 Ⓕ Ⓖ Ⓗ Ⓙ Ⓚ	60 Ⓕ Ⓖ Ⓗ Ⓙ Ⓚ

TEST 3: READING

1 Ⓐ Ⓑ Ⓒ Ⓓ	8 Ⓕ Ⓖ Ⓗ Ⓙ	15 Ⓐ Ⓑ Ⓒ Ⓓ	22 Ⓕ Ⓖ Ⓗ Ⓙ	29 Ⓐ Ⓑ Ⓒ Ⓓ	36 Ⓕ Ⓖ Ⓗ Ⓙ
2 Ⓕ Ⓖ Ⓗ Ⓙ	9 Ⓐ Ⓑ Ⓒ Ⓓ	16 Ⓕ Ⓖ Ⓗ Ⓙ	23 Ⓐ Ⓑ Ⓒ Ⓓ	30 Ⓕ Ⓖ Ⓗ Ⓙ	37 Ⓐ Ⓑ Ⓒ Ⓓ
3 Ⓐ Ⓑ Ⓒ Ⓓ	10 Ⓕ Ⓖ Ⓗ Ⓙ	17 Ⓐ Ⓑ Ⓒ Ⓓ	24 Ⓕ Ⓖ Ⓗ Ⓙ	31 Ⓐ Ⓑ Ⓒ Ⓓ	38 Ⓕ Ⓖ Ⓗ Ⓙ
4 Ⓕ Ⓖ Ⓗ Ⓙ	11 Ⓐ Ⓑ Ⓒ Ⓓ	18 Ⓕ Ⓖ Ⓗ Ⓙ	25 Ⓐ Ⓑ Ⓒ Ⓓ	32 Ⓕ Ⓖ Ⓗ Ⓙ	39 Ⓐ Ⓑ Ⓒ Ⓓ
5 Ⓐ Ⓑ Ⓒ Ⓓ	12 Ⓕ Ⓖ Ⓗ Ⓙ	19 Ⓐ Ⓑ Ⓒ Ⓓ	26 Ⓕ Ⓖ Ⓗ Ⓙ	33 Ⓐ Ⓑ Ⓒ Ⓓ	40 Ⓕ Ⓖ Ⓗ Ⓙ
6 Ⓕ Ⓖ Ⓗ Ⓙ	13 Ⓐ Ⓑ Ⓒ Ⓓ	20 Ⓕ Ⓖ Ⓗ Ⓙ	27 Ⓐ Ⓑ Ⓒ Ⓓ	34 Ⓕ Ⓖ Ⓗ Ⓙ	
7 Ⓐ Ⓑ Ⓒ Ⓓ	14 Ⓕ Ⓖ Ⓗ Ⓙ	21 Ⓐ Ⓑ Ⓒ Ⓓ	28 Ⓕ Ⓖ Ⓗ Ⓙ	35 Ⓐ Ⓑ Ⓒ Ⓓ	

TEST 4: SCIENCE

1 Ⓐ Ⓑ Ⓒ Ⓓ	8 Ⓕ Ⓖ Ⓗ Ⓙ	15 Ⓐ Ⓑ Ⓒ Ⓓ	22 Ⓕ Ⓖ Ⓗ Ⓙ	29 Ⓐ Ⓑ Ⓒ Ⓓ	36 Ⓕ Ⓖ Ⓗ Ⓙ
2 Ⓕ Ⓖ Ⓗ Ⓙ	9 Ⓐ Ⓑ Ⓒ Ⓓ	16 Ⓕ Ⓖ Ⓗ Ⓙ	23 Ⓐ Ⓑ Ⓒ Ⓓ	30 Ⓕ Ⓖ Ⓗ Ⓙ	37 Ⓐ Ⓑ Ⓒ Ⓓ
3 Ⓐ Ⓑ Ⓒ Ⓓ	10 Ⓕ Ⓖ Ⓗ Ⓙ	17 Ⓐ Ⓑ Ⓒ Ⓓ	24 Ⓕ Ⓖ Ⓗ Ⓙ	31 Ⓐ Ⓑ Ⓒ Ⓓ	38 Ⓕ Ⓖ Ⓗ Ⓙ
4 Ⓕ Ⓖ Ⓗ Ⓙ	11 Ⓐ Ⓑ Ⓒ Ⓓ	18 Ⓕ Ⓖ Ⓗ Ⓙ	25 Ⓐ Ⓑ Ⓒ Ⓓ	32 Ⓕ Ⓖ Ⓗ Ⓙ	39 Ⓐ Ⓑ Ⓒ Ⓓ
5 Ⓐ Ⓑ Ⓒ Ⓓ	12 Ⓕ Ⓖ Ⓗ Ⓙ	19 Ⓐ Ⓑ Ⓒ Ⓓ	26 Ⓕ Ⓖ Ⓗ Ⓙ	33 Ⓐ Ⓑ Ⓒ Ⓓ	40 Ⓕ Ⓖ Ⓗ Ⓙ
6 Ⓕ Ⓖ Ⓗ Ⓙ	13 Ⓐ Ⓑ Ⓒ Ⓓ	20 Ⓕ Ⓖ Ⓗ Ⓙ	27 Ⓐ Ⓑ Ⓒ Ⓓ	34 Ⓕ Ⓖ Ⓗ Ⓙ	
7 Ⓐ Ⓑ Ⓒ Ⓓ	14 Ⓕ Ⓖ Ⓗ Ⓙ	21 Ⓐ Ⓑ Ⓒ Ⓓ	28 Ⓕ Ⓖ Ⓗ Ⓙ	35 Ⓐ Ⓑ Ⓒ Ⓓ	

The ACT® *Sample Answer Document*

EXAMINEE STATEMENTS, CERTIFICATION, AND SIGNATURE

1. **Statements**: I understand that by registering for, launching, starting, or submitting answer documents for an ACT® test, I am agreeing to comply with and be bound by the *Terms and Conditions: Testing Rules and Policies for the ACT® Test* ("Terms").

I UNDERSTAND AND AGREE THAT THE TERMS PERMIT ACT TO CANCEL MY SCORES IN CERTAIN CIRCUMSTANCES. THE TERMS ALSO LIMIT DAMAGES AVAILABLE TO ME AND REQUIRE ARBITRATION OF CERTAIN DISPUTES. BY AGREEING TO ARBITRATION, ACT AND I BOTH WAIVE THE RIGHT TO HAVE THOSE DISPUTES HEARD BY A JUDGE OR JURY.

I understand that ACT owns the test questions and responses, and I will not share them with anyone by any form of communication before, during, or after the test administration. I understand that taking the test for someone else may violate the law and subject me to legal penalties. I consent to the collection and processing of personally identifying information I provide, and its subsequent use and disclosure, as described in the ACT Privacy Policy (www.act.org/privacy.html). If I am taking the test outside of the United States, I also permit ACT to transfer my personally identifying information to the United States, to ACT, or to a third-party service provider, where it will be subject to use and disclosure under the laws of the United States, including being accessible to law enforcement or national security authorities.

2. **Certification**: Copy the italicized certification below, then sign and date in the spaces provided.

*I agree to the **Statements** above and certify that I am the person whose information appears on this form.*

____

____

____
Your Signature   Today's Date

Do NOT mark in this shaded area.

USE A NO. 2 PENCIL ONLY.
(Do NOT use a mechanical pencil, ink, ballpoint, correction fluid, or felt-tip pen.)

A — **NAME, MAILING ADDRESS, AND TELEPHONE**
(Please print.)

Last Name   First Name   MI (Middle Initial)

House Number & Street (Apt. No.); or PO Box & No.; or RR & No.

City   State/Province   ZIP/Postal Code

Area Code   Number   Country

ACT, Inc.—Confidential Restricted when data present

ALL examinees must complete block A – please print.

Blocks B, C, and D are required for all examinees. Find the MATCHING INFORMATION on your ticket. Enter it EXACTLY the same way, even if any of the information is missing or incorrect. Fill in the corresponding ovals. If you do not complete these blocks to match your previous information EXACTLY, your scores will be **delayed up to 8 weeks**.

ACT®

PO BOX 168, IOWA CITY, IA 52243-0168

B MATCH NAME
(First 5 letters of last name)

C MATCH NUMBER

D DATE OF BIRTH

Month	Day	Year
January		
February		
March		
April		
May		
June		
July		
August		
September		
October		
November		
December		

PAGE 2

Marking Directions: Mark only **one** oval for each question. Fill in response completely. Erase errors cleanly without smudging.

Correct mark: ○ ● ○ ○

- -

Do NOT use these *incorrect* **or** *bad* **marks.**

Incorrect marks: ⊘ ⊗ ● ◉
Overlapping mark: ○ ○ ◐ ◑
Cross-out mark: ○ ● ● ○
Smudged erasure: ○ ○ ● ○
Mark is too light: ◌ ○ ○ ○

BOOKLET NUMBER

FORM

Print your 5-character **Test Form** in the boxes at the right <u>and</u> fill in the corresponding ovals.

TEST 1: ENGLISH

1 Ⓐ Ⓑ Ⓒ Ⓓ	14 Ⓕ Ⓖ Ⓗ Ⓙ	27 Ⓐ Ⓑ Ⓒ Ⓓ	40 Ⓕ Ⓖ Ⓗ Ⓙ	53 Ⓐ Ⓑ Ⓒ Ⓓ	66 Ⓕ Ⓖ Ⓗ Ⓙ
2 Ⓕ Ⓖ Ⓗ Ⓙ	15 Ⓐ Ⓑ Ⓒ Ⓓ	28 Ⓕ Ⓖ Ⓗ Ⓙ	41 Ⓐ Ⓑ Ⓒ Ⓓ	54 Ⓕ Ⓖ Ⓗ Ⓙ	67 Ⓐ Ⓑ Ⓒ Ⓓ
3 Ⓐ Ⓑ Ⓒ Ⓓ	16 Ⓕ Ⓖ Ⓗ Ⓙ	29 Ⓐ Ⓑ Ⓒ Ⓓ	42 Ⓕ Ⓖ Ⓗ Ⓙ	55 Ⓐ Ⓑ Ⓒ Ⓓ	68 Ⓕ Ⓖ Ⓗ Ⓙ
4 Ⓕ Ⓖ Ⓗ Ⓙ	17 Ⓐ Ⓑ Ⓒ Ⓓ	30 Ⓕ Ⓖ Ⓗ Ⓙ	43 Ⓐ Ⓑ Ⓒ Ⓓ	56 Ⓕ Ⓖ Ⓗ Ⓙ	69 Ⓐ Ⓑ Ⓒ Ⓓ
5 Ⓐ Ⓑ Ⓒ Ⓓ	18 Ⓕ Ⓖ Ⓗ Ⓙ	31 Ⓐ Ⓑ Ⓒ Ⓓ	44 Ⓕ Ⓖ Ⓗ Ⓙ	57 Ⓐ Ⓑ Ⓒ Ⓓ	70 Ⓕ Ⓖ Ⓗ Ⓙ
6 Ⓕ Ⓖ Ⓗ Ⓙ	19 Ⓐ Ⓑ Ⓒ Ⓓ	32 Ⓕ Ⓖ Ⓗ Ⓙ	45 Ⓐ Ⓑ Ⓒ Ⓓ	58 Ⓕ Ⓖ Ⓗ Ⓙ	71 Ⓐ Ⓑ Ⓒ Ⓓ
7 Ⓐ Ⓑ Ⓒ Ⓓ	20 Ⓕ Ⓖ Ⓗ Ⓙ	33 Ⓐ Ⓑ Ⓒ Ⓓ	46 Ⓕ Ⓖ Ⓗ Ⓙ	59 Ⓐ Ⓑ Ⓒ Ⓓ	72 Ⓕ Ⓖ Ⓗ Ⓙ
8 Ⓕ Ⓖ Ⓗ Ⓙ	21 Ⓐ Ⓑ Ⓒ Ⓓ	34 Ⓕ Ⓖ Ⓗ Ⓙ	47 Ⓐ Ⓑ Ⓒ Ⓓ	60 Ⓕ Ⓖ Ⓗ Ⓙ	73 Ⓐ Ⓑ Ⓒ Ⓓ
9 Ⓐ Ⓑ Ⓒ Ⓓ	22 Ⓕ Ⓖ Ⓗ Ⓙ	35 Ⓐ Ⓑ Ⓒ Ⓓ	48 Ⓕ Ⓖ Ⓗ Ⓙ	61 Ⓐ Ⓑ Ⓒ Ⓓ	74 Ⓕ Ⓖ Ⓗ Ⓙ
10 Ⓕ Ⓖ Ⓗ Ⓙ	23 Ⓐ Ⓑ Ⓒ Ⓓ	36 Ⓕ Ⓖ Ⓗ Ⓙ	49 Ⓐ Ⓑ Ⓒ Ⓓ	62 Ⓕ Ⓖ Ⓗ Ⓙ	75 Ⓐ Ⓑ Ⓒ Ⓓ
11 Ⓐ Ⓑ Ⓒ Ⓓ	24 Ⓕ Ⓖ Ⓗ Ⓙ	37 Ⓐ Ⓑ Ⓒ Ⓓ	50 Ⓕ Ⓖ Ⓗ Ⓙ	63 Ⓐ Ⓑ Ⓒ Ⓓ	
12 Ⓕ Ⓖ Ⓗ Ⓙ	25 Ⓐ Ⓑ Ⓒ Ⓓ	38 Ⓕ Ⓖ Ⓗ Ⓙ	51 Ⓐ Ⓑ Ⓒ Ⓓ	64 Ⓕ Ⓖ Ⓗ Ⓙ	
13 Ⓐ Ⓑ Ⓒ Ⓓ	26 Ⓕ Ⓖ Ⓗ Ⓙ	39 Ⓐ Ⓑ Ⓒ Ⓓ	52 Ⓕ Ⓖ Ⓗ Ⓙ	65 Ⓐ Ⓑ Ⓒ Ⓓ	

TEST 2: MATHEMATICS

1 Ⓐ Ⓑ Ⓒ Ⓓ Ⓔ	11 Ⓐ Ⓑ Ⓒ Ⓓ Ⓔ	21 Ⓐ Ⓑ Ⓒ Ⓓ Ⓔ	31 Ⓐ Ⓑ Ⓒ Ⓓ Ⓔ	41 Ⓐ Ⓑ Ⓒ Ⓓ Ⓔ	51 Ⓐ Ⓑ Ⓒ Ⓓ Ⓔ
2 Ⓕ Ⓖ Ⓗ Ⓙ Ⓚ	12 Ⓕ Ⓖ Ⓗ Ⓙ Ⓚ	22 Ⓕ Ⓖ Ⓗ Ⓙ Ⓚ	32 Ⓕ Ⓖ Ⓗ Ⓙ Ⓚ	42 Ⓕ Ⓖ Ⓗ Ⓙ Ⓚ	52 Ⓕ Ⓖ Ⓗ Ⓙ Ⓚ
3 Ⓐ Ⓑ Ⓒ Ⓓ Ⓔ	13 Ⓐ Ⓑ Ⓒ Ⓓ Ⓔ	23 Ⓐ Ⓑ Ⓒ Ⓓ Ⓔ	33 Ⓐ Ⓑ Ⓒ Ⓓ Ⓔ	43 Ⓐ Ⓑ Ⓒ Ⓓ Ⓔ	53 Ⓐ Ⓑ Ⓒ Ⓓ Ⓔ
4 Ⓕ Ⓖ Ⓗ Ⓙ Ⓚ	14 Ⓕ Ⓖ Ⓗ Ⓙ Ⓚ	24 Ⓕ Ⓖ Ⓗ Ⓙ Ⓚ	34 Ⓕ Ⓖ Ⓗ Ⓙ Ⓚ	44 Ⓕ Ⓖ Ⓗ Ⓙ Ⓚ	54 Ⓕ Ⓖ Ⓗ Ⓙ Ⓚ
5 Ⓐ Ⓑ Ⓒ Ⓓ Ⓔ	15 Ⓐ Ⓑ Ⓒ Ⓓ Ⓔ	25 Ⓐ Ⓑ Ⓒ Ⓓ Ⓔ	35 Ⓐ Ⓑ Ⓒ Ⓓ Ⓔ	45 Ⓐ Ⓑ Ⓒ Ⓓ Ⓔ	55 Ⓐ Ⓑ Ⓒ Ⓓ Ⓔ
6 Ⓕ Ⓖ Ⓗ Ⓙ Ⓚ	16 Ⓕ Ⓖ Ⓗ Ⓙ Ⓚ	26 Ⓕ Ⓖ Ⓗ Ⓙ Ⓚ	36 Ⓕ Ⓖ Ⓗ Ⓙ Ⓚ	46 Ⓕ Ⓖ Ⓗ Ⓙ Ⓚ	56 Ⓕ Ⓖ Ⓗ Ⓙ Ⓚ
7 Ⓐ Ⓑ Ⓒ Ⓓ Ⓔ	17 Ⓐ Ⓑ Ⓒ Ⓓ Ⓔ	27 Ⓐ Ⓑ Ⓒ Ⓓ Ⓔ	37 Ⓐ Ⓑ Ⓒ Ⓓ Ⓔ	47 Ⓐ Ⓑ Ⓒ Ⓓ Ⓔ	57 Ⓐ Ⓑ Ⓒ Ⓓ Ⓔ
8 Ⓕ Ⓖ Ⓗ Ⓙ Ⓚ	18 Ⓕ Ⓖ Ⓗ Ⓙ Ⓚ	28 Ⓕ Ⓖ Ⓗ Ⓙ Ⓚ	38 Ⓕ Ⓖ Ⓗ Ⓙ Ⓚ	48 Ⓕ Ⓖ Ⓗ Ⓙ Ⓚ	58 Ⓕ Ⓖ Ⓗ Ⓙ Ⓚ
9 Ⓐ Ⓑ Ⓒ Ⓓ Ⓔ	19 Ⓐ Ⓑ Ⓒ Ⓓ Ⓔ	29 Ⓐ Ⓑ Ⓒ Ⓓ Ⓔ	39 Ⓐ Ⓑ Ⓒ Ⓓ Ⓔ	49 Ⓐ Ⓑ Ⓒ Ⓓ Ⓔ	59 Ⓐ Ⓑ Ⓒ Ⓓ Ⓔ
10 Ⓕ Ⓖ Ⓗ Ⓙ Ⓚ	20 Ⓕ Ⓖ Ⓗ Ⓙ Ⓚ	30 Ⓕ Ⓖ Ⓗ Ⓙ Ⓚ	40 Ⓕ Ⓖ Ⓗ Ⓙ Ⓚ	50 Ⓕ Ⓖ Ⓗ Ⓙ Ⓚ	60 Ⓕ Ⓖ Ⓗ Ⓙ Ⓚ

TEST 3: READING

1 Ⓐ Ⓑ Ⓒ Ⓓ	8 Ⓕ Ⓖ Ⓗ Ⓙ	15 Ⓐ Ⓑ Ⓒ Ⓓ	22 Ⓕ Ⓖ Ⓗ Ⓙ	29 Ⓐ Ⓑ Ⓒ Ⓓ	36 Ⓕ Ⓖ Ⓗ Ⓙ
2 Ⓕ Ⓖ Ⓗ Ⓙ	9 Ⓐ Ⓑ Ⓒ Ⓓ	16 Ⓕ Ⓖ Ⓗ Ⓙ	23 Ⓐ Ⓑ Ⓒ Ⓓ	30 Ⓕ Ⓖ Ⓗ Ⓙ	37 Ⓐ Ⓑ Ⓒ Ⓓ
3 Ⓐ Ⓑ Ⓒ Ⓓ	10 Ⓕ Ⓖ Ⓗ Ⓙ	17 Ⓐ Ⓑ Ⓒ Ⓓ	24 Ⓕ Ⓖ Ⓗ Ⓙ	31 Ⓐ Ⓑ Ⓒ Ⓓ	38 Ⓕ Ⓖ Ⓗ Ⓙ
4 Ⓕ Ⓖ Ⓗ Ⓙ	11 Ⓐ Ⓑ Ⓒ Ⓓ	18 Ⓕ Ⓖ Ⓗ Ⓙ	25 Ⓐ Ⓑ Ⓒ Ⓓ	32 Ⓕ Ⓖ Ⓗ Ⓙ	39 Ⓐ Ⓑ Ⓒ Ⓓ
5 Ⓐ Ⓑ Ⓒ Ⓓ	12 Ⓕ Ⓖ Ⓗ Ⓙ	19 Ⓐ Ⓑ Ⓒ Ⓓ	26 Ⓕ Ⓖ Ⓗ Ⓙ	33 Ⓐ Ⓑ Ⓒ Ⓓ	40 Ⓕ Ⓖ Ⓗ Ⓙ
6 Ⓕ Ⓖ Ⓗ Ⓙ	13 Ⓐ Ⓑ Ⓒ Ⓓ	20 Ⓕ Ⓖ Ⓗ Ⓙ	27 Ⓐ Ⓑ Ⓒ Ⓓ	34 Ⓕ Ⓖ Ⓗ Ⓙ	
7 Ⓐ Ⓑ Ⓒ Ⓓ	14 Ⓕ Ⓖ Ⓗ Ⓙ	21 Ⓐ Ⓑ Ⓒ Ⓓ	28 Ⓕ Ⓖ Ⓗ Ⓙ	35 Ⓐ Ⓑ Ⓒ Ⓓ	

TEST 4: SCIENCE

1 Ⓐ Ⓑ Ⓒ Ⓓ	8 Ⓕ Ⓖ Ⓗ Ⓙ	15 Ⓐ Ⓑ Ⓒ Ⓓ	22 Ⓕ Ⓖ Ⓗ Ⓙ	29 Ⓐ Ⓑ Ⓒ Ⓓ	36 Ⓕ Ⓖ Ⓗ Ⓙ
2 Ⓕ Ⓖ Ⓗ Ⓙ	9 Ⓐ Ⓑ Ⓒ Ⓓ	16 Ⓕ Ⓖ Ⓗ Ⓙ	23 Ⓐ Ⓑ Ⓒ Ⓓ	30 Ⓕ Ⓖ Ⓗ Ⓙ	37 Ⓐ Ⓑ Ⓒ Ⓓ
3 Ⓐ Ⓑ Ⓒ Ⓓ	10 Ⓕ Ⓖ Ⓗ Ⓙ	17 Ⓐ Ⓑ Ⓒ Ⓓ	24 Ⓕ Ⓖ Ⓗ Ⓙ	31 Ⓐ Ⓑ Ⓒ Ⓓ	38 Ⓕ Ⓖ Ⓗ Ⓙ
4 Ⓕ Ⓖ Ⓗ Ⓙ	11 Ⓐ Ⓑ Ⓒ Ⓓ	18 Ⓕ Ⓖ Ⓗ Ⓙ	25 Ⓐ Ⓑ Ⓒ Ⓓ	32 Ⓕ Ⓖ Ⓗ Ⓙ	39 Ⓐ Ⓑ Ⓒ Ⓓ
5 Ⓐ Ⓑ Ⓒ Ⓓ	12 Ⓕ Ⓖ Ⓗ Ⓙ	19 Ⓐ Ⓑ Ⓒ Ⓓ	26 Ⓕ Ⓖ Ⓗ Ⓙ	33 Ⓐ Ⓑ Ⓒ Ⓓ	40 Ⓕ Ⓖ Ⓗ Ⓙ
6 Ⓕ Ⓖ Ⓗ Ⓙ	13 Ⓐ Ⓑ Ⓒ Ⓓ	20 Ⓕ Ⓖ Ⓗ Ⓙ	27 Ⓐ Ⓑ Ⓒ Ⓓ	34 Ⓕ Ⓖ Ⓗ Ⓙ	
7 Ⓐ Ⓑ Ⓒ Ⓓ	14 Ⓕ Ⓖ Ⓗ Ⓙ	21 Ⓐ Ⓑ Ⓒ Ⓓ	28 Ⓕ Ⓖ Ⓗ Ⓙ	35 Ⓐ Ⓑ Ⓒ Ⓓ	

Practice Test 3

EXAMINEE STATEMENTS, CERTIFICATION, AND SIGNATURE

1. **Statements:** I understand that by registering for, launching, starting, or submitting answer documents for an ACT® test, I am agreeing to comply with and be bound by the *Terms and Conditions: Testing Rules and Policies for the ACT® Test* ("Terms").

   I UNDERSTAND AND AGREE THAT THE TERMS PERMIT ACT TO CANCEL MY SCORES IN CERTAIN CIRCUMSTANCES. THE TERMS ALSO LIMIT DAMAGES AVAILABLE TO ME AND REQUIRE ARBITRATION OF CERTAIN DISPUTES. BY AGREEING TO ARBITRATION, ACT AND I BOTH WAIVE THE RIGHT TO HAVE THOSE DISPUTES HEARD BY A JUDGE OR JURY.

   I understand that ACT owns the test questions and responses, and I will not share them with anyone by any form of communication before, during, or after the test administration. I understand that taking the test for someone else may violate the law and subject me to legal penalties.

   I consent to the collection and processing of personally identifying information I provide, and its subsequent use and disclosure, as described in the ACT Privacy Policy (www.act.org/privacy.html). If I am taking the test outside of the United States, I also permit ACT to transfer my personally identifying information to the United States, to ACT, or to a third-party service provider, where it will be subject to use and disclosure under the laws of the United States, including being accessible to law enforcement or national security authorities.

2. **Certification:** Copy the italicized certification below, then sign, date, and print your name in the spaces provided.

   *I agree to the **Statements** above and certify that I am the person whose information appears on this form.*

____

____

Your Signature _______________   Today's Date _______   Print Your Name

Directions

This booklet contains tests in English, mathematics, reading, and science. These tests measure skills and abilities highly related to high school course work and success in college. **Calculators may be used on the mathematics test only.**

The questions in each test are numbered, and the suggested answers for each question are lettered. On the answer document, the rows of ovals are numbered to match the questions, and the ovals in each row are lettered to correspond to the suggested answers.

For each question, first decide which answer is best. Next, locate on the answer document the row of ovals numbered the same as the question. Then, locate the oval in that row lettered the same as your answer. Finally, fill in the oval completely. Use a soft lead pencil and make your marks heavy and black. **Do not use ink or a mechanical pencil.**

Mark only one answer to each question. If you change your mind about an answer, erase your first mark thoroughly before marking your new answer. For each question, make certain that you mark in the row of ovals with the same number as the question.

Only responses marked on your answer document will be scored. Your score on each test will be based only on the number of questions you answer correctly during the time allowed for that test. You will **not** be penalized for guessing. **It is to your advantage to answer every question even if you must guess.**

You may work on each test **only** when the testing staff tells you to do so. If you finish a test before time is called for that test, you should use the time remaining to reconsider questions you are uncertain about in that test. You may **not** look back to a test on which time has already been called, and you may **not** go ahead to another test. To do so will disqualify you from the examination.

Lay your pencil down immediately when time is called at the end of each test. You may **not** for any reason fill in or alter ovals for a test after time is called for that test. To do so will disqualify you from the examination.

Do not fold or tear the pages of your test booklet.

DO NOT OPEN THIS BOOKLET
UNTIL TOLD TO DO SO.

The ONLY Official Prep Guide from the Makers of the ACT

1 ■ ■ ■ ■ ■ ■ ■ ■ 1

ENGLISH TEST
35 Minutes—50 Questions

DIRECTIONS: In the passages that follow, certain words and phrases are underlined and numbered. In the right-hand column, you will find alternatives for the underlined part. You are to choose the best answer to each question. If you think the original version is best, choose "**No Change.**"

You will also find questions about a section of the passage, or about the passage as a whole. These questions do not refer to an underlined portion of the passage, but rather are identified by a number or numbers in a box.

For each question, choose the alternative you consider best and fill in the corresponding oval on your answer document. Read each passage through once before you begin to answer the questions that accompany it. For many of the questions, you must read several sentences beyond the question to determine the answer. Be sure that you have read far enough ahead each time you choose an alternative.

PASSAGE I

Double the Manta Rays

When Andrea Marshall began studying manta rays off the coast of Mozambique, she didn't expect to identify an entirely new species. During her research she observed intriguing physical <u>variations, in the mantas</u> she swam
₁
amongst. She began to suspect that the one recognized species of manta might in fact be two species.

[1] To investigate, Marshall began collecting data. [2] Other data required a closer look. [3] The skin of all mantas, for example, <u>is</u> embedded with tiny, toothlike
₂
"denticles." [4] Marshall found that denticles on some mantas were randomly spaced and occasionally overlapped, whereas denticles on other mantas were evenly spaced and never overlapped. [5] Another discovery was that some mantas had egg-shaped masses at the base of their tail fins. [6] | 3 |

1. Which choice makes the sentence most grammatically acceptable?

  A. No Change
  B. variations—in the mantas
  C. variations, in the mantas,
  D. variations in the mantas

2. Which choice make the sentence most grammatically acceptable?

  F. No Change
  G. happen to be
  H. were
  J. are

3. The writer wants to add the following sentence to this paragraph:

    Some of the data were basic, such as manta coloration and size.

The sentence would most logically be placed:

  A. after Sentence 1.
  B. after Sentence 2.
  C. after Sentence 3.
  D. after Sentence 4.

GO ON TO THE NEXT PAGE.

1 ▪ ▪ ▪ ▪ ▪ ▪ ▪ ▪ ▪ 1

In 2009, Marshall announced, with two other
<u>scientists,</u> that indeed there are two manta species.
The more common *Manta alfredi* thrives in shallow
water. In contrast, the giant *Manta birostris* favors deep
water. That such gentle giants went undifferentiated for
so long highlights how little scientists know about them.
<u>At the moment, manta ray populations face an array
of threats worldwide.</u>

4. Which choice best conveys that Marshall's announce-
ment was backed by scientific data?
   - **F. No Change**
   - **G.** surprised many scientists by announcing
   - **H.** had the evidence to announce
   - **J.** at long last announced

5. Which of the following true statements best concludes
this paragraph and the essay by suggesting that the scientific study of manta rays will continue?
   - **A. No Change**
   - **B.** A 2009 documentary film about Dr. Marshall
   related the story of her manta-species discovery.
   - **C.** Dr. Marshall once described the manta ray as "like
   the largest, most beautiful underwater bird."
   - **D.** Fortunately, mantas have a devoted and expert
   researcher in Dr. Marshall.

PASSAGE II

Origins of Aspirin

When a plant is attacked by bacteria, fungi, or insects,
it produces chemicals, called salicylates, that help the
plant produce enzymes or toxins capable of destroying the
plant's attackers. Salicylates may also play a role in the
plant's ability to regulate its <u>temperature; in effect, helping</u>
the plant tolerate heat and cold. And humans
have long used the salicylic acids found in

<u>plants, particularly in the bark</u> of the willow
tree, to fight disease and to reduce fevers.

The first known references to willow bark's
medicinal use date from ancient Egypt and Sumeria.
On a Sumerian stone tablet from 3000 BC, willow is
listed among dozens of plants used to treat illnesses.
An Egyptian papyrus from about 1534 BC refers to
willow's use as an all-purpose medicine.

6. Which choice makes the sentence or sentences most
grammatically acceptable?
   - **F. No Change**
   - **G.** temperature. As a result, helping
   - **H.** temperature, this helps
   - **J.** temperature, helping

7. Which choice makes the sentence most grammatically
acceptable?
   - **A. No Change**
   - **B.** plants—particularly in the bark—
   - **C.** plants; particularly in the bark
   - **D.** plants particularly, in the bark

GO ON TO THE NEXT PAGE.

1 ▪ ▪ ▪ ▪ ▪ ▪ ▪ ▪ ▪ 1

Though willow trees are often found near water
<u>8</u>
and have become religious symbols in many cultures,
<u>8</u>
its medicinal use gradually fell out of favor in Europe.

Apothecaries increasingly preferred the imported bark of

South American cinchona trees as a fever reducer, even

though willow grew abundantly throughout Europe.

Importing cinchona <u>bark however,</u> was expensive.
<u>9</u>

<u>Consequently,</u> in the mid-1700s, English minister Edward
<u>10</u>

Stone <u>had began</u> to seek a substitute. He noted that
<u>11</u>
the bitter taste of willow bark was reminiscent of the

bitter taste of cinchona bark. Believing that the two

plants must share similar qualities, Stone pulverized

some willow bark and <u>adds its</u> powder to a liquid.
<u>12</u>

<u>He administered the medicine</u> to people suffering
<u>13</u>

from <u>fevers, he then noted that</u> it worked.
<u>14</u>
    As the field of medicine evolved, so did

the use of willow bark. Searching for a way

to make the salicylic acid in willow bark less

abrasive to the stomach, in 1853 French chemist

Charles von Gerhardt created a synthetic version.

8. Given that all the choices are true, which one would provide the most logical transition to the new subject of this paragraph?

  F. No Change
  G. While the use of willow bark remained a common-place method to reduce aches, pains, and fevers around the world,
  H. Though the ancient Egyptian physician Imhotep was worshipped as a god of healing and thought to have used willow bark,
  J. Despite the fact that possible side effects to using willow bark could sometimes include stomach aches and dizziness,

9. Which choice makes the sentence most grammatically acceptable?

  A. No Change
  B. bark; however,
  C. bark, however,
  D. bark, however

10. Which transition word is most logical in context?

  F. No Change
  G. Nevertheless,
  H. Furthermore,
  J. Likewise,

11. Which choice makes the sentence most grammatically acceptable?

  A. No Change
  B. would have began
  C. begun
  D. began

12. Which choice makes the sentence most grammatically acceptable?

  F. No Change
  G. then added it's
  H. added its
  J. adds it's

13. Which choice best emphasizes the experimental nature of the liquid Stone created?

  A. No Change
  B. He tested his new concoction on
  C. The liquid was given to benefit
  D. He decided to give the drink to

14. Which choice makes the sentence or sentences most grammatically acceptable?

  F. No Change
  G. fevers, he was elated to find that
  H. fevers which
  J. fevers. It

GO ON TO THE NEXT PAGE.

Decades later, German chemist Felix Hoffmann combined synthetic salicylic acid with acetic acid, inventing a consumer-friendly powdered formula that would come to be known as aspirin.

> Question 15 asks about the preceding passage as a whole.

15. Suppose the writer's primary purpose had been to outline the development of a common medicine. Would this essay accomplish that purpose?
    A. Yes, because the essay describes how Egyptians used to administer willow bark and how this process evolved from ancient Sumerian practices.
    B. Yes, because the essay documents the historical use of willow bark as a medicine and traces its gradual refinement into modern aspirin.
    C. No, because the essay primarily explains the function of salicylates in willow bark and how aspirin affects the human body.
    D. No, because the essay primarily compares the use of willow bark to the use of cinchona bark in eighteenth-century European medicine.

Good Vibrations

In his studio in Dusseldorf, Germany, paint is what photographer Martin Klimas carefully pours onto a
<u>16</u>
rubber membrane placed on top of an audio speaker. The paint collects in a puddle of colors: rich oranges and powder blues, hot pinks and electric yellows. Klimas attaches his camera to a tripod and he positions the camera so it is level with the paint puddle. He then
<u>17</u>
sets a sound trigger on his camera. Finally, he inserts Daft Punk's *Homework* CD into a stereo, cranks up the volume to ten, and pushes Play.

The result is what Klimas calls a "sonic sculpture." The vibrations produced by Daft Punk's dance anthem "Around the World" cause the paint to
<u>18</u>
rise and fall, to string and swirl, to splatter and stretch.

16. Which choice makes the sentence most grammatically correct?
    F. **No Change**
    G. there is paint carefully being poured by photographer Martin Klimas
    H. paint is carefully poured by Martin Klimas, a photographer,
    J. photographer Martin Klimas carefully pours paint

17. Which choice is clearest and most precise in context?
    A. **No Change**
    B. eye-to-eye with
    C. the same as
    D. equal to

18. Which choice makes the sentence most grammatically acceptable?
    F. **No Change**
    G. has caused
    H. is causing
    J. causes

GO ON TO THE NEXT PAGE.

1 ▪ ▪ ▪ ▪ ▪ ▪ ▪ ▪ **1**

It is this image that Klimas's camera captures—sound
                                          19
visually rendered by the effects of the vibrations on the

paint. Although Klimas's photographs only capture an

instant erupting of the paint in arcs of color, each of the

photographs is unique to a given song. "I leave the
                                                20
creation of the picture to the sound itself," Klimas says.
              20

19. Which choice most effectively maintains the essay's tone?

  A. **No Change**
  B. pic, frozen in time's embrace that Klimas's camera has snapped—
  C. picture that Klimas's photographic paraphernalia has managed to catch—
  D. snapshot that Klimas's photographic machine snares—

20. Which of the following quotations from Klimas provides the most relevant information at this point in the essay?

  F. **No Change**
  G. "The most annoying thing was cleaning up the set thoroughly after every single shot,"
  H. "In general, I use normal photographic equipment and common music stuff,"
  J. "The shooting is mostly about repeating the process again and again,"

Building and Rebuilding "the King of Roads"

[1]

Separating Oregon from Washington, the Columbia

River Gorge is eighty-five miles of flowing water,

tree-covered bluffs, and roaring waterfalls. These striking

features daunted would-be road builders until 1913. That
         21
year, Samuel Hill and Samuel Lancaster, a businessman

and an engineer, respectively, began constructing a road

through the gorge to connect the towns along the river.

[A] Their design went beyond practicalities it showcased
                                    22
the scenic grandeur of the gorge.

21. Which choice most clearly indicates that the features of the Columbia River Gorge intimidated road builders and kept them from constructing the highway?

  A. **No Change**
  B. posed problems for
  C. slowed potential
  D. challenged

22. Which choice makes the sentence most grammatically acceptable?

  F. **No Change**
  G. practicalities: and
  H. practicalities:
  J. practicalities,

GO ON TO THE NEXT PAGE.

1

[2]

Featuring seven viaducts and eighteen bridges, the Columbia River Highway was a marvel. [B] Roadside overlooks with benches for sitting by the road offered
<u>23</u>
travelers the chance to take in a view of the river or a waterfall. Guardrails made of local rock lined the route and blurred the distinction between that and environment.
<u>24</u>

[C] Engineers created 25 openings in the side of one tunnel, enabling motorists surrounded by rock to glimpse the river below. Completed in 1922, the highway earned the local nickname "the King of Roads."

[3]

Impressive as it was, the highway was soon outmoded because of increased traffic and larger vehicles. In time,
<u>26</u>
Oregon built a new road along the Columbia, much of the highway was destroyed to make room; other stretches were abandoned. By 1954, only the western third of the original road was still in use, mainly by tourists seeking waterfalls. [D]

23. Which choice is least redundant in context?

  A. **No Change**
  B. alongside the road
  C. for travelers
  D. **Delete** the underlined portion.

24. Which choice makes the sentence most grammatically acceptable?

  F. **No Change**
  G. this and the
  H. road and
  J. it and it's

25. At this point, the writer is considering adding the following accurate phrase:

    an unprecedented five

Should the writer make this addition here?

  A. Yes, because it adds a detail that highlights the impressive design of the highway.
  B. Yes, because it hints at how the engineers were able to make openings in the tunnel.
  C. No, because it provides information that is unrelated to the sentence.
  D. No, because it suggests that creating intricate tunnels was easy for road engineers.

26. Which choice makes the sentence most grammatically acceptable?

  F. **No Change**
  G. When
  H. Soon
  J. **Delete** the underlined portion.

GO ON TO THE NEXT PAGE.

1 ■ ■ ■ ■ ■ ■ ■ ■ **1**

[4]

In the 1980s, however, local people's interest in the original highway abounded. In 1981, the
₂₇
National Park Service offered suggestions for restoring parts of the road and repurposing unused sections of it as a trail. Since then, crumbling stone guardrails along the roadside have been repaired. Damaged bridges and viaducts have been rebuilt. Tunnels, now empty and strong, had rubble removed from them. Today, hikers
₂₈
and bikers on the Historic Columbia River Highway

Trail experience a site that became a National Historic Landmark in 2000.
₂₉

27. Which choice most clearly conveys that people's interest in the original Columbia River Highway was not a new phenomenon?

   A. **No Change**
   B. took hold.
   C. rekindled.
   D. set in.

28. Which choice most closely maintains the sentence pattern the writer has established in the previous two sentences?

   F. **No Change**
   G. Rubble-filled tunnels have been emptied and strengthened.
   H. The tunnels have had the rubble removed from them, and people have strengthened them.
   J. Once filled with rubble, tunnels have been emptied and strengthened.

29. Given that all the choices are accurate, which one best concludes the essay by referring back to the first paragraph?

   A. **No Change**
   B. the gorge on sections of the road where it wasn't feasible to restore motor vehicle traffic.
   C. the splendor of the highway that Hill and Lancaster envisioned over one hundred years ago.
   D. a beautiful path that has become a popular tourist destination.

> Question 30 asks about the preceding passage as a whole.

30. The writer wants to add the following sentence to the essay:

> The rest of the highway fell into disrepair.

The sentence would most logically be placed at:

   F. Point A in Paragraph 1.
   G. Point B in Paragraph 2.
   H. Point C in Paragraph 2.
   J. Point D in Paragraph 3.

GO ON TO THE NEXT PAGE.

PASSAGE V

The Object of Love

[1]

[A] I was waiting at the veterinarian's office recently with my cat when a young woman came in. After she sat $\underset{31}{}$ down next to me, she asked if I would mind if she took her pet iguana out of its carrier. It was just a baby, she said, and it liked being held. [B]

[2]

Now, I'm not fond of iguanas. [C] They're strange, unpredictable creatures that belong deep in a rain forest, walking on the ground or resting high in the $\underset{32}{}$ trees, which are hidden in the canopy. Wishing to be $\underset{33}{}$ polite, but with reluctance in my voice, I told the woman that I didn't mind. She thanked me as she popped open the plastic carrier and pulled the iguana out, onto her lap.

[3]

I guardedly examined the animal: A dinosaur-like thing, it was the size of a cat but armored in gray-green scales, with a black-striped, whiplike tail two feet long. It had a spine with tiny spikes, and its muscular limbs $\underset{34}{}$ ended with what resembled crinkly leather gloves drawn tightly over fine-boned human hands. When I looked more closely, I saw a tiny claw at the tip of each slender finger.

31. Which choice is least redundant in context?
   A. **No Change**
   B. into the veterinarian's office where I was.
   C. in, and there I was, waiting in the office.
   D. in while I was waiting there.

32. Which choice provides the most vivid description of iguanas on the floor of a rain forest?
   F. **No Change**
   G. scuttling through dank undergrowth
   H. living underneath the treetops
   J. moving about down low

33. Which choice makes the sentence most grammatically acceptable?
   A. **No Change**
   B. trees, they are
   C. trees,
   D. trees;

34. Given that all the choices are accurate, which one provides the most precise description of the pattern of spikes on the iguana's spine?
   F. **No Change**
   G. I saw spikes that looked like they were just beginning to develop,
   H. There were small spikes on its armored back,
   J. Rows of budding spikes lined its spine,

GO ON TO THE NEXT PAGE.

1 ■ ■ ■ ■ ■ ■ ■ ■ ■ 1

[4]

The woman began to pet the iguana under its chin, and the little dragon arched its neck and closed its eyes. The reptile's calmness amazed me, as did the caress that was <u>given tenderly from the woman to her pet</u>
                                                    35
and watched it peacefully rest. With a twinge of pity, I thought how sad it was for the woman to lavish so much affection on something that couldn't love her back.

[5]

At that moment, the iguana slowly opened its eyes, which shone <u>large and bright, from</u> its scaly face. [D] Head
                        36
slightly cocked, it regarded me, steadily and fixedly, like a

judge <u>delivering</u> a verdict.
        37

[6]

"Who are you," it seemed to ask me, "to name the proper object of love?"

[7]

The veterinary assistant called for my cat and me from the hallway that leads to the examination area. A bit unsettled, I rose and picked up my cat carrier. As I walked from the waiting room into the hall, I glanced back and saw the iguana snuggle down into the young woman's lap, <u>looking</u> as content as a kitten, and close its eyes again.
  38

35. Which choice makes the sentence most grammatically acceptable?

   A. No Change
   B. tenderness with which the woman caressed her pet
   C. woman caressing her pet tenderly
   D. tenderness the woman showed

36. Which choice makes the sentence most grammatically acceptable?

   F. No Change
   G. large and bright from,
   H. large, and bright from
   J. large and bright from

37. Which choice makes the sentence most grammatically acceptable?

   A. No Change
   B. having a delivery of
   C. in deliverance with
   D. deliver

38. Which choice best avoids wordiness and redundancy in context?

   F. No Change
   G. like as if it was giving off the impression of being
   H. appearing something like
   J. sort of like it was

GO ON TO THE NEXT PAGE.

39. Upon reviewing the essay and finding that some information has been left out, the writer composes the following sentence incorporating that information:

> She told me that her iguana especially liked attention when it was in unfamiliar surroundings, and that this was its first trip to the veterinarian.

If the writer were to add this sentence to the essay, it would most logically be placed at:

A. Point A in Paragraph 1.
B. Point B in Paragraph 1.
C. Point C in Paragraph 2.
D. Point D in Paragraph 5.

40. Suppose the writer's primary purpose had been to describe a moment in which a person notices something unexpected while observing his or her surroundings. Would this essay accomplish that purpose?

F. Yes, because it describes what the narrator, while waiting at the vet, perceived to be a surprising bond between a woman and her pet iguana.
G. Yes, because it recounts a moment when the narrator, while waiting at the vet, realized people often don't know when they're being impolite.
H. No, because it instead tells the story of why the narrator doesn't like iguanas.
J. No, because it instead focuses on providing information about the physical characteristics of iguanas and their habitat.

PASSAGE VI

Selling Hip-Hop

One night in the late seventies, at a popular club in New York City, singer and music producer Sylvia Robinson had a revelation. At the time, hip-hop subculture—based on the graffiti, breakdancing, deejaying, and rapping art forms—was emerging as a phenomenon. Robinson watched as DJ Lovebug Starski spun records for the crowd and rapped over the instrumental breaks in the music. Every time the DJ chanted, "Throw your hands in the air," everyone obeyed. Robinson could hear the enthusiasm shared between the hip-hop performer and his audience. She knew she had to capture that excitement on record.

41. Which choice makes the sentence most grammatically acceptable?

A. **No Change**
B. singer, and music producer, Sylvia Robinson,
C. singer and music producer, Sylvia Robinson,
D. singer, and music producer Sylvia Robinson

42. Which choice best avoids wordiness and redundancy in context?

F. **No Change**
G. obeyed by throwing their hands in the air.
H. heeded the DJ's call and obeyed him.
J. did what he said and obeyed.

GO ON TO THE NEXT PAGE.

1 ⬛ ⬛ ⬛ ⬛ ⬛ ⬛ ⬛ ⬛ ⬛ **1**

Robinson wasted no time in recruiting three aspiring rappers—Big Bank Hank, Master Gee, and Wonder Mike—to record on her label as the Sugarhill Gang. [43] Wanting to recreate the feel-good vibe of the music she'd heard, an upbeat disco record provided the background that the rappers rhymed over. The resulting track, "Rapper's Delight," sold fourteen million copies; Robinson had produced the first rap record to break into the charts.

Robinson's musical instincts, and business savvy had served her well with the Sugarhill Gang. However, there was more to hip-hop music than party-ready club anthems. She hoped to capitalize on her success by expanding the genre, Robinson signed Grandmaster Flash and the Furious Five, a group that already had a following, to her label.

43. At this point, the writer is considering adding the following true statement:

> Robinson and her husband would go on to form other record labels as well.

Should the writer make this addition here?

A. Yes, because it suggests that the Sugarhill Gang was able to choose where they wanted to record "Rapper's Delight."
B. Yes, because it helps explain why Big Bank Hank, Master Gee, and Wonder Mike decided to record with Robinson.
C. No, because it interrupts the paragraph's discussion of how "Rapper's Delight" was created.
D. No, because it fails to specify the time period in which Robinson and her husband started their labels.

44. Which choice makes the sentence most grammatically acceptable?

F. No Change
G. an upbeat disco record provided by Robinson was rhymed over by the rappers.
H. rhymes were created by the rappers over an upbeat disco record.
J. Robinson had the rappers rhyme over an upbeat disco record.

45. Which choice makes the sentence most grammatically acceptable?

A. No Change
B. instincts, and, business savvy
C. instincts and business savvy,
D. instincts and business savvy

46. Which choice makes the sentence most grammatically acceptable?

F. No Change
G. She was hoping
H. The hope was
J. Hoping

GO ON TO THE NEXT PAGE.

Robinson <u>allowed</u> the group to record a track that
₄₇
studio musician Edward Fletcher had written. The track,

titled "The Message," covered new commercial hip-hop

ground by addressing the harsh realities of inner-city life.

It was a far cry from the more digestible singles the group

had previously <u>released because</u> the rappers were hesitant
₄₈
to record it. But Robinson believed it was a surefire hit.

In the <u>opposite fashion,</u> Fletcher and Melle Mel (one of
₄₉
the Furious Five) recorded the track, which became the

group's biggest hit. Its <u>socially conscious</u> rhymes
₅₀
helped usher in a new generation of artists and

secured Robinson's legacy in the landscape of

commercial hip-hop.

47. Which choice most effectively indicates that Robinson
had to convince Grandmaster Flash and the Furious
Five to record "The Message"?

   A. No Change
   B. pressured
   C. helped
   D. asked

48. Which choice is clearest and most logical in context?

   F. No Change
   G. released although
   H. released, for
   J. released, so

49. Which transition word or phrase is most logical in
context?

   A. No Change
   B. first place,
   C. same way,
   D. end,

50. Which choice makes the sentence most grammatically
acceptable?

   F. No Change
   G. Its socially conscience
   H. It's socially conscious
   J. It's socially conscience

END OF TEST 1

STOP! DO NOT TURN THE PAGE UNTIL TOLD TO DO SO.

2   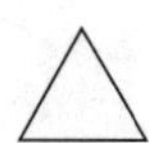  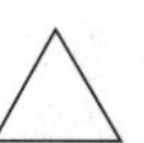      **2**

MATHEMATICS TEST

50 Minutes—45 Questions

DIRECTIONS: Solve each problem, choose the correct answer, and then fill in the corresponding oval on your answer document.

Do not linger over problems that take too much time. Solve as many as you can; then return to the others in the time you have left for this test.

You are permitted to use a calculator on this test. You may use your calculator for any problems you choose, but some of the problems may best be done without using a calculator.

Note: Unless otherwise stated, all of the following should be assumed.

1. Illustrative figures are **not** necessarily drawn to scale.
2. Geometric figures lie in a plane.
3. The word "line" indicates a straight line.
4. The word "average" indicates arithmetic mean.

---

1. A function, f, is defined by $f(x,y) = 3x^2 - 4y$. What is the value of $f(3,2)$?

   A. 0
   B. 10
   C. 19
   D. 24

2. In the figure, $\angle BAC$ measures $35°$, $\angle ABC$ measures $95°$, and points B, C, and D are collinear. What is the measure of $\angle ACD$?

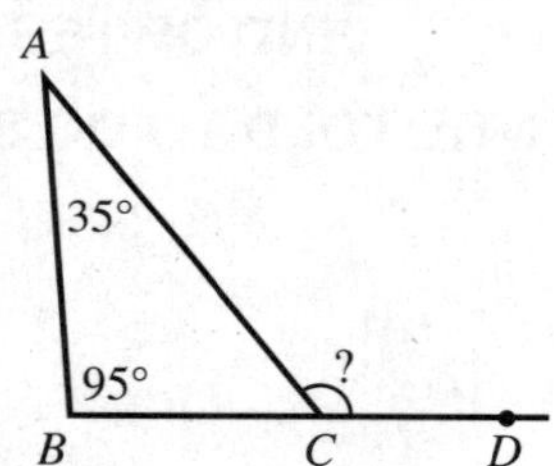

   F. 125°
   G. 130°
   H. 140°
   J. 145°

3. For all nonzero values of x and y, which of the following expressions is equivalent to $-\dfrac{36x^4y^3}{4xy}$?

   A. $-40x^3y^2$
   B. $-32x^3y^2$
   C. $-9x^5y^4$
   D. $-9x^3y^2$

DO YOUR FIGURING HERE.

GO ON TO THE NEXT PAGE.

2 △ △ △ △ △ △ △ △ △ **2**

4. At a certain airline company, the cost to transfer mileage points from one account to another is $0.75 for every 100 mileage points transferred plus a onetime $20 processing fee. What is the cost to transfer 7,000 mileage points from one account to another?

F. $25.25
G. $67.50
H. $72.50
J. $95.00

5. For $x = -5$, what is the value of $4x^2 - 11x$?

A. −84
B. −45
C. 84
D. 155

6. Taho earns his regular pay of $11 per hour for up to 40 hours of work per week. For each hour over 40 hours of work per week, Taho earns $1\frac{1}{2}$ times his regular pay. How much does Taho earn in a week in which he works 50 hours?

F. $550
G. $605
H. $625
J. $825

7. A science class has 8 juniors and 4 seniors. The teacher will randomly select 2 students, one at a time, to represent the class in a committee at the school. Given that the first student selected is a junior, what is the probability that the second student selected will be a senior?

A. $\frac{1}{11}$

B. $\frac{1}{4}$

C. $\frac{1}{3}$

D. $\frac{4}{11}$

8. The total cost of renting a car is $35.00 per day plus 42.5¢ for each mile the car is driven. What is the total cost of renting the car for 6 days and driving 350 miles?

(Note: No sales tax is involved.)

F. $154.75
G. $224.88
H. $358.75
J. $420.00

GO ON TO THE NEXT PAGE.

2          **2**

DO YOUR FIGURING HERE.

9. In the standard (x,y) coordinate plane, what is the slope of the line that passes through $(-6,4)$ and $(1,3)$?

A. $-\frac{7}{5}$

B. $-\frac{1}{5}$

C. $-\frac{1}{7}$

D. $\frac{1}{7}$

10. One morning at a coffee shop, each customer ordered either decaf or regular coffee, and each ordered it either with milk or without milk. The number of customers who ordered each type of coffee with or without milk is listed in the table.

Order	Decaf	Regular	Total
With milk	12	8	20
Without milk	6	10	16
Total	18	18	36

A customer will be randomly selected from all 36 customers for a prize. What is the probability that the selected customer will have ordered a regular coffee without milk?

F. $\frac{1}{6}$

G. $\frac{5}{18}$

H. $\frac{5}{13}$

J. $\frac{1}{2}$

11. Which of the following inequalities describes the solution set for $3x - 5 < 2x + 1$?

A. $x < -4$

B. $x > -\frac{4}{5}$

C. $x < \frac{6}{5}$

D. $x < 6$

12. Which of the following expressions is equivalent to $4(x + 2) + 3(2x - 1)$?

F. $3x + 8$
G. $5(2x + 1)$
H. $10(x + 1)$
J. $15x$

GO ON TO THE NEXT PAGE.

2 △ △ △ △ △ △ △ △ △ **2**

DO YOUR FIGURING HERE.

13. What is 4% of 1.36×10^4?

   A. 340
   B. 544
   C. 3,400
   D. 5,440

14. The point (3,27) is labeled on the graph of $f(x) = x^3$ in the given standard (x,y) coordinate plane. The graph of $f(x)$ will be translated 3 coordinate units to the left. Which of the following points will be on the image of the graph after the translation?

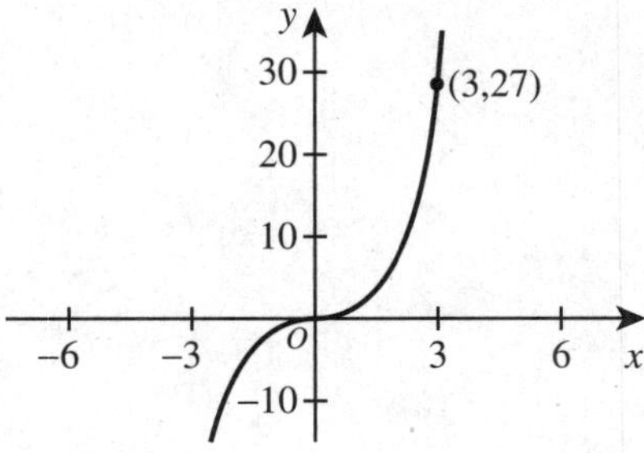

   F. (0,27)
   G. (3,24)
   H. (3,30)
   J. (6,27)

15. In the standard (x,y) coordinate plane, what is the midpoint of the line segment that has endpoints (−6,9) and (2,5)?

   A. (−4,−4)
   B. (−2,7)
   C. (4,−2)
   D. (8,−4)

16. What value of x satisfies the equation $\dfrac{x^2 + 2x}{x + 2} = 2$?

   F. −4
   G. −2
   H. 1
   J. 2

17. In the figure shown, all angles are right angles, and the side lengths given are in centimeters. What is the area, in square centimeters, of the figure?

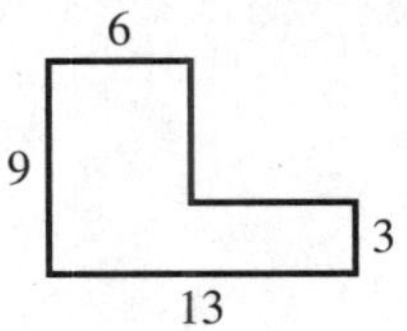

   A. 42
   B. 75
   C. 93
   D. 117

GO ON TO THE NEXT PAGE.

2 △ △ △ △ △ △ △ △ △ **2**

18. In the given figure, E is on $\overline{CA}$, and the measures of $\angle BED$ and $\angle AEB$ are 90° and 145°, respectively. What is the measure of $\angle CED$?

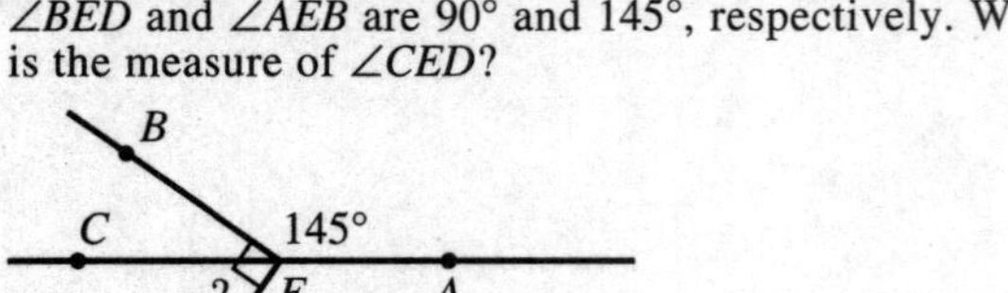

F. 35°
G. 45°
H. 55°
J. 80°

DO YOUR FIGURING HERE.

19. In the standard (x,y) coordinate plane, the graph of the function $y = 5\sin(x) - 7$ undergoes a single translation such that the equation of its image is $y = 5\sin(x) - 14$. Which of the following describes this translation?

A. Up 7 coordinate units
B. Down 7 coordinate units
C. Left 7 coordinate units
D. Right 14 coordinate units

20. What is the value of $\left(9^{\frac{1}{2}} + 16^{\frac{1}{2}}\right)^2$?

F. 7
G. 25
H. 49
J. 337

21. A right triangle is shown in the figure. What is the value of $\sin\theta$?

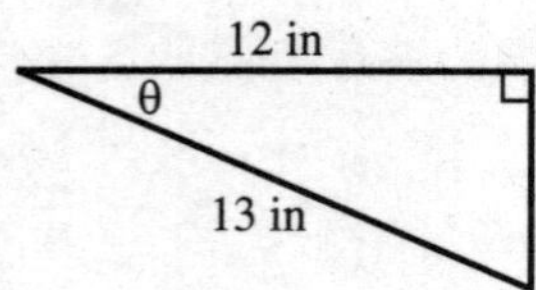

A. $\frac{5}{13}$

B. $\frac{5}{12}$

C. $\frac{12}{13}$

D. $\frac{13}{12}$

GO ON TO THE NEXT PAGE.

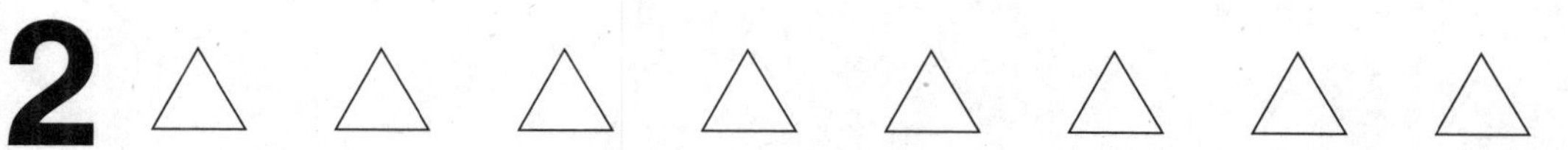

2 △ △ △ △ △ △ △ △ △ **2**

DO YOUR FIGURING HERE.

22. All the values in the equation are exact. What value of c makes the equation true?

$$(4.25 \times 10^{2c+4})(6 \times 10^7) = 255$$

F. -7
G. -6.5
H. -5
J. -4.5

23. Which of the following inequalities is true for all positive integers m?

A. $m \le \frac{1}{m}$

B. $m \le \sqrt{m}$

C. $m \ge m^2$

D. $m \le m + 1$

24. Graphed in the standard (x,y) coordinate plane is a right triangle with vertices $(0,0)$, $(-40,0)$, and $(0,30)$. What is the length, in coordinate units, of the hypotenuse of the triangle?

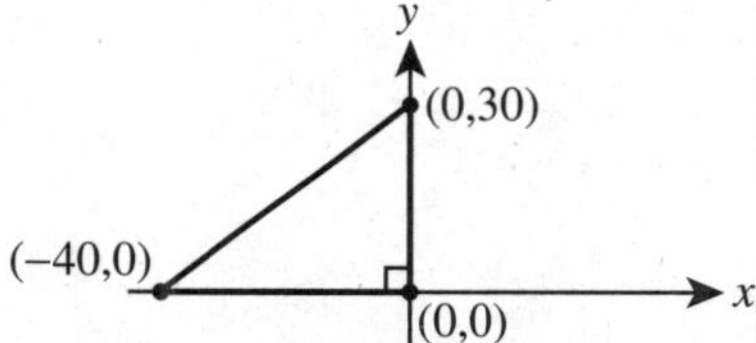

F. 30
G. 40
H. 50
J. 70

25. In the standard (x,y) coordinate plane, the graph of $y = 30(x + 17)^2 - 42$ is a parabola. What are the coordinates of the vertex of the parabola?

A. $(-30,-42)$
B. $(-17,-42)$
C. $(17,-42)$
D. $(17,42)$

26. One side of square $ABCD$ has a length of 15 meters. A certain rectangle whose area is equal to the area of $ABCD$ has a width of 10 meters. What is the length, in meters, of the rectangle?

F. 15
G. 20
H. 22.5
J. 37.5

GO ON TO THE NEXT PAGE.

Taking Additional Practice Tests

2 △ △ △ △ △ △ △ △ △ **2**

27. The total amount of a certain substance present in a laboratory experiment is given by the formula $A = A_0\left(2^{\frac{h}{5}}\right)$, where A is the total amount of the substance h hours after initial amount (A_0) of the substance began accumulating. Which of the following expressions gives the number of hours it will take an initial amount of 10 grams of this substance to accumulate to 100 grams?

   A. 5
   B. 25
   C. $5\log_2(10)$
   D. $5\log_{20}(100)$

28. For all values of x greater than 3, which of the following expressions is equivalent to $\dfrac{x^2 - x - 6}{x^2 - 9}$?

   F. $\dfrac{x-2}{x-3}$
   G. $\dfrac{x-2}{x+3}$
   H. $\dfrac{x+2}{x-3}$
   J. $\dfrac{x+2}{x+3}$

29. If the positive integers x and y are relatively prime (their greatest common factor is 1) and $\frac{1}{2} + \frac{1}{3} \cdot \frac{1}{4} \div \frac{1}{5} = \frac{x}{y}$, then $x + y = ?$

   A. 23
   B. 49
   C. 91
   D. 132

30. What is the 358th digit after the decimal point in the repeating decimal $0.\overline{3178}$?

   F. 3
   G. 1
   H. 7
   J. 8

GO ON TO THE NEXT PAGE.

2 △ △ △ △ △ △ △ △ △ **2**

31. To promote a new brand of shoes, a shoe store will run a promotion using a jar containing 3 red balls marked "10% off," 2 white balls marked "30% off," and 1 green ball marked "60% off." Each customer will randomly select 1 ball from the jar to determine the discount that the customer will receive on any single pair of the new brand of shoes. Given that the new brand of shoes regularly costs $60 per pair, what is the average discount amount, in dollars, that the store can expect to give each customer due to this promotion?

   A. $6
   B. $10
   C. $15
   D. $20

32. Anela and Jacob plan to attend a concert in Brady. Anela will drive 375 km to Brady at a constant speed of 75 km/hr, stopping 1 time for a 30-minute break. Jacob will start 600 km from Brady and will drive at a constant speed of 90 km/hr for 2 hours. He will take a 1-hour break and then drive to Brady at a constant speed of 70 km/hr. To the nearest 0.1 hour, Jacob must leave how much earlier than Anela in order for them to arrive in Brady at the same time?

   F. 2.5
   G. 3.1
   H. 3.5
   J. 4.0

33. For all $x \neq 0$, which of the following is equal to $\frac{3x+5}{2x} - \frac{7x-3}{2x}$?

   A. $-4x + 8$

   B. $-4x + 2$

   C. $-2x + 1$

   D. $\frac{-2x+4}{x}$

34. A rectangular stage is 90 feet long and 30 feet wide. What is the area, in square **yards**, of this stage?

   F. 300
   G. 675
   H. 900
   J. 2,700

DO YOUR FIGURING HERE.

GO ON TO THE NEXT PAGE.

2 △ △ △ △ △ △ △ △ △ **2**

DO YOUR FIGURING HERE.

35. A rectangle, with its vertex coordinates labeled, is graphed in the standard (x,y) coordinate plane shown. A lattice point is a point with coordinates that are both integers. A lattice point inside but **not** on the rectangle will be chosen at random. What is the probability that the sum of the x-coordinate and the y-coordinate of the chosen lattice point will be odd?

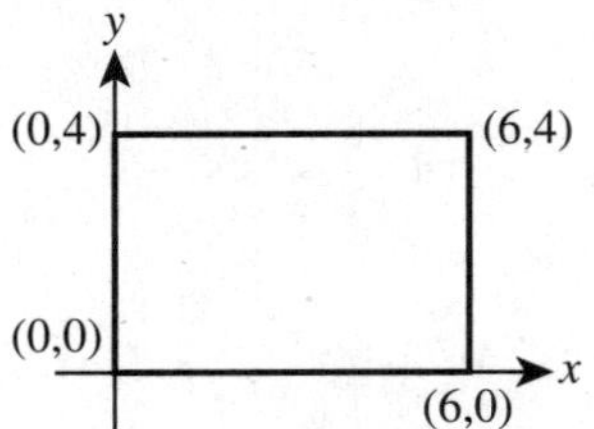

A. $\frac{1}{5}$

B. $\frac{7}{15}$

C. $\frac{17}{35}$

D. $\frac{1}{2}$

36. The nth term of an arithmetic progression is given by the formula $a_n = a_1 + (n-1)d$, where d is the common difference and a_1 is the first term. If the third term of an arithmetic progression is $\frac{5}{2}$ and the sixth term is $\frac{1}{4}$, what is the seventh term?

F. $-\frac{1}{2}$

G. $\frac{1}{2}$

H. $\frac{3}{4}$

J. 1

37. The probability of Jamie being chosen to bat first in the lineup for his baseball team is $\frac{1}{9}$. What are the odds in favor of Jamie being chosen to bat first?

(Note: The odds in favor of an event are defined as the ratio of the probability that the event will happen to the probability that the event will **not** happen.)

A. $\frac{1}{8}$

B. $\frac{1}{9}$

C. $\frac{8}{1}$

D. $\frac{9}{1}$

GO ON TO THE NEXT PAGE.

2 △ △ △ △ △ △ △ △ △ 2

38. A 120-liter solution that is 5% salt is mixed with an 80-liter solution that is 15% salt. The combined solution is what percent salt?

   F. 8%
   G. 9%
   H. 10%
   J. 12%

39. A 50-foot-long rectangular swimming pool with vertical sides is 3 feet deep at the shallow end and 10 feet deep at the deep end. The bottom of the pool slopes downward at a constant angle from horizontal along the length of the pool. Which of the following expressions gives this constant angle?

(Note: For $-\frac{\pi}{2} < x < \frac{\pi}{2}$, $y = \tan x$ if and only if $x = \tan^{-1} y$.)

   A. $\tan^{-1}\left(\frac{7}{50}\right)$

   B. $\tan^{-1}\left(\frac{13}{50}\right)$

   C. $\tan^{-1}\left(\frac{7}{10}\right)$

   D. $\tan^{-1}\left(\frac{50}{13}\right)$

40. A hyperbola that has vertices (1,2) and (3,2) and that passes through the origin is shown in the standard (x,y) coordinate plane. The hyperbola has which of the following equations?

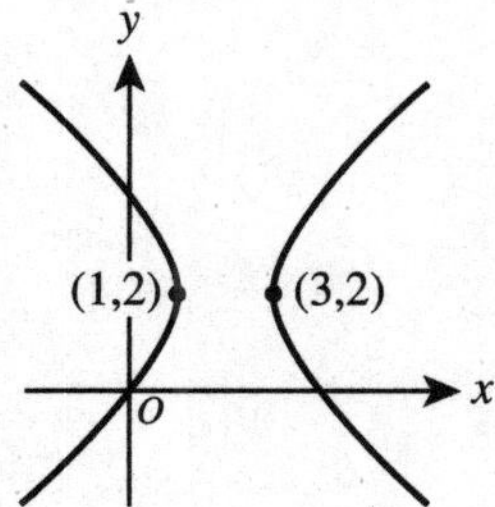

   F. $\dfrac{(x-2)^2}{1} - \dfrac{3(y-2)^2}{4} = 1$

   G. $\dfrac{(x+2)^2}{1} - \dfrac{3(y+2)^2}{4} = 1$

   H. $\dfrac{(x-2)^2}{1} + \dfrac{3(y-2)^2}{4} = 1$

   J. $\dfrac{(x+2)^2}{1} + \dfrac{3(y+2)^2}{4} = 1$

GO ON TO THE NEXT PAGE.

2 △ △ △ △ △ △ △ △ △ **2**

41. As shown, Alli walked her dog 250 feet due east from the entrance of a dog park to a trash can and then walked 700 feet in a straight line 25° north of east to a bench. Which of the following expressions is equal to the distance, in feet, between the entrance and the bench?

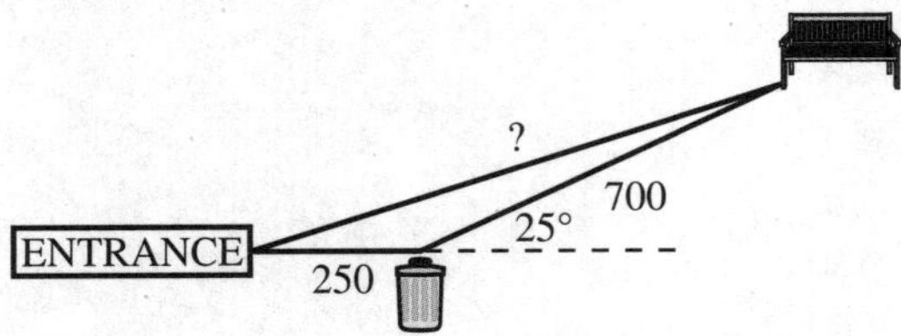

A. $\dfrac{250}{\cos 25°} + 700$

B. $\dfrac{250}{\sin 155°} + 700$

C. $\sqrt{700^2 + 250^2 - 2(700)(250)\cos 25°}$

D. $\sqrt{700^2 + 250^2 - 2(700)(250)\cos 155°}$

42. Kenji and Mary are members of a school committee that will be meeting this afternoon. The 6 members of the committee will be seated randomly around a circular table. What is the probability that Kenji and Mary will **not** sit next to each other at the meeting?

F. $\dfrac{1}{5}$

G. $\dfrac{1}{3}$

H. $\dfrac{3}{5}$

J. $\dfrac{4}{5}$

43. The digit in the ones place of 2^{88} is 6. What is the digit in the ones place of 2^{90}?

A. 2
B. 4
C. 6
D. 8

GO ON TO THE NEXT PAGE.

2 △ △ △ △ △ △ △ △ △ 2

44. Which of the following expressions represents the area, in square coordinate units, of $\triangle RST$ shown in the standard (x,y) coordinate plane?

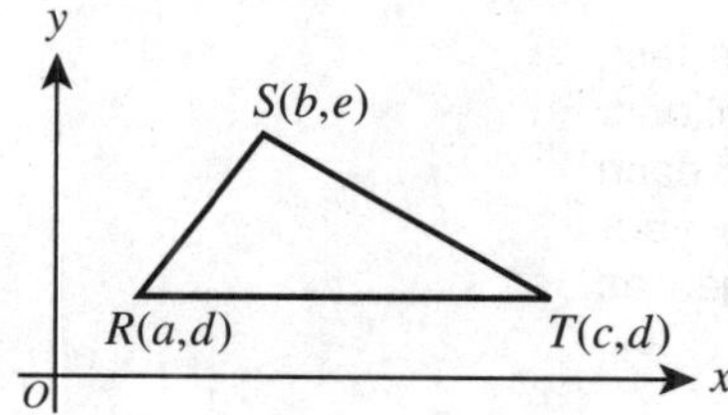

F. $\frac{1}{2}(c-a)(e-d)$

G. $\frac{1}{2}e(c-a)$

H. $\frac{1}{2}\left((e-d)^2+(b-a)^2\right)\left((e-d)^2+(b-c)^2\right)$

J. $\frac{1}{2}\left(\sqrt{(e-d)^2+(b-a)^2}\right)\left(\sqrt{(e-d)^2+(b-c)^2}\right)$

45. In the complex numbers, where $i^2=-1$, what complex number x is a solution to the equation $x(2+3i)=1$?

A. $\frac{2}{13}-\frac{3}{13}i$

B. $\frac{2}{5}+\frac{3}{5}i$

C. 1

D. -1

END OF TEST 2

STOP! DO NOT TURN THE PAGE UNTIL TOLD TO DO SO.

DO NOT RETURN TO THE PREVIOUS TEST.

3

3

READING TEST

40 Minutes—36 Questions

DIRECTIONS: There are several passages in this test. Each passage is accompanied by several questions. After reading a passage, choose the best answer to each question and fill in the corresponding oval on your answer document. You may refer to the passages as often as necessary.

Passage I

LITERARY NARRATIVE: This passage is adapted from the novel *Love Marriage* by V. V. Ganeshananthan (©2008 by Vasugi Ganeshananthan).

He met her, my mother, in New York City, and the Heart said plaintively: *Thump thump thump.* That was not the sound of illness. Theirs was an auspicious meet-ing, although no one had troubled to check the align-
5 ment of the stars; the young woman was twenty-seven—old for a prospective bride?—but she did not look it. She had a generous face, he said to himself.

He liked her glossy sheaf of dark hair, her sparse
10 brows, her pronounced chin, her full lower lip. She smiled with her mouth closed because she did not like her teeth. He could already see within the structure of her face how she would become thinner, that her bones would give her older face a certain elegance, a chiseled
15 and austere severity. He liked her precision in even the smallest of tasks, like arranging hibiscus in a vase. Her reserve, her inability to say anything truly personal in public. He thought she might be full of secrets and wanted to know them. She never raised her voice, but
20 she did not speak softly. *How are you? That's a beauti-ful sari. How are the children? I like this rice.* She liked her food steaming and spicy, as he did. She made her own clothes, staying up late into the night, her foot on the pedal of a sewing machine that had belonged to her
25 mother and had crossed the ocean with her. Her hem-lines suited both the times and her young pale slimness, which reminded him of a flowering tree by his home in Jaffna. He never caught her admitting she was wrong; her words clambered around that impossibility, but so
30 sheepishly that he found it endearing. In a noisy room he learned to tell the clear bell sound of her bangles apart from the rest.

Suddenly, he was no longer thinking about widows or about repeating his own father's collapse. It was as
35 though an invisible conductor was directing the pulling of strings to draw them together. Whether it was Murali who managed to get introduced to Vani or the other way around, no one else really remembers. And they will never admit which one of them was responsible.
40 And yet, it was this simple: a friend of his noticed that they were staying near each other. Perhaps Murali could give Vani a ride home? Yes, yes, two heads

nodded. They left the party they were at too quickly to say all their good-byes. After the door closed behind
45 them the space where they had been was filled with the laughter of friends.

He took her home. She boarded with a family in Brooklyn. During the car ride they were silent. It was a strange and comfortable silence for two people who had
50 waited for so long to be alone. The thrum of the motor was loud because the car was old. When they turned around the corner he pulled over and turned the engine off and there was a quiet as loud as the motor had been. He walked her to her door and she thanked him. She did
55 not ask him in for a cup of coffee; it was not her house. But it was out of his way and both of them knew it. She forgot that she did not like her teeth and bared them at him. Her smile, for once, was not self-conscious. She watched him drive away, waving from the window.

60 The Sri Lankan elders of New York City were all too eager to play parents to the couple. She was Proper: smart and polite and a good cook and lovely. Vani had a job, and more important than any of these things, she had grace, which was something that could not be
65 taught. Murali, of course, was the Beloved Parentless Boy; their favorite bachelor-doctor whom they took into their homes and bosoms and tried to smother with welcome and curry. Occasions were arranged; even the very rooms seemed to conspire to make the two end up
70 next to each other. And then one day something was suggested by one of those elders. And somehow the pair of them were *talking* about it. To each other. Directly.

Which was a faux pas. But neither of them minded.

75 Oceans away, families exploded. True to form, his family's discord faded quickly. But her family almost did not consent: afraid of the Improper, they questioned his intentions, his failure to observe certain formalities, his ancestry, his habits and his character. He heard
80 about what they had said and turned to her, his eyes full of questions.

They may not know these things about you, she said, but I do.

Are you sure? he asked her. The unsaid: they may
85 not forgive you for this.

GO ON TO THE NEXT PAGE.

3

3

Positive, she answered. Countries away, Vani's brother crashed into Murali's brother's house, yelling: *Who* is this doctor who wants to marry my *sister*? *Who* is this doctor who is *in love with my sister*?

90   The nerve of Murali, they thought. In Love? These were not words they were used to saying.

1. The third paragraph (lines 33–46) marks a shift from the second paragraph's focus on Murali's impressions of Vani to the rest of the passage's focus on:

A. Murali's life as a married man.
B. Murali's concerns about marriage.
C. Murali and Vani's courtship and its effects on others.
D. Murali's characteristics and his family conflicts.

2. Details in the second paragraph (lines 9–32) primarily characterize Vani as:

F. reserved but self-assured.
G. severe and impolite.
H. intelligent and apologetic.
J. beautiful but unkempt.

3. Which of the following events mentioned in the passage occurred first chronologically?

A. The elders organized occasions during which Vani and Murali would be together.
B. A friend suggested that Murali drive Vani home.
C. Vani smiled at Murali without thinking about her teeth.
D. Vani's brother burst into Murali's brother's home.

4. As it is presented in the passage, the italicized portion "*How are you? That's a beautiful sari. How are the children? I like this rice*" (lines 20–21) most likely indicates:

F. the types of pleasantries Murali prepares in his head before meeting someone new.
G. parts of a conversation between Murali and Vani when they were first introduced.
H. comments typical of the kind that Vani makes in public.
J. secret thoughts that Murali imagines Vani to be thinking.

5. According to the passage, one similarity between Murali and Vani is that both:

A. enjoy eating spicy food.
B. were born in New York City.
C. have a passion for cooking.
D. work at a medical clinic.

6. In the context of the passage, the statement "And they will never admit which one of them was responsible" (lines 38–39) most strongly suggests that:

F. neither Murali nor Vani remembers who first sought to be introduced to the other.
G. both Murali and Vani refuse to confess to initiating their introduction to each other.
H. Murali initiated contact with Vani, though he would stubbornly deny that he did so.
J. each of Murali and Vani's friends claims to have been the one who introduced them.

7. In the passage, the narrator makes clear that Vani didn't ask Murali in for coffee because Vani:

A. felt extremely self-conscious in Murali's presence.
B. did not want to invite Murali into someone else's house.
C. assumed that Murali wanted to get home at a reasonable hour.
D. did not want to further burden Murali with her requests.

8. The passage indicates that the description of Vani in lines 61–65 most closely reflects the perspective of:

F. Murali.
G. Vani's family in Sri Lanka.
H. Murali's friends in New York City.
J. the Sri Lankan elders in New York City.

9. As it is used in line 78, the word *observe* most nearly means:

A. study.
B. follow.
C. express.
D. perceive.

GO ON TO THE NEXT PAGE.

3   3

Passage II

INFORMATIONAL: Passage A is adapted from the article "Our Vanishing Night" by Verlyn Klinkenborg (©2008 by National Geographic Society, Inc.). Passage B is adapted from the book *The End of Night: Searching for Natural Darkness in an Age of Artificial Light* by Paul Bogard (©2013 by Paul Bogard).

Passage A by Verlyn Klinkenborg

For most of human history, the phrase "light pollution" would have made no sense. Imagine walking toward London on a moonlit night around 1800, when it was Earth's most populous city. Nearly a million
5 people lived there, making do, as they always had, with candles and rushlights and torches and lanterns. Only a few houses were lit by gas, and there would be no public gaslights in the streets or squares for another seven years. From a few miles away, you would have
10 been as likely to *smell* London as to see its dim collective glow.

Now most of humanity lives under intersecting domes of reflected, refracted light, of scattering rays from overlit cities and suburbs, from light-flooded
15 highways and factories. Nearly all of nighttime Europe is a nebula of light, as is most of the United States and all of Japan. In the south Atlantic the glow from a single fishing fleet—squid fishermen luring their prey with metal halide lamps—can be seen from space, burn
20 ing brighter, in fact, than Buenos Aires or Rio de Janeiro.

In most cities the sky looks as though it has been emptied of stars, leaving behind a vacant haze that mirrors our fear of the dark. We've grown so used to this
25 pervasive orange haze that the original glory of an unlit night—dark enough for the planet Venus to throw shadows on Earth—is wholly beyond our experience. And yet above the city's pale ceiling lies the rest of the universe, utterly undiminished by the light we waste—a
30 bright shoal of stars and planets and galaxies, shining in seemingly infinite darkness.

We've lit up the night as if it were an unoccupied country, when nothing could be further from the truth. Among mammals alone, the number of nocturnal spe
35 cies is astonishing. Light is a powerful biological force, and on many species it acts as a magnet, a process being studied by researchers such as Travis Longcore and Catherine Rich. The effect is so powerful that scientists speak of songbirds and seabirds being "cap
40 tured" by searchlights on land or by the light from gas flares on marine oil platforms, circling and circling in the thousands.

Passage B by Paul Bogard

Unless Vincent Van Gogh's *The Starry Night* from 1889 is traveling as part of an exhibition, it hangs at
45 home on its wall at the Museum of Modern Art (MoMA) in Manhattan as fifty million people pass by every year. On a Saturday morning I stand near Van Gogh's scene of stars and moon and sleeping town,

talking with its guardian for the day, Joseph, as he
50 repeats, "No flash, no flash," "Two feet away," and "Too close, too close" again and again as people from around the world crowd near. "What's the appeal of this painting?" I ask. "It's beautiful," he says. "What more can you say than that?"

55 You could rightly leave it at that. But I love the story this painting tells, of a small dark town, a few yellow-orange gaslights in house windows, under a giant swirling and waving blue-green sky. This is a painting of our world from before night had been
60 pushed back to the forest and the seas, from back when sleepy towns slept without streetlights. People are too quick, I think, to imagine the story of this painting— and especially this sky—is simply that of "a werewolf of energy," as Joachim Pissarro, curator at the MoMA
65 exhibition Van Gogh and the Colors of the Night, would tell me. While Van Gogh certainly had his troubles, this painting looks as it does in part because it's of a time that no longer exists, a time when the night sky would have looked a lot more like this. Does Van Gogh
70 use his imagination? Of course, but this is an imagined sky inspired by a real sky of a kind few of the fifty million MoMA visitors have ever seen. It's an imagined sky inspired by the real sky over a town much darker than the towns we live in today. So a painting of a night
75 imagined? Sure. But unreal?

In our age, yes. But Van Gogh lived in a time before electric light. In a letter from the summer of 1888, he described what he'd seen while walking a southern French beach:

80 The deep blue sky was flecked with clouds of a
   blue deeper than the fundamental blue of
   intense cobalt, and others of a clearer blue, like
   the blue whiteness of the Milky Way. In the
   blue depth the stars were sparkling, greenish,
85 yellow, white, pink, more brilliant, more sparkling gemlike than at home—even in Paris:
   opals you might call them, emeralds, lapis
   lazuli, rubies, sapphires.

It's remarkable to modern eyes, first of all, that
90 Van Gogh would reference the stars over Paris—no one has seen a sky remotely close to this over Paris for at least fifty years. But stars of different colors? It's true.

10. The main idea of the first paragraph of Passage A is that:

   F. before electricity, it was difficult to travel to London at night.
   G. light pollution is a relatively recent phenomenon in human history.
   H. gas lighting existed long before it was widely used.
   J. because of its large population, London has had light pollution for centuries.

GO ON TO THE NEXT PAGE.

3   3

11. In the third paragraph of Passage A (lines 22–31), the author makes a contrast between the:

- **A.** hazy night sky over cities today and the bright stars and planets that exist above it.
- **B.** gray night sky over cities and the various colors of the stars.
- **C.** brightness of the planet Venus on an unlit night and the comparative dimness of the stars.
- **D.** appreciation that people once had for stars and the apathy that is pervasive today.

12. It can reasonably be inferred from Passage A that an animal "captured" by light is most nearly one that:

- **F.** has lost the ability to search for food in dark areas.
- **G.** is irresistibly drawn to artificial light at night.
- **H.** is confined to limited dark areas at night.
- **J.** has lost its natural habitat to urban expansion.

13. Compared to what Joseph appreciates about *The Starry Night*, the author of Passage B is more appreciative of the:

- **A.** painting's vivid colors.
- **B.** story the painting tells.
- **C.** beauty of the painting.
- **D.** technique used in the painting.

14. Based on Passage B, which of the following statements best summarizes the passage author's point about Van Gogh's use of imagination while painting *The Starry Night*?

- **F.** Van Gogh had to rely heavily on his imagination because he usually painted during the daytime.
- **G.** Van Gogh's work is almost entirely imagined because the painting's stars have colors that are unlike actual stars.
- **H.** Van Gogh used his imagination in part, but his painting was also inspired by the real night sky he observed.
- **J.** Van Gogh barely used his imagination at all; he tried to depict the vivid night sky exactly as it was.

15. As it is used in line 91, the phrase *remotely close to* most nearly means:

- **A.** exactly similar to.
- **B.** anything like.
- **C.** anywhere nearby.
- **D.** somewhat adjacent to.

16. Which of the following statements best captures the main difference in the information presented in the two passages?

- **F.** Passage A summarizes the process by which light at night became common, whereas Passage B explores one person's reaction to Van Gogh's *The Starry Night*.
- **G.** Passage A offers suggestions for restoring darkness to today's night, whereas Passage B compares the night skies of several Van Gogh paintings.
- **H.** Passage A discusses the problems of today's bright night sky, whereas Passage B explains how people in Van Gogh's time used light at night.
- **J.** Passage A gives an overview of the issue of light at night, whereas Passage B examines the matter of light at night through a discussion of Van Gogh's *The Starry Night*.

17. One similarity between the passages is that, in order to make a point about light at night, both authors discuss:

- **A.** how dark large cities once were.
- **B.** the opinions of scientific researchers.
- **C.** well-known works of art.
- **D.** personal memories of when night was darker.

18. Compared to Passage B, Passage A offers more information about the:

- **F.** effects lighting up the night sky can have on animals.
- **G.** colorful appearance stars had prior to electric lights.
- **H.** interaction between nature and the imagination.
- **J.** places where night's original darkness remains.

GO ON TO THE NEXT PAGE.

3   3

Passage III

INFORMATIONAL: This passage is adapted from the essay "On Places, Photographs, and Memory" by Chris Engman (©2012 by Chris Engman).

Recently I visited a place that I knew intimately in childhood, a waterfall with cliffs on both sides and a pool of cold water below. We used to jump from those cliffs despite our parents' concerns. I loved this place,
5 and revisiting it I am amazed by all that I can remember. Bends in trails, sap stains on bark, crooks in branches, the intricate web of root structures—all are startlingly unchanged and I remember them precisely. A small tree is in the middle of the trail. I put my hand
10 on it for support and drops of moisture fall on my back from above, and I realize: I have done this before. Standing on a rock ledge getting ready to jump, I reach for a handhold so I can lean over the edge and prepare myself for what I am about to do. The shape of the rock
15 where my hand touches it is known to me: I have performed this ritual.

Places hold memories better than people and better than photographs. Family, or people from our past who may remind us of events in our lives and with whom we
20 may reminisce, are themselves constantly changing, as is their version of events. Conversations with others about shared experiences of the past can seem to augment memory but quite often they operate in the opposite way: they alter or even replace our own
25 memories with those of another. Whatever the event, one's memory of it is inevitably altered through conversation.

Photographs act on us in a similar fashion. Whatever their apparent precision or correctness, photo-
30 graphs inaccurately reflect experience from the start. They convert the three dimensions of space into two and eliminate the third spatial dimension and time. Also sacrificed are smell, touch, sound, and context. In a word, a photograph is an abstraction of experience. Yet
35 we take them compulsively. We fill scrapbooks and hard drives with family outings, vacations, and ballgames in the hope of freezing time, making experience tangible for future reference, preserving memory. I do it, too. But it is well to realize that photographs do not
40 preserve memory, they replace memory. Just as photographs are an abstraction of experience, they are even more so an abstraction of memory—a dangerously compelling abstraction. Memories are fragile and impressionable. They cannot hold up against the
45 seemingly irrefutable factuality of a photograph. It isn't that what is in a photograph is false: a photograph's version of events did happen, what is in a picture did indeed pass before the lens. The problem is that photographs only tell such a small part of any story. And
50 while they may be technically correct, nonetheless they deceive. Does a smile in a photograph mean that a person is happy? Was the fish I caught really bigger than my uncle's, or did I cleverly, intentionally hold mine closer to the lens? Photographs deceive in another
55 respect. Whatever the event one wishes to preserve, snapshots are most commonly a break from that event.

The moment that a photograph is taken is experienced as a moment taking a photograph, not as a moment engaged in the activity implied by the resulting image.
60 Time taken to make photographs is time subtracted from the experience of the thing being photographed. What photographs most accurately record, ultimately, is nothing more than the act of photography, itself.

To be sure, photographs can form a record of our
65 lives that has value. But as image-makers and consumers, which all of us are these days, there is also value to be had in a recognition of the limits of photography to the facility of memory—in an understanding of what images can and cannot offer us in this regard. Moreover
70 it is precisely the deceitfulness of photography as it pertains to memory that gives the medium its unique platform to address the nature of memory itself: its malleability, its unreliability, its elusiveness. It seems to me that no conversation or photograph can make
75 memory so vivid or recognizable, so physically palpable, as the return to a place.

19. The passage as a whole can best be described as:
    A. a summary of a childhood incident followed by reflections on how the memory of that incident has changed.
    B. a description of an experience followed by consideration of a topic raised by that experience.
    C. an account of the author's lifelong interest in a hobby.
    D. an explanation of why the author's opinions on a topic have changed.

20. Which of the following statements best represents the passage's central claim?
    F. The accuracy of most memories is improved by viewing photographs related to the memories.
    G. Revisiting a place evokes clearer and more accurate memories than conversations or photographs.
    H. The truth represented by a photograph is only as accurate as your memory of the event in the photograph.
    J. Memories are sustained over time only through a combination of conversations, photographs, and visits to places.

21. The author's tone when recounting his visit to the waterfall can best be described as:
    A. joking.
    B. gloomy.
    C. pleading.
    D. reverent.

GO ON TO THE NEXT PAGE.

3   **3**

22. The main idea of the second paragraph (lines 17–27) is
that:

   F. over time, some memories fade.
   G. frequently, reminiscing with other people changes
one's memories.
   H. reminiscing with other people helps preserve one's
memories.
   J. family members better evoke one's memories than
nonfamily members.

23. When the author states "What photographs most accurately record, ultimately, is nothing more than the act
of photography, itself" (lines 62–63), he most nearly
means that:

   A. the quality of a photograph reflects the skill of the
photographer.
   B. when viewing a photograph, people forget that the
photographer is an unseen participant in the scene.
   C. photographs by nature are records of brief
moments.
   D. photographs tend to depict people stopping an
activity and posing for the photographer.

24. It can most reasonably be inferred that immediately
after the events described in the first paragraph, the
author:

   F. hikes back down the cliffs.
   G. sits on the rock ledge.
   H. jumps into the water below.
   J. takes a photograph of the scene.

25. Which of the following details does the author use to
support his claim that photographs don't accurately
reflect experiences?

   A. Photographs are usually only taken by adults.
   B. People take photographs without considering the
best way to photograph an event.
   C. Photographs don't record the passage of time.
   D. The human eye can discern more detail than a pho-
tograph can capture.

26. The phrase "seemingly irrefutable factuality" (line 45)
mainly serves to emphasize that photographs:

   F. convey an impression of objective truth.
   G. help clarify the events being photographed.
   H. record details that can't be proven.
   J. imply a story beyond what they actually depict.

27. As it is used in line 72, the word *nature* most nearly
means:

   A. temperament.
   B. essence.
   C. scenery.
   D. environment.

GO ON TO THE NEXT PAGE.

3   **3**

Passage IV

INFORMATIONAL: This passage is adapted from the article "Reinventing the Leaf" by Antonio Regalado (©2010 by Scientific American, a division of Nature America, Inc.).

Nathan S. Lewis has been giving a lecture on the energy crisis that is both terrifying and exhilarating. To avoid potentially debilitating global warming, the chemist says civilization must be able to generate more

5 than 10 trillion watts of clean, carbon-free energy by 2050. That level is three times the U.S.'s average energy demand of 3.2 trillion watts.

Before Lewis's crowds get too depressed, he tells them there is one source of salvation: the sun pours

10 more energy onto the earth every hour than humankind uses in a year. But to be saved, humankind needs a radical breakthrough in solar-fuel technology: artificial leaves that will capture solar rays and churn out chemical fuel on the spot, much as plants do. We can burn the

15 fuel, as we do oil or natural gas, to power cars, create heat or generate electricity, and we can store the fuel for use when the sun is down.

Lewis's lab is one of several that are crafting prototype leaves, not much larger than computer chips,

20 designed to produce hydrogen fuel from water, rather than the glucose fuel that natural leaves create. Unlike fossil fuels, hydrogen burns clean. Other researchers are working on competing ideas for capturing the sun's energy, such as algae that has been genetically altered

25 to pump out biofuels, or on new biological organisms engineered to excrete oil. All these approaches are intended to turn sunlight into chemical energy that can be stored, shipped and easily consumed. Lewis argues, however, that the man-made leaf option is the most

30 likely to scale up to the industrial levels needed to power civilization.

Although a few lab prototypes have produced small amounts of direct solar fuel—or electrofuel, as the chemicals are sometimes called—the technology

35 has to be improved so the fuel can be manufactured on a massive scale, very inexpensively. To power the U.S., Lewis estimates the country would need to manufacture thin, flexible solar-fuel films, instead of discrete chiplike devices, that roll off high-speed production lines

40 the way newsprint does. The films would have to be as cheap as wall-to-wall carpeting and eventually cover an area the size of South Carolina.

Far from being a wild dream, direct solar-fuel technology has been advancing in fits and starts ever

45 since President Jimmy Carter's push for alternative energy sources during the 1970s oil shocks. Now, with a new energy and climate crunch looming, solar fuel is suddenly gaining attention.

In photosynthesis, green leaves use the energy in

50 sunlight to rearrange the chemical bonds of water and carbon dioxide, producing and storing fuel in the form of sugars. "We want to make something as close to a leaf as possible," Lewis says, meaning devices that

work as simply, albeit producing a different chemical

55 output. The artificial leaf Lewis is designing requires two principal elements: a collector that converts solar energy (photons) into electrical energy (electrons) and an electrolyzer that uses the electron energy to split water into oxygen and hydrogen. A catalyst—a chemi-

60 cal or metal—is added to help achieve the splitting. Existing photovoltaic cells already create electricity from sunlight, and electrolyzers are used in various commercial processes, so the trick is marrying the two into cheap, efficient solar films.

65 Bulky prototypes have been developed just to demonstrate how the marriage would work. Engineers at a Japanese automaker, for example, have built a box that stands taller than a refrigerator and is covered with photovoltaic cells. An electrolyzer, inside, uses the

70 solar electricity to break water molecules. The box releases the resulting oxygen to the ambient air and compresses and stores the remaining hydrogen, which the automaker would like to use to recharge fuel-cell cars.

75 In principle, the scheme could solve global warming: only sunlight and water are needed to create energy, the by-product is oxygen, and the exhaust from burning the hydrogen later in a fuel cell is water. The problem is that commercial solar cells contain expen-

80 sive silicon crystals. And electrolyzers are packed with platinum, to date the best material for catalyzing the water-splitting reaction, but it costs $1,500 an ounce.

Lewis calculates that to meet global energy demand, future solar-fuel devices would have to cost

85 less than $1 per square foot of sun-collecting surface and be able to convert 10 percent of that light energy into chemical fuel. Fundamentally new, massively scalable technology such as films or carpets made from inexpensive materials are needed.

28. The main function of the seventh and eighth paragraphs (lines 65–82) is to:

F. suggest that solar technology has advanced but still faces problems that prevent it from being a viable power source on a large scale.

G. introduce the information that under specific laboratory conditions electrolyzers can be used to release energy from water molecules.

H. establish that the United States and Japan are collaborating on research efforts regarding new energy sources.

J. question whether the auto industry will be a leader in the race to develop new sources of energy.

GO ON TO THE NEXT PAGE.

3   **3**

29. Based on the passage, whose opinion is it that there is a need for "more than 10 trillion watts of clean, carbon-free energy by 2050" (lines 4–6)?

   A. Researchers in South Carolina who are developing a form of artificial algae
   B. An unidentified chemist whom Lewis challenges in his lectures
   C. Lewis, as expressed in lectures he gives on the subject of world energy needs
   D. The author before attending a lecture by Lewis that changed the author's mind

30. Based on the passage, what is the relationship between the "radical breakthrough" referred to in line 12 and the capabilities described in lines 14–17?

   F. The breakthrough has been made based on the capabilities.
   G. The breakthrough will make the capabilities possible.
   H. Both were made possible as a result of Lewis's work in his lab.
   J. Both serve as examples for Lewis of the energy industry's misguided focus on consumption.

31. According to the passage, one challenge facing Lewis in developing his energy solution is the:

   A. high price of the silicon crystals and platinum that are integral to the process.
   B. lack of technology to split water into hydrogen and oxygen.
   C. diminishing availability of federal funding for his research.
   D. public's reluctance to embrace new technology.

32. According to Lewis, compared to the amount of energy the sun pours onto the earth in one hour, what amount of energy does humankind use in one year?

   F. A smaller amount
   G. The same amount
   H. Twice the amount
   J. Ten times the amount

33. As it is used in line 25, the phrase *pump out* most nearly means:

   A. remove.
   B. drain.
   C. produce.
   D. siphon.

34. According to the passage, what physical form does Lewis imagine his artificial leaves will ideally take?

   F. Chiplike devices
   G. Thin, flexible films
   H. Rigid miniature solar panels
   J. Refrigerated photovoltaic cells

35. The passage states that the two principal elements of Lewis's artificial leaf technology are:

   A. a fuel cell and ambient air.
   B. solar electricity and a catalyst.
   C. platinum and silicon.
   D. a collector and an electrolyzer.

36. According to the passage, what is one outcome of the process of burning hydrogen in a fuel cell?

   F. The electron energy splits silicon crystals.
   G. The hydrogen bonds with oxygen.
   H. The fuel cell's lining deteriorates.
   J. The exhaust produced is water.

END OF TEST 3

STOP! DO NOT TURN THE PAGE UNTIL TOLD TO DO SO.

DO NOT RETURN TO A PREVIOUS TEST.

4 ○ ○ ○ ○ ○ ○ ○ ○ ○ 4

SCIENCE TEST

40 Minutes—40 Questions

DIRECTIONS: There are several passages in this test. Each passage is followed by several questions. After reading a passage, choose the best answer to each question and fill in the corresponding oval on your answer document. You may refer to the passages as often as necessary.

You are **not** permitted to use a calculator on this test.

Passage I

The *molar volume* of a gas is the volume occupied by 1 mole (mol; 6×10^{23} atoms or molecules) of that gas at a given pressure and temperature.

Table 1 shows how the molar volume, in L, of each of 6 gases—helium (He), neon (Ne), argon (Ar), hydrogen (H_2), nitrogen (N_2), and oxygen (O_2)—varies with pressure, in atmospheres (atm), at a temperature of 273 kelvins (K).

Table 2 shows how the molar volume of each of the 6 gases varies with temperature at a pressure of 1.00 atm.

	Table 1					
Pressure (atm)	Molar volume (L) at 273 K of:					
	He	Ne	Ar	H_2	N_2	O_2
0.500	44.825	44.810	44.774	44.818	44.781	44.773
1.00	22.424	22.409	22.374	22.417	22.380	22.372
5.00	4.503	4.488	4.453	4.496	4.459	4.451
10.0	2.262	2.248	2.213	2.256	2.219	2.211
50.0	0.471	0.456	0.421	0.465	0.430	0.420
100.0	0.247	0.233	0.200	0.242	0.210	0.198

	Table 2					
Temperature (K)	Molar volume (L) at 1.00 atm of:					
	He	Ne	Ar	H_2	N_2	O_2
223	18.321	18.304	18.257	18.312	18.263	18.256
323	26.504	26.513	26.486	26.521	26.492	26.485
373	30.670	30.617	30.595	30.625	30.601	30.594
573	47.041	47.031	47.022	47.040	47.028	47.021
773	63.453	63.443	63.440	63.452	63.446	63.440

GO ON TO THE NEXT PAGE.

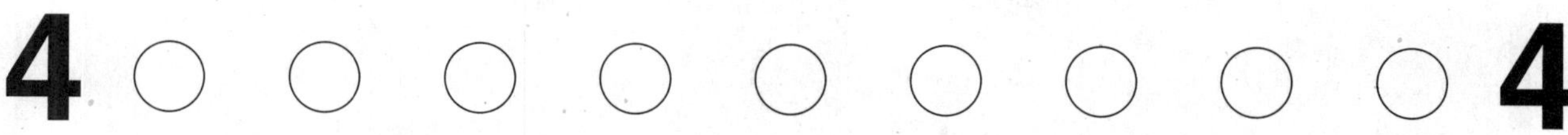

4 ◯ ◯ ◯ ◯ ◯ ◯ ◯ ◯ ◯ 4

1. Based on Table 1, for H_2 at 273 K, the absolute value of the difference between the molar volume at 5.00 atm and the molar volume at 10.0 atm is approximately:

   A. 1.8 L.
   B. 2.2 L.
   C. 4.0 L.
   D. 5.0 L.

2. Consider the molar volumes of He, Ar, H_2, and N_2 listed in Table 2 at 323 K. What is the order of these gases from the gas having the smallest molar volume to the gas having the largest molar volume?

   F. Ar, He, N_2, H_2
   G. Ar, N_2, He, H_2
   H. H_2, He, N_2, Ar
   J. H_2, N_2, He, Ar

3. An ideal gas has a molar volume of 63.429 L at 1.00 atm and 773 K. At 1.00 atm and 773 K, how many of the gases listed in Table 2 have a *smaller* molar volume than that of an ideal gas?

   A. 0
   B. 2
   C. 4
   D. 6

4. In a gas sample, collisions between gas particles are common. The average time a gas particle spends between one collision and the next is called the mean free time. In general, mean free time decreases as a sample's volume decreases. Based on Table 1, the mean free time would be *least* for a 1 mol sample of which gas at which pressure?

   F. He at 0.500 atm
   G. O_2 at 0.500 atm
   H. He at 100.0 atm
   J. O_2 at 100.0 atm

5. Consider 2 separate 1 mol samples of O_2, each at a pressure of 1 atm. One sample has a volume of about 18 L, and the other has a volume of about 63 L. Based on Table 2, the average kinetic energy of the O_2 molecules is more likely greater in which sample?

   A. The 18 L sample, because it's at the lower temperature.
   B. The 18 L sample, because it's at the higher temperature.
   C. The 63 L sample, because it's at the lower temperature.
   D. The 63 L sample, because it's at the higher temperature.

GO ON TO THE NEXT PAGE.

4 ◯ ◯ ◯ ◯ ◯ ◯ ◯ ◯ ◯ **4**

Passage II

Scientists conducted 3 experiments to study the transfer of bacteria from one surface to another by 2 species of flies: *Musca domestica* and *Sarcophaga carnaria*.

Experiment 1

A group of 10 *M. domestica* was tested using this procedure:

1. Each fly was placed in a separate enclosure containing *Escherichia coli* (a type of bacteria) and allowed to walk on the *E. coli* for 5 min.

2. Each fly was then immediately placed in a separate petri dish containing sterile nutrient agar. Five minutes later, the flies were removed from the dishes.

3. The dishes were incubated at 37°C for 24 hr so that each *E. coli* cell on the dish divided to form a separate colony, and then the number of *E. coli* colonies on each dish was counted.

4. The average number of colonies per dish was calculated.

This procedure was also used to test a group of 10 *S. carnaria*. The results are shown in Figure 1.

Figure 1

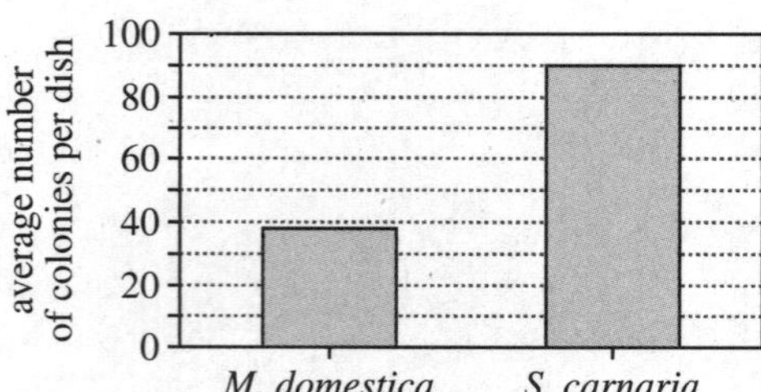

Experiment 2

The procedure from Experiment 1 was repeated with each of 3 groups of 10 *S. carnaria* except that the flies in each group were allowed to walk on the *E. coli* for a different period of time—5 min, 30 min, or 60 min—before each fly was placed in a separate petri dish containing nutrient agar. The results are shown in Figure 2.

Figure 2

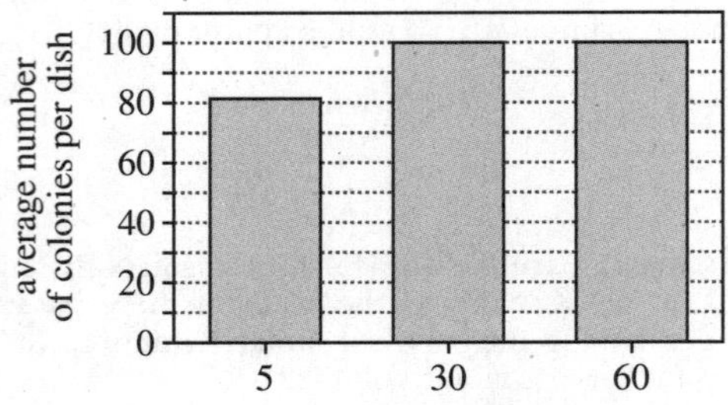

Experiment 3

The procedure from Experiment 1 was repeated with each of 3 groups of 10 *S. carnaria* except that, after Step 1, the flies in each group were allowed a different period of time—0 min, 30 min, or 60 min—to clean themselves before each fly was placed in a separate petri dish containing sterile nutrient agar. The results are shown in Figure 3.

Figure 3

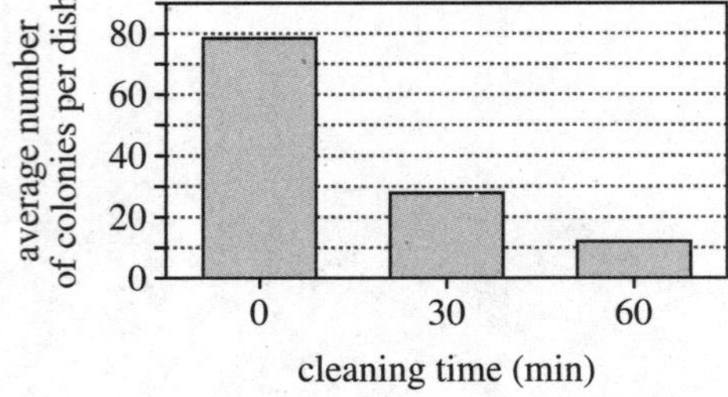

Figures adapted from Julie J. Shaffer, Kasey Jo Warner, and W. Wyatt Hoback, "Filthy Flies? Experiments to Test Flies as Vectors of Bacterial Disease." ©2007 by National Association of Biology Teachers.

6. As the amount of cleaning time increased, the average number of colonies per dish:

F. increased only.
G. decreased only.
H. increased and then decreased.
J. decreased and then increased.

GO ON TO THE NEXT PAGE.

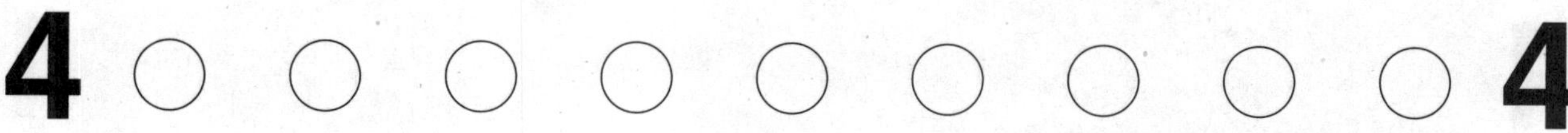

7. What was the total number of flies tested in Experiment 3?

A. 5
B. 10
C. 24
D. 30

8. A scientist claimed that some species of flies spread bacterial diseases. Are the results of Experiment 1 consistent with this claim?

F. Yes; based on Figure 1, the flies transferred bacteria from one surface to another.
G. Yes; based on Figure 1, *M. domestica* transferred bacteria to *S. carnaria*.
H. No; based on Figure 1, the flies did not transfer bacteria from one surface to another.
J. No; based on Figure 1, *M. domestica* did not transfer bacteria to *S. carnaria*.

9. In the experiments, why was it necessary for the nutrient agar in the petri dishes to be sterile until the flies were placed in the dishes?

A. To ensure that any colonies that formed came from bacteria present in the nutrient agar before the flies were placed in the dishes
B. To ensure that any colonies that formed came from bacteria transferred to the nutrient agar by the flies
C. To ensure that the nutrient agar contained all the nutrients necessary for the flies to reproduce
D. To ensure that the nutrient agar contained all the nutrients necessary for the bacteria to reproduce

10. A student claimed that Species X flies would transfer more *E. coli* cells to a petri dish containing nutrient agar than would either *M. domestica* or *S. carnaria*. Which of the following experiments would best test the student's claim?

F. Repeat Experiment 1 except include a group of 10 Species X flies.
G. Repeat Experiment 1 except with a different species of bacteria.
H. Repeat Experiment 2 except include a group of 10 Species X flies.
J. Repeat Experiment 2 except with a different species of bacteria.

11. Which of the following statements gives the most likely hypothesis for Experiment 3?

A. *S. carnaria* remove bacteria when they clean themselves.
B. The longer *S. carnaria* are exposed to bacteria, the more bacteria they transfer between surfaces.
C. *M. domestica* transfer more bacteria between surfaces than do *S. carnaria*.
D. *M. domestica* are better at removing bacteria during cleaning than are *S. carnaria*.

GO ON TO THE NEXT PAGE.

4 ○ ○ ○ ○ ○ ○ ○ ○ ○ **4**

Passage III

Forest fires require oxygen (O_2) to burn. Figure 1 shows the number of paleowildfires (large forest fires known from the rock record) for each 10-million-year interval of the Mesozoic era (250–65 million years ago, mya). Figure 1 also shows a model of the percent O_2 by volume (%O_2) in Earth's atmosphere from 250 mya to 70 mya.

Figure 1

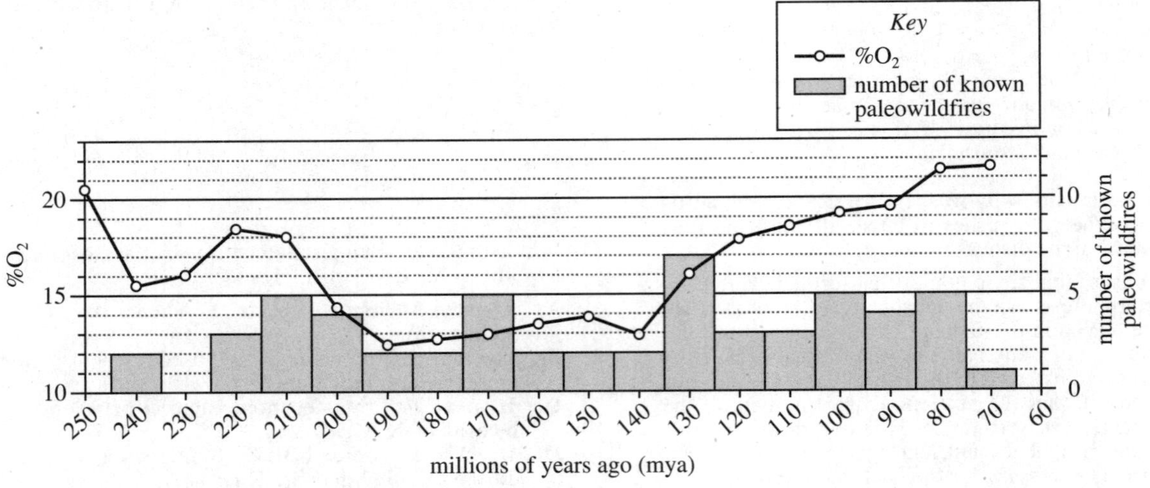

To study how %O_2 affects burning, scientists attempted to ignite 7 samples of each of 4 different materials, 1 sample at a time, in a chamber. For each set of samples of the same material, the initial %O_2 in the chamber ranged from 12% to 18%. Figure 2 shows, for each sample that ignited, the duration of the sample's flame.

Figure 2

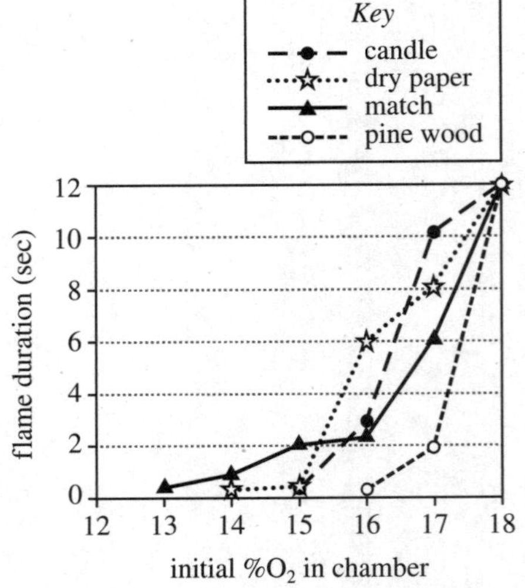

Note: At an initial %O_2 of 18, all samples burned to ash in 12 seconds.

GO ON TO THE NEXT PAGE.

4 ○ ○ ○ ○ ○ ○ ○ ○ 4

12. The $\%O_2$ in Earth's atmosphere today is about 21. Based on Figure 1, at which of the following times during the Mesozoic era was the $\%O_2$ in Earth's atmosphere closest to the $\%O_2$ in Earth's atmosphere today?

  F. 250 mya
  G. 200 mya
  H. 150 mya
  J. 100 mya

13. Based on Figure 2, at an initial $\%O_2$ of 17, approximately how many seconds greater was the flame duration for dry paper than the flame duration for pine wood?

  A. 2
  B. 4
  C. 6
  D. 8

14. A scientist claimed that paleowildfires could only have occurred when the $\%O_2$ was higher than 15. For which of the following time intervals during the Mesozoic era are the data in Figure 1 **inconsistent** with this claim?

  F. 250–230 mya
  G. 180–160 mya
  H. 120–100 mya
  J. 90–70 mya

15. Based on Figure 2, what is the order of the 4 materials tested, from the material that required the highest initial $\%O_2$ to ignite to the material that required the lowest initial $\%O_2$ to ignite?

  A. Match, pine wood, dry paper, candle
  B. Match, dry paper, pine wood, candle
  C. Pine wood, candle, dry paper, match
  D. Pine wood, dry paper, candle, match

16. Based on Figure 1, how many paleowildfires are known from the rock record between 95 mya and 85 mya?

  F. 4
  G. 9
  H. 14
  J. 19

GO ON TO THE NEXT PAGE.

4 ○ ○ ○ ○ ○ ○ ○ ○ **4**

Passage IV

The tensile strength of a paper towel (PT) is the force per unit width required to break the PT when it is clamped and stretched (see diagram).

diagram

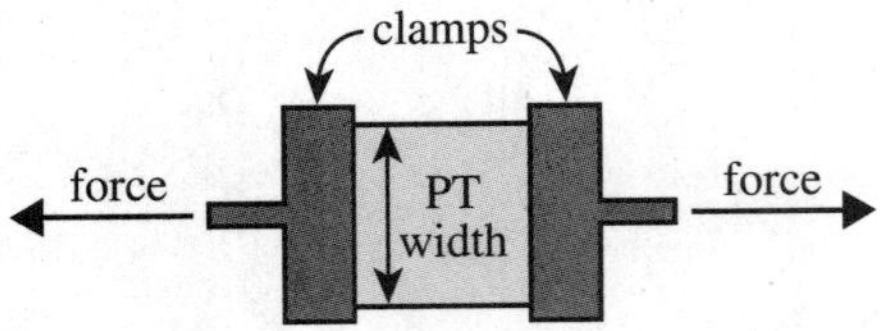

Dry strength is the tensile strength of a dry PT, and wet strength is the tensile strength of a PT that has been submerged in water. The wet strength can be increased by treating the PT with certain chemicals.

Students conducted 2 experiments to study the wet strengths of identical PTs, each 20 cm × 20 cm, treated with glutaraldehyde (GLA) or with GLA and zinc nitrate.

Experiment 1

First, the dry strengths of 5 PTs were measured, in newtons per meter (N/m), and the average of the measurements, D, was calculated. Then, Steps 1–5 were performed on each of 100 other PTs:

1. A PT was submerged for 30 sec in water (if the PT was to be a control) or in a test solution containing GLA.

2. The PT was dried on a hot plate at 85°C for 4 min.

3. The PT was heated in an oven for 3 min at a certain temperature—25°C for a control PT and 25°C, 110°C, 120°C, 130°C, or 140°C for a treated PT.

4. The PT was submerged in water for 10 min, 2 hr, or 24 hr.

5. The wet strength of the PT was measured in N/m.

The wet strengths of PTs that had been subjected to identical conditions were averaged. Each average wet strength, W, was divided by D and then multiplied by 100. The resulting $\frac{W}{D}$ values are shown in Figure 1.

Figure 1

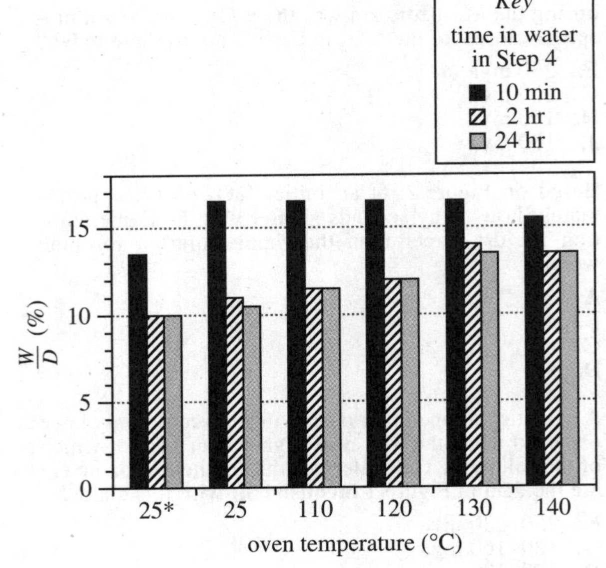

*controls

Experiment 2

Steps 1–5 were repeated with 100 other PTs, except that the test solution contained both GLA and zinc nitrate (see Figure 2).

Figure 2

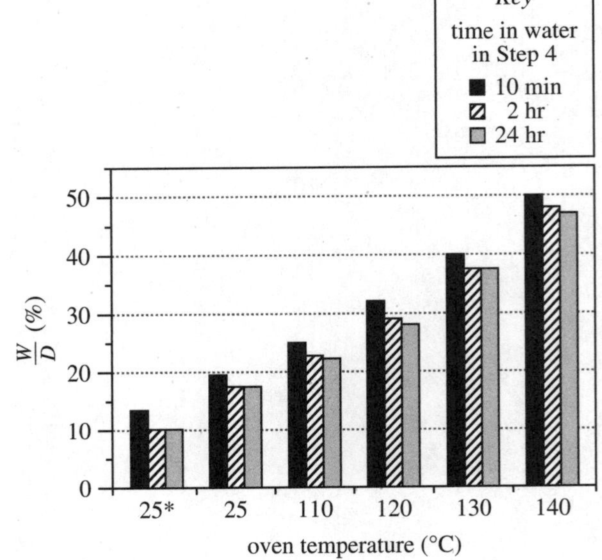

*controls

Figures 1 and 2 adapted from Gordon Guozhong Xu, Charles Qixiang Yang, and Yulin Deng, "Applications of Bifunctional Aldehydes to Improve Paper Wet Strength." ©2002 by John Wiley & Sons, Inc.

GO ON TO THE NEXT PAGE.

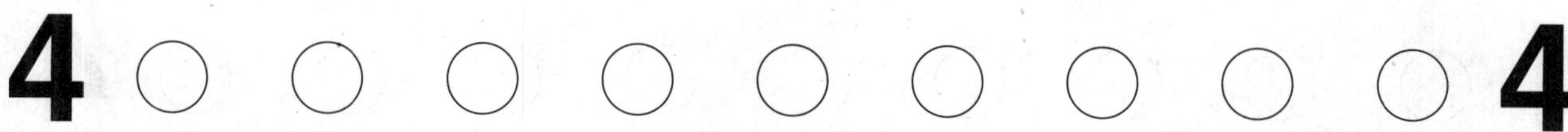

4 ○ ○ ○ ○ ○ ○ ○ ○ ○ **4**

17. In Experiment 2, for PTs that were submerged in water for 2 hr, as the oven temperature increased from 110°C through 140°C, the $\frac{W}{D}$ value:

   A. increased only.
   B. decreased only.
   C. remained the same.
   D. varied, but with no general trend.

18. In Step 1 of Experiment 1, the PTs that would become controls were submerged in what liquid, and in Step 3 of Experiment 1, these control PTs were heated in an oven at what temperature?

   F. Liquid: water
   Temperature: 25°C

   G. Liquid: water
   Temperature: 85°C

   H. Liquid: GLA solution
   Temperature: 25°C

   J. Liquid: GLA solution
   Temperature: 85°C

19. In which of Experiments 1 and 2, if either, did the students measure the wet strengths of PTs that had been submerged in water for a total of 18 hr?

   A. Experiment 1 only
   B. Experiment 2 only
   C. Both Experiment 1 and Experiment 2
   D. Neither Experiment 1 nor Experiment 2

20. Which of the following statements comparing the $\frac{W}{D}$ value of the PTs that were submerged in water for 2 hr with the $\frac{W}{D}$ value of the PTs that were submerged in water for 10 min is supported by the results of Experiment 1?

   F. For all the oven temperatures, the $\frac{W}{D}$ value at 2 hr was greater than the $\frac{W}{D}$ value at 10 min.
   G. For all the oven temperatures, the $\frac{W}{D}$ value at 2 hr was less than the $\frac{W}{D}$ value at 10 min.
   H. For all the oven temperatures, the $\frac{W}{D}$ value at 2 hr was the same as the $\frac{W}{D}$ value at 10 min.
   J. For some of the oven temperatures, the $\frac{W}{D}$ value at 2 hr was greater than the $\frac{W}{D}$ value at 10 min; at the other oven temperatures, the $\frac{W}{D}$ value at 2 hr was less than the $\frac{W}{D}$ value at 10 min.

21. One of the students predicted that the wet strengths of PTs would **not** increase after treating the PTs with a solution containing both GLA and zinc nitrate. The results of which experiment better refute or support this prediction? The results of:

   A. Experiment 1 better refute this prediction.
   B. Experiment 1 better support this prediction.
   C. Experiment 2 better refute this prediction.
   D. Experiment 2 better support this prediction.

22. Based on the results of the experiments, is the dry strength of a paper towel greater than or less than the wet strength of the paper towel?

   F. Greater; each average wet strength, W, was greater than 100% of D.
   G. Greater; each average wet strength, W, was less than 100% of D.
   H. Less; each average wet strength, W, was greater than 100% of D.
   J. Less; each average wet strength, W, was less than 100% of D.

Taking Additional Practice Tests

GO ON TO THE NEXT PAGE.

4 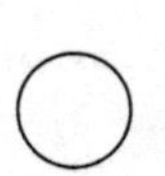 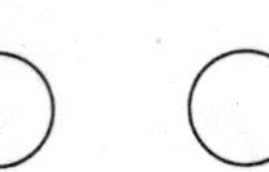 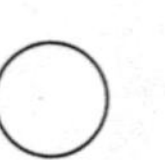  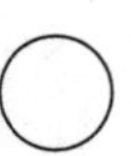 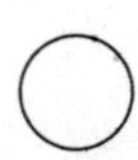 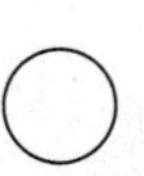 **4**

Passage V

Four students observed that in a population of land plants, Population A, a plant could have a green stem or a purple stem. Each student proposed an explanation for this observation.

Student 1

All plants in Population A produce the green pigment chlorophyll. If a plant receives 8 hr or more of sunlight each day, it also produces a purple pigment, causing its stem to be purple. If a plant receives less than 8 hr of sunlight each day, it does not produce this purple pigment, so its stem is green. All plants in Population A are genetically identical, so they all have the ability to produce both pigments.

Student 2

All plants in Population A produce the green pigment chlorophyll. If a plant receives too little phosphorus (a nutrient), it also produces a purple pigment, causing its stem to be purple. If a plant receives enough phosphorus, it does not produce this purple pigment, so its stem is green. All plants in Population A are genetically identical, so they all have the ability to produce both pigments. The amount of sunlight received by a plant does not affect stem color.

Student 3

All plants in Population A produce the green pigment chlorophyll. The production of purple pigment is determined by Gene Q, which has 2 alleles (Q and q) and 3 possible genotypes (QQ, Qq, and qq). A plant with either the Gene Q genotype QQ or the Gene Q genotype Qq produces the purple pigment, causing its stem to be purple. A plant with the Gene Q genotype qq does not produce this purple pigment, so its stem is green. The amount of sunlight or nutrients received by a plant does not affect stem color.

Student 4

All plants in Population A produce the green pigment chlorophyll. The production of purple pigment is determined by Gene Q, which has 2 alleles (Q and q) and 3 possible genotypes (QQ, Qq, and qq). A plant with the Gene Q genotype qq produces the purple pigment, causing its stem to be purple. A plant with either the Gene Q genotype QQ or the Gene Q genotype Qq does not produce this purple pigment, so its stem is green. The amount of sunlight or nutrients received by a plant does not affect stem color.

23. Suppose it were found that the presence of the purple pigment in some plant tissues protects those tissues from being damaged by sunlight. Would this finding better support the explanation of Student 1 or the explanation of Student 2?

   A. Student 1, because Student 1 indicated that the plants receiving the most sunlight will have purple stems.

   B. Student 1, because Student 1 indicated that the plants receiving the most sunlight will have green stems.

   C. Student 2, because Student 2 indicated that the plants receiving the most sunlight will have purple stems.

   D. Student 2, because Student 2 indicated that the plants receiving the most sunlight will have green stems.

24. All 4 of the students' explanations are consistent with which of the following statements? In Population A:

   F. both green-stemmed plants and purple-stemmed plants produce a pigment that can be used for photosynthesis.

   G. only green-stemmed plants produce a pigment that can be used for photosynthesis.

   H. only purple-stemmed plants produce a pigment that can be used for photosynthesis.

   J. neither green-stemmed plants nor purple-stemmed plants produce a pigment that can be used for photosynthesis.

25. Which of the students, if any, would be likely to agree that providing a purple-stemmed plant from Population A with additional sunlight will cause its stem to become green?

   A. Student 1 only
   B. Students 1 and 3 only
   C. Students 3 and 4 only
   D. None of the students

GO ON TO THE NEXT PAGE.

4 ○ ○ ○ ○ ○ ○ ○ ○ **4**

26. Suppose 2 of the purple-stemmed plants in the population were crossed and 52 purple-stemmed and 15 green-stemmed offspring were produced. If all the parents and offspring in the cross were grown under the same conditions, these results would best support the explanation of which student?

F. Student 1
G. Student 2
H. Student 3
J. Student 4

27. Based on Student 4's explanation, if a purple-stemmed plant and a green-stemmed plant from Population A are crossed and they produce both purple-stemmed offspring and green-stemmed offspring, the Gene Q genotype of the parent with the:

A. purple stem must be QQ.
B. purple stem must be Qq.
C. green stem must be QQ.
D. green stem must be Qq.

28. Which of the students would be likely to agree that a plant receiving 9 hr of sunlight each day could have either a purple stem or a green stem?

F. Student 1 only
G. Student 2 only
H. Students 3 and 4 only
J. Students 2, 3, and 4 only

GO ON TO THE NEXT PAGE.

4 ◯ ◯ ◯ ◯ ◯ ◯ ◯ ◯ ◯ 4

Passage VI

Liquid H_2O can be broken down into hydrogen gas (H_2) and oxygen gas (O_2) by electrolysis according to the following chemical equation:

$$2H_2O \rightarrow 2H_2 + O_2$$

A scientist performed an experiment to study the electrolysis of H_2O using electricity generated from sunlight.

Experiment

Steps 1–5 were performed daily for 12 months:

1. A tank fitted with 2 electrodes—an anode (where O_2 would be produced) and a cathode (where H_2 would be produced)—was assembled. Each electrode was suspended in an inverted plastic tube, and each tube was marked to allow gas volume to be measured.

2. Four liters (4.0 L) of a 25% by mass aqueous solution of sodium hydroxide (NaOH) was added to the tank. As a result, the tubes were completely filled with the solution.

3. At 8:00 a.m., a rectangular solar cell was attached to the electrodes and placed next to a particular south-facing window for 8 hr. (Figure 1 shows the apparatus at the initiation of electrolysis.)

Figure 1

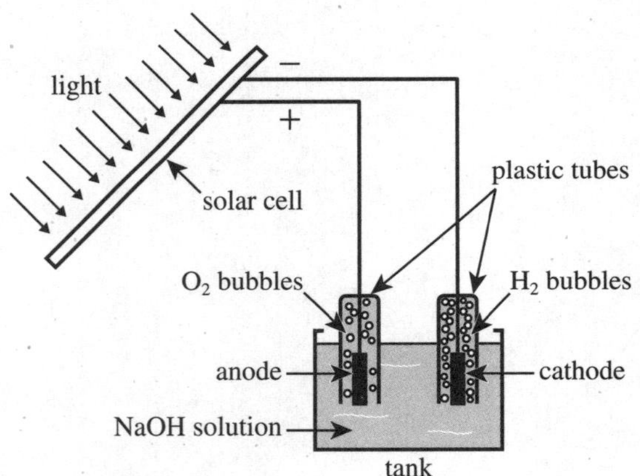

4. Eight hours later, the solar cell was detached from the electrodes, and the amount of H_2 that had been produced was measured.

5. The tank, tubes, and electrodes were cleaned and dried for reuse.

Figure 2 shows the total volume of H_2 produced (in L) in each month of the experiment. Table 1 shows the average solar irradiance (power per unit area), in watts per square meter (W/m^2), at the location of the solar cell during each month of the experiment.

Figure 2

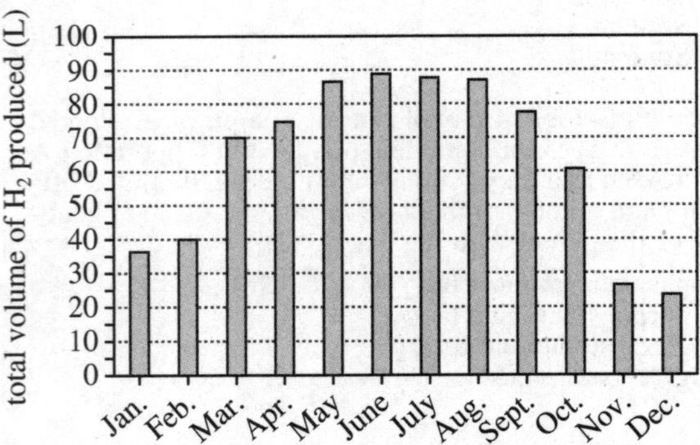

Table 1	
Month	Average solar irradiance (W/m^2)
January	77.8
February	106.4
March	153.8
April	170.7
May	197.5
June	213.1
July	206.4
August	198.7
September	183.1
October	137.1
November	59.9
December	52.3

GO ON TO THE NEXT PAGE.

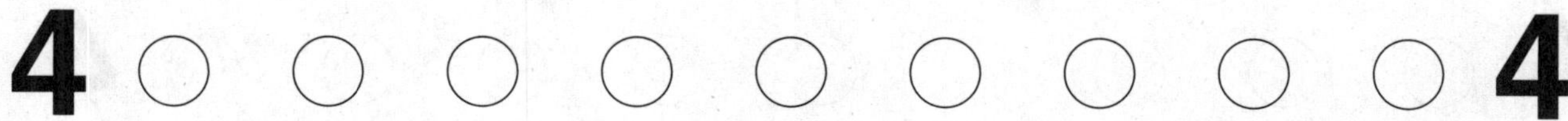

29. Based on Figure 2 and Table 1, during the month in which a total of 70 L of H_2 was produced, the average solar irradiance was:

A. 77.8 W/m².
B. 153.8 W/m².
C. 197.5 W/m².
D. 206.4 W/m².

30. Based on the description of the experiment, at 4:00 p.m. on each day, did the scientist measure the amount of gas produced at the anode or the cathode?

F. The anode, because the anode is where H_2 was produced.
G. The anode, because the anode is where O_2 was produced.
H. The cathode, because the cathode is where H_2 was produced.
J. The cathode, because the cathode is where O_2 was produced.

31. Consider the percent by mass of NaOH in the solution added to the tank in Step 2. Approximately what mass of NaOH was in 200 g of this solution?

A. 25 g
B. 50 g
C. 200 g
D. 225 g

32. Based on the chemical equation and Figure 2, approximately how many liters of O_2 (NOT H_2) were produced in February?

F. 20 L
G. 40 L
H. 80 L
J. 100 L

33. Based on the description of the experiment, in the month of June how many total liters of NaOH solution were added to the tank?

A. 4.0 L, because Step 2 was performed once in June, on June 1.
B. 8.0 L, because Step 2 was performed twice in June, once on June 1 and once on June 30.
C. 120 L, because Step 2 was performed 30 times in June, once each day.
D. 240 L, because Step 2 was performed 60 times in June, twice each day.

34. Suppose the experiment was repeated, except that the scientist added only pure liquid H_2O to the tank in Step 2. Based on the description of the experiment, would this change have more likely resulted in more H_2 being produced or less H_2 being produced?

F. More H_2; pure liquid H_2O has more ions and thus higher electrical conductivity than does an aqueous NaOH solution.
G. More H_2; pure liquid H_2O has fewer ions and thus lower electrical conductivity than does an aqueous NaOH solution.
H. Less H_2; pure liquid H_2O has more ions and thus higher electrical conductivity than does an aqueous NaOH solution.
J. Less H_2; pure liquid H_2O has fewer ions and thus lower electrical conductivity than does an aqueous NaOH solution.

GO ON TO THE NEXT PAGE.

4 ○ ○ ○ ○ ○ ○ ○ ○ ○ **4**

Passage VII

A *standing wave* on a taut string is a wave that appears to vibrate without traveling along the string. Such waves are called the string's *harmonics*. Each harmonic has a characteristic number of *nodes*: locations between the ends of the string that do not move (the ends of the string do not count as nodes). Figure 1 illustrates a harmonic and also the apparatus that a student used to perform 2 experiments on standing waves.

Figure 1

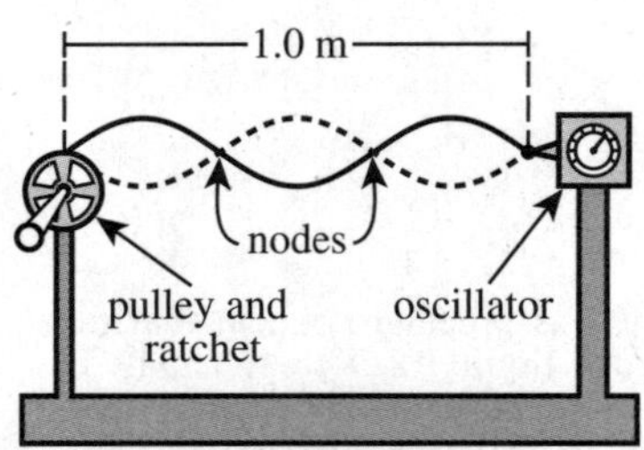

Note: Figure not drawn to scale.

A string having a mass per unit length of μ was attached on one end to an *oscillator* (a motor that vibrates) and on the other end to a pulley and ratchet. The student could select the frequency, f (the number of cycles per second), of the oscillator's vibration. By cranking the ratchet, the student could vary the force of tension, T, in the string.

Experiment 1

With 0.10 newtons (N) of tension in String X ($\mu = 0.02$ g/cm), the student varied f. She noted that standing waves occurred only at certain values of f. The student sketched the first 5 harmonics and recorded f (in hertz, Hz) for each. She repeated this procedure for String Y ($\mu = 0.08$ g/cm) and for String Z ($\mu = 0.16$ g/cm). See Table 1.

Table 1				
		f (Hz) for String		
Harmonic	Sketch	X	Y	Z
1st		11.2	5.59	3.95
2nd		22.4	11.2	7.91
3rd		33.5	16.8	11.9
4th		44.7	22.4	15.8
5th		55.9	28.0	19.8

Experiment 2

Beginning again with String X, the student set the oscillator to vibrate at $f = 25.0$ Hz. She then varied T, and noted that standing waves occurred only at certain values of T. The student recorded T for the first 5 harmonics. She repeated this procedure for Strings Y and Z. See Table 2.

Table 2			
	T (N) in String:		
Harmonic	X	Y	Z
1st	0.50	2.00	4.00
2nd	0.13	0.50	1.00
3rd	0.06	0.22	0.44
4th	0.03	0.13	0.25
5th	0.02	0.08	0.16

GO ON TO THE NEXT PAGE.

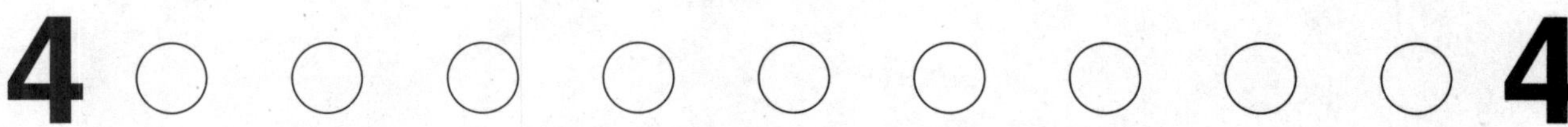

4 ○ ○ ○ ○ ○ ○ ○ ○ ○ **4**

35. Based on the sketches made in Experiment 1, the string shown in Figure 1 is vibrating in which harmonic?

A. 1st
B. 2nd
C. 3rd
D. 4th

36. In a new trial, the student made the following sketch of a standing wave on String Z.

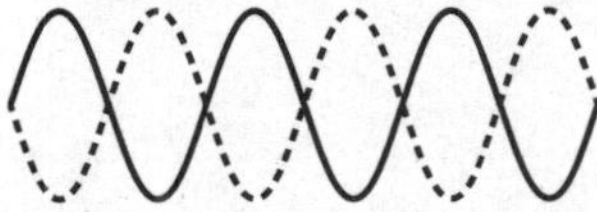

Based on the results of Experiments 1 and 2, this standing wave occurred at which approximate values of f and T?

F. $f = 0.10$ Hz and $T = 0.11$ N
G. $f = 0.10$ Hz and $T = 23.7$ N
H. $f = 25.0$ Hz and $T = 0.11$ N
J. $f = 25.0$ Hz and $T = 23.7$ N

37. A piece of String Y that is 1 cm in length would have the same mass as a piece of:

A. String X that is 1 cm in length.
B. String X that is 4 cm in length.
C. String Z that is 1 cm in length.
D. String Z that is 4 cm in length.

38. For a string at constant tension, let f_n represent the frequency of the nth harmonic (f_1 is the frequency of the 1st harmonic, f_2 is the frequency of the 2nd harmonic, f_3 is the frequency of the 3rd harmonic, and so on). Which of the following equations for f_n is consistent with the results of Experiment 1 for String X?

F. $f_n = n + f_1$
G. $f_n = n - f_1$
H. $f_n = n \times f_1$
J. $f_n = n \div f_1$

39. Suppose that a string having a mass per unit length of 0.32 g/cm had been tested in Experiment 2. The 4th harmonic of this string would most likely have occurred at a tension:

A. less than 0.03 N.
B. between 0.03 N and 0.13 N.
C. between 0.13 N and 0.25 N.
D. greater than 0.25 N.

40. Based on the results of Experiments 1 and 2, for a given harmonic, as μ increased, did f increase or decrease, and did T increase or decrease?

F. f: increased
   T: increased

G. f: increased
   T: decreased

H. f: decreased
   T: increased

J. f: decreased
   T: decreased

END OF TEST 4

STOP! DO NOT RETURN TO ANY OTHER TEST.

You may wish to photocopy these sample answer document pages to respond to the practice ACT Writing Test.

Please enter the information at the right before beginning the writing test.

Use a No. 2 pencil only. Do NOT use a mechanical pencil, ink, ballpoint, or felt-tip pen.

WRITING TEST BOOKLET NUMBER

Print your 9-digit **Booklet Number** in the boxes at the right.

WRITING TEST FORM

Print your 5-character **Test Form** in the boxes at the right <u>and</u> fill in the corresponding ovals.

Begin WRITING TEST here.

If you need more space, please continue on the next page.

1

WRITING TEST

If you need more space, please continue on the back of this page.

The ONLY Official Prep Guide from the Makers of the ACT

WRITING TEST

If you need more space, please continue on the next page.

The ONLY Official Prep Guide from the Makers of the ACT

WRITING TEST

STOP here with the writing test.

4

Practice Writing Test Prompt 3

Your Signature: _______________________________
(Do not print.)

Print Your Name Here: _______________________________

Your Date of Birth:

	–		–	
Month		Day		Year

Form 22WT9

The **ACT®** WRITING TEST BOOKLET

You must take the multiple-choice tests before you take the writing test.

Directions

This is a test of your writing skills. You will have **forty (40)** minutes to read the prompt, plan your response, and write an essay in English. Before you begin working, read all material in this test booklet carefully to understand exactly what you are being asked to do.

You will write your essay on the lined pages in the **answer document** provided. Your writing on those pages will be scored. You may use the unlined pages in this test booklet to plan your essay. Your work on these pages will not be scored.

Your essay will be evaluated based on the evidence it provides of your ability to:

- clearly state your own perspective on a complex issue and analyze the relationship between your perspective and at least one other perspective
- develop and support your ideas with reasoning and examples
- organize your ideas clearly and logically
- communicate your ideas effectively in standard written English

Lay your pencil down immediately when time is called.

DO NOT OPEN THIS BOOKLET UNTIL TOLD TO DO SO.

PO Box 168
Iowa City, IA 52243-0168

The ONLY Official Prep Guide from the Makers of the ACT

Field Trips

In elementary school, class trips to visit museums, science laboratories, zoos, and historical sites are relatively common. Such field trips can provide unique educational opportunities and connect what is learned in the classroom to the world beyond school. But field trips are not as common in the high school setting. Most classes tend to be limited to the school grounds—in a classroom or computer lab. Given the benefits they provide, should field trips be a standard part of the high school experience?

Read and carefully consider these perspectives. Each suggests a particular way of thinking about the question above.

Perspective One

Confining students to the classroom stifles their academic development. Field trips encourage motivation and interest among students, which enhances their learning.

Perspective Two

High school students require structure and discipline, which are not available in a field trip setting. Students treat it as an opportunity to socialize rather than a chance to learn.

Perspective Three

Field trips cost money, and many school budgets are strained. A high school's limited resources should be spent at the school.

Essay Task

Write a unified, coherent essay in which you address the question of whether field trips should be a standard part of the high school experience. In your essay, be sure to:

- clearly state your own perspective and analyze the relationship between your perspective and at least one other perspective
- develop and support your ideas with reasoning and examples
- organize your ideas clearly and logically
- communicate your ideas effectively in standard written English

Your perspective may be in full agreement with any of those given, in partial agreement, or completely different.

Planning Your Essay

Your work on these prewriting pages will not be scored.

Use the space below and on the back cover to generate ideas and plan your essay. You may wish to consider the following as you think critically about the task:

Strengths and weaknesses of different perspectives on the issue
- What insights do they offer, and what do they fail to consider?
- Why might they be persuasive to others, or why might they fail to persuade?

Your own knowledge, experience, and values
- What is your perspective on this issue, and what are its strengths and weaknesses?
- How will you support your perspective in your essay?

If you need more space to plan, please continue on the following page.

The ONLY Official Prep Guide from the Makers of the ACT

Planning Your Essay

Use this page to continue planning your essay. Your work on this page will not be scored.

Passage I

Question 1. The best answer is D because it does not include any unnecessary punctuation.

The best answer is NOT:

A because it has an unnecessary comma after *variations*.

B because it has an unnecessary dash after *variations*.

C because it has two unnecessary commas that incorrectly set off "in the mantas" from the rest of the sentence.

Question 2. The best answer is F because it is the only option with correct subject-verb agreement. The singular subject *skin* must have a singular verb.

The best answer is NOT:

G because *happen* is a plural verb, and the subject of the sentence is singular.

H because *were* is a plural verb, and the subject of the sentence is singular.

J because *are* is a plural verb, and the subject of the sentence is singular.

Question 3. The best answer is A because after Sentence 1 is the only logical place to add information that refers to the basic data Marshall began collecting.

The best answer is NOT:

B because Sentence 2 begins with "Other data," which refers to the phrase "Some of the data" in the new sentence, so it would be illogical to place the new sentence after Sentence 2.

C because placing the sentence after Sentence 3 would interrupt the discussion of the manta denticles.

D because placing the sentence after Sentence 4 would interrupt the introduction of another discovery Marshall made about the mantas.

Taking Additional Practice Tests

Question 4. The best answer is H because it best expresses the idea specified in the question. The word choice in this option (*evidence*) best conveys that the announcement was backed by scientific data.

The best answer is NOT:

F because the wording doesn't clearly indicate that the announcement was backed by scientific data.

G because the wording doesn't clearly indicate that the announcement was backed by scientific data.

J because the wording doesn't clearly indicate that the announcement was backed by scientific data.

Question 5. The best answer is D because it is the only option that clearly supports the suggestion that the scientific study of manta rays will continue: it is because Dr. Marshall, an expert researcher, is so devoted to manta rays.

The best answer is NOT:

A because the fact that the current manta ray population faces an array of threats across the world does not support the suggestion that the scientific study of manta rays will continue.

B because the fact that a documentary film about Dr. Marshall was released in 2009 does not support the suggestion that the scientific study of manta rays will continue.

C because the fact that Dr. Marshall once described the manta ray as a large and beautiful underwater bird does not support the suggestion that the scientific study of manta rays will continue.

Passage II

Question 6. The best answer is J because it is the only option that has correct sentence structure. It correctly uses a comma to connect the independent clause to the participial phrase.

The best answer is NOT:

F because it inserts a semicolon after *temperature*, which creates a sentence fragment because what comes after the semicolon is a participial phrase.

G because it inserts a period after *temperature*, which creates a sentence fragment because what comes after the period is a participial phrase.

H because the comma after *temperature* is separating two independent clauses, which creates a run-on sentence.

Question 7. **The best answer is** A because it provides the appropriate punctuation (commas) to set off the adverbial phrase "particularly in the bark of the willow tree."

The best answer is NOT:

B because it contains misplaced and inconsistent punctuation, creating an unclear sentence. The second dash after *bark* interrupts the adverbial phrase. In addition, an adverbial phrase should be set off by the same punctuation on both sides, either commas or dashes, but not both.

C because a semicolon should not be used to introduce an adverbial phrase.

D because it contains misplaced punctuation, creating an unclear sentence. The first comma should precede, not follow, the word *particularly*.

Question 8. **The best answer is** G because it is the only option that provides a logical transition to the information presented in the paragraph it introduces.

The best answer is NOT:

F because the information in this clause does not logically connect to the information in the rest of the paragraph.

H because the information in this clause does not logically connect to the information in the rest of the paragraph.

J because the information in this clause does not logically connect to the information in the rest of the paragraph.

Question 9. **The best answer is** C because it provides the appropriate punctuation (commas) to set off the conjunctive adverb *however.*

The best answer is NOT:

A because it lacks a comma before *however.*

B because a semicolon creates a sentence fragment.

D because it lacks a comma after *however.*

Question 10. **The best answer is F** because it provides the most logical transition word to connect this sentence with the preceding one. The word *consequently* provides a resolution to the earlier word *however* in the previous sentence, helping to explain the pivot away from cinchona bark to willow bark.

The best answer is NOT:

G because the word *nevertheless* is illogical in relation to the previous sentence.

H because the word *furthermore* is illogical in relation to the previous sentence.

J because the word *likewise* is illogical in relation to the previous sentence.

Question 11. **The best answer is D** because the word *began*, the simple past tense, is the correct form of the verb as it is used in this sentence.

The best answer is NOT:

A because the past tense is appropriate here, not the past perfect. Additionally, the past-perfect tense is "had begun," not "had began."

B because the past tense is appropriate here, not the past-perfect subjunctive mood. Additionally, the past-perfect subjunctive mood is "would have begun," not "would have began."

C because *began* is the correct form of the past tense, not *begun*.

Question 12. **The best answer is H** because it is the only choice that uses the correct verb tense and the correct form of the possessive pronoun *its*.

The best answer is NOT:

F because *adds* is the incorrect tense of the verb as it is used in this sentence.

G because *it's* is the incorrect form of the possessive pronoun.

J because *adds* is the incorrect tense of the verb as it is used in this sentence, and *it's* is the incorrect form of the possessive pronoun.

Question 13. **The best answer is B** because it best expresses the idea specified in the question. *Tested* emphasizes that the medicine was experimental in nature.

The best answer is NOT:

A because the wording doesn't clearly indicate that the medicine was experimental in nature.

C because the wording doesn't clearly indicate that the medicine was experimental in nature.

D because the wording doesn't clearly indicate that the medicine was experimental in nature.

Question 14. **The best answer is J** because it is the only option that has correct sentence structure. It creates two independent sentences.

The best answer is NOT:

F because it creates two independent clauses that are separated by a comma, which is a run-on sentence.

G because it creates two independent clauses that are separated by a comma, which is a run-on sentence.

H because a comma is needed before a nonrestrictive relative clause introduced by *which*.

Question 15. **The best answer is B** because this option clearly indicates why the essay does fulfill the writer's primary purpose. The essay outlines the development of a common medicine by documenting the historical use of willow bark as a medicine and tracing its gradual refinement into modern aspirin.

The best answer is NOT:

A because the essay does not focus on how the Egyptians and Sumerians administered willow bark.

C because the essay does not focus on the function of salicylates and how aspirin affects the human body.

D because the essay does not focus on comparing the use of willow bark to that of cinchona bark in the eighteenth century.

Passage III

Question 16. **The best answer is J** because it is the only option that creates a clear sentence. It correctly places "painter Martin Klimas" immediately after the introductory phrase "in his studio in Dusseldorf, Germany," which correctly provides an antecedent for the word *his*.

The best answer is NOT:

F because it delays introducing the antecedent for *his* to the point of making an unclear sentence.

G because it delays introducing the antecedent for *his* to the point of making an unclear sentence.

H because it delays introducing the antecedent for *his* to the point of making an unclear sentence.

Question 17. The best answer is A because "level with" is precise and appropriately conveys how the camera is positioned relative to the paint puddle.

The best answer is NOT:

B because the phrase "eye-to-eye with" isn't appropriate in this context, as neither the camera nor the puddle has eyes.

C because "the same as" falsely equates the camera to the paint puddle. They are different things.

D because the phrase "equal to" indicates that the camera and the paint puddle are somehow equal, which doesn't make sense.

Question 18. The best answer is F because it is the only option with correct subject-verb agreement. The plural subject *vibrations* must have a plural verb.

The best answer is NOT:

G because "has caused" is a singular verb, and the subject of the sentence is plural.

H because "is causing" is a singular verb, and the subject of the sentence is plural.

J because *causes* is a singular verb, and the subject of the sentence is plural.

Question 19. The best answer is A because it maintains the overall style and tone of the essay. The language here is neither overly informal nor too formal.

The best answer is NOT:

B because the phrase "frozen in time's embrace" is too flowery compared with the rest of the essay, and the words *pic* and *snapped* are too casual.

C because the wording is too informal compared with the rest of the essay.

D because the wording is too informal compared with the rest of the essay.

Question 20. The best answer is **F** because at this point, the writer is discussing how Klimas's photos are unique to each song. The quotation about letting the sound of the music create the picture is therefore the most relevant.

The best answer is NOT:

G because this quotation is about how annoying it was to clean up after each shot, which is not relevant at this point in the essay.

H because a quotation about using normal photographic equipment and common music is less relevant at this point than the quotation in **F** is.

J because this quotation is about the repetitive nature of the process, which is less relevant at this point than the quotation in **F** is.

Passage IV

Question 21. The best answer is **A** because it best expresses the idea specified in the question. The phrase "daunted would-be" best indicates that the builders who intended to construct the highway were intimidated by the features of the gorge.

The best answer is NOT:

B because the wording doesn't clearly indicate that the builders who intended to construct the highway were intimidated by the features of the gorge.

C because the wording doesn't clearly indicate that the builders who intended to construct the highway were intimidated by the features of the gorge.

D because the wording doesn't clearly indicate that the builders who intended to construct the highway were intimidated by the features of the gorge.

Question 22. The best answer is **H** because it provides appropriate punctuation (a colon) to connect two independent clauses and indicate the relationship between them. In this sentence, the information in the second clause ("showcased the scenic grandeur") illustrates and expands on information in the first clause ("design went beyond practicalities").

The best answer is NOT:

F because no punctuation between two independent clauses creates a run-on sentence.

G because the coordinating conjunction *and* should not be used with a colon to join two independent clauses.

J because a comma between two independent clauses creates a run-on sentence.

Taking Additional Practice Tests

Question 23. The best answer is D because deleting the underlined portion provides the clearest, most concise wording.

The best answer is NOT:

A because it is redundant and wordy; the location of the benches is referenced earlier in the sentence, and benches are typically for sitting.

B because it is redundant and wordy; the location of the benches is referenced earlier in the sentence.

C because it is redundant; that the benches were for travelers' use is referenced later in the sentence.

Question 24. The best answer is H because it is the only option that is clear. The word *road* clearly indicates that the distinction that was blurred was between "road and environment," which prevents ambiguity regarding what the writer is referring to at this point in the sentence.

The best answer is NOT:

F because the pronoun *that* is ambiguous, lacking a clear antecedent.

G because the pronoun *this* is ambiguous, lacking a clear antecedent.

J because the pronoun *it* is ambiguous, lacking a clear antecedent. In addition, the word *it's* is the incorrect form of the possessive pronoun.

Question 25. The best answer is A because it clearly explains why the phrase should be added to the sentence. The detail helps develop and support the overarching idea in the paragraph that the design of the Columbia River Highway was impressive, with five tunnels previously being unheard of in such a design.

The best answer is NOT:

B because the phrase, though it should be added, does not imply how the engineers were able to make openings in the tunnel.

C because the phrase, which should be added, makes clear that there were several openings in the side of one tunnel; this relates to information in the sentence about motorists' ability to glimpse the river below.

D because the phrase, which should be added, does not suggest that creating intricate tunnels was easy for engineers.

Question 26. The best answer is **G** because it is the only option that has correct sentence structure. It uses a subordinating conjunction to begin the introductory dependent clause that links to an independent clause, which creates a complete sentence.

The best answer is NOT:

F because it creates a run-on sentence. "In time" is a prepositional phrase, not a subordinating conjunction. "In time, Oregon built a new road along the Columbia" is an independent clause.

H because it creates a run-on sentence. The word *soon* is an adverb, not a subordinating conjunction. "Soon Oregon built a new road along the Columbia" is an independent clause.

J because it creates a run-on sentence. "Oregon built a new road along the Columbia" is an independent clause.

Question 27. The best answer is **C** because it best expresses the idea specified in the question. The word *rekindled* clearly conveys that people's interest in the Columbia River Highway in the 1980s was a renewal of earlier interest in the original highway.

The best answer is NOT:

A because the wording doesn't clearly convey that people's interest in the Columbia River Highway in the 1980s was a renewal of earlier interest in the original highway.

B because the wording doesn't clearly convey that people's interest in the Columbia River Highway in the 1980s was a renewal of earlier interest in the original highway.

D because the wording doesn't clearly convey that people's interest in the Columbia River Highway in the 1980s was a renewal of earlier interest in the original highway.

Question 28. The best answer is **G** because it maintains the sentence pattern the writer has established in the previous two sentences by using simple sentence structure, passive voice, present-perfect tense, and similar ordering of words and phrases. This approach creates a sense of repetition and emphasis for stylistic effect.

The best answer is NOT:

F because it does not maintain the sentence pattern the writer has established in the previous two sentences.

H because it does not maintain the sentence pattern the writer has established in the previous two sentences.

J because it does not maintain the sentence pattern the writer has established in the previous two sentences.

Question 29. The best answer is C because it is the only option that clearly refers to information in the first paragraph, which mentions that Hill and Lancaster began constructing the road in 1913 and that their design showcased the splendor of the gorge.

The best answer is NOT:

A because the first paragraph does not state that the site became a National Historic Landmark in 2000.

B because the first paragraph does not discuss uses for sections of the road where it was not feasible to restore motor traffic.

D because the idea that the Historic Columbia River Highway Trail has become a popular tourist destination is not referred to in the first paragraph.

Question 30. The best answer is J because Point D in Paragraph 3 is the most logical place to add information about the eventual disrepair of what remained of the original Columbia River Highway. Paragraph 3 as a whole focuses on the highway's decrease in use and resulting decline, so a sentence about the highway's condition fits logically at Point D and helps overall understanding of the paragraph.

The best answer is NOT:

F because placing the sentence at Point A would interrupt the discussion of Hill and Lancaster's role in designing and constructing the original Columbia River Highway.

G because placing the sentence at Point B would interrupt the introduction of the discussion of particular design features of the original Columbia River Highway.

H because placing the sentence at Point C would interrupt the list of design features of the original Columbia River Highway.

Passage V

Question 31. The best answer is A because it clearly and succinctly indicates that the young woman arrived at the same location where the narrator was waiting.

The best answer is NOT:

B because it unnecessarily repeats the first part of the sentence, explaining again that the narrator is waiting in a veterinarian's office.

C because it unnecessarily repeats that the narrator is waiting in the office. This information has already been established in the first part of the sentence, "I was waiting in the veterinarian's office."

D because it unnecessarily repeats that the narrator is there in the office. This information is already established in the first part of the sentence, "I was waiting in the veterinarian's office."

Question 32. **The best answer is G** because the verb *scuttling* provides a vivid description of the iguana's movement. This choice also provides a description of the iguana's rain forest environment, "dank undergrowth."

The best answer is NOT:

F because "walking on the ground" does not satisfy the requirement in the question that the choice be a vivid description. "Walking on the ground" indicates what the iguana does but is not a vivid description of the iguana's action or environment.

H because "living underneath the treetops" states an obvious point about iguanas and nearly restates the next part of the sentence, "resting high in the trees." No vivid modifiers or verbs are used.

J because the words "down low" are repetitive and the expression "moving about down low" is vague and imprecise.

Question 33. **The best answer is C** because the comma after *trees* indicates that the iguanas, not the canopy itself, are hidden in the trees.

The best answer is NOT:

A because it is nonsensical given the context of the sentence. The comma after *trees* followed by "which are hidden in the canopy" indicates that the trees themselves are hidden in the canopy.

B because it is a comma splice. "They're . . . trees" is an independent clause. "They are hidden in the canopy" is another independent clause. Two independent clauses cannot be joined using only a comma.

D because the semicolon is incorrectly placed between an independent clause and an explanatory phrase in a simple sentence. Semicolons are used to join two independent clauses.

Question 34. **The best answer is J** because the *rows* specified in the response indicate the pattern of spikes that appear on the reptile. The word *lined* also indicates the position and pattern of the spikes.

The best answer is NOT:

F because "it had a spine with tiny spikes" indicates the size of the spikes but not the pattern of the spikes.

G because the spikes "just beginning to develop again" indicates the potential size of the spikes and their development but not the arrangement or pattern of the spikes as stipulated in the question.

H because "there were small spikes on its armored back" indicates the size of the spikes and provides a visual description of the appearance and texture of the reptile's back but does not indicate the pattern of the spikes.

Question 35. **The best answer is B** because it creates a clear, logical, and parallel sentence (the verbs *caressed* and *watched* are parallel in form). The pronoun *it* later in the sentence also has a clear and logical antecedent, *pet*.

The best answer is NOT:

A because it is overly wordy and does not fit with the rest of the sentence. The underlined text is not parallel with the phrase "and watched it" later in the sentence, and the pronoun *it* has no clear antecedent.

C because the verb *caressing* is in the ongoing present tense, which is inconsistent with the past tense *watched* later in the sentence. This creates a confusing sequence of time when part of the action is an ongoing present action, *caressing*, and part of the action occurred in the past, *watched*.

D because it results in an illogical and ungrammatical transition to the rest of the sentence. The pronoun *it* in the remaining sentence also has no clear antecedent.

Question 36. **The best answer is J** because no comma is needed to separate the modifiers describing the iguana's eyes and how they shone and the prepositional phrase.

The best answer is NOT:

F because there is an unnecessary comma between a modifier and a prepositional phrase. No comma is needed to set off the prepositional phrase "from its scaly face."

G because there is an unnecessary comma between a preposition (*from*) and its object ("its scaly face").

H because there is an unnecessary comma between modifiers joined by the conjunction *and*. No comma is needed here because *and* is joining two adjectives, not two independent clauses.

Question 37. The best answer is **A** because it clearly indicates that the narrator is comparing the iguana's actions to a judge delivering (or giving) the verdict.

The best answer is NOT:

B because the phrase "having a delivery of a verdict" is awkward and wordy, and it does not make sense in the given context. Without an explanation, it's hard to imagine how an iguana's actions could be like a judge *having* a delivery of a verdict.

C because the phrase "in deliverance with a verdict" does not make sense in this context (a judge delivers a verdict; she does not deliver the verdict with the verdict). The intended meaning of this action is unclear, especially when likened to the actions of the iguana.

D because the plural verb form *deliver* does not agree with the singular noun *judge*.

Question 38. The best answer is **F** because the word *looking* offers a concise and effective choice to compare the appearance of the iguana and the appearance of a kitten.

The best answer is NOT:

G because the phrase "like as if it was" offers a wordy and repetitive description of the iguana. This repetition is distracting and unnecessary. It is also overly informal given the style and tone of the rest of the essay.

H because the phrase "appearing something like" is wordy and vague. The phrase also does a poor job of setting up the comparison in the sentence "appearing something like as content as a kitten, and close its eyes again." The meaning here is unclear.

J because the phrase "sort of like it was" is wordy and vague, which makes the comparison in the sentence less clear. The phrase is also overly informal for the style and tone of the essay.

Question 39. The best answer is **B** because placing the sentence at Point B further explains the young woman's statement that the iguana liked being held. The sentence is a logical extension of the preceding sentence.

The best answer is NOT:

A because neither the woman nor her pet iguana has entered the office yet, so placing the sentence at Point A is incorrect. The pronoun *she* in the added sentence would have no antecedent, so it would be unclear who is speaking.

C because placing the sentence at Point C interrupts the logical flow between the narrator's statement that she dislikes iguanas and her reasons for disliking the creatures.

D because placing the sentence at Point D interrupts the narrative flow between the iguana opening its eyes and its staring at the narrator.

Question 40. The best answer is F because the essay focuses on the narrator's surprise that the iguana is pampered and loved by its owner. The iguana is lovingly caressed by its owner, which the narrator finds both amazing and unsettling.

The best answer is NOT:

G because there is no indication in the essay that the narrator believes the woman is impolite. The woman politely asks the narrator if she can let the reptile out of its carrier, and the narrator gives her approval. The narrator's guarded response comes from her awe at the relationship between owner and pet, not from annoyance.

H because the essay makes it clear that the narrator does not like iguanas, but it does not tell the story of why the narrator dislikes the creatures. The essay is primarily about the narrator's observation of a bond between the iguana and its owner on a particular day at the veterinary clinic.

J because the essay focuses on the narrator's observations of one iguana in a veterinary clinic. Only a brief mention is given to where iguanas live. Any physical descriptions in the essay focus on one pet iguana, not iguanas in general or as a species.

Passage VI

Question 41. The best answer is A because the name "Sylvia Robinson" is an essential element and should not be set off in the sentence.

The best answer is NOT:

B because "Sylvia Robinson" is an essential element and should not be set off with commas.

C because "Sylvia Robinson" is an essential element and should not be set off with commas.

D because it adds a comma after *singer*, which is incorrect.

Question 42. The best answer is F because it provides the clearest, most concise wording.

The best answer is NOT:

G because it is redundant; the sentence already indicates the action people were taking when they obeyed the directive from the DJ.

H because it is redundant; "heeded the DJ's call" and "obeyed him" mean the same thing.

J because it is redundant; "did what he said" is redundant with *obeyed*.

Question 43. The best answer is C because it clearly explains why the new sentence should not be added. The information about Robinson and her husband forming other record labels is not relevant to the paragraph's discussion of how "Rapper's Delight" was created.

The best answer is NOT:

A because the suggested addition refers to the future labels Robinson would form, which logically had no bearing on where the Sugarhill Gang chose to record at the time being referenced.

B because the suggested addition refers to the future labels Robinson would form, and since the three rappers had already signed with Robinson at the time being referenced, it is illogical to say Robinson's future labels had any effect on why they decided to record with her.

D because the time period in which Robinson and her husband started other record labels is not relevant to the paragraph's discussion of how "Rapper's Delight" was created.

Question 44. The best answer is J because it is the only option that has correct sentence structure. The introductory phrase correctly modifies *Robinson*, because Robinson wanted to "recreate the feel-good vibe of the music."

The best answer is NOT:

F because it creates a dangling modifier; the introductory phrase incorrectly modifies "an upbeat disco record" as if the record were "wanting to recreate the feel-good vibe of the music."

G because it creates a dangling modifier; the introductory phrase incorrectly modifies "an upbeat disco record" as if the record were "wanting to recreate the feel-good vibe of the music."

H because it creates a dangling modifier; the introductory phrase incorrectly modifies *rhymes* as if the rhymes were "wanting to recreate the feel-good vibe of the music."

Question 45. The best answer is D because it does not include any unnecessary punctuation.

The best answer is NOT:

A because it has an unnecessary comma after *instincts*.

B because it has two unnecessary commas that incorrectly set off the word *and* from the rest of the sentence.

C because it has an unnecessary comma after *savvy*.

Question 46. **The best answer is J** because it is the only option that has correct sentence structure. It uses a participle to begin the introductory participial phrase that links to an independent clause, which creates a complete sentence.

The best answer is NOT:

F because it creates two independent clauses that are separated by a comma, which creates a run-on sentence.

G because it creates two independent clauses that are separated by a comma, which creates a run-on sentence.

H because it creates two independent clauses that are separated by a comma, which creates a run-on sentence.

Question 47. **The best answer is B** because it best expresses the idea specified in the question. The word option in this choice (*pressured*) most effectively indicates that Robinson had to be convincing.

The best answer is NOT:

A because the wording doesn't effectively indicate that Robinson had to be convincing.

C because the wording doesn't effectively indicate that Robinson had to be convincing.

D because the wording doesn't effectively indicate that Robinson had to be convincing.

Question 48. **The best answer is J** because it provides the most logical conjunction to connect the ideas presented in this sentence. The song's focus was weightier and very different from other singles the group had released, and this caused them to be hesitant to record it.

The best answer is NOT:

F because the subordinating conjunction *because* is not logical in context; the song wasn't different from previous singles because of the rappers' hesitancy to record it.

G because the subordinating conjunction *although* is not logical in context; the song wasn't different from previous singles despite the rappers' hesitancy to record it.

H because the coordinating conjunction *for* is not logical in context; the song wasn't different from previous singles because of the rappers' hesitancy to record it.

Question 49. The best answer is **D** because it provides the most logical transitional phrase in context. The preceding sentences describe the tension between Robinson's determination to record "The Message" and the group's hesitancy to record it. But eventually, or "in the end," two group members recorded the song, and it became a success.

The best answer is NOT:

A because the phrase "in the opposite fashion" signals that what follows in the sentence presents a contrast to the idea in the preceding sentences, which is incorrect.

B because the phrase "in the first place" is illogical when the sentence is in fact describing the outcome of the situation described in the preceding sentences.

C because the phrase "in the same way" indicates that what follows in the sentence is similar to the idea described in the preceding sentences, which is incorrect.

Question 50. The best answer is **F** because the possessive adjective *its* and the adjective *conscious* are the correct words to use in this context.

The best answer is NOT:

G because the noun *conscience* is incorrect in this context. It should be the adjective *conscious*.

H because the contraction *it's* is incorrect in this context. It should be the possessive adjective *its*.

J because the noun *conscience* and the contraction *it's* are both incorrect in this context.

Question 1. The correct answer is C. Substitute 3 for x and 2 for y to get $3(3^2) - 4(2) = 3(9) - 8 = 27 - 8$, or 19. If you chose **A**, you may have substituted 2 for x and 3 for y to get $3(2^2) - 4(3) = 3(4) - 12 = 12 - 12$, or 0. If you chose **B**, you may have substituted 3 for x and 2 for y and multiplied the exponent to get $3(3)(2) - 4(2) = 3(6) - 8 = 18 - 8$, or 10. If you chose **D**, you may have substituted 2 for x and 3 for y and then squared the product of 2 and 3 before applying the exponent to get $[3(2)]^2 - 4(3) = (6^2) - 12 = 36 - 12$, or 24.

Question 2. The correct answer is G. Use the exterior angle theorem to determine that the measure of $\angle ACD$ is the sum of the measures of the interior angles $\angle BAC$ and $\angle ABC$: $35° + 95° = 130°$. If you chose **F**, you may have added $35° + 90°$ to get $125°$. If you chose **H**, you may have added $90° + 180° - 35° - 95° = 90° + 50°$ to get $140°$. If you chose **J**, you may have subtracted the measure of $\angle BAC$ from $180°$ to get $180° - 35°$, or $145°$.

Question 3. The correct answer is D. First, divide the constants to get $-\frac{36}{4}$, or -9. Then, apply the exponent rule for division to get $x^{4-1}y^{3-1}$, or x^3y^2. By combining the constant and the variable expression, you get $-9x^3y^2$. If you chose **A**, you may have added the constants, $-(36 + 4) = -40$, and correctly applied the exponent rule for division to get $-40x^3y^2$. If you chose **B**, you may have subtracted the constants, $-(36 - 4) = -32$, and correctly applied the exponent rule for division to get $-32x^3y^2$. If you chose **C**, you may have correctly calculated the constant as -9, but then incorrectly applied the exponent rule for division and added the exponents to get $x^{4+1}y^{3+1}$, or x^5y^4, thus obtaining $-9x^5y^4$.

Question 4. The correct answer is H. Find how many batches of 100 mileage points are in 7,000: $\frac{7,000}{100} = 70$. Multiply that number by $0.75: (70)(\$0.75) = \$52.50$. Finally, add $\$20.00$ to get $\$72.50$. If you chose **F**, you may have incorrectly calculated $\frac{7,000}{100}$ as 7, multiplied the 7 by $0.75 to get $5.25, and then added $20.00 to get $25.25. If you chose **G**, you may have correctly calculated that there were $\frac{7,000}{100} = 70$ batches of 100 points in 7,000, added 70 and 20 to get 90, and then multiplied 90 by $0.75 to get $67.50. If you chose **J**, you may have multiplied $0.75 by 100 to get $75.00 and then added $20.00 to get $95.00.

Question 5. The correct answer is D. Substitute -5 for x to get $4(-5)^2 - 11(-5) = 4(25) + 55 = 100 + 55 = 155$. If you chose **A**, you may have correctly substituted $4(-5)^2 - 11(-5)$ but then simplified as $-100 + 11 + 5$ to get -84. If you chose **B**, you may have correctly substituted but then simplified as $-100 + 55$ to get -45. If you chose **C**, you may have correctly substituted but then simplified as $100 - 11 - 5$ to get 84.

Question 6. The correct answer is G. Set up an expression that represents the sum of regular pay and overtime pay, with one addend for the regular hourly rate and one addend for the over-40-hours rate: $11(40) + 11(1.5)(50 - 40)$. This yields $440 + 165$, or $605. If you chose **F**, you may have multiplied the regular hourly rate by the total number of hours: $11(50) = \$550$. If you chose **H**, you may have multiplied the total number of hours by the sum of 11 and 1.5 to get $50(12.5)$, or $625. If you chose **J**, you may have multiplied the over-40-hours rate by the total number of hours: $11(1.5)(50) = \$825$.

Question 7. The correct answer in D. Since a junior has already been selected, that leaves 11 students: 4 seniors and 7 juniors. The probability of a senior being selected is the number of seniors divided by the total number of students left, or $\frac{4}{11}$. If you chose **A**, you may have thought the probability was the number of students being selected divided by the total number of students left, or $\frac{1}{11}$. If you chose **B**, you may have thought the probability was the number of students being selected over the number of seniors, or $\frac{1}{4}$. If you chose C, you may have thought the first student selected was a senior and the probability was the number of students being selected over the number of seniors left, or $\frac{1}{3}$.

Question 8. The correct answer is H. The total cost of the car rental is equal to the sum of the total daily rental fee (the product of the number of days the car is rented and the daily rental fee) and the total mileage fee (the product of the number of miles the car is driven and the per-mile fee), $6(35) + 350(0.425) = 210 + 158.75$, or \$358.75. If you chose **F**, you may have added 6 to the product of the number of miles the car is driven and the per-mile fee to get $6 + 350(0.425) = 6 + 148.75$, or \$154.75. If you chose **G**, you may have multiplied 35 by the sum of 6 and 0.425 to get $35(6 + 0.425)$, or \$224.88. If you chose **J**, you may have calculated twice the product of 6 and 35 to get $2(6)(35.00)$, or \$420.00.

Question 9. The correct answer is C. Slope is defined as $\frac{y_1 - y_2}{x_1 - x_2}$. For these 2 points, it is $\frac{4-3}{-6-1}$, or $-\frac{1}{7}$. If you chose **A**, you may have added instead of subtracted to get $\frac{4+3}{-6+1}$, or $-\frac{7}{5}$. If you chose **B**, you may have subtracted the y terms and added the x terms to get $\frac{4-3}{-6+1}$, or $-\frac{1}{5}$. If you chose **D**, you may have subtracted the y terms in one order and the x terms in the opposite order to get $\frac{4-3}{1-(-6)}$, or $\frac{1}{7}$.

Question 10. The correct answer is G. To find the probability of the selected customer having ordered regular coffee without milk, first find the number in the cell where the Regular column and the Without milk row meet. Then place that number over the total number of customers to get $\frac{10}{36}$, or $\frac{5}{18}$. If you chose **F**, you may have found the cell where the Decaf column and the Without milk row meet and then put that number over the total number of customers to get $\frac{6}{36}$, or $\frac{1}{6}$. If you chose **H**, you may have found the cell where the Regular column and the Without milk row meet and then put that number over the customer total minus that number to get $\frac{10}{36-10} = \frac{10}{26}$, or $\frac{5}{13}$. If you chose **J**, you may have found the cell where the Regular column and the Total row meet and then put that number over the total number of customers to get $\frac{18}{36}$, or $\frac{1}{2}$.

Question 11. The correct answer is D. To solve the inequality, subtract $2x$ and add 5 to both sides to get $3x - 2x < 1 + 5$, or $x < 6$. If you chose **A**, you may have subtracted $2x$ and added -5 to get $3x - 2x < 1 - 5$, or $x < -4$. If you chose **B**, you may have added $2x$ and -5 to get $3x + 2x < 1 - 5$, or $5x < -4$, or $x > -\frac{4}{5}$. If you chose **C**, you may have added $2x$ and 5 to get $3x + 2x < 1 + 5$, or $5x < 6$, or $x < \frac{6}{5}$.

Question 12. The correct answer is G. To simplify the expression, distribute the multiplication inside the parentheses to $4x + 8 + 6x - 3$, or $10x + 5$, which factors to $5(2x + 1)$. If you chose **F**, you may have added all the terms to get $4 + x + 2 + 3 + 2x - 1$, or $3x + 8$. If you chose **H**, you may have distributed and added all the expressions to get $4x + 8 + 6x + 3$, or $10x + 11$, and then you factored incorrectly to get $10(x + 11 - 10)$, or $10(x + 1)$. If you chose **J**, you may have combined the expressions in the parentheses and then multiplied to get $4(3x) + 3(x)$, or $15x$.

Question 13. The correct answer is B. Convert the percentage to a decimal and the scientific notation to standard form and then multiply $0.04(13{,}600)$ to get 544. If you chose **A**, you may have divided by 4 to get $\frac{1.36}{4}$, or 0.34, decreased the exponent by 1, and then multiplied the exponential part to get $0.34(1{,}000)$, or 340. If you chose **C**, you may have divided by 0.4 to get $\frac{1.36}{0.4}$, or 3.4, decreased the exponent by 1, and then multiplied to get $3.4(1{,}000)$, or 3,400. If you chose **D**, you may have multiplied by 0.4 to get $0.4(13{,}600)$, or 5,440.

Question 14. The correct answer is F. Translating a graph 3 coordinate units to the left means that you need to subtract 3 from the x-coordinate to get $(3 - 3, 27)$, or $(0, 27)$. If you chose **G**, you may have subtracted 3 from the y-coordinate to get $(3, 27 - 3)$, or $(3, 24)$. If you chose **H**, you may have added 3 to the y-coordinate to get $(3, 27 + 3)$, or $(3, 30)$. If you chose **J**, you may have added 3 to the x-coordinate to get $(3 + 3, 27)$, or $(6, 27)$.

Question 15. The correct answer is B. To find the midpoint, average the x-coordinates and the y-coordinates to get $\left(\frac{-6 + 2}{2}, \frac{9 + 5}{2}\right)$, or $(-2, 7)$. If you chose **A**, you may have subtracted the first point's coordinates from the second point's coordinates but thought that a negative number, when subtracted, is still negative, yielding $(2 - 6, 5 - 9)$, or $(-4, -4)$. If you chose **C**, you may have subtracted the first point's coordinates from the second point's coordinates and divided by 2 to get $\left(\frac{2 - (-6)}{2}, \frac{5 - 9}{2}\right)$, or $(4, -2)$. If you chose **D**, you may have subtracted the first point's coordinates from the second point's coordinates to get $(2 - (-6), 5 - 9)$, or $(8, -4)$.

Question 16. The correct answer is J. Simplifying the fraction on the left to x yields $\frac{x(x+2)}{x+2} = 2$, or $x = 2$. If you chose **F**, you may have multiplied incorrectly to get $x^2 + 2x = x + 4$ and then subtracted incorrectly to get $x^2 + 3x - 4 = 0$; next, you factored the left side as $(x + 4)(x - 1) = 0$; then, setting the factor equal to 0 and solving for x, you got $x = -4$. If you chose **G**, you may have set the denominator equal to 0 to get $x + 2 = 0$, or $x = -2$. If you chose **H**, you may have rewritten the left side as $\frac{x^2}{x} + \frac{2x}{2} = x + x = 2x$, and then you set that side equal to the right side to get $2x = 2$, or $x = 1$.

Question 17. The correct answer is B. Decompose the composite figure into 2 rectangles by extending the partial vertical line segment to the base to create a 6-by-9 rectangle and a 3-by-7 rectangle (see Figure 1). The 7-centimeter-long side is found by calculating $13 - 6 = 7$. The area of the 6-by-9 rectangle is 54 square centimeters, and the area of the 3-by-7 rectangle is 21 square centimeters. Therefore, the figure's total area is 75 square centimeters because $54 + 21 = 75$. An alternative method is to find the area of the larger 9-by-13 rectangle and then to subtract the area of the 6-by-7 rectangle that is not part of the original figure (see Figure 2). The 6-centimeter-long side of the rectangle shown shaded is found by calculating $9 - 3 = 6$. The total area is 75 square centimeters because $9(13) - 6(7) = 75$. If you chose **A**, you may have reasoned that the composite figure was a 9-by-13 rectangle with a 6-by-7 rectangle removed and then calculated the area of the removed rectangle instead of the area of the composite rectangle: $6(7) = 42$. If you chose **C**, you may have added the areas of a 6-by-9 rectangle and a 13-by-3 rectangle but did not subtract the overlapped area: $54 + 39 = 93$. If you chose **D**, you may have calculated the area of a 9-by-13 rectangle but did not subtract the 6-by-7 rectangle: $9(13) = 117$.

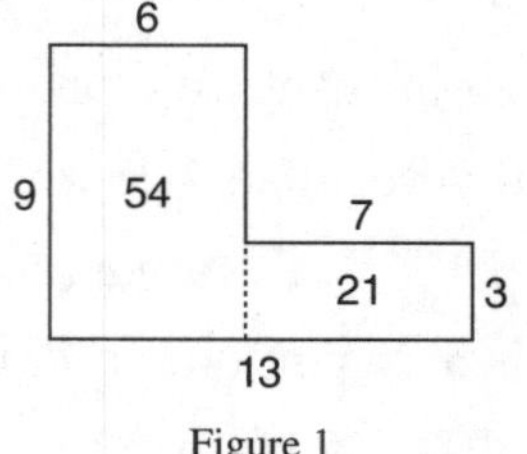

Figure 1

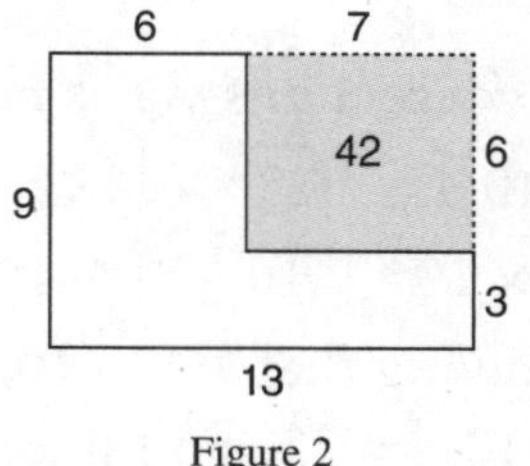

Figure 2

Question 18. The correct answer is H. Because $\angle BEC$ and $\angle AEB$ form a line, $m\angle BEC + m\angle AEB = 180°$. Solve for $m\angle BEC$: $m\angle BEC = 180° - 145° = 35°$. The sum of the measures of adjacent angles is equal to the measure of the angle they form, so $m\angle BEC + m\angle CED = m\angle BED$. Substitute the values of the known angles: $35° + m\angle CED = 90°$. Then, solve for $m\angle CED$: $m\angle CED = 90° - 35° = 55°$. If you chose **F**, you may have calculated $m\angle BEC$ instead of $m\angle CED$. If you chose **G**, you may have incorrectly thought that that $\overrightarrow{EC}$ bisected $\angle BED$ and then calculated $m\angle CED = \frac{90°}{2} = 45°$. If you chose **J**, you may have known that the angle appeared to be between 45° and 90° according to the diagram but did not know how to calculate it correctly.

Question 19. **The correct answer is B.** Let $f(x) = 5\sin(x) - 7$. Since $5\sin(x) - 14 = 5\sin(x) - 7 - 7$, we can write the image of $f(x)$ after the transformation to be $f(x) - 7$. This is a translation down 7 coordinate units. If you chose **A**, you may have thought the image of the transformation was $f(x) + 7$. If you chose **C**, you may have confused the negative direction on the x-axis with the negative direction on the y-axis. If you chose **D**, you may not have compared the subtracted 14 and the subtracted 7. You may have thought the image of the transformation was $f(x - 14)$.

Question 20. **The correct answer is H.** Because $9^{\frac{1}{2}} = \sqrt{9} = 3$ and $16^{\frac{1}{2}} = \sqrt{16} = 4$, then $\left(9^{\frac{1}{2}} + 16^{\frac{1}{2}}\right)^2 = (3 + 4)^2 = 7^2 = 49$. If you chose **F**, you may have calculated $9^{\frac{1}{2}} + 16^{\frac{1}{2}} = 7$ correctly but not squared the result. If you chose **G**, you may have added the bases to get $\left((9 + 16)^{\frac{1}{2}}\right)^2$ and then simplified to get $(\sqrt{25})^2$. If you chose **J**, you may have incorrectly simplified $\left(9^{\frac{1}{2}} + 16^{\frac{1}{2}}\right)^2$ to get $9^2 + 16^2$ or $81 + 256$.

Question 21. **The correct answer is A.** The sine of an angle in a right triangle is the ratio of the length of the side opposite that angle to the length of the hypotenuse of the triangle. To find the sine of θ, we need to calculate the length of the side opposite the angle by using the Pythagorean theorem, $a^2 + b^2 = c^2$. For the given triangle, $a^2 + 12^2 = 13^2$, so $a = \sqrt{13^2 - 12^2} = 5$. The length of the side opposite angle θ is 5 inches. Therefore, the sine of θ is $\frac{5}{13}$. If you chose **B**, you may have calculated $\tan\theta$, the ratio of the length of the opposite side to the length of the adjacent side. If you chose **C**, you may have calculated $\cos\theta$, the ratio of the length of the adjacent side to the length of the hypotenuse. If you chose **D**, you may have calculated $\sec\theta$, the ratio of the length of the hypotenuse to the length of the adjacent side.

Question 22. **The correct answer is H.** By the commutative property of multiplication, $(4.25 \times 10^{2c+4})(6 \times 10^7) = 4.25 \times 6 \times 10^{2c+4} \times 10^7$. Because $4.25 \times 6 = 25.5$ and $10^{2c+4} \times 10^7 = 10^{2c+4+7}$, then $(4.25 \times 10^{2c+4})(6 \times 10^7) = 25.5 \times 10^{2c+11}$. Because $25.5 \times 10^1 = 255$, we know that $2c + 11 = 1$, implying that $2c = -10$, or $c = -5$. If you chose **F**, you may have incorrectly thought that $25.5 \times 10^{-3} = 255$ and then calculated the solution to $2c + 11 = -3$. If you chose **G**, you may have incorrectly thought that $25.5 \times 10^{-2} = 255$ and then calculated the solution to $2c + 11 = -2$. If you chose **J**, you may have incorrectly thought that $25.5 \times 10^2 = 255$ and then calculated the solution to $2c + 11 = 2$.

Question 23. **The correct answer is D.** The value of $m + 1$ is always 1 more than m; thus $m + 1$ is always greater than m. If you chose one of the other choices, you may have been unable to produce a counterexample. Consider the following counterexamples: We know that $m \le \frac{1}{m}$ (choice **A**) is false because $2 > \frac{1}{2}$. We know that $m \le \sqrt{m}$ (choice **B**) is false because $4 > \sqrt{4} = 2$. We know that $m \ge m^2$ (choice **C**) is false because $3 < 3^2 = 9$.

Question 24. The correct answer is **H**. The length of the horizontal leg is 40 coordinate units, which can be calculated by subtracting $0 - (-40)$. The length of the vertical leg is 30 coordinate units, which can be calculated by subtracting $30 - 0$. To find the length of the hypotenuse, c, when you know the lengths of the 2 legs, a and b, use the Pythagorean theorem: $c^2 = a^2 + b^2$. So, $c^2 = 40^2 + 30^2$ and $c = \sqrt{1600 + 900}$, which simplifies to $c = 50$. If you chose **F**, you may have calculated the length of the vertical leg. If you chose **G**, you may have calculated the length of the horizontal leg. If you chose **J**, you may have calculated the sum of the leg lengths: $30 + 40$.

Question 25. The correct answer is **B**. A parabola with vertex (h, k) has equation $y = a(x - h)^2 + k$. The given equation is equivalent to $y = 30(x - (-1)7)^2 + (-42)$, which means $h = -17$ and $k = -42$. Therefore, the vertex is given by $(-17, -42)$. If you chose **A**, which represents $(-a, k)$, you may have thought the x-coordinate of the vertex is equal to the opposite of a, the coefficient of the squared term. If you chose **C**, which represents $(-h, k)$, you may have thought that the vertex form of a parabola was $y = a(x + h)^2 + k$, forgetting that h, the x-coordinate of the vertex, is subtracted from x. If you chose **D**, which represents $(-h, -k)$, you may have divided -42 by -1.

Question 26. The correct answer is **H**. First, find the area of square $ABCD$. For any square, all sides are congruent, so the length and width of square $ABCD$ are both 15 meters. The area of any square or rectangle is the product of its length and width, so the area of square $ABCD$ is 225 square meters. We are told that the area of the rectangle is equal to the area of the square, so the area of the rectangle is also 225 square meters. We then divide the area of the rectangle by its width, 10 meters, to calculate its length, $225 \div 10 = 22.5$ meters.

If you chose **F**, you may have assumed that the length of the rectangle was equal to the length of the square. If you chose G, you may have thought that the perimeters—not the areas—of the square and rectangle were equal: $2(15 + 15) = 2(10 + 20)$. If you chose **J**, you may have calculated the product of the given lengths and then divided by 4: $\frac{15 \cdot 10}{4} = 37.5$.

Question 27. The correct answer is **C**. Substitute 10 and 100 for A and A_0, respectively: $100 = 10\left(2^{\frac{h}{5}}\right)$. To solve for h, first, divide both sides by 10 to isolate the power: $10 = \left(2^{\frac{h}{5}}\right)$. Rewrite this exponential equation as an equivalent equation in logarithmic form: $\log_2 10 = \frac{h}{5}$. Finally, multiply both sides by 5 to get $5\log_2 10 = h$. If you chose **A**, you may have incorrectly rewritten $100 = 10\left(2^{\frac{h}{5}}\right)$ by taking 10^2 first, resulting in $100 = 100^{\frac{h}{5}}$, and then solved for h. If you chose **B**, you may have incorrectly rewritten $100 = 10\left(2^{\frac{h}{5}}\right)$ as if the exponent were a factor, resulting in $100 = 10(2)\left(\frac{h}{5}\right)$, and then solved for h. If you chose **D**, you may have incorrectly multiplied the 10 and 2 on the right side before rewriting the equation in logarithmic form, $100 = 20^{\frac{h}{5}} \rightarrow \log_{20} 100 = \frac{h}{5}$, and then solved for h.

Question 28. The correct answer is J. Both the numerator and the denominator of the given fraction can be factored into 2 binomials: $\frac{(x-3)(x+2)}{(x-3)(x+3)}$. The identical binomials $(x-3)$ cancel from the numerator and denominator, leaving the fraction $\frac{x+2}{x+3}$. If you chose **F**, you may have factored incorrectly: $\frac{(x+3)(x-2)}{(x+3)(x-3)}$. If you chose **G**, you may have factored incorrectly: $\frac{(x+3)(x-2)}{(x+3)(x+3)}$. If you chose **H**, you may have factored incorrectly: $\frac{(x+3)(x+2)}{(x+3)(x-3)}$.

Question 29. The correct answer is A. According to the order of operations, multiplication and division must be performed before addition, so begin by multiplying $\frac{1}{3} \cdot \frac{1}{4} : \frac{1}{2} + \frac{1}{3} \cdot \frac{1}{4} \div \frac{1}{5} = \frac{x}{y} \rightarrow \frac{1}{2} + \frac{1}{12} \div \frac{1}{5} = \frac{x}{y}$. Then, because dividing by $\frac{1}{5}$ is equivalent to multiplying by 5, multiply $5\left(\frac{1}{12}\right) = \frac{5}{12}$ to yield $\frac{1}{2} + \frac{5}{12} = \frac{x}{y}$. To add the fractions on the left side of the equation, get a common denominator: $\frac{1}{2} + \frac{5}{12} = \frac{6}{12} + \frac{5}{12} = \frac{11}{12}$. Because $\frac{11}{12} = \frac{x}{y}$ and 11 and 12 are relatively prime, $x = 11$ and $y = 12$. Therefore, $x + y = 23$. If you chose **B**, you may have added $\frac{1}{2} + \frac{1}{3} = \frac{5}{6}$ before multiplying: $\frac{5}{6} \cdot \frac{1}{4} \cdot \frac{5}{1} = \frac{25}{24}$. Then, you may have added $x + y = 25 + 24 = 49$. If you chose **C**, you may have multiplied by $\frac{1}{5}$ instead of multiplying by its reciprocal: $\frac{1}{2} + \frac{1}{12}\left(\frac{1}{5}\right) = \frac{1}{2} + \frac{1}{60} = \frac{31}{60}$. Then, $x + y = 31 + 60 = 91$. If you chose **D**, you may have correctly solved for $x = 11$ and $y = 12$ but found their product instead of their sum: $x(y) = 11(12) = 132$.

Question 30. The correct answer is G. Any number divided by another number, n, will be equivalent to $r \bmod n$, where r is the remainder upon division by n. For example, 7 is equivalent to 3 mod 4 because 7 divided by 4 has a remainder of 3. For this problem, note that $\frac{358}{4}$ has a remainder of 2 and so is equivalent to 2 mod 4. Because the digits repeat every 4 digits, any digit in a position corresponding to 2 mod4 will be the same as the 2nd digit after the decimal place, which is 1. Therefore, the 358th digit after the decimal place will be 1. If you chose **F**, you may have thought 358 was equivalent to 1mod4 and chosen the 1st digit after the decimal place. If you chose **H**, you may have thought 358 was equivalent to 3mod4 and chosen the 3rd digit after the decimal place. If you chose **J**, you may have thought that 358 was 4mod4 (which is the same as 0mod4, or being evenly divisible by 4) and chosen the 4th digit after the decimal place.

Question 31. The correct answer is C. Let the discount amount per customer, measured in dollars, be a random variable. The value of the random variable depends on the color of the ball selected: $\$60(0.10) = \$6$ for red, $\$60(0.30) = \$18$ for white, and $\$60(0.60) = \$36$ for green. To calculate the expected value, multiply each value by its probability of occurring and then add the products. There is a $\frac{3}{6}$ probability of a red selection (a \$6 discount), a $\frac{2}{6}$ probability of a white selection (an \$18 discount), and a $\frac{1}{6}$ probability of a green selection (a \$36 discount). The expected value is $\$6\left(\frac{3}{6}\right) + \$18\left(\frac{2}{6}\right) + \$36\left(\frac{1}{6}\right) = \$15$. If you chose **A**, you may have found the value of the random variable for red: $\$60(0.10) = \$6$. If you chose **B**, you may have divided the sum of the 3 possible discount amounts by the number of balls in the jar: $\frac{\$6 + \$18 + \$36}{6}$. If you chose **D**, you may have averaged the 3 possible discount amounts: $\frac{\$6 + \$18 + \$36}{3}$.

Question 32. The correct answer is H. To find Anela's driving time, divide her total distance by her speed: $\frac{375 \text{ km}}{75 \frac{\text{km}}{\text{hr}}}$ 5 hours + 0.5 hours = 5.5 hours. To find Jacob's total driving time, start by finding the distance that he drove before his 1 hour break. Before the break, he drove $\frac{90 \text{ km}}{\text{hr}} \cdot 2\text{hrs} = 180$ km. This means he will drive 600 km − 180 km = 420 km after his break. Because he drives $70 \frac{\text{km}}{\text{hr}}$, it will take him $\frac{420 \text{ km}}{70 \frac{\text{km}}{\text{hr}}} = 6$ hours. Therefore, Jacob's total trip time will be 2 + 1 + 6 = 9 hours. Jacob will need to leave 9 − 5.5 = 3.5 hours earlier than Anela in order for them to arrive in Brady at the same time. If you chose **F**, you may have forgotten to add Jacob's break time to his travel time, so you thought he only traveled 8 hours. Then, subtracting Jacob and Anela's total trip time yields 8 − 5.5 = 2.5. If you chose **G**, you may have divided Jacob's starting distance from Brady by his speed after the break, $\frac{600 \text{ km}}{70 \frac{\text{km}}{\text{hr}}} \approx 8.6\text{hrs}$, and subtracted Anela's total trip time from that: 8.6 − 5.5 = 3.1. If you chose **J**, you may have forgotten to add Anela's break time to her driving time and so subtracted only 5 hours from Jacob's total trip time: 9 − 5 = 4.

Question 33. The correct answer is D. The difference of two rational expressions with a common denominator will be the difference of the numerators divided by the common denominator: $\frac{(3x + 5) - (7x - 3)}{2x} = \frac{3x + 5 - 7x + 3}{2x} = \frac{-4x + 8}{2x}$. Then, factor and cancel the common factor of 2 from the numerator and denominator: $\frac{2(-2x + 4)}{2x} = \frac{-2x + 4}{x}$. If you chose **A**, you may have found the difference of the numerators, −4x + 8, but thought that the denominators cancel because they are identical. If you chose **B**, you may have subtracted 3 instead of subtracting −3 when finding the difference of the numerators: 3x + 5 − 7x − 3 = −4x + 2. Then, you may have also thought the denominators cancel because they are identical. If you chose **C**, you may have subtracted 3 instead of subtracting −3 when finding the difference of the numerators: 3x + 5 − 7x − 3 = −4x + 2. Then, you may have thought that canceling a common factor of 2 in the numerator and denominator canceled the denominator entirely: $\frac{2(-2x + 1)}{2x} \rightarrow -2x + 1$.

Question 34. The correct answer is F. To find the area of the rectangular stage in square yards, first convert its length and width from feet to yards. Since there are 3 feet per yard, the stage is $\frac{90}{3} = 30$ yards long and $\frac{30}{3} = 10$ yards wide. The area of a rectangle is its length times its width. So, the area of the stage is 30 yards · 10 yards = 300 square yards. If you chose **G**, you may have divided the area in square feet by the number of sides of the stage: $\frac{90 \cdot 30}{4}$. If you chose **H**, you may have divided the area in square feet by 3—the number of feet in 1 yard—to try to convert square feet into square yards: $\frac{90 \cdot 30}{3}$. If you chose **J**, you may have calculated the area in square feet, not square yards: 90 · 30.

Question 35. The correct answer is B. There are 15 lattice points inside the rectangle: $(1, 1)$, $(1, 2)$, $(1, 3)$, $(2, 1)$, $(2, 2)$, $(2, 3)$, $(3, 1)$, $(3, 2)$, $(3, 3)$, $(4, 1)$, $(4, 2)$, $(4, 3)$, $(5, 1)$, $(5, 2)$, and $(5, 3)$. Seven of these lattice points have coordinates whose sum is odd: $(1, 2)$, $(2, 1)$, $(2, 3)$, $(3, 2)$, $(4, 1)$, $(4, 3)$, and $(5, 2)$. So, the probability that the chosen lattice point will have coordinates with an odd-numbered sum is $\frac{7}{15}$. If you chose **A**, you may have divided the number of lattice points that would be randomly chosen, 1, by the number of different odd x- and y-coordinates of lattice points within the rectangle, $x = 1, 3, 5$ and $y = 1, 3$. If you chose **C**, you may have divided the number of lattice points that lie on and inside the rectangle, resulting in an odd-numbered sum of coordinates, 17, divided by the total number of lattice points that lie on and inside the rectangle, 35. If you chose **D**, you may have thought that since an integer is either odd or even, half of the lattice points would have an odd-numbered sum of coordinates.

Question 36. The correct answer is F. One method for finding the answer starts with two equations. First, use the given formula to write an equation to describe the third term ($n = 3$): $\frac{5}{2} = a_1 + 2d$. Second, use the given formula to write an equation to describe the sixth term ($n = 6$): $\frac{1}{4} = a_1 + 5d$. Subtract the second equation from the first equation to yield $\frac{9}{4} = -3d$, or $d = -\frac{3}{4}$. Now, add the common difference of $-\frac{3}{4}$ to the sixth term to calculate the seventh term: $\frac{1}{4} + \left(-\frac{3}{4}\right) = -\frac{2}{4} = -\frac{1}{2}$. If you chose **G**, you may have subtracted the sixth term from the opposite of d: $\frac{3}{4} - \frac{1}{4}$. If you chose **H**, you may have selected the fraction that resembled the common difference but thought you did not need to include the negative sign. If you chose **J**, you may have subtracted the common difference from sixth term instead of adding: $\frac{1}{4} - \left(-\frac{3}{4}\right)$.

Question 37. The correct answer is A. The probability that Jamie will be chosen to bat first is $\frac{1}{9}$. The probability that Jamie will **not** be chosen to bat first is $1 - \frac{1}{9} = \frac{8}{9}$. According to the note in the question, the odds in favor of Jamie being chosen to bat first is $\frac{\frac{1}{9}}{\frac{8}{9}} = \frac{1}{8}$. If you chose **B**, you may have thought the **probability** of Jamie being chosen to bat first was equal to the **odds** in favor of Jamie being chosen to bat first. If you chose **C**, you most likely calculated the odds against Jamie being chosen to bat first: $\frac{\frac{8}{9}}{\frac{1}{9}}$. If you chose **D**, you may have thought the odds in favor of Jamie being chosen to bat first was the reciprocal of the probability of Jamie being chosen to bat first.

Question 38. The correct answer is G. Calculate the total amount of salt by adding 5% of 120 liters and 15% of 80 liters: $0.05(120) + 0.15(80) = 6 + 12 = 18$. Divide the 18 liters of salt by the 200-liter total: $\frac{18}{200} = 0.09$. Finally, convert 0.09 to a percentage. If you chose **F**, you may have guessed that a possible solution would be between 5% and 15% but closer to 5%. If you chose **H**, you may have found the average of the given percentages: $\frac{5\% + 15\%}{2}$. If you chose **J**, you may have guessed that a possible solution would be between 5% and 15% but closer to 15%.

Question 39. The correct answer is A. Draw a trapezoid to represent a cross section of the pool: from a 50-foot horizontal line representing the length of the pool, extend lines to be the vertical bases of 3 feet representing the shallow end and 10 feet representing the deep end of the pool. Then, draw a sloped bottom side of the trapezoid to represent the sloped bottom of the pool. Find the point where the sloped bottom meets the 3-foot vertical base and label it X. Beginning at X, draw a 50-foot horizontal line segment through the trapezoid to the 10-foot base to form a right triangle. The acute angle X is opposite the side of length 7 feet (found from $10 - 3$) and is adjacent to the side of length 50 feet. Therefore, $\tan X = \frac{7}{50}$. To solve for X, take the inverse tangent of both sides of the equation.

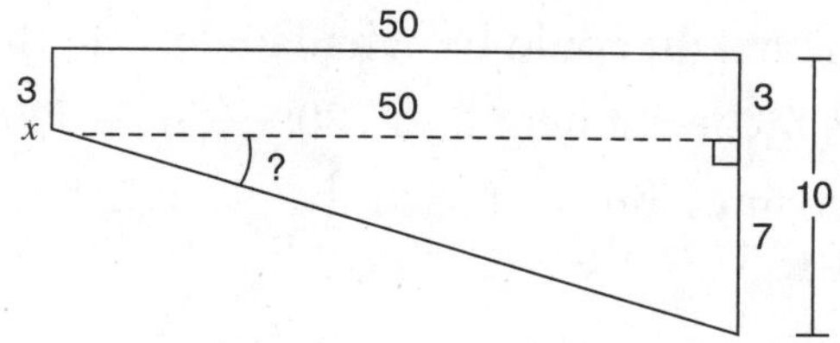

If you chose B, you may have added 10 feet and 3 feet instead of subtracting them. You may have thought $\tan X = \frac{10 + 3}{50}$. If you chose **C**, you may have made a ratio of the difference in depths to the greater depth equal to the tangent of the angle: $\tan X = \frac{10 - 3}{10}$. If you chose **D**, you may have added 10 feet and 3 feet instead of subtracting them and also thought that the tangent ratio is the adjacent side over the opposite side instead of the opposite side over the adjacent side: $\tan X = \frac{50}{10 + 3}$.

Question 40. The correct answer is F. The standard form of a hyperbola is $\frac{(x - h)^2}{a^2} - \frac{(y - k)^2}{b^2} = 1$, where the center of the hyperbola is (h, k), the vertices are at $(h \pm a, k)$, and the equations of the asymptotes are $y - k = \pm\frac{b}{a}(x - h)$. The center of the given hyperbola is $(2, 2)$ and the vertices are at $(2 + 1, 2)$ and $(2 - 1, 2)$. The answer should look like $\frac{(x - 2)^2}{1^2} - \frac{(y - 2)^2}{b^2} = 1$. From the graph, the slope of the asymptote with a positive slope is greater than 1. This means that $\frac{b}{a} > 1 \leftrightarrow b > a$. Of the answer choices, only **F** is possible. Rewrite **F** in standard form as $\frac{(x - 2)^2}{1^2} - \frac{(y - 2)^2}{\left(\sqrt{\frac{4}{3}}\right)^2} = 1$. In the equation, $a = 1$ and $b = \sqrt{\frac{4}{3}}$. The equation of asymptotes would be $y - 2 = \sqrt{\frac{4}{3}}(x - 2)$ which is reasonable based on the graph. If you chose **G**, you may have forgotten that h and k are subtracted from x and y. If you chose **H**, you may have forgotten that the second fraction in standard form is subtracted instead of added. If you chose **J**, you may have forgotten that h and k are subtracted from x and y and forgotten that the second fraction in standard form is subtracted instead of added.

Question 41. The correct answer is D. Note that you are asked to find the length of the side opposite the obtuse angle of the triangle. The obtuse angle forms a linear pair with the 25° angle, so the measure of the obtuse angle must be 180° − 25° = 155°. To find the third side length of a triangle when you know the opposite angle measure and the other two side lengths, apply the law of cosines: $c^2 = a^2 + b^2 - 2(a)(b) \cos C$. Substitute 700 for a, 250 for b, and 155° for c to get $c^2 = 700^2 + 250^2 - 2(700)(250) \cos 155°$. Finally, take the square root of both sides to isolate c, the unknown side length. If you chose **A**, you may have thought the height could be calculated using the formula $\cos 25° = \frac{250}{h}$. You may have then added this height to 700: $\frac{250}{\cos 25°} + 700$. If you chose **B**, you may have calculated the relevant obtuse angle to be 155° and thought the height could be calculated using the formula: $\sin 155° = \frac{250}{h}$. You may have then added this incorrect height to 700: $\frac{250}{\sin 155°} + 700$. If you chose **C**, you may have known to use the law of cosines, but you used the given 25° angle instead of the relevant interior angle measure of 155°.

Question 42. The correct answer is H. The committee is made up of Kenji, Mary, and 4 others. Imagine that Mary is seated. Someone will be randomly seated to her right. The probability that the person seated to Mary's right is not Kenji is $\frac{4}{5}$ because 4 of the 5 people not seated yet are not Kenji. Now imagine that someone who is not Kenji is seated to Mary's right, and someone else will now be randomly seated to Mary's left. The probability that the person seated to Mary's left is not Kenji is $\frac{3}{4}$ because 3 of the 4 people not seated yet are not Kenji. Recall $P(A \text{ and } B) = P(A) \cdot P(B|A)$: the probability that events A and B occur is equal to the probability of A times the probability of B given that A has occurred. Therefore, find the product of $\frac{4}{5}$ and $\frac{3}{4}$: $\frac{3}{5}$. Alternately, find the probability of the complement—that Kenji and Mary are seated next to each other—and subtract that probability from 1. Imagine that Mary is seated. There are 5 positions in which Kenji can sit, 2 of which are next to Mary. So the probability that Kenji is seated next to Mary is $\frac{2}{5}$. Therefore, the probability that Kenji is **not** seated next to Mary is $1 - \frac{2}{5}$: $\frac{3}{5}$. If you chose **F**, you may have considered Mary to be seated; then you considered Kenji to be 1 of 5 (the total number of people who are not seated). If you chose **G**, you may have considered Kenji and Mary to be 2 of 6 (the total number of people). If you chose **J**, you may have thought that the probability that Kenji is seated next to Mary is $\frac{1}{5}$ and then subtracted $\frac{1}{5}$ from 1.

Question 43. The correct answer is B. Note that 2^{90} is the product of 2^{88} and $2^2 = 4$; therefore, you can multiply 2^{88} by 4 to get 2^{90}. The question states that 2^{88} has a 6 in the ones place. Multiply the 6 in the ones place by 4 to get 24, which will result in a 4 in the ones place. If you chose **A**, **C**, or **D**, you may have chosen one of the possible digits other than 0 that could be in the ones place of a power of 2.

Question 44. **The correct answer is F.** The area of a triangle with base b and height h is given by $\frac{1}{2}bh$. Recall that b and h must be perpendicular. The bottom side of given triangle RST is horizontal because the endpoints both have a y-coordinate of d. Consider this side to be the base of the triangle, b, and find the length of this base by subtracting the x-coordinates: $c - a$. Now imagine the altitude of the triangle drawn from point (b, e) down to the base at point (b, d). This altitude would be vertical, making the x-coordinates of the endpoints both b. To find the altitude's length or height, h, subtract the y-coordinates: $e - d$. In the expression $\frac{1}{2}bh$, substitute $(c - a)$ for b and $(e - d)$ for h. If you chose **G**, you may have used just e for the height instead of $e - d$. If you chose **H**, you may have assumed that sides $\overline{RS}$ and $\overline{ST}$ were perpendicular and then tried to use the distance formula to represent their lengths; however, you forgot to take the square root of the sums of the squares. If you chose **J**, you may have assumed that sides $\overline{RS}$ and $\overline{ST}$ were perpendicular and then used the distance formula to represent their lengths.

Question 45. **The correct answer is A.** To solve for x, divide both sides of the equation by $(2 + 3i)$. This gives the solution $\frac{1}{2 + 3i}$. To find which of the given answer choices is equivalent to this solution, multiply the numerator and denominator of the fraction by $2 - 3i$, the conjugate of the denominator: $\frac{1(2 - 3i)}{(2 + 3i)(2 - 3i)}$. Distribute terms to get $\frac{2 - 3i}{4 - 6i + 6i - 9i^2}$, and then simplify the denominator: $\frac{2 - 3i}{13}$. Finally, decompose the fraction into addends using the numerator addends. If you chose **B**, you may have simplified $\frac{2 - 3i}{4 - 6i + 6i - 9i^2}$ as $\frac{2 - 3i}{4 - 9}$ instead of $\frac{2 - 3i}{4 + 9}$; then, you may have incorrectly simplified $\frac{2 - 3i}{-5}$ as $\frac{2}{5} + \frac{3i}{5}$. If you chose **C**, you may have thought that the number to the right of the equal sign of the given equation was the solution. If you chose **D**, you may have thought that $i = -1$ and then simplified $\frac{1}{2 + 3i}$ as $\frac{1}{2 - 3}$.

Passage I

Question 1. The best answer is C because the paragraphs that follow describe Murali and Vani's growing closeness with each other as they become a "couple" (line 61). The passage implies that the two were "talking" (line 72) about their future plans for marriage. Lines 76–91 recount the negative reactions of their respective families.

The best answer is NOT:

A because the passage does not depict a time in which Murali is yet married.

B because although the passage alludes to Murali's previously "thinking about widows or about repeating his own father's collapse" (lines 33–34), nowhere does the passage indicate that Murali has specific reservations about marriage.

D because although Murali is indirectly characterized in the narration, this is not the main focus of the paragraphs that follow. Murali's family conflicts are not specifically characterized in the passage.

Question 2. The best answer is F because the paragraph describes Vani's "reserve" (line 17). The passage also notes that "she did not speak softly" (line 20), denoting her certainty about speaking and indicating that her reserve was not caused by a lack of confidence. The description of Vani sewing her own clothes (lines 22–25) suggests a determined self-reliance.

The best answer is NOT:

G because although Murali anticipates that Vani's face may take on an "austere severity" (line 15) when older, her manner is not described as being harsh or severe. Nowhere does the paragraph indicate that Vani is impolite.

H because the paragraph does not directly characterize Vani's intelligence, nor does it describe Vani as apologetic. The paragraph notes her avoidance of "admitting she was wrong" (line 28), which suggests that Vani may be unlikely to be especially apologetic.

J because although the paragraph describes qualities Murali admires, no specific claims are made about Vani's beauty. There is no support in the passage for the idea that Vani's appearance was unkempt. Murali notes Vani's "precision in even the smallest of tasks" (lines 15–16), which may extend to indicate precision in her personal style, as well.

Question 3. **The best answer is B** because, in recounting who "was responsible" (line 39) for the introduction, the paragraph indicates that the friend's suggestion that Murali drive Vani home provided the introduction that drew the two together.

The best answer is NOT:

A because the elders were "eager to play parents" (line 61) only after Murali and Vani were known as a "couple" (line 61).

C because Vani smiled with her teeth (lines 57–59) after she'd exited Murali's car at the conclusion of the drive to her home.

D because Vani's brother burst into Murali's brother's home after learning that Murali wanted to marry his sister (lines 86–89).

Question 4. **The best answer is H** because the quoted dialogue immediately follows the description of Vani's manner of speaking (lines 19–20), and the italicized portion serves to exemplify her calmly confident speech in public.

The best answer is NOT:

F because the passage does not provide any information that suggests Murali rehearses comments to himself in advance of speaking with someone previously unknown to him.

G because, as the passage indicates, before Murali drove Vani home, the two had admired each other but hadn't yet been introduced (lines 34–39). During the car ride home, which served as their introduction to each other, "they were silent" (line 48).

J because although Murali thought Vani "might be full of secrets and wanted to know them" (lines 18–19), he does not speculate about what those secrets are.

Question 5. **The best answer is A** because as the passage states, Vani "liked her food steaming and spicy" (lines 21–22), as Murali did.

The best answer is NOT:

B because although the passage states that Vani and Murali met in New York City (line 1), it does not indicate that they were born there.

C because the passage doesn't indicate if either Vani or Murali had a passion for cooking.

D because although the passage states that "Vani had a job" (lines 62–63), it does not indicate where she worked. The passage describes Murali as a "bachelor-doctor" (line 66) but does not specifically indicate his place of work.

Question 6. **The best answer is G** because, as the passage indicates in lines 34–42, neither Murali nor Vani initiated direct contact with the other, and therefore neither of them would falsely claim or "admit" (line 39) responsibility.

The best answer is NOT:

F because the passage does not indicate that either Murali or Vani have forgotten, but rather that "no one else" (line 38) other than Murali and Vani remembers.

H because Murali did not initiate contact with Vani, but rather, as the passage relates in lines 41– 42, Murali and Vani had their first direct contact after a friend suggested that Murali could give Vani a ride home.

J because the passage doesn't indicate that a friend claims responsibility; aside from Murali and Vani, "no one else really remembers" (line 38).

Question 7. **The best answer is B** because, as the passage states, Vani "did not ask him in for a cup of coffee; it was not her house" (lines 54–55).

The best answer is NOT:

A because the silence of their ride home is described as "comfortable" (line 49), and there is no evidence to suggest Vani was self-conscious or uncomfortable.

C because the passage does not indicate at what time Vani and Murali left the party or whether it was late.

D because, as the passage states, Murali gave Vani a ride home in response to a friend's suggestion (lines 41–42), rather than from a request from Vani.

Question 8. **The best answer is J** because the description of Vani serves to illustrate why the elders may have been "eager to play parents to the couple" (lines 60–61).

The best answer is NOT:

F because although Murali admired Vani, he was drawn by specific traits outlined in the second paragraph (lines 9–32), rather than the more generic virtues of being polite or being a good cook (line 62).

G because although the passage describes Vani's family's negative reaction to news of Murali's interest in Vani (lines 75–81), the passage does not indicate how the family regards Vani herself.

H because the passage's indication that a friend of Murali's suggested Murali could give Vani a ride home (lines 41–42) is the passage's only reference to a New York friend of Murali.

Question 9. **The best answer is B** because *follow* is a synonym of *observe* in the context of adhering to certain traditions and practices. In this usage, the passage describes the family's perception that Murali has failed to follow the rules required by "certain formalities" (line 78).

The best answer is NOT:

A because although *study* can be a synonym for *observe*, the passage describes that the family is disappointed by Murali's failure to act in a traditional way (lines 77–80), rather than by a failure to study certain traditions.

C because *express* and *observe* have different meanings, and *express* would not make sense in the context of the passage.

D because although *perceive* can be a synonym for *observe*, the passage describes that the family is disappointed by Murali's failure to act in a traditional way (line 78), rather than by a failure of his perception.

Passage II

Question 10. **The best answer is G** because the first paragraph of Passage A states that "for most of human history, the phrase 'light pollution' would have made no sense" (lines 1–2). The details that follow describing the darkness of London, "Earth's most populous city" (line 4) in 1800, support this idea that light pollution created by artificial light is a relatively recent phenomenon.

The best answer is NOT:

F because although the paragraph relates the invitation to "imagine walking toward London on a moonlit night" (lines 2–3), it does not include a specific claim about travel difficulty, nor does it include a claim about the impact of electricity.

H because although the paragraph mentions gas lighting (lines 6–9), these details further emphasize how dark London was in 1800.

J because although the paragraph describes London as "Earth's most populous city" (line 4) in 1800, the darkness of such a populous city further illustrates the overall lack of light pollution.

Question 11. The best answer is A because the third paragraph of Passage A begins by stating that "in most cities the sky looks as though it has been emptied of stars, leaving behind a vacant haze" (lines 22–23). The third paragraph of Passage A concludes by describing the universe above "the city's pale ceiling" (line 28) as "a bright shoal of stars and planets and galaxies, shining in seemingly infinite darkness" (lines 29–31).

The best answer is NOT:

B because the paragraph does not describe the colors of stars.

C because although the paragraph refers to the planet Venus in lines 26–27, this reference serves to illustrate the darkness of the sky, and no comparison of the brightness of Venus to that of the stars is made.

D because although the paragraph states that people have "grown so used to this pervasive orange haze" (lines 24–25), it does not mention people's lost appreciation for stars or a pervasive apathy for stars today.

Question 12. The best answer is G because Passage A describes light as "a powerful biological force" (line 35) that can act "as a magnet" (line 36). Passage A gives the example of songbirds and seabirds "circling and circling in the thousands" (lines 41–42) because of being drawn by the artificial light emitted by searchlights and gas flares.

The best answer is NOT:

F because Passage A does not refer to any animal's food-searching abilities, nor does it indicate that darkness would diminish those abilities.

H because Passage A states that light "is a powerful biological force" (line 35) that can act "as a magnet" (line 36) that draws animals. It does not indicate whether light levels drive animals to dark areas.

J because Passage A does not refer to the natural habitats of animals or to urban expansion.

Question 13. The best answer is B because the author of Passage B states: "I love the story this painting tells, of a small dark town, a few yellow-orange gaslights in house windows, under a giant swirling and waving blue-green sky" (lines 55–58). In contrast, Joseph doesn't mention the story of the painting. "It's beautiful" (line 53), Joseph states, adding, "What more can you say than that?" (lines 53–54).

The best answer is NOT:

A because although the author of Passage B notes the "yellow-orange" (line 57) and "blue-green" (line 58) colors in the painting, the author focuses in greater detail on "the story this painting tells" (lines 55–56).

C because Passage B indicates in lines 53–55 that both the author and Joseph admire the painting's beauty.

D because Passage B does not include any information about the technique Van Gogh used to paint *The Starry Night*.

Question 14. The best answer is H because the author of Passage B states, "Does Van Gogh use his imagination? Of course, but this is an imagined sky inspired by a real sky" (lines 69–71). The excerpt from Van Gogh's letter in lines 80–88 then describes the bright and colorful night sky that he observed in 1888.

The best answer is NOT:

F because Passage B does not establish the time of day in which Van Gogh painted.

G because the excerpt from Van Gogh's 1888 letter establishes that the artist witnessed a night sky with such vibrant colors that he compared the stars to jewels: "opals you might call them, emeralds, lapis lazuli, rubies, sapphires" (lines 87–88).

J because the author of Passage B argues that Van Gogh did use his imagination to paint *The Starry Night*, stating, "Does Van Gogh use his imagination? Of course, but this is an imagined sky inspired by a real sky" (lines 69–71).

Question 15. The best answer is B because in Passage B, Van Gogh's description of the stars as "more brilliant, more sparkling gemlike than at home—even in Paris" (lines 85–86) indicates that the stars over Paris would have been quite bright even in that "time before electric light" (lines 76–77). That this brightness would be "remarkable to modern eyes" (line 89) helps establish that in recent times, the night sky in Paris is much duller. Therefore, no one has recently seen "anything like" the night sky over Paris mentioned in Van Gogh's letter.

The best answer is NOT:

A because Passage B establishes a stark contrast between the two night skies in Paris rather than a strong similarity between them.

C because Passage B does not establish a spatial relationship between the two night skies in Paris.

D because Passage B does not establish a spatial relationship between the two night skies in Paris.

Question 16. The best answer is J because Passage A explores the issue of light at night, noting how "most of humanity" (line 12) lives beneath artificial light, positing that "in most cities the sky looks as though it has been emptied of stars" (lines 22–23) and that "we've lit up the night as if it were an unoccupied country" (lines 32–33). Passage B presents the issue of light at night by discussing the depiction of the night sky in Van Gogh's *The Starry Night*, describing it as "a painting of our world from before night had been pushed back to the forest and the seas, from back when sleepy towns slept without streetlights" (lines 58–61).

The best answer is NOT:

F because Passage A does not present a summary of the circumstances that led to light being common at night.

G because Passage A does not offer suggestions for restoring darkness to today's night. Additionally, Passage B provides information only about Van Gogh's *The Starry Night*.

H because Passage B does not provide an explanation for how people in Van Gogh's time used light at night.

Question 17. **The best answer is A** because the first paragraph of Passage A discusses the darkness of night in London in 1800. From the references to the bright stars of Paris in lines 84–88 of Passage B, it can be inferred that the night sky over the city of Paris was dark during Van Gogh's lifetime.

The best answer is NOT:

B because neither of the passage authors discuss the opinions of scientific researchers.

C because the author of Passage A does not discuss any well-known works of art.

D because neither of the passage authors discuss personal memories of when night was darker.

Question 18. **The best answer is F** because the last paragraph of Passage A describes the effects of artificial light on animals in lines 34–42, whereas Passage B does not mention animals at all.

The best answer is NOT:

G because in lines 80–92, Passage B provides information on the colorful appearance of stars prior to electric lights, whereas Passage A does not refer to star color at all.

H because Passage B makes the argument that Van Gogh's *The Starry Night* is both a reflection of nature and a work of imagination in lines 69–75, whereas Passage A does not refer to the imagination at all.

J because Passage B refers to night having "been pushed back to the forest and the seas" (lines 59–60), places where night's original darkness remains.

Passage III

Question 19. **The best answer is B** because the passage begins in lines 1–16 by recounting the author's experience returning to a once-familiar place and experiencing memories. This first paragraph provides an example of how "places hold memories" (line 17). The author proceeds to consider how personal memories can be affected by photographs and other factors.

The best answer is NOT:

A because although the passage alludes to a childhood experience in lines 1–16, the passage does not describe a specific incident.

C because although the author self-identifies as belonging to the "image-makers and consumers" (lines 65–66), the passage does not relate a specific narrative of the author's lifelong hobby of photography.

D because the passage does not indicate that the author's opinions on a topic have changed.

Question 20. **The best answer is G** because the author claims that "places hold memories better than people and better than photographs" (lines 17–18). Lines 21–25 describe how conversations may alter or replace memories, and the passage continues by exploring how "photographs do not preserve memory" (lines 39–40) but instead "replace memory" (line 40).

The best answer is NOT:

F because the author claims in lines 21–25 that conversations may alter or replace memories and states that "photographs inaccurately reflect experience from the start" (lines 29–30).

H because the passage makes no claim that a person's memory of an event has any effect on the truth of a photograph depicting that event.

J because the passage does not establish that conversation, photographs, and visits to places are the exclusive sustainers of memories.

Question 21. **The best answer is D** because the author states, "I loved this place" (line 4) and describes himself as "amazed" (line 5). The reference to "this ritual" (line 16) also suggests an earnest seriousness.

The best answer is NOT:

A because the author's tone is sincere, rather than joking, in recounting how the place remains "startingly unchanged" (line 8).

B because the waterfall reminds the author of positive childhood memories..

C because the author does not make a request.

Question 22. **The best answer is G** because the details in the second paragraph support the claim that conversations about shared memories may "alter or even replace our own memories with those of another" (lines 24–25).

The best answer is NOT:

F because instead of focusing on the loss of the memory, the second paragraph focuses on how memories may be changed as a result of interactions with others.

H because in lines 18–27, reminiscing is portrayed as an activity that alters or replaces memories, rather than preserving them.

J because although the second paragraph identifies both "family" (line 18) and "people from our past who may remind us of events in our lives and with whom we may reminisce" (lines 18–20), it makes no distinction between how well family members or non-family members evoke memories.

Question 23. **The best answer is D** because the prior sentence describes how "snapshots are most commonly a break from that event" (line 56), in which people pause to allow a photo to be taken. The moment captured in the photograph, therefore, "is experienced as a moment taking a photograph" (lines 57–58) rather than a moment in the experience being documented.

The best answer is NOT:

A because the quotation focuses on the act of photography itself, rather than the skill of the photographer.

B because the author's description of a photograph being taken in lines 51–55 focuses on the experience of being photographed and does not focus on the photographer as a participant in the action.

C because the author questions the degree to which photographs can be considered accurate records of experience, noting that "photographs only tell such a small part of any story" (lines 48–49) and that "they deceive" (line 50–51).

Question 24. **The best answer is H** because in the first paragraph the author states that he was "getting ready to jump" (line 12), leaning over the edge of the cliff to "prepare myself for what I am about to do" (lines 13–14). He describes the action he is about to take as "this ritual" (line 16), suggesting the repetition of the childhood action of when the author "used to jump from those cliffs" (lines 3–4).

The best answer is NOT:

F because the first paragraph does not mention the possibility of hiking back down, and the author instead describes "getting ready to jump" (line 12) from the cliff.

G because the first paragraph does not mention the possibility of sitting, and the author instead describes "getting ready to jump" (line 12) from the cliff.

J because the first paragraph does not indicate whether the author was in possession of a camera or intended to take a photograph.

Question 25. The best answer is **C** because in the third paragraph the author states that "photographs inaccurately reflect experience" (lines 29–30), partly as a result of "eliminat[ing] . . . time" (line 32).

The best answer is NOT:

A because the author makes no reference to the age of people taking photographs.

B because although the author provides examples in lines 35–37 of different events a photograph might depict, the author does not indicate that there is a best way to photograph an event.

D because the author does not make a comparison between the ability of the human eye to capture detail and that of a photograph.

Question 26. The best answer is **F** because "objective truth" has a similar meaning as "irrefutable factuality" (line 45) and "seemingly" (line 45) suggests something that appears to be true but isn't necessarily so—something that "conveys an impression." Further clarity is provided by the statement that "a photograph's version of events did happen" (lines 46–47) but only tells a "small part of any story" (line 49).

The best answer is NOT:

G because the author argues that "photographs are an abstraction of experience" (lines 40–41) and "an abstraction of memory" (line 42), which, it can be inferred, would serve to make events less clear.

H because although the passage states that "a photograph's version of events did happen" (lines 46–47), lines 48–51 state that the image can be deceptive by telling only a small part of the story.

J because the author claims that photographic depictions "only tell such a small part of any story" (line 49) and "deceive" (line 51), rather than imply a story beyond the actual depiction.

Question 27. The best answer is **B** because *essence* is a synonym of nature in the context of the author's defining key qualities of memory in lines 72–73.

The best answer is NOT:

A because although *temperament* can be a synonym for nature, the word is usually used to describe the mood or behavior of a living entity, making this a contextually inappropriate choice to modify "memory" in lines 72–73.

C because although *scenery* may sometimes be used to refer to natural surroundings or landscapes, the word would not make sense in the context of defining the key qualities or "nature" of memory in lines 72–73.

D because although *environment* may sometimes be used to refer to natural settings, the word would not make sense in the context of defining the key qualities or "nature" of memory in lines 72–73.

Passage IV

Question 28. The best answer is **F** because lines 65–78 describe how a certain type of solar technology that uses electrolyzers demonstrates that the technology could work, "in principle" (line 75). The passage notes, however, that the models are "bulky" (line 65), and key components such as silicon crystals (line 80) and platinum (lines 81–82) are too expensive for use in large-scale implementation.

The best answer is NOT:

G because although the seventh paragraph states that an electrolyzer "uses the solar electricity to break water molecules" (lines 69–70), this detail is given in support of the paragraph's overall explanation of the technology.

H because although the seventh and eighth paragraphs (lines 65–82) describe a prototype made by a Japanese automaker, they do not indicate that the United States and Japan are working collaboratively on research.

J because although the seventh and eighth paragraphs (lines 65–82) describe a prototype made by a Japanese automaker, they do not question any aspect of the auto industry.

Question 29. The best answer is **C** because Nathan S. Lewis is identified as the speaker "giving a lecture" (line 1), and lines 4–6 present a paraphrase of the lecture's key claim.

The best answer is NOT:

A because although the passage mentions that "other researchers" (line 22) are researching uses of algae, this is given as an example of alternate research approaches, and the researchers' location is not given.

B because the passage attributes the claim in lines 4–6 to "the chemist" (lines 3–4) that is giving the lecture. Nathan S. Lewis was introduced in the preceding sentence (lines 1–2) as the speaker giving the lecture.

D because the passage author prefaces the claim in lines 4–6 with "the chemist says" (lines 3–4), indicating that what follows is the opinion of "the chemist," Nathan S. Lewis, and not the opinion of the author.

Question 30. The best answer is **G** because the passage states that "humankind needs a radical breakthrough in solar fuel technology" (lines 11–12), indicating that a technological breakthrough is necessary but has not yet occurred. The passage then indicates that such a breakthrough would involve using solar technology to "create heat or generate electricity" (lines 15–16) and "store the fuel for use when the sun is down" (lines 16–17).

The best answer is NOT:

F because the passage states that "humankind needs a radical breakthrough in solar fuel technology" (lines 11–12), indicating that a technological breakthrough has not yet occurred. The description of Lewis's research that follows in lines 18–22 suggests early progress toward the goal of "artificial leaves" (lines 12–13), but this work is too preliminary to have a broad impact.

H because the passage states that "humankind needs a radical breakthrough in solar fuel technology" (lines 11–12), indicating that the breakthrough has not yet occurred. In addition, the passage suggests that the capabilities described in lines 14–17 will be the result of the radical breakthrough, not the cause.

J because the passage does not indicate that Lewis believes that either the breakthrough or the capabilities are misguided. The passage does not refer to the energy industry focusing on consumption.

Question 31. **The best answer is A** because the passage states that "commercial solar cells contain expensive silicon crystals" (lines 79–80) and that platinum is "to date the best material for catalyzing the water-splitting reaction, but it costs $1,500 an ounce" (lines 81–82). The passage goes on to explain that, according to Lewis, "future solar-fuel devices would have to cost less than $1 per square foot of sun-collecting surface" (lines 84–85), suggesting that cheaper materials will be needed to implement solar technology on a large scale.

The best answer is NOT:

B because the passage relates that a device called an "electrolyzer" (line 58) can "split water into oxygen and hydrogen" (lines 58–59). The passage then goes on to explain that "electrolyzers are used in various commercial processes" (lines 62–63), indicating that a device capable of splitting water into hydrogen and oxygen already exists.

C because the passage does not refer to federal funding research for solar technology research, nor does it specifically indicate that Lewis lacks the federal funding necessary for his research.

D because the passage does not indicate that the public is reluctant to embrace new technology. Rather, it claims that "with a new energy and climate crunch looming, solar fuel is suddenly gaining attention" (lines 46–48).

Question 32. **The best answer is F** because, as the passage indicates in a paraphrase of Lewis's lectures, he tells his crowds that "the sun pours more energy onto the earth every hour than humankind uses in a year" (lines 9–11).

The best answer is NOT:

G because, as the passage indicates in a paraphrase of Lewis's lectures, he tells his crowds that "the sun pours more energy onto the earth every hour than humankind uses in a year" (lines 9–11).

H because, as the passage indicates in a paraphrase of Lewis's lectures, he tells his crowds that "the sun pours more energy onto the earth every hour than humankind uses in a year" (lines 9–11).

J because, as the passage indicates in a paraphrase of Lewis's lectures, he tells his crowds that "the sun pours more energy onto the earth every hour than humankind uses in a year" (lines 9–11).

Question 33. **The best answer is C** because lines 24–26 describe projects that seek to "capture solar rays and churn out chemical fuel" (lines 13–14) and "turn sunlight into chemical energy that can be stored" (lines 27– 28). In this context, when the passage states that the algae "has been genetically altered to pump out biofuels" (lines 24–25), it can be inferred that "to pump out" means "to produce."

The best answer is NOT:

A because when the passage states that the algae "has been genetically altered to pump out biofuels" (lines 24–25), it can be inferred that the goal is for the algae to produce, rather than to remove, fuel to use as an energy source.

B because when the passage states that the algae "has been genetically altered to pump out biofuels" (lines 24–25), it can be inferred that the goal is for the algae to produce, rather than to drain or diminish, fuel to use as an energy source.

D because when the passage states that the algae "has been genetically altered to pump out biofuels" (lines 24–25), it can be inferred that the goal is for the algae to produce, rather than to siphon or drain away, fuel to use as an energy source.

Question 34. **The best answer is G** because the passage states that Lewis estimates the need to "manufacture thin, flexible solar-fuel films" (lines 37–38) that would "roll off high-speed production lines the way newsprint does" (lines 39–40).

The best answer is NOT:

F because, although the passage describes Lewis's initial prototypes as "not much larger than computer chips" (line 19), it paraphrases Lewis's prediction of the need for "thin, flexible solar-fuel films, instead of discrete chip-like devices" (lines 38–39).

H because the passage does not indicate that Lewis imagines small, rigid solar panels as the ideal, but rather "thin, flexible solar-fuel films" (line 38).

J because, although the passage does describe a Japanese prototype that is "taller than a refrigerator and is covered with photovoltaic cells" (lines 68–69), the passage does not relate this research to Lewis's ideals for energy innovation. Instead, the passage states that Lewis argues that "the man-made leaf option is the most likely" (lines 29–30) to provide a large-scale solar energy solution, which he imagines as being manufactured as "thin, flexible solar-fuel films" (line 38).

Question 35. **The best answer is D** because the passage states that Lewis's artificial leaf technology "requires two principal elements: a collector that converts solar energy (photons) into electrical energy (electrons) and an electrolyzer" (lines 55–58).

The best answer is NOT:

A because the passage does not indicate that either ambient air or fuel cells are the principal elements of Lewis's artificial leaves. Rather, the passage explains that the principal elements of Lewis's leaves are a collector and an electrolyzer (lines 55–59).

B because, while the passage indicates that a catalyst is needed to help an electrolyzer split oxygen and hydrogen (lines 59–60) and explains that an electrolyzer uses solar electricity to break water molecules (lines 69–70), it does not indicate that these are the principal elements of Lewis's artificial leaves. Rather, the passage explains that the principal elements of Lewis's leaves are a collector and an electrolyzer (lines 55–59).

C because, while the passage does indicate that commercial solar cells contain silicon crystals (lines 79–80), and that electrolyzers contain platinum (lines 80–81), it does not indicate that these are the principal elements of Lewis's artificial leaves. Rather, the passage explains that the principal elements of Lewis's leaves are a collector and an electrolyzer (lines 55–59).

Question 36. **The best answer is J** because the passage states that "the exhaust from burning the hydrogen later in a fuel cell is water" (lines 77–78).

The best answer is NOT:

F because the passage does not claim that burning hydrogen in a fuel cell creates electron energy that splits silicon crystals. Instead, the passage states that "the exhaust from burning the hydrogen later in a fuel cell is water" (lines 77–78).

G because the passage does not claim that burning hydrogen in a fuel cell causes the hydrogen to bond with oxygen. Instead, the passage states that "the exhaust from burning the hydrogen later in a fuel cell is water" (lines 77–78).

H because the passage does not claim that burning hydrogen in a fuel cell causes the fuel cell's lining to deteriorate. Instead, the passage states that "the exhaust from burning the hydrogen later in a fuel cell is water" (lines 77–78).

Passage I

Question 1. The best answer is B. According to Table 1, at 273 K, the molar volume of H_2 at 5.00 atm is 4.496 L, and the molar volume of H_2 at 10.0 atm is 2.256 L. The absolute value of the difference between the two molar volumes is 2.240 L. Therefore, **B** is correct. **A**, **C**, and **D** are incorrect; the difference is closest to 2.2 L.

Question 2. The best answer is G. According to Table 2, at 323 K, the molar volume of Ar was the smallest at 26.486 L, followed by N_2 with a molar volume of 26.492 L, then He with a molar volume of 26.504 L, and finally H_2 with the largest molar volume of 26.521 L. Therefore, **G** is correct. **F** is incorrect; the molar volume of He is greater than the molar volume of N_2. **H** and **J** are incorrect; Ar has the smallest molar volume, and H_2 has the greatest molar volume.

Question 3. The best answer is A. According to Table 2, at 1.00 atm and 773 K, the molar volumes of the gases range from 63.440 L to 63.453 L; none of these values are smaller than the molar volume of an ideal gas. Therefore, **A** is correct. **B**, **C**, and **D** are incorrect; none of the gases listed in Table 2 have a molar volume less than the molar volume of an ideal gas.

Question 4. The best answer is J. Because the mean free time decreases as a sample's volume decreases, the mean free time would be least for a 1 mol sample of the gas with the smallest molar volume. According to Table 1, O_2 at 100.0 atm has a molar volume of 0.198 L. This is the smallest molar volume listed in Table 1. Therefore, **J** is correct. **F**, **G**, and **H** are incorrect; these gas samples do not have the smallest molar volume.

Question 5. The best answer is D. To answer this item, the examinee must know that the average kinetic energy of the molecules in a sample of O_2 increases as the temperature increases. Based on Table 2, a 1 mol sample of O_2 with a volume of 18 L has a temperature of approximately 223 K, and a 1 mol sample of O_2 with a volume of 63 L has a temperature of approximately 773 K. The sample with the volume of 63 L has a higher temperature, and therefore the average kinetic energy of the molecules in this sample is greater. Therefore, **D** is correct. **A** and **B** are incorrect; the molecules in the sample with a volume of 63 L are more likely to have a greater average kinetic energy. **C** is incorrect; the average kinetic energy of the molecules in the 63 L sample is more likely greater because it is at the higher temperature not the lower temperature.

Passage II

Question 6. The best answer is G. According to Figure 3, as cleaning time increased from 0 minutes to 30 minutes and then to 60 minutes, the corresponding average number of colonies per dish went from 79 to 29 and then to 12. Therefore, **G** is correct. **F** is incorrect; the trend consistently decreases not increases with increasing cleaning time. **H** and **J** are incorrect; the average number of colonies trend did not start in one direction and then change to the opposite direction.

Question 7. The best answer is D. The description of Experiment 3 states that 3 groups of 10 *S. carnaria* flies were used. Therefore, there were a total of 30 flies used in Experiment 3. Therefore, **D** is correct. **A, B,** and **C** are incorrect; 5, 10, and 24 flies are less than the actual number of flies used in Experiment 3.

Question 8. The best answer is F. The first paragraph states that the experiments were conducted to study the transfer of bacteria from one surface to another by flies. It is true that the bacteria being transferred could be disease-causing and be spread by the flies after walking in the enclosure containing *E. coli*. Figure 1 shows that after the flies walked in an enclosure containing *E. coli* and were then placed on sterile nutrient agar, bacteria were transferred and grew on the nutrient agar plates. Therefore, **F** is correct. **G** is incorrect; the 2 species of flies were examined in separate procedures. There was no interaction between the 2 species in the experiments, and Figure 1 does not show the results of such an interaction. **H** is incorrect; Figure 1 shows that both species of flies transferred *E. coli* from the enclosure to the nutrient agar. **J** is incorrect; the experiments did not mix flies of the 2 species and did not study whether one species of fly transferred bacteria to the other species, and Figure 1 does not show the results of such an interaction.

Question 9. The best answer is B. The experiments were done to determine if flies transferred bacteria from one surface to another. To ensure the flies were the only source of the bacteria colonies that grew on the nutrient agar, the agar had to be sterilized before the flies and any bacteria they carried were placed on the agar. Therefore, **B** is correct. **A** is incorrect; the agar was sterilized to be sure all bacteria on the agar were killed before the flies were placed in the dishes. **C** is incorrect; the agar was not a food source for the flies, and sterilizing the agar would have done nothing to ensure that it had nutrients even if it were a food source. **D** is incorrect; the nutrient agar already contained the necessary nutrients for bacteria growth. The sterilization process kills any bacteria on the agar; it does not affect the bacteria nutrients that were already there.

Question 10. The best answer is F. To see if the new species (Species X) transferred more bacteria than either of the 2 species in the experiments, Species X flies would have to be subjected to the same procedures as the other 2 species. Only Experiment 1 used both original species of flies. Adding a group of Species X flies to that experiment would allow a comparison of the number of colonies transferred by each of the 3 species. These data would allow the student's claim to be evaluated. Therefore, **F** is correct. **G** is incorrect; just changing the kind of bacteria in Experiment 1 would still include only the original 2 species of flies; no Species X flies would be included. There would be no data for Species X that could be used to evaluate the claim. **H** is incorrect; Experiment 2 included only 1 of the 2 original species of flies. To evaluate the claim, data for all 3 species would need to be collected. The design of Experiment 2 would not provide those data. **J** is incorrect; just changing the kind of bacteria in Experiment 2 would still include only 1 of the original 2 species of flies; in addition, no Species X flies would be included. Data for all 3 species would need to be collected to evaluate the claim.

Question 11. The best answer is A. In Experiment 3, *S. carnaria* flies were allowed to walk in an enclosure containing *E. coli* and then allowed various lengths of time to clean themselves before being placed on nutrient agar. This experiment tested whether cleaning time affected the average number of colonies per dish. Therefore, **A** is correct. **B** is incorrect; Experiment 3 used the procedures from Experiment 1, where the flies were allowed to walk in the *E. coli* enclosure for exactly 5 minutes. Since exposure time was held constant, this experiment would not be able to test a hypothesis about the effect of varying exposure time. **C** and **D** are incorrect; Experiment 3 used only *S. carnaria* flies. Without the second species of fly included, Experiment 3 cannot test whether one species transferred more bacteria or removed bacteria better than the other species.

Passage III

Question 12. The best answer is F. Figure 1 displays a plot line representing the $\%O_2$ in Earth's atmosphere from 250 mya to 64 mya. The single data point along that line that is closest to 21% is at the *x*-axis value of 250 mya (a value of approximately 20.5%). Therefore, **F** is correct. **G** is incorrect; the $\%O_2$ value at 200 mya is approximately 14.5%, much less than 21%. **H** is incorrect; the $\%O_2$ value at 150 mya is approximately 13.9%, much less than 21%. **J** is incorrect; the $\%O_2$ value at 100 mya is approximately 19.1%, less than 21% and not as close to 21% as the data point at 250 mya.

Question 13. The best answer is C. Figure 2 shows that at an initial $\%O_2$ of 17%, the flame duration for dry paper is approximately 8 sec and the flame duration for pine wood is approximately 2 sec. The difference is closest to 6 sec. Therefore, **C** is correct. **A** and **B** are incorrect; the values 2 sec and 4 sec are less than the actual difference of approximately 6 sec. **D** is incorrect; the value of 8 sec is greater than the actual difference of approximately 6 sec.

Question 14. The best answer is G. In Figure 1, there are 7 time periods, covering 200 mya–140 mya, in which paleowildfires occurred, but the %O_2 values were all less than 15%. Any interval within that range would have data that are inconsistent with the claim. Therefore, **G** is correct. **F** is incorrect; 250 mya–230 mya had paleowildfires, but the %O_2 was greater than 15%. Those data are consistent, not inconsistent, with the claim. **H** and **J** are incorrect; both 120 mya–100 mya and 90 mya–70 mya had paleowildfires, but the %O_2 was greater than 15%. Those data are consistent, not inconsistent, with the claim.

Question 15. The best answer is C. Figure 2 shows that the lowest initial %O_2 values at which each of the materials ignited are 13% for the match, 14% for the dry paper, 15% for the candle, and 16% for the pine wood. The order of the materials from highest initial %O_2 to ignite to lowest initial %O_2 to ignite is pine wood, candle, dry paper, and match. Therefore, **C** is correct. **A** and **B** are incorrect; match would be last in the order, as it had the lowest initial %O_2 to ignite. **D** is incorrect; candle should come before dry paper in the order since the candle had a higher initial %O_2 to ignite than did the dry paper.

Question 16. The best answer is F. Figure 1 shows bars representing the number of paleowildfires for each of several time periods, each covering a 10-million-year interval, starting 5 million years before the labeled year, and ending 5 million years after the labeled year (e.g., the bar labeled 140 mya represents the period 145 mya–135 mya). The question asks about the data for 95 mya–85 mya, which corresponds to the bar labeled 90 mya. That bar shows there were 4 paleowildfires over that time interval. Therefore, **F** is correct. **G**, **H**, and **J** are incorrect; the values 9, 14, and 19 are too high. The value 14 corresponds to the incorrect y-axis in Figure 1.

Passage IV

Question 17. The best answer is A. According to Figure 2, as the oven temperature increased from 110°C to 140°C, the *W/D* value for PTs submerged in water for 2 hr increased from approximately 23% to 48%. Therefore, **A** is correct. **B**, **C**, and **D** are incorrect; the *W/D* value increased steadily as the temperature increased.

Question 18. The best answer is F. According to the passage, in Step 1 the control PTs were submerged in water and in Step 3 the control PTs were heated in an oven at 25°C. Therefore, **F** is correct. **G** is incorrect; the oven temperature was 25°C. **H** and **J** are incorrect; the PTs were submerged in water.

Question 19. The best answer is D. According to the passage, in both Experiments 1 and 2 the PTs were soaked in water for 10 min, 2 hr, or 24 hr. None of the PTs were soaked in water for 18 hr. Therefore, **D** is correct. **A**, **B**, and **C** are incorrect; PTs were not soaked for 18 hr in either experiment.

Question 20. The best answer is G. According to Figure 1, the PTs submerged in water for 10 min had a higher W/D value at all oven temperatures than did the PTs submerged in water for 2 hr. Therefore, **G** is correct. **F** is incorrect; the W/D value at 2 hr was less than the W/D value at 10 min. **H** is incorrect; the W/D values were not the same. **J** is incorrect; the W/D value at 10 min was always greater than the W/D value at 2 hr.

Question 21. The best answer is C. The results of Experiment 2 show that the wet strength of PTs treated with both GLA and zinc nitrate was greater than the wet strength of PTs treated with water. Because the results show that treatment with GLA and zinc nitrate did increase the wet strength of the PTs, the results of Experiment 2 refute the prediction. Therefore, **C** is correct. **A** and **B** are incorrect; Experiment 1 did not investigate the effect of treating the PTs with GLA and zinc nitrate. **D** is incorrect; Experiment 2 does not support the prediction.

Question 22. The best answer is G. In both experiments the wet strength of the PTs is expressed as a percentage of the dry strength. Because this percentage is less than 100%, the dry strength is greater than the wet strength. Therefore, **G** is correct. **F** is incorrect; the wet strength was less than 100% of the dry strength. **H** and **J** are incorrect; the dry strength was greater than the wet strength.

Passage V

Question 23. The best answer is A. Student 1 claimed that plants receiving 8 hr or more of sunlight each day had purple stems, which is consistent with the finding that the presence of the purple pigment in plant tissues protects the tissues from being damaged by sunlight. Student 2 claimed that the amount of sunlight a plant receives does not affect the stem color; this is not consistent with the finding. Therefore, **A** is correct. **B** is incorrect; Student 1 indicated that plants receiving the most sunlight will have purple stems, not green stems. **C** and **D** are incorrect; the finding better supports the explanation of Student 1.

Question 24. The best answer is F. To answer this item, the examinee must know that the green pigment, chlorophyll, can be used for photosynthesis. All 4 of the students stated that all plants in Population A produce the green pigment chlorophyll. The explanations of all 4 students are therefore consistent with the statement that both green-stemmed and purple-stemmed plants produce a pigment that can be used for photosynthesis. Therefore, **F** is correct. **G**, **H**, and **J** are incorrect; all 4 students stated that all the plants in Population A produce a pigment that can be used for photosynthesis.

Question 25. The best answer is D. Only Student 1 claimed that sunlight affects the plants' stem color; however, Student 1 stated that if a plant receives 8 hr or more of sunlight each day, then it produces the purple pigment, and its stem will be purple. Student 1 would therefore not agree that providing a purple-stemmed plant with additional sunlight will change the stem color to green. Students 2, 3, and 4 would not be likely to agree that sunlight would affect the stems' color in any way. Therefore, **D** is correct. **A**, **B**, and **C** are incorrect; none of the students would be likely to agree that providing a purple-stemmed plant with additional sunlight will cause its stem to become green.

Question 26. The best answer is H. To answer this item, the examinee must know how to work a genetic cross. According to Student 3's explanation, a plant with either the Gene Q genotype Qq or the Gene Q genotype QQ will produce the purple pigment, and therefore will have a purple stem. A plant with the Gene Q genotype qq will produce the green pigment, and therefore will have a green stem. If the 2 purple-stemmed plants that were crossed had the Qq genotype, then their offspring would be approximately 25% green-stemmed with the qq genotype, and approximately 75% purple-stemmed with either the QQ genotype or the Qq genotype. Therefore, **H** is correct. **F** is incorrect; based on Student 1's explanation, because the stem color depends on exposure to sunlight, plants grown under the same conditions would have the same stem color. **G** is incorrect; based on Student 2's explanation, because the stem color depends on the amount of phosphorous received by the plants, plants grown under the same conditions would have the same stem color. **J** is incorrect; Student 4 claimed that purple-stemmed plants have the Gene Q genotype qq, and therefore all the offspring of 2 purple-stemmed plants would have purple stems.

Question 27. The best answer is D. To answer this item, the examinee must know how to work a genetic cross. Student 4 claimed that purple-stemmed plants have the Gene Q genotype qq and green-stemmed plants have either the Gene Q genotype Qq or QQ. A cross between a plant with the qq genotype (a purple-stemmed plant) and the Qq genotype (a green-stemmed plant) would produce some green-stemmed offspring with the Qq genotype and some purple-stemmed offspring with the qq genotype. Therefore, **D** is correct. **A** and **B** are incorrect; based on Student 4's explanation, the Gene Q genotype of the purple-stemmed parent must be qq. **C** is incorrect; a cross between a purple-stemmed plant with the qq genotype and a green-stemmed plant with the QQ genotype would produce only green-stemmed offspring with the Qq genotype.

Question 28. The best answer is J. Student 1 claimed that plants that receive sunlight for 8 hr or more each day have a purple stem. All plants that receive 9 hr of sunlight per day would therefore have a purple stem, and none would have a green stem. Student 2, Student 3, and Student 4 all agreed that the amount of sunlight received by a plant does not affect the stem color, and therefore a plant receiving 9 hr of sunlight could have either a purple stem or a green stem. Therefore, **J** is correct. **F** is incorrect; Student 1 would not agree with the statement. **G** is incorrect; while Student 2 likely would agree, Students 3 and 4 would also agree with the statement. **H** is incorrect; while Students 3 and 4 likely would agree, Student 2 would also agree with the statement.

Passage VI

Question 29. The best answer is B. According to Figure 2, March was the month in which a total of 70 L of H_2 was produced. According to Table 1, the average solar irradiance in the month of March was 153.8 W/m^2. Therefore, **B** is correct. **A** is incorrect; 77.8 W/m^2 was the average solar irradiance in January, not March. **C** is incorrect; 197.5 W/m^2 was the average solar irradiance in May, not March. **D** is incorrect; 206.4 W/m^2 was the average solar irradiance in July, not March.

Question 30. The best answer is H. According to Figure 1, O_2 is produced at the anode and H_2 is produced at the cathode during electrolysis. According to Step 3 of the experiment, electrolysis was initiated at 8:00 a.m. Then, eight hours later (at 4:00 p.m.), in Step 4, the amount of H_2 that had been produced was measured. Therefore, **H** is correct. **F** is incorrect; H_2 was not produced at the anode. **G** is incorrect; the amount of O_2 gas was not measured each day. **J** is incorrect; O_2 gas was not produced at the cathode and was not measured each day.

Question 31. The best answer is B. According to the passage, a 25% by mass aqueous solution of NaOH was added to the tank in Step 2 of the experiment. In 200 g of this solution, 25% of the mass would be NaOH: 25% × 200 g = 50 g. Therefore, **B** is correct. **A** is incorrect; 25 g is 12.5% of 200 g. **C** is incorrect; 200 g of an aqueous solution of NaOH cannot contain 200 g of NaOH because that would not be a solution, it would be pure NaOH. **D** is incorrect; the mass of NaOH in the 200 g of solution cannot exceed the total mass of the solution.

Question 32. The best answer is F. To answer this item, the examinee must know that, for balanced chemical equations involving gases, the coefficients may be interpreted in terms of gas volumes. The balanced equation for the electrolysis reaction is $2H_2O \rightarrow 2H_2 + O_2$. So, for every 2 L of H_2 gas produced, 1 L of O_2 gas will be produced. According to Figure 2, 40 L of H_2 gas was produced in February. Therefore, the number of liters of O_2 produced was (40 L)/2 = 20 L. Therefore, **F** is correct. **G** is incorrect; 40 L of H_2 were produced in February, and only half that amount of O_2 would have been produced. **H** is incorrect; this is twice the amount of H_2 that was produced, and according to the chemical equation only half as much O_2 would be produced. **J** is incorrect; the largest volume of H_2 produced in a month during the experiment was less than 90 L, so 100 L of O_2 could not have been produced in February since only half as much O_2 as H_2 could be produced each month.

Question 33. The best answer is C. According to the description of the experiment, Steps 1–5 were performed daily. Step 2 states that 4.0 L of NaOH solution were added to the tank. There are 30 days in June, so 30 days × 4.0L/day = 120 L of NaOH solution was added in June. Therefore, **C** is correct. **A**, **B**, and **D** are incorrect; Step 2 was performed once daily for 30 days in June.

Question 34. The best answer is J. To answer this item, the examinee must know that an aqueous NaOH solution has more ions than pure liquid H_2O, and that solutions with more ions have higher electrical conductivity. Since the H_2 gas is produced by the electrolysis of H_2O, the higher the conductivity the more H_2 produced. Therefore, **J** is correct. **F** is incorrect; pure liquid H_2O does not contain more ions than aqueous NaOH solution and does not have higher conductivity. **G** is incorrect; while pure liquid H_2O does have fewer ions and thus lower electrical conductivity than aqueous NaOH, that would result in less H_2, not more. **H** is incorrect; pure liquid H_2O would produce less H_2 because it has fewer ions, not more ions, than aqueous NaOH and thus has a lower electrical conductivity.

Passage VII

Question 35. The best answer is C. Figure 1 shows a vibrating string with 2 nodes, which matches the sketch in Table 1 for the 3rd harmonic. Therefore, **C** is correct. **A** is incorrect; the sketch in Table 1 for the 1st harmonic shows 0 nodes, and Figure 1 shows a string with 2 nodes. **B** is incorrect; the sketch in Table 1 for the 2nd harmonic shows 1 node, and Figure 1 shows a string with 2 nodes. **D** is incorrect; the sketch in Table 1 for the 4th harmonic shows 3 nodes, and Figure 1 shows a string with 2 nodes.

Question 36. The best answer is H. The sketch made in the new trial shows the vibrating string with 5 nodes. Based on the sketches shown in Table 1, the number of nodes on a vibrating string is always one more than the number of the harmonic. There are 4 nodes shown for the 5th harmonic, so a string having 5 nodes must correspond to the 6th harmonic. According to the results of Experiment 1 for String Z, as the number of the harmonic increases, the frequency increases by about 4 Hz. So, the frequency of the 6th harmonic should be greater than 19.8 Hz, or approximately 19.8 Hz + 4 Hz = 23.8 Hz. According to the results of Experiment 2, as the number of the harmonic increases, the tension, T, decreases. For String Z, the tension required for the 5th harmonic was 0.16 N, so the tension for the 6th harmonic should be less. Therefore, **H** is correct. **F** is incorrect; f should be greater than 19.8 Hz. **G** is incorrect; f should be greater than 19.8 Hz, and T should be less than 0.16 N. **J** is incorrect; T should be less than 0.16 N.

Question 37. The best answer is B. For String Y, $\mu = 0.08$ g/cm. The mass of a piece of string is equal to its length multiplied by μ, so a piece of String Y that is 1 cm in length will have a mass of 1 cm × 0.08 g/cm. For String X, $\mu = 0.02$ g/cm, and for String Z, $\mu = 0.16$ g/cm. So, for a piece of String X to have the same mass as the piece of String Y, it would have to be 4 times as long, and for a piece of String Z to have the same mass it would have to be half the length. Therefore, **B** is correct. **A** and **C** are incorrect; String X and String Z have different values of μ than String Y, so 1 cm lengths of those strings would not have the same mass as a 1 cm length of String Y. **D** is incorrect; String Z has a greater value of μ than String Y, so a length greater than 1 cm would not have the same mass.

Question 38. The best answer is H. For String X, Table 1 lists 11.2 Hz as the frequency for the 1st harmonic (f_1). For String X, the frequency for the 2nd harmonic (n = 2) was 22.4 Hz (exactly twice f_1), and for the 3rd harmonic (n = 3) was 33.5 (approximately 3 times f_1). The rest of the data for String X follows the same pattern, indicating that the equation $f_n = n \times f_1$ is most consistent with the results of Experiment 1 for String X. Therefore, **H** is correct. **F** is incorrect; for the 2nd harmonic, the equation $f_n = n + f_1$ yields $f_n = 2 + 11.2 = 13.2$ Hz, which does not match the 2nd harmonic frequency (22.4 Hz) given in Table 1. **G** is incorrect; for the 2nd harmonic, the equation $f_n = n - f_1$ yields $f_n = 2 - 11.2 = -9.2$ Hz, and negative frequencies do not exist. This also does not match the 2nd harmonic frequency (22.4 Hz) given in Table 1. **J** is incorrect; for the 2nd harmonic, the equation $f_n = n \div f_1$ yields $f_n = 2 \div 11.2 = 0.179$ Hz, which does not match the 2nd harmonic frequency (22.4 Hz) given in Table 1.

Question 39. The best answer is D. According to the description of the experiments, for String X, $\mu = 0.02$ g/cm; for String Y, $\mu = 0.08$ g/cm; and for String Z, $\mu = 0.16$ g/cm. Table 2 shows that as μ increased from string to string, the tension increased, with String Z requiring a tension of 0.25 N for the 4th harmonic. A string with a mass per unit length, μ, of 0.32 g/cm would require a tension greater than 0.25 N. Therefore, **D** is correct. **A**, **B**, and **C** are incorrect; the indicated tensions are lower than 0.25 N, so they would not be great enough.

Question 40. The best answer is H. According to the description of the experiments, μ increased from String X to String Y, to String Z. Considering the results of Experiment 1 for the 3rd harmonic, f decreased from string to string, going from 33.5 Hz for String X to 16.8 Hz for String Y to 11.9 Hz for String Z. The results of Experiment 2 show that the tension, T, for the 3rd harmonic increased from string to string, going from 0.06 N for String X to 0.22 N for String Y to 0.44 N for String Z. Therefore, **H** is correct. **F** is incorrect; f decreased as μ increased. **G** is incorrect; f decreased, and T increased as μ increased. **J** is incorrect; T increased as μ increased.

The ACT® *Sample Answer Document*

EXAMINEE STATEMENTS, CERTIFICATION, AND SIGNATURE

1. Statements: I understand that by registering for, launching, starting, or submitting answer documents for an ACT® test, I am agreeing to comply with and be bound by the *Terms and Conditions: Testing Rules and Policies for the ACT® Test* ("Terms").

I UNDERSTAND AND AGREE THAT THE TERMS PERMIT ACT TO CANCEL MY SCORES IN CERTAIN CIRCUMSTANCES. THE TERMS ALSO LIMIT DAMAGES AVAILABLE TO ME AND REQUIRE ARBITRATION OF CERTAIN DISPUTES. BY AGREEING TO ARBITRATION, ACT AND I BOTH WAIVE THE RIGHT TO HAVE THOSE DISPUTES HEARD BY A JUDGE OR JURY.

I understand that ACT owns the test questions and responses, and I will not share them with anyone by any form of communication before, during, or after the test administration. I understand that taking the test for someone else may violate the law and subject me to legal penalties. I consent to the collection and processing of personally identifying information I provide, and its subsequent use and disclosure, as described in the ACT Privacy Policy (www.act.org/privacy.html). If I am taking the test outside of the United States, I also permit ACT to transfer my personally identifying information to the United States, to ACT, or to a third-party service provider, where it will be subject to use and disclosure under the laws of the United States, including being accessible to law enforcement or national security authorities.

2. Certification: Copy the italicized certification below, then sign and date in the spaces provided.

*I agree to the **Statements** above and certify that I am the person whose information appears on this form.*

Your Signature   Today's Date

Do NOT mark in this shaded area.

USE A NO. 2 PENCIL ONLY.
(Do NOT use a mechanical pencil, ink, ballpoint, correction fluid, or felt-tip pen.)

A   NAME, MAILING ADDRESS, AND TELEPHONE
(Please print.)

Last Name   First Name   MI (Middle Initial)

House Number & Street (Apt. No.); or PO Box & No.; or RR & No.

City   State/Province   ZIP/Postal Code

Area Code   Number   Country

ACT, Inc.—Confidential Restricted when data present

ALL examinees must complete block A – please print.

Blocks B, C, and D are required for all examinees. Find the MATCHING INFORMATION on your ticket. Enter it EXACTLY the same way, even if any of the information is missing or incorrect. Fill in the corresponding ovals. If you do not complete these blocks to match your previous information EXACTLY, your scores will be **delayed up to 8 weeks**.

B   MATCH NAME (First 5 letters of last name)

C   MATCH NUMBER

D   DATE OF BIRTH

Month	Day	Year
January		
February		
March		
April		
May		
June		
July		
August		
September		
October		
November		
December		

ACT®

PO BOX 168, IOWA CITY, IA 52243-0168

          01121525W   (A)204361-001:654321   ISD39683   Printed in the US.

PAGE 2

Marking Directions: Mark only **one** oval for each question. Fill in response completely. Erase errors cleanly without smudging.

Correct mark: ○ ● ○ ○

Do NOT use these *incorrect* **or** *bad* **marks.**

Incorrect marks: ⊘ ⊗ ◐ ⊙
Overlapping mark: ○ ○ ◑ ◖
Cross-out mark: ○ ◐ ○ ○
Smudged erasure: ○ ○ ◐ ○
Mark is too light: ◯ ○ ○ ○

BOOKLET NUMBER

① ① ① ① ① ① ① ① ①
② ② ② ② ② ② ② ② ②
③ ③ ③ ③ ③ ③ ③ ③ ③
④ ④ ④ ④ ④ ④ ④ ④ ④
⑤ ⑤ ⑤ ⑤ ⑤ ⑤ ⑤ ⑤ ⑤
⑥ ⑥ ⑥ ⑥ ⑥ ⑥ ⑥ ⑥ ⑥
⑦ ⑦ ⑦ ⑦ ⑦ ⑦ ⑦ ⑦ ⑦
⑧ ⑧ ⑧ ⑧ ⑧ ⑧ ⑧ ⑧ ⑧
⑨ ⑨ ⑨ ⑨ ⑨ ⑨ ⑨ ⑨ ⑨
⓪ ⓪ ⓪ ⓪ ⓪ ⓪ ⓪ ⓪ ⓪

Print your 5-character **Test Form** in the boxes at the right and fill in the corresponding ovals.

FORM

① ① Ⓜ Ⓒ ①
② ②   ②
  ③   ③
  ④   ④
  ⑤   ⑤
  ⑥   ⑥
  ⑦   ⑦
  ⑧   ⑧
  ⑨   ⑨
  ⓪   ⓪

TEST 1: ENGLISH

1 Ⓐ Ⓑ Ⓒ Ⓓ	14 Ⓕ Ⓖ Ⓗ Ⓙ	27 Ⓐ Ⓑ Ⓒ Ⓓ	40 Ⓕ Ⓖ Ⓗ Ⓙ	53 Ⓐ Ⓑ Ⓒ Ⓓ	66 Ⓕ Ⓖ Ⓗ Ⓙ
2 Ⓕ Ⓖ Ⓗ Ⓙ	15 Ⓐ Ⓑ Ⓒ Ⓓ	28 Ⓕ Ⓖ Ⓗ Ⓙ	41 Ⓐ Ⓑ Ⓒ Ⓓ	54 Ⓕ Ⓖ Ⓗ Ⓙ	67 Ⓐ Ⓑ Ⓒ Ⓓ
3 Ⓐ Ⓑ Ⓒ Ⓓ	16 Ⓕ Ⓖ Ⓗ Ⓙ	29 Ⓐ Ⓑ Ⓒ Ⓓ	42 Ⓕ Ⓖ Ⓗ Ⓙ	55 Ⓐ Ⓑ Ⓒ Ⓓ	68 Ⓕ Ⓖ Ⓗ Ⓙ
4 Ⓕ Ⓖ Ⓗ Ⓙ	17 Ⓐ Ⓑ Ⓒ Ⓓ	30 Ⓕ Ⓖ Ⓗ Ⓙ	43 Ⓐ Ⓑ Ⓒ Ⓓ	56 Ⓕ Ⓖ Ⓗ Ⓙ	69 Ⓐ Ⓑ Ⓒ Ⓓ
5 Ⓐ Ⓑ Ⓒ Ⓓ	18 Ⓕ Ⓖ Ⓗ Ⓙ	31 Ⓐ Ⓑ Ⓒ Ⓓ	44 Ⓕ Ⓖ Ⓗ Ⓙ	57 Ⓐ Ⓑ Ⓒ Ⓓ	70 Ⓕ Ⓖ Ⓗ Ⓙ
6 Ⓕ Ⓖ Ⓗ Ⓙ	19 Ⓐ Ⓑ Ⓒ Ⓓ	32 Ⓕ Ⓖ Ⓗ Ⓙ	45 Ⓐ Ⓑ Ⓒ Ⓓ	58 Ⓕ Ⓖ Ⓗ Ⓙ	71 Ⓐ Ⓑ Ⓒ Ⓓ
7 Ⓐ Ⓑ Ⓒ Ⓓ	20 Ⓕ Ⓖ Ⓗ Ⓙ	33 Ⓐ Ⓑ Ⓒ Ⓓ	46 Ⓕ Ⓖ Ⓗ Ⓙ	59 Ⓐ Ⓑ Ⓒ Ⓓ	72 Ⓕ Ⓖ Ⓗ Ⓙ
8 Ⓕ Ⓖ Ⓗ Ⓙ	21 Ⓐ Ⓑ Ⓒ Ⓓ	34 Ⓕ Ⓖ Ⓗ Ⓙ	47 Ⓐ Ⓑ Ⓒ Ⓓ	60 Ⓕ Ⓖ Ⓗ Ⓙ	73 Ⓐ Ⓑ Ⓒ Ⓓ
9 Ⓐ Ⓑ Ⓒ Ⓓ	22 Ⓕ Ⓖ Ⓗ Ⓙ	35 Ⓐ Ⓑ Ⓒ Ⓓ	48 Ⓕ Ⓖ Ⓗ Ⓙ	61 Ⓐ Ⓑ Ⓒ Ⓓ	74 Ⓕ Ⓖ Ⓗ Ⓙ
10 Ⓕ Ⓖ Ⓗ Ⓙ	23 Ⓐ Ⓑ Ⓒ Ⓓ	36 Ⓕ Ⓖ Ⓗ Ⓙ	49 Ⓐ Ⓑ Ⓒ Ⓓ	62 Ⓕ Ⓖ Ⓗ Ⓙ	75 Ⓐ Ⓑ Ⓒ Ⓓ
11 Ⓐ Ⓑ Ⓒ Ⓓ	24 Ⓕ Ⓖ Ⓗ Ⓙ	37 Ⓐ Ⓑ Ⓒ Ⓓ	50 Ⓕ Ⓖ Ⓗ Ⓙ	63 Ⓐ Ⓑ Ⓒ Ⓓ	
12 Ⓕ Ⓖ Ⓗ Ⓙ	25 Ⓐ Ⓑ Ⓒ Ⓓ	38 Ⓕ Ⓖ Ⓗ Ⓙ	51 Ⓐ Ⓑ Ⓒ Ⓓ	64 Ⓕ Ⓖ Ⓗ Ⓙ	
13 Ⓐ Ⓑ Ⓒ Ⓓ	26 Ⓕ Ⓖ Ⓗ Ⓙ	39 Ⓐ Ⓑ Ⓒ Ⓓ	52 Ⓕ Ⓖ Ⓗ Ⓙ	65 Ⓐ Ⓑ Ⓒ Ⓓ	

TEST 2: MATHEMATICS

1 Ⓐ Ⓑ Ⓒ Ⓓ Ⓔ	11 Ⓐ Ⓑ Ⓒ Ⓓ Ⓔ	21 Ⓐ Ⓑ Ⓒ Ⓓ Ⓔ	31 Ⓐ Ⓑ Ⓒ Ⓓ Ⓔ	41 Ⓐ Ⓑ Ⓒ Ⓓ Ⓔ	51 Ⓐ Ⓑ Ⓒ Ⓓ Ⓔ
2 Ⓕ Ⓖ Ⓗ Ⓙ Ⓚ	12 Ⓕ Ⓖ Ⓗ Ⓙ Ⓚ	22 Ⓕ Ⓖ Ⓗ Ⓙ Ⓚ	32 Ⓕ Ⓖ Ⓗ Ⓙ Ⓚ	42 Ⓕ Ⓖ Ⓗ Ⓙ Ⓚ	52 Ⓕ Ⓖ Ⓗ Ⓙ Ⓚ
3 Ⓐ Ⓑ Ⓒ Ⓓ Ⓔ	13 Ⓐ Ⓑ Ⓒ Ⓓ Ⓔ	23 Ⓐ Ⓑ Ⓒ Ⓓ Ⓔ	33 Ⓐ Ⓑ Ⓒ Ⓓ Ⓔ	43 Ⓐ Ⓑ Ⓒ Ⓓ Ⓔ	53 Ⓐ Ⓑ Ⓒ Ⓓ Ⓔ
4 Ⓕ Ⓖ Ⓗ Ⓙ Ⓚ	14 Ⓕ Ⓖ Ⓗ Ⓙ Ⓚ	24 Ⓕ Ⓖ Ⓗ Ⓙ Ⓚ	34 Ⓕ Ⓖ Ⓗ Ⓙ Ⓚ	44 Ⓕ Ⓖ Ⓗ Ⓙ Ⓚ	54 Ⓕ Ⓖ Ⓗ Ⓙ Ⓚ
5 Ⓐ Ⓑ Ⓒ Ⓓ Ⓔ	15 Ⓐ Ⓑ Ⓒ Ⓓ Ⓔ	25 Ⓐ Ⓑ Ⓒ Ⓓ Ⓔ	35 Ⓐ Ⓑ Ⓒ Ⓓ Ⓔ	45 Ⓐ Ⓑ Ⓒ Ⓓ Ⓔ	55 Ⓐ Ⓑ Ⓒ Ⓓ Ⓔ
6 Ⓕ Ⓖ Ⓗ Ⓙ Ⓚ	16 Ⓕ Ⓖ Ⓗ Ⓙ Ⓚ	26 Ⓕ Ⓖ Ⓗ Ⓙ Ⓚ	36 Ⓕ Ⓖ Ⓗ Ⓙ Ⓚ	46 Ⓕ Ⓖ Ⓗ Ⓙ Ⓚ	56 Ⓕ Ⓖ Ⓗ Ⓙ Ⓚ
7 Ⓐ Ⓑ Ⓒ Ⓓ Ⓔ	17 Ⓐ Ⓑ Ⓒ Ⓓ Ⓔ	27 Ⓐ Ⓑ Ⓒ Ⓓ Ⓔ	37 Ⓐ Ⓑ Ⓒ Ⓓ Ⓔ	47 Ⓐ Ⓑ Ⓒ Ⓓ Ⓔ	57 Ⓐ Ⓑ Ⓒ Ⓓ Ⓔ
8 Ⓕ Ⓖ Ⓗ Ⓙ Ⓚ	18 Ⓕ Ⓖ Ⓗ Ⓙ Ⓚ	28 Ⓕ Ⓖ Ⓗ Ⓙ Ⓚ	38 Ⓕ Ⓖ Ⓗ Ⓙ Ⓚ	48 Ⓕ Ⓖ Ⓗ Ⓙ Ⓚ	58 Ⓕ Ⓖ Ⓗ Ⓙ Ⓚ
9 Ⓐ Ⓑ Ⓒ Ⓓ Ⓔ	19 Ⓐ Ⓑ Ⓒ Ⓓ Ⓔ	29 Ⓐ Ⓑ Ⓒ Ⓓ Ⓔ	39 Ⓐ Ⓑ Ⓒ Ⓓ Ⓔ	49 Ⓐ Ⓑ Ⓒ Ⓓ Ⓔ	59 Ⓐ Ⓑ Ⓒ Ⓓ Ⓔ
10 Ⓕ Ⓖ Ⓗ Ⓙ Ⓚ	20 Ⓕ Ⓖ Ⓗ Ⓙ Ⓚ	30 Ⓕ Ⓖ Ⓗ Ⓙ Ⓚ	40 Ⓕ Ⓖ Ⓗ Ⓙ Ⓚ	50 Ⓕ Ⓖ Ⓗ Ⓙ Ⓚ	60 Ⓕ Ⓖ Ⓗ Ⓙ Ⓚ

TEST 3: READING

1 Ⓐ Ⓑ Ⓒ Ⓓ	8 Ⓕ Ⓖ Ⓗ Ⓙ	15 Ⓐ Ⓑ Ⓒ Ⓓ	22 Ⓕ Ⓖ Ⓗ Ⓙ	29 Ⓐ Ⓑ Ⓒ Ⓓ	36 Ⓕ Ⓖ Ⓗ Ⓙ
2 Ⓕ Ⓖ Ⓗ Ⓙ	9 Ⓐ Ⓑ Ⓒ Ⓓ	16 Ⓕ Ⓖ Ⓗ Ⓙ	23 Ⓐ Ⓑ Ⓒ Ⓓ	30 Ⓕ Ⓖ Ⓗ Ⓙ	37 Ⓐ Ⓑ Ⓒ Ⓓ
3 Ⓐ Ⓑ Ⓒ Ⓓ	10 Ⓕ Ⓖ Ⓗ Ⓙ	17 Ⓐ Ⓑ Ⓒ Ⓓ	24 Ⓕ Ⓖ Ⓗ Ⓙ	31 Ⓐ Ⓑ Ⓒ Ⓓ	38 Ⓕ Ⓖ Ⓗ Ⓙ
4 Ⓕ Ⓖ Ⓗ Ⓙ	11 Ⓐ Ⓑ Ⓒ Ⓓ	18 Ⓕ Ⓖ Ⓗ Ⓙ	25 Ⓐ Ⓑ Ⓒ Ⓓ	32 Ⓕ Ⓖ Ⓗ Ⓙ	39 Ⓐ Ⓑ Ⓒ Ⓓ
5 Ⓐ Ⓑ Ⓒ Ⓓ	12 Ⓕ Ⓖ Ⓗ Ⓙ	19 Ⓐ Ⓑ Ⓒ Ⓓ	26 Ⓕ Ⓖ Ⓗ Ⓙ	33 Ⓐ Ⓑ Ⓒ Ⓓ	40 Ⓕ Ⓖ Ⓗ Ⓙ
6 Ⓕ Ⓖ Ⓗ Ⓙ	13 Ⓐ Ⓑ Ⓒ Ⓓ	20 Ⓕ Ⓖ Ⓗ Ⓙ	27 Ⓐ Ⓑ Ⓒ Ⓓ	34 Ⓕ Ⓖ Ⓗ Ⓙ	
7 Ⓐ Ⓑ Ⓒ Ⓓ	14 Ⓕ Ⓖ Ⓗ Ⓙ	21 Ⓐ Ⓑ Ⓒ Ⓓ	28 Ⓕ Ⓖ Ⓗ Ⓙ	35 Ⓐ Ⓑ Ⓒ Ⓓ	

TEST 4: SCIENCE

1 Ⓐ Ⓑ Ⓒ Ⓓ	8 Ⓕ Ⓖ Ⓗ Ⓙ	15 Ⓐ Ⓑ Ⓒ Ⓓ	22 Ⓕ Ⓖ Ⓗ Ⓙ	29 Ⓐ Ⓑ Ⓒ Ⓓ	36 Ⓕ Ⓖ Ⓗ Ⓙ
2 Ⓕ Ⓖ Ⓗ Ⓙ	9 Ⓐ Ⓑ Ⓒ Ⓓ	16 Ⓕ Ⓖ Ⓗ Ⓙ	23 Ⓐ Ⓑ Ⓒ Ⓓ	30 Ⓕ Ⓖ Ⓗ Ⓙ	37 Ⓐ Ⓑ Ⓒ Ⓓ
3 Ⓐ Ⓑ Ⓒ Ⓓ	10 Ⓕ Ⓖ Ⓗ Ⓙ	17 Ⓐ Ⓑ Ⓒ Ⓓ	24 Ⓕ Ⓖ Ⓗ Ⓙ	31 Ⓐ Ⓑ Ⓒ Ⓓ	38 Ⓕ Ⓖ Ⓗ Ⓙ
4 Ⓕ Ⓖ Ⓗ Ⓙ	11 Ⓐ Ⓑ Ⓒ Ⓓ	18 Ⓕ Ⓖ Ⓗ Ⓙ	25 Ⓐ Ⓑ Ⓒ Ⓓ	32 Ⓕ Ⓖ Ⓗ Ⓙ	39 Ⓐ Ⓑ Ⓒ Ⓓ
5 Ⓐ Ⓑ Ⓒ Ⓓ	12 Ⓕ Ⓖ Ⓗ Ⓙ	19 Ⓐ Ⓑ Ⓒ Ⓓ	26 Ⓕ Ⓖ Ⓗ Ⓙ	33 Ⓐ Ⓑ Ⓒ Ⓓ	40 Ⓕ Ⓖ Ⓗ Ⓙ
6 Ⓕ Ⓖ Ⓗ Ⓙ	13 Ⓐ Ⓑ Ⓒ Ⓓ	20 Ⓕ Ⓖ Ⓗ Ⓙ	27 Ⓐ Ⓑ Ⓒ Ⓓ	34 Ⓕ Ⓖ Ⓗ Ⓙ	
7 Ⓐ Ⓑ Ⓒ Ⓓ	14 Ⓕ Ⓖ Ⓗ Ⓙ	21 Ⓐ Ⓑ Ⓒ Ⓓ	28 Ⓕ Ⓖ Ⓗ Ⓙ	35 Ⓐ Ⓑ Ⓒ Ⓓ	

The ACT® *Sample Answer Document*

EXAMINEE STATEMENTS, CERTIFICATION, AND SIGNATURE

1. Statements: I understand that by registering for, launching, starting, or submitting answer documents for an ACT® test, I am agreeing to comply with and be bound by the *Terms and Conditions: Testing Rules and Policies for the ACT® Test* ("Terms").

I UNDERSTAND AND AGREE THAT THE TERMS PERMIT ACT TO CANCEL MY SCORES IN CERTAIN CIRCUMSTANCES. THE TERMS ALSO LIMIT DAMAGES AVAILABLE TO ME AND REQUIRE ARBITRATION OF CERTAIN DISPUTES. BY AGREEING TO ARBITRATION, ACT AND I BOTH WAIVE THE RIGHT TO HAVE THOSE DISPUTES HEARD BY A JUDGE OR JURY.

I understand that ACT owns the test questions and responses, and I will not share them with anyone by any form of communication before, during, or after the test administration. I understand that taking the test for someone else may violate the law and subject me to legal penalties. I consent to the collection and processing of personally identifying information I provide, and its subsequent use and disclosure, as described in the ACT Privacy Policy (www.act.org/privacy.html). If I am taking the test outside of the United States, I also permit ACT to transfer my personally identifying information to the United States, to ACT, or to a third-party service provider, where it will be subject to use and disclosure under the laws of the United States, including being accessible to law enforcement or national security authorities.

2. Certification: Copy the italicized certification below, then sign and date in the spaces provided.

*I agree to the **Statements** above and certify that I am the person whose information appears on this form.*

____

____

Your Signature   Today's Date

Do NOT mark in this shaded area.

USE A NO. 2 PENCIL ONLY.
(Do NOT use a mechanical pencil, ink, ballpoint, correction fluid, or felt-tip pen.)

A NAME, MAILING ADDRESS, AND TELEPHONE
(Please print.)

Last Name   First Name   MI (Middle Initial)

House Number & Street (Apt. No.); or PO Box & No.; or RR & No.

City   State/Province   ZIP/Postal Code

Area Code   Number   Country

ACT, Inc.—Confidential Restricted when data present

ALL examinees must complete block A – please print.

Blocks B, C, and D are required for all examinees. Find the MATCHING INFORMATION on your ticket. Enter it EXACTLY the same way, even if any of the information is missing or incorrect. Fill in the corresponding ovals. If you do not complete these blocks to match your previous information EXACTLY, your scores will be **delayed up to 8 weeks**.

ACT®

PO BOX 168, IOWA CITY, IA 52243-0168

B MATCH NAME
(First 5 letters of last name)

C MATCH NUMBER

D DATE OF BIRTH

Month	Day	Year
January		
February		
March		
April		
May		
June		
July		
August		
September		
October		
November		
December		

The ONLY Official Prep Guide from the Makers of the ACT

PAGE 2

Marking Directions: Mark only **one** oval for each question. Fill in response completely. Erase errors cleanly without smudging.

Correct mark: ○ ● ○ ○

Do NOT use these *incorrect* or *bad* **marks.**

Incorrect marks: ⊘ ⊗ ⊖ ⊙
Overlapping mark:
Cross-out mark:
Smudged erasure:
Mark is too light:

BOOKLET NUMBER

Print your 5-character **Test Form** in the boxes at the right <u>and</u> fill in the corresponding ovals.

FORM

TEST 1: ENGLISH

1 Ⓐ Ⓑ Ⓒ Ⓓ	14 Ⓕ Ⓖ Ⓗ Ⓙ	27 Ⓐ Ⓑ Ⓒ Ⓓ	40 Ⓕ Ⓖ Ⓗ Ⓙ	53 Ⓐ Ⓑ Ⓒ Ⓓ	66 Ⓕ Ⓖ Ⓗ Ⓙ
2 Ⓕ Ⓖ Ⓗ Ⓙ	15 Ⓐ Ⓑ Ⓒ Ⓓ	28 Ⓕ Ⓖ Ⓗ Ⓙ	41 Ⓐ Ⓑ Ⓒ Ⓓ	54 Ⓕ Ⓖ Ⓗ Ⓙ	67 Ⓐ Ⓑ Ⓒ Ⓓ
3 Ⓐ Ⓑ Ⓒ Ⓓ	16 Ⓕ Ⓖ Ⓗ Ⓙ	29 Ⓐ Ⓑ Ⓒ Ⓓ	42 Ⓕ Ⓖ Ⓗ Ⓙ	55 Ⓐ Ⓑ Ⓒ Ⓓ	68 Ⓕ Ⓖ Ⓗ Ⓙ
4 Ⓕ Ⓖ Ⓗ Ⓙ	17 Ⓐ Ⓑ Ⓒ Ⓓ	30 Ⓕ Ⓖ Ⓗ Ⓙ	43 Ⓐ Ⓑ Ⓒ Ⓓ	56 Ⓕ Ⓖ Ⓗ Ⓙ	69 Ⓐ Ⓑ Ⓒ Ⓓ
5 Ⓐ Ⓑ Ⓒ Ⓓ	18 Ⓕ Ⓖ Ⓗ Ⓙ	31 Ⓐ Ⓑ Ⓒ Ⓓ	44 Ⓕ Ⓖ Ⓗ Ⓙ	57 Ⓐ Ⓑ Ⓒ Ⓓ	70 Ⓕ Ⓖ Ⓗ Ⓙ
6 Ⓕ Ⓖ Ⓗ Ⓙ	19 Ⓐ Ⓑ Ⓒ Ⓓ	32 Ⓕ Ⓖ Ⓗ Ⓙ	45 Ⓐ Ⓑ Ⓒ Ⓓ	58 Ⓕ Ⓖ Ⓗ Ⓙ	71 Ⓐ Ⓑ Ⓒ Ⓓ
7 Ⓐ Ⓑ Ⓒ Ⓓ	20 Ⓕ Ⓖ Ⓗ Ⓙ	33 Ⓐ Ⓑ Ⓒ Ⓓ	46 Ⓕ Ⓖ Ⓗ Ⓙ	59 Ⓐ Ⓑ Ⓒ Ⓓ	72 Ⓕ Ⓖ Ⓗ Ⓙ
8 Ⓕ Ⓖ Ⓗ Ⓙ	21 Ⓐ Ⓑ Ⓒ Ⓓ	34 Ⓕ Ⓖ Ⓗ Ⓙ	47 Ⓐ Ⓑ Ⓒ Ⓓ	60 Ⓕ Ⓖ Ⓗ Ⓙ	73 Ⓐ Ⓑ Ⓒ Ⓓ
9 Ⓐ Ⓑ Ⓒ Ⓓ	22 Ⓕ Ⓖ Ⓗ Ⓙ	35 Ⓐ Ⓑ Ⓒ Ⓓ	48 Ⓕ Ⓖ Ⓗ Ⓙ	61 Ⓐ Ⓑ Ⓒ Ⓓ	74 Ⓕ Ⓖ Ⓗ Ⓙ
10 Ⓕ Ⓖ Ⓗ Ⓙ	23 Ⓐ Ⓑ Ⓒ Ⓓ	36 Ⓕ Ⓖ Ⓗ Ⓙ	49 Ⓐ Ⓑ Ⓒ Ⓓ	62 Ⓕ Ⓖ Ⓗ Ⓙ	75 Ⓐ Ⓑ Ⓒ Ⓓ
11 Ⓐ Ⓑ Ⓒ Ⓓ	24 Ⓕ Ⓖ Ⓗ Ⓙ	37 Ⓐ Ⓑ Ⓒ Ⓓ	50 Ⓕ Ⓖ Ⓗ Ⓙ	63 Ⓐ Ⓑ Ⓒ Ⓓ	
12 Ⓕ Ⓖ Ⓗ Ⓙ	25 Ⓐ Ⓑ Ⓒ Ⓓ	38 Ⓕ Ⓖ Ⓗ Ⓙ	51 Ⓐ Ⓑ Ⓒ Ⓓ	64 Ⓕ Ⓖ Ⓗ Ⓙ	
13 Ⓐ Ⓑ Ⓒ Ⓓ	26 Ⓕ Ⓖ Ⓗ Ⓙ	39 Ⓐ Ⓑ Ⓒ Ⓓ	52 Ⓕ Ⓖ Ⓗ Ⓙ	65 Ⓐ Ⓑ Ⓒ Ⓓ	

TEST 2: MATHEMATICS

1 Ⓐ Ⓑ Ⓒ Ⓓ Ⓔ	11 Ⓐ Ⓑ Ⓒ Ⓓ Ⓔ	21 Ⓐ Ⓑ Ⓒ Ⓓ Ⓔ	31 Ⓐ Ⓑ Ⓒ Ⓓ Ⓔ	41 Ⓐ Ⓑ Ⓒ Ⓓ Ⓔ	51 Ⓐ Ⓑ Ⓒ Ⓓ Ⓔ
2 Ⓕ Ⓖ Ⓗ Ⓙ Ⓚ	12 Ⓕ Ⓖ Ⓗ Ⓙ Ⓚ	22 Ⓕ Ⓖ Ⓗ Ⓙ Ⓚ	32 Ⓕ Ⓖ Ⓗ Ⓙ Ⓚ	42 Ⓕ Ⓖ Ⓗ Ⓙ Ⓚ	52 Ⓕ Ⓖ Ⓗ Ⓙ Ⓚ
3 Ⓐ Ⓑ Ⓒ Ⓓ Ⓔ	13 Ⓐ Ⓑ Ⓒ Ⓓ Ⓔ	23 Ⓐ Ⓑ Ⓒ Ⓓ Ⓔ	33 Ⓐ Ⓑ Ⓒ Ⓓ Ⓔ	43 Ⓐ Ⓑ Ⓒ Ⓓ Ⓔ	53 Ⓐ Ⓑ Ⓒ Ⓓ Ⓔ
4 Ⓕ Ⓖ Ⓗ Ⓙ Ⓚ	14 Ⓕ Ⓖ Ⓗ Ⓙ Ⓚ	24 Ⓕ Ⓖ Ⓗ Ⓙ Ⓚ	34 Ⓕ Ⓖ Ⓗ Ⓙ Ⓚ	44 Ⓕ Ⓖ Ⓗ Ⓙ Ⓚ	54 Ⓕ Ⓖ Ⓗ Ⓙ Ⓚ
5 Ⓐ Ⓑ Ⓒ Ⓓ Ⓔ	15 Ⓐ Ⓑ Ⓒ Ⓓ Ⓔ	25 Ⓐ Ⓑ Ⓒ Ⓓ Ⓔ	35 Ⓐ Ⓑ Ⓒ Ⓓ Ⓔ	45 Ⓐ Ⓑ Ⓒ Ⓓ Ⓔ	55 Ⓐ Ⓑ Ⓒ Ⓓ Ⓔ
6 Ⓕ Ⓖ Ⓗ Ⓙ Ⓚ	16 Ⓕ Ⓖ Ⓗ Ⓙ Ⓚ	26 Ⓕ Ⓖ Ⓗ Ⓙ Ⓚ	36 Ⓕ Ⓖ Ⓗ Ⓙ Ⓚ	46 Ⓕ Ⓖ Ⓗ Ⓙ Ⓚ	56 Ⓕ Ⓖ Ⓗ Ⓙ Ⓚ
7 Ⓐ Ⓑ Ⓒ Ⓓ Ⓔ	17 Ⓐ Ⓑ Ⓒ Ⓓ Ⓔ	27 Ⓐ Ⓑ Ⓒ Ⓓ Ⓔ	37 Ⓐ Ⓑ Ⓒ Ⓓ Ⓔ	47 Ⓐ Ⓑ Ⓒ Ⓓ Ⓔ	57 Ⓐ Ⓑ Ⓒ Ⓓ Ⓔ
8 Ⓕ Ⓖ Ⓗ Ⓙ Ⓚ	18 Ⓕ Ⓖ Ⓗ Ⓙ Ⓚ	28 Ⓕ Ⓖ Ⓗ Ⓙ Ⓚ	38 Ⓕ Ⓖ Ⓗ Ⓙ Ⓚ	48 Ⓕ Ⓖ Ⓗ Ⓙ Ⓚ	58 Ⓕ Ⓖ Ⓗ Ⓙ Ⓚ
9 Ⓐ Ⓑ Ⓒ Ⓓ Ⓔ	19 Ⓐ Ⓑ Ⓒ Ⓓ Ⓔ	29 Ⓐ Ⓑ Ⓒ Ⓓ Ⓔ	39 Ⓐ Ⓑ Ⓒ Ⓓ Ⓔ	49 Ⓐ Ⓑ Ⓒ Ⓓ Ⓔ	59 Ⓐ Ⓑ Ⓒ Ⓓ Ⓔ
10 Ⓕ Ⓖ Ⓗ Ⓙ Ⓚ	20 Ⓕ Ⓖ Ⓗ Ⓙ Ⓚ	30 Ⓕ Ⓖ Ⓗ Ⓙ Ⓚ	40 Ⓕ Ⓖ Ⓗ Ⓙ Ⓚ	50 Ⓕ Ⓖ Ⓗ Ⓙ Ⓚ	60 Ⓕ Ⓖ Ⓗ Ⓙ Ⓚ

TEST 3: READING

1 Ⓐ Ⓑ Ⓒ Ⓓ	8 Ⓕ Ⓖ Ⓗ Ⓙ	15 Ⓐ Ⓑ Ⓒ Ⓓ	22 Ⓕ Ⓖ Ⓗ Ⓙ	29 Ⓐ Ⓑ Ⓒ Ⓓ	36 Ⓕ Ⓖ Ⓗ Ⓙ
2 Ⓕ Ⓖ Ⓗ Ⓙ	9 Ⓐ Ⓑ Ⓒ Ⓓ	16 Ⓕ Ⓖ Ⓗ Ⓙ	23 Ⓐ Ⓑ Ⓒ Ⓓ	30 Ⓕ Ⓖ Ⓗ Ⓙ	37 Ⓐ Ⓑ Ⓒ Ⓓ
3 Ⓐ Ⓑ Ⓒ Ⓓ	10 Ⓕ Ⓖ Ⓗ Ⓙ	17 Ⓐ Ⓑ Ⓒ Ⓓ	24 Ⓕ Ⓖ Ⓗ Ⓙ	31 Ⓐ Ⓑ Ⓒ Ⓓ	38 Ⓕ Ⓖ Ⓗ Ⓙ
4 Ⓕ Ⓖ Ⓗ Ⓙ	11 Ⓐ Ⓑ Ⓒ Ⓓ	18 Ⓕ Ⓖ Ⓗ Ⓙ	25 Ⓐ Ⓑ Ⓒ Ⓓ	32 Ⓕ Ⓖ Ⓗ Ⓙ	39 Ⓐ Ⓑ Ⓒ Ⓓ
5 Ⓐ Ⓑ Ⓒ Ⓓ	12 Ⓕ Ⓖ Ⓗ Ⓙ	19 Ⓐ Ⓑ Ⓒ Ⓓ	26 Ⓕ Ⓖ Ⓗ Ⓙ	33 Ⓐ Ⓑ Ⓒ Ⓓ	40 Ⓕ Ⓖ Ⓗ Ⓙ
6 Ⓕ Ⓖ Ⓗ Ⓙ	13 Ⓐ Ⓑ Ⓒ Ⓓ	20 Ⓕ Ⓖ Ⓗ Ⓙ	27 Ⓐ Ⓑ Ⓒ Ⓓ	34 Ⓕ Ⓖ Ⓗ Ⓙ	
7 Ⓐ Ⓑ Ⓒ Ⓓ	14 Ⓕ Ⓖ Ⓗ Ⓙ	21 Ⓐ Ⓑ Ⓒ Ⓓ	28 Ⓕ Ⓖ Ⓗ Ⓙ	35 Ⓐ Ⓑ Ⓒ Ⓓ	

TEST 4: SCIENCE

1 Ⓐ Ⓑ Ⓒ Ⓓ	8 Ⓕ Ⓖ Ⓗ Ⓙ	15 Ⓐ Ⓑ Ⓒ Ⓓ	22 Ⓕ Ⓖ Ⓗ Ⓙ	29 Ⓐ Ⓑ Ⓒ Ⓓ	36 Ⓕ Ⓖ Ⓗ Ⓙ
2 Ⓕ Ⓖ Ⓗ Ⓙ	9 Ⓐ Ⓑ Ⓒ Ⓓ	16 Ⓕ Ⓖ Ⓗ Ⓙ	23 Ⓐ Ⓑ Ⓒ Ⓓ	30 Ⓕ Ⓖ Ⓗ Ⓙ	37 Ⓐ Ⓑ Ⓒ Ⓓ
3 Ⓐ Ⓑ Ⓒ Ⓓ	10 Ⓕ Ⓖ Ⓗ Ⓙ	17 Ⓐ Ⓑ Ⓒ Ⓓ	24 Ⓕ Ⓖ Ⓗ Ⓙ	31 Ⓐ Ⓑ Ⓒ Ⓓ	38 Ⓕ Ⓖ Ⓗ Ⓙ
4 Ⓕ Ⓖ Ⓗ Ⓙ	11 Ⓐ Ⓑ Ⓒ Ⓓ	18 Ⓕ Ⓖ Ⓗ Ⓙ	25 Ⓐ Ⓑ Ⓒ Ⓓ	32 Ⓕ Ⓖ Ⓗ Ⓙ	39 Ⓐ Ⓑ Ⓒ Ⓓ
5 Ⓐ Ⓑ Ⓒ Ⓓ	12 Ⓕ Ⓖ Ⓗ Ⓙ	19 Ⓐ Ⓑ Ⓒ Ⓓ	26 Ⓕ Ⓖ Ⓗ Ⓙ	33 Ⓐ Ⓑ Ⓒ Ⓓ	40 Ⓕ Ⓖ Ⓗ Ⓙ
6 Ⓕ Ⓖ Ⓗ Ⓙ	13 Ⓐ Ⓑ Ⓒ Ⓓ	20 Ⓕ Ⓖ Ⓗ Ⓙ	27 Ⓐ Ⓑ Ⓒ Ⓓ	34 Ⓕ Ⓖ Ⓗ Ⓙ	
7 Ⓐ Ⓑ Ⓒ Ⓓ	14 Ⓕ Ⓖ Ⓗ Ⓙ	21 Ⓐ Ⓑ Ⓒ Ⓓ	28 Ⓕ Ⓖ Ⓗ Ⓙ	35 Ⓐ Ⓑ Ⓒ Ⓓ	

Practice Test 4

EXAMINEE STATEMENTS, CERTIFICATION, AND SIGNATURE

1. **Statements:** I understand that by registering for, launching, starting, or submitting answer documents for an ACT® test, I am agreeing to comply with and be bound by the *Terms and Conditions: Testing Rules and Policies for the ACT® Test* ("Terms").

   I UNDERSTAND AND AGREE THAT THE TERMS PERMIT ACT TO CANCEL MY SCORES IN CERTAIN CIRCUMSTANCES. THE TERMS ALSO LIMIT DAMAGES AVAILABLE TO ME AND REQUIRE ARBITRATION OF CERTAIN DISPUTES. BY AGREEING TO ARBITRATION, ACT AND I BOTH WAIVE THE RIGHT TO HAVE THOSE DISPUTES HEARD BY A JUDGE OR JURY.

   I understand that ACT owns the test questions and responses, and I will not share them with anyone by any form of communication before, during, or after the test administration. I understand that taking the test for someone else may violate the law and subject me to legal penalties.

   I consent to the collection and processing of personally identifying information I provide, and its subsequent use and disclosure, as described in the ACT Privacy Policy (www.act.org/privacy.html). If I am taking the test outside of the United States, I also permit ACT to transfer my personally identifying information to the United States, to ACT, or to a third-party service provider, where it will be subject to use and disclosure under the laws of the United States, including being accessible to law enforcement or national security authorities.

2. **Certification:** Copy the italicized certification below, then sign, date, and print your name in the spaces provided.

   *I agree to the **Statements** above and certify that I am the person whose information appears on this form.*

   ____

   ____

| Your Signature | Today's Date | Print Your Name |

The ACT® Form 25MC4
2026 | 2027

Directions

This booklet contains tests in English, mathematics, reading, and science. These tests measure skills and abilities highly related to high school course work and success in college. **Calculators may be used on the mathematics test only.**

The questions in each test are numbered, and the suggested answers for each question are lettered. On the answer document, the rows of ovals are numbered to match the questions, and the ovals in each row are lettered to correspond to the suggested answers.

For each question, first decide which answer is best. Next, locate on the answer document the row of ovals numbered the same as the question. Then, locate the oval in that row lettered the same as your answer. Finally, fill in the oval completely. Use a soft lead pencil and make your marks heavy and black. **Do not use ink or a mechanical pencil.**

Mark only one answer to each question. If you change your mind about an answer, erase your first mark thoroughly before marking your new answer. For each question, make certain that you mark in the row of ovals with the same number as the question.

Only responses marked on your answer document will be scored. Your score on each test will be based only on the number of questions you answer correctly during the time allowed for that test. You will **not** be penalized for guessing. **It is to your advantage to answer every question even if you must guess.**

You may work on each test **only** when the testing staff tells you to do so. If you finish a test before time is called for that test, you should use the time remaining to reconsider questions you are uncertain about in that test. You may **not** look back to a test on which time has already been called, and you may **not** go ahead to another test. To do so will disqualify you from the examination.

Lay your pencil down immediately when time is called at the end of each test. You may **not** for any reason fill in or alter ovals for a test after time is called for that test. To do so will disqualify you from the examination.

Do not fold or tear the pages of your test booklet.

**DO NOT OPEN THIS BOOKLET
UNTIL TOLD TO DO SO.**

The ONLY Official Prep Guide from the Makers of the ACT

1 ■ ■ ■ ■ ■ ■ ■ ■ 1

ENGLISH TEST
35 Minutes—50 Questions

DIRECTIONS: In the passages that follow, certain words and phrases are underlined and numbered. In the right-hand column, you will find alternatives for the underlined part. You are to choose the best answer to each question. If you think the original version is best, choose "**No Change**."

You will also find questions about a section of the passage, or about the passage as a whole. These questions do not refer to an underlined portion of the passage, but rather are identified by a number or numbers in a box.

For each question, choose the alternative you consider best and fill in the corresponding oval on your answer document. Read each passage through once before you begin to answer the questions that accompany it. For many of the questions, you must read several sentences beyond the question to determine the answer. Be sure that you have read far enough ahead each time you choose an alternative.

PASSAGE I

A Mouthful of Music

Mouth music is the name for the many ways of imitating the sounds of musical instruments with the human voice. Forms of mouth music are performed around the world, but the genre <u>being</u> particularly

[1]

popular in England, Ireland, and Scotland.

Celtic mouth music exists to accompany dancing. Instead of using traditional lyrics, singers often produce nonsense <u>syllables, called vocables to</u>

[2]

represent specific instrumental sounds, such as those of bagpipes or violins. The results are songs that rarely make literal sense—they focus instead on rhythm and sound—but nevertheless flow in a way that is easy to dance to.

Because of this, one Scottish form of mouth music, *puirt-a-beul*, is performed entirely in the Gaelic language and accompanies traditional dance steps.

1. Which choice makes the sentence most grammatically acceptable?
   A. **No Change**
   B. was being
   C. is
   D. **Delete** the underlined portion.

2. Which choice makes the sentence most grammatically acceptable?
   F. **No Change**
   G. syllables called vocables,
   H. syllables, called vocables,
   J. syllables called, vocables,

GO ON TO THE NEXT PAGE.

The <u>often tongue-twisting</u> lyrics require much practice
₃
to perfect.

[4] Instruments were prohibitively expensive and

thus scarce in isolated Scottish villages. In order to fill

the void, mouth music emerged and provided residents

with the music they wanted for dancing. Additionally,

puirt-a-beul gave anyone <u>whomever</u> didn't read music
₅
a way to learn and pass on traditional songs.

3. If the writer were to delete the underlined portion, the sentence would primarily lose:
   A. a description that emphasizes the difficulty of puirt-a-beul.
   B. information about writing lyrics for puirt-a-beul.
   C. an indication of how often puirt-a-beul is performed in Celtic culture.
   D. an example of a training exercise puirt-a-beul singers use to practice lyrics.

4. Given that all the following statements are true, which one, if added here, would most effectively introduce the subject of the paragraph?
   F. Puirt-a-beul was most likely invented out of necessity.
   G. Mouth music singers must have a good sense of rhythm.
   H. Celtic mouth music, including puirt-a-beul, has influenced jazz scat singing.
   J. Another form of mouth music that originated in Scotland is the waulking song.

5. Which choice makes the sentence most grammatically acceptable?
   A. No Change
   B. which
   C. whom
   D. who

Making the Desert Bloom

More than two thousand years ago, a people the

<u>Romans, called the Garamantes,</u> created a complex
₆
civilization in one of the world's driest places—the

Sahara Desert. Beginning around 500 BCE, they built

towns and villages, <u>cloth was manufactured there and</u>
₇
jewelry, and traded throughout North Africa and the

Mediterranean. They also grew a variety of crops,

including wheat, dates, palms, grapes, figs, and melons.

6. Which choice makes the sentence most grammatically acceptable?
   F. No Change
   G. Romans called the Garamantes,
   H. Romans called: the Garamantes
   J. Romans called the Garamantes

7. Which choice makes the sentence most grammatically acceptable?
   A. No Change
   B. the manufacture of cloth took place
   C. manufactured cloth
   D. cloth

GO ON TO THE NEXT PAGE.

1 ■ ■ ■ ■ ■ ■ ■ ■ ■ **1**

The survival of their civilization depended on hundreds of miles of underground tunnels. These tunnels carried water to desert settlements from an aquifer, an underground water source, in the distant mountains. The water ran through sloping, hand-dug tunnels [8] called foggaras, which could be as deep as one hundred thirty feet below ground. These tunnels were connected to the surface by ventilation shafts every thirty feet or so. When the tunnels reached a town or field, the water flowed into more easily accessible surface canals or reservoirs. Having left no clues, archaeologists don't [9] know how the Garamantes learned to build foggaras. Other such tunnels exist in Iran, Algeria, Tunisia, and elsewhere.

Because the canals were underground, the water they carried stayed clean and didn't evaporate. And because the water came from an aquifer rather then from its rainfall, [10] the supply was unaffected by drought. The Garamantes

could of relied on a constant supply of water for drinking, [11]

washing, and irrigation. Moreover, the cold, damp air of [12] the foggaras lowered the temperature inside the homes that were built over them, resulting in an ancient form of air-conditioning.

8. Which choice best indicates the method used to build the tunnels?
   F. **No Change**
   G. underground
   H. dimly lit
   J. desert

9. Which choice makes the sentence most grammatically acceptable?
   A. **No Change**
   B. A genuine puzzle to scientists, archaeologists
   C. Giving no indication, archaeologists
   D. Archaeologists

10. Which choice makes the sentence most grammatically acceptable?
    F. **No Change**
    G. than from
    H. then
    J. by

11. Which choice makes the sentence most grammatically acceptable?
    A. **No Change**
    B. had to of relied
    C. could rely
    D. relies

12. Which transition word or phrase is most logical in context?
    F. **No Change**
    G. Nevertheless,
    H. In contrast,
    J. Even so,

GO ON TO THE NEXT PAGE.

1 ■ ■ ■ ■ ■ ■ ■ ■ ■ **1**

The Garamantes thrived until about 500 CE, when some archaeologists believe they began to deplete the aquifer. As the foggaras supplied less
13
and less water, the Garamantes' population declined. Their civilization eventually collapsed. However, at least six hundred of the ancient foggaras survive. The stone mounds that mark their ventilation shafts are still visible in what is now southwestern Libya, where they can be seen even now.
14

13. Which choice is clearest and most precise in context?
   A. **No Change**
   B. As to when
   C. Whereas
   D. Though

14. Which choice is least redundant in context?
   F. **No Change**
   G. a place where visitors can see these amazing signs of an ancient civilization.
   H. the location that continues to present visitors with a view of these remnants of a time gone by.
   J. **Delete** the underlined portion and end the sentence with a period.

> Question 15 asks about the preceding passage as a whole.

15. Suppose the writer's primary purpose had been to present information about a civilization's efforts to overcome a natural obstacle in order to survive. Would this essay accomplish that purpose?
   A. Yes, because it explains that the Garamantes traded throughout North Africa and the Mediterranean.
   B. Yes, because it describes the Garamantes' method of bringing water to an otherwise dry area, allowing the Garamantes to thrive there.
   C. No, because the foggaras were not naturally occurring tunnels.
   D. No, because the foggaras ultimately led to the downfall of the Garamantes' civilization.

GO ON TO THE NEXT PAGE.

1 ▪ ▪ ▪ ▪ ▪ ▪ ▪ ▪ ▪ 1

PASSAGE III

Faith Ringgold's Quilting Bee

The artist Faith Ringgold has made a name for herself with her "story quilts," lively combinations of painting, quilting, and storytelling. Each artwork consists of a painting framed by quilted squares of fabric and story panels. One of these artworks, *The Sunflowers Quilting Bee at Arles*, depicts a scene of women at work on a quilt in a field of towering yellow flowers that eight African American women sit around the quilt that covers their laps. Who are these people stitching among the flowers? What brings them so close that their shoulders touch?

Thus, the answers to these questions can be found in the artwork itself. Ringgold has told the story of this gathering on two horizontal panels of text. One panel is sewn into the piece's top border, the other into it's bottom border. These eight women, the story explains, strove in their various ways to support the cause of justice in the world.

In reality, these women never met to piece together a quilt. The scene comes out of the artists imagination as a statement of the unity of purpose that she perceives in their lives.

16. Which choice makes the sentence or sentences most grammatically acceptable?
   - **F. No Change**
   - **G.** flowers and eight
   - **H.** flowers. Eight
   - **J.** flowers, eight

17. Which transition word, if any, is most logical in context?
   - **A. No Change**
   - **B.** Instead, the
   - **C.** Furthermore, the
   - **D.** The

18. Which choice makes the sentence most grammatically acceptable?
   - **F. No Change**
   - **G.** its'
   - **H.** its
   - **J.** their

19. Which transition word is most logical in context?
   - **A. No Change**
   - **B.** summary,
   - **C.** addition,
   - **D.** contrast,

20. Which choice makes the sentence most grammatically acceptable?
   - **F. No Change**
   - **G.** artist's imagination
   - **H.** artists' imagination
   - **J.** artists imagination,

GO ON TO THE NEXT PAGE.

1 ■ ■ ■ ■ ■ ■ ■ ■ ■ 1

Sojourner Truth and Harriet Tubman fought to abolish slavery and, later, were active in the crusade for suffrage. Newspaper journalist Ida B. Wells courageously spoke out for social and racial justice
21
in the late nineteenth and early twentieth centuries.
21

Establishing her own hair products business herself
22
in the first decade of the twentieth century, Madam C. J. Walker later bequeathed millions of dollars to charities and educational institutions. Among the schools that benefited from this generosity, were
23
those that Mary McLeod Bethune opened and ran in order to provide a better education for Black students. And Fannie Lou Hamer, Ella Baker, and Rosa Parks showed leadership and strength during the civil rights movement, it happened in the 1950s and 1960s.
24
     In the artwork, Ringgold has surrounded these women with bright sunflowers. The flowers seem to celebrate the women's accomplishments and the beauty of their shared vision. [25]

21. Given that all the choices are true, which one provides the most relevant information at this point in the essay?
   A. **No Change**
   B. married Ferdinand Barnett, editor of the first Black newspaper in Chicago, the *Chicago Conservator*.
   C. wrote for newspapers in Memphis, New York City, and finally, Chicago.
   D. was born in Holly Springs, Mississippi, in 1862, the eldest of eight children.

22. Which choice is least redundant in context?
   F. **No Change**
   G. business belonging to her
   H. business, herself,
   J. business

23. Which choice makes the sentence most grammatically acceptable?
   A. **No Change**
   B. generosity; were
   C. generosity were
   D. generosity were:

24. Which choice makes the sentence most grammatically acceptable?
   F. **No Change**
   G. movement, it took place in
   H. movement, that happened in
   J. movement of

25. If the writer were to delete the preceding sentence, the essay would primarily lose:
   A. an interpretation of the artwork that serves to summarize the essay.
   B. a reflection on the women depicted in the artwork that compares them to Ringgold.
   C. a description of a brushwork technique that refers back to the essay's opening.
   D. an evaluation of Ringgold's artistic talent that places her in a historical context.

GO ON TO THE NEXT PAGE.

1 ■ ■ ■ ■ ■ ■ ■ ■ **1**

PASSAGE IV

Neutrinos on Ice

At the IceCube Neutrino Observatory in Antarctica, eighty-six cables descend 2,500 meters into the glacial terrain. Each cable is equipped with sixty digital optical modules (DOMs), which, are programmed, to detect
₂₆
a faint blue flash known as Cherenkov radiation. This radiation—a veritable shock wave of photonic energy—is emitted when subatomic particles called neutrinos collide with electrons in the molecules of ice. Although there are countless neutrinos in the universe (fifty trillion neutrinos pass through your body
₂₇
every second), actually detecting them is a formidable
₂₇
task. Neutrinos carry no electrical charge, are practically weightless, and travel at nearly the speed of light. Neutrinos are rarely affected by matter or electromagnetic fields. For this purpose, many neutrinos have been
₂₈
traveling through space unimpeded for billions of years.

On some occasions, however, neutrinos do collide with other particles. `29`

26. Which choice makes the sentence most grammatically acceptable?

  F. No Change
  G. (DOMs), which are programmed
  H. (DOMs): which are programmed
  J. (DOMs); which are programmed

27. If the writer were to delete the underlined portion (adjusting the punctuation as needed), the essay would primarily lose information that:

  A. specifies why neutrinos are practically weightless.
  B. explains how neutrinos pass through matter.
  C. indicates why there are so many neutrinos.
  D. emphasizes how numerous neutrinos are.

28. Which transition word or phrase is most logical in context?

  F. No Change
  G. In contrast,
  H. Besides,
  J. In fact,

29. At this point, the writer is considering adding the following true sentence:

> In 1956, during the Cowan–Reines neutrino experiment, a neutrino was detected for the first time.

Should the writer make this addition?

  A. Yes, because the information is relevant to the history of neutrino detection outlined in the paragraph.
  B. Yes, because the information indicates that sub-zero altitude is essential to the detection of neutrinos.
  C. No, because the information is unrelated to the discussion of why scientists selected the location of the IceCube Neutrino Observatory.
  D. No, because the information is unrelated to why the detection of neutrinos is facilitated by zero-gravity conditions.

GO ON TO THE NEXT PAGE.

Scientists specifically selected the site of the IceCube

Neutrino <u>Observatory to</u> facilitate the detection of such
     30

a collision. Not only is the Antarctic subterranean ice

exceptionally clear, it is also less pressurized due to

<u>its</u> subzero altitude. These factors increase the chance
 31
of DOMs detecting the blue flash that signifies a neutrino

collision. Once this detection occurs, data are gathered

and transferred to laboratories at the University of

Wisconsin. Here, scientists determine the origin of

each of these neutrinos by analyzing the direction

and intensity of the flash.

    <u>Determining neutrinos' origins could provide</u>
               32
<u>scientists with new insights into the universe.</u> For
               32
instance, some neutrinos are produced during supernovae

(the collapsing of stars). The origins of these neutrinos

could give us <u>opulent</u> information about how, when,
          33
and why stars collapse. Scientists are optimistic that

the neutrinos detected at IceCube could lead to new

ways of looking at <u>our galaxy—and galaxies beyond.</u>
                  34

30. Which choice makes the sentence or sentences most grammatically acceptable?

  F. No Change
  G. Observatory, and to
  H. Observatory. To
  J. Observatory; to

31. Which choice makes the sentence most grammatically acceptable?

  A. No Change
  B. their
  C. it's
  D. its'

32. Which of the following true sentences best introduces the main idea of the paragraph?

  F. No Change
  G. For decades, scientists have been trying to learn more about gamma rays through the study of supernovae.
  H. Recently, scientists at IceCube discovered two neutrinos, which they now refer to as Bert and Ernie.
  J. Neutrinos can now be created in laboratories using a particle accelerator called a Super Proton Synchrotron.

33. Which choice is clearest and most precise in context?

  A. No Change
  B. invaluable
  C. upscale
  D. lavish

34. The writer wants to emphasize that information garnered from the neutrinos detected at IceCube could have dramatic effects on how scientists study the universe. Which choice best accomplishes that goal?

  F. No Change
  G. phenomena that have puzzled scientists over the last decade.
  H. common occurrences in space.
  J. the world around us.

GO ON TO THE NEXT PAGE.

Taking Additional Practice Tests

1 ▪ ▪ ▪ ▪ ▪ ▪ ▪ ▪ ▪ 1

Question 35 asks about the preceding passage as a whole.

35. Suppose the writer's primary purpose had been to outline a scientific theory concerning the origins of a particle found in nature. Would this essay accomplish that goal?
    A. Yes, because it explains how scientists are discovering new reasons why neutrinos emit a blue flash known as Cherenkov radiation.
    B. Yes, because it summarizes how DOMs at the IceCube Neutrino Observatory track neutrinos to their origins despite neutrinos' numerous collisions with matter and electromagnetic forces.
    C. No, because it describes instead how neutrinos are detected at an observatory and how these detections could benefit future scientific research.
    D. No, because it details instead how new research on neutrinos could potentially contradict a commonly held theory about supernovae.

PASSAGE V

Clinton Hill's Found Artist

[1]

At the Urban Vintage, my favorite café here in Clinton Hill, Brooklyn, I found a table by the window and checked the day's news on my laptop. On the *New York Times* home page, I noticed an article about Rafael Leonardo Black, a 64-year-old Clinton Hill artist who had just been discovered. [A]

[2]

Black, a native of Aruba, has been creating art in his New York City studio apartment for over three decades. Until recently, few people had seen his work.

36. Which choice makes the sentence most grammatically acceptable?
    F. **No Change**
    G. of whom
    H. which
    J. whom

37. Which choice is least redundant in context?
    A. **No Change**
    B. originally from Aruba, for more than half his life
    C. living in Clinton Hill but a native of Aruba,
    D. a newly found artist originally from Aruba,

GO ON TO THE NEXT PAGE.

1 ■ ■ ■ ■ ■ ■ ■ ■ ■ **1**

I wondered why—and learned he simply never cared to share it. Black has worked as a typist, a salesperson, and a receptionist. However, in May of 2013, art dealer Francis Naumann, directed to Black's art by one of Black's longtime friends, displayed sixteen of the artist's drawings in a solo show.
<u>38</u>

Within days, ten of Black's pieces <u>sold for, prices</u>
<u>39</u>
ranging from $16,000 to $28,000. [B]

[3]

Black draws collages in black No. 2 pencil on white board. They're packed with <u>depictions, in the</u> <u>form of drawings,</u> of ancient myths, historical events,
<u>40</u>
and popular culture. I found a collage titled *Seven Lamps* in a quick search online. [C] It features a representation of a British psychedelic poster, a portrayal of Danish surrealist <u>painter, Wilhelm Freddie,</u> at work, and a tiny
<u>41</u>
figure of Los Angeles architect Simon Rodia. The images are stacked, forming a surreal tower. I wasn't sure how the drawings in *Seven Lamps*—so detailed that I could see the folds in Rodia's clothing—fit together logically, but <u>I liked that there was so much for me to puzzle over.</u>
<u>42</u>

38. Given that all the choices are accurate, which one provides the best transition to the information in the following sentence?
  F. **No Change**
  G. was taking down an artist's long-running exhibition at his Manhattan gallery.
  H. became aware that Black had never shown his drawings, formally or otherwise.
  J. recognized that no one in the New York City art world had heard of Black.

39. Which choice makes the sentence most grammatically acceptable?
  A. **No Change**
  B. sold—for
  C. sold; for
  D. sold for:

40. Which choice is least redundant in context?
  F. **No Change**
  G. black pencil drawings that depict
  H. drawings that create collages of
  J. depictions of

41. Which choice makes the sentence most grammatically acceptable?
  A. **No Change**
  B. painter Wilhelm Freddie,
  C. painter, Wilhelm Freddie
  D. painter Wilhelm Freddie

42. If the writer were to delete the underlined portion (adjusting the punctuation as needed), the essay would primarily lose a:
  F. claim arguing that the reason Naumann chose to show Black's art is that the art offers so much for a viewer to reflect upon and analyze.
  G. detail indicating that the narrator appreciated Black's collage even though he or she might not have understood its overall intent.
  H. comment suggesting that though the narrator enjoys only some of Black's art, he or she is glad that Black has been discovered.
  J. statement revealing the narrator's belief that the best modern art is understood only by the artist who created it.

GO ON TO THE NEXT PAGE.

1 ▪ ▪ ▪ ▪ ▪ ▪ ▪ ▪ 1

Maybe this complexity in May helps explain why
                    43
Black's work created such a stir.

[4]

I read that Black observes the sudden interest in
                      44
his drawings. [D] He says he's always been an artist,

regardless of who knew it. Now that I know about him,

I'll keep checking the *Times* for word of his next show.

When I walk home from the Urban Vintage tonight, I

wonder if I'll pass the brownstone building where Black

creates his fascinating, newly found art.

43. The best placement for the underlined portion would be:

A. where it is now.
B. after the word *Maybe*.
C. after the word *explain*.
D. after the word *stir* (and before the period).

44. The writer wants to clearly establish that the newspaper article claims Black is unmoved by the sudden interest in his art. Which choice best accomplishes that goal?

F. **No Change**
G. is nearly a celebrity in Clinton Hill due to
H. has benefited financially from
J. gives little thought to

Question 45 asks about the preceding passage as a whole.

45. The writer is considering adding the following sentence to the essay:

> Fortunately, the web page included a key that identified the people, places, and events—most of which I had never even heard of—that Black portrays in this piece.

If the writer were to add this sentence, it would most logically be placed at:

A. Point A in Paragraph 1.
B. Point B in Paragraph 2.
C. Point C in Paragraph 3.
D. Point D in Paragraph 4.

Cher Ami, Pigeon Hero

In many urban areas, pigeons are considered little

more than, "rats with wings," blamed for spreading
    46

disease and despoiling statues. For example,
                                 47
one species, the homing pigeon, is among

the best navigators of the natural world.

46. Which choice makes the sentence most grammatically acceptable?

F. **No Change**
G. than—
H. than;
J. than

47. Which transition word or phrase is most logical in context?

A. **No Change**
B. Similarly,
C. However,
D. Thus,

GO ON TO THE NEXT PAGE.

There navigational ability has earned the homely
— 48 —
pigeon an undeniable place in history.

The most famous avian war hero is perhaps Cher
Ami, whose name means *dear friend*. One of six hundred
birds used by the US Army Signal Corps in France during
World War I, all twelve of Cher Ami's missions were
— 49 —
deemed successful. His last was instrumental in saving
— 49 —
hundreds of lives.

Near Verdun, France, the 77th Infantry Division
became separated from US forces. The men were
surrounded by German troops and were rapidly running
out of rations. They were separated from other US forces.
— 50 —
They had but one link to headquarters: homing pigeons.
Major Whittlesey wrote a note about the 77th's location,
placed it in a canister attached to the pigeon's leg, and
watched as the bird flew out in the midst of battle.
Despite being wounded in flight, Cher Ami managed
to deliver the message to headquarters; the unit known
as "the Lost Battalion" would be rescued.

48. Which choice makes the sentence most grammatically
acceptable?
F. **No Change**
G. They're
H. It's
J. Its

49. Which choice makes the sentence most grammatically
acceptable?
A. **No Change**
B. the twelve missions Cher Ami flew were successful.
C. successful missions by Cher Ami numbered twelve.
D. Cher Ami flew twelve successful missions.

50. Which choice is least redundant in context?
F. **No Change**
G. German troops were all around them.
H. They would soon be out of rations.
J. **Delete** the underlined portion.

END OF TEST 1

STOP! DO NOT TURN THE PAGE UNTIL TOLD TO DO SO.

2 △ △ △ △ △ △ △ △ △ 2

MATHEMATICS TEST
50 Minutes—45 Questions

DIRECTIONS: Solve each problem, choose the correct answer, and then fill in the corresponding oval on your answer document.

Do not linger over problems that take too much time. Solve as many as you can; then return to the others in the time you have left for this test.

You are permitted to use a calculator on this test. You may use your calculator for any problems you choose, but some of the problems may best be done without using a calculator.

Note: Unless otherwise stated, all of the following should be assumed.

1. Illustrative figures are **not** necessarily drawn to scale.
2. Geometric figures lie in a plane.
3. The word "line" indicates a straight line.
4. The word "average" indicates arithmetic mean.

---

1. The parallelogram shown has consecutive angles with measures $x°$ and $25°$. What is the value of x?

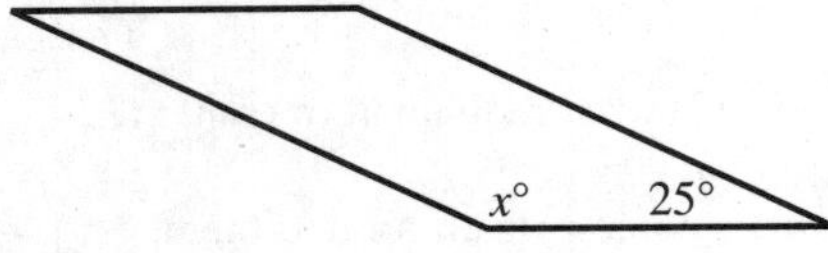

   A. 100
   B. 115
   C. 130
   D. 155

2. A retail sales associate's daily commission during 1 week was \$30 on Monday and Tuesday and \$70 on Wednesday, Thursday, and Friday. What was the associate's average daily commission for these 5 days?

   F. \$50
   G. \$51
   H. \$54
   J. \$55

3. What is the greatest common factor of 45, 50, and 84?

   A. 0
   B. 1
   C. 2
   D. 3

4. For what value of x is the equation $2(x - 12) + x = 36$ true?

   F. 4
   G. 8
   H. 16
   J. 20

DO YOUR FIGURING HERE.

GO ON TO THE NEXT PAGE.

2 △ △ △ △ △ △ △ △ △ 2

5. A bag contains exactly 22 solid-colored buttons: 4 red, 6 blue, and 12 white. What is the probability of randomly selecting 1 button that is **not** white?

- **A.** $\frac{5}{11}$
- **B.** $\frac{5}{6}$
- **C.** $\frac{1}{22}$
- **D.** $\frac{1}{10}$

6. On a map, $\frac{1}{2}$ inch represents 12 miles. Two towns that are 5 inches apart on this map are how many miles apart?

- **F.** 120
- **G.** 60
- **H.** 30
- **J.** 24

7. An on-demand movie service charges \$5 per month, plus \$2 for each movie rented. Which of the following equations models the relationship between M, the number of movies rented per month, and T, the total monthly charge, in dollars, for the service?

- **A.** $M = 5 + 2T$
- **B.** $M = 2 + 5T$
- **C.** $T = 5 + 2M$
- **D.** $T = 2 + 5M$

8. What are the solutions to the quadratic equation $(2x + 5)(3x - 4) = 0$?

- **F.** -5 and 4
- **G.** $-\frac{5}{2}$ and $-\frac{4}{3}$
- **H.** $-\frac{5}{2}$ and $\frac{4}{3}$
- **J.** $\frac{5}{2}$ and $-\frac{4}{3}$

GO ON TO THE NEXT PAGE.

2 △ △ △ △ △ △ △ △ △ **2**

DO YOUR FIGURING HERE.

9. In a class of tenth graders, no student participated in more than 1 of the following extracurricular activities: $\frac{2}{3}$ of the class played in the band; $\frac{1}{6}$ sang in the chorus; $\frac{1}{10}$ played football; and $\frac{1}{60}$ played basketball. What fraction of the class did **not** participate in any 1 of these 4 activities?

A. 0

B. $\frac{1}{20}$

C. $\frac{74}{79}$

D. $\frac{57}{60}$

10. In $\triangle ABC$ shown, $\sin C = \frac{2}{3}$, and the length of $\overline{AB}$ is 6 inches. What is the length, in inches, of $\overline{AC}$?

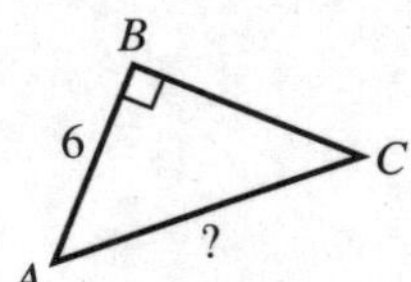

F. $\sqrt{5}$
G. $\sqrt{13}$
H. 4
J. 9

11. The table shows the first 5 terms of an arithmetic sequence. Which of the following is a general expression for the nth term?

Term position (n)	nth term
1	1
2	5
3	9
4	13
5	17

A. $2n - 1$
B. $3n - 2$
C. $4n - 3$
D. $5n - 4$

GO ON TO THE NEXT PAGE.

DO YOUR FIGURING HERE.

12. So far this basketball season, Sherita has made 46 of her first 60 free throws, which gives her a free throw average of about 76.7%. What is the minimum number of free throws she would need to make from now on in order to have a free throw average of at least 80%?

F. 2
G. 3
H. 10
J. 14

13. Two functions are defined as $f(x) = 2x - 1$ and $g(x) = x^2 + 1$. Which of the following expressions represents $f(g(x))$?

A. $x^2 + 2x$
B. $2x^2 + 1$
C. $2x^2 + 2$
D. $4x^2 - 4x + 2$

14. Dataset A consists of the 8 numbers listed. Dataset B consists of the 8 numbers in A and a 9th number that is greater than 90. How will the mean and the median of B compare to the mean and the median of A?

62, 76, 76, 80, 82, 87, 94, 96

F. The mean and the median of B will each be greater than the mean and the median of A, respectively.
G. The mean and the median of B will each be less than the mean and the median of A, respectively.
H. The mean of B will be the same as the mean of A, and the median of B will be greater than the median of A.
J. The mean of B will be greater than the mean of A, and the median of B will be the same as the median of A.

15. A truck traveling at 35 mph has a leaky radiator that is losing 4 fluid ounces per minute. If the radiator held 480 fluid ounces when it began to leak, how many **miles** will the truck travel before the radiator is empty?

A. 17.5
B. 35.0
C. 70.0
D. 120.0

16. In the standard (x,y) coordinate plane, what is the midpoint of the line segment that has endpoints $(-5,8)$ and $(3,-1)$?

F. $(-2,-9)$

G. $\left(-1, \frac{7}{2}\right)$

H. $\left(4, -\frac{9}{2}\right)$

J. $(8,-9)$

GO ON TO THE NEXT PAGE.

2 △ △ △ △ △ △ △ △ △ **2**

17. The ordered pairs (x,y) in one of the following tables belong to a linear function. Which one?

A.

x	y
0	2
1	1
2	1
3	0

C.

x	y
0	0
1	1
2	0
3	1

B.

x	y
0	3
1	2
2	1
3	0

D.

x	y
0	0
1	1
2	4
3	9

18. In $\triangle ABC$ shown, $m\angle A = x°$, $m\angle B = (2x)°$, $m\angle C = (3x)°$, $AB = c$ inches, $AC = b$ inches, and $BC = a$ inches. Which of the following inequalities correctly relates the side lengths of $\triangle ABC$?

(Note: $m\angle A$ denotes the measure of $\angle A$, and AB denotes the length of $\overline{AB}$. The triangle is NOT drawn to scale.)

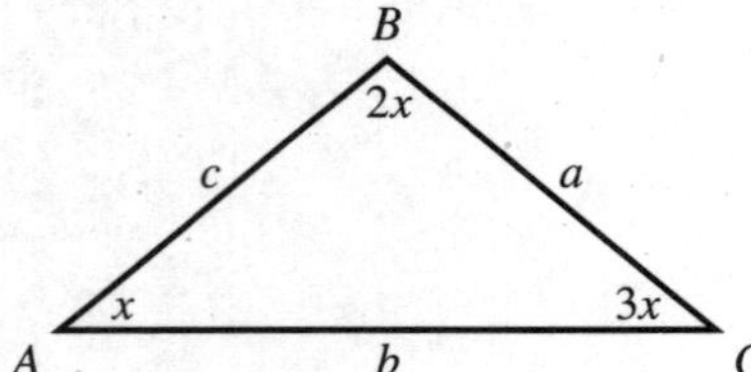

F. $a < b < c$
G. $a < c < b$
H. $b < a < c$
J. $c < b < a$

19. What is the slope of the line that passes through $(1,5)$ and $(17,7)$ in the standard (x,y) coordinate plane?

A. $\frac{1}{8}$

B. $\frac{2}{3}$

C. $\frac{3}{2}$

D. 8

GO ON TO THE NEXT PAGE.

2 △ △ △ △ △ △ △ △ △ **2**

20. The perimeter of a particular rectangle is 36 centimeters. The longer sides of the rectangle are each 2 centimeters longer than each of the shorter sides of the rectangle. What is the length, in centimeters, of one of the longer sides of this rectangle?

F. 8
G. 9
H. 10
J. 18

DO YOUR FIGURING HERE.

21. One side of square $ABCD$ has a length of 18 meters. A rectangle whose area is equal to the area of $ABCD$ has a width of 6 meters. What is the length, in meters, of that rectangle?

A. 18
B. 24
C. 27
D. 54

22. The 2×2 matrices A and B are related to matrix C by the equation $C = 2A - 3B$. What is matrix C?

$$A = \begin{bmatrix} 3 & 5 \\ -2 & 1 \end{bmatrix} \quad B = \begin{bmatrix} -4 & 5 \\ 2 & 1 \end{bmatrix}$$

F. $\begin{bmatrix} 18 & -5 \\ -10 & -1 \end{bmatrix}$

G. $\begin{bmatrix} 10 & 5 \\ -6 & 1 \end{bmatrix}$

H. $\begin{bmatrix} 6 & -1 \\ -5 & -1 \end{bmatrix}$

J. $\begin{bmatrix} -6 & 25 \\ 2 & 5 \end{bmatrix}$

23. In the United States, phone numbers begin with a 3-digit area code. Now, there are restrictions on some of the digits, but in the future, as more and more area codes are needed, the restrictions may need to be lifted. If, and when, there are no restrictions and each of the 3 digits can be any integer from 0 through 9, how many area codes will be possible?

A. 30
B. 720
C. 729
D. 1,000

GO ON TO THE NEXT PAGE.

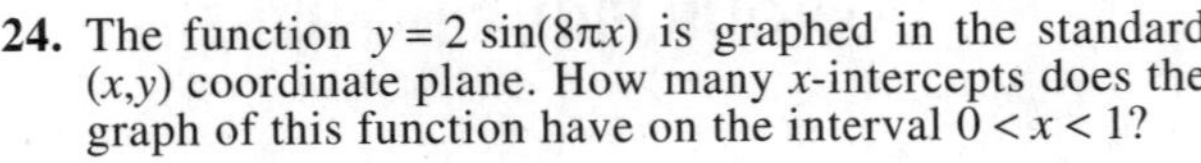

2

DO YOUR FIGURING HERE.

24. The function $y = 2\sin(8\pi x)$ is graphed in the standard (x,y) coordinate plane. How many x-intercepts does the graph of this function have on the interval $0 < x < 1$?

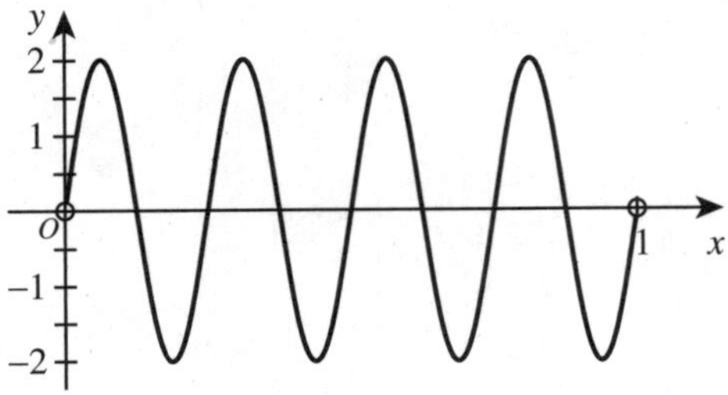

   F. 4
   G. 7
   H. 8
   J. 9

25. If both x and $\left(\frac{x}{3} + \frac{x}{7} + \frac{x}{9}\right)$ are positive integers, what is the least possible value of x?

   A. 21
   B. 27
   C. 36
   D. 63

26. Which of the following expressions is equal to $(a + \sqrt{b})(a - 2\sqrt{b})$ for all positive real numbers a and b?

   F. $a^2 - 3a\sqrt{b}$
   G. $a^2 - a\sqrt{b} - 2b$
   H. $a^2 - a\sqrt{b} - 2\sqrt{2b}$
   J. $a^2 - 3a\sqrt{b} - 2b$

27. The track for a model railroad display is set up as 2 circles that are tangent to one another and have diameters of 30 feet and 50 feet, as shown. The engine of the train travels at a constant rate of 75 feet per minute. To the nearest minute, how many minutes does the engine take to go in a figure-8 pattern around the entire track exactly 1 time?

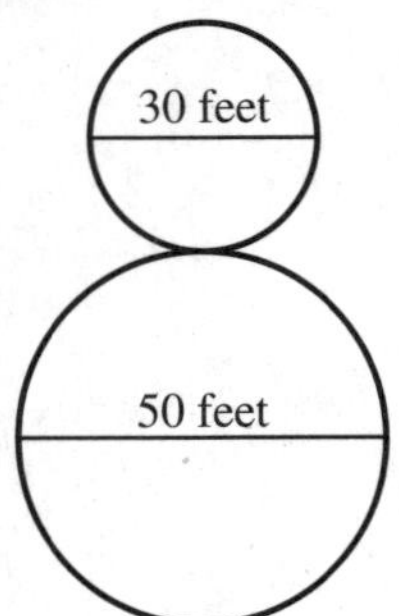

   A. 1
   B. 2
   C. 3
   D. 4

GO ON TO THE NEXT PAGE.

2 △ △ △ △ △ △ △ △ △ 2

28. $\left(\frac{4}{5}\right)^{-\frac{3}{2}} = ?$

DO YOUR FIGURING HERE.

F. $\frac{5}{2}$

G. $\frac{5\sqrt{5}}{8}$

H. $\frac{4\sqrt{2}}{5}$

J. $\frac{\sqrt{5}}{2}$

29. What is the value of the positive real number x such that $\log_x\left(\frac{1}{25}\right) = -2$?

A. 5

B. 50

C. $\frac{1}{50}$

D. $\frac{1}{5}$

30. The points $(-4,-5)$, $(0,-3)$, and $(6,0)$ lie on a line in the standard (x,y) coordinate plane. Which of the following points also lies on that line?

F. $(-3,-4)$
G. $(-1,-4)$
H. $(1,-2)$
J. $(4,-1)$

31. The CFO of Math King Enterprises estimates that if the company sells its new product for x cents per unit, the weekly profit will be modeled by $p(x) = 1{,}600x - 4x^2$, where $0 \le x \le 400$. According to this model, for which of the following values of x will the weekly profit for this product be the greatest?

A. 40
B. 100
C. 200
D. 400

32. Given consecutive positive integers a, b, c, and d such that $a < b < c < d$, which of the following expressions has the greatest value?

F. $\frac{b}{c}$

G. $\frac{c}{d}$

H. $\frac{a+b}{b+c}$

J. $\frac{b+c}{c+d}$

GO ON TO THE NEXT PAGE.

2 △ △ △ △ △ △ △ △ △ **2**

DO YOUR FIGURING HERE.

33. The ratio of the perimeters of two squares is 2:3. If the area of the larger square is 324 square feet, what is the length, in feet, of the side of the smaller square?

A. 12
B. 18
C. 24
D. 36

34. What is the set of all integer solutions for the inequality $-1 \le x - \sqrt{5} < 4$?

F. $\{3, 4, 5\}$
G. $\{2, 3, 4, 5, 6\}$
H. $\{2, 3, 4, 5\}$
J. $\{1, 2, 3, 4, 5, 6\}$

35. Wind blowing against a flat surface exerts a maximum force equal to kSv^2, where S is the area of the surface, v is the wind's velocity, and k is a constant. If a 40-mile-per-hour (mph) wind can exert a maximum force of 50 pounds on a 1-square-foot flat surface, what is the maximum force, in pounds, that an 80 mph wind can exert on a 2-square-foot flat surface?

A. 100
B. 200
C. 400
D. 1,600

36. Roger is pouring concrete to make a sidewalk with the dimensions, in feet, shown in the figure. He pours the concrete to a depth of 4 **inches**. One bag of concrete mix makes 0.6 cubic feet of concrete. What is the least whole number of bags of concrete mix that Roger needs in order to make the sidewalk?

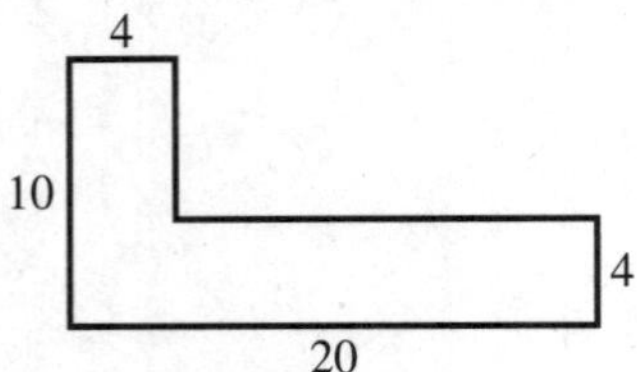

F. 44
G. 50
H. 58
J. 67

GO ON TO THE NEXT PAGE.

2 △ △ △ △ △ △ △ △ △ **2**

37. Radius $\overline{OA}$ of the circle shown is perpendicular to $\overline{AP}$. The circle intersects $\overline{OP}$ at B. The length of $\overline{AP}$ is 12 centimeters, and the measure of $\angle APO$ is 20°. Which of the following values is closest to the length, in centimeters, of $\overline{BP}$?

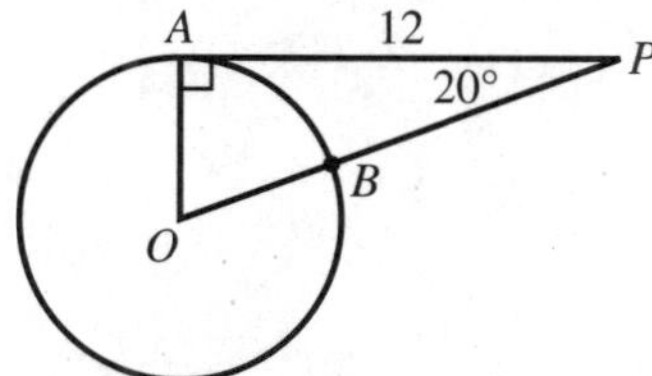

(Note: sin 20° ≈ 0.342, cos 20° ≈ 0.940, and tan 20° ≈ 0.364)

A. 4.4
B. 6.9
C. 7.6
D. 8.4

DO YOUR FIGURING HERE.

38. The average of 10 test scores is x. When the highest score and lowest score are removed from the 10 scores, the average is y. Which of the following is an expression for the average of the highest score and lowest score?

F. $10x - 8y$

G. $\dfrac{x+y}{2}$

H. $\dfrac{10x + 8y}{2}$

J. $\dfrac{10x - 8y}{2}$

39. Which of the following is the solution set of $27^{n^2} = 9^{5n-4}$?

A. $\left\{-4, \dfrac{2}{3}\right\}$

B. $\left\{-1, \dfrac{8}{3}\right\}$

C. $\left\{-\dfrac{2}{3}, 4\right\}$

D. $\left\{\dfrac{4}{3}, 2\right\}$

GO ON TO THE NEXT PAGE.

2 △ △ △ △ △ △ △ △ △ **2**

40. Each face of 2 cubes with faces numbered from 1 through 6 has a $\frac{1}{6}$ chance of landing faceup when the 2 cubes are tossed. What is the probability that the sum of the numbers on the faces landing faceup will be less than 6?

F. $\frac{13}{36}$

G. $\frac{5}{12}$

H. $\frac{5}{18}$

J. $\frac{5}{36}$

41. At 2:00 p.m., Louisa leaves Kansas City in her car traveling east on I-70 toward St. Louis at an average speed of 68 mph. At precisely the same time, Antonio leaves St. Louis in his car traveling west on I-70 toward Kansas City at an average speed of 57 mph. The driving distance from St. Louis to Kansas City is 240 miles. At what time, to the nearest minute, will Louisa and Antonio drive past each other on I-70?

A. 3:46 p.m.
B. 3:53 p.m.
C. 3:55 p.m.
D. 4:06 p.m.

42. There are 10 points in a plane, and no 3 of the points are collinear. These 10 points, taken 2 points at a time, determine how many distinct lines?

F. 10
G. 20
H. 45
J. 90

43. The expression $n!$ (read as "n factorial") is defined as the product of all positive integers up to and including n whenever n is a positive integer. For example, $4! = 1 \cdot 2 \cdot 3 \cdot 4$. Whenever n is a positive integer, which of the following is equivalent to $\frac{(n+1)!6!}{n!3!}$?

A. $120(n+1)$

B. 120

C. $\frac{2(n+1)}{n}$

D. $\frac{(6n+6)!}{(3n)!}$

GO ON TO THE NEXT PAGE.

2 △ △ △ △ △ △ △ △ △ **2**

44. When $(x + 1)^4$ is expanded and like terms are combined, what is the coefficient of x^2?

F. 0
G. 1
H. 4
J. 6

DO YOUR FIGURING HERE.

45. A hill makes an angle of 20° with the horizontal, $\overrightarrow{AD}$, as shown in the figure. A taut guy wire, $\overline{AB}$, extends from the base of the hill, point A, to point B on a vertical pole. Point B is 25 ft directly above where the pole is inserted into the ground at point C. Given that the length of $\overline{AC}$ is 60 ft, which of the following expressions represents the length, in feet, of the guy wire?

(Note: For a triangle with sides of lengths a, b, and c that are opposite angles $\angle A$, $\angle B$, and $\angle C$, respectively, $\frac{\sin \angle A}{a} = \frac{\sin \angle B}{b} = \frac{\sin \angle C}{c}$ and $c^2 = a^2 + b^2 - 2ab \cos \angle C$.)

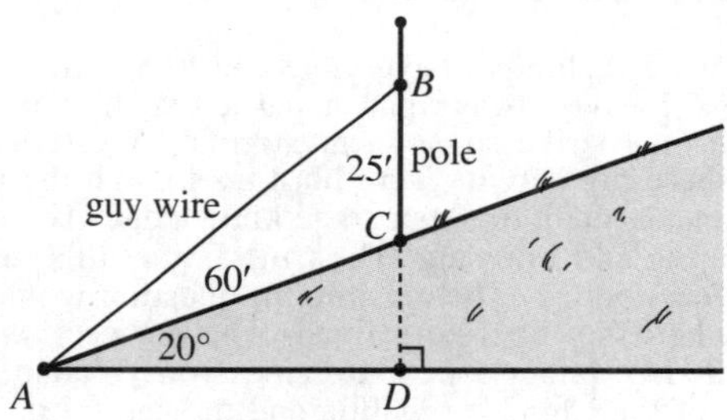

A. $\dfrac{25 \sin 60°}{\sin 20°}$

B. $\dfrac{25 \sin 70°}{\sin 20°}$

C. $\sqrt{60^2 + 25^2 - 2(60)(25) \cos 70°}$

D. $\sqrt{60^2 + 25^2 - 2(60)(25) \cos 110°}$

END OF TEST 2
STOP! DO NOT TURN THE PAGE UNTIL TOLD TO DO SO.
DO NOT RETURN TO THE PREVIOUS TEST.

3

READING TEST
40 Minutes—36 Questions

DIRECTIONS: There are several passages in this test. Each passage is accompanied by several questions. After reading a passage, choose the best answer to each question and fill in the corresponding oval on your answer document. You may refer to the passages as often as necessary.

Passage I

LITERARY NARRATIVE: Passage A is adapted from the essay "Touring Home" by Susan Power (©1996 by Susan Power). Passage B is adapted from the memoir *Beyond the Narrow Gate: The Journey of Four Chinese Women from the Middle Kingdom to Middle America* by Leslie Chang (©1999 by Leslie Chang).

Passage A by Susan Power

My mother tells me stories every day: while she cleans, while she cooks, on our way to the library, standing in the checkout line at the supermarket. I like to share her stories with other people and chatter away
5   when I am able to command adult attention.

"She left the reservation when she was sixteen years old," I tell my audience. Sixteen sounds very old to me, but I always state the number because it seems integral to my recitation. "She had never been on a train
10   before or used a telephone. She left Standing Rock to take a job in Chicago so she could help out the family during the War. She was so petrified of the new surroundings, she stayed in her seat all the way from McLaughlin, South Dakota, to Chicago, Illinois, and
15   didn't move once."

I usually laugh after saying this because I cannot imagine my mother being afraid of anything. She is so tall, a true Dakota woman; she rises against the sun like a skyscraper, and when I draw her picture in my note-
20   book, she takes up the entire page. She talks politics and attends sit-ins and says what's on her mind.

I am her small shadow and witness. I am the timid daughter who can rage only on paper.

We don't have much money, but Mom takes me
25   from one end of the city to the other, on foot, on buses. I will grow up believing that Chicago belongs to me, because it was given to me by my mother.

Some days we haunt the Art Institute, and my mother pauses before a Picasso. "He did this during his
30   blue period," she tells me.

I squint at the blue man holding a blue guitar. "Was he very sad?" I ask.

"Yes, I think he was." My mother takes my hand and looks away from the painting. I can see a story
35   developing behind her eyes, and I tug on her arm to release the words. She will tell me why Picasso was blue, what his thoughts were as he painted this canvas. She relates anecdotes I will never find in books, never see footnoted in a biography of the master artist. I don't
40   even bother to check these references because I like my mother's version best.

Passage B by Leslie Chang

Water belongs to everyone and to no one. For this reason, I have always had a particular affinity for it, which may strike some as mysterious. Westerners ask
45   me where my parents were born, as though the answer will enable them to glean some knowledge. The answer is Beijing and Luoyang. The truth is that this response signifies nothing. The meaningful question would be to ask where my ancestors lived. The answer to that is
50   inland. My father's people came from Wuhan, birthplace of the Chinese republic and the capital of Hubei, that sweltering province sandwiched between Sichuan and Anhui. My mother's father was from Inner Mongolia, land of desert and grassy plains.

55   Yet water calls to me. I remain convinced that I would find peace if I could only have a house by the ocean. I insisted on being married near the sea. This bond, I know, comes from my mother.

She longs for a view more than anything else.
60   Once, staying at a hotel in San Francisco, she insisted on seeing three different rooms before she found one with which she was satisfied. It was on a floor so high it made me dizzy, with a corner window overlooking the bay. Even so, my mother spent most of her time on
65   the bridge linking the elevator bank to our wing. The bridge consisted almost entirely of windows. It offered a view in either direction that was brilliant and blinding. If there had been a chair, she could have sat forever, letting the gold sun and blue sea overwhelm her through
70   the glass.

My mother may have descended from inland people, but they were also nomads. Her father once rode his horse practically the length of China, from Inner Mongolia to Guangzhou, a distance of some
75   twelve hundred miles. My mother could only become a

GO ON TO THE NEXT PAGE.

3   **3**

nomad herself—forever moving, changing and going,
yet always retaining some essential part of her being,
recognizable and intact in spite of all the places she has
been. In this, she is like water, not dead water but fear-
80 somely alive. When she gazes out on its shimmering
expanse, she sees her own reflection. When I gaze out,
I see her, my mother, always pulling away, returning
and pulling away again. I drink from her, and she slips
between my fingertips. She has borne me all this way. I
85 cannot decide whether I want her to stay or go. When
she is here, I wish she would leave. When she is gone, I
wish she would return. She pulls away again, a force as
elemental as the ebbing tide. I remain a child on the
shore, eagerly collecting the sea glass and driftwood
90 she has left behind.

1. In Passage A, the narrator directly compares her mother
to a:

  A. Picasso painting.
  B. shadow and witness.
  C. story behind someone's eyes.
  D. skyscraper against the sun.

2. The narrator of Passage A most strongly suggests that
the reason she began to believe Chicago belongs to her
is that she:

  F. could eventually take several different routes to
travel from one end of the city to the other without
getting lost.
  G. had watched her mother directly influence the politics of the city.
  H. felt she could move about the city almost unseen,
like a small shadow.
  J. initially explored the city with her mother as her
affirming guide, so her connection to the city
seemed familial.

3. It can most reasonably be inferred from Passage A that
the narrator doesn't bother to verify that her mother's
ideas about Picasso and his work are accurate primarily because the narrator:

  A. doesn't know which references would be best for
her to consult.
  B. is confident that what her mother says about the
artist is accurate and feels that checking references
would be a waste of time.
  C. doesn't care whether her mother is accurate given
how much the narrator likes what her mother says
about the artist.
  D. wants to hold to her own ideas about the artist,
regardless of what her mother says about him.

4. In Passage B, the narrator most strongly suggests that
she believes her answer to which of the following
questions does not provide significant information
about her background?

  F. How is your mother like your other ancestors?
  G. Where did your ancestors live?
  H. Where were your parents born?
  J. Why does water call to you?

5. As they are used in Passage B, the word *blinding*
(line 67) and the word *overwhelm* (line 69) both have a
connotation that most strongly suggests a feeling of:

  A. fright.
  B. awe.
  C. regret.
  D. quietness.

6. The last sentence of Passage B can best be described
as a:

  F. metaphor for the narrator's feelings as her mother
goes away from her.
  G. memory of childhood and of her mother that the
narrator holds dear.
  H. literal explanation of the way the narrator reacts to
her mother's actions.
  J. reference to a set of objects that the narrator as a
child often found on the shore.

7. Which of the following actions do the narrators of both
passages closely connect with their mothers?

  A. Traveling and moving
  B. Exploring Chicago streets
  C. Speaking openly and boldly
  D. Staying at hotels in cities

8. The narrator of Passage B would be more likely than the
narrator of Passage A to describe her relationship with
her mother as being marked by:

  F. moments of lively conversation and pure joy.
  G. years of fierce competition and debate.
  H. displays of physical affection and warmth.
  J. feelings of distance and tension.

9. In both Passage A and Passage B, the narrator of the
passage shares information about her mother's:

  A. personal history.
  B. physical appearance.
  C. academic interests.
  D. relationship to the narrator's father.

GO ON TO THE NEXT PAGE.

3   **3**

Passage II

INFORMATIONAL: This passage is adapted from *The Frozen-Water Trade: A True Story* by Gavin Weightman (©2003 by Gavin Weightman).

When the first comprehensive report on the ice industry of the United States was commissioned in 1879 as part of a national census, it was estimated that about eight million tons were harvested annually,
5 though the business was so extensive and production so poorly documented that this was, at best, a well-informed guess. The figures were put together by one Henry Hall, who signed himself "special agent" and gave an account of the great growth of the industry in
10 the preceding ten years. Of the eight million tons of ice harvested, about five million reached the consumer—the rest melted during shipment and storage. By far the biggest market was in New York, and none of its ice was manufactured artificially: it was all cut in winter
15 and stored in hundreds of timber warehouses that lined the lakes and rivers and had a capacity of up to fifty thousand tons each. Between New York and Albany, 150 miles up the Hudson River, there were 135 ice-houses, but even this was not enough to supply the
20 metropolis, which relied heavily on imports. In fact, in the year of the great ice census, New York and Phila-delphia suffered one of their recurrent ice "famines," when unseasonably warm weather destroyed the harvest on the Hudson and local lakes, and the price of ice rose
25 from $4 to $5 a ton. That year the ice was fifteen to twenty inches thick in Maine, a top-quality crop, and it could be shipped down to New York at an estimated cost of $1.50 a ton. This produced a frenzy of harvest-ing on the Kennebec, Penobscot, and Sheepscot Rivers,
30 and two thousand cargoes of ice packed in hay and saw-dust were shipped south to New York, Philadelphia, and other more southern cities, where they were sold for a total of around $1.5 million.

Though the demand for ice rose annually, the New
35 York suppliers did not explore the use of artificial refrigeration. Instead, they began to buy up sections of the Kennebec River shoreline and to erect great wooden warehouses there, transforming the landscape of the river for many miles. It was the same farther inland,
40 where ice companies bought up shoreline along the lakes and put up storehouses to supply the meat indus-try of Chicago and the brewers of Milwaukee, as well as millions of domestic consumers.

The first real crisis in the natural-ice trade was
45 caused not by competition from artificial manufacture, but by pollution. As the cities grew, they encroached on the rivers and lakes from which the ice was cut, and soon there were health scares. This produced a search for cleaner supplies away from towns, and stimulated
50 the search for a means of manufacturing ice with pure water. The realization that the bacteria that cause dis-eases such as typhoid were not killed off in frozen water added to the urgency of finding safer forms of refrigeration.

55   The natural-ice trade began to decline from the early decades of the twentieth century, though in more remote areas of North America where electric power was not available but lake ice was abundant in winter, it survived as late as the 1950s. As ice harvesting died
60 out, the evidence of its former vast scale rapidly disap-peared. There was no alternative use for the great ice-houses, many of which simply burned down, often set alight by a spark from a steam train—they were surpris-ingly flammable, as most were made of wood and kept
65 as dry as possible to better preserve the blocks of ice they housed. But the majority were demolished or simply rotted away.

Over a wide area of the northern states, young diving enthusiasts with no knowledge of the former ice
70 trade still emerge from lakes and rivers clutching an impressive variety of odd implements—plows and chis-els and scrapers that fell through the ice during the har-vesting. One or two museums keep small displays of these tools, and collectors have preserved manufactur-
75 ers' catalogs that proudly present their versions of the ice plow, the ice saw, the grapple, the Jack grapple, the breaking-off bar, the caulk bar, the packing chisel, the house bar, the fork bar, the float hook, the line marker, and many other specialist implements the use
80 of which has long been forgotten.

The inner-city icehouses have also gone, and the ice wagon and the iceman are rapidly fading memories. All that is left in America of this once-great industry is the water itself, which provided a continuously renew-
85 able supply of ice each winter. There are few memori-als on the banks of the rivers and lakes that once produced such a vital crop.

---

10. Which of the following events referred to in the passage occurred last chronologically?

  F. The first comprehensive report on the ice industry of the United States was commissioned.
  G. Divers emerged from lakes and rivers clutching ice industry implements.
  H. Two thousand cargoes of ice were sold for around $1.5 million.
  J. The price of ice rose from $4 to $5 a ton.

11. The passage states that, in terms of the natural-ice industry, the decade from 1869 to 1879 was character-ized by:

  A. significant growth.
  B. damaging publicity.
  C. high shipping prices.
  D. mildly declining demand.

GO ON TO THE NEXT PAGE.

3 〓〓〓〓〓〓〓〓〓〓〓〓〓〓 **3**

12. As it is used in lines 19–20, the phrase *the metropolis* most likely refers to:

    F. Albany.
    G. New York City.
    H. Philadelphia.
    J. the average US city of the 1870s.

13. Based on the passage, the 1879 Maine ice that was fifteen to twenty inches thick can best be described as:

    A. a top-quality crop that was shipped to New York City, Philadelphia, and destinations farther south.
    B. sufficient for local demand but not a solution to the problem of the ice "famine" in the South.
    C. typical of Maine crops of ice until the ice "famine" struck.
    D. remarkable but surpassed in size and quality by crops the following year.

14. The main idea of the fourth paragraph (lines 55–67) is that:

    F. the natural-ice industry declined over several decades, leaving few traces of its magnitude.
    G. the arrival of the steam train signaled the demise of ice harvesting.
    H. icehouses were extremely flammable and therefore few remain.
    J. in the 1950s, the natural-ice industry experienced a short-lived revival.

15. The author most clearly indicates that the contents of the manufacturers' catalogs referred to in the fifth paragraph (lines 68–80) typify the natural-ice industry's:

    A. rapid response to market changes.
    B. ability to erect icehouses quickly.
    C. wide array of tools.
    D. simple work.

16. On which of the following points does the author contradict himself elsewhere in the passage?

    F. "Of the eight million tons of ice harvested, about five million reached the consumer" (lines 10–11).
    G. "The New York suppliers did not explore the use of artificial refrigeration" (lines 34–36).
    H. "There was no alternative use for the great icehouses" (lines 61–62).
    J. "All that is left in America of this once-great industry is the water itself" (lines 83–84).

17. According to the passage, in the time period referred to in the first paragraph, how much of New York City's ice was made artificially?

    A. The vast majority
    B. About half
    C. About ten percent
    D. None

18. The passage indicates that the first real crisis in the natural-ice industry can be attributed to:

    F. polluted water.
    G. weather pattern changes.
    H. the advent of refrigeration.
    J. the Great Depression.

GO ON TO THE NEXT PAGE.

3 3

Passage III

INFORMATIONAL: This passage is adapted from the article "Read My Lips" by Chiara Barzini (©2012 by the Harper's Magazine Foundation).

In the passage, dubbing primarily refers to providing a film with a new soundtrack, especially dialogue in a different language.

Filmmakers have debated the respective merits of subtitles and dubbing since the earliest sound films. In "The Impossible Life of Clark Costa," published in 1940 in the film journal *Cinema*, director Michelangelo
5 Antonioni wrote that Romolo Costa, the person who dubbed all of actor Clark Gable's performances, was a "hybrid individual born out of a chemical combination." This "half Clark, half Costa" was unbearable to Antonioni, who considered dubbing to be a mere
10 "acoustic surrogate" of acting. To him, dubbing compromised the intention of the director, leading to an artificial product that lacked artistic unity. Director Pier Paolo Pasolini, who called both dubbing and subtitles "evils," said that, between the two, dubbing was the
15 less harmful, since it allowed you to see the picture in full. Director Jean Renoir called dubbing a "monstrosity, a challenge to human and divine laws."

Director Federico Fellini didn't agree with any of them. Dubbing was an extension of his shoots, a tech-
20 nique he would use to retouch and rewrite. He mercilessly dubbed over his actors, changing dialogue in postproduction, sometimes having worked without a script. (He reportedly instructed his actors to count aloud in front of the camera so that he could insert new
25 dialogue afterward.) Renato Cortesi, a veteran Fellini dubber, told me that, during the filming of *Amarcord* (1973), he witnessed Fellini ask an old Neapolitan lady to tell him a sad story. Over footage of this woman recounting a tragic tale about her grandson, Fellini
30 added a new sound track about war and hunger recorded by an actor from Emilia-Romagna, combining the vivid expressiveness of the South with his favorite northern accent.

If you visit a dubbing studio, the over-the-top zest
35 of the actors is evident in everything from their melodramatic speech to their movements; standing in front of the microphone, they coil and twitch. I asked Cortesi whether this was a consequence of having to focus one's lifelong talent into the few centimeters between
40 mouth and microphone, a kind of bodily rebellion to the condition of being heard but not seen, and he laughed. "Of course it isn't easy to spend a life in the darkness, but this is hardly the reason why they twitch and turn! Dubbers are used to reciting while trying to re-create
45 the bodily sensations of what they see on the screen before them. If there is running in the film, they will run on their feet. The moving," he explained, "is the result of re-creating large movements in small spaces."

There are still few options for those seeking to
50 watch subtitled, original-language films at a movie house in Italy. The Metropolitan cinema on Via del Corso closed recently after a long battle involving intel-
lectuals, show-business people, and American and British expats in Rome, to be replaced with a clothing
55 store. Italians remain hooked on dubbing—perhaps because of simple affection. Familiar voices yield emotional attachment.

Francesco Vairano, a dubber and dubbing director known for adapting foreign films considered to be
60 "undubbable," such as the French box office hit *Bienvenue chez les Ch'tis* ("Welcome to the Sticks," 2008), which relies on linguistic misunderstandings for much of its comedy, explained that actors become just as attached to their parts as audiences do. Vairano has
65 been one of the few directors to break the habit of matching the same Italian dubber to a foreign actor for all his films, preferring instead to select the dubber according to the requirements of the role, and, he admits, he was hated by all the prima donna dubbers for
70 this. "If you take that actor away from them," he told me, "they will insult you."

In 2007, I met dubber Luca Ward, who provided the voice of the narrator for a romantic comedy I co-wrote, *Scusa ma Ti Chiamo Amore* ("Sorry but I
75 Love You"). What I didn't then know was that everyone Ward met wanted him to recite actor Samuel L. Jackson's Ezekiel 25:17 passage from the film *Pulp Fiction*, and that I should consider it an honor that he would offer a performance to a stranger. When he
80 finally did recite the monologue, it was astonishing, every dramatic pause carefully timed and every word perfectly enunciated. I understood that, if anybody took Samuel L. Jackson away from Ward, it would have meant taking away a part of his soul; he was, as
85 Antonioni would say, half Ward, half Jackson. Leaving the day's recording session, Ward told me he was off to have dinner with actress Meg Ryan, before raising an eyebrow and clarifying, "With Meg Ryan's *dubber* . . . I am having dinner with Meg Ryan's voice."

19. The last sentence of the passage primarily serves to illustrate the passage author's central claim that:

A. dubbers want others in the film industry to respect the actors they usually dub.
B. the work of Ryan's dubber is as effective as that of Jackson's dubber.
C. dubbers begin to seem almost like hybrids of themselves and the actors they dub.
D. Ward is unlike most dubbers in that he prefers to dub many different actors.

20. It can reasonably be inferred from the passage that regarding whether dubbing is useful or valuable, Vairano would most strongly sympathize with the views of:

F. Antonioni.
G. Fellini.
H. Pasolini.
J. Renoir.

GO ON TO THE NEXT PAGE.

3 ▃▃▃▃▃▃▃▃▃▃▃▃▃▃▃▃▃▃▃▃▃▃▃▃▃▃ **3**

21. The main function of the second paragraph (lines 18–33) is for the passage author to present:

   A. her own ideas as an example of a contemporary perspective on the merits of dubbing.
   B. a perspective on dubbing that bluntly counters those outlined in the first paragraph.
   C. Fellini's personal, direct response to Renoir's criticism of his work.
   D. a claim, centered on Fellini's work, that strengthens the argument she makes in the first paragraph.

22. The anecdote about Fellini's footage of a woman recounting a tragic tale (lines 25–33) primarily serves to:

   F. explain why Fellini preferred to feature voices with northern accents in his films.
   G. provide a famous example of Fellini closely following scripted dialogue.
   H. illustrate the extent to which dubbing was a part of Fellini's craft.
   J. show why Fellini preferred his actors to follow a script rather than tell their own stories.

23. As Cortesi is presented in the passage, does he agree with the passage author's assumptions about the reason for dubbers' "over-the-top zest" (line 34)?

   A. Yes, and he thinks she should visit his dubbing studio to see how he works.
   B. Yes, and he suggests that the reason is a dubber's condition of being heard but not seen.
   C. No, and he gruffly makes clear his belief that she does not at all understand a dubber's work.
   D. No, and he corrects her misinterpretation with an explanation of his own.

24. It can most reasonably be inferred from the passage that the Metropolitan cinema on Via del Corso was known for showing films that had been:

   F. dubbed only.
   G. subtitled only.
   H. both dubbed and subtitled.
   J. neither dubbed nor subtitled.

25. The passage indicates that a foreign film with which of the following characteristics is particularly difficult to dub?

   A. Linguistic misunderstanding that creates comedy
   B. Dramatic action that advances the plot
   C. Reverse chronology that provides context
   D. Extensive monologues that further characterization

26. According to the passage, the work of dubbing director Vairano differs from that of most other Italian directors in that Vairano:

   F. focuses on dubbing French films into Italian.
   G. does not match the same Italian dubber to the same foreign actor for all his films.
   H. works mostly with "prima donna" dubbers.
   J. does not believe that dialogue should be rewritten during a dubbing session.

27. As it is used in line 17, the phrase *a challenge to* most nearly means:

   A. an assault on.
   B. a declaration of.
   C. a question for.
   D. an offer to.

GO ON TO THE NEXT PAGE.

3 — 3

Passage IV

INFORMATIONAL: This passage is adapted from the essay "Making Stuff: From Bacon to Bakelite" by Philip Ball (©2010 by Philip Ball).

During the Industrial Revolution, the high price of steel meant that many large engineering projects were carried out that used instead cast iron, which is brittle and prone to failure. This was why Henry Bessemer's
5 new process for making steel was greeted with jubilation: the details, announced at a meeting of the British Association in 1856, were published in full in *The Times*. Bessemer himself was lauded not just as an engineer but as a scientist, being elected a Fellow of the
10 Royal Society in 1879.

Bessemer's process controlled the amount of carbon mixed with iron to make steel. That the proportion of carbon governs the hardness was first noted in 1774 by the Swedish metallurgist Torbern Bergmann.
15 Bergmann made an extensive study of the propensity of different chemical elements to combine with one another—a property known as elective affinity, central to the eighteenth-century notion of chemical reactivity.

Oxygen, as a component of air, was the key to the
20 Bessemer process. It offered a way of removing impurities from pig iron and adjusting its carbon content during conversion to steel. A blast of air through the molten metal turned impurities such as silicon into light silica slag (a collection of compounds removed from
25 metal in the smelting process), and removed carbon in the form of volatile carbon dioxide. Pig iron contains as much as 4 per cent carbon; steels have only around 0.3–2 per cent.

It was long known that steel can be improved with
30 a spice of other elements. A dash of the metal manganese helps to remove oxygen and sulphur from the iron. Manganese also makes steel stronger, while nickel and chromium improve its hardness. And chromium is the key additive in stainless steel—in a proportion of more
35 than about 11 per cent, it makes the metal rust-resistant. Most modern steels are therefore alloys blended to give the desired properties.

But is this science? Some of the early innovations in steel alloys were chance discoveries, often due to
40 impurities incorporated by accident. In this respect, metallurgy has long retained the air of an artisan craft, akin to the trial-and-error explorations of dyers, glassmakers and potters. But the reason for this empiricism is not that the science of metallurgy is trivial; it
45 is because it is so difficult. According to Rodney Cotterill, a remarkable British physicist whose expertise stretched from the sciences of materials to that of the brain, "metallurgy is one of our most ancient arts, but is often referred to as one of the youngest
50 sciences."

One of the principal difficulties in understanding the behaviour of materials such as steel is that this depends on its structure over a wide range of length scales, from the packing of individual atoms to the size
55 and shape of grains micrometres or even millimetres in size. Science has trouble dealing with such a span of scales. One might regard this difficulty as akin to that in the social sciences, where social behaviour is governed by how individuals behave but also how we inter-
60 act on the scale of families and neighbourhoods, within entire cities, and at a national level.

The mechanical properties of metals depend on how flaws in the crystal structure, called defects, move and interact. These defects are produced by almost
65 inevitable imperfections in the regular stacking of atoms in the crystalline material. The most common type of stacking fault is called a dislocation. Metals bend, rather than shattering like porcelain, because dislocations can shift around and accommodate the defor-
70 mation. But if dislocations accumulate and get entangled, restricting their ability to move, the metal becomes brittle. Dislocations can also get trapped at the boundaries between the fine, microscopic grains that divide a metal into mosaics of crystallites. The arrest of
75 dislocations at grain edges means that metals may be made harder by reducing the size of their grains, a useful trick for modifying their mechanical behaviour.

28. The main purpose of the passage is to:
   F. explain in detail the various experiments Bessemer conducted in order to develop a better steel.
   G. provide an overview of some of the scientific principles that apply to the creation and behavior of steel.
   H. describe some of the philosophical questions concerning metallurgy.
   J. illustrate the differences between pig iron and cast iron.

29. The author most likely includes details about the initial response to Bessemer's new steel-making process in order to:
   A. emphasize that Bessemer's new process was a significant achievement for industry.
   B. provide support for the author's opinion that Bessemer's new process was prone to failure.
   C. describe Bessemer's qualifications as an engineer.
   D. provide specific examples of the criticism that Bessemer's new process received.

30. According to the passage, which of the following conversions is a direct result of adding oxygen to molten pig iron?
   F. Light silica slag is converted into carbon dioxide.
   G. Carbon dioxide is converted into carbon.
   H. Silicon is converted into light silica slag.
   J. Impurities in the metal are converted into silicon.

GO ON TO THE NEXT PAGE.

3   3

31. In the context of the passage, the main effect of the word "spice" (line 30) is to emphasize that:

   A. elements must be gradually mixed into steel in order to produce the desired effect.
   B. adding certain elements to steel can enrich the steel's quality.
   C. manganese, chromium, and nickel are used sparingly in steel because of their expense.
   D. blending elements is a trial-and-error process that has not yet yielded positive results.

32. Based on the passage, with which of the following statements would the author most likely agree?

   F. Metallurgy is not an art because it requires too much scientific knowledge.
   G. Metallurgy is too difficult to be considered a science.
   H. Metallurgy is a science as well as an art.
   J. Metallurgy is a trivial science.

33. The passage most strongly suggests that the study of the behavior of materials and the study of the social sciences are similar because they:

   A. require analyses that span a wide range of scales.
   B. are based on trial-and-error experimentation.
   C. involve examination of the size and shape of individual atoms.
   D. produce results that must be interpreted by both scientists and artists.

34. The main idea of the last paragraph is that:

   F. defects in the crystal structure of a metal determine that metal's mechanical properties.
   G. dislocations are the most common type of stacking fault in a metal.
   H. the mechanical behavior of a metal can be modified by increasing the size of a metal's grains.
   J. microscopic grains divide a metal into mosaics of crystallites.

35. As it is used in line 47, the word *stretched* most nearly means:

   A. strained.
   B. exaggerated.
   C. extended.
   D. amplified.

36. According to the passage, reducing the size of a metal's grains can make the metal:

   F. more rust-resistant.
   G. more brittle.
   H. finer.
   J. harder.

END OF TEST 3

STOP! DO NOT TURN THE PAGE UNTIL TOLD TO DO SO.

DO NOT RETURN TO A PREVIOUS TEST.

4 ◯ ◯ ◯ ◯ ◯ ◯ ◯ ◯ ◯ 4

SCIENCE TEST

40 Minutes—40 Questions

DIRECTIONS: There are several passages in this test. Each passage is followed by several questions. After reading a passage, choose the best answer to each question and fill in the corresponding oval on your answer document. You may refer to the passages as often as necessary.

You are **not** permitted to use a calculator on this test.

Passage I

The termite *Reticulitermes flavipes* consumes wood and bark. A study examined whether the consumption of wood or bark mulch by *R. flavipes* varies with the type of mulch or the age of the mulch. Separate portions of each of 5 types of mulch were aged (allowed to decay) for 1, 24, and 48 weeks. Then, 2 g of each type of 1-week-old mulch were put into a box, 2 g of each type of 24-week-old mulch were put into a second box, and 2 g of each type of 48-week-old mulch were put into a third box. Next, 1 g of *R. flavipes* was added to each box. After 15 days, the mass of mulch consumed, in milligrams (mg), was determined for each type and age of mulch (see figure).

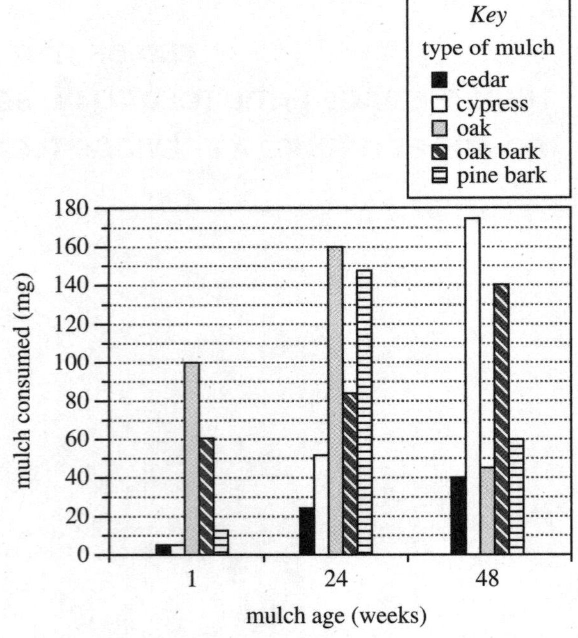

Figure adapted from O. P. Pinzon, R. M. Houseman, and C. J. Starbuck, "Feeding, Weight Change, Survival, and Aggregation of *Reticulitermes flavipes* (Kollar) (Isoptera: Rhinotermitidae) in Seven Varieties of Differentially-Aged Mulch." ©2006 by the Horticultural Research Institute.

1. Of the following combinations of type of mulch and mulch age, which combination resulted in the greatest mass of mulch consumed by *R. flavipes*?

   A. Type of mulch: oak
   Mulch age: 24 weeks

   B. Type of mulch: pine bark
   Mulch age: 24 weeks

   C. Type of mulch: oak
   Mulch age: 48 weeks

   D. Type of mulch: pine bark
   Mulch age: 48 weeks

2. Which of the following statements about the effect of mulch age on the consumption of mulch by *R. flavipes* is consistent with the figure? As mulch age increased from 1 week through 48 weeks, the mass of mulch consumed by *R. flavipes*:

   F. decreased only for all 5 types of mulch.
   G. increased only for all 5 types of mulch.
   H. initially decreased for all 5 types of mulch and then increased for some of the 5 types of mulch.
   J. initially increased for all 5 types of mulch and then decreased for some of the 5 types of mulch.

3. Based on the passage, would *R. flavipes* be classified as an autotroph or as a detritivore, and why?

   A. Autotroph, because *R. flavipes* produces its own energy without consuming organic material.
   B. Autotroph, because *R. flavipes* obtains its energy by consuming decaying organic material.
   C. Detritivore, because *R. flavipes* produces its own energy without consuming organic material.
   D. Detritivore, because *R. flavipes* obtains its energy by consuming decaying organic material.

GO ON TO THE NEXT PAGE.

4 ○ ○ ○ ○ ○ ○ ○ ○ 4

4. Which of the following statements comparing the consumption by *R. flavipes* of 1-week-old oak mulch, 24-week-old oak mulch, and 48-week-old oak mulch is supported by the figure?

   F. More 1-week-old mulch was consumed than 24-week-old mulch, and more 24-week-old mulch was consumed than 48-week-old mulch.

   G. Less 1-week-old mulch was consumed than 24-week-old mulch, and less 24-week-old mulch was consumed than 48-week-old mulch.

   H. More 1-week-old mulch was consumed than 24-week-old mulch, and less 24-week-old mulch was consumed than 48-week-old mulch.

   J. Less 1-week-old mulch was consumed than 24-week-old mulch, and more 24-week-old mulch was consumed than 48-week-old mulch.

5. What mass, in grams (**not** milligrams), of the 48-week-old oak bark mulch was consumed by *R. flavipes*?

   A. 0.06 g
   B. 0.14 g
   C. 0.6 g
   D. 1.4 g

GO ON TO THE NEXT PAGE.

4 ○ ○ ○ ○ ○ ○ ○ ○ 4

Passage II

Samples of Species C bacteria must often be transported from the areas in which they are collected. During transport, the samples are typically packed in ice to keep them alive. However, ice is not always available where the samples are collected.

Scientists studied how lyophilization (a freeze-drying process that doesn't require ice) followed by incubation affects the survival of 2 strains (Strain E and Strain V2) of Species C bacteria.

Experiment 1

The scientists placed a $100\,\mu L$ $(1\,\mu L = 10^{-3}\,mL)$ sample of a nutrient medium containing 4×10^6 Strain E elementary bodies into each of 8 sterile test tubes. An elementary body is the infective form of Species C. The sample in each of the tubes was then lyophilized, and each tube was sealed. Two of the tubes were incubated at 4°C, 2 were incubated at 20°C, 2 were incubated at 30°C, and 2 were incubated at 37°C.

One week after the start of incubation, the *percent survival* (the percent of the elementary bodies that survived) was determined for the sample in 1 of the 2 tubes at each temperature. Then, 1 month after the start of incubation, the percent survival was determined for the sample in the remaining tube at each temperature. The results are shown in Table 1.

	Table 1		
Strain	Incubation temperature (°C)	Percent (%) survival at:	
		1 week	1 month
E	4	52	51
	20	69	42
	30	5	4
	37	0	0

Experiment 2

The scientists repeated Experiment 1, except with Strain V2 instead of Strain E. The results are shown in Table 2.

	Table 2		
Strain	Incubation temperature (°C)	Percent (%) survival at:	
		1 week	1 month
V2	4	59	6
	20	29	4
	30	2	2
	37	0	0

Tables adapted from the article DOI: 10.1128/JCM.00968-06 by Adrian Eley et al. (©2006 by American Society for Microbiology).

6. Which of the following statements describes a difference between Experiment 1 and Experiment 2?

   F. A different incubation temperature was tested in Experiment 1 than in Experiment 2.
   G. A different strain of Species C was tested in Experiment 1 than in Experiment 2.
   H. Samples in Experiment 1 were lyophilized before being transported, whereas samples in Experiment 2 were transported on ice.
   J. Samples in Experiment 1 were incubated for 1 week before being transported, whereas samples in Experiment 2 were incubated for 1 month before being transported.

GO ON TO THE NEXT PAGE.

4 ○ ○ ○ ○ ○ ○ ○ ○ **4**

7. Suppose that in Experiment 2 the scientists had determined the percent survival for a sample incubated at 25°C for 1 week. The percent survival of the Strain V2 elementary bodies in the sample would most likely have been:

- **A.** 0%.
- **B.** between 2% and 29%.
- **C.** between 29% and 59%.
- **D.** greater than 59%.

8. Which of the following questions was **not** addressed by the experiments?

- **F.** Does incubation time affect the percent survival of Strain E and Strain V2 elementary bodies after lyophilization?
- **G.** Does temperature affect the percent survival of Strain E and Strain V2 elementary bodies after lyophilization?
- **H.** Does the number of Strain E or Strain V2 elementary bodies present in a sample before lyophilization affect their percent survival?
- **J.** Do Strain E elementary bodies have a greater percent survival than Strain V2 elementary bodies after lyophilization and incubation?

9. One week after the start of incubation, which of the 4 samples of Strain V2 elementary bodies would have been least likely to infect another organism that came into contact with the samples?

- **A.** The sample that had been incubated at 4°C
- **B.** The sample that had been incubated at 10°C
- **C.** The sample that had been incubated at 20°C
- **D.** The sample that had been incubated at 37°C

10. Suppose that a scientist wants to transport a lyophilized sample of Strain E elementary bodies. Based on the results of Experiment 1, which of the following combinations of temperature and transportation time would most likely ensure the greatest percent survival of the elementary bodies?

- **F.** 4°C and 1 week
- **G.** 4°C and 1 month
- **H.** 20°C and 1 week
- **J.** 20°C and 1 month

11. Consider the rating system in the table below for the percent survival of elementary bodies after lyophilization.

Rating	Percent survival
Excellent	> 90%
Good	≥ 30% and ≤ 90%
Poor	< 30%

Based on this table, what is the total number of tubes in Experiment 1 that contained samples having a poor percent survival?

- **A.** 2
- **B.** 4
- **C.** 6
- **D.** 8

GO ON TO THE NEXT PAGE.

4 ○ ○ ○ ○ ○ ○ ○ ○ **4**

Passage III

When an object is submerged in a fluid, the object displaces a volume of fluid equal to the object's submerged volume. The fluid exerts an upward buoyant force on the object that is equal in magnitude to the weight of the displaced fluid. The object floats if the buoyant force equals the object's weight.

A group of students conducted 2 studies on buoyant forces using 3 fluids—water, Fluid A, and Fluid B—having densities of 1.0 g/cm^3, 1.25 g/cm^3, and 1.50 g/cm^3, respectively.

Study 1

The students placed a 10 cm long cylinder in a container of water and measured the length of the portion of the cylinder that was submerged. They then repeated this procedure with a container of Fluid A and a container of Fluid B (see Figure 1).

Figure 1

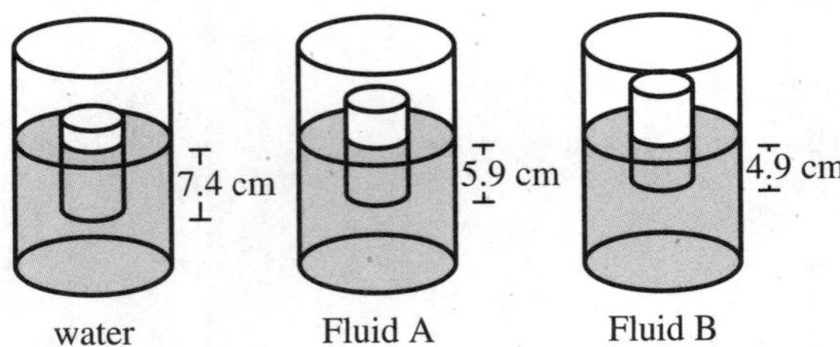

Study 2

The students placed a stone—either Stone X, Stone Y, or Stone Z—in a net that was tied to a spring balance. They recorded the force measured by the balance as the stone's weight, W. They then submerged the stone in water and again recorded the force measured by the balance (see Figure 2).

Figure 2

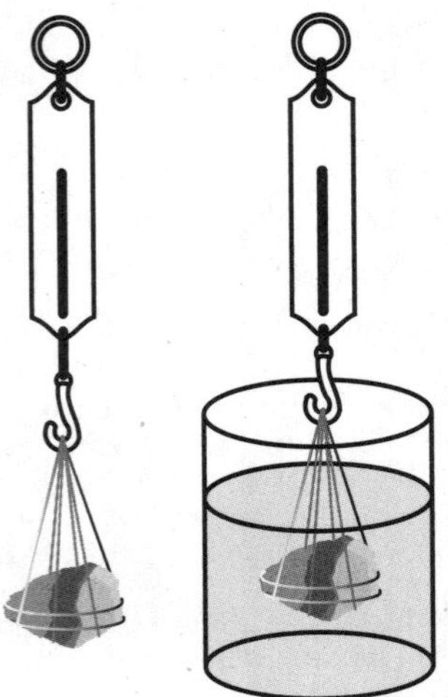

The students calculated the buoyant force on the stone in water as W minus the force that was measured when the stone was submerged. They repeated this procedure to test all 3 stones in all 3 fluids. Table 1 lists each stone's volume, in cm^3, and W, in newtons (N), as well as the buoyant force, in N, on each stone in the fluid.

Table 1					
			Buoyant force (N) in:		
Stone	Volume (cm^3)	W (N)	water	Fluid A	Fluid B
X	48	1.50	0.47	0.59	0.70
Y	96	1.50	0.94	1.18	1.41
Z	96	3.00	0.94	1.18	1.41

GO ON TO THE NEXT PAGE.

4 ◯ ◯ ◯ ◯ ◯ ◯ ◯ ◯ 4

12. Based on the results of Study 2, as the density of the fluid in which Stone X was submerged increased, the buoyant force on Stone X:

F. decreased only.
G. increased only.
H. decreased and then increased.
J. varied with no general trend.

13. Based on the results of Study 2, for Stone Y, what was the difference between the buoyant force in Fluid A and the buoyant force in Fluid B?

A. 0.11 N
B. 0.23 N
C. 0.47 N
D. 0.71 N

14. Suppose the students decide to study whether a cylinder's volume determines the submerged length of the cylinder in a given fluid. Which of the following procedural changes should the students make to Study 1? The students should test:

F. multiple cylinders with a single fluid; the cylinders should have different weights but the same volume.
G. multiple cylinders with a single fluid; the cylinders should have different volumes but the same density.
H. a single cylinder with multiple fluids; the fluids should have different densities.
J. a single cylinder with multiple fluids; the fluids should each have the same density as the cylinder.

15. In Study 1, did the cylinder displace a greater volume of water or a greater volume of Fluid A?

A. Water, because the cylinder's submerged length was greater in water than in Fluid A.
B. Water, because the cylinder's submerged length was greater in Fluid A than in water.
C. Fluid A, because the cylinder's submerged length was greater in water than in Fluid A.
D. Fluid A, because the cylinder's submerged length was greater in Fluid A than in water.

16. Suppose that in Study 2 the students had tested a stone having the same weight as Stone Z but a larger volume than Stone Z. Which of the following statements about the buoyant force on this submerged stone would be correct? The buoyant force on this stone in:

F. water would have been less than 0.94 N.
G. Fluid A would have been less than 1.18 N.
H. Fluid B would have been greater than 1.41 N.
J. water would have been greater than the buoyant force on this stone in Fluid A.

17. Assume that Atlantic Ocean water has a density of 1.01 g/cm^3 and that Pacific Ocean water has a density of 1.03 g/cm^3. Based on the results of Study 1, in which ocean would a given iceberg more likely have the greater submerged volume?

A. The Atlantic Ocean, because the results of Study 1 indicate that submerged volume increases as fluid density decreases.
B. The Atlantic Ocean, because the results of Study 1 indicate that submerged volume decreases as fluid density decreases.
C. The Pacific Ocean, because the results of Study 1 indicate that submerged volume increases as fluid density decreases.
D. The Pacific Ocean, because the results of Study 1 indicate that submerged volume decreases as fluid density decreases.

GO ON TO THE NEXT PAGE.

4 ◯ ◯ ◯ ◯ ◯ ◯ ◯ ◯ ◯ 4

Passage IV

Chemical reactions that release heat are exothermic reactions. The amount of heat released depends on the number of moles of reactants consumed in the reaction. A mole of any substance is 6×10^{23} molecules or formula units of the substance.

When sodium hypochlorite (NaClO) and sodium iodide (NaI) are dissolved in acidic H_2O, an exothermic reaction occurs:

$$NaClO + NaI \rightarrow products + heat$$

Students did an experiment to study this reaction.

Experiment

In each of 8 trials, the students performed Steps 1–5:

1. A known volume of a 0.2 mole/L aqueous NaClO solution was poured into a foam coffee cup. A lid was placed on the cup.

2. A thermometer was placed into the solution through a hole in the lid. The solution's initial temperature, T_i, of 22.0°C was recorded.

3. The lid was lifted, and a known volume of a 0.2 mole/L aqueous NaI solution, also at a T_i of 22.0°C, was poured into the cup. The lid was put back on the cup, and the solution was swirled.

4. The solution's final (maximum) temperature, T_f, was measured.

5. The change in temperature, ΔT, was calculated:

$$\Delta T = T_f - T_i$$

The data for each trial are shown in Table 1.

	Table 1			
Trial	Volume of NaClO solution (mL)	Volume of NaI solution (mL)	T_f (°C)	ΔT (°C)
1	0	100	22.0	0.0
2	25	75	25.5	3.5
3	50	50	29.0	7.0
4	70	30	31.7	9.7
5	75	25	32.5	10.5
6	80	20	30.6	8.6
7	90	10	26.2	4.2
8	100	0	22.0	0.0

The students plotted ΔT versus the volume of NaClO solution for each trial (see Figure 1).

Figure 1

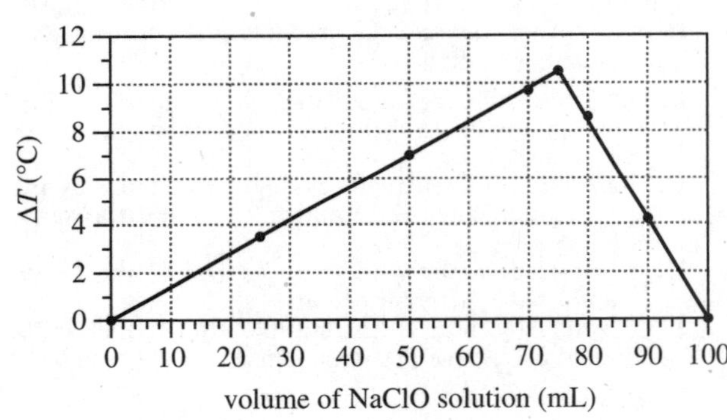

Then they identified the trial for which ΔT had its greatest value. The ratio of the volume of the NaClO solution to the volume of the NaI solution for this trial is the mole ratio for the reaction.

Table and figure adapted from M. Jerome Bigelow, "Thermochemistry of Hypochlorite Oxidations." ©1969 by Division of Chemical Education, Inc., American Chemical Society.

GO ON TO THE NEXT PAGE.

4 ○ ○ ○ ○ ○ ○ ○ ○ **4**

18. Before the experiment, a student predicted that ΔT for Trial 2 would be greater than ΔT for Trial 6. Do the results shown in Table 1 support this prediction?

- **F.** No; ΔT for Trial 2 was 5.1°C less than ΔT for Trial 6.
- **G.** No; ΔT for Trial 2 was 8.6°C less than ΔT for Trial 6.
- **H.** Yes; ΔT for Trial 2 was 5.1°C greater than ΔT for Trial 6.
- **J.** Yes; ΔT for Trial 2 was 8.6°C greater than ΔT for Trial 6.

19. In each trial, the total volume of solution poured into the cup was:

- **A.** 25 mL.
- **B.** 50 mL.
- **C.** 75 mL.
- **D.** 100 mL.

20. Consider the trial for which the volume of NaClO was 4 times as great as the volume of NaI. For this trial, T_f was:

- **F.** 25.5°C.
- **G.** 26.2°C.
- **H.** 30.6°C.
- **J.** 32.5°C.

21. Suppose a trial had been performed with 20 mL of NaClO solution and 80 mL of NaI solution. Based on Figure 1, ΔT for this new trial would most likely have been closest to which of the following?

- **A.** 1°C
- **B.** 3°C
- **C.** 5°C
- **D.** 7°C

22. Which of the following statements best explains why ΔT was 0.0°C for Trial 8? The volume of solution added was 0 mL for one of the:

- **F.** products, NaClO, so no reaction had occurred.
- **G.** products, NaI, so no reaction had occurred.
- **H.** reactants, NaClO, so no reaction had occurred.
- **J.** reactants, NaI, so no reaction had occurred.

23. Suppose that the reaction studied had been endothermic. As the endothermic reaction progressed, would the solution temperature more likely have decreased or increased?

- **A.** Decreased, because the reaction would have released heat.
- **B.** Decreased, because the reaction would have absorbed heat.
- **C.** Increased, because the reaction would have released heat.
- **D.** Increased, because the reaction would have absorbed heat.

GO ON TO THE NEXT PAGE.

4 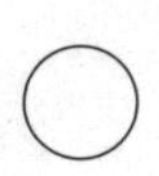 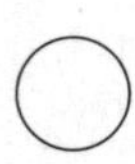 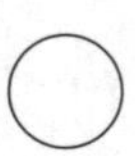 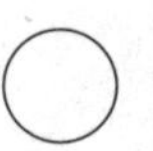     **4**

Passage V

Tomato plants grow poorly in high-salt environments. This effect is caused by 2 processes:

- A net movement of H_2O between the cytoplasm of the plants' cells and the environment via osmosis

- An increase in the cytoplasmic Na^+ concentration

The plant *Arabidopsis thaliana* carries a gene, *AtNHX1*. The product of this gene, VAC, facilitates uptake of cytoplasmic Na^+ by the plant's vacuoles.

A researcher created 4 genetically identical lines of tomato plants (L1–L4). An *AtNHX1* gene from *Arabidopsis thaliana* was isolated and 2 identical copies of this gene were incorporated into L1's genome. This process was repeated with L2 and L3 using a different *AtNHX1* allele for each line, so that L1, L2, and L3 had different genotypes for *AtNHX1*. The researcher then did an experiment.

Experiment

Fifty seedlings from each of the 4 lines were grown in 10 L of nutrient solution for 80 days. The 10 L nutrient solution contained H_2O, 12 g of fertilizer, and 3 g of NaCl. The nutrient solution was replaced every 5 days. After 80 days, average height, average mass (without fruit), and average fruit mass (per plant) were measured (see Table 1).

Table 1			
3 g of NaCl/10 L nutrient solution			
Line	Height (cm)	Mass (kg)	Fruit mass (kg)
L1	124	1.2	2.1
L2	128	1.2	2.0
L3	120	1.2	2.1
L4	124	1.2	2.0

This process was repeated except the 10 L nutrient solution contained 60 g of NaCl instead of 3 g of NaCl (see Table 2).

Table 2			
60 g of NaCl/10 L nutrient solution			
Line	Height (cm)	Mass (kg)	Fruit mass (kg)
L1	119	1.1	1.9
L2	121	1.1	1.9
L3	61	0.4	1.1
L4	63	0.5	1.0

The process was repeated again except the 10 L nutrient solution contained 120 g of NaCl instead of 3 g of NaCl (see Table 3).

Table 3			
120 g of NaCl/10 L nutrient solution			
Line	Height (cm)	Mass (kg)	Fruit mass (kg)
L1	118	1.0	1.8
L2	115	1.0	1.7
L3	34	0.2	0
L4	36	0.3	0

GO ON TO THE NEXT PAGE.

4 ○ ○ ○ ○ ○ ○ ○ ○ ○ 4

24. One plant produced no fruit and had a height of 21 cm. Which of the following most likely describes this plant?

  F. It was from L2 and was grown in a 10 L nutrient solution containing 60 g of NaCl.

  G. It was from L2 and was grown in a 10 L nutrient solution containing 120 g of NaCl.

  H. It was from L4 and was grown in a 10 L nutrient solution containing 60 g of NaCl.

  J. It was from L4 and was grown in a 10 L nutrient solution containing 120 g of NaCl.

25. During osmosis, water migrates through a semipermeable barrier. The osmosis referred to in the passage occurs through which of the following structures?

  A. Chromosomes
  B. Nuclear envelope
  C. Cell membrane
  D. Rough endoplasmic reticulum

26. For each line, as the concentration of salt in the nutrient solutions increased, average plant mass:

  F. increased only.
  G. decreased only.
  H. increased and then decreased.
  J. decreased and then increased.

27. Which of the following was an independent variable in the experiment?

  A. Whether a line received *AtNHX1*
  B. Whether a tomato plant was used
  C. Plant mass without fruit
  D. Plant height

28. Suppose the data for all of the plants were plotted on a graph with height on the x-axis and mass (without fruit) on the y-axis. Suppose also that the best-fit line for these data was determined. Which of the following would most likely characterize the slope of this line?

  F. The line would not have a slope, because the line would be vertical.

  G. The slope of the line would be zero.

  H. The slope of the line would be negative.

  J. The slope of the line would be positive.

29. The researchers included 1 of the 4 lines to serve as a control. This line was most likely which one?

  A. L1
  B. L2
  C. L3
  D. L4

GO ON TO THE NEXT PAGE.

4 ◯ ◯ ◯ ◯ ◯ ◯ ◯ ◯ ◯ **4**

Passage VI

When rocks are melted at very high temperatures beneath Earth's surface, magma (molten rock) is formed. The gases CO_2 and H_2O can dissolve in magma. Figure 1 shows, for 4 different magmas (leucitite, basanite, rhyolite, and tholeiitic basalt), how the solubility of CO_2 in the magma at 1,150°C varies with pressure (in megapascals, MPa).

Figure 1

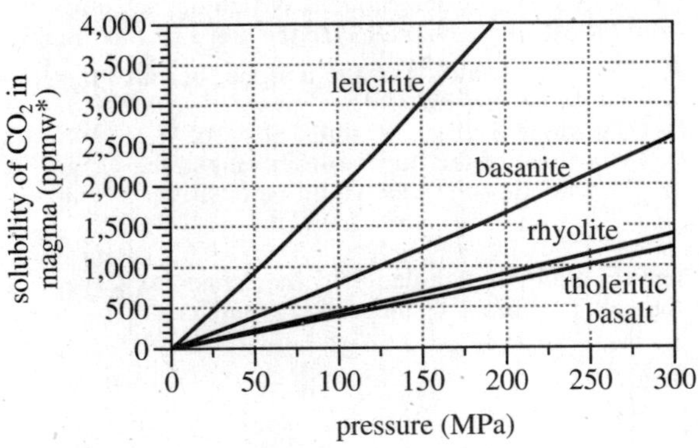

*parts per million by weight

Figure 2 shows, at 3 different pressures, how the solubility of CO_2 in rhyolite magma varies with temperature.

Figure 2

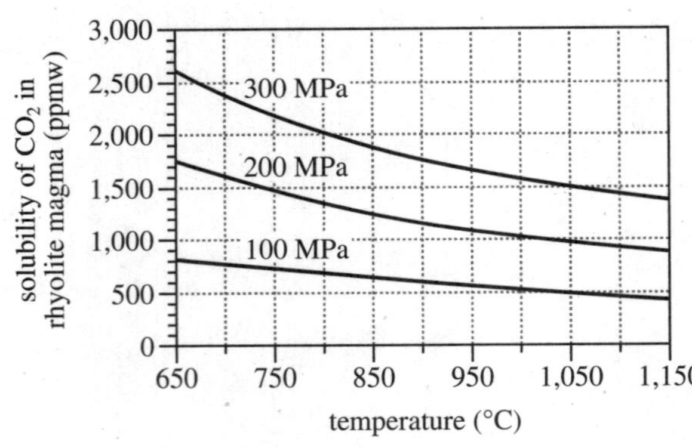

Figure 3 shows, at 4 different pressures, how the solubility of CO_2 in rhyolite magma at 750°C varies with the weight percent of H_2O in the magma.

Figure 3

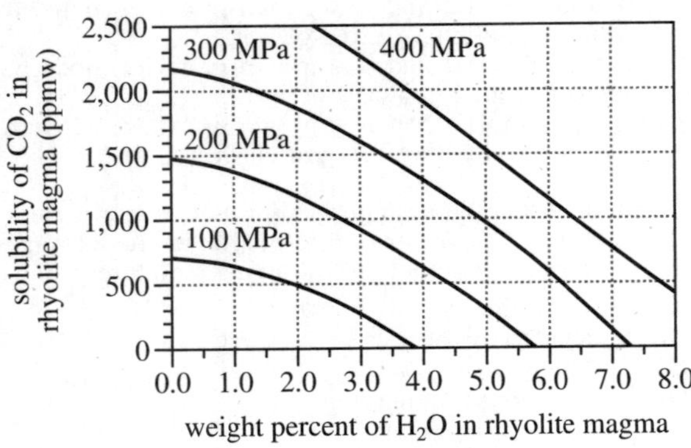

Figures 1 and 3 adapted from Jacob B. Lowenstern, "Carbon Dioxide in Magmas and Implications for Hydrothermal Systems." ©2001 by Springer-Verlag.

Figure 2 adapted from Robert A. Fogel and Malcolm J. Rutherford, "The Solubility of Carbon Dioxide in Rhyolitic Melts: A Quantitative FTIR Study." ©1990 by the Mineralogical Society of America.

30. Based on Figure 2, at 300 MPa, the solubility of CO_2 in rhyolite magma is closest to 2,000 ppmw at which of the following temperatures?

F. 700°C
G. 750°C
H. 800°C
J. 850°C

GO ON TO THE NEXT PAGE.

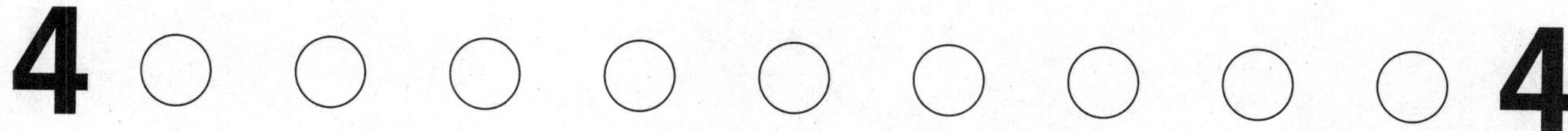

31. Based on Figure 1, at 1,150°C, the solubility of CO_2 in basanite magma and the solubility of CO_2 in tholeiitic basalt magma are closest in value at which of the following pairs of pressures?

   A. Basanite magma: 50 MPa
       Tholeiitic basalt magma: 200 MPa

   B. Basanite magma: 50 MPa
       Tholeiitic basalt magma: 250 MPa

   C. Basanite magma: 125 MPa
       Tholeiitic basalt magma: 200 MPa

   D. Basanite magma: 125 MPa
       Tholeiitic basalt magma: 250 MPa

32. Based on Figure 1, at 1,150°C and 150 MPa, the solubility of CO_2 in leucitite magma is approximately how much greater than or less than the solubility of CO_2 in rhyolite magma?

   F. 1,750 ppmw greater
   G. 2,300 ppmw greater
   H. 1,750 ppmw less
   J. 2,300 ppmw less

33. Based on Figure 2, increasing the temperature from 650°C to 1,150°C has the lesser effect on the solubility of CO_2 in rhyolite magma at which pressure, 100 MPa or 300 MPa?

   A. 100 MPa; the solubility of CO_2 decreases by about 400 ppmw.
   B. 100 MPa; the solubility of CO_2 decreases by about 1,300 ppmw.
   C. 300 MPa; the solubility of CO_2 decreases by about 400 ppmw.
   D. 300 MPa; the solubility of CO_2 decreases by about 1,300 ppmw.

34. Consider the solubility of CO_2 in rhyolite magma at 750°C and 200 MPa, as shown in Figure 2. Based on Figure 3, this rhyolite magma has a weight percent of H_2O closest to which of the following?

   F. 0.0%
   G. 2.0%
   H. 4.0%
   J. 6.0%

GO ON TO THE NEXT PAGE.

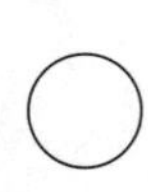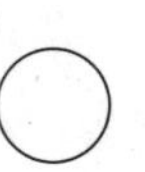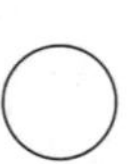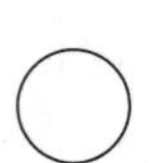

Passage VII

When viewed from Earth, the other planets in the solar system usually appear to move prograde (eastward relative to the stars). Occasionally, however, each planet appears to briefly move retrograde (westward relative to the stars). For example, Figure 1 shows Mars's position relative to the stars on 9 dates between July 24, 2005, and February 26, 2006.

Figure 1

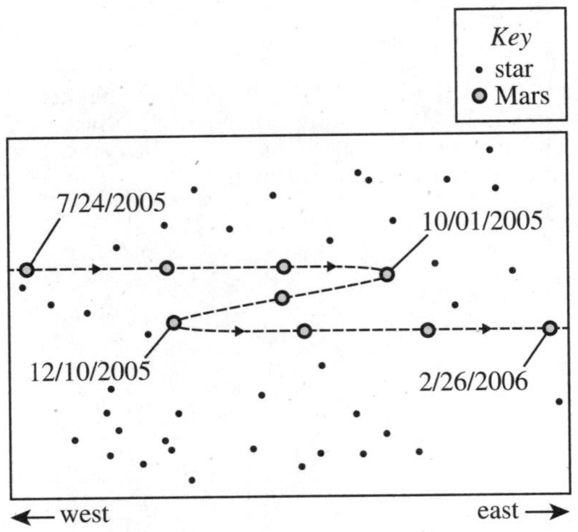

Two hypotheses were proposed to explain why the planets occasionally appear to move retrograde.

Hypothesis 1

Earth is the solar system's central body, and the other bodies move around Earth in looped orbits. Each body (except Earth) has 2 circles associated with it: a deferent and an epicycle. Both circles rotate counterclockwise, and their combined motions result in a body following a looped orbit. In Figure 2, the left panel shows Mars's deferent and epicycle, and the right panel shows Mars's orbit.

Figure 2

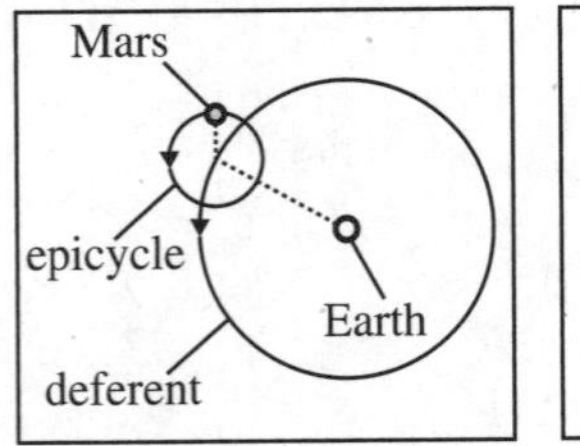

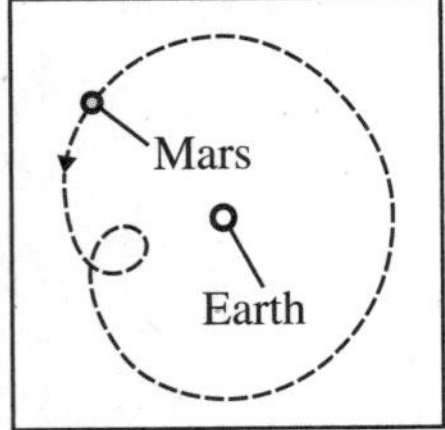

As a body passes through a loop, the body's motion changes from prograde to retrograde and back. The larger a body's deferent, the more loops in the body's orbit, and the more often that body passes through a loop.

Hypothesis 2

The Sun is the solar system's central body, and the planets move counterclockwise around the Sun in elliptical orbits. The larger a planet's orbit, the more time the planet takes to complete a revolution around the Sun. As a result, the line of sight from Earth to a given planet drifts over time. Figure 3 shows the orbits of Earth and Mars, and the positions of Earth and Mars, on each of the 4 dates labeled in Figure 1. For each date, the line of sight from Earth to Mars is projected onto a view of the sky.

There are 2 rules for apparent retrograde motion:

- A planet with an orbit larger than Earth's appears to move retrograde whenever Earth passes between the Sun and that planet. The larger that planet's orbit, the more often a pass occurs.

- A planet with an orbit smaller than Earth's appears to move retrograde whenever that planet passes between the Sun and Earth. The smaller that planet's orbit, the more often a pass occurs.

Figure 3

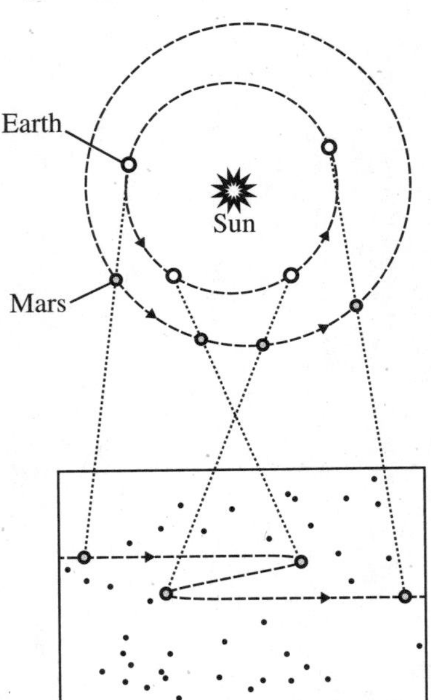

GO ON TO THE NEXT PAGE.

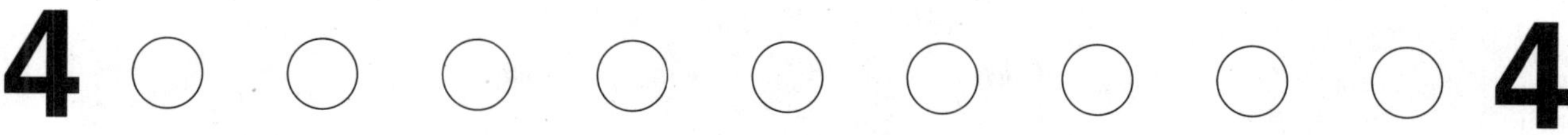

4 ○ ○ ○ ○ ○ ○ ○ ○ **4**

35. Which of the following statements best describes a primary difference between the two hypotheses? Hypothesis 1 claims that all planets follow:

  A. looped orbits around Earth, whereas Hypothesis 2 claims that all planets follow elliptical orbits around the Sun.
  B. looped orbits around Earth, whereas Hypothesis 2 claims that all planets follow elliptical orbits around Earth.
  C. elliptical orbits around the Sun, whereas Hypothesis 2 claims that all planets follow looped orbits around the Sun.
  D. elliptical orbits around the Sun, whereas Hypothesis 2 claims that all planets follow looped orbits around Earth.

36. Assume that Figures 2 and 3 are drawn to scale. Which of the figures, if either, implies that the distance between Earth and Mars varies with time?

  F. Figure 2 only
  G. Figure 3 only
  H. Both Figure 2 and Figure 3
  J. Neither Figure 2 nor Figure 3

37. Consider both the interval of time represented in Figures 1 and 3 and the reason that, according to Hypothesis 2, the line of sight from Earth to Mars drifts over time. Is the top portion of Figure 3 consistent with that reason?

  A. Yes; Earth is shown as having the smaller orbit and as having completed a greater percentage of its revolution around the Sun than is Mars.
  B. Yes; Earth is shown as having the larger orbit and as having completed a greater percentage of its revolution around the Sun than is Mars.
  C. No; Earth is shown as having the smaller orbit and as having completed a greater percentage of its revolution around the Sun than is Mars.
  D. No; Earth is shown as having the larger orbit and as having completed a greater percentage of its revolution around the Sun than is Mars.

38. Based on Figure 1, as viewed from Earth, for approximately how many days between July 2005 and February 2006 did Mars move retrograde?

  F. 30
  G. 70
  H. 150
  J. 220

39. A supporter of Hypothesis 1 and a supporter of Hypothesis 2 would both be likely to agree with which of the following statements? When viewed from Earth, if a planet appears to be moving prograde, that planet is actually moving:

  A. clockwise around Earth.
  B. clockwise around the central body in the solar system.
  C. counterclockwise around the Sun.
  D. counterclockwise around the central body in the solar system.

40. Based on Figures 1 and 3, if Hypothesis 2 is correct, which of the following figures most likely shows the positions of Earth and Mars on November 7, 2005?

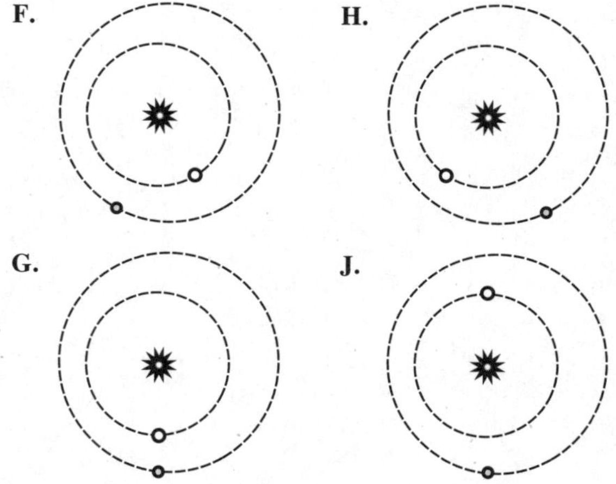

END OF TEST 4

STOP! DO NOT RETURN TO ANY OTHER TEST.

You may wish to photocopy these sample answer document pages to respond to the practice ACT Writing Test.

Please enter the information at the right before beginning the writing test.

Use a No. 2 pencil only. Do NOT use a mechanical pencil, ink, ballpoint, or felt-tip pen.

WRITING TEST BOOKLET NUMBER

Print your 9-digit **Booklet Number** in the boxes at the right.

WRITING TEST FORM

Print your 5-character **Test Form** in the boxes at the right <u>and</u> fill in the corresponding ovals.

Begin WRITING TEST here.

If you need more space, please continue on the next page.

The ONLY Official Prep Guide from the Makers of the ACT

WRITING TEST

If you need more space, please continue on the back of this page.

2

WRITING TEST

If you need more space, please continue on the next page.

3

WRITING TEST

STOP here with the writing test.

Practice Writing Test Prompt 4

Your Signature: ____
(Do not print.)

Print Your Name Here: ____

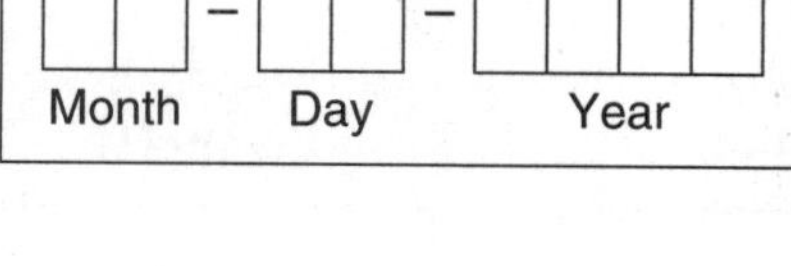

Your Date of Birth:

☐☐ – ☐☐ – ☐☐☐☐
Month   Day   Year

Form 23WT2

The **ACT**® WRITING TEST
BOOKLET

You must take the multiple-choice tests before you take the writing test.

Directions

This is a test of your writing skills. You will have **forty** (40) minutes to read the prompt, plan your response, and write an essay in English. Before you begin working, read all material in this test booklet carefully to understand exactly what you are being asked to do.

You will write your essay on the lined pages in the **answer document** provided. Your writing on those pages will be scored. You may use the unlined pages in this test booklet to plan your essay. Your work on these pages will not be scored.

Your essay will be evaluated based on the evidence it provides of your ability to:

- clearly state your own perspective on a complex issue and analyze the relationship between your perspective and at least one other perspective
- develop and support your ideas with reasoning and examples
- organize your ideas clearly and logically
- communicate your ideas effectively in standard written English

Lay your pencil down immediately when time is called.

DO NOT OPEN THIS BOOKLET UNTIL TOLD TO DO SO.

PO Box 168
Iowa City, IA 52243-0168

The ONLY Official Prep Guide from the Makers of the ACT

Spirit Week

Spirit Week, whether centered on homecoming or simply celebrating the school and its student body, is common in US high schools. Students participate in a wide range of activities, including assemblies, costume or dress-up days, games and competitions, and parades. But all these activities take a lot of time, and all the commotion can be distracting. Such an environment makes it easier for students to turn their attention away from academics and toward social and athletic events. Should schools continue the practice of Spirit Week?

Read and carefully consider these perspectives. Each suggests a particular way of thinking about the question above.

Perspective One	**Perspective Two**	**Perspective Three**
Academics should be the highest priority of every school. Events such as Spirit Week send the message that putting fun before work is acceptable.	Team spirit and goodwill are essential to the survival of any community. Spirit events bring students closer together and create a friendly, harmonious environment.	Many students have interests other than those represented by Spirit Week. Such events force those students to engage in a type of activity they would rather avoid.

Essay Task

Write a unified, coherent essay in which you address the question of whether schools should continue the practice of Spirit Week. In your essay, be sure to:

- clearly state your own perspective and analyze the relationship between your perspective and at least one other perspective
- develop and support your ideas with reasoning and examples
- organize your ideas clearly and logically
- communicate your ideas effectively in standard written English

Your perspective may be in full agreement with any of those given, in partial agreement, or completely different.

Planning Your Essay

Your work on these prewriting pages will not be scored.

Use the space below and on the back cover to generate ideas and plan your essay. You may wish to consider the following as you think critically about the task:

Strengths and weaknesses of different perspectives on the issue
- What insights do they offer, and what do they fail to consider?
- Why might they be persuasive to others, or why might they fail to persuade?

Your own knowledge, experience, and values
- What is your perspective on this issue, and what are its strengths and weaknesses?
- How will you support your perspective in your essay?

If you need more space to plan, please continue on the back of this page.

The ONLY Official Prep Guide from the Makers of the ACT

Planning Your Essay

Use this page to continue planning your essay. Your work on this page will not be scored.

Passage I

Question 1. **The best answer is** C because it provides the appropriate verb form and tense (*is*) for the second independent clause in this sentence.

The best answer is NOT:

A because the participle *being* leaves the second independent clause without a predicate.

B because the verb "was being" creates an illogical shift in verb tense. The first clause of the sentence uses present tense, so the second clause should also use present tense.

D because a deletion would leave the second independent clause without a predicate.

Question 2. **The best answer is** H because it provides the appropriate punctuation (commas) to set off the nonessential element "called vocables."

The best answer is NOT:

F because it is missing the second comma to set off the nonessential element.

G because it is missing the first comma to set off the nonessential element.

J because the comma after *called* is misplaced; it should be after *syllables* to set off the nonessential element.

Question 3. **The best answer is** A because the phrase "often tongue-twisting," which describes the lyrics of puirt-abeul, suggests a sequence of words or sounds that are difficult to pronounce.

The best answer is NOT:

B because "tongue-twisting" is not related to writing lyrics; the phrase describes words or sounds that are difficult to pronounce.

C because "often" refers to the frequency with which the puirt-a-beul lyrics are "tongue-twisting," not the frequency with which puirt-a-beul is performed.

D because there is no mention of any training exercises for puirt-a-beul.

Question 4. **The best answer is F** because it is the only option that introduces a discussion about how puirt-a-beul was invented out of necessity, which is the main focus of the paragraph.

The best answer is NOT:

G because the main focus of the paragraph is why puirt-a-beul was invented, not how mouth music singers must have good rhythm.

H because the main focus of the paragraph is why puirt-a-beul was invented, not how it has influenced jazz scat singing.

J because the main focus of the paragraph is why puirt-a-beul was invented, not where another form of mouth music originated.

Question 5. **The best answer is D** because it uses the appropriate pronoun case. The nominative pronoun *who* is used to introduce a clause about a person, and in this instance, the person is *anyone*.

The best answer is NOT:

A because the pronoun *whomever* is in the objective case, and the sentence requires a nominative pronoun because of the verb "didn't read."

B because the pronoun *which* is used for things, not people.

C because the pronoun *whom* is in the objective case, and the sentence requires a nominative case.

Passage II

Question 6. **The best answer is J** because it is the only option that does not add unnecessary and confusing punctuation.

The best answer is NOT:

F because the phrase "called the Garamantes" is an essential element that should not be separated from the rest of the clause.

G because it adds an unnecessary comma before the phrase beginning with the word *created*.

H because the colon after the word *called* is incorrect, as it breaks up the complete predicate in this clause.

Question 7. The best answer is **C** because it is the only option that provides parallel verb structure.

The best answer is NOT:

A because it shifts to passive voice; the other verbs are in active voice.

B because it disrupts the parallelism with the other elements in this sentence.

D because it is not a verb and so is not parallel with the other elements.

Question 8. The best answer is **F** because it is the only option that indicates the method for building the tunnels.

The best answer is NOT:

G because the word *underground* does not indicate the method for building the tunnels.

H because the phrase "dimly lit" does not indicate the method for building the tunnels.

J because the word *desert* does not indicate the method for building the tunnels.

Question 9. The best answer is **D** because it is the only option that does not create a misplaced or dangling modifier.

The best answer is NOT:

A because the introductory phrase inaccurately modifies the archaeologists, suggesting that they were the ones who "left no clues."

B because the introductory phrase inaccurately modifies the archaeologists, suggesting that they were a "genuine puzzle."

C because the introductory phrase inaccurately modifies the archaeologists, suggesting that they were the ones who gave "no indication."

Question 10. The best answer is **G** because the word *than* is the correct word to use in this context; it is a conjunction used to make a comparison, which this sentence does. It also creates a Standard English idiom.

The best answer is NOT:

F because the word *then* is not the correct word to use in this context; the phrase "rather then" is not a Standard English idiom. In addition, "its" has no logical antecedent.

H because the word *then* is not the correct word to use in this context; the phrase "rather then" is not a Standard English idiom.

J because the word *by* is not the correct word to use in this context; the phrase "rather by" is not a Standard English idiom.

Question 11. The best answer is C because it is the only option that uses the appropriate verb form. The water from the aquifer meant that the Garamantes "could rely" on "a constant supply of water."

> **The best answer is NOT:**

A because it is not a proper verb form.

B because it is not a proper verb form.

D because the singular verb form *relies* does not agree with its plural subject, *Garamantes*.

Question 12. The best answer is F because it provides the most logical transitional word to connect this sentence with the preceding one. The word *moreover* means *furthermore*, and this sentence provides further information about the benefits of the underground canals.

> **The best answer is NOT:**

G because the transitional word *nevertheless* suggests contrasting ideas, but the information in this sentence does not contrast with the idea in the preceding sentence.

H because the transitional phrase "in contrast" suggests contrasting ideas, but the information in this sentence does not contrast with the idea in the preceding sentence.

J because the transitional phrase "even so" suggests contrasting ideas, but the information in this sentence does not contrast with the idea in the preceding sentence.

Question 13. The best answer is A because it provides the most logical subordinating conjunction to introduce the dependent clause in this sentence. The conjunction *as* is used to indicate that something happens during the time when something else is taking place.

> **The best answer is NOT:**

B because the phrase "as to when" is unclear and unnecessarily wordy.

C because the word *whereas* indicates contrast or comparison; this sentence is making a connection, not a comparison.

D because the word *though* results in an illogical statement.

Question 14. The best answer is **J** because deleting the underlined portion avoids redundancy with information elsewhere in the paragraph.

The best answer is NOT:

F because it is redundant; preceding information notes that the ventilation shafts are visible.

G because it is redundant and wordy; preceding information notes that the ventilation shafts are visible.

H because it is redundant and wordy; preceding information notes that the ventilation shafts are visible.

Question 15. The best answer is **B** because this option clearly indicates why the essay does fulfill the writer's primary purpose. The main focus of the essay is describing how the Garamantes were able to meet their need for water in a dry area.

The best answer is NOT:

A because trade is mentioned only briefly in the first paragraph, and it has nothing to do with overcoming a natural obstacle.

C because the fact that the foggaras were not naturally occurring does support the primary purpose of explaining how the Garamantes overcame a natural obstacle.

D because the lack of water, not the foggaras, led to the Garamantes' downfall; in fact, the foggaras aided the Garamantes by moving the water from the mountains to their settlements.

Passage III

Question 16. The best answer is **H** because the meaning here is clearest when the ideas are divided into two sentences, with the first sentence giving a general description of the artwork and the second describing the eight women in the artwork more specifically.

The best answer is NOT:

F because the relative pronoun *that* should be used to connect an adjectival clause to a main clause, not to connect two main clauses. *That* in this position would logically refer to the immediately preceding noun, *flowers*, which makes no sense here.

G because the coordinating conjunction *and* creates a rambling sentence in which it's difficult to tell where one thought ends and the next begins, especially without a comma before *and*.

J because using only a comma after the word *flowers* to join two independent clauses creates a comma splice.

Question 17. The best answer is **D** because no transition word is necessary here to link the two questions posed at the end of the essay's first paragraph with the answers that unfold beginning in the second paragraph.

The best answer is NOT:

A because the word *thus* illogically suggests that the fact that the answers to the questions posed at the end of the essay's first paragraph can be found in the artwork itself is a result of the questions being posed.

B because the word *instead* illogically sets up a contrast between the questions posed at the end of the essay's first paragraph and the fact that the answers can be found in the artwork itself.

C because the word *furthermore* illogically suggests that something additional but similar to the questions posed at the end of the essay's first paragraph is coming next (mostly likely, more questions), when in fact the essay switches to discussing the answers to the questions.

Question 18. The best answer is **H** because *its* is the correct form of the singular possessive pronoun and agrees with its singular antecedent, *piece*.

The best answer is NOT:

F because *it's* is a contraction meaning "it is" rather than the singular possessive pronoun *its*, which is needed here.

G because *its'* is an incorrect form of the singular possessive pronoun *its*, which is needed here.

J because *their* is the plural possessive pronoun, which doesn't agree with its singular antecedent, *piece*.

Question 19. The best answer is **A** because the rest of the paragraph explains that the women depicted in the artwork lived at different times and so couldn't have sat together and made a quilt.

The best answer is NOT:

B because the phrase "in summary" illogically suggests that the sentence summarizes the preceding text, which it does not do.

C because the phrase "in addition" illogically suggests that the sentence directly adds to the preceding text, which it does not do.

D because the phrase "in contrast" illogically suggests that the sentence provides a direct contrast to the preceding text, which it does not do.

Question 20. The best answer is **G** because Ringgold is the only artist being referred to at this point; the singular possessive form of the noun, *artist's*, is therefore required.

The best answer is NOT:

F because *artists* is a plural noun, not the singular possessive form, *artist's*, that is required.

H because *artists'* is a plural possessive form of the noun, not the singular possessive form, *artist's*, that is required.

J because the phrase "artists imagination" uses the plural form of the noun, *artists*, instead of the singular possessive, *artist's*, that is required, and because **J** includes an unnecessary comma after the word *imagination*.

Question 21. The best answer is **A** because information about Wells speaking out for social and racial justice is highly relevant given that the paragraph focuses on the causes championed by the women, including Wells, who are depicted in Ringgold's artwork.

The best answer is NOT:

B because information about the man Wells married is only marginally relevant to the topic of the paragraph: the historical reality behind Ringgold's artwork.

C because information about which newspapers Wells wrote for isn't as relevant to the topic of the paragraph as the information in **A**.

D because information about Wells's birthplace, birth year, and siblings is only marginally relevant to the topic of the paragraph.

Question 22. The best answer is **J** because the word *business* is sufficient, together with the words *her own* earlier in the sentence, to indicate that Madam C. J. Walker established her own business.

The best answer is NOT:

F because the intensive pronoun *herself* is awkward and redundant with *her own*.

G because the phrase "belonging to her" is awkward and redundant with "her own."

H because the intensive pronoun *herself* is awkward and redundant with "her own," and because an intensifier, even when appropriate in a sentence, doesn't need to be set off from the rest of the sentence with commas.

Question 23. The best answer is C because no punctuation is warranted in this underlined portion. "Among the schools that benefited from this generosity" is an introductory adverbial phrase that immediately precedes the verb it modifies; therefore, it should not be set off by a comma. Had the sentence elements been arranged in the more typical subject-verb-object order ("Those [schools] that Mary McLeod Bethune opened and ran in order to provide a better education for Black students were among the schools that benefited from this generosity"), it would've been more obvious that no internal punctuation is required.

The best answer is NOT:

A because the comma after the word *generosity* is an unwarranted break between the

prepositional phrase and the verb it modifies.

B because the semicolon after the word *generosity* creates two inappropriate sentence fragments, as neither what precedes nor what follows the semicolon is an independent clause.

D because the colon after the word *were* is unwarranted; what precedes the colon is not a grammatically complete sentence.

Question 24. The best answer is J because the phrase "movement of " creates a clear, complete sentence, with the preposition *of* heading the phrase *of the 1950s and 1960s.*

The best answer is NOT:

F because "movement, it happened in" forms a second independent clause joined to the original independent clause by only a comma, creating a comma splice.

G because "movement, it took place in" forms a second independent clause joined to the original independent clause by only a comma, creating a comma splice.

H because "movement, that happened in" forms a second independent clause joined to the original independent clause by only a comma, creating a comma splice.

Question 25. The best answer is A because the sentence under consideration interprets what the flowers represent ("seem to celebrate") and makes a concluding reference to the main focus of the essay ("the women's accomplishments and the beauty of their shared vision").

The best answer is NOT:

B because the sentence under consideration makes no comparison between Ringgold and the women depicted in the artwork.

C because the sentence under consideration says nothing about a brushwork technique.

D because the sentence under consideration offers no evaluation of Ringgold's artistic talent, only an interpretation of what the flowers represent ("seem to celebrate").

Passage IV

Question 26. **The best answer is G** because it provides the appropriate punctuation for this sentence. A comma is needed after *(DOMs)* to separate the two clauses in this sentence.

The best answer is NOT:

F because the verb "are programmed" is essential and should not be set off with commas.

H because a colon should not be used to separate an independent clause from a relative clause.

J because the semicolon creates a sentence fragment.

Question 27. **The best answer is D** because the phrase "fifty trillion neutrinos" in the underlined portion is an enormous number meant to emphasize how numerous neutrinos are.

The best answer is NOT:

A because even though the underlined portion implies that neutrinos have little weight, it does not specify why this is so.

B because even though the underlined portion notes that neutrinos pass through a body, it does not explain how this happens.

C because even though the underlined portion notes that there are "fifty trillion neutrinos," it does not explain why this number is so high.

Question 28. **The best answer is J** because it provides the most logical transition to connect this sentence with the preceding one. The phrase "in fact" is used to emphasize the assertion that "Neutrinos are rarely affected by matter or electromagnetic fields."

The best answer is NOT:

F because the transitional phrase "for this purpose" does not logically link the idea in this sentence with the idea in the preceding one.

G because the transitional phrase "in contrast" suggests two opposing ideas, which does not characterize the ideas in these two sentences.

H because the transitional word *besides* means "in addition to," but the idea in the second sentence emphasizes what is asserted in the first sentence; it does not add another assertion.

Question 29. The best answer is **C** because it clearly explains why the new sentence should not be added. The information in the first two sentences about neutrinos colliding and the selection of the site to detect those collisions would be interrupted by irrelevant information on a completely different topic.

The best answer is NOT:

A because the suggested addition is not relevant to the discussion of colliding neutrinos.

B because the suggested addition says nothing about subzero altitude.

D because zero-gravity conditions are not mentioned later in the paragraph; therefore, this is not a logical reason for not adding the sentence.

Question 30. The best answer is **F** because it is the only option that has correct sentence structure.

The best answer is NOT:

G because it creates an awkward sentence with faulty coordination.

H because it creates a sentence fragment.

J because it creates a sentence fragment.

Question 31. The best answer is **A** because it provides the appropriate singular possessive pronoun for this sentence. The singular *its* refers to the singular noun *ice* that appears earlier in the sentence.

The best answer is NOT:

B because it is a plural possessive pronoun, not a singular possessive pronoun.

C because it is a contraction, not a singular possessive pronoun.

D because it is not a correct form of possessive pronoun.

Question 32. The best answer is **F** because it is the only option that introduces the discussion of the origins of neutrinos, which is the main focus of the paragraph.

The best answer is NOT:

G because the main focus of the paragraph is the origins of neutrinos, not scientists learning more about gamma rays.

H because the main focus of the paragraph is the origins of neutrinos, not the discovery of the specific neutrinos Bert and Ernie.

J because the main focus of the paragraph is the origins of neutrinos, not the particle accelerator.

Question 33. The best answer is B because it provides the most precise wording for this sentence. The word *invaluable* means "extremely useful" and accurately describes the information that could be obtained by learning more about the origins of neutrinos.

The best answer is NOT:

A because it means "luxurious or lavish," which is not contextually appropriate.

C because it means "high-priced or posh," which is not contextually appropriate.

D because it means "marked by profusion or excess," which is not contextually appropriate.

Question 34. The best answer is F because it is the only option that emphasizes how information gleaned from neutrinos could have dramatic effects on how scientists study the universe.

The best answer is NOT:

G because it does not indicate how information gained from neutrinos could impact scientists' study of the universe.

H because it does not indicate how information gained from neutrinos could impact scientists' study of the universe.

J because it does not indicate how information gained from neutrinos could impact scientists' study of the universe.

Question 35. The best answer is C because this option clearly indicates why the essay does not meet the writer's primary purpose. The main focus of the essay is how scientists at the IceCube Neutrino Observatory detect neutrinos and how this could benefit future research; the essay does not outline any scientific theory.

The best answer is NOT:

A because Cherenkov radiation is mentioned only briefly in the first paragraph; it is not the main focus of the essay.

B because DOMs are mentioned only briefly in the first paragraph; they are not the main focus of the essay.

D because the essay suggests that research on neutrinos could lead to new discoveries; it does not suggest that this research might contradict existing theories.

Passage V

Question 36. **The best answer is F** because it uses the appropriate pronoun case. The nominative pronoun *who* is used to introduce a clause about a person, and in this instance, the person is "a 64-year-old Clinton Hill artist."

The best answer is NOT:

G because "of whom" is a genitive form of the relative pronoun *who*, which is the wrong pronoun case for this sentence.

H because the pronoun *which* is used for things, not people.

J because *whom* is the objective pronoun case, which is the wrong pronoun case for this sentence.

Question 37. **The best answer is A** because it provides the clearest, most concise wording and avoids redundancy.

The best answer is NOT:

B because it is redundant; if Black, who is 64, has been creating art "for over three decades," he has been doing so for more than half his life.

C because it is redundant; the preceding paragraph notes that Black lives in Clinton Hill.

D because it is redundant; the preceding paragraph notes that Black had recently been discovered.

Question 38. **The best answer is F** because information about Naumann's decision to display Black's drawings is the best transition to the fact that "ten of Black's pieces sold."

The best answer is NOT:

G because information about how "ten of Black's pieces sold" within days makes no sense if it is not preceded by information about where and how they sold.

H because information about how "ten of Black's pieces sold" within days makes no sense if it is not preceded by information about where and how they sold.

J because information about how "ten of Black's pieces sold" within days makes no sense if it is not preceded by information about where and how they sold.

Question 39. **The best answer is B** because it provides the most appropriate punctuation to set off the nonessential element in this sentence; the dash is used to emphasize the prices buyers paid for Black's work.

The best answer is NOT:

A because the comma after the word *for* incorrectly interrupts the prepositional phrase.

C because a semicolon should not separate an independent clause from a prepositional phrase.

D because the colon after the word *for* incorrectly interrupts the prepositional phrase.

Question 40. **The best answer is J** because it provides the clearest, most concise wording for this sentence and avoids redundancy.

The best answer is NOT:

F because it is redundant; preceding information notes that the pieces Black produces are drawings.

G because it is redundant; preceding information notes that the drawings are done in pencil.

H because it is redundant: preceding information notes that the drawings are collages.

Question 41. **The best answer is D** because the name "Wilhelm Freddie" is an essential element and should not be set off in the sentence.

The best answer is NOT:

A because the commas are incorrect; "Wilhelm Freddie" is essential and should not be set off with commas.

B because it adds an incorrect comma after *Freddie*.

C because it adds an incorrect comma after *painter*.

Question 42. The best answer is G because the underlined portion states that the narrator liked how much there was to puzzle over, which indicates the narrator's appreciation as well as suggests that the narrator did not understand the overall intent of the collage.

The best answer is NOT:

F because the underlined portion does not make an argument or discuss Naumann in any way.

H because the underlined portion in no way refers to Black being discovered as an artist.

J because the underlined portion reveals the narrator's thoughts about one collage; it does not discuss modern art in general.

Question 43. The best answer is D because the best placement for the phrase "in May" is at the end of the sentence, since Black's work created "a stir" in May.

The best answer is NOT:

A because the phrase "this complexity in May" illogically reads as though Black's work was complex only in May.

B because the phrase "Maybe in May this complexity helps explain" illogically reads as though the complexity is making the explanation in May.

C because the phrase "Maybe this complexity helps explain in May" illogically reads as though the complexity in Black's work can be explained only in May.

Question 44. The best answer is J because it is the only option that establishes that Black is "unmoved" by the interest in his art.

The best answer is NOT:

F because the word *observes* does not indicate Black was unmoved by the sudden interest in his art as clearly as J does.

G because it describes Black's celebrity status rather than indicating his response to the sudden interest in his art.

H because it describes the financial benefits to Black rather than indicating his response to the sudden interest in his art.

Question 45. **The best answer is C** because it provides the most logical transition between the two sentences. It explains how the narrator learned about the people and images that are represented in Black's collage titled *Seven Lamps*.

The best answer is NOT:

A because the added sentence includes a reference to "this piece," but none of Black's pieces have been discussed yet in the passage.

B because the added sentence is unrelated to the paragraph, which discusses why few people had seen Black's work and how his work came to be more widely known.

D because the added sentence is unrelated to the paragraph's discussion of Black's disinterest in his newfound fame and the narrator's desire to see more of Black's work.

Passage VI

Question 46. **The best answer is J** because it is the only option that does not add unnecessary and confusing punctuation.

The best answer is NOT:

F because it is incorrect to use a comma in the middle of a comparative phrase.

G because it is incorrect to use a dash in the middle of a comparative phrase.

H because the semicolon after the word *than* creates two sentence fragments.

Question 47. **The best answer is C** because it provides the most logical transition to connect this sentence with the preceding one. The word *however* signals two opposing ideas, which is accurate here. Pigeons are first described as nuisances, but one species of pigeon is not a nuisance. Rather, it is a great navigator.

The best answer is NOT:

A because the transitional phrase "for example" should logically be followed by an example of a disease-spreading pigeon, but it is followed by an example of a valued pigeon.

B because the transitional word *similarly* signals two ideas that are essentially the same, which does not occur in the two linked sentences.

D because the transitional word *thus* signals a cause-effect relationship between ideas, which is not the case here.

Question 48. **The best answer is J** because it provides the appropriate possessive pronoun for this sentence. The singular *its* refers to the singular noun *pigeon* that appears later in the sentence.

The best answer is NOT:

F because it is an adverb, not a possessive pronoun.

G because it is a contraction, not a possessive pronoun.

H because it is a contraction, not a possessive pronoun.

Question 49. **The best answer is D** because it correctly places the modifiers in the sentence. The introductory phrase refers to a bird that was one of six hundred used in World War I, so the noun immediately after that phrase must be *Cher Ami*, the bird to which the phrase refers.

The best answer is NOT:

A because the introductory phrase should modify *Cher Ami*, not Cher Ami's twelve missions.

B because the introductory phrase should modify *Cher Ami*, not Cher Ami's twelve missions.

C because the introductory phrase should modify *Cher Ami*, not Cher Ami's twelve missions.

Question 50. **The best answer is J** because deleting the underlined portion avoids redundancy with information elsewhere in the paragraph.

The best answer is NOT:

F because it repeats information that is already given in the first sentence of the paragraph.

G because it repeats information that is already given in the second sentence of the paragraph.

H because it repeats information that is already given in the second sentence of the paragraph.

Question 1. The correct answer is D. A parallelogram consists of 2 pairs of parallel lines. Any 2 consecutive angles in the parallelogram are supplementary. Because the angle that measures $x°$ and the angle that measures 25° are consecutive, these 2 angles are supplementary: $x° + 25° = 180°$. Solve this equation by subtracting 25° from each side to get $x° = 155°$. If you chose **A**, you may have multiplied 25° by 4 to get $x°$. If you chose **B**, you may have added 25° to 90°. If you chose **C**, you may have subtracted 25° from 180° twice instead of once.

Question 2. The correct answer is H. The retail sales associate's commission was \$30 on Monday, \$30 on Tuesday, \$70 on Wednesday, \$70 on Thursday, and \$70 on Friday. To calculate the associate's total commission for these 5 days, add these 5 values together: \$30 + \$30 + \$70 + \$70 + \$70 = \$270. To calculate the average daily commission for these 5 days, divide the total commission by the number of days, 5. The associate's average daily commission is then $\frac{\$270}{5} = \$54$. If you chose **F**, you may have calculated the average of \$30 and \$70. If you chose **G**, you may have calculated the average of \$30 and \$70 and then added \$1. If you chose **J**, you may have correctly calculated \$54 and then added \$1.

Question 3. The correct answer is B. Because $45 = 3^2 \cdot 5$, the factors of 45 are 1, 3, 5, 9, 15, and 45. Because $50 = 2 \cdot 5^2$, the factors of 50 are 1, 2, 5, 10, 25, and 50. Because $84 = 2^2 \cdot 3 \cdot 7$, the factors of 84 are 1, 2, 3, 4, 6, 7, 12, 14, 21, 28, 42, and 84. Note that 45, 50, and 84 share only the common factor 1. This means the greatest common factor of 45, 50, and 84 is 1. If you chose **A**, you may have thought that 45, 50, and 84 share no common factor. If you chose **C**, you may have considered the greatest common factor of only 50 and 84. If you chose **D**, you may have considered the greatest common factor of only 45 and 84.

Question 4. The correct answer is J. To solve the equation $2(x - 12) + x = 36$, isolate the variable x. Use the distributive property to obtain the equivalent equation $2x - 2 \cdot 12 + x = 36$. Multiply 2 by 12 on the left side of the equation: $2x - 24 + x = 36$. Add 24 to both sides to obtain the equivalent equation $2x + x = 36 + 24$. Add like terms together on both sides of the equation: $3x = 60$. Divide both sides of the equation by 3 to get $x = 20$. If you chose **F**, you may have subtracted 24 from one side and added 24 to the other side instead of adding 24 to both sides. If you chose **G**, you may have distributed the 2 only to the x and then added 12 to one side and subtracted it from the other side instead of adding 12 to both sides. If you chose **H**, you may have distributed 2 to only the first term.

Question 5. The correct answer is A. There are 12 white buttons and 22 total buttons. Thus, there are $22 - 12 = 10$ buttons that are not white. The probability of selecting 1 button that is not white is the fraction in which the numerator is the number of buttons that are not white and the denominator is the total number of buttons. Therefore, the probability of selecting 1 button that is not white is $\frac{10}{22} = \frac{5}{11}$. If you chose **B**, you may have added the number of red buttons to the number of blue buttons and then divided by the number of white buttons: $\frac{4+6}{12} = \frac{10}{12} = \frac{5}{6}$. If you chose **C**, you may have divided 1 by the total number of buttons. If you chose **D**, you may have divided 1 by the number of buttons that are not white.

Question 6. The correct answer is F. Because $\frac{1}{2}$ inch represents 12 miles, and because 5 is $\frac{5}{\frac{1}{2}} = 10$ times as long as $\frac{1}{2}$, then 5 inches represents $10(12) = 120$ miles. If you chose **G**, you may have multiplied 12 by 5. If you chose **H**, you may have multiplied 12 by 5 by $\frac{1}{2}$. If you chose **J**, you may have multiplied 12 by 2.

Question 7. The correct answer is C. Because T represents the total monthly charge, and because the monthly charge is \$5 plus \$2 per movie rented, the relationship can be modeled by $T = 5 + 2M$. If you chose **A**, you may have switched the values of T and M. If you chose **B**, you may have switched the values of T and M and also thought the monthly charge was \$2 per month and \$5 per movie rented. If you chose **D**, you may have thought the monthly charge was \$2 per month and \$5 per movie rented.

Question 8. The correct answer is H. The equation $(2x + 5)(3x - 4) = 0$ is given. According to the zero factor theorem, this is only true if $2x + 5 = 0$ or $3x - 4 = 0$. If we solve both equations, the two solutions to the original equation are $x = -\frac{5}{2}$ and $x = \frac{4}{3}$. If you chose **F**, you may have taken the opposite of the constants in the original equation. If you chose **G**, or **J**, you may have solved the two equations incorrectly.

Question 9. The correct answer is B. Each fraction represents a portion of the class that participated in band, chorus, football, or basketball. The sum of these fractions represents the portion of the entire class that participated in the 4 extracurricular activities. No student participated in more than 1 activity, so there is no overlap; in other words, none of the students who played in the band also sang in the chorus, and so on. To add these fractions, express them as equivalent fractions with common denominators: $\left(\frac{2}{3}\right)\left(\frac{20}{20}\right) + \left(\frac{1}{6}\right)\left(\frac{10}{10}\right) + \left(\frac{1}{10}\right)\left(\frac{6}{6}\right) + \frac{1}{60} = \frac{40}{60} + \frac{10}{60} + \frac{6}{60} + \frac{1}{60} = \frac{57}{60}$. The item asks for the fraction of the class who did **not** participate in any of the 4 activities, so subtract $\frac{57}{60}$ from 1 to get a difference of $\frac{3}{60}$. An equivalent form of $\frac{3}{60}$ is $\frac{3 \div 3}{60 \div 3} = \frac{1}{20}$. If you chose **A**, you may have interpreted "no student participated in more than 1 of the following extracurricular activities" in the first sentence to mean that 0 students participated in the activities. If you chose **C**, you may have added all the numerators and all the denominators $\left(\frac{2 + 1 + 1 + 1}{3 + 6 + 10 + 60} = \frac{5}{79}\right)$ and then subtracted that sum from 1 to get $\frac{74}{79}$. If you chose **D**, you chose the total fraction of students who participated in any of the 4 activities.

Question 10. **The correct answer is J.** The sine ratio of a non-right angle of a right triangle is the ratio of the length of the side opposite the angle to the length of the hypotenuse, or $\frac{\text{opposite}}{\text{hypotenuse}}$. The length of the side opposite angle C is given (6 inches), and the length of the hypotenuse is unknown. The sine ratio of C is also given $\left(\frac{2}{3}\right)$. Let x be the length of the hypotenuse, and use the proportion $\frac{2}{3} = \frac{6}{x}$ to solve for x. Cross multiplying gives $2x = (3)(6)$, or $2x = 18$. Divide both sides of the equation by 2 to find the value of x: $\frac{2x}{2} = \frac{18}{2}$, or $x = 9$. If you chose **F**, you may have calculated the square root of the difference of 3^2 and 2^2. If you chose **G**, you may have calculated the square root of the sum of 3^2 and 2^2. If you chose **H**, you may have calculated $\frac{2}{3}$ of 6.

Question 11. **The correct answer is C.** In an arithmetic sequence, the difference between any two consecutive terms is constant. This is called the common difference. Here, the common difference between any two consecutive terms is 4: $17 - 13 = 4; 13 - 9 = 4; 9 - 5 = 4$; and $5 - 1 = 4$. In the general expression, the common difference is the coefficient of n, where n is the term position. This is because every time n increases by 1, the nth term increases by 4. So, the general expression must include $4n$. To find the constant in the expression, find the nth term for term position $n = 0$. The nth term for term position 1 is 1. To find the nth term for term position 0, subtract the common difference, 4, from 1: $1 - 4 = -3$. The constant in the expression is -3. So, the general expression is $4n - 3$. If you chose **A**, **B**, or **D**, you chose an expression that works only for the first pair of numbers in the table.

Question 12. **The correct answer is H.** Divide 46 by 60 to verify that the quotient $\frac{46}{60} = 0.7\overline{6}$ rounds to 76.7%. Sherita has made $\frac{46}{60}$ of her free throws—the numerator is the number of successful free throws, and the denominator is the total number of attempted free throws. Sherita is going to make more free throw attempts to increase her free throw average. Let x be the minimum number of free throws Sherita must make from now on to have a free throw average of 80%. Add x to both the numerator (the number of successful free throws) and the denominator (the total number of attempted free throws): $\frac{46 + x}{60 + x}$. Her desired free throw average of at least 80% can then be expressed as $\frac{46 + x}{60 + x} \geq 0.8$, or $\frac{46 + x}{60 + x} \geq \frac{8}{10}$. The minimum value can be calculated by solving the equation $\frac{46 + x}{60 + x} = \frac{8}{10}$ for x. Cross multiply to get $8(60 + x) = 10(46 + x)$. Use the distributive property to simplify: $480 + 8x = 460 + 10x$. Use the addition property of equality to isolate the x terms on one side and the numbers on the other side: $480 + (-460) = 10x + (-8x)$. Combine like terms: $20 = 2x$. Divide both sides by 2 to get $10 = x$. If you chose **F**, you may have subtracted 46 from $(60)(0.8) = 48$. If you chose **G**, you may have subtracted 76.7 from 80 and rounded down. If you chose **J**, you may have subtracted 46 from 60.

Question 13. The correct answer is B. Substitute the expression equal to $g(x)$ for the x in the expression for $f(x)$: $2(x^2 + 1) - 1$. Then, use the distributive property to simplify: $(2)(x^2) + (2)(1) - 1 = 2x^2 + 2 - 1$. Finally, combine like terms: $2x^2 + 1$. If you chose **A**, you may have added the expressions equal to $f(x)$ and $g(x)$. If you chose **C**, you may have substituted the expression equal to $g(x)$ for the x in the expression for $f(x)$ but did not subtract 1. If you chose **D**, you may have substituted the expression equal to $g(x)$ for x in the expression for $f(x)$ and obtained $g(f(x))$.

Question 14. The correct answer is F. The mean of a set of data is the sum of all the data points divided by the number of data points in the set. Dataset A has 8 numbers, and so has a mean of $\frac{62 + 76 + 76 + 80 + 82 + 87 + 94 + 96}{8} = \frac{653}{8} = 81.625$. Dataset B has 9 numbers: all the numbers of dataset A and an additional number that is greater than 90. If the 9th number were 90, the mean of dataset B would be $\frac{653 + 90}{9} = 82.\overline{5}$, which is greater than the mean of dataset A, 81.625. It follows that because the 9th number is greater than 90, the mean of dataset B will be greater than $82.\overline{5}$, which is greater than the mean of dataset A. For example, $\frac{653 + 91}{9} = 82.\overline{6}$; $\frac{653 + 92}{9} = 82.\overline{7}$; etc. When a dataset has an even number of data points, the median is the average of the middle two data points after the data points are listed in order (ascending or descending). The median of dataset A is $\frac{80 + 82}{2} = 81$. When a dataset has an odd number of data points, the median is the middle number after the data points are in listed order (ascending or descending). Dataset B has an odd number of data points: the 8 numbers in dataset A and an additional 9th number greater than 90. The 9th number could be in three different positions among the 8 dataset A numbers in order. Let X represent the 9th number:

Position 1: 62, 76, 76, 80, 82, 87, X, 94, 96

Position 2: 62, 76, 76, 80, 82, 87, 94, X, 96

Position 3: 62, 76, 76, 80, 82, 87, 94, 96, X

Whatever position the 9th number is in, 82 is the median because it is the 5th (the middle) of the 9 numbers listed in order. Because 82 is greater than 81, the median of dataset B will be greater than the median of dataset A. If you chose **G**, you may have confused dataset A for dataset B, reversing the relationships between the means and the medians of both sets. If you chose **H**, you may have noticed that adding a number greater than 90 would change the median from 81 to 82, but you may have assumed that because the 9th number was the last number added to the data set, it would not change the mean of the set. If you chose **J**, you may have noticed that adding a number greater than 90 would change the mean from 81.625 to a value greater than $82.\overline{5}$, but you may have assumed that because the 9th number was the last number added to the data set, it would not change the median of the set.

Question 15. The correct answer is C. Since the truck is losing 4 fluid ounces of radiator fluid per minute and there are 60 minutes in 1 hour, the truck will lose $(60)(4) = 240$ fluid ounces per hour. The truck's radiator holds 480 fluid ounces, so it will take $480 \div 240 = 2$ hours for the tank to be empty. The truck is traveling at 35 miles per hour, so in 2 hours it will have traveled $(35)(2) = 70$ miles. If you chose **A**, you may have divided the speed of the truck by 2. If you chose **B**, you may have selected the speed of the truck. If you chose **D**, you may have divided 480 by 4.

Question 16. The correct answer is G. The midpoint of a line segment that has endpoints at (x_1, y_1) and (x_2, y_2) is $\left(\frac{x_1 + x_2}{2}, \frac{y_1 + y_2}{2}\right)$. The midpoint of this segment is thus $\left(\frac{-5 + 3}{2}, \frac{8 + (-1)}{2}\right) = \left(-1, \frac{7}{2}\right)$. If you chose **F**, you may have added the x_1-value and subtracted the y_1-value, and you may have forgotten to divide by 2: $(-5 + 3, -1 - 8) = (-2, -9)$. If you chose **H**, you may have subtracted the x_1- and y_1-values instead of adding: $\left(\frac{3 - (-5)}{2}, \frac{-1 - 8}{2}\right) = \left(4, -\frac{9}{2}\right)$. If you chose **J**, you may have subtracted the x_1- and y_1-values instead of adding, and you may have forgotten to divide by 2: $(3 - (-5), -1 - 8) = (8, -9)$.

Question 17. The correct answer is B. A linear function has a constant rate of change, $\frac{y_2 - y_1}{x_2 - x_1}$, for all points (x_1, y_1) and (x_2, y_2). Because **B** is the only choice where the rate of change is constant for all the given points, it must be the linear function. Notice $\frac{2-3}{1-0} = \frac{1-2}{2-1} = \frac{0-1}{3-2} = -1$, so -1 is the constant rate of change. If you chose **A**, you may not have realized that because $\frac{1-2}{1-0} \neq \frac{1-1}{2-1}$, the function is not linear. If you chose **C**, you may not have realized that because $\frac{1-0}{1-0} \neq \frac{0-1}{2-1}$, the function is not linear. If you chose **D**, you may not have realized that because $\frac{1-0}{1-0} \neq \frac{4-1}{2-1}$, the function is not linear.

Question 18. The correct answer is F. The longest side of a triangle is opposite the angle of greatest measure, and the shortest side of a triangle is opposite the angle of least measure. Because $x < 2x < 3x$, it follows that $m\angle A < m\angle B < m\angle C$. Because the side lengths of the sides opposite $\angle A, \angle B,$ and $\angle C$ are a inches, b inches, and c inches, respectively, it follows that $a < b < c$. If you chose **G**, you may have correctly realized that side a was shortest but incorrectly ordered sides b and c. If you chose **H**, you may have correctly realized that side c was longest but incorrectly ordered sides b and a. If you chose **J**, you may have ordered the side lengths from longest to shortest instead of shortest to longest.

Question 19. The correct answer is A. The slope of a line through points (x_1, y_1) and (x_2, y_2) is $m = \frac{y_2 - y_1}{x_2 - x_1}$. The slope of this line is thus $m = \frac{7 - 5}{17 - 1} = \frac{2}{16} = \frac{1}{8}$. If you chose **B**, you may have added the values in the formula instead of subtracting: $m = \frac{7 + 5}{17 + 1} = \frac{12}{18} = \frac{2}{3}$. If you chose **C**, you may have added the values in the formula instead of subtracting and mixed up the numerator and denominator: $\frac{17 + 1}{7 + 5} = \frac{18}{12} = \frac{3}{2}$. If you chose **D**, you may have mixed up the numerator and denominator: $\frac{17 - 1}{7 - 5} = \frac{16}{2} = 8$.

Question 20. The correct answer is H. Let the length of the shorter side of the rectangle be x centimeters. The longer side is then $x + 2$ centimeters. The perimeter of the rectangle is then $2x + 2(x + 2)$ centimeters. Solve the equation $2x + 2(x + 2) = 36$ for x: $2x + 2x + 4 = 36 \rightarrow 4x + 4 = 36 \rightarrow 4x = 32 \rightarrow x = 8$. The length of the shorter side of the rectangle is 8 centimeters. The length of the longer side is then $8 + 2 = 10$ centimeters. If you chose **F**, you may have calculated the length of the shorter side instead of the longer side. If you chose **G**, you may have thought the rectangle was a square and thus the length of all sides was equal to $\frac{36}{4} = 9$ centimeters. If you chose **J**, you may have divided the two numbers given in the question: $\frac{36}{2} = 18$.

Question 21. The correct answer is D. The area of square $ABCD$ is $18^2 = 324$ square meters. Since the width of the rectangle is 6 meters and the area is 324 square meters, the length is calculated by solving the equation $L(6) = 324$. The length is thus $L = \frac{324}{6} = 54$ meters. If you chose **A**, you may have thought that the length of the rectangle must be equal to the length of $ABCD$. If you chose **B**, you may have added the length of the square to the width of the rectangle: $18 + 6 = 24$. If you chose **C**, you may have divided the area by 2(6) instead of 6: $L = \frac{324}{2(6)} = 27$.

Question 22. The correct answer is F. Substitute the matrices into the equation: $C = 2\begin{bmatrix} 3 & 5 \\ -2 & 1 \end{bmatrix} - 3\begin{bmatrix} -4 & 5 \\ 2 & 1 \end{bmatrix}$. Multiply by the scalars to get $C = \begin{bmatrix} 6 & 10 \\ -4 & 2 \end{bmatrix} - \begin{bmatrix} -12 & 15 \\ 6 & 3 \end{bmatrix}$. Finally, subtract the matrices to get $C = \begin{bmatrix} 6 - (-12) & 10 - 15 \\ -4 - 6 & 2 - 3 \end{bmatrix} = \begin{bmatrix} 18 & -5 \\ -10 & -1 \end{bmatrix}$. If you chose **G**, you may not have multiplied matrix B by 3 and instead found $2A - B$. If you chose **H**, you may have added 2 to the elements in matrix A and added 3 to the elements in matrix B instead of multiplying them by the scalars: $\begin{bmatrix} 3 + 2 & 5 + 2 \\ -2 + 2 & 1 + 2 \end{bmatrix} - \begin{bmatrix} -4 + 3 & 5 + 3 \\ 2 + 3 & 1 + 3 \end{bmatrix}$. Then, you may have subtracted these incorrect matrices: $\begin{bmatrix} 5 & 7 \\ 0 & 3 \end{bmatrix} - \begin{bmatrix} -1 & 8 \\ 5 & 4 \end{bmatrix} = \begin{bmatrix} 5 - (-1) & 7 - 8 \\ 0 - 5 & 3 - 4 \end{bmatrix}$. If you chose **J**, you may have found $2A + 3B$ instead of $2A - 3B$.

Question 23. The correct answer is D. Each of the 3 digits has 10 possible integer choices, 0 through 9. In order to calculate the number of combinations, multiply by the number of possible values for each digit: $10 \times 10 \times 10 = 1,000$. If you chose **A**, you may have added: $10 + 10 + 10 = 30$. If you chose **B**, you may have decreased the possible values for each successive digit: $10 \times 9 \times 8 = 720$. If you chose **C**, you may have only used 9 possible integers instead of 10: $9 \times 9 \times 9 = 729$.

Question 24. The correct answer is G. An x-intercept is located where the graph crosses the x-axis or where $y = 0$. The number of x-intercepts on the interval may be found by counting them on the graph. Another method is to find them algebraically by solving $2\sin(8\pi x) = 0 \rightarrow \sin(8\pi x) = 0$. Sine functions are cyclic and are equal to zero whenever you calculate the sine of πk such that k is an integer. Solve $8\pi x = \pi k \rightarrow x = \frac{k}{8}$. Recall that $0 < x < 1$, so the only values of k that satisfy $x = \frac{k}{8}$ and the domain restriction for x values are $\frac{1}{8}, \frac{2}{8}, \frac{3}{8}, \frac{4}{8}, \frac{5}{8}, \frac{6}{8}$, and $\frac{7}{8}$. If you chose **F**, you may have calculated $\frac{8\pi}{2\pi}$. If you chose **H**, you may have calculated $2\left(\frac{8\pi}{2\pi}\right)$. If you chose **J**, you may have calculated $2\left(\frac{8\pi}{2\pi}\right) + 1$.

Question 25. The correct answer is D. First, find the least common multiple (LCM) of the denominators: Given $\frac{x}{3} + \frac{x}{7} + \frac{x}{9}$, the LCM is $3 \times 3 \times 7$ or 63. Therefore, $\frac{x}{3} + \frac{x}{7} + \frac{x}{9} = \frac{21x}{63} + \frac{9x}{63} + \frac{7x}{63} = \frac{37x}{63}$. In order for $\frac{37x}{63}$ to be an integer, $37x$ **must** be divisible by 63. Because 37 is a prime number, the least positive integer value of x that satisfies this condition is $x = 63$. If you chose **A**, you may have used 3(7) as the LCM. If you chose **B**, you may have used 3(9) as the LCM. If you chose **C**, you may have used 4(9) as the LCM.

Question 26. The correct answer is G. First, multiply the terms using the distributive property, which is sometimes called FOIL, for binomials: $a^2 - 2a\sqrt{b} + a\sqrt{b} - 2(\sqrt{b})^2$. Then, combine like terms: $a^2 - a\sqrt{b} - 2(\sqrt{b})^2$. Next, simplify the power and root term: $a^2 - a\sqrt{b} - 2b$. If you chose **F** or **H**, you may have incorrectly calculated the product of the last terms of the binomials. For **F**, you may have simplified $a^2 - 2a\sqrt{b} + a\sqrt{b} - 2a\sqrt{b}$. For **H**, you may have simplified $a^2 - 2a\sqrt{b} + a\sqrt{b} - 2(\sqrt{2b})$. If you chose **J**, you may have made a sign error when multiplying the inner terms of the binomials: $a^2 - 2a\sqrt{b} - a\sqrt{b} - 2(\sqrt{b})^2$.

Question 27. The correct answer is C. First, find the distance the engine will travel around both circles. The circumference of a circle is $C = 2\pi r$. Therefore, the total distance, in feet, that the train travels is $2\pi\left(\frac{30}{2}\right) + 2\pi\left(\frac{50}{2}\right)$ or 80π. Next, divide the total distance by the constant rate the train travels: $\frac{80\pi \text{ feet}}{75\frac{\text{feet}}{\text{min}}} \approx 3.4$ minutes. If you chose **A**, you may have calculated $\frac{30 + 50}{75}$. If you chose **B**, you may have calculated $\frac{\frac{30 + 50}{2}\pi}{75}$. If you chose **D**, you may have incorrectly rounded 3.4 up to the nearest integer.

Question 28. The correct answer is G. To simplify an expression with a negative fractional exponent, apply the positive of the exponent to the reciprocal of the base of the expression. Thus, $\left(\frac{4}{5}\right)^{-\frac{3}{2}} = \left(\frac{5}{4}\right)^{\frac{3}{2}}$. To simplify an expression with a fractional exponent, use the exponent rule $x^{\frac{m}{n}} = \sqrt[n]{x^m}$. Therefore, $\left(\frac{5}{4}\right)^{\frac{3}{2}} = \sqrt[2]{\left(\frac{5}{4}\right)^3} = \sqrt{\frac{125}{64}} = \frac{\sqrt{125}}{\sqrt{64}} = \frac{\sqrt{25 \cdot 5}}{8}$. If you chose **F**, you picked the value equal to $\frac{4^{-\frac{1}{2}}}{5^{-1}} = \frac{5}{4^{\frac{1}{2}}}$. If you chose **H**, you picked the value equal to $\left(\frac{4}{5}\right)\left(\sqrt{2}\right)$. If you chose **J**, you picked the value equal to $\left(\frac{4}{5}\right)^{-\frac{1}{2}} = \left(\frac{5}{4}\right)^{\frac{1}{2}} = \sqrt{\frac{5}{4}}$.

Question 29. The correct answer is A. The logarithmic equation $\log_x\left(\frac{1}{25}\right) = -2$ is equivalent to the exponential equation $x^{-2} = \frac{1}{25}$. Because $x^{-2} = \frac{1}{x^2}$ and $\frac{1}{25} = \frac{1}{5^2}$, it follows that $x = 5$. If you chose **B**, you may have thought $x^{-2} = \frac{2}{x}$, so that $\frac{2}{x} = \frac{1}{25}$. If you chose **C**, you may have thought the logarithmic equation $\log_x\left(\frac{1}{25}\right) = -2$ was equivalent to the equation $2x = \frac{1}{25}$. If you chose **D**, you may have thought the logarithmic equation $\log_x\left(\frac{1}{25}\right) = -2$ was equivalent to the equation $x^2 = \frac{1}{25}$.

Question 30. The correct answer is J. The line has an x-intercept at $(6, 0)$ and a y-intercept at $(0, -3)$. The slope of the line passing through these intercepts is equal to $\frac{-3 - 0}{0 - 6} = \frac{-3}{-6} = \frac{1}{2}$. Thus, the equation of the line in slope-intercept form is given by $y = \frac{1}{2}x - 3$. The only point in the options given that satisfies this equation is $(4, -1)$. If you chose **F**, you may have added 1 to each of the coordinates of the point $(-4, -5)$. If you chose **G**, you may have subtracted 1 from each of the coordinates of the point $(0, -3)$. If you chose **H**, you may have added 1 to each of the coordinates of the point $(0, -3)$.

Question 31. The correct answer is C. For $0 \le x \le 400$, the profit function $p(x) = 1{,}600x - 4x^2 = -4x^2 + 1{,}600x$ is quadratic and attains its maximum value at the vertex of the function. The value of x for which the weekly profit will be the greatest is then $x = -\frac{b}{2a} = -\frac{1{,}600}{2(-4)} = 200$. If you chose **A**, you may have picked the value equivalent to $\sqrt{1{,}600}$. If you chose **B**, you may have picked the value equivalent to $\frac{1{,}600}{4^2}$. If you chose **D**, you may have picked the greatest value of x.

Question 32. The correct answer is G. Because a, b, c, and d are consecutive positive integers such that $a < b < c < d$, it follows that $\frac{a}{b} < \frac{b}{c} < \frac{c}{d}$. Consider the inequality $\frac{a}{b} + 1 < \frac{b}{c} + 1$. Combining the fractions gives $\frac{a}{b} + \frac{b}{b} < \frac{b}{c} + \frac{c}{c}$, or $\frac{a+b}{b} < \frac{b+c}{c}$. Multiplying both sides of this new inequality by $\frac{b}{b+c}$ gives $\frac{a+b}{b+c} < \frac{b}{c}$. Note that $\frac{a+b}{b+c} < \frac{b}{c} < \frac{c}{d}$. Similarly, $\frac{b}{c} + 1 < \frac{c}{d} + 1 = \frac{b+c}{c} < \frac{c+d}{d}$, and $\frac{b+c}{c+d} < \frac{c}{d}$. Among the answer choices, $\frac{c}{d}$ has the greatest value. If you chose **F**, **H**, or **J**, consider a counterexample in which $a = 1$, $b = 2$, $c = 3$, and $d = 4$. In this example, $\frac{2}{3} < \frac{3}{4}$, which disproves **F**; $\frac{1+2}{2+3} = \frac{3}{5} < \frac{3}{4}$, which disproves **H**; and $\frac{2+3}{3+4} = \frac{5}{7} \approx 0.7 < \frac{3}{4}$, which disproves **J**.

Question 33. The correct answer is A. The area of the larger square is 324 square feet, so the length, in feet, of the side of the larger square is $\sqrt{324} = 18$ feet. The ratio of the perimeters of the two squares is 2:3, so the ratio of the side lengths of the two squares is x:18, where x is the length, in feet, of the smaller square. It follows that $\frac{2}{3} = \frac{x}{18}$; $3x = 2(18)$; $3x = 36$; $x = 12$. If you chose **B**, you picked the value that is the length of the larger square. If you chose **C**, you picked the value that is twice the length of the smaller square. If you chose **D**, you may have solved the equation $\frac{2}{18} = \frac{x}{324}$.

Question 34. The correct answer is G. Consider the inequality $-1 \le x - \sqrt{5} < 4$. Adding $\sqrt{5}$ to all three parts of the inequality gives $-1 + \sqrt{5} \le x < 4 + \sqrt{5}$. Because the inequality $4 < 5 < 9$ is true, it is also true that $\sqrt{4} < \sqrt{5} < \sqrt{9}$, or $2 < \sqrt{5} < 3$. Adding -1 to all three parts of this inequality gives $1 < -1 + \sqrt{5} < 2$. Similarly, adding 4 to all three parts of the inequality gives $6 < 4 + \sqrt{5} < 7$. It follows that the integers that satisfy the inequality $-1 + \sqrt{5} \le x < 4 + \sqrt{5}$ also satisfy the inequality $2 \le x < 7$. If you chose **F**, you may have used $<$ on both ends of the inequality, replaced $\sqrt{5}$ with 3 on the lower bound of the inequality, and replaced $\sqrt{5}$ with 2 on the upper bound of the inequality: $2 = -1 + 3 < x < 4 + 2 = 6$. If you chose **H**, you may have followed the process described for **F** but used $\le$ on the left side of the inequality: $2 \le x < 6$. If you chose **J**, you may have used a lower bound of $0 < -1 + \sqrt{5} < x$ and an upper bound of $x < 4 + \sqrt{5} < 7$.

Question 35. The correct answer is C. For the 40 mph wind, $kSv^2 = k(1)(40^2) = 50$, so $k = \frac{50}{1,600} = \frac{1}{32}$. It follows that for the 80 mph wind, $\frac{1}{32}(2)(80^2) = 400$. If you chose **A**, you may have calculated the force the 40 mph wind exerts on a 2-square-foot flat surface: $\frac{1}{32}(2)(40^2) = 100$. If you chose **B**, you may have calculated the force the 80 mph wind exerts on a 1-square-foot flat surface: $\frac{1}{32}(1)(80^2) = 200$. If you chose **D**, you picked the value that is equivalent to $\frac{80^2}{2^2} = \frac{6,400}{4}$.

Question 36. **The correct answer is H.** The area of the sidewalk will be $20(10) - 6(16) = 200 - 96 = 104$ square feet. The volume of concrete needed to make the sidewalk is $104 \cdot \left(4 \text{ in} \cdot \frac{1 \text{ ft}}{12 \text{ in}}\right) = \frac{104}{3}$ cubic feet. The number of bags of concrete needed to make the sidewalk is $\frac{104}{3} \div 0.6 = \frac{104}{1.8} \approx 57.8$, or 58 whole bags. If you chose **F**, you may have calculated the volume of the sidewalk as $104 \div 4 = 26$ square feet and the number of bags as $26 \div 0.6 \approx 43.3$, or 44 whole bags. If you chose **G**, you may have calculated the area of the sidewalk as $4(10) + 4(20) = 40 + 80 = 120$ square feet, the volume as $120 \cdot \left(\frac{1 \text{ ft}}{4 \text{ in}}\right) = 30$ cubic feet, and the number of bags as $30 \div 0.6 = 50$ whole bags. If you chose **J**, you may have calculated the area of the sidewalk as 120 square feet as in **G**, the volume as $120 \cdot \left(4 \text{ in} \cdot \frac{1 \text{ ft}}{12 \text{ in}}\right) = 40$ cubic feet, and the number of bags as $40 \div 0.6 \approx 66.7$, or 67 whole bags.

Question 37. **The correct answer is D.** Let r be the radius of the circle. Since $\triangle OAP$ is a right triangle, $\tan 20° = \frac{r}{12}$, or $r = 12 \tan 20° \approx 4.368$ with the approximation given in the note of the question. Let x be the length of $\overline{BP}$ in centimeters. Since $\triangle OAP$ is a right triangle, use the Pythagorean theorem to create the equation $r^2 + 12^2 = (r + x)^2$, which can be rewritten as $x^2 + 2rx - 144 = 0$. Use the approximation for $r\,(r \approx 4.368)$ in the equation: $x^2 + 2(4.368)x - 144 = 0 = x^2 + 8.736x - 144 = 0$. Then, solve for x using the quadratic formula: $x \approx \frac{-8.736 \pm \sqrt{8.736^2 - 4(1)(-144)}}{2} \to x \approx 8.402$ or $x \approx -17.138$. As x represents a length, the positive value is the only one that makes sense in context. If you chose **A**, you may have found the length of the radius and assumed that it was the length of the desired segment. If you chose **B**, you may have assumed $r = x$ and solved the equation $x^2 + 144 = (2x)^2$ to get $x^2 + 144 = 4x^2 \to 3x^2 = 144 \to x^2 = 48$ or $x \approx 6.9$. If you chose **C**, you may have correctly determined the length of the radius and then subtracted that from the given length of $\overline{AP}$, $12 - 4.368 = 7.632$.

Question 38. **The correct answer is J.** The average of the 10 test scores is x, so the total sum of the scores is $10x$. Let H be the highest score and L be the lowest score. Then $y = \frac{10x - (H + L)}{8} \to 8y = 10x - (H + L)$, or $H + L = 10x - 8y$. Therefore, the average of the highest and lowest scores is $\frac{H + L}{2} = \frac{10x - 8y}{2}$. If you chose **F**, you may have correctly calculated the sum of the highest and lowest values, but you forgot to average the two. If you chose **G**, you may have calculated the average of the two given averages, x and y. If you chose **H**, you may have incorrectly changed a sign when solving for the sum of the highest and lowest values: $y = \frac{10x - (H + L)}{8} \to H + L = 10x + 8y$.

Question 39. The correct answer is D. Both sides of the given equation can be written as a power of 3, as follows: $(3^3)^{n^2} = (3^2)^{5n-4} \rightarrow 3^{3n^2} = 3^{2(5n-4)}$. Since both sides of the equation have the same base, their exponents must be equal. Hence, the equation to solve is $3n^2 = 10n - 8$, or $3n^2 - 10n + 8 = 0$. Factoring this quadratic equation yields $(3n - 4)(n - 2) = 0$, so the solutions are $3n - 4 = 0 \rightarrow n = \frac{4}{3}$ and $n - 2 = 0 \rightarrow n = 2$. Thus the solution set is $\left\{\frac{4}{3}, 2\right\}$. If you chose **A**, you may have correctly determined the equivalent exponents but incorrectly factored the quadratic expression $3n^2 - 10n + 8$ as $(3n - 2)(n + 4)$. If you chose **B**, you may have identified the common base of 3 but rewritten the original equation as $3^{3n^2} = 3^{5n+8}$ and thus solved the quadratic equation $3n^2 - 5n - 8 = 0 \rightarrow (3n - 8)(n + 1) = 0$. If you chose **C**, you may have correctly determined equivalent exponents but changed a sign in the quadratic equation you needed to solve: $3n^2 - 10n - 8 = 0 \rightarrow (3n + 2)(n - 4)$.

Question 40. The correct answer is H. There are 36 possible outcomes from rolling 2 dice and recording the numbers that land face up: $\{(1, 1), (1, 2), (1, 3), (1, 4), \ldots, (6, 3), (6, 4), (6, 5)(6, 6)\}$. Adding the 2 numbers in each ordered pair of outcomes gives the following list: $\{2, 3, 4, 5, 6, 7, 3, 4, 5, 6, 7, 8, 4, 5, 6, 7, 8, 9, 5, 6, 7, 8, 9, 10, 6, 7, 8, 9, 10, 11, 7, 8, 9, 10, 11, 12\}$. There are 10 outcomes in this list that are less than 6. Thus, the probability is $\frac{10}{36} = \frac{5}{18}$. If you chose **F**, you may have miscounted the number of outcomes less than 6 to be 13 but correctly determined the number of possible outcomes to be 36. The probability would then be $\frac{13}{36}$. If you chose **G**, you may have counted the number of outcomes less than or equal to 6, which is 15, and divided by the total number of outcomes for the 2 dice. If you chose **J**, you may have counted the number of possibilities less than 6 for a single die and divided by the total number of outcomes for the 2 dice.

Question 41. The correct answer is C. Let t be the amount of time, in hours, both drivers have been traveling. Louisa has driven $68t$ miles, and Antonio has driven $57t$ miles. At the time they pass each other, they will have driven a combined 240 miles; that is, $68t + 57t = 240$. The solution for t in this equation is 1.92, which is approximately 1 hour plus an additional $0.92\text{hrs} \times \frac{60 \text{ min}}{1\text{hr}} = 55.2$ minutes. Thus, they pass each other approximately 1 hour 55 minutes after 2:00 p.m., or 3:55 p.m. If you chose **A**, you may have used 68 mph for both drivers, solving $68t + 68t = 240$. If you chose **B**, you may have divided $\frac{240}{68} \approx 3.529$ and incorrectly thought that this was 3:53 p.m. If you chose **D**, you may have used 57 mph for both drivers, solving $57t + 57t = 240$.

Question 42. The correct answer is H. Selecting every possible pair of points from among 10 points is, by definition, calculating the combination of 10 objects taken 2 at a time: $\binom{10}{2} = \frac{10!}{(10-2)!2!} = \frac{10 \cdot 9 \cdot 8!}{8!2!} = \frac{10 \cdot 9}{2} = 45$. If you chose **F**, you may have thought 10 points would determine 10 lines. If you chose **G**, you may have thought 10 points taken 2 at a time would determine $10 \cdot 2 = 20$ lines. If you chose **J**, you may have counted each line twice by counting 10 choices for the first point and 9 choices for the second point. Since switching the order of 2 points will still determine the same line, each possibility is counted twice here.

Question 43. The correct answer is A. Using the given definition, manipulate the fraction to obtain an equivalent expression: $\frac{(n+1)!6!}{n!3!} = \frac{(n+1)n!6 \cdot 5 \cdot 4 \cdot 3!}{n!3!} = (n+1)6 \cdot 5 \cdot 4 = 120(n+1)$. If you chose **B**, you may have calculated $\frac{6!}{3!}$, ignoring n. If you chose **C**, you may have ignored the factorials and simplified. If you chose **D**, you may have incorrectly thought that multiplication and factorials can be interchanged: $n!m! = (nm)!$.

Question 44. The correct answer is J. The expanded form of $(x+1)^4$ is $(x+1)^2(x+1)^2 = (x^2 + 2x + 1)(x^2 + 2x + 1) = x^4 + 4x^3 + 6x^2 + 4x + 1$. The coefficient of x^2 is 6. If you chose **F**, you may have thought the expansion of $(x+1)^4$ was $x^4 + 1$, so there was no x^2 term. If you chose **G**, you may have thought the expansion of $(x+1)^4$ was $x^4 + x^3 + x^2 + x + 1$, so the coefficient of x^2 was 1. If you chose **H**, you may have thought the expansion of $(x+1)^4$ was $x^4 + 2x^3 + 4x^2 + 2x + 1$, so the coefficient of x^2 was 4.

Question 45. The correct answer is D. In the diagram, $\triangle ADC$ is a right triangle, so $m\angle ACD = 90° - 20° = 70°$. By the property of supplementary angles, $m\angle ACB = 180° - 70° = 110°$. In $\triangle ACB$, two sides and the included angle are known, so the measure of the remaining side can be calculated using the law of cosines. Let $g = $ the length of the guy wire. Then $g^2 = 60^2 + 25^2 - 2(60)(25) \cos 110°$. Taking the square root of both sides gives the desired result. If you chose **A**, you may have incorrectly assumed $m\angle BAC = 20°$ and $m\angle ACB = 60°$, then calculated the length of the guy wire using the law of sines: $\frac{\sin 60°}{g} = \frac{\sin 20°}{25}$. If you chose **B**, you may have incorrectly assumed $m\angle BAC = 20°$ and $m\angle ACB = 70°$, then calculated the length of the guy wire using the law of sines: $\frac{\sin 70°}{g} = \frac{\sin 20°}{25}$. If you chose **C**, you may have thought that $m\angle ACB = 90° - 20° = 70°$, then correctly used the law of cosines: $g^2 = 60^2 + 25^2 - 2(60)(25)\cos 70°$.

Passage I

Question 1. The best answer is D because the narrator states that her mother "rises against the sun like a skyscraper" (lines 18–19).

The best answer is NOT:

A because although the narrator and her mother view a Picasso painting (lines 28–29), the narrator does not compare her mother to a Picasso painting.

B because when the narrator refers to shadow and witness, she is talking about herself, not her mother. Line 22: "I am her small shadow and witness."

C because "a story developing behind her eyes" (lines 34-35) is the narrator's description of something she sees in her mother rather than a comparison between her mother and something else.

Question 2. The best answer is J because after explaining that her mother took her all around Chicago, the narrator states that the city "was given to me by my mother" (line 27).

The best answer is NOT:

F because although the narrator describes traveling "from one end of the city to the other" (line 25), she does not mention her ability to do so without getting lost.

G because although the narrator notes that her mother talks about politics (line 20), she does not indicate that her mother influenced city politics.

H because although the narrator refers to herself as a small shadow (line 22), she does so in the context of describing herself in relation to her mother, not in the context of her relationship to Chicago.

Question 3. The best answer is C because the narrator explains that the reason she doesn't verify her mother's ideas about Picasso is because "I like my mother's version best" (lines 40–41).

The best answer is NOT:

A because there is no indication in the passage that the narrator doesn't know which references to check; she indicates that the reason she doesn't check them is because she prefers her mother's anecdotes to others she might find (lines 39–41).

B because the narrator does not indicate that she believes her mother's anecdotes are accurate; she simply prefers them (lines 39–41).

D because it contradicts the narrator's statement that "I like my mother's version best" (lines 40–41).

Question 4. **The best answer is H** because the narrator states that the answer to the question of where her parents were born "signifies nothing" (line 48) about understanding the narrator and her family.

The best answer is NOT:

F because the narrator makes no reference to questions regarding how her mother may have been like the narrator's other ancestors.

G because the narrator states that "the meaningful question would be to ask where my ancestors lived" (lines 48–49).

J because the answer to the question would provide significant information about the narrator's background. She notes that her connection to water "comes from my mother" (line 58).

Question 5. **The best answer is B** because in the context of the passage, "blinding" (line 67) and "overwhelm" (line 69) serve to illustrate the sense of reverence the narrator's mother feels for the power and beauty of the sea as she observes it.

The best answer is NOT:

A because there is no indication in the passage that the narrator's mother felt fright in response to watching the sea; rather, it was an experience she sought out. Line 59: "She longs for a view more than anything else."

C because there is no indication in the passage that the narrator's mother felt regret in response to watching the sea; rather, she was drawn to the sea and went to great lengths to acquire a good view of it (lines 59–70).

D because there is no indication in the passage that the narrator's mother experienced quietness in response to watching the sea; rather, the narrator's use of "blinding" (line 67) and "overwhelm" (line 69) suggest a dramatic and thrilling experience.

Question 6. **The best answer is F** because the last sentence of the passage is part of the narrator's metaphor likening her mother to water (lines 88–90). In the sentence, the narrator depicts herself as a child collecting sea glass and driftwood, or what her mother leaves behind when she goes away.

The best answer is NOT:

G because the narrator does not make any reference to memory; the child in the sentence represents the narrator at the time she is writing as an adult.

H because the sentence is not a literal explanation of what the narrator is doing but rather a metaphorical description of how she reacts when her mother goes away.

J because the sentence is not a literal description of what the narrator found as a child but rather a metaphorical description of how she reacts when her mother goes away.

Question 7. The best answer is **A** because traveling and moving are referenced in both passages. Passage A, lines 24–25: "We don't have much money, but Mom takes me from one end of the city to the other, on foot, on buses." Passage B, lines 75–79: "My mother could only become a nomad herself—forever moving, changing and going, yet always retaining some essential part of her being, recognizable and intact in spite of all the places she has been."

The best answer is NOT:

B because Chicago is referenced in Passage A (line 14 and line 26) but not in Passage B.

C because speaking openly and boldly is referenced in Passage A (lines 20–21) but not in Passage B.

D because staying at a hotel is referenced in Passage B (line 60) but not in Passage A.

Question 8. The best answer is **J** because in Passage B, the narrator uses language that evokes distance and tension to describe the conflicted feelings she has about her mother. Lines 81–87: "When I gaze out, I see her, my mother, always pulling away, returning and pulling away again. I drink from her, and she slips between my fingertips. She has borne me all this way. I cannot decide whether I want her to stay or go. When she is here, I wish she would leave. When she is gone, I wish she would return."

The best answer is NOT:

F because there is no reference in either passage to lively conversation or joy experienced by the narrators. There are no examples of conversation in Passage B, and those referenced in Passage A are one-sided and/or brief. Lines 32–33: " 'Was he very sad?' I ask. 'Yes, I think he was.' "

G because there is no reference in either passage to fierce competition or debate between the narrator and her mother.

H because there is no reference in either passage to physical affection or warmth from the narrator's mother.

Question 9. The best answer is A because both passages include information about the narrators' mothers' lives. Passage A, lines 9–15: "She had never been on a train before or used a telephone. She left Standing Rock to take a job in Chicago so she could help out the family during the War. She was so petrified of the new surroundings, she stayed in her seat all the way from McLaughlin, South Dakota, to Chicago, Illinois, and didn't move once." Passage B, lines 44–47: "Westerners ask me where my parents were born, as though the answer will enable them to glean some knowledge. The answer is Beijing and Luoyang." Passage B, lines 53–54: "My mother's father was from Inner Mongolia, land of desert and grassy plains."

The best answer is NOT:

B because although in passage A the narrator describes her mother's height (lines 17–18), in passage B, the narrator does not describe her mother's physical appearance at all.

C because there is no mention in either passage of the narrator's mother's academic interests.

D because while in passage B the narrator describes where her father was from (lines 50–53), there is no mention in passage A of the narrator's father at all, and there is no mention in either passage of the relationship between the narrator's mother and father.

Passage II

Question 10. The best answer is G because the passage states that young diving enthusiasts "still emerge" with implements "of the former ice trade" (lines 68–70), which indicates that the action continues in the present day, long after the ice trade's end.

The best answer is NOT:

F because the passage states that the "first comprehensive report on the ice industry of the United States was commissioned in 1879" (lines 1–3).

H because the passage indicates that this sale took place "in the year of the great ice census" (lines 20–21), which was commissioned in 1879 (lines 2–3).

J because the passage indicates that this was the price of ice "in the year of the great ice census" (lines 20–21), which was commissioned in 1879 (lines 2–3).

Question 11. **The best answer is A** because the passage states that the 1879 national census reported "an account of the great growth of the [ice] industry in the preceding ten years" (lines 9–10).

The best answer is NOT:

B because there is no indication in the passage that damaging publicity affected the natural-ice industry in this period.

C because although the passage mentions an estimated shipping cost of $1.50 per ton (lines 27–28) the passage does not indicate whether this was considered a high price.

D because although the passage notes the decline of the natural ice industry, it states that the decline began in "the early decades of the twentieth century" (lines 55–56).

Question 12. **The best answer is G** because the passage states that "by far the biggest market was in New York" (lines 12–13), and it can reasonably be inferred that New York was the metropolis subsequently described as being supplied by imports and icehouses (lines 17–20).

The best answer is NOT:

F because although the passage states that there were 135 icehouses between New York and Albany (lines 17–19), the passage does not indicate that Albany was a large ice market.

H because although the passage mentions the city of Philadelphia, it is in reference to the city's ice shortage after "unseasonably warm weather" (lines 21–23).

J because the passage does not mention or make generalizations about average US cities of the 1870s.

Question 13. **The best answer is A** because the passage describes the fifteen-to-twenty-inch ice in Maine as "a top-quality crop" (line 26) and states that two thousand cargoes of this ice "were shipped south to New York, Philadelphia, and other more southern cities" (lines 31–32).

The best answer is NOT:

B because the passage indicates that the ice was shipped south to various locations, rather than remaining in Maine to meet local demand.

C because the passage does not indicate that the ice "famine" negatively affected the 1879 Maine ice crop.

D because although the passage states that "the demand for ice rose annually" (line 34), it does not indicate that the size or quality of the ice changed in the subsequent year.

Question 14. The best answer is **F** because the paragraph states that the "natural-ice trade began to decline from the early decades of the twentieth century" (lines 55–56 and claims that much of the "evidence of its former vast scale rapidly disappeared" (lines 60–61) with the loss of the icehouses.

The best answer is NOT:

G because although the paragraph mentions that sparks from steam trains occasionally caused icehouses to burn down (lines 62–63), it does not suggest that the steam train signaled the demise of ice harvesting.

H because although the paragraph notes that icehouses easily caught fire (lines 62–63), this is a subordinate detail in the paragraph and not the main idea.

J because although the paragraph states that the natural ice industry survived into the late 1950s in remote areas (lines 57–59), this is not characterized as a short-lived revival of the industry.

Question 15. The best answer is **C** because the fifth paragraph describes the "impressive variety of odd implements" (line 71) found in waters formerly utilized by the ice industry. The range of "many other specialist implements" (line 79) found in industry catalogues supports the inference that these were typical ice industry tools.

The best answer is NOT:

A because the paragraph does not refer to the natural-ice industry's ability to respond rapidly to market changes.

B because the paragraph does not refer to the natural-ice industry's ability to erect icehouses quickly.

D because the paragraph does not indicate that ice harvesting was simple work.

Question 16. The best answer is **J** because the passage indicates that artifacts of the natural ice-industry remain, stating that divers "still emerge from lakes and rivers clutching an impressive variety of odd implements—plows and chisels and scrapers that fell through the ice during the harvesting" (lines 69–73). The passage also notes that "one or two museums keep small displays of these tools" (lines 73–74) and that "collectors have preserved manufacturers' catalogs" (lines 74–75).

The best answer is NOT:

F because the author does not contradict this statement elsewhere in the passage.

G because the author does not contradict this statement elsewhere in the passage.

H because the author does not contradict the statement elsewhere in the passage.

Question 17. The best answer is **D** because the passage states that "the biggest market was in New York, and none of its ice was manufactured artificially" (lines 12–14).

The best answer is NOT:

A because the passage states that "none of its ice was manufactured artificially" (lines 13–14).

B because the passage states that "none of its ice was manufactured artificially" (lines 13–14).

C because the passage states that "none of its ice was manufactured artificially" (lines 13–14).

Question 18. The best answer is **F** because the passage states that "The first real crisis in the natural-ice trade was caused not by competition from artificial manufacture, but by pollution" (lines 44–46).

The best answer is NOT:

G because the passage does not state that weather pattern changes caused the first crisis in the natural-ice industry.

H because although the passage mentions artificial refrigeration (lines 35–36) it does not claim that artificial refrigeration caused the first crisis in the natural-ice industry.

J because the passage does not refer to the impact of the Great Depression on the natural-ice industry.

Passage III

Question 19. The best answer is **C** because the passage explores the claim that dubbing is a hybrid form that incorporates the artistry of both the actor and dubber, beginning with Antonioni's description of Romolo Costa as "a hybrid individual born out of a chemical combination" (lines 7–8). The hybrid identities of dubbers are indicated in Vairano's account of how some dubbers were associated with particular actors. The passage describes dubber Luca Ward's connection to actor Samuel L. Jackson: "as Antonioni would say, half Ward, half Jackson" (line 84-85). Ward conflates the identities of Meg Ryan and her dubber (lines 86–89), further emphasizing the idea of hybridity between the dubber and actor.

The best answer is NOT:

A because the passage does not describe how dubbers want to be regarded by actors.

B because the passage does not compare the work of these two dubbers.

D because although the passage discusses some of the dubbing work Ward has done (lines 73-78), it does not indicate that he prefers to dub many different actors.

Question 20. The best answer is **G** because the comparison to Fellini accurately reflects Variano's point of view that dubbing can be useful. The passage describes how dubbing was part of Fellini's creative process. Lines 19–20: "Dubbing was an extension of his shoots, a technique he would use to retouch and rewrite." The passage describes how Vairano selects dubbers according to who would perform best in the particular role, which is similar to how Fellini used dubbing creatively.

The best answer is NOT:

F because the passage notes that Antonioni disapproved of dubbing. "This 'half Clark, half Costa' was unbearable to Antonioni, who considered dubbing to be a mere 'acoustic surrogate' of acting" (lines 8–10).

H because the passage notes that Pasolini also disapproved of dubbing. "Director Pier Paolo Pasolini, who called both dubbing and subtitles evils" (lines 12–14).

J because the passage notes that Renoir also disapproved of dubbing. "Director Jean Renoir called dubbing a 'monstrosity, a challenge to human and divine laws.' " (lines 16–17).

Question 21. The best answer is **B** because the second paragraph describes Fellini's extensive use of dubbing. The first paragraph of the passage recounts the perspectives of directors critical of dubbing. Lines 18–20: "Director Frederico Fellini didn't agree with any of them. Dubbing was an extension of his shoots, a technique he would use to retouch and rewrite."

The best answer is NOT:

A because the paragraph does not relate the author's perspective on dubbing.

C because although the passage notes that Renoir was critical of dubbing, his comments are about dubbing in general, not in reference to Fellini's work. Lines 16–17: "Director Jean Renoir called dubbing a 'monstrosity, a challenge to human and divine laws.' "

D because the paragraph's focus on Fellini does not function to support an argument made in the first paragraph. The first paragraph presents perspectives of directors who were against the use of dubbing; this paragraph presents an opposing perspective. Line 18–20: "Director Frederico Fellini didn't agree with any of them."

Question 22. The best answer is H because the anecdote mainly provides an example of how dubbing was an integral part of Fellini's creative process.

The best answer is NOT:

F because although the passage mentions that Fellini favored the northern accent (lines 32–33), this is a detail from the anecdote, rather than its main function.

G because the anecdote is unclear about whether Fellini followed a scripted dialogue in this instance. The passage notes that Fellini did not always follow a script. Lines 20–23: "He mercilessly dubbed over his actors, changing dialogue in postproduction, sometimes having worked without a script."

J because the passage notes that Fellini did not always follow a script. Lines 20–23: "He mercilessly dubbed over his actors, changing dialogue in postproduction, sometimes having worked without a script."

Question 23. The best answer is D because the passage makes clear that Cortesi disagrees with the author's assumptions, offering his own explanation. Lines 44–46: "Dubbers are used to reciting while trying to recreate the bodily sensations of what they see on the screen before them."

The best answer is NOT:

A because the passage indicates that Cortesi disagrees with the author (lines 42–48).

B because the passage indicates that Cortesi disagrees with the author (lines 42–48).

C because although the passage indicates that Cortesi disagrees with the author (lines 42–48), Cortesi's response is not characterized as gruff.

Question 24. The best answer is G because the details in the passage suggest that the Metropolitan cinema was a place to watch subtitled films. "There are still few options for those seeking to watch subtitled, original language films at a movie house in Italy. The Metropolitan cinema on Via del Corso closed recently after a long battle" (lines 49–52).

The best answer is NOT:

F because the passage does not indicate that the Metropolitan cinema was a place to watch dubbed films.

H because the details in the passage suggest that the Metropolitan cinema was a place to watch subtitled films only.

J because the details in the passage suggest that the Metropolitan cinema was a place to watch subtitled films.

Question 25. The best answer is A because in the passage, the film *Bien-venu chez le Ch'tis* is provided as an example of a film considered undubbable due to its comedic reliance on linguistic misunderstanding. Lines 58–63: "Francesco Vairano, a dubber and dubbing director known for adapting foreign films considered to be 'undubbable,' such as the French box office hit *Bien-venu chez le Ch'tis* ('Welcome to the Sticks,' 2008), which relies on linguistic misunderstandings for much of its comedy."

The best answer is NOT:

B because there is no mention in the passage of dramatic action that advances plot.

C because there is no mention in the passage of reverse chronology that provides context.

D because there is no mention in the passage of extensive monologues that further characterization.

Question 26. The best answer is G because the passage explains that Vairano uses different dubbers with different actors. Lines 64–67: "Vairano has been one of the few directors to break the habit of matching the same Italian dubber to a foreign actor for all his films."

The best answer is NOT:

F because although the passage identifies one French film that Vairano dubbed (lines 60–61), it does not say that dubbing French films is Vairano's focus.

H because the passage does not indicate that Vairano mostly worked with "prima donna" dubbers and even notes that Vairano "was hated by all the prima donna dubbers" (line 69).

J because there is no indication in the passage of whether Vairona thinks dialogue should be rewritten during dubbing.

Question 27. The best answer is A because *assault* is a synonym of *challenge*. The negative connotation of the word *assault* is consistent with the negative connotation of the word *monstrosity* (lines 16–17) in the same sentence. "An assault on" can be substituted for the phrase "a challenge to" without changing the meaning of the sentence.

The best answer is NOT:

B because "a declaration of" has a different meaning than "a challenge to," and it would not make sense in the context of the sentence.

C because although *question* can be a synonym for *challenge* the phrase "a question for human and divine laws" would not be contextually appropriate in this sentence.

D because "an offer to" and "a challenge to" have different meanings, and it would not make sense in the context of the sentence.

Passage IV

Question 28. The best answer is **G** because the passage focuses on presenting information about various scientific aspects of the creation and behavior of steel.

The best answer is NOT:

F because although the passage discusses Bessemer's process for improving steel, it does not discuss the various experiments Bessemer conducted to develop the process.

H because although the fifth paragraph (lines 38–50) addresses philosophical questions about metallurgy, these questions function as subordinate details that contribute to the main focus of the passage.

J because although both cast iron and pig iron are mentioned in the passage, they are not directly compared, and an illustration of their differences is not a central element of the passage.

Question 29. The best answer is **A** because the description of the initial response to Bessemer's process helps the author establish its success and impact in the manufacturing industry. Lines 1–6: "During the Industrial Revolution, the high price of steel meant that many large engineering projects were carried out that used instead cast iron, which is brittle and prone to failure. This was why Henry Bessemer's new process for making steel was greeted with jubilation."

The best answer is NOT:

B because the author does not assert an opinion that Bessemer's process was prone to failure.

C because although the author states that Bessemer was lauded as an engineer (lines 8–9), the description of the initial response to Bessemer's process does not relate directly to his qualifications as an engineer.

D because the author does not provide specific examples of criticism that Bessemer's new process received.

Question 30. The best answer is H because the passage directly states that adding oxygen to molten pig iron results in silicon being converted into light silica slag. Lines 19–24: "Oxygen, as a component of air, was the key to the Bessemer process. It offered a way of removing impurities from pig iron and adjusting its carbon content during conversion to steel. A blast of air through the molten metal turned impurities such as silicon into light silica slag."

The best answer is NOT:

F because although the passage mentions light silica slag as a by-product of the Bessemer process (lines 22–24), it does not indicate that the slag is converted to carbon dioxide.

G because the passage indicates that carbon is removed in the form of volatile carbon dioxide (lines 25–26), not that it is converted.

J because the passage indicates that silicon is one of the impurities that are converted and does not indicate that impurities are converted into silicon. Lines 22–24: "A blast of air through the molten metal turned impurities such as silicon into light silica slag."

Question 31. The best answer is B because, in the context of the passage, the word *spice* (line 30), in conjunction with the word *dash* in the following sentence, is used to suggest something added to enhance something else, which is a main focus of the discussion of steel in the fourth paragraph (lines 29–37). Lines 29–31: "It was long known that steel can be improved with a spice of other elements. A dash of the metal manganese helps."

The best answer is NOT:

A because there is no indication in the passage that elements need to be added to steel gradually to produce the desired effect.

C because there is no indication in the passage that manganese, chromium, and nickel are expensive.

D because the positive results of blending elements are discussed in the fourth paragraph (lines 29–37). The passage indicates that adding a specific proportion of chromium (lines 34–35) makes steel rust-resistant, which contradicts the idea that blending elements has not yet yielded positive results.

Question 32. **The best answer is H** because although the author indicates that there have been questions raised about whether metallurgy is a science or an art, he suggests his view that it is both. Lines 40–45: "In this respect, metallurgy has long retained the air of an artisan craft…it is because it is so difficult." He includes a quote from a well-respected physicist to support his view. Lines 45–50: "According to Rodney Cotterill, a remarkable British physicist whose expertise stretched from the sciences of materials to that of the brain, 'metallurgy is one of our most ancient arts, but is often referred to as one of the youngest sciences.' "

The best answer is NOT:

F because it contradicts the idea that metallurgy is both an art and a science, which the author puts forth in the fifth paragraph (lines 38–50).

G because although the author states that metallurgy is difficult, he does not do so to suggest that this is the reason why metallurgy is not considered a science. Lines 43–45: "But the reason for this empiricism is not that the science of metallurgy is trivial; it is because it is so difficult."

J because it directly contradicts a statement by the author. Lines 43–45: "But the reason for this empiricism is not that the science of metallurgy is trivial; it is because it is so difficult."

Question 33. **The best answer is A** because in comparing the behavior of materials to the study of the social sciences, the passage suggests that both require the study of a wide range of scales. Lines 56–61: "Science has trouble dealing with such a span of scales. One might regard this difficulty as akin to that in the social sciences, where social behaviour is governed by how individuals behave but also how we interact on the scale of families and neighborhoods, within entire cities, and at a national level."

The best answer is NOT:

B because the passage does not suggest that the study of the social sciences is based on trial-and-error experimentation.

C because the passage explains that the study of the social sciences involves the study of people (lines 57–61). The passage does not suggest that the study of social sciences involves the examination of individual atoms.

D because the passage does not indicate that either field of study produces results that must be interpreted by both scientist and artists.

Question 34. The best answer is **F** because the paragraph as a whole describes the way various defects in the crystal structure of a metal influence its behavior, as introduced in the first sentence of the paragraph. Lines 62–64: "The mechanical properties of metals depend on how flaws in the crystal structure, called defects, move and interact."

The best answer is NOT:

G because although the paragraph notes dislocations as the most common fault (lines 66–67), this is a subordinate detail in the paragraph and not the main idea.

H because the paragraph does not describe how increasing a metal's grain size would modify its behavior.

J because although the paragraph mentions that grains may divide into crystallite mosaics, (lines 72–74), this is a subordinate detail in the paragraph and not the main idea.

Question 35. The best answer is **C** because *stretched* can mean *extended*, and this meaning is contextually appropriate in the description of the wide range of Cotterill's expertise. Lines 45–48: "According to Rodney Cotterill, a remarkable British physicist whose expertise stretched from the sciences of materials to that of the brain."

The best answer is NOT:

A because although *stretched* can mean *strained*, it is not contextually appropriate to say that "Cotterill's expertise strained from the sciences of materials to that of the brain."

B because although *stretched* can mean *exaggerated*, it is not contextually appropriate to say that "Cotterill's expertise exaggerated from the sciences of materials to that of the brain."

D because although *stretched* can mean *amplified*, it is not contextually appropriate to say that "Cotterill's expertise amplified from the sciences of materials to that of the brain."

Question 36. **The best answer is J** because the passage directly states that reducing the size of a metal's grains can make the metal harder. Lines 74–77: "The arrest of dislocations at grain edges means that metals may be made harder by reducing the size of their grains, a useful trick for modifying their mechanical behaviour."

The best answer is NOT:

F because the passage does not state that reducing the size of a metal's grains can make the metal more rust-resistant.

G because the passage does not state that reducing the size of a metal's grains can make the metal more brittle.

H because the passage does not state that reducing the size of a metal's grain can make the metal finer.

Passage I

Question 1. The best answer is **A**. According to the figure, 160 mg of 24-week-old oak mulch was consumed, 148 mg of 24-week-old pine bark mulch was consumed, 45 mg of 48-week-old oak mulch was consumed, and 60 mg of 48-week-old pine bark was consumed. The greatest mass of these is that of the 24-week-old oak mulch. Therefore, **A** is correct. **B**, **C**, and **D** are incorrect; 160 mg of 24-week-old oak mulch was consumed, which is more than any other combination of mulch and mulch age listed.

Question 2. The best answer is **J**. According to Figure 1, as mulch age increased, the consumption of cedar, cypress, and oak bar mulches increased. As mulch age increased, the consumption of oak and pine bark mulches increased and then decreased. **J** is correct; the mass of mulch consumed initially increased for all 5 types of mulch and then continued to increase for 3 types and decreased for 2 types. **F** is incorrect; the mass of mulch consumed did not decrease for any of the types of mulch. **G** is incorrect; the mass of mulch consumed increased for only 3 types of mulch. **H** is incorrect; the mass of mulch consumed did not initially decrease for any of the types of mulch.

Question 3. The best answer is **D**. To answer this item, you must know that detritivores, and not autotrophs, obtain energy by consuming dead and decaying plant matter. According to the passage, the mulch was allowed to decay before the termites consumed it. Because the termites consumed decaying plant matter, they are detritivores. Therefore, **D** is correct. **A** and **B** are incorrect; the termites are not autotrophs. **C** is incorrect; the termites consumed decaying organic material.

Question 4. The best answer is **J**. According to the figure, 100 mg of 1-week-old oak mulch was consumed, 160 mg of 24-week-old oak mulch was consumed, and approximately 45 mg of 48-week-old oak mulch was consumed. Therefore, **J** is correct. **F** is incorrect; more 24-week-old mulch was consumed than 1-week-old mulch. **G** is incorrect; more 24-week-old mulch was consumed than 48-week-old mulch. **H** is incorrect; less 1-week-old mulch was consumed than 24-week-old mulch.

Question 5. The best answer is **B**. To answer this item, you must know that 1 g = 1,000 mg. According to Figure 1, 140 mg of 48-week-old oak bark mulch was consumed.

$$140 \text{ mg} \times (1 \text{ g}/1000 \text{ mg}) = 0.14 \text{ g}$$

Therefore, **B** is correct. **A**, **C**, and **D** are incorrect; 0.14 g of 48-week-old oak bar mulch was consumed.

Passage II

Question 6. The best answer is G. According to the passage, Experiment 2 followed the same procedure as Experiment 1 except that a different strain of Species C was used. **G** is correct; Strain E was studied in Experiment 1, and Strain V2 was studied in Experiment 2. **F** is incorrect; the same incubation temperatures were tested in both experiments. **H** is incorrect; samples from both experiments were lyophilized, and none were transported on ice. **J** is incorrect; incubations times were the same for both experiments.

Question 7. The best answer is B. According to Table 2, as the incubation temperature increased, the percent survival at 1 week decreased. At an incubation temperature of 20°C, Strain V2 had 29% survival at 1 week. At an incubation temperature of 30°C, Strain V2 had 2% survival at 1 week. One would predict that at an incubation temperature of 25°C, Strain V2 would have a percent survival between 2% and 29% at 1 week. Therefore, **B** is correct. **A** is incorrect; the survival would be greater than 2%. **C** and **D** are incorrect; the survival would be less than 29%.

Question 8. The best answer is H. According to the passage, Strain E was studied in Experiment 1 and Strain V2 was studied in Experiment 2. The bacteria were lyophilized in both experiments. The incubation time and temperature were varied in both experiments, and the percent survival was determined. Therefore, **H** is correct; the number of elementary bodies present was not varied in either experiment. **F** is incorrect; the incubation time was varied in both experiments. **G** is incorrect; the temperature was varied in both experiments. **J** is incorrect; two different strains were studied in the experiments.

Question 9. The best answer is D. According to Table 2, after 1 week the sample incubated at 37°C had a 0% survival rate and therefore would not have been able to infect another organism. Therefore, **D** is correct. **A** is incorrect; the sample that had been incubated at 4°C had 59% survival. **B** is incorrect; the sample that had been incubated at 20°C had 29% survival. **C** is incorrect; the sample that had been incubated at 30°C had 2% survival.

Question 10. The best answer is H. According to Table 1, the sample incubated at 20°C for 1 week had the highest percent survival (69%). Therefore, **H** is correct. **F** is incorrect; the sample incubated at 4°C for 1 week had a survival rate of 52%. **G** is incorrect; the sample incubated at 4°C for 1 month had a survival rate of 51%. **J** is incorrect; the sample incubated at 20°C for 1 month had a survival rate of 42%.

Question 11. The best answer is B. According to Table 1, the two samples incubated at 30°C and the two samples incubated at 37°C all had a percent survival less than 30%. The percent survival for the samples incubated at 4°C and 20°C were all greater than 30%. Therefore, **B** is correct. **A**, **C**, and **D** are incorrect; 4 samples had percent survival less than 30%.

Passage III

Question 12. The best answer is G. According to the passage, of the fluids studied, water was the least dense and Fluid B was the most dense. Table 1 shows that the buoyant force on Stone X was greatest in Fluid B and lowest in water. The buoyant force on Stone X increased as the density of the fluid in which it was submerged increased. Therefore, **G** is correct. **F** is incorrect; the buoyant force increased. **H** is incorrect; the buoyant force increased only. **J** is incorrect; there was a trend—the buoyant force increased.

Question 13. The best answer is B. According to Table 1, the buoyant force for Stone Y was 1.18 N in Fluid A and 1.41 N in Fluid B. The difference was 1.41 N – 1.18 N = 0.23 N. Therefore, **B** is correct. **A**, **C**, and **D** are incorrect; the difference was 0.23 N.

Question 14. The best answer is G. To determine the effect of the cylinder's volume on the submerged length of the cylinder in a given fluid, the students must use multiple cylinders with different volumes and then measure the submerged length of each cylinder. Therefore, **G** is correct. **F** is incorrect; the students must use multiple cylinders with different volumes, not weights. **H** and **J** are incorrect; the students must use multiple cylinders, each with a different volume.

Question 15. The best answer is A. Based on the passage, as the length of the portion of the cylinder that was submerged increased, the amount of water that was displaced also increased. Figure 1 also shows that the submerged length was greatest when the cylinder was placed in water, and therefore the amount of fluid that was displaced was greatest in water. Therefore, **A** is correct. **B** is incorrect; the submerged length was greater in water than in Fluid A. **C** and **D** are incorrect; a greater volume of water was displaced than Fluid A.

Question 16. The best answer is H. A stone with a volume larger than that of Stone Z would displace more water than did Stone Z. According to the passage, the buoyant force exerted on the submerged stone is equal in magnitude to the weight of the displaced fluid. Because more fluid would be displaced, the buoyant force on the new stone would be greater than the buoyant force on Stone Z. **H** is correct; in Fluid B the buoyant force on Stone Z was 1.41 N. The buoyant force on the larger stone would be greater than 1.41 N. **F** is incorrect; in water the buoyant force on Stone Z was 0.94 N. The buoyant force on the larger stone would be greater than 0.94 N. **G** is incorrect; in Fluid A the buoyant force on Stone Z was 1.18 N. The buoyant force on the larger stone would be greater than 1.18 N. **J** is incorrect; because water is less dense than Fluid A, the weight of the displaced water (and therefore the buoyant force in water) would be less than the weight of displaced Fluid A (and therefore the buoyant force in Fluid A).

Question 17. The best answer is A. According to the passage and Figure 1, the submerged length increased as density decreased. It follows that the iceberg would have the greatest submerged volume in the less dense Atlantic Ocean. Therefore, **A** is correct. **B** is incorrect; submerged volume increased as fluid density decreased. **C** and **D** are incorrect; the iceberg would most likely have the greatest submerged volume in the Atlantic Ocean.

Passage IV

Question 18. The best answer is F. According to Table 1, ΔT = 3.5°C for Trial 2 and ΔT = 8.6°C for Trial 6, so ΔT was 5.1°C less for Trial 2 than Trial 6. The results do not support the student's prediction. Therefore, **F** is correct. **G** is incorrect; ΔT = 8.6°C for Trial 6, and the difference between Trials 2 and 6 was 5.1°C. **H** and **J** are incorrect; the results do not support the prediction because ΔT for Trial 2 was less than ΔT for Trial 6.

Question 19. The best answer is D. According to Table 1, for each trial the sum of the volume of NaClO solution and the volume of NaI solution was equal to 100 mL. Therefore, **D** is correct. **A**, **B**, and **C** are incorrect; the total volume of solution used was 100 mL.

Question 20. The best answer is H. According to Table 1, 80 mL of NaClO and 20 mL of NaI were used in Trial 6 (80 mL = 4 × 20 mL), and T_f = 30.6°C. Therefore, **H** is correct. **F**, **G**, and **J** are incorrect; T_f = 30.6°C in Trial 6 when the volume of NaClO (80 mL) was 4 times as great as the volume of NaI (20 mL).

Question 21. The best answer is B. According to Figure 1, when 20 mL of NaClO solution was used, ΔT was just under 3°C. Therefore, **B** is correct. **A**, **C**, and **D** are incorrect; Figure 1 shows that ΔT is closest to 3°C.

Question 22. The best answer is J. To answer this item, you must understand how to read chemical equations. Table 1 shows that in Trial 8, 0 mL of NaI was added. According to the equation shown in the passage, NaI is a reactant in the chemical reaction. Without both reactants present, the reaction will not proceed, and no heat will be generated, resulting in ΔT = 0°C. Therefore, **J** is correct. **F** and **G** are incorrect; 0 mL of NaI was added and NaI is a reactant. **H** is incorrect; 100 mL of NaClO was used.

Question 23. The best answer is B. To answer this item, you must know that heat is absorbed during an endothermic reaction. If the reaction had been endothermic, then the reaction would have absorbed heat from the surroundings and the temperature of the solution would have decreased. Therefore, **B** is correct. **A** is incorrect; as stated in the passage, heat is released in an exothermic reaction. **C** and **D** are incorrect; the solution temperature increases when the reaction is exothermic, as is illustrated in the results of the experiment.

Passage V

Question 24. The best answer is J. The plant in question has a height of only 21 cm, and it produced no fruit. According to the results of the experiment, these properties are most consistent with the data shown for the L4 plants that were grown in a nutrient solution containing 120 g of NaCl. The L2 and L4 plants grown in nutrient solutions containing 60 g of NaCl had both greater average plant heights and nonzero average fruit masses. The same is true for the L2 plants grown in a nutrient solution containing 120 g of NaCl. Therefore, **J** is correct, and **F**, **G**, and **H** are incorrect.

Question 25. The best answer is C. To answer this item, you must know that the cell membrane separates the cell's cytoplasm from the environment. According to the passage, the H_2O moved between the cytoplasm of the plants' cells and the environment. If the H_2O passed from the cell to the environment, then it passed through the cell membrane. Therefore, **C** is correct. **A**, **B**, and **D** are incorrect; for water to pass between the cytoplasm into the environment, it must pass through the cell membrane.

Question 26. The best answer is G. To answer this item, you must know that NaCl is a salt. According to Tables 1, 2, and 3, as the amount of NaCl added to the nutrient solution increased, the plant mass decreased. Therefore, **G** is correct. **F** is incorrect; the mass did not increase. **H** and **J** are incorrect; the plant mass decreased only.

Question 27. The best answer is A. The researchers controlled which lines received the *AtNHX1* gene. Therefore, **A** is correct. **B** is incorrect; only tomato plants were used, so this was not a variable. **C** is incorrect; the plant mass was a dependent variable. **D** is incorrect; the plant height was a dependent variable.

Question 28. The best answer is J. According to the information in Tables 1, 2, and 3, as the height decreased, the mass decreased. A plot of this data would result in a line with a positive slope. Therefore, **J** is correct. **F** and **G** are incorrect; the line would have a slope because the mass changed as the height changed. **H** is incorrect; the line would have a positive slope because the mass increased as the height increased.

Question 29. The best answer is D. L1, L2, and L3 all had *AtNHX1* introduced. L4 did not have *AtNHX1* introduced; L4 was the control. Therefore, **D** is correct; L4 was not altered. **A**, **B**, and **C** are incorrect; L1, L2, and L3 all contained different genotypes for *AtNHX1*.

Passage VI

Question 30. The best answer is H. According to Figure 2, at 300 MPa the solubility of CO_2 in rhyolite magma is 2,000 ppmw at 800°C. Therefore, **H** is correct. **F** is incorrect; the solubility is approximately 2,350 ppmw at 700°C. **G** is incorrect; the solubility is approximately 2,200 ppmw at 750°C. **J** is incorrect; the solubility is approximately 1,875 ppmw at 850°C.

Question 31. **The best answer is D**. According to Figure 1, at 1,150°C and 50 MPa, the solubility of CO_2 in basanite magma was 300 ppmw, and at 1,150°C and 125 MPa, the solubility was 1,000 ppmw. At 1,150°C and 200 MPa, the solubility of CO_2 in tholeiitic basalt magma was 700 ppmw, and at 1,150°C and 250 MPa, the solubility of CO_2 was 1,000 ppmw. The CO_2 solubilities were closest in value when basanite magma was at 125 MPa and tholeiitic basalt magma was at 250 Mpa. Therefore, **D** is correct. **A**, **B**, and **C** are incorrect; the CO_2 solubilities for both types of magma were 1,000 ppmw at 125 Mpa for basanite magma and 250 Mpa for tholeiitic basalt magma.

Question 32. **The best answer is G**. According to Figure 1, at 1,150°C and 150 Mpa, the solubility of CO_2 in leucite magma was 3,000 ppmw and the solubility of CO_2 in rhyolite magma was 700 ppmw. The solubility in leucite magma was 2,300 ppmw greater. Therefore, **G** is correct. **F** is incorrect; the solubility is 2,300 ppmw greater in leucite magma. **H** and **J** are incorrect; the solubility was greater in the leucite magma than in the rhyolite magma.

Question 33. **The best answer is A**. According to Figure 2, as the temperature increased from 650°C to 1,150°C, the solubility of CO_2 in rhyolite magma at 100 MPa decreased from 800 ppmw to 400 ppmw and the solubility at 300 MPa decreased from 2,600 ppmw to 1,300 ppmw. Increasing the temperature had a smaller effect on the solubility of CO_2 at 100 MPa. Therefore, **A** is correct. **B** is incorrect; the solubility decreased by only 400 ppmw, from 800 ppmw to 400 ppmw. **C** and **D** are incorrect; a greater effect was seen at 300 Mpa.

Question 34. **The best answer is F**. According to Figure 2, at 750°C and 200 Mpa, the solubility of CO_2 in rhyolite magma is 1,500 ppmw. Figure 3 shows that at 200 Mpa and a CO_2 solubility of 1,500 ppmw, rhyolite magma contains 0% H_2O. Therefore, **F** is correct. **G** is incorrect; rhyolite magma with 2% H_2O has a CO_2 solubility of 1,250 ppmw at 200 Mpa. **H** is incorrect; rhyolite magma with 4% H_2O has a CO_2 solubility of 700 ppmw at 200 Mpa. **J** is incorrect; CO_2 is insoluble in rhyolite magma with 6% H_2O at 200 Mpa.

Passage VII

Question 35. **The best answer is A**. According to Hypothesis 1, Earth is the solar system's central body and other bodies move around Earth in looped orbits. Hypothesis 2 states that the Sun is the solar system's central body and the planets move around the Sun in elliptical orbits. Therefore, **A** is correct. **B** is incorrect; Hypothesis 2 claims that the planets follow elliptical orbits around the Sun, not Earth. **C** and **D** are incorrect; Hypothesis 1 claims that the planets follow looped orbits.

Question 36. **The best answer is H**. According to Figure 2, as Mars loops, the distance between Earth and Mars varies. Figure 3 shows that as Earth and Mars orbit the Sun, the distance between them varies. This is obvious because they are relatively near one another on 10/01/2005 and 12/10/2005 and farther apart on 7/24/2005 and 2/26/2006. Therefore, **H** is correct. **F**, **G**, and **J** are incorrect; both Figures 2 and 3 imply that the distance between Earth and Mars varies.

Question 37. The best answer is A. The top portion of Figure 3 is consistent with Hypothesis 2, showing that, over time, Earth will move a greater percentage of its smaller orbit than will Mars. Therefore, **A** is correct. **B** is incorrect; Earth is shown as having a smaller orbit. **C** and **D** are incorrect; the top portion is consistent with the reasoning presented in Hypothesis 2.

Question 38. The best answer is G. According to the passage, Mars appears to move retrograde when it is moving westward relative to the stars. Figure 1 shows that Mars is moving westward, and therefore retrograde, between 10/01/2005 and 12/10/2005, a period of 70 days. Therefore, **G** is correct. **F**, **H**, and **J** are incorrect; Mars is retrograde for 70 days.

Question 39. The best answer is D. Figure 2 shows that Mars's deferent is a counterclockwise circle around Earth, the central body of the solar system according to Hypothesis 1. Figure 3 shows that Mars moves in a counterclockwise circle around the Sun, the central body of the solar system according to Hypothesis 2. Therefore, **D** is correct. **A** and **B** are incorrect; according to the hypotheses, Mars moves in a counterclockwise direction around the central body of the solar system. **C** is incorrect; Hypothesis 1 states that Mars orbits Earth.

Question 40. The best answer is G. According to Figure 1, the first position shown on Figure 3 corresponds to 7/24/2005, the second corresponds to 10/01/2005, and the third corresponds to 12/10/2005. On November 7, 2005, the positions of Earth and Mars would be between those found on 10/01/2005 and 12/10/2005. Therefore, **G** is correct; this figure best shows the likely positions of Earth and Mars in November. **F** is incorrect; this figure illustrates the position of Mars in October and that of Earth in December. **H** is incorrect; this figure illustrates the position of Earth in October and that of Mars in December. **J** is incorrect; this figure illustrates the likely position of Earth around April or May.

Chapter 11: Scoring the Additional Practice Tests

After taking any of the ACT practice tests in Chapter 10, you are ready to score the test to see how you did. In this chapter, you learn how to determine your raw score, convert raw scores to scale scores, compute your Composite score, determine your estimated percentile ranks for each of your scale scores, and score your practice writing test essay.

Assuming you already scored practice test 1 (see chapter 3), you should be familiar with the scoring procedures.

When scoring each practice test and reviewing your scores, remember that your scores on the practice tests are only estimates of the scores that you will obtain on the ACT. If your score isn't as high as you expected, the cause could be related to any number of factors. Maybe you need to review important content and skills. Maybe you should work a little faster, or more slowly and carefully, when taking the test. Perhaps you simply weren't doing your best work on the test. Or maybe you need to take more challenging courses to be better prepared. Keep in mind that a test score is just one indicator of your level of academic knowledge and skills. You know your own strengths and weaknesses better than anyone else, so keep them in mind as you evaluate your performance.

Scoring Your Practice Tests

For the multiple-choice tests (English, mathematics, reading, and science), the number of questions you answer correctly is called a *raw* score. To figure out your raw scores use the scoring key for each test to score your answer document for the sections in the practice test. Mark a "1" in the blank for each question you answered correctly and add up the total number correct for each test. Do not count correct answers for gray cells, as those are for field test items not included in converting raw scores to scale scores. Please note: the placement of these field test questions varies across different test forms, and will NOT remain in the same test item slots each test administration. Then you can convert your raw scores into *scale* scores. Scale scores are the scores that ACT reports to students, high schools, colleges, and scholarship agencies. Raw scores are converted to a common scale score to enhance score interpretation and allow comparability across different forms. After you've converted your raw scores for the practice tests to scale scores, you'll want to convert your scale scores to percentile ranks. Percentile ranks, which are explained in the following pages, are useful for interpreting your scores relative to the scores of others who have taken the ACT.

If you took the optional practice writing test, use the analytic rubric in chapter 3 (pages 107–108) to evaluate your essay and estimate your writing test score. Being objective about one's own work is difficult, and you have not had the extensive training provided to actual readers of the ACT writing test. However, it is to your advantage to read your own writing critically. Becoming your own editor helps you grow as a writer and as a reader, so it makes sense for you to evaluate your own practice essay. That having been said, it may also be helpful for you to give your practice essay to another reader to get another perspective: perhaps that of a classmate, a parent, or an English teacher, for example. To rate your essay, you and your reader should be familiar with the analytic rubric in chapter 3 and the sample essays and scoring explanations in chapter 9, and then assign your practice essay a score of 1 (low) through 6 (high) in each of the four writing domains (Ideas and Analysis, Development and Support, Organization, and Language Use and Conventions).

Your writing test should be based on two ratings, so you may either multiply your own rating times two, or sum your rating and another reader's rating to calculate your domain scores (2–12 for each domain). Your writing test score is the average of your domain scores and will be in a range of 2–12.

Scoring Practice Test 2

Scoring the Multiple-Choice Tests

To score your multiple-choice practice tests, starting with the English test, follow these six steps:

STEP 1. Mark a "1" in the blank for each question you answered correctly and add up the total number correct for each test. Do not count correct answers for gray cells, as those are for field test items not included in converting raw scores to scale scores. An example is provided in the following box:

	Key		Your answer was
1.	A	–	Incorrect
2.	J	1	Correct
3.	B	1	Correct
4.	G	–	Incorrect

English ▪ Scoring Key ▪ Practice Test 2

Key			Key			Key	
1.	D		18.	J		35.	D
2.	H		19.	D		36.	F
3.	A		20.	F		37.	B
4.	F		21.	D		38.	J
5.	A		22.	G		39.	B
6.	H		23.	B		40.	J
7.	A		24.	F		41.	A
8.	G		25.	B		42.	H
9.	C		26.	H		43.	A
10.	G		27.	A		44.	J
11.	B		28.	G		45.	D
12.	H		29.	B		46.	J
13.	A		30.	G		47.	A
14.	H		31.	C		48.	G
15.	A		32.	H		49.	B
16.	G		33.	D		50.	H
17.	D		34.	G			

STEP 2. Add the numbers you entered in step 1 and write this total in the following shaded box. This is your raw score.

Number Correct (Raw Score) for:

English Test (40 questions) ______________

STEP 3. Repeat steps 1 and 2 for the ACT mathematics, reading, and science tests using the scoring keys on the following pages.

Mathematics ■ Scoring Key ■ Practice Test 2

	Key			Key			Key	
1.	A	______	16.	H	______	31.	D	______
2.	G	______	17.	C	______	32.	H	______
3.	C	______	18.	J	______	33.	B	______
4.	G	______	19.	C	______	34.	G	______
5.	D	______	20.	H	______	35.	C	______
6.	G	______	21.	B	______	36.	F	______
7.	B	______	22.	J	______	37.	C	______
8.	H	______	23.	A	______	38.	G	______
9.	D	______	24.	F	______	39.	C	______
10.	F	______	25.	C	______	40.	J	______
11.	D	______	26.	G	______	41.	C	______
12.	J	______	27.	B	______	42.	H	______
13.	C	______	28.	H	______	43.	D	______
14.	F	______	29.	B	______	44.	F	______
15.	B	______	30.	H	______	45.	C	______

Number Correct (Raw Score) for:

Mathematics Test (41 questions) ______________

Reading ■ Scoring Key ■ Practice Test 2

	Key			Key			Key	
1.	A		13.	B		25.	C	
2.	G		14.	J		26.	J	
3.	D		15.	A		27.	B	
4.	G		16.	H		28.	G	
5.	A		17.	B		29.	A	
6.	H		18.	H		30.	H	
7.	A		19.	D		31.	B	
8.	J		20.	J		32.	H	
9.	C		21.	B		33.	D	
10.	J		22.	G		34.	F	
11.	C		23.	C		35.	A	
12.	F		24.	F		36.	H	

Number Correct (Raw Score) for:

Reading Test (27 questions) ______________

Science ■ Scoring Key ■ Practice Test 2

	Key			Key			Key	
1.	B		15.	B		29.	B	
2.	H		16.	G		30.	H	
3.	C		17.	D		31.	A	
4.	G		18.	H		32.	F	
5.	A		19.	B		33.	B	
6.	G		20.	G		34.	F	
7.	D		21.	D		35.	A	
8.	H		22.	F		36.	J	
9.	B		23.	B		37.	C	
10.	F		24.	G		38.	F	
11.	A		25.	C		39.	C	
12.	H		26.	F		40.	J	
13.	A		27.	D				
14.	F		28.	G				

Number Correct (Raw Score) for:

Science Test (34 questions) ______________

STEP 4. On each of the four tests, the total number of correct responses yields a raw score. Use the conversion table on the following page to convert your raw scores to scale scores. For each of the four tests, locate and circle your raw score or the range of raw scores that includes it in the conversion table. Then, read across to either outside column of the table and circle the scale score that corresponds to that raw score. As you determine your scale scores, enter them in the blanks provided below. The highest possible scale score for each test is 36. The lowest possible scale score for any of the four tests is 1.

	Your Scale Scores
English	_______________
Mathematics	_______________
Reading	_______________
Science	_______________
Sum of Scores	_______________

STEP 5. Compute your Composite score by averaging the four scale scores. To do this, add your four scale scores and divide the sum by 4. If the resulting number ends in a fraction, round it off to the nearest whole number. (Round down any fraction less than one-half; round up any fraction that is one-half or more.) Enter this number in the appropriate blank below. This is your Composite score. The highest possible Composite score is 36. The lowest possible Composite score is 1.

	Your Scale Scores
English	_______________
Mathematics	_______________
Reading	_______________
Science	_______________
Sum of Scores	_______________
Composite Score (sum ÷ 4)	_______________

Scale Score Conversion Table: Practice Test 2

Scale Score	Raw Score				Scale Score
	English	Mathematics	Reading	Science	
36	40	40–41	27	34	36
35	38–39	39	26	33	35
34	37	38	25	32	34
33	–	37	–	31	33
32	36	36	24	–	32
31	–	35	–	30	31
30	35	34	23	29	30
29	34	33	–	28	29
28	–	32	22	27	28
27	33	30–31	–	26	27
26	32	29	21	24–25	26
25	31	27–28	20	23	25
24	29–30	26	19	20–22	24
23	28	25	18	18–19	23
22	26–27	24	–	17	22
21	25	22–23	17	16	21
20	23–24	21	16	15	20
19	22	20	15	14	19
18	21	18–19	14	13	18
17	20	15–17	13	12	17
16	19	12–14	–	11	16
15	17–18	10–11	12	10	15
14	16	7–9	11	–	14
13	15	6	9–10	9	13
12	13–14	5	8	8	12
11	11–12	4	7	7	11
10	8–10	3	6	5–6	10
9	7	–	5	–	9
8	6	2	4	4	8
7	5	–	–	3	7
6	4	–	3	–	6
5	3	1	–	2	5
4	2	–	2	–	4
3	–	–	1	1	3
2	1	–	–	–	2
1	0	0	0	0	1

STEP 6. Use the table on the following page to determine your estimated percentile ranks (percent at or below) for each of your scale scores. In the far left column of the table, circle your scale score for the English test (from the preceding page). Then read across to the percentile rank column for that test; circle or put a checkmark beside the corresponding percentile rank. Use the same procedure for the other four tests (from the preceding page). Using the right-hand column of scale scores for your science test and Composite scores may be easier. As you mark your percentile ranks, enter them in the blanks provided. You may also find it helpful to compare your performance with the national mean (average) score for each of the five tests and the Composite as shown at the bottom of the table.

National Norms for ACT Test Scores
Reported During the 2025–2026 Reporting Year

Score	ACT Score National Ranks						Score
	English	Math	Reading	Science	Composite	STEM	
36	100	100	100	100	100	100	36
35	99	99	98	99	99	99	35
34	97	99	97	99	99	99	34
33	96	98	95	98	98	98	33
32	95	98	93	97	97	98	32
31	94	97	91	96	96	97	31
30	93	96	89	95	94	95	30
29	91	94	87	93	92	94	29
28	90	93	85	92	91	92	28
27	88	91	83	91	88	90	27
26	86	88	80	89	86	88	26
25	84	85	78	86	83	85	25
24	81	81	75	82	80	81	24
23	77	77	71	76	76	77	23
22	73	74	66	70	72	73	22
21	69	71	60	65	68	68	21
20	63	68	55	59	63	63	20
19	58	64	50	53	57	58	19
18	53	60	46	47	52	51	18
17	49	53	41	40	46	44	17
16	46	45	37	33	40	35	16
15	40	32	32	26	34	26	15
14	33	20	27	19	27	17	14
13	27	10	21	14	20	10	13
12	22	5	16	10	12	4	12
11	17	3	9	6	5	2	11
10	11	1	4	3	2	1	10
9	6	1	2	2	1	1	9
8	3	1	1	1	1	1	8
7	2	1	1	1	1	1	7
6	1	1	1	1	1	1	6
5	1	1	1	1	1	1	5
4	1	1	1	1	1	1	4
3	1	1	1	1	1	1	3
2	1	1	1	1	1	1	2
1	1	1	1	1	1	1	1
Mean	18.6	19.0	20.1	19.6	19.2	19.5	
SD	7.0	5.6	7.1	5.8	6.1	5.4	

Note: These ranks are reported as "US Rank" on ACT score reports during the 2025–2026 reporting year (September 2025 through August 2026). The ranks are based on ACT-tested high school graduates of 2023, 2024, and 2025.

Scoring Your Practice Writing Test 2 Essay

To score your practice writing test essay, follow these steps:

STEP 1. Use the guidelines from the writing test analytic rubric in chapter 3 (pages 107–108) to score your essay. Because many essays do not fit the exact description at each score point, read each description and try to determine which paragraph in the rubric best describes most of the characteristics of your essay.

STEP 2. Because your writing test domain scores are the sum of two readers' ratings of your essay, multiply your own 1–6 rating from step 1 by 2. Or, have both you and someone else read and score your practice essay, add those ratings together, and record the total in the Domain Score column in step 3.

STEP 3. Enter your writing test domain scores in the following box:

		Domain Score
Ideas and Analysis	__________	x 2 = __________
Development and Support	__________	x 2 = __________
Organization	__________	x 2 = __________
Language Use and Convention	__________	x 2 = __________

STEP 4. Enter the sum of the second-column scores here ______.

STEP 5. Divide sum by 4[†] (range 2–12). This is your Writing Subject score.

[†]Round value to the nearest whole number. Round down any fraction less than one-half; round up any fraction that is one-half or more.

STEP 6. Use the table below to determine your estimated percentile rank (percent at or below) for your writing subject score.

National Norms for ACT Writing Scores
Reported During the 2025–2026 Reporting Year

Score	ACT Score National Ranks	
	ELA	Writing
36	100	
35	99	
34	99	
33	99	
32	99	
31	99	
30	98	
29	97	
28	96	
27	94	
26	92	
25	90	
24	87	
23	84	
22	80	
21	76	
20	71	
19	65	
18	59	
17	53	
16	47	
15	40	
14	34	
13	27	
12	21	100
11	15	99
10	10	99
9	7	97
8	4	93
7	2	74
6	1	61
5	1	34
4	1	21
3	1	9
2	1	4
1	1	
Mean	17.5	6.1
SD	5.7	1.8

Note: These ranks are reported as "US Rank" on ACT score reports during the 2025–2026 reporting year (September 2025 through August 2026). The ranks are based on ACT-tested high school graduates of 2023, 2024, and 2025 who took the ACT Writing test.

Scoring Practice Test 3

Scoring the Multiple-Choice Tests

To score each of your multiple-choice practice tests, starting with the English test, follow these steps:

STEP 1. Mark a "1" in the blank for each question you answered correctly and add up the total number correct for each test. Do not count correct answers for gray cells, as those are for field test items not included in converting raw scores to scale scores. An example is provided in the following box:

	Key		Your answer was
1.	A	___	Incorrect
2.	J	1	Correct
3.	B	1	Correct
4.	G	___	Incorrect

English ■ Scoring Key ■ Practice Test 3

	Key			Key			Key	
1.	D	_____	18.	F	_____	35.	B	
2.	F	_____	19.	A	_____	36.	J	
3.	A	_____	20.	F	_____	37.	A	
4.	H	_____	21.	A	_____	38.	F	
5.	D	_____	22.	H	_____	39.	B	
6.	J	_____	23.	D	_____	40.	F	
7.	A	_____	24.	H	_____	41.	A	_____
8.	G	_____	25.	A	_____	42.	F	_____
9.	C	_____	26.	G	_____	43.	C	_____
10.	F	_____	27.	C	_____	44.	J	_____
11.	D	_____	28.	G	_____	45.	D	_____
12.	H	_____	29.	C	_____	46.	J	_____
13.	B	_____	30.	J	_____	47.	B	_____
14.	J	_____	31.	A		48.	J	_____
15.	B	_____	32.	G		49.	D	_____
16.	J	_____	33.	C		50.	F	_____
17.	A	_____	34.	J				

STEP 2. Add the numbers you entered in step 1 and write this total in the following shaded box. This is your raw score.

> **Number Correct (Raw Score) for:**
>
> **English test (40 questions)**   ___________

STEP 3. Repeat steps 1 and 2 for the ACT mathematics, reading, and science tests using the scoring keys on the following pages.

Mathematics ■ Scoring Key ■ Practice Test 3

	Key			Key			Key	
1.	C	_______	16.	J	_______	31.	C	_______
2.	G	_______	17.	B	_______	32.	H	_______
3.	D	_______	18.	H	_______	33.	D	_______
4.	H	_______	19.	B	_______	34.	F	_______
5.	D	_______	20.	H	_______	35.	B	_______
6.	G	_______	21.	A	_______	36.	F	_______
7.	D	_______	22.	H	_______	37.	A	_______
8.	H	_______	23.	D	_______	38.	G	_______
9.	C	_______	24.	H	_______	39.	A	_______
10.	G	_______	25.	B	_______	40.	F	_______
11.	D	_______	26.	H	_______	41.	D	_______
12.	G	_______	27.	C	_______	42.	H	_______
13.	B	_______	28.	J	_______	43.	B	_______
14.	F	_______	29.	A	_______	44.	F	_______
15.	B	_______	30.	G	_______	45.	A	_______

> **Number Correct (Raw Score) for:**
>
> **Math test (41 questions)**   ___________

Reading ■ Scoring Key ■ Practice Test 3

	Key			Key			Key	
1.	C	_____	13.	B	_____	25.	C	_____
2.	F	_____	14.	H	_____	26.	F	_____
3.	B	_____	15.	B	_____	27.	B	_____
4.	H	_____	16.	J	_____	28.	F	_____
5.	A	_____	17.	A	_____	29.	C	_____
6.	G	_____	18.	F	_____	30.	G	_____
7.	B	_____	19.	B	_____	31.	A	_____
8.	J	_____	20.	G	_____	32.	F	_____
9.	B	_____	21.	D	_____	33.	C	_____
10.	G	_____	22.	G	_____	34.	G	_____
11.	A	_____	23.	D	_____	35.	D	_____
12.	G	_____	24.	H	_____	36.	J	_____

Number Correct (Raw Score) for:

Reading test (27 questions)   _____________

Science ■ Scoring Key ■ Practice Test 3

	Key			Key			Key	
1.	B	_____	15.	C	_____	29.	B	_____
2.	G	_____	16.	F	_____	30.	H	_____
3.	A	_____	17.	A	_____	31.	B	_____
4.	J	_____	18.	F	_____	32.	F	_____
5.	D	_____	19.	D	_____	33.	C	_____
6.	G	_____	20.	G	_____	34.	J	_____
7.	D	_____	21.	C	_____	35.	C	_____
8.	F	_____	22.	G	_____	36.	H	_____
9.	B	_____	23.	A	_____	37.	B	_____
10.	F	_____	24.	F	_____	38.	H	_____
11.	A	_____	25.	D	_____	39.	D	_____
12.	F	_____	26.	H	_____	40.	H	_____
13.	C	_____	27.	D	_____			
14.	G	_____	28.	J	_____			

Number Correct (Raw Score) for:

Science test (34 questions)   _____________

STEP 4. On each of the four tests, the total number of correct responses yields a raw score. Use the conversion table on the following page to convert your raw scores to scale scores. For each of the four tests, locate and circle your raw score or the range of raw scores that includes it in the conversion table. Then, read across to either outside column of the table and circle the scale score that corresponds to that raw score. As you determine your scale scores, enter them in the blanks provided below. The highest possible scale score for each test is 36. The lowest possible scale score for any of the four tests is 1.

	Your Scale Scores
English	____________
Mathematics	____________
Reading	____________
Science	____________
Sum of Scores	____________

STEP 5. Compute your Composite score by averaging the four scale scores. To do this, add your four scale scores and divide the sum by 4. If the resulting number ends in a fraction, round it off to the nearest whole number. (Round down any fraction less than one-half; round up any fraction that is one-half or more.) Enter this number in the appropriate blank below. This is your Composite score. The highest possible Composite score is 36. The lowest possible Composite score is 1.

	Your Scale Scores
English	____________
Mathematics	____________
Reading	____________
Science	____________
Sum of Scores	____________
Composite Score (sum ÷ 4)	____________

Scale Score Conversion Table:
Practice Test 3

Scale Score	Raw Score				Scale Score
	English	Mathematics	Reading	Science	
36	40	40–41	27	34	36
35	38–39	38–39	26	33	35
34	36–37	36–37	–	32	34
33	–	35	25	31	33
32	35	–	–	–	32
31	–	34	24	30	31
30	34	33	–	29	30
29	33	32	23	28	29
28	32	31	22	27	28
27	31	30	21	26	27
26	30	28–29	–	25	26
25	29	27	20	23–24	25
24	27–28	26	18–19	21–22	24
23	26	–	17	20	23
22	24–25	25	16	18–19	22
21	22–23	24	15	17	21
20	21	23	–	16	20
19	20	22	14	15	19
18	19	20–21	13	14	18
17	18	17–19	12	13	17
16	17	15–16	–	11–12	16
15	15–16	12–14	11	10	15
14	14	8–11	10	–	14
13	13	6–7	9	9	13
12	12	5	–	8	12
11	11	4	7–8	6–7	11
10	8–10	–	6	5	10
9	7	3	5	4	9
8	6	–	–	–	8
7	5	2	4	3	7
6	4	–	3	–	6
5	3	–	–	2	5
4	2	1	2	–	4
3	–	–	–	1	3
2	1	–	1	–	2
1	0	0	0	0	1

STEP 6. Use the table on the following page to determine your estimated percentile ranks (percent at or below) for each of your scale scores. In the far left column of the table, circle your scale score for the English test (from the preceding page). Then read across to the percentile rank column for that test; circle or put a checkmark beside the corresponding percentile rank. Use the same procedure for the other three tests (from the preceding page). Using the right-hand column of scale scores for your science test and Composite scores may be easier. As you mark your percentile ranks, enter them in the blanks provided. You may also find it helpful to compare your performance with the national mean (average) score for each of the four tests and the Composite as shown at the bottom of the table.

National Norms for ACT Test Scores
Reported During the 2025–2026 Reporting Year

Score	ACT Score National Ranks						Score
	English	Math	Reading	Science	Composite	STEM	
36	100	100	100	100	100	100	36
35	99	99	98	99	99	99	35
34	97	99	97	99	99	99	34
33	96	98	95	98	98	98	33
32	95	98	93	97	97	98	32
31	94	97	91	96	96	97	31
30	93	96	89	95	94	95	30
29	91	94	87	93	92	94	29
28	90	93	85	92	91	92	28
27	88	91	83	91	88	90	27
26	86	88	80	89	86	88	26
25	84	85	78	86	83	85	25
24	81	81	75	82	80	81	24
23	77	77	71	76	76	77	23
22	73	74	66	70	72	73	22
21	69	71	60	65	68	68	21
20	63	68	55	59	63	63	20
19	58	64	50	53	57	58	19
18	53	60	46	47	52	51	18
17	49	53	41	40	46	44	17
16	46	45	37	33	40	35	16
15	40	32	32	26	34	26	15
14	33	20	27	19	27	17	14
13	27	10	21	14	20	10	13
12	22	5	16	10	12	4	12
11	17	3	9	6	5	2	11
10	11	1	4	3	2	1	10
9	6	1	2	2	1	1	9
8	3	1	1	1	1	1	8
7	2	1	1	1	1	1	7
6	1	1	1	1	1	1	6
5	1	1	1	1	1	1	5
4	1	1	1	1	1	1	4
3	1	1	1	1	1	1	3
2	1	1	1	1	1	1	2
1	1	1	1	1	1	1	1
Mean	18.6	19.0	20.1	19.6	19.2	19.5	
SD	7.0	5.6	7.1	5.8	6.1	5.4	

Note: These ranks are reported as "US Rank" on ACT score reports during the 2025–2026 reporting year (September 2025 through August 2026). The ranks are based on ACT-tested high school graduates of 2023, 2024, and 2025.

Scoring Your Practice Writing Test 3 Essay

To score your practice writing test essay, follow these steps:

STEP 1. Use the guidelines from the writing test analytic rubric in chapter 3 (pages 107–108) to score your essay. Because many essays do not fit the exact description at each score point, read each description and try to determine which paragraph in the rubric best describes most of the characteristics of your essay.

STEP 2. Because your writing test domain scores are the sum of two readers' ratings of your essay, multiply your own 1–6 rating from step 1 by 2. Or, have both you and someone else read and score your practice essay, add those ratings together, and record the total in the Domain Score column in step 3.

STEP 3. Enter your writing test domain scores in the following box.

		Domain Score
Ideas and Analysis	__________ × 2 =	__________
Development and Support	__________ × 2 =	__________
Organization	__________ × 2 =	__________
Language Use and Conventions	__________ × 2 =	__________

STEP 4. Enter the sum of the second-column scores here _______.

STEP 5. Divide sum by 4[†] (range 2–12). This is your Writing Subject score.

[†]Round value to the nearest whole number. Round down any fraction less than one-half; round up any fraction that is one-half or more.

STEP 6. Use the table below to determine your estimated percentile rank (percent at or below) for your writing subject score.

National Norms for ACT Writing Scores Reported During the 2025–2026 Reporting Year

| | ACT Score National Ranks | |
Score	ELA	Writing
36	100	
35	99	
34	99	
33	99	
32	99	
31	99	
30	98	
29	97	
28	96	
27	94	
26	92	
25	90	
24	87	
23	84	
22	80	
21	76	
20	71	
19	65	
18	59	
17	53	
16	47	
15	40	
14	34	
13	27	
12	21	100
11	15	99
10	10	99
9	7	97
8	4	93
7	2	74
6	1	61
5	1	34
4	1	21
3	1	9
2	1	4
1	1	
Mean	17.5	6.1
SD	5.7	1.8

Note: These ranks are reported as "US Rank" on ACT score reports during the 2025–2026 reporting year (September 2025 through August 2026). The ranks are based on ACT-tested high school graduates of 2023, 2024, and 2025 who took the ACT Writing test.

Scoring Practice Test 4

Scoring Your Multiple-Choice Practice Tests

To score your multiple-choice practice tests, follow these eight steps:

STEP 1. Mark a "1" in the blank for each question you answered correctly and add up the total number correct for each test. Do not count correct answers for gray cells, as those are for field test items not included in converting raw scores to scale scores. An example is provided in the box below:

	Key		Your answer was
1.	A	__	Incorrect
2.	J	1	Correct
3.	B	1	Correct
4.	G	__	Incorrect

English ■ Scoring Key ■ Practice Test 4

	Key			Key			Key	
1.	C	_____	18.	H		35.	C	_____
2.	H	_____	19.	A		36.	F	_____
3.	A	_____	20.	G		37.	A	_____
4.	F	_____	21.	A		38.	F	_____
5.	D	_____	22.	J		39.	B	_____
6.	J	_____	23.	C		40.	J	_____
7.	C	_____	24.	J		41.	D	_____
8.	F	_____	25.	A		42.	G	_____
9.	D	_____	26.	G	_____	43.	D	_____
10.	G	_____	27.	D	_____	44.	J	_____
11.	C	_____	28.	J	_____	45.	C	_____
12.	F	_____	29.	C	_____	46.	J	_____
13.	A	_____	30.	F	_____	47.	C	_____
14.	J	_____	31.	A	_____	48.	J	_____
15.	B	_____	32.	F	_____	49.	D	_____
16.	H		33.	B	_____	50.	J	_____
17.	D		34.	F	_____			

STEP 2. Add the numbers you entered in step 1 and write this total in the following shaded box. This is your raw score.

Number Correct (Raw Score) for:

Total Number Correct for English Test (40 questions) ___________

STEP 3. Repeat Steps 1 and 2 for the ACT mathematics, reading, and science tests using the scoring keys on the following pages.

Mathematics ■ Scoring Key ■ Practice Test 4

	Key			Key			Key	
1.	D	_______	16.	G	_______	31.	C	_______
2.	H	_______	17.	B	_______	32.	G	_______
3.	B	_______	18.	F	_______	33.	A	_______
4.	J	_______	19.	A	_______	34.	G	_______
5.	A	_______	20.	H	_______	35.	C	_______
6.	F	_______	21.	D	_______	36.	H	_______
7.	C	_______	22.	F	_______	37.	D	_______
8.	H	_______	23.	D	_______	38.	J	_______
9.	B	_______	24.	G	_______	39.	D	_______
10.	J	_______	25.	D	_______	40.	H	_______
11.	C	_______	26.	G	_______	41.	C	_______
12.	H	_______	27.	C	_______	42.	H	_______
13.	B	_______	28.	G	_______	43.	A	_______
14.	F	_______	29.	A	_______	44.	J	_______
15.	C	_______	30.	J	_______	45.	D	_______

Number Correct (Raw Score) for:

Total Number Correct for Math Test (41 questions) ___________

Reading ■ Scoring Key ■ Practice Test 4

	Key			Key			Key	
1.	D		13.	A		25.	A	
2.	J		14.	F		26.	G	
3.	C		15.	C		27.	A	
4.	H		16.	J		28.	G	
5.	B		17.	D		29.	A	
6.	F		18.	F		30.	H	
7.	A		19.	C		31.	B	
8.	J		20.	G		32.	H	
9.	A		21.	B		33.	A	
10.	G		22.	H		34.	F	
11.	A		23.	D		35.	C	
12.	G		24.	G		36.	J	

Number Correct (Raw Score) for:

Total Number Correct for Reading Test (27 questions) ______________

Science ■ Scoring Key ■ Practice Test 4

	Key			Key			Key	
1.	A		15.	A		29.	D	
2.	J		16.	H		30.	H	
3.	D		17.	A		31.	D	
4.	J		18.	F		32.	G	
5.	B		19.	D		33.	A	
6.	G		20.	H		34.	F	
7.	B		21.	B		35.	A	
8.	H		22.	J		36.	H	
9.	D		23.	B		37.	A	
10.	H		24.	J		38.	G	
11.	B		25.	C		39.	D	
12.	G		26.	G		40.	G	
13.	B		27.	A				
14.	G		28.	J				

Number Correct (Raw Score) for:

Total Number Correct for Science Test (34 questions) ______________

STEP 4. On each of the four tests, the total number of correct responses yields a raw score. Use the conversion table on the following page to convert your raw scores to scale scores. For each of the four tests, locate and circle your raw score or the range of raw scores that includes it in the conversion table. Then, read across to either outside column of the table and circle the scale score that corresponds to that raw score. As you determine your scale scores, enter them in the blanks provided below. The highest possible scale score for each test is 36. The lowest possible scale score for any of the four tests is 1.

	Your Scale Scores
English	__________
Mathematics	__________
Reading	__________
Science	__________
Sum of Scores	__________

STEP 5. Compute your Composite score by averaging the four scale scores. To do this, add your four scale scores and divide the sum by 4. If the resulting number ends in a fraction, round it off to the nearest whole number. (Round down any fraction less than one-half; round up any fraction that is one-half or more.) Enter this number in the appropriate blank below. This is your Composite score. The highest possible Composite score is 36. The lowest possible Composite score is 1.

	Your Scale Scores
English	__________
Mathematics	__________
Reading	__________
Science	__________
Sum of Scores	__________
Composite Score (sum ÷ 4)	__________

Scale Score Conversion Table: Practice Test 4

Scale Score	Raw Score				Scale Score
	English	Mathematics	Reading	Science	
36	40	40–41	27	34	36
35	38–39	38–39	26	33	35
34	37	36–37	–	32	34
33	36	35	25	–	33
32	–	34	–	31	32
31	35	33	24	30	31
30	–	32	23	–	30
29	34	31	–	29	29
28	33	29–30	22	28	28
27	–	28	21	27	27
26	32	27	20	26	26
25	31	25–26	19	24–25	25
24	30	24	18	22–23	24
23	28–29	23	17	20–21	23
22	27	22	16	19	22
21	26	21	15	18	21
20	24–25	20	14	17	20
19	23	19	–	15–16	19
18	22	17–18	13	14	18
17	21	15–16	12	13	17
16	20	13–14	–	11–12	16
15	18–19	11–12	11	10	15
14	16–17	7–10	10	9	14
13	15	6	9	8	13
12	14	5	–	7	12
11	12–13	4	7–8	6	11
10	9–11	–	6	5	10
9	7–8	3	5	4	9
8	6	–	–	–	8
7	5	2	4	3	7
6	4	–	3	2	6
5	3	1	–	–	5
4	–	–	2	1	4
3	2	–	–	–	3
2	1	–	1	–	2
1	0	0	0	0	1

STEP 6. Use the table on the following page to determine your estimated percentile ranks (percent at or below) for each of your scale scores. In the far left column of the table, circle your scale score for the English test (from the preceding page). Then read across to the percentile rank column for that test; circle or put a checkmark beside the corresponding percentile rank. Use the same procedure for the other three tests (from the preceding page). Using the right-hand column of scale scores for your science test and Composite scores may be easier. As you mark your percentile ranks, enter them in the blanks provided. You may also find it helpful to compare your performance with the national mean (average) score for each of the four tests and the Composite as shown at the bottom of the table.

National Norms for ACT Test Scores
Reported During the 2025–2026 Reporting Year

Score	ACT Score National Ranks						Score
	English	Math	Reading	Science	Composite	STEM	
36	100	100	100	100	100	100	36
35	99	99	98	99	99	99	35
34	97	99	97	99	99	99	34
33	96	98	95	98	98	98	33
32	95	98	93	97	97	98	32
31	94	97	91	96	96	97	31
30	93	96	89	95	94	95	30
29	91	94	87	93	92	94	29
28	90	93	85	92	91	92	28
27	88	91	83	91	88	90	27
26	86	88	80	89	86	88	26
25	84	85	78	86	83	85	25
24	81	81	75	82	80	81	24
23	77	77	71	76	76	77	23
22	73	74	66	70	72	73	22
21	69	71	60	65	68	68	21
20	63	68	55	59	63	63	20
19	58	64	50	53	57	58	19
18	53	60	46	47	52	51	18
17	49	53	41	40	46	44	17
16	46	45	37	33	40	35	16
15	40	32	32	26	34	26	15
14	33	20	27	19	27	17	14
13	27	10	21	14	20	10	13
12	22	5	16	10	12	4	12
11	17	3	9	6	5	2	11
10	11	1	4	3	2	1	10
9	6	1	2	2	1	1	9
8	3	1	1	1	1	1	8
7	2	1	1	1	1	1	7
6	1	1	1	1	1	1	6
5	1	1	1	1	1	1	5
4	1	1	1	1	1	1	4
3	1	1	1	1	1	1	3
2	1	1	1	1	1	1	2
1	1	1	1	1	1	1	1
Mean	18.6	19.0	20.1	19.6	19.2	19.5	
SD	7.0	5.6	7.1	5.8	6.1	5.4	

Note: These ranks are reported as "US Rank" on ACT score reports during the 2025–2026 reporting year (September 2025 through August 2026). The ranks are based on ACT-tested high school graduates of 2023, 2024, and 2025.

Scoring Your Practice Writing Test 4 Essay

To score your practice writing test essay, follow these steps:

STEP 1. Use the guidelines from the writing test analytic rubric in chapter 3 (pages 107–108) to score your essay. Because many essays do not fit the exact description at each score point, read each description and try to determine which paragraph in the rubric best describes most of the characteristics of your essay.

STEP 2. Because your writing test domain scores are the sum of two readers' ratings of your essay, multiply your own 1–6 rating from step 1 by 2. Or, have both you and someone else read and score your practice essay, add those ratings together, and record the total in the Domain Score column in step 3.

STEP 3. Enter your writing test domain scores in the following box.

		Domain Score
Ideas and Analysis	__________ × 2 =	__________
Development and Support	__________ × 2 =	__________
Organization	__________ × 2 =	__________
Language Use and Conventions	__________ × 2 =	__________

STEP 4. Enter the sum of the second-column scores here ________.

STEP 5. Divide sum by 4† (range 2–12). This is your Writing test score.

†Round value to the nearest whole number. Round down any fraction less than one-half; round up any fraction that is one-half or more.

STEP 6. Use the table below to determine your estimated percentile rank (percent at or below) for your Writing test score.

National Norms for ACT Writing Scores
Reported During the 2025–2026 Reporting Year

Score	ACT Score National Ranks	
	ELA	Writing
36	100	
35	99	
34	99	
33	99	
32	99	
31	99	
30	98	
29	97	
28	96	
27	94	
26	92	
25	90	
24	87	
23	84	
22	80	
21	76	
20	71	
19	65	
18	59	
17	53	
16	47	
15	40	
14	34	
13	27	
12	21	100
11	15	99
10	10	99
9	7	97
8	4	93
7	2	74
6	1	61
5	1	34
4	1	21
3	1	9
2	1	4
1	1	
Mean	17.5	6.1
SD	5.7	1.8

Note: These ranks are reported as "US Rank" on ACT score reports during the 2025–2026 reporting year (September 2025 through August 2026). The ranks are based on ACT-tested high school graduates of 2023, 2024, and 2025 who took the ACT Writing test.

12

Chapter 12: Interpreting Your ACT Test Scores and Ranks

After taking any test, students are eager to see how they've done. Assuming you took and scored ACT practice test 1 in chapter 3 or took other practice tests in chapter 10 and scored them in chapter 11, you have a great deal of information to consider when determining how well you did.

- **Raw scores:** ACT does not provide raw scores, but you have raw scores for the practice tests in this book.

- **Scale scores** are the scores that ACT reports to students, high schools, colleges, and scholarship agencies.

- **Composite score** is a scale score that reflects your overall performance on *all* of the multiple choice tests—English, math, reading, and science.

- **Ranks** indicate the approximate percentage of ACT-tested students who scored at or below each of your scores; for example, if your mathematics rank is 85%, then you scored as well as or better than 85% of the other students who took the mathematics test.

If you take the ACT you receive the *ACT Student Report*, which includes scale scores, the Composite score, and the rank for each score. You can visit www.act.org to view samples of this report as well as the High School and College reports.

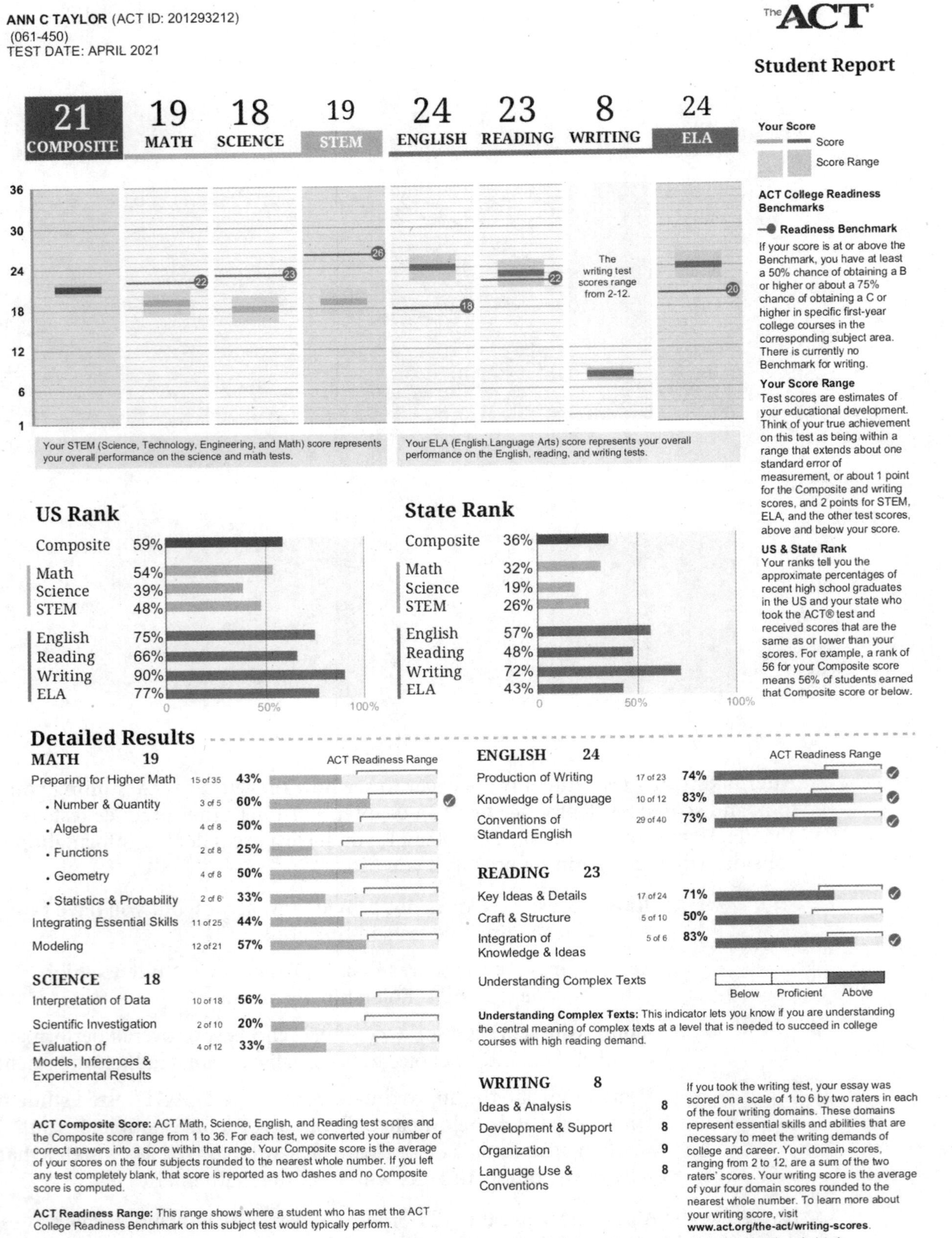

ACT College Readiness Benchmarks

Readiness Benchmark

If your score is at or above the Benchmark, you have at least a 50% chance of obtaining a B or higher or about a 75% chance of obtaining a C or higher in specific first-year college courses in the corresponding subject area. There is currently no Benchmark for writing.

Your Score Range

Test scores are estimates of your educational development. Think of your true achievement on this test as being within a range that extends about one standard error of measurement, or about 1 point for the Composite and writing scores, and 2 points for STEM, ELA, and the other test scores, above and below your score.

US & State Rank

Your ranks tell you the approximate percentages of recent high school graduates in the US and your state who took the ACT® test and received scores that are the same as or lower than your scores. For example, a rank of 56 for your Composite score means 56% of students earned that Composite score or below.

US Rank

Composite	59%	
Math	54%	
Science	39%	
STEM	48%	
English	75%	
Reading	66%	
Writing	90%	
ELA	77%	

0   50%   100%

State Rank

Composite	36%	
Math	32%	
Science	19%	
STEM	26%	
English	57%	
Reading	48%	
Writing	72%	
ELA	43%	

0   50%   100%

Detailed Results

MATH   19   ACT Readiness Range

Preparing for Higher Math	15 of 35	43%
. Number & Quantity	3 of 5	60%
. Algebra	4 of 8	50%
. Functions	2 of 8	25%
. Geometry	4 of 8	50%
. Statistics & Probability	2 of 6	33%
Integrating Essential Skills	11 of 25	44%
Modeling	12 of 21	57%

SCIENCE   18

Interpretation of Data	10 of 18	56%
Scientific Investigation	2 of 10	20%
Evaluation of Models, Inferences & Experimental Results	4 of 12	33%

ENGLISH   24   ACT Readiness Range

Production of Writing	17 of 23	74%
Knowledge of Language	10 of 12	83%
Conventions of Standard English	29 of 40	73%

READING   23

Key Ideas & Details	17 of 24	71%
Craft & Structure	5 of 10	50%
Integration of Knowledge & Ideas	5 of 6	83%

Understanding Complex Texts

Below   Proficient   Above

Understanding Complex Texts: This indicator lets you know if you are understanding the central meaning of complex texts at a level that is needed to succeed in college courses with high reading demand.

WRITING   8

Ideas & Analysis	8
Development & Support	8
Organization	9
Language Use & Conventions	8

If you took the writing test, your essay was scored on a scale of 1 to 6 by two raters in each of the four writing domains. These domains represent essential skills and abilities that are necessary to meet the writing demands of college and career. Your domain scores, ranging from 2 to 12, are a sum of the two raters' scores. Your writing score is the average of your four domain scores rounded to the nearest whole number. To learn more about your writing score, visit **www.act.org/the-act/writing-scores**.

ACT Composite Score: ACT Math, Science, English, and Reading test scores and the Composite score range from 1 to 36. For each test, we converted your number of correct answers into a score within that range. Your Composite score is the average of your scores on the four subjects rounded to the nearest whole number. If you left any test completely blank, that score is reported as two dashes and no Composite score is computed.

ACT Readiness Range: This range shows where a student who has met the ACT College Readiness Benchmark on this subject test would typically perform.

Dashes (-) indicate information was not provided or could not be calculated.

In this chapter, we explain how to interpret your scores and use them as a tool to help inform your education and career decisions. We encourage you to look at your ACT test scores and ranks with additional information to help guide your future education and career planning.

Understanding Your ACT Test Results

Your scores, Composite score, and ranks provide a good indication of how well you did on the test, but you can interpret these scores on a deeper level to find out more about how well prepared you are to tackle a certain course of studies or pursue a specific career. In the following sections, we help you put your scores and ranks in perspective to make them more meaningful and relevant to your education and career planning.

How ACT Scores Your Multiple-Choice Tests

ACT scores the multiple-choice tests the same way you scored your ACT practice tests in chapters 3 and 11. The first step is to do exactly what you did for your practice tests: count the number of questions you answered correctly to determine your raw score. No points are deducted for incorrect answers.

The raw score is converted to a scale score to enhance score interpretation and allow comparability across different forms. Scale scores range from 1 (low) to 36 (high) for each of the four individual tests and for the Composite score.

How ACT Scores Your Writing Test

Two trained readers score each writing test based on the analytic rubric presented on pages 107–108. Each reader scores your essay on a scale from 1 (low) to 6 (high) on each domain. If their scores differ by more than 1 point on any of the four domains, a third reader scores your essay to resolve the discrepancy. This method is designed to be as impartial as possible. The writing score is calculated from your domain scores and is reported on a 2-to-12 scale.

Recognizing That Test Scores Are Estimates of Educational Achievement

No test, including the ACT, is an exact measure of your educational achievement. We estimate the amount of imprecision using the "standard error of measurement." On the ACT, the standard error of measurement (SEM) is 2 points for each of the multiple-choice tests, 1 point for the writing test, and 1 point for the Composite score.

Because no test score is an exact measure of your achievement, think of each of your ACT scores as a range of scores rather than as a precise number. The SEM can be used to estimate ranges for your scores. To do this, just add the SEM to, and subtract it from, each of your scores. For example, if your score on the English test is 22, your true achievement is likely in the score range of 20 to 24 (22 plus or minus 2 points). Beginning with the September 2020 national test date, students who have taken the ACT test more than once will have a Superscore calculated on their behalf by ACT. Superscoring allows students to utilize their highest individual section scores across all of their test events for ACT to calculate the best possible Composite score. Students will

Taking Additional Practice Tests

have the option to send an individual full battery Composite score or a Superscore to colleges or scholarship agencies.

Using Ranks to Interpret Your Scores

The US and state ranks for a score tell you how your scores compare to those earned by recent high school graduates who took the ACT. The numbers indicate the cumulative percent of students who scored at or below a given score. For example, if your rank is 63%, then 63% of recent high school graduates who took the ACT scored at or below your score.

Comparing Your Test Scores to Each Other

Another way to interpret your ACT test scores is by comparing them to each other using the ranks. You may find it interesting, for example, to compare your ranks for the science and mathematics tests to your ranks for the reading and English tests. Perhaps you felt more comfortable and successful in some subject areas than in others. Making comparisons among your ACT test ranks can be especially helpful as you make decisions about the courses you will take in high school and college. A high rank in a particular area indicates that you compare well to other ACT test-takers in that subject. A low rank may indicate that you need to develop your skills more in that area.

Keep in mind, however, that scale scores from the different individual tests can't be directly compared to each other. Scoring 23 on the ACT English and mathematics tests, for example, doesn't necessarily mean that your levels of skill and knowledge in English are the same as they are in mathematics. The percentile ranks corresponding to the scores—not the scores themselves—are probably best for making comparisons among subject areas.

Comparing Your Scores and Ranks to Your High School Grades

After you take the ACT and receive your student report, compare your scores and ranks to your high school grades. Are your highest grades and highest ACT test scores and ranks in the same content areas? If so, you might want to consider college majors that would draw on your areas of greatest strength or seek to improve your knowledge and skills in weaker subject areas. However, if your grades and scores differ significantly, talk with your counselor about possible reasons for the differences.

Comparing Your Scores to Those of Enrolled First-Year College Students

Another way to understand your ACT test scores and ranks is by comparing them to those of students enrolled at colleges or universities you're interested in attending. This information can be very useful as you make decisions about applying for college. Keep in mind that admissions offices use a number of measures—including high school grades, recommendations, and extracurricular activities—to determine how students are likely to perform at their schools. Still, knowing that your ACT test scores are similar to those of students already enrolled at a college or university you're considering may make you more confident in applying for admission there.

Using ACT College and Career Readiness Standards to Help You Understand Your ACT Scores

After you calculate your scores, you may wonder what your test scores mean regarding how well you are prepared to tackle college-level courses. In other words, what do your test scores tell you about your knowledge and skills in English, math, reading, and science? One way to understand this is to consider your scores from the perspective of what students who have that score are likely to know and be able to do. ACT developed the College and Career Readiness Standards to tell you exactly that.

What Are the ACT College and Career Readiness Standards?

The ACT College and Career Readiness Standards are sets of statements that describe what students are *likely* to know and be able to do in each content area based on their scores on each of the tests (English, mathematics, reading, science, and writing). The statements serve as score descriptors and reflect a progression of skills and knowledge in a particular content area. The College and Career Readiness Standards are reported in terms of score range, so that the statements describe the knowledge and skills that students *typically* demonstrate who score in these different ranges on the multiple-choice tests: 13–15, 16–19, 20–23, 24–27, 28–32, 33–36. A score of 1–12 indicates the student is most likely beginning to develop the knowledge and skills described in the 13–15 score range for that particular test. All the College and Career Readiness Standards are cumulative, meaning that students typically can also demonstrate the skills and knowledge described in the score ranges below the range in which they scored.

How Can the ACT College and Career Readiness Standards Help You?

The purpose of the ACT College and Career Readiness Standards is to help you and others better understand what your ACT scores indicate about the knowledge and skills you likely have and what areas might need further development for you to be better prepared for college.

Because the ACT College and Career Readiness Standards provide statements that describe what you are *likely* to know and be able to do, you can use that information to help zero in on what specific steps you should take to further develop your college readiness. If, for example, you scored in the 16–19 range on the English test, you might infer that you likely have the skills and knowledge described in the 13–15 and in the 16–19 range. You might choose to take a closer look at the standards in the 20–23 and higher score ranges to see what courses to take, or what instruction you might need, to develop those particular areas in order to be better prepared for college. In other words, you can use the ACT College and Career Readiness Standards to help you select courses and instruction that will focus on preparing you for college.

ACT College Readiness Benchmarks

ACT has identified the minimum score needed on each ACT test to indicate a 50% chance of obtaining a B or higher or about a 75% chance of obtaining a C or higher in the corresponding first-year college course. Your score report will have a visual representation of where you scored compared to the ACT College Readiness Benchmark.

ACT Test	ACT Benchmark Score	College Course
English	18	English Composition
Mathematics	22	Algebra
Reading	22	Social Sciences/Humanities
Science	23	Biology

To increase your college readiness, consider taking additional rigorous course work before you enter college. When you meet with your academic advisor to plan your first-year college courses, select courses that are appropriate for your academic background and reflect your planned curriculum.

Planning Your Education and Career

The *ACT Student Report* includes a College and Career Planning section that helps you explore college majors and occupations, consider your options, and develop plans. The information in this section is all about you. Majors and occupations you may want to explore have been listed here, because they are related to the interests you expressed or occupations you said you were considering.

Seeking Additional Information and Guidance

Your *ACT Student Report* will provide additional information to help you understand your ACT test results and use them to make important decisions about college and to explore possible future careers.

As you approach decisions about college and careers, be sure to take advantage of all the assistance you can find. Talk to your parents, counselors, and teachers; visit your local library; and talk directly to personnel at colleges in which you're interested. The more you can find out about all the educational options available to you and the level of your academic skills and knowledge (using such information as your ACT test results), the better prepared you'll be to make informed college and career choices.

ACT College and Career Readiness Standards—English

These standards describe what students who score in specific score ranges on the English test are likely to know and be able to do.

- Students who score in the 1–12 range are most likely beginning to develop the knowledge and skills assessed in the other ranges.

- The ACT College Readiness Benchmark for English is 18. Students who achieve this score on the ACT English test have a 50% likelihood of achieving a B or better in a first-year English composition course at a typical college. The knowledge and skills highly likely to be demonstrated by students who meet the benchmark are shaded.

Score Range	Production of Writing: Topic Development in Terms of Purpose and Focus (TOD)
13–15	TOD 201. Delete material because it is obviously irrelevant in terms of the topic of the essay
16–19	TOD 301. Delete material because it is obviously irrelevant in terms of the focus of the essay TOD 302. Identify the purpose of a word or phrase when the purpose is simple (e.g., identifying a person, defining a basic term, using common descriptive adjectives) TOD 303. Determine whether a simple essay has met a straightforward goal
20–23	TOD 401. Determine relevance of material in terms of the focus of the essay TOD 402. Identify the purpose of a word or phrase when the purpose is straightforward (e.g., describing a person, giving examples) TOD 403. Use a word, phrase, or sentence to accomplish a straightforward purpose (e.g., conveying a feeling or attitude)
24–27	TOD 501. Determine relevance of material in terms of the focus of the paragraph TOD 502. Identify the purpose of a word, phrase, or sentence when the purpose is fairly straightforward (e.g., identifying traits, giving reasons, explaining motivations) TOD 503. Determine whether an essay has met a specified goal TOD 504. Use a word, phrase, or sentence to accomplish a fairly straightforward purpose (e.g., sharpening an essay's focus, illustrating a given statement)

(continued)

Score Range	Production of Writing: Topic Development in Terms of Purpose and Focus (TOD) *(continued)*
28–32	TOD 601. Determine relevance when considering material that is plausible but potentially irrelevant at a given point in the essay TOD 602. Identify the purpose of a word, phrase, or sentence when the purpose is subtle (e.g., supporting a later point, establishing tone) or when the best decision is to delete the text in question TOD 603. Use a word, phrase, or sentence to accomplish a subtle purpose (e.g., adding emphasis or supporting detail, expressing meaning through connotation)
33–36	TOD 701. Identify the purpose of a word, phrase, or sentence when the purpose is complex (e.g., anticipating a reader's need for background information) or requires a thorough understanding of the paragraph and essay TOD 702. Determine whether a complex essay has met a specified goal TOD 703. Use a word, phrase, or sentence to accomplish a complex purpose, often in terms of the focus of the essay

Score Range	Production of Writing: Organization, Unity, and Cohesion (ORG)
13–15	ORG 201. Determine the need for transition words or phrases to establish time relationships in simple narrative essays (e.g., *then*, *this time*)
16–19	ORG 301. Determine the most logical place for a sentence in a paragraph ORG 302. Provide a simple conclusion to a paragraph or essay (e.g., expressing one of the essay's main ideas)
20–23	ORG 401. Determine the need for transition words or phrases to establish straightforward logical relationships (e.g., first, afterward, in response) ORG 402. Determine the most logical place for a sentence in a straightforward essay ORG 403. Provide an introduction to a straightforward paragraph ORG 404. Provide a straightforward conclusion to a paragraph or essay (e.g., summarizing an essay's main idea or ideas) ORG 405. Rearrange the sentences in a straightforward paragraph for the sake of logic

18

Score Range	Production of Writing: Organization, Unity, and Cohesion (ORG) *(continued)*
24–27	**ORG 501.** Determine the need for transition words or phrases to establish subtle logical relationships within and between sentences (e.g., *therefore*, *however*, *in addition*)
	ORG 502. Provide a fairly straightforward introduction or conclusion to or transition within a paragraph or essay (e.g., supporting or emphasizing an essay's main idea)
	ORG 503. Rearrange the sentences in a fairly straightforward paragraph for the sake of logic
	ORG 504. Determine the best place to divide a paragraph to meet a particular rhetorical goal
	ORG 505. Rearrange the paragraphs in an essay for the sake of logic
28–32	**ORG 601.** Determine the need for transition words or phrases to establish subtle logical relationships within and between paragraphs
	ORG 602. Determine the most logical place for a sentence in a fairly complex essay
	ORG 603. Provide a subtle introduction or conclusion to or transition within a paragraph or essay (e.g., echoing an essay's theme or restating the main argument)
	ORG 604. Rearrange the sentences in a fairly complex paragraph for the sake of logic and coherence
33–36	**ORG 701.** Determine the need for transition words or phrases, basing decisions on a thorough understanding of the paragraph and essay
	ORG 702. Provide a sophisticated introduction or conclusion to or transition within a paragraph or essay, basing decisions on a thorough understanding of the paragraph and essay (e.g., linking the conclusion to one of the essay's main images)

Score Range	Knowledge of Language (KLA)
13–15	**KLA 201.** Revise vague, clumsy, and confusing writing that creates obvious logic problems
16–19	**KLA 301.** Delete obviously redundant and wordy material **KLA 302.** Revise expressions that deviate markedly from the style and tone of the essay
20–23	**KLA 401.** Delete redundant and wordy material when the problem is contained within a single phrase (e.g., "alarmingly startled," "started by reaching the point of beginning") **KLA 402.** Revise expressions that deviate from the style and tone of the essay **KLA 403.** Determine the need for conjunctions to create straightforward logical links between clauses **KLA 404.** Use the word or phrase most appropriate in terms of the content of the sentence when the vocabulary is relatively common
24–27	**KLA 501.** Revise vague, clumsy, and confusing writing **KLA 502.** Delete redundant and wordy material when the meaning of the entire sentence must be considered **KLA 503.** Revise expressions that deviate in subtle ways from the style and tone of the essay **KLA 504.** Determine the need for conjunctions to create logical links between clauses **KLA 505.** Use the word or phrase most appropriate in terms of the content of the sentence when the vocabulary is uncommon
28–32	**KLA 601.** Revise vague, clumsy, and confusing writing involving sophisticated language **KLA 602.** Delete redundant and wordy material that involves fairly sophisticated language (e.g., "the outlook of an aesthetic viewpoint") or that sounds acceptable as conversational English **KLA 603.** Determine the need for conjunctions to create subtle logical links between clauses **KLA 604.** Use the word or phrase most appropriate in terms of the content of the sentence when the vocabulary is fairly sophisticated
33–36	**KLA 701.** Delete redundant and wordy material that involves sophisticated language or complex concepts or where the material is redundant in terms of the paragraph or essay as a whole **KLA 702.** Use the word or phrase most appropriate in terms of the content of the sentence when the vocabulary is sophisticated

18

Score Range	Conventions of Standard English: Sentence Structure and Formation (SST)
13–15	SST 201. Determine the need for punctuation or conjunctions to join simple clauses SST 202. Recognize and correct inappropriate shifts in verb tense between simple clauses in a sentence or between simple adjoining sentences
16–19	SST 301. Determine the need for punctuation or conjunctions to correct awkward-sounding fragments and fused sentences as well as obviously faulty subordination and coordination of clauses SST 302. Recognize and correct inappropriate shifts in verb tense and voice when the meaning of the entire sentence must be considered
20–23	SST 401. Recognize and correct marked disturbances in sentence structure (e.g., faulty placement of adjectives, participial phrase fragments, missing or incorrect relative pronouns, dangling or misplaced modifiers, lack of parallelism within a simple series of verbs)
24–27	SST 501. Recognize and correct disturbances in sentence structure (e.g., faulty placement of phrases, faulty coordination and subordination of clauses, lack of parallelism within a simple series of phrases) SST 502. Maintain consistent and logical verb tense and pronoun person on the basis of the preceding clause or sentence
28–32	SST 601. Recognize and correct subtle disturbances in sentence structure (e.g., danglers where the intended meaning is clear but the sentence is ungrammatical, faulty subordination and coordination of clauses in long or involved sentences) SST 602. Maintain consistent and logical verb tense and voice and pronoun person on the basis of the paragraph or essay as a whole
33–36	SST 701. Recognize and correct very subtle disturbances in sentence structure (e.g., weak conjunctions between independent clauses, run-ons that would be acceptable in conversational English, lack of parallelism within a complex series of phrases or clauses)

18

Taking Additional Practice Tests

Score Range	Conventions of Standard English: Usage Conventions (USG)
13–15	**USG 201.** Form the past tense and past participle of irregular but commonly used verbs **USG 202.** Form comparative and superlative adjectives
16–19	**USG 301.** Determine whether an adjective form or an adverb form is called for in a given situation **USG 302.** Ensure straightforward subject-verb agreement **USG 303.** Ensure straightforward pronoun-antecedent agreement **USG 304.** Use idiomatically appropriate prepositions in simple contexts **USG 305.** Use the appropriate word in frequently confused pairs (e.g., *there* and *their*, *past* and *passed*, *led* and *lead*)
20–23	**USG 401.** Use the correct comparative or superlative adjective or adverb form depending on context (e.g., "He is the oldest of my three brothers") **USG 402.** Ensure subject-verb agreement when there is some text between the subject and verb **USG 403.** Use idiomatically appropriate prepositions, especially in combination with verbs (e.g., *long for*, *appeal to*) **USG 404.** Recognize and correct expressions that deviate from idiomatic English
24–27	**USG 501.** Form simple and compound verb tenses, both regular and irregular, including forming verbs by using *have* rather than *of* (e.g., "would have gone," not "would of gone") **USG 502.** Ensure pronoun-antecedent agreement when the pronoun and antecedent occur in separate clauses or sentences **USG 503.** Recognize and correct vague and ambiguous pronouns
28–32	**USG 601.** Ensure subject-verb agreement in some challenging situations (e.g., when the subject-verb order is inverted or when the subject is an indefinite pronoun) **USG 602.** Correctly use reflexive pronouns, the possessive pronouns *its* and *your*, and the relative pronouns *who* and *whom* **USG 603.** Use the appropriate word in less-common confused pairs (e.g., *allude* and *elude*)
33–36	**USG 701.** Ensure subject-verb agreement when a phrase or clause between the subject and verb suggests a different number for the verb **USG 702.** Use idiomatically and contextually appropriate prepositions in combination with verbs in situations involving sophisticated language or complex concepts

18

Score Range	Conventions of Standard English: Punctuation Conventions (PUN)
13–15	PUN 201. Delete commas that create basic sense problems (e.g., between verb and direct object)
16–19	PUN 301. Delete commas that markedly disturb sentence flow (e.g., between modifier and modified element)
	PUN 302. Use appropriate punctuation in straightforward situations (e.g., simple items in a series)
20–23	PUN 401. Delete commas when an incorrect understanding of the sentence suggests a pause that should be punctuated (e.g., between verb and direct object clause)
	PUN 402. Delete apostrophes used incorrectly to form plural nouns
	PUN 403. Use commas to avoid obvious ambiguity (e.g., to set off a long introductory element from the rest of the sentence when a misreading is possible)
	PUN 404. Use commas to set off simple parenthetical elements
24–27	PUN 501. Delete commas in long or involved sentences when an incorrect understanding of the sentence suggests a pause that should be punctuated (e.g., between the elements of a compound subject or compound verb joined by *and*)
	PUN 502. Recognize and correct inappropriate uses of colons and semicolons
	PUN 503. Use punctuation to set off complex parenthetical elements
	PUN 504. Use apostrophes to form simple possessive nouns
28–32	PUN 601. Use commas to avoid ambiguity when the syntax or language is sophisticated (e.g., to set off a complex series of items)
	PUN 602. Use punctuation to set off a nonessential/nonrestrictive appositive or clause
	PUN 603. Use apostrophes to form possessives, including irregular plural nouns
	PUN 604. Use a semicolon to link closely related independent clauses
33–36	PUN 701. Delete punctuation around essential/restrictive appositives or clauses
	PUN 702. Use a colon to introduce an example or an elaboration

18

Taking Additional Practice Tests

ACT College and Career Readiness Standards—Mathematics

These standards describe what students who score in specific score ranges on the mathematics test are likely to know and be able to do.

- Students who score in the 1–12 range are most likely beginning to develop the knowledge and skills assessed in the other ranges.

- The ACT College Readiness Benchmark for mathematics is 22. Students who achieve this score on the ACT mathematics test have a 50% likelihood of achieving a B or better in a first-year college algebra course at a typical college. The knowledge and skills highly likely to be demonstrated by students who meet the benchmark are shaded.

Score Range	Number and Quantity (N)
13–15	N 201. Perform one-operation computation with whole numbers and decimals N 202. Recognize equivalent fractions and fractions in lowest terms N 203. Locate positive rational numbers (expressed as whole numbers, fractions, decimals, and mixed numbers) on the number line
16–19	N 301. Recognize one-digit factors of a number N 302. Identify a digit's place value N 303. Locate rational numbers on the number line Note: A matrix as a representation of data is treated here as a basic table.
20–23	N 401. Exhibit knowledge of elementary number concepts such as rounding, the ordering of decimals, pattern identification, primes, and greatest common factor N 402. Write positive powers of 10 by using exponents N 403. Comprehend the concept of length on the number line, and find the distance between two points N 404. Understand absolute value in terms of distance N 405. Find the distance in the coordinate plane between two points with the same x-coordinate or y-coordinate N 406. Add two matrices that have whole number entries
24–27	N 501. Order fractions N 502. Find and use the least common multiple N 503. Work with numerical factors N 504. Exhibit some knowledge of the complex numbers N 505. Add and subtract matrices that have integer entries

Score Range	Number and Quantity (N) (*continued*)
28–32	N 601. Apply number properties involving prime factorization
	N 602. Apply number properties involving even/odd numbers and factors/multiples
	N 603. Apply number properties involving positive/negative numbers
	N 604. Apply the facts that π is irrational and that the square root of an integer is rational only if that integer is a perfect square
	N 605. Apply properties of rational exponents
	N 606. Multiply two complex numbers
	N 607. Use relations involving addition, subtraction, and scalar multiplication of vectors and of matrices
33–36	N 701. Analyze and draw conclusions based on number concepts
	N 702. Apply properties of rational numbers and the rational number system
	N 703. Apply properties of real numbers and the real number system, including properties of irrational numbers
	N 704. Apply properties of complex numbers and the complex number system
	N 705. Multiply matrices
	N 706. Apply properties of matrices and properties of matrices as a number system

Because algebra and functions are closely connected, some standards apply to both categories.

Score Range	Algebra (A)	Functions (F)
13–15	AF 201. Solve problems in one or two steps using whole numbers and using decimals in the context of money	
	A 201. Exhibit knowledge of basic expressions (e.g., identify an expression for a total as $b + g$) A 202. Solve equations in the form $x + a = b$, where a and b are whole numbers or decimals	F 201. Extend a given pattern by a few terms for patterns that have a constant increase or decrease between terms
16–19	AF 301. Solve routine one-step arithmetic problems using positive rational numbers, such as single-step percent	
	AF 302. Solve some routine two-step arithmetic problems	
	AF 303. Relate a graph to a situation described qualitatively in terms of familiar properties such as before and after, increasing and decreasing, higher and lower	
	AF 304. Apply a definition of an operation for whole numbers (e.g., $a \bullet b = 3a - b$)	

(*continued*)

(continued)

Score Range	Algebra (A)	Functions (F)
	A 301. Substitute whole numbers for unknown quantities to evaluate expressions A 302. Solve one-step equations to get integer or decimal answers A 303. Combine like terms (e.g., $2x + 5x$)	F 301. Extend a given pattern by a few terms for patterns that have a constant factor between terms
20–23	AF 401. Solve routine two-step or three-step arithmetic problems involving concepts such as rate and proportion, tax added, percentage off, and estimating by using a given average value in place of actual values AF 402. Perform straightforward word-to-symbol translations AF 403. Relate a graph to a situation described in terms of a starting value and an additional amount per unit (e.g., unit cost, weekly growth)	
	A 401. Evaluate algebraic expressions by substituting integers for unknown quantities A 402. Add and subtract simple algebraic expressions A 403. Solve routine first-degree equations A 404. Multiply two binomials A 405. Match simple inequalities with their graphs on the number line (e.g., $x > -3$) A 406. Exhibit knowledge of slope	F 401. Evaluate linear and quadratic functions, expressed in function notation, at integer values
24–27	AF 501. Solve multistep arithmetic problems that involve planning or converting common derived units of measure (e.g., feet per second to miles per hour) AF 502. Build functions and write expressions, equations, or inequalities with a single variable for common pre-algebra settings (e.g., rate and distance problems and problems that can be solved by using proportions) AF 503. Match linear equations with their graphs in the coordinate plane	

Score Range	Algebra (A)	Functions (F)
	A 501. Recognize that when numerical quantities are reported in real-world contexts, the numbers are often rounded	F 501. Evaluate polynomial functions, expressed in function notation, at integer values
	A 502. Solve real-world problems by using first-degree equations	F 502. Find the next term in a sequence described recursively
	A 503. Solve first-degree inequalities when the method does not involve reversing the inequality sign	F 503. Build functions and use quantitative information to identify graphs for relations that are proportional or linear
	A 504. Match compound inequalities with their graphs on the number line (e.g., $-10.5 < x < 20.3$)	F 504. Attend to the difference between a function modeling a situation and the reality of the situation
	A 505. Add, subtract, and multiply polynomials	F 505. Understand the concept of a function as having a well-defined output value at each valid input value
	A 506. Identify solutions to simple quadratic equations	F 506. Understand the concept of domain and range in terms of valid input and output, and in terms of function graphs
	A 507. Solve quadratic equations in the form $(x + a)(x + b) = 0$, where a and b are numbers or variables	F 507. Interpret statements that use function notation in terms of their context
	A 508. Factor simple quadratics (e.g., the difference of squares and perfect square trinomials)	F 508. Find the domain of polynomial functions and rational functions
	A 509. Work with squares and square roots of numbers	F 509. Find the range of polynomial functions
	A 510. Work with cubes and cube roots of numbers	F 510. Find where a rational function's graph has a vertical asymptote
	A 511. Work with scientific notation	F 511. Use function notation for simple functions of two variables
	A 512. Work problems involving positive integer exponents	
	A 513. Determine when an expression is undefined	
	A 514. Determine the slope of a line from an equation	

(continued)

The ONLY Official Prep Guide from the Makers of the ACT

(continued)

Score Range	Algebra (A)	Functions (F)
28–32	AF 601. Solve word problems containing several rates, proportions, or percentages AF 602. Build functions and write expressions, equations, and inequalities for common algebra settings (e.g., distance to a point on a curve and profit for variable cost and demand) AF 603. Interpret and use information from graphs in the coordinate plane AF 604. Given an equation or function, find an equation or function whose graph is a translation by a specified amount up or down	
	A 601. Manipulate expressions and equations A 602. Solve linear inequalities when the method involves reversing the inequality sign A 603. Match linear inequalities with their graphs on the number line A 604. Solve systems of two linear equations A 605. Solve quadratic equations A 606. Solve absolute value equations	F 601. Relate a graph to a situation described qualitatively in terms of faster change or slower change F 602. Build functions for relations that are inversely proportional F 603. Find a recursive expression for the general term in a sequence described recursively F 604. Evaluate composite functions at integer values
33–36	AF 701. Solve complex arithmetic problems involving percent of increase or decrease or requiring integration of several concepts (e.g., using several ratios, comparing percentages, or comparing averages) AF 702. Build functions and write expressions, equations, and inequalities when the process requires planning and/or strategic manipulation AF 703. Analyze and draw conclusions based on properties of algebra and/or functions AF 704. Analyze and draw conclusions based on information from graphs in the coordinate plane AF 705. Identify characteristics of graphs based on a set of conditions or on a general equation such as $y = ax^2 + c$ AF 706. Given an equation or function, find an equation or function whose graph is a translation by specified amounts in the horizontal and vertical directions	

Score Range	Algebra (A)	Functions (F)
	A 701. Solve simple absolute value inequalities A 702. Match simple quadratic inequalities with their graphs on the number line A 703. Apply the remainder theorem for polynomials, that $P(a)$ is the remainder when $P(x)$ is divided by $(x - a)$	F 701. Compare actual values and the values of a modeling function to judge model fit and compare models F 702. Build functions for relations that are exponential F 703. Exhibit knowledge of geometric sequences F 704. Exhibit knowledge of unit circle trigonometry F 705. Match graphs of basic trigonometric functions with their equations F 706. Use trigonometric concepts and basic identities to solve problems F 707. Exhibit knowledge of logarithms F 708. Write an expression for the composite of two simple functions

Score Range	Geometry (G)
13–15	G 201. Estimate the length of a line segment based on other lengths in a geometric figure G 202. Calculate the length of a line segment based on the lengths of other line segments that go in the same direction (e.g., overlapping line segments and parallel sides of polygons with only right angles) G 203. Perform common conversions of money and of length, weight, mass, and time within a measurement system (e.g., dollars to dimes, inches to feet, and hours to minutes)
16–19	G 301. Exhibit some knowledge of the angles associated with parallel lines G 302. Compute the perimeter of polygons when all side lengths are given G 303. Compute the area of rectangles when whole number dimensions are given G 304. Locate points in the first quadrant

(continued)

Taking Additional Practice Tests

Score Range	Geometry (G) (*continued*)
20–23	**G 401.** Use properties of parallel lines to find the measure of an angle **G 402.** Exhibit knowledge of basic angle properties and special sums of angle measures (e.g., 90°, 180°, and 360°) **G 403.** Compute the area and perimeter of triangles and rectangles in simple problems **G 404.** Find the length of the hypotenuse of a right triangle when only very simple computation is involved (e.g., 3–4–5 and 6–8–10 triangles) **G 405.** Use geometric formulas when all necessary information is given **G 406.** Locate points in the coordinate plane **G 407.** Translate points up, down, left, and right in the coordinate plane
24–27	**G 501.** Use several angle properties to find an unknown angle measure **G 502.** Count the number of lines of symmetry of a geometric figure **G 503.** Use symmetry of isosceles triangles to find unknown side lengths or angle measures **G 504.** Recognize that real-world measurements are typically imprecise and that an appropriate level of precision is related to the measuring device and procedure **G 505.** Compute the perimeter of simple composite geometric figures with unknown side lengths **G 506.** Compute the area of triangles and rectangles when one or more additional simple steps are required **G 507.** Compute the area and circumference of circles after identifying necessary information **G 508.** Given the length of two sides of a right triangle, find the third when the lengths are Pythagorean triples **G 509.** Express the sine, cosine, and tangent of an angle in a right triangle as a ratio of given side lengths **G 510.** Determine the slope of a line from points or a graph **G 511.** Find the midpoint of a line segment **G 512.** Find the coordinates of a point rotated 180° around a given center point

22

Score Range	Geometry (G) (*continued*)
28–32	G 601. Use relationships involving area, perimeter, and volume of geometric figures to compute another measure (e.g., surface area for a cube of a given volume and simple geometric probability)
	G 602. Use the Pythagorean theorem
	G 603. Apply properties of 30°–60°–90°, 45°–45°–90°, similar, and congruent triangles
	G 604. Apply basic trigonometric ratios to solve right-triangle problems
	G 605. Use the distance formula
	G 606. Use properties of parallel and perpendicular lines to determine an equation of a line or coordinates of a point
	G 607. Find the coordinates of a point reflected across a vertical or horizontal line or across $y = x$
	G 608. Find the coordinates of a point rotated 90° about the origin
	G 609. Recognize special characteristics of parabolas and circles (e.g., the vertex of a parabola and the center or radius of a circle)
33–36	G 701. Use relationships among angles, arcs, and distances in a circle
	G 702. Compute the area of composite geometric figures when planning and/or visualization is required
	G 703. Use scale factors to determine the magnitude of a size change
	G 704. Analyze and draw conclusions based on a set of conditions
	G 705. Solve multistep geometry problems that involve integrating concepts, planning, and/or visualization

Score Range	Statistics and Probability (S)
13–15	S 201. Calculate the average of a list of positive whole numbers
	S 202. Extract one relevant number from a basic table or chart, and use it in a single computation
16–19	S 301. Calculate the average of a list of numbers
	S 302. Calculate the average given the number of data values and the sum of the data values
	S 303. Read basic tables and charts
	S 304. Extract relevant data from a basic table or chart and use the data in a computation
	S 305. Use the relationship between the probability of an event and the probability of its complement

(continued)

Taking Additional Practice Tests

Score Range	Statistics and Probability (S) (*continued*)
20–23	S 401. Calculate the missing data value given the average and all data values but one
	S 402. Translate from one representation of data to another (e.g., a bar graph to a circle graph)
	S 403. Determine the probability of a simple event
	S 404. Describe events as combinations of other events (e.g., using *and*, *or*, and *not*)
	S 405. Exhibit knowledge of simple counting techniques
24–27	S 501. Calculate the average given the frequency counts of all the data values
	S 502. Manipulate data from tables and charts
	S 503. Compute straightforward probabilities for common situations
	S 504. Use Venn diagrams in counting
	S 505. Recognize that when data summaries are reported in the real world, results are often rounded and must be interpreted as having appropriate precision
	S 506. Recognize that when a statistical model is used, model values typically differ from actual values
28–32	S 601. Calculate or use a weighted average
	S 602. Interpret and use information from tables and charts, including two-way frequency tables
	S 603. Apply counting techniques
	S 604. Compute a probability when the event and/or sample space are not given or obvious
	S 605. Recognize the concepts of conditional and joint probability expressed in real-world contexts
	S 606. Recognize the concept of independence expressed in real-world contexts
33–36	S 701. Distinguish among mean, median, and mode for a list of numbers
	S 702. Analyze and draw conclusions based on information from tables and charts, including two-way frequency tables
	S 703. Understand the role of randomization in surveys, experiments, and observational studies
	S 704. Exhibit knowledge of conditional and joint probability
	S 705. Recognize that part of the power of statistical modeling comes from looking at regularity in the differences between actual values and model values

ACT College and Career Readiness Standards—Reading

These standards describe what students who score in specific score ranges on the reading test are likely to know and be able to do.

- Students who score in the 1–12 range are most likely beginning to develop the knowledge and skills assessed in the other ranges.

- The ACT College Readiness Benchmark for reading is 22. Students who achieve this score on the ACT reading test have a 50% likelihood of achieving a B or better in a first-year social science course at a typical college. The knowledge and skills highly likely to be demonstrated by students who meet the benchmark are shaded.

Score Range	Key Ideas and Details: Close Reading (CLR)
13–15	CLR 201. Locate basic facts (e.g., names, dates, events) clearly stated in a passage
	CLR 202. Draw simple logical conclusions about the main characters in somewhat challenging literary narratives
16–19	CLR 301. Locate simple details at the sentence and paragraph level in somewhat challenging passages
	CLR 302. Draw simple logical conclusions in somewhat challenging passages
20–23	CLR 401. Locate important details in somewhat challenging passages
	CLR 402. Draw logical conclusions in somewhat challenging passages
	CLR 403. Draw simple logical conclusions in more challenging passages
	CLR 404. Paraphrase some statements as they are used in somewhat challenging passages
24–27	CLR 501. Locate and interpret minor or subtly stated details in somewhat challenging passages
	CLR 502. Locate important details in more challenging passages
	CLR 503. Draw subtle logical conclusions in somewhat challenging passages
	CLR 504. Draw logical conclusions in more challenging passages
	CLR 505. Paraphrase virtually any statement as it is used in somewhat challenging passages
	CLR 506. Paraphrase some statements as they are used in more challenging passages

22

(continued)

The ONLY Official Prep Guide from the Makers of the ACT

Score Range	Key Ideas and Details: Close Reading (CLR) *(continued)*
28–32	CLR 601. Locate and interpret minor or subtly stated details in more challenging passages CLR 602. Locate important details in complex passages CLR 603. Draw subtle logical conclusions in more challenging passages CLR 604. Draw simple logical conclusions in complex passages CLR 605. Paraphrase virtually any statement as it is used in more challenging passages
33–36	CLR 701. Locate and interpret minor or subtly stated details in complex passages CLR 702. Locate important details in highly complex passages CLR 703. Draw logical conclusions in complex passages CLR 704. Draw simple logical conclusions in highly complex passages CLR 705. Draw complex or subtle logical conclusions, often by synthesizing information from different portions of the passage CLR 706. Paraphrase statements as they are used in complex passages

Score Range	Key Ideas and Details: Central Ideas, Themes, and Summaries (IDT)
13–15	IDT 201. Identify the topic of passages and distinguish the topic from the central idea or theme
16–19	IDT 301. Identify a clear central idea in straightforward paragraphs in somewhat challenging literary narratives
20–23	IDT 401. Infer a central idea in straightforward paragraphs in somewhat challenging literary narratives IDT 402. Identify a clear central idea or theme in somewhat challenging passages or their paragraphs IDT 403. Summarize key supporting ideas and details in somewhat challenging passages
24–27	IDT 501. Infer a central idea or theme in somewhat challenging passages or their paragraphs IDT 502. Identify a clear central idea or theme in more challenging passages or their paragraphs IDT 503. Summarize key supporting ideas and details in more challenging passages

22

Score Range	Key Ideas and Details: Central Ideas, Themes, and Summaries (IDT) (*continued*)
28–32	IDT 601. Infer a central idea or theme in more challenging passages or their paragraphs
	IDT 602. Summarize key supporting ideas and details in complex passages
33–36	IDT 701. Identify or infer a central idea or theme in complex passages or their paragraphs
	IDT 702. Summarize key supporting ideas and details in highly complex passages

Score Range	Key Ideas and Details: Relationships (REL)
13–15	REL 201. Determine when (e.g., *first, last, before, after*) an event occurs in somewhat challenging passages
	REL 202. Identify simple cause-effect relationships within a single sentence in a passage
16–19	REL 301. Identify clear comparative relationships between main characters in somewhat challenging literary narratives
	REL 302. Identify simple cause-effect relationships within a single paragraph in somewhat challenging literary narratives
20–23	REL 401. Order simple sequences of events in somewhat challenging literary narratives
	REL 402. Identify clear comparative relationships in somewhat challenging passages
	REL 403. Identify clear cause-effect relationships in somewhat challenging passages
24–27	REL 501. Order sequences of events in somewhat challenging passages
	REL 502. Understand implied or subtly stated comparative relationships in somewhat challenging passages
	REL 503. Identify clear comparative relationships in more challenging passages
	REL 504. Understand implied or subtly stated cause-effect relationships in somewhat challenging passages
	REL 505. Identify clear cause-effect relationships in more challenging passages

(continued)

22

Score Range	Key Ideas and Details: Relationships (REL) (*continued*)
28–32	REL 601. Order sequences of events in more challenging passages REL 602. Understand implied or subtly stated comparative relationships in more challenging passages REL 603. Identify clear comparative relationships in complex passages REL 604. Understand implied or subtly stated cause-effect relationships in more challenging passages REL 605. Identify clear cause-effect relationships in complex passages
33–36	REL 701. Order sequences of events in complex passages REL 702. Understand implied or subtly stated comparative relationships in complex passages REL 703. Identify clear comparative relationships in highly complex passages REL 704. Understand implied or subtly stated cause-effect relationships in complex passages REL 705. Identify clear cause-effect relationships in highly complex passages

Score Range	Craft and Structure: Word Meanings and Word Choice (WME)
13–15	WME 201. Understand the implication of a familiar word or phrase and of simple descriptive language
16–19	WME 301. Analyze how the choice of a specific word or phrase shapes meaning or tone in somewhat challenging passages when the effect is simple WME 302. Interpret basic figurative language as it is used in a passage
20–23	WME 401. Analyze how the choice of a specific word or phrase shapes meaning or tone in somewhat challenging passages WME 402. Interpret most words and phrases as they are used in somewhat challenging passages, including determining technical, connotative, and figurative meanings

22

Score Range	Craft and Structure: Word Meanings and Word Choice (WME) (*continued*)
24–27	WME 501. Analyze how the choice of a specific word or phrase shapes meaning or tone in somewhat challenging passages when the effect is subtle
	WME 502. Analyze how the choice of a specific word or phrase shapes meaning or tone in more challenging passages
	WME 503. Interpret virtually any word or phrase as it is used in somewhat challenging passages, including determining technical, connotative, and figurative meanings
	WME 504. Interpret most words and phrases as they are used in more challenging passages, including determining technical, connotative, and figurative meanings
28–32	WME 601. Analyze how the choice of a specific word or phrase shapes meaning or tone in complex passages
	WME 602. Interpret virtually any word or phrase as it is used in more challenging passages, including determining technical, connotative, and figurative meanings
	WME 603. Interpret words and phrases in a passage that makes consistent use of figurative, general academic, domain-specific, or otherwise difficult language
33–36	WME 701. Analyze how the choice of a specific word or phrase shapes meaning or tone in passages when the effect is subtle or complex
	WME 702. Interpret words and phrases as they are used in complex passages, including determining technical, connotative, and figurative meanings
	WME 703. Interpret words and phrases in a passage that makes extensive use of figurative, general academic, domain-specific, or otherwise difficult language

Score Range	Craft and Structure: Text Structure (TST)
13–15	TST 201. Analyze how one or more sentences in passages relate to the whole passage when the function is stated or clearly indicated
16–19	TST 301. Analyze how one or more sentences in somewhat challenging passages relate to the whole passage when the function is simple
	TST 302. Identify a clear function of straightforward paragraphs in somewhat challenging literary narratives

(continued)

Taking Additional Practice Tests

Score Range	Craft and Structure: Text Structure (TST) (*continued*)
20–23	TST 401. Analyze how one or more sentences in somewhat challenging passages relate to the whole passage TST 402. Infer the function of straightforward paragraphs in somewhat challenging literary narratives TST 403. Identify a clear function of paragraphs in somewhat challenging passages TST 404. Analyze the overall structure of somewhat challenging passages
24–27	TST 501. Analyze how one or more sentences in somewhat challenging passages relate to the whole passage when the function is subtle TST 502. Analyze how one or more sentences in more challenging passages relate to the whole passage TST 503. Infer the function of paragraphs in somewhat challenging passages TST 504. Identify a clear function of paragraphs in more challenging passages TST 505. Analyze the overall structure of more challenging passages
28–32	TST 601. Analyze how one or more sentences in complex passages relate to the whole passage TST 602. Infer the function of paragraphs in more challenging passages TST 603. Analyze the overall structure of complex passages
33–36	TST 701. Analyze how one or more sentences in passages relate to the whole passage when the function is subtle or complex TST 702. Identify or infer the function of paragraphs in complex passages TST 703. Analyze the overall structure of highly complex passages

Score Range	Craft and Structure: Purpose and Point of View (PPV)
13–15	PPV 201. Recognize a clear intent of an author or narrator in somewhat challenging literary narratives
16–19	PPV 301. Recognize a clear intent of an author or narrator in somewhat challenging passages
20–23	PPV 401. Identify a clear purpose of somewhat challenging passages and how that purpose shapes content and style PPV 402. Understand point of view in somewhat challenging passages

Score Range	Craft and Structure: Purpose and Point of View (PPV) *(continued)*
24–27	PPV 501. Infer a purpose in somewhat challenging passages and how that purpose shapes content and style PPV 502. Identify a clear purpose of more challenging passages and how that purpose shapes content and style PPV 503. Understand point of view in more challenging passages
28–32	PPV 601. Infer a purpose in more challenging passages and how that purpose shapes content and style PPV 602. Understand point of view in complex passages
33–36	PPV 701. Identify or infer a purpose in complex passages and how that purpose shapes content and style PPV 702. Understand point of view in highly complex passages

Score Range	Integration of Knowledge and Ideas: Arguments (ARG)
13–15	ARG 201. Analyze how one or more sentences in passages offer reasons for or support a claim when the relationship is clearly indicated
16–19	ARG 301. Analyze how one or more sentences in somewhat challenging passages offer reasons for or support a claim when the relationship is simple
20–23	ARG 401. Analyze how one or more sentences in somewhat challenging passages offer reasons for or support a claim ARG 402. Identify a clear central claim in somewhat challenging passages
24–27	ARG 501. Analyze how one or more sentences in more challenging passages offer reasons for or support a claim ARG 502. Infer a central claim in somewhat challenging passages ARG 503. Identify a clear central claim in more challenging passages
28–32	ARG 601. Analyze how one or more sentences in complex passages offer reasons for or support a claim ARG 602. Infer a central claim in more challenging passages
33–36	ARG 701. Analyze how one or more sentences in passages offer reasons for or support a claim when the relationship is subtle or complex ARG 702. Identify or infer a central claim in complex passages ARG 703. Identify a clear central claim in highly complex passages

Score Range	Integration of Knowledge and Ideas: Multiple Texts (SYN)
13–15	SYN 201. Make simple comparisons between two passages
16–19	SYN 301. Make straightforward comparisons between two passages
20–23	SYN 401. Draw logical conclusions using information from two literary narratives
24–27	SYN 501. Draw logical conclusions using information from two informational texts
28–32	SYN 601. Draw logical conclusions using information from multiple portions of two literary narratives
33–36	SYN 701. Draw logical conclusions using information from multiple portions of two informational texts

Text Complexity Rubric—Reading

This rubric describes reading passages for ACT® Aspire® Grade 8, ACT® Aspire® Early High School, and the ACT.

Literary Narratives: Stories and Literary Nonfiction

	Somewhat Challenging Literary Narratives	More Challenging Literary Narratives	Complex Literary Narratives	Highly Complex Literary Narratives
Purpose/Levels of Meaning	• Have a largely straightforward purpose (chiefly literary nonfiction) • Contain literal and inferential levels of meaning (chiefly stories)	• Have a largely straightforward to somewhat complex purpose (chiefly literary nonfiction) • Contain literal, inferential, and interpretive levels of meaning (chiefly stories)	• Have a somewhat complex to complex purpose; apparent purpose may differ from real purpose (chiefly literary nonfiction) • Contain literal, inferential, and interpretive levels of meaning (chiefly stories)	• Have a complex purpose; apparent purpose may differ from real purpose (chiefly literary nonfiction) • Contain literal, inferential, and interpretive levels of meaning (chiefly stories)

	Somewhat Challenging Literary Narratives	More Challenging Literary Narratives	Complex Literary Narratives	Highly Complex Literary Narratives
Structure	• Use a mostly straightforward structure and a wide range of transitions (chiefly literary nonfiction) • Offer insights into people, situations, and events (e.g., motives) • May contain subplots, flashbacks, and flash-forwards (chiefly stories) • Explore largely straightforward conflicts that may be internal or external (chiefly stories) • May have multiple narrators, with switches clearly signaled; main characters exhibit growth and change (chiefly stories)	• Use a somewhat complex structure and a full range of transitions (chiefly literary nonfiction) • Offer deep insights into people, situations, and events (e.g., motives in conflict) • May contain numerous subplots, flashbacks, and flash-forwards as well as parallel and nonlinear plots; may lack clear resolution (chiefly stories) • Explore subtle conflicts that may be internal or external (chiefly stories) • May have multiple narrators; main characters are well rounded (chiefly stories)	• Use a complex structure (chiefly literary nonfiction) • Offer sophisticated and profound insights into people, situations, and events (e.g., philosophical commentary) • May contain numerous subplots, flashbacks, and flash-forwards as well as parallel and nonlinear plots; may lack clear resolution (chiefly stories) • Explore complex conflicts that are largely internal and lack an obvious or easy resolution (e.g., moral dilemmas) (chiefly stories) • May have multiple and/or unreliable narrator(s); main characters are well rounded (chiefly stories)	• Use a highly complex structure (chiefly literary nonfiction) • Offer sophisticated and profound insights into people, situations, and events (e.g., philosophical commentary) • Contain plots that are intricate, nonlinear, and/or difficult to discern; may lack resolution or may not be plot driven (chiefly stories) • Explore complex conflicts that are largely internal and lack an obvious or easy resolution (e.g., moral dilemmas) (chiefly stories) • May have multiple and/or unreliable narrator(s); main characters are well rounded (chiefly stories)

(continued)

Taking Additional Practice Tests

The ONLY Official Prep Guide from the Makers of the ACT

(continued)

	Somewhat Challenging Literary Narratives	**More Challenging Literary Narratives**	**Complex Literary Narratives**	**Highly Complex Literary Narratives**
Language	• Use some uncommon words and phrases (e.g., general academic [tier 2] words, archaic words, dialect) • Use varied sentence structures significantly more or less formal than in everyday language • Use some somewhat challenging nonliteral and figurative language and literary devices (e.g., symbols, irony) • Observe language conventions (e.g., standard paragraph breaks) (chiefly stories)	• Use some uncommon words and phrases (e.g., general academic [tier 2] words, archaic words, dialect) • Use varied, often complex, and formal sentence structures, with texts from earlier time periods containing structures uncommon in more modern reading • Consistently use somewhat challenging nonliteral and figurative language and literary devices (e.g., symbols, irony) • Largely observe language conventions, with some unconventional elements possible (e.g., dialogue marked with dashes) (chiefly stories)	• Consistently use uncommon words and phrases (e.g., general academic [tier 2] words, archaic words, dialect) • Use varied, often complex, and formal sentence structures, with texts from earlier time periods containing structures uncommon in more modern reading • Consistently use challenging nonliteral and figurative language and literary devices (e.g., extended metaphors, satire, parody) • May use unconventional language structures (e.g., stream-of-consciousness)	• Extensively use uncommon words and phrases (e.g., general academic [tier 2] words, archaic words, dialect) • Use varied, often complex, and formal sentence structures, with texts from earlier time periods containing structures uncommon in more modern reading • Extensively use challenging nonliteral and figurative language and literary devices (e.g., extended metaphors, satire, parody) • Use unconventional language structures (e.g., stream-of-consciousness)

	Somewhat Challenging Literary Narratives	More Challenging Literary Narratives	Complex Literary Narratives	Highly Complex Literary Narratives
Abstractness (chiefly literary nonfiction)	• Depict some abstract ideas and concepts that may be important to understanding the text	• Depict several abstract ideas and concepts that are essential to understanding the text	• Depict numerous abstract ideas and concepts that are essential to understanding the text	• Depict numerous abstract ideas and concepts that are essential to understanding the text
Density (chiefly literary nonfiction)	• Have moderate information/ concept density	• Have moderately high information/ concept density	• Have high information/ concept density	• Have very high information/ concept density
Knowledge Demands: Textual Analysis, Life Experiences, Cultural and Literary Knowledge	• Assume readers can read on literal and inferential levels • Assume readers can handle somewhat challenging themes and subject matter with some maturity and objectivity • Assume readers can relate to experiences outside of their own • Call on cultural or literary knowledge to some extent	• Assume readers can read on literal, inferential, and interpretive levels • Assume readers can handle somewhat challenging themes and subject matter with some maturity and objectivity • Assume readers can relate to experiences distinctly different from their own	• Assume readers can read on literal, inferential, and interpretive levels • Assume readers can handle challenging themes and subject matter with maturity and objectivity • Assume readers can relate to experiences distinctly different from their own • Call on cultural or literary knowledge to some extent	• Assume readers can read on literal, inferential, and interpretive levels • Assume readers can handle complex themes and subject matter with maturity and objectivity • Assume readers can relate to experiences distinctly different from their own • Require cultural or literary knowledge for full comprehension

(continued)

(continued)

	Somewhat Challenging Literary Narratives	More Challenging Literary Narratives	Complex Literary Narratives	Highly Complex Literary Narratives
	• Have low intertextuality (i.e., make no/few or unimportant connections to other texts); drawing connections between texts at the level of theme may enhance understanding and appreciation	• Call on cultural or literary knowledge to some extent • Have moderate intertextuality (i.e., make some important connections to other texts); drawing connections between texts may enhance understanding and appreciation	• Have moderate intertextuality (i.e., make some important connections to other texts); drawing connections between texts may enhance understanding and appreciation	• Have high intertextuality (i.e., make many important connections to other texts); drawing connections between texts is essential for full understanding and appreciation

Informational Texts: Social Science, Humanities, and Natural Science

	Somewhat Challenging Informational Texts	More Challenging Informational Texts	Complex Informational Texts	Highly Complex Informational Texts
Purpose	• Have a largely straightforward purpose	• Have a largely straightforward to somewhat complex purpose	• Have a somewhat complex to complex purpose; apparent purpose may differ from real purpose	• Have a complex purpose; apparent purpose may differ from real purpose

	Somewhat Challenging Informational Texts	More Challenging Informational Texts	Complex Informational Texts	Highly Complex Informational Texts
Structure	• Use a mostly straightforward structure and a wide range of transitions • Exhibit norms and conventions of a general discipline (e.g., natural science)	• Use a somewhat complex structure and a full range of transitions • Exhibit norms and conventions of a general discipline (e.g., natural science	• Use a complex structure • Exhibit norms and conventions of a general discipline (e.g., natural science)	• Use a highly complex and possibly highly formalized structure (e.g., journal article) • Exhibit norms and conventions of a specific discipline (e.g., biology)
Language	• Use some general academic [tier 2] and domain-specific [tier 3] words and phrases • Use varied and some long and complicated sentence structures	• Consistently use general academic [tier 2] and domain-specific [tier 3] words and phrases • Use varied and often complex sentence structures, with consistent use of long and complicated structures	• Consistently use general academic [tier 2] and domain-specific [tier 3] words and phrases • Use varied and often complex sentence structures, with consistent use of long and complicated structures	• Extensively use general academic [tier 2] and domain-specific [tier 3] words and phrases • Use varied and often complex sentence structures, with consistent use of long and complicated structures
Abstractness	• Depict some abstract ideas and concepts that may be important to understanding the text	• Depict several abstract ideas and concepts that are essential to understanding the text	• Depict numerous abstract ideas and concepts that are essential to understanding the text	• Depict numerous abstract ideas and concepts that are essential to understanding the text
Density	• Have moderate information/concept density	• Have moderately high information/concept density	• Have high information/concept density	• Have very high information/concept density

(*continued*)

Taking Additional Practice Tests

(continued)

	Somewhat Challenging Informational Texts	More Challenging Informational Texts	Complex Informational Texts	Highly Complex Informational Texts
Knowledge Demands: Textual Analysis, Life Experiences, Content and Discipline Knowledge	• Assume readers can read on literal and inferential levels • Assume readers can handle somewhat challenging subject matter, including perspectives, values, and ideas unlike their own, with some maturity and objectivity • Assume readers have everyday knowledge and some broad content knowledge, with texts at the high end of the range assuming some content knowledge • Have low intertextuality (i.e., make no/few or unimportant connections to other texts); drawing connections between texts at the level of general concept may enhance understanding	• Assume readers can read on literal, inferential, and evaluative levels • Assume readers can handle somewhat challenging subject matter, including perspectives, values, and ideas unlike their own, with some maturity and objectivity • Assume readers have some content knowledge, with texts at the high end of the range assuming some discipline-specific content knowledge • Have moderate intertextuality (i.e., make some important connections to other texts); drawing connections between texts may enhance understanding	• Assume readers can read on literal, inferential, and evaluative levels • Assume readers can handle challenging subject matter, including perspectives, values, and ideas in opposition to their own, with maturity and objectivity • Assume readers have some discipline-specific content knowledge • Have moderate intertextuality (i.e., make some important connections to other texts); drawing connections between texts may enhance understanding	• Assume readers can read on literal, inferential, and evaluative levels • Assume readers can handle complex subject matter, including perspectives, values, and ideas in opposition to their own, with maturity and objectivity • Assume readers have extensive discipline-specific content knowledge, often in specialized subjects or areas • Have high intertextuality (i.e., make many important connections to other texts); drawing connections between texts is essential for full understanding

ACT College and Career Readiness Standards—Science

These standards describe what students who score in specific score ranges on the science test are likely to know and be able to do.

- Students who score in the 1–12 range are most likely beginning to develop the knowledge and skills assessed in the other ranges.

- The ACT College Readiness Benchmark for science is 23. Students who achieve this score on the ACT science test have a 50% likelihood of achieving a B or better in a first-year biology course at a typical college. The knowledge and skills highly likely to be demonstrated by students who meet the benchmark are shaded.

Score Range	Interpretation of Data (IOD)
13–15	**IOD 201.** Select one piece of data from a simple data presentation (e.g., a simple food web diagram)
	IOD 202. Identify basic features of a table, graph, or diagram (e.g., units of measurement)
	IOD 203. Find basic information in text that describes a simple data presentation
16–19	**IOD 301.** Select two or more pieces of data from a simple data presentation
	IOD 302. Understand basic scientific terminology
	IOD 303. Find basic information in text that describes a complex data presentation
	IOD 304. Determine how the values of variables change as the value of another variable changes in a simple data presentation
20–23	**IOD 401.** Select data from a complex data presentation (e.g., a phase diagram)
	IOD 402. Compare or combine data from a simple data presentation (e.g., order or sum data from a table)
	IOD 403. Translate information into a table, graph, or diagram
	IOD 404. Perform a simple interpolation or simple extrapolation using data in a table or graph
24–27	**IOD 501.** Compare or combine data from two or more simple data presentations (e.g., categorize data from a table using a scale from another table)
	IOD 502. Compare or combine data from a complex data presentation
	IOD 503. Determine how the values of variables change as the value of another variable changes in a complex data presentation
	IOD 504. Determine and/or use a simple (e.g., linear) mathematical relationship that exists between data
	IOD 505. Analyze presented information when given new, simple information

(continued)

Taking Additional Practice Tests

Score Range	Interpretation of Data (IOD) (*continued*)
28–32	IOD 601. Compare or combine data from a simple data presentation with data from a complex data presentation
	IOD 602. Determine and/or use a complex (e.g., nonlinear) mathematical relationship that exists between data
	IOD 603. Perform a complex interpolation or complex extrapolation using data in a table or graph
33–36	IOD 701. Compare or combine data from two or more complex data presentations
	IOD 702. Analyze presented information when given new, complex information

Score Range	Scientific Investigation (SIN)
13–15	SIN 201. Find basic information in text that describes a simple experiment
	SIN 202. Understand the tools and functions of tools used in a simple experiment
16–19	SIN 301. Understand the methods used in a simple experiment
	SIN 302. Understand the tools and functions of tools used in a complex experiment
	SIN 303. Find basic information in text that describes a complex experiment
20–23	SIN 401. Understand a simple experimental design
	SIN 402. Understand the methods used in a complex experiment
	SIN 403. Identify a control in an experiment
	SIN 404. Identify similarities and differences between experiments
	SIN 405. Determine which experiments used a given tool, method, or aspect of design
24–27	SIN 501. Understand a complex experimental design
	SIN 502. Predict the results of an additional trial or measurement in an experiment
	SIN 503. Determine the experimental conditions that would produce specified results
28–32	SIN 601. Determine the hypothesis for an experiment
	SIN 602. Determine an alternate method for testing a hypothesis
33–36	SIN 701. Understand precision and accuracy issues
	SIN 702. Predict the effects of modifying the design or methods of an experiment
	SIN 703. Determine which additional trial or experiment could be performed to enhance or evaluate experimental results

23

Score Range	Evaluation of Models, Inferences, and Experimental Results (EMI)
13–15	EMI 201. Find basic information in a model (conceptual)
16–19	EMI 301. Identify implications in a model EMI 302. Determine which models present certain basic information
20–23	EMI 401. Determine which simple hypothesis, prediction, or conclusion is, or is not, consistent with a data presentation, model, or piece of information in text EMI 402. Identify key assumptions in a model EMI 403. Determine which models imply certain information EMI 404. Identify similarities and differences between models
24–27	EMI 501. Determine which simple hypothesis, prediction, or conclusion is, or is not, consistent with two or more data presentations, models, and/or pieces of information in text EMI 502. Determine whether presented information, or new information, supports or contradicts a simple hypothesis or conclusion, and why EMI 503. Identify the strengths and weaknesses of models EMI 504. Determine which models are supported or weakened by new information EMI 505. Determine which experimental results or models support or contradict a hypothesis, prediction, or conclusion
28–32	EMI 601. Determine which complex hypothesis, prediction, or conclusion is, or is not, consistent with a data presentation, model, or piece of information in text EMI 602. Determine whether presented information, or new information, supports or weakens a model, and why EMI 603. Use new information to make a prediction based on a model
33–36	EMI 701. Determine which complex hypothesis, prediction, or conclusion is, or is not, consistent with two or more data presentations, models, and/or pieces of information in text EMI 702. Determine whether presented information, or new information, supports or contradicts a complex hypothesis or conclusion, and why

Taking Additional Practice Tests

ACT College and Career Readiness Standards for science are measured in rich and authentic contexts based on science content that students encounter in science courses. This content includes the following:

Life Science/Biology

- Animal behavior
- Animal development and growth
- Body systems
- Cell structure and processes
- Ecology
- Evolution
- Genetics
- Homeostasis
- Life cycles
- Molecular basis of heredity
- Origin of life
- Photosynthesis
- Plant development, growth, structure
- Populations
- Taxonomy

Physical Science/Chemistry, Physics

- Atomic structure
- Chemical bonding, equations, nomenclature, reactions
- Electrical circuits
- Elements, compounds, mixtures
- Force and motions
- Gravitation
- Heat and work
- Kinetic and potential energy
- Magnetism
- Momentum
- The periodic table
- Properties of solutions
- Sound and light
- States, classes, and properties of matter
- Waves

Earth and Space Science

- Earthquakes and volcanoes
- Earth's atmosphere
- Earth's resources
- Fossils and geological time
- Geochemical cycles
- Groundwater
- Lakes, rivers, oceans
- Mass movements
- Plate tectonics
- Rocks, minerals
- Solar system
- Stars, galaxies, and the universe
- Water cycle
- Weather and climate
- Weathering and erosion

ACT College & Career Readiness Standards
Writing

These Standards describe what students who score in specific score ranges on the writing section of the ACT® college readiness assessment are likely to know and be able to do.

SCORE RANGE	Ideas and Analysis (I&A)
3–4	**I&A 201.** Understanding the task and writing with purpose A score in this range indicates that the writer is able to: — Generate a thesis that is unclear or not entirely related to the given issue — Respond weakly to other perspectives on the issue **I&A 202.** Analyzing critical elements of an issue and differing perspectives on it A score in this range indicates that the writer is able to: — Provide analysis that is incomplete or largely irrelevant
5–6	**I&A 301.** Understanding the task and writing with purpose A score in this range indicates that the writer is able to: — Generate a somewhat clear thesis that establishes a perspective on a contemporary issue — Respond to other perspectives on the issue **I&A 302.** Analyzing critical elements of an issue and differing perspectives on it A score in this range indicates that the writer is able to: — Establish a limited or tangential context for analysis — Provide analysis that is simplistic or somewhat unclear
7–8	**I&A 401.** Understanding the task and writing with purpose A score in this range indicates that the writer is able to: — Generate a clear thesis that establishes a perspective on a contemporary issue — Engage with other perspectives on the issue **I&A 402.** Analyzing critical elements of an issue and differing perspectives on it A score in this range indicates that the writer is able to: — Establish and employ a relevant context for analysis — Recognize implications, complexities and tensions, and/or underlying values and assumptions
9–10	**I&A 501.** Understanding the task and writing with purpose A score in this range indicates that the writer is able to: — Generate a precise thesis that establishes a perspective on a contemporary issue — Engage productively with other perspectives on the issue **I&A 502.** Analyzing critical elements of an issue and differing perspectives on it A score in this range indicates that the writer is able to: — Establish and employ a thoughtful context for analysis — Address implications, complexities and tensions, and/or underlying values and assumptions
11–12	**I&A 601.** Understanding the task and writing with purpose A score in this range indicates that the writer is able to: — Generate a nuanced, precise thesis that establishes a perspective on a contemporary issue — Engage critically with other perspectives on the issue **I&A 602.** Analyzing critical elements of an issue and differing perspectives on it A score in this range indicates that the writer is able to: — Establish and employ an insightful context for analysis — Examine implications, complexities and tensions, and/or underlying values and assumptions

Scores below 3 do not permit useful generalizations about students' writing abilities.

Taking Additional Practice Tests

1

The ONLY Official Prep Guide from the Makers of the ACT

ACT College & Career Readiness Standards
Writing

ACT®

SCORE RANGE	Development and Support (D&S)
3–4	**D&S 201.** Building and strengthening the argument A score in this range indicates that the writer is able to: — Arrive at a weak understanding of the issue and differing perspectives on it through inadequate reasoning and examples — Offer a rationale that fails to clarify the argument — Provide elaboration of ideas and analysis that is illogical, disjointed, or circular
5–6	**D&S 301.** Building and strengthening the argument A score in this range indicates that the writer is able to: — Make use of mostly relevant reasoning and examples to support the thesis and arrive at a general or simplistic understanding of the issue — Offer a rationale that largely clarifies the argument — Provide elaboration of ideas and analysis that is somewhat repetitive or imprecise
7–8	**D&S 401.** Building and strengthening the argument A score in this range indicates that the writer is able to: — Make use of clear reasoning and examples to arrive at an understanding of the issue and differing perspectives on it — Adequately convey reasons why the argument is worth considering — Extend ideas and analysis by considering factors that complicate the writer's own perspective — Anticipate objections by qualifying the argument
9–10	**D&S 501.** Building and strengthening the argument A score in this range indicates that the writer is able to: — Make purposeful use of reasoning and examples to support the thesis and arrive at a deeper understanding of the issue — Capably convey reasons why the argument is worth considering — Enrich ideas and analysis by considering factors that complicate the writer's own perspective — Anticipate objections by qualifying the argument
11–12	**D&S 601.** Building and strengthening the argument A score in this range indicates that the writer is able to: — Make skillful use of reasoning and examples to broaden the context for analysis, support the thesis, and arrive at deeper insight into the issue — Effectively convey reasons why the argument is worth considering — Enrich and strengthen ideas and analysis by considering factors that complicate the writer's own perspective — Anticipate objections by qualifying the argument

> Scores below 3 do not permit useful generalizations about students' writing abilities.

The ONLY Official Prep Guide from the Makers of the ACT

ACT College & Career Readiness Standards
Writing

SCORE RANGE	Organization (ORG)
3–4	**ORG 201. Grouping and connecting ideas** A score in this range indicates that the writer is able to: — Group ideas with little consistency or clarity — Use misleading and poorly formed transitions **ORG 202. Employing an organizational strategy** A score in this range indicates that the writer is able to: — Provide a minimal organizational structure in which some ideas are grouped locally
5–6	**ORG 301. Grouping and connecting ideas** A score in this range indicates that the writer is able to: — Group most ideas logically — Use transitions between and within paragraphs to clarify some relationships among ideas **ORG 302. Employing an organizational strategy** A score in this range indicates that the writer is able to: — Provide a basic organizational structure are grouped locally
7–8	**ORG 401. Grouping and connecting ideas** A score in this range indicates that the writer is able to: — Group and sequence ideas logically — Use transitions between and within paragraphs to clarify relationships among ideas **ORG 402. Employing an organizational strategy** A score in this range indicates that the writer is able to: — Make use of an emergent controlling idea or purpose to shape the argument
9–10	**ORG 501. Grouping and connecting ideas** A score in this range indicates that the writer is able to: — Group and sequence ideas logically to increase the effectiveness of the argument — Use transitions between and within paragraphs to consistently clarify relationships among ideas **ORG 502. Employing an organizational strategy** A score in this range indicates that the writer is able to: — Make use of a controlling idea or purpose to unify the argument
11–12	**ORG 601. Grouping and connecting ideas** A score in this range indicates that the writer is able to: — Group and sequence ideas logically, creating a progression that increases the effectiveness of the argument — Use transitions between and within paragraphs to strengthen the relationships among ideas **ORG 602. Employing an organizational strategy** A score in this range indicates that the writer is able to: — Make use of a controlling idea or purpose to unify and focus the argument

Scores below 3 do not permit useful generalizations about students' writing abilities.

Taking Additional Practice Tests

3

The ONLY Official Prep Guide from the Makers of the ACT

ACT College & Career Readiness Standards
Writing

SCORE RANGE	Language Use and Conventions (L&C)
3–4	**L&C 201. Using language to enhance meaning** A score in this range indicates that the writer is able to: — Make word choices that are rudimentary and frequently imprecise — Make stylistic choices, including voice, tone, and diction, that are inconsistent and are not always appropriate for the given writing purpose and topic **L&C 202. Applying the conventions of standard written English** A score in this range indicates that the writer is able to: — Compose sentences that sometimes have clear structures — Produce writing that has distracting errors in grammar, usage, and mechanics and only sometimes conveys meaning clearly
5–6	**L&C 301. Using language to enhance meaning** A score in this range indicates that the writer is able to: — Make word choices that are general and occasionally imprecise — Make stylistic choices, including voice, tone, and diction, that are not always appropriate for the given writing purpose and topic **L&C 302. Applying the conventions of standard written English** A score in this range indicates that the writer is able to: — Compose sentences that usually have clear structures but show little variety — Produce writing that has distracting errors in grammar, usage, and mechanics but, in most instances, conveys meaning clearly
7–8	**L&C 401. Using language to enhance meaning** A score in this range indicates that the writer is able to: — Make adequate word choices that convey the argument with clarity — Make stylistic choices, including voice, tone, and diction, that are appropriate for the given writing purpose and topic **L&C 402. Applying the conventions of standard written English** A score in this range indicates that the writer is able to: — Compose sentences with clear and occasionally varied structures — Produce writing that has errors in grammar, usage, and mechanics but conveys meaning clearly
9–10	**L&C 501. Using language to enhance meaning** A score in this range indicates that the writer is able to: — Make precise word choices that work in service of the argument — Make stylistic choices, including voice, tone, and diction, that are effective for the given writing purpose and topic **L&C 502. Applying the conventions of standard written English** A score in this range indicates that the writer is able to: — Compose sentences with clear and often varied structures — Produce writing that has only minor errors in grammar, usage, and mechanics
11–12	**L&C 601. Using language to enhance meaning** A score in this range indicates that the writer is able to: — Make skillful and precise word choices that enhance the argument — Make stylistic choices, including voice, tone, and diction, that are strategic and effective for the given writing purpose and topic **L&C 602. Applying the conventions of standard written English** A score in this range indicates that the writer is able to: — Compose sentences with clear and consistently varied structures — Produce writing that is free of all but a few minor errors in grammar, usage, and mechanics

Scores below 3 do not permit useful generalizations about students' writing abilities.

The ONLY Official Prep Guide from the Makers of the ACT

Part Five: Moving Forward to Test Day

In This Part

Even when you are fully prepared, mentally and physically, to take the ACT, you may need additional guidance to handle the logistics of arriving at the test center on time and with the necessary items. This part helps you avoid any unpleasant surprises on test day that might cause confusion and anxiety, which could negatively affect your performance. Specifically, in this part, you learn how to do the following:

- Register for a convenient test date and test center in plenty of time to have your scores reported to the colleges and scholarship agencies of your choice by their deadlines.

- Map a route and choose a means of travel that ensure you arrive at the test center on time.

- Dress for comfort to ensure that you are not too hot or too cold when taking the test.

- Pack everything you need for test day, so you are admitted to the testing room and have the items you need to take the test.

- Find out what to expect at the test center in terms of check-in procedures, rules, and maintaining your composure and energy.

- Obtain additional information you may need, including how to void your test on test day, retake the test, and gather additional information.

Chapter 13: Registering, Planning, and Packing for Test Day

When you feel ready to take the actual ACT, the time has come to register, plan, and pack for the upcoming day. Your goal is to avoid any unpleasant surprises on test day, such as getting lost on the way to the test center, showing up without a valid ID, or wearing the wrong clothing and being physically uncomfortable during the entire test. Such surprises distract you from what should be your sole focus on test day—doing your very best on the test.

In this chapter, we help you register for the ACT, avoid the most common pitfalls that test-takers encounter leading up to test day, offer guidance on how to dress and what to pack for test day, explain what you can expect at the test center, and give you a heads up about posttest concerns, such as voiding your test on test day, retaking the test, and reporting your scores.

National Testing Program Versus State and District Testing

ACT makes the test available via national testing centers and through certain school districts or states. Registration for and administration of the test varies accordingly. For example, if your district or state offers the test, you do not need to register for that test. Instead, your district or state registers for the test and chooses a school day on which to administer it. If you want to take the test at a national test center on a Saturday, you will need to register yourself for that test. Check with your counselor to find out whether your school offers the ACT or whether you must register individually to take the ACT at a national testing center.

Registering for the ACT

If your district or state offers the ACT for your grade level test, you can skip ahead to the section "Planning and Packing for Test Day." Your district or state will take the first two registration steps for you:

- Selects a test date (typically a school day)

- Chooses whether students will take the ACT with or without the writing test

Note: If you have a diagnosed disability or are an English language learner, and have documentation of receiving an accommodation or support in school, you *may* be eligible to take the ACT with that accommodation or support. Work with your school counselor or accommodations coordinator to determine if they have submitted the required documentation.

If your school does not offer the ACT, you must register for it through the ACT national testing program. In the following sections, we lead you through the process of choosing a national test date and test option (ACT with or without the writing test) and registering for the test. We also address special circumstances that could affect your registration.

Selecting a National Testing Date and Location

Prior to registering for the ACT through the ACT national testing program, choose the date on which you want to take the test. When choosing a date, consider the following:

- Available test dates and test centers near you

- College and scholarship application deadlines

- Where you stand in your high school coursework

- Whether you may want to take the ACT more than once

Let's look at each of these considerations in turn.

Checking Available Test Dates and Test Centers

The ACT is offered nationally and internationally several times a year. However, it's not offered at every test center on each test date. If you need to take the ACT on a day other than Saturday (for religious reasons), you'll want to be especially attentive in selecting a test date when a test center near you is open on a non-Saturday date.

One of the first things you should find out, then, is where and when the ACT is being offered in your area. A quick and easy way to access available test dates and find test centers is to visit ACT's website at www.actstudent.org. Search for **test dates and deadlines** to find test dates and registration deadlines. You can also look at nearby ACT test centers by searching for **ACT test centers**.

Note: You may *not* receive scores from more than one test taken on a scheduled national or international test date *and* one of the alternate test dates associated with that date. For example, suppose you take the test on Saturday *and* then again on the non-Saturday date associated with that Saturday. We will report only the scores from the first test. The second set of scores will be cancelled without refund.

Considering College and Scholarship Application Deadlines

Colleges and scholarship agencies may require that ACT test scores be submitted sometime during your junior year of high school. Find out what these deadlines are and then make absolutely sure that you take the test early enough to ensure that the colleges and scholarship agencies you're applying to receive your ACT test scores by those deadlines.

Score reports are usually ready about 2 to 8 weeks after the test date. To be on the safe side, consider taking your ACT at least 10 weeks prior to the earliest deadline.

You may not be certain yet which school or program you'll decide on. That's okay. Just be sure you're doing everything, including taking the ACT, early enough to keep all options open.

Gauging Where You Stand in Your High School Coursework and Whether You May Want to Take the ACT More Than Once

Another consideration in deciding when to take the ACT is where you stand in your high school coursework. If you're in a college-prep program and taking a lot of courses in English, mathematics, and science in your sophomore and junior years, taking the ACT in your junior year, while those subjects are still fresh in your memory, is probably best.

Perhaps you'll decide to take the ACT more than once, in hopes of improving your score. In that case, it's better to take the exam early in the spring of your junior year to allow time for a second try. If you find you're studying a significant amount of material covered on the ACT during your senior year, you may plan on retaking the ACT in your senior year, based on the reasonable assumption that your scores will reflect your improved knowledge and skills.

Taking the ACT in your junior year has several advantages:

- You probably will have completed much of the coursework corresponding to the material covered on the ACT.

- You will have your ACT scores and other information in time to help make decisions about your final year of high school coursework. (For example, you may decide to take additional classes in an area in which your test score was lower than you wanted it to be.)

- Colleges will know of your interest and have your scores in time to contact you during the summer before your senior year, when many of them like to send information about admissions, scholarships, advanced placement, and special programs to prospective students.

- You'll have your ACT scores and information from colleges in time to make decisions about visiting campuses or contacting schools.

- You'll have the opportunity to take the ACT again if you feel your scores don't accurately reflect your achievement.

Selecting a Test Option

When you register, you must choose one of two test options—the ACT (which includes the four multiple-choice tests: English, mathematics, reading, and science), or the ACT with the optional writing test (which includes the four multiple-choice tests plus a 40-minute writing test). Taking the writing test does not affect your composite score.

Not all institutions require the ACT writing test. Check directly with the institutions you are considering to find out their requirements, or ask your high school counselor which test option you should take.

Registering

The fastest and easiest way to register to take the ACT through its national testing program is online at www.actstudent.org. When you register on the web, you will know immediately if your preferred test center has space for you, and you can print your admission ticket. Read all the information on your admission ticket carefully to make sure it is correct.

You are guaranteed a seat and test booklet at a test center only if you register by the deadline for a test date. If you miss the late registration deadline, you can try to test as a "standby" examinee. Testing as a standby costs more and does not guarantee you a seat or test booklet. If you decide to take your chance as a standby, be sure to follow the instructions for standby testing on the ACT website. You must bring acceptable identification to be admitted. Standby examinees will be admitted only after all registered students have been seated for their test option.

However you register, you are encouraged to create your free ACT web account. You can use your ACT web account to do several things:

- View your scores and score report on the web at no charge.

- Send your scores to additional colleges.

- Receive email updates from ACT about changes to your registration.

- Make changes to your student profile.

- Print your admission ticket.

Registering under Special Circumstances

See the website or our online registration brochure for instructions if special circumstances apply to you—for example, if your religious beliefs prevent you from taking the exam on Saturday and no test centers in your area offer non-Saturday test dates or if you have a diagnosed disability or are an English language learner and require accommodations or supports.

If you have a diagnosed disability, or are an English language learner, and have documentation of receiving an accommodation or support in school, you *may* be eligible to take the ACT with that accommodation or support. Details about the procedures for applying to test with accommodations and supports are provided on the ACT website.

Planning and Packing for Test Day

At least one week before your scheduled test date, start planning and packing for test day. You need to know where you're going, how you're getting there, how much time the trip will take you, how to dress, and what to pack. In the following sections, we help you plan and pack for test day.

Getting to the Test Center

If your school is administering the ACT on a school day, you simply need to arrive at your school at the start of the school day. Testing will be the first activity of the day.

Under no circumstances will you be admitted to the test after the test booklets have been distributed, so be sure to arrive on time.

If you registered to take the test through the ACT national testing program, you'll be asked to report to the test center by 8:00 a.m. on your test date. Under no circumstances will you be admitted after the test booklets have been distributed, so be sure to arrive on time by 8:00 a.m.

You may need to walk a few blocks to get to the test center or drive several hours, perhaps to an unfamiliar city. Whatever your situation, be certain to allow plenty of time. We recommend that you plan to arrive 15 to 30 minutes early just in case you experience an unexpected delay.

Test centers vary considerably. You may be taking the ACT in your own high school, at a local community college, or in a large building on a nearby university campus. Your surroundings may be quite familiar or they may be new. If they're new, allow yourself a few extra minutes to get acclimated. Then try to forget about your surroundings so that you can concentrate on the test.

To ensure that you arrive on time, map your route to the test center and choose a means of travel—car, train, bus, taxi, bicycle, carpool with a friend . . . whatever works best for you.

One week prior to test day, travel to the testing center using the selected means of travel. By doing a test run on the same day and at the same time (but a week early), you gain a better sense of what traffic will be like, what your parking options will be, whether the buses are running during those times, and so on.

Dressing for Test Day

The night before the test, set out the clothes you want to wear. Dress in layers so that you can adjust to the temperature in your testing room.

Keep in mind that you're going to be sitting in the same place for more than three hours. Wearing something you're especially comfortable in may make you better able to relax and concentrate on the test. For many people, what they're wearing can make a difference in how they feel about themselves. Picking something you like and feel good wearing may boost your confidence.

Packing for Test Day: What to Bring

Bring with you only what you'll need that morning, because other materials will be in your way and may be prohibited in the test room. Be sure to bring these:

- **Your paper admission ticket** (if you are taking the test on a national or international ACT test date). Failure to bring your admission ticket will delay your scores. If your district or state is administering the test, you will not receive (or need) an admission ticket.

- **Acceptable photo identification.** Examples of acceptable identification include current identification issued by your city/state/federal government or school, on which both your name and current photograph appear (for example, driver's license or passport). Without acceptable identification, you will not be allowed to take the test. (See www.actstudent.org for details on what constitutes acceptable and unacceptable identification.)

- Several sharpened **soft-lead No. 2 pencils with good erasers** (no mechanical pencils or ink pens). Test the erasers to make sure they erase cleanly without leaving any residue.

- **A watch *without* an alarm function** to pace yourself. If your watch has an alarm function and the alarm goes off, it will disturb the other students, you will be dismissed, and your answer document will not be scored. Although the test supervisor will announce when 5 minutes remain on each test, not all test rooms have wall clocks for pacing yourself in the meantime.

- **A permitted calculator** if you wish to use one *on the mathematics test only* (for a list of permitted and prohibited calculators, visit www.actstudent.org). You are solely responsible for knowing whether a particular calculator is permitted.

- **A snack and a drink** to consume outside the test room only during the break.

Obtaining Additional Test Details

On certain national test dates, if you test at a national test center, you may request and pay for a copy of the multiple-choice test questions used to determine your scores, a list of your answers, and the answer key. If you take the writing test, you will also receive a copy of the writing prompt, scoring guidelines, and the scores assigned to your essay. You'll also get information about requesting a photocopy of your answer document for an additional fee. These services are not offered for all test dates, so if you're interested in receiving any of these services, you'll need to check the dates on ACT's website (www.actstudent.org) to be sure you're choosing a test date on which the desired service is available.

At the Test Center

Knowing ahead of time what to expect at the test center can alleviate any anxiety you may feel, ensure that you do everything ACT requires in terms of checking in and obeying the rules, and help you maintain your composure. In the following sections, we describe the check-in procedure, present the rules, encourage you to communicate with the testing staff (if necessary), and provide tips on maintaining your composure and energy level.

Checking In

The way **check-in procedures** are handled may vary from location to location. You may find that all students are met at a central location and directed from there to different classrooms. Signs may be posted, telling you that everyone whose last name falls between certain letters should report directly to a particular room. However this part of the check-in is handled at your location, you can anticipate that certain check-in procedures will be performed, including verification of your identity.

In the room you'll be directed to a seat by a member of the testing staff. If you are left-handed, let the testing staff know so that an appropriate desk or table may be made available to you.

Following the Rules

*The below text was pulled from the Terms and Conditions: Testing Rules and Policies for the ACT®
Test at the time of publishing.*

The following behaviors are prohibited. You may be dismissed and/or your test may not be
scored, at ACT's sole discretion, if you are found:

- Filling in or altering responses to any multiple-choice questions or continuing
  to write or alter the essay after time has been called. This means that you cannot
  make any changes to a test section outside of the designated time for that section,
  even to fix a stray mark or accidental keystroke.

- Looking back at a test section on which time has already been called.

- Looking ahead in the test.

- Looking at another person's test or answers.

- Giving or receiving assistance by any means.

- Discussing or sharing test questions, answers, or test form identification numbers
  at any time, including during test administration, during breaks, or after the test.

- Attempting to photograph, copy, or memorize test-related information or remove
  test materials, including questions or answers, from the test room in any way or at
  any time.

- Disclosing test questions or answers, in whole or in part, in any way or at any time,
  including through social media.

- Using a prohibited calculator (www.act.org/calculator-policy.html).

- Using a calculator on any test section other than mathematics.

- Sharing a calculator with another person.

- Wearing a watch during test administration. All watches must be removed and
  placed face up on the desk.

- Using a watch with recording, internet, communication, or calculator capabilities
  (e.g., a smart watch or fitness band).

- Accessing any electronic device other than an approved calculator or watch. **All**
  other electronic devices, including cell phones and other wearable devices, must
  be powered off and stored out of sight from the time you are admitted to your
  testing room until you are dismissed at the end of the test.

- Using highlighter pens, colored pens or pencils, notes, dictionaries, or other aids.

- Using scratch paper. **

- Not following instructions or abiding by the rules of the test center.

- Not following the rules of the test administration.

- Exhibiting confrontational, threatening, or unruly behavior.

- Violating any laws. If ACT suspects you have engaged in criminal activities in connection with a test, such activities may be reported to law enforcement agencies.

- Allowing an alarm on a personal item to sound in the test room or creating any other disturbance.

** If you are taking the ACT online, some use of ACT-provided scratch paper or dry erase surface may be permitted; all such use must be in accordance with ACT policies and procedures.

ACT may restrict the items you bring into the test center. All items brought into the test center, such as hats, purses, backpacks, cell phones, calculators, watches, and other electronic devices, may be searched at the discretion of ACT and its testing staff. Searches may include the use of tools, such as handheld metal detectors, that detect prohibited devices. ACT and its testing staff may confiscate and retain for a reasonable period of time any item suspected of having been used, or capable of being used, in violation of these prohibited behaviors. ACT may also provide such items to and permit searches by third parties in connection with an investigation conducted by ACT or others. ACT and its testing staff shall not be responsible for lost, stolen, or damaged items that you bring to a test center. Your test center may also have additional procedures with which you must comply.

Dismissal for Prohibited Behavior

Examinees who are dismissed because of prohibited behavior forfeit their registration for that test date. There are no options for refunds or appeals in situations involving prohibited behavior.

Eating, drinking, and the use of tobacco are not allowed in the test room. You may bring a snack to eat or drink before the test or during the break, but any food or beverage you bring must be put away during testing and must be consumed outside the test room.

Communicating with the Testing Staff

Although you are required to work silently during the test, you may need to communicate with the testing staff under certain circumstances, such as the following:

- **If you have problems with the testing environment, let the testing staff know immediately.** Possible problems include being seated below, over, or next to a heating or cooling vent that is making you too warm or too cold; having a defective chair or desk; poor lighting that makes reading difficult; or excessive noise.

- **If any aspect of the test-taking procedure is not perfectly clear to you, request clarification.** Testing staff will be available throughout the exam. In fact, they'll be moving quietly around the room while you're working. If you have a question about the administration of the test (not about any of the test questions), raise your hand and quietly ask for information.

- **If you need to use the restroom, ask.** Bathroom breaks are permitted during the test or between tests, but you're not allowed to make up the lost time.

- **If you become ill during the test, you may turn in your test materials and leave, if necessary.** Let the testing staff know that you are ill and whether you wish to have your answer document scored. One caution: Once you leave the test center, you won't be allowed to return and continue—so be sure that leaving is what you want to do. You might try closing your eyes or putting your head on the desk for a minute first; then if you feel better, you'll be able to continue.

Maintaining Your Composure and Energy

While you're waiting for the test to begin, you may find yourself getting anxious or jittery. That's perfectly normal. Most of us get nervous in new situations. People handle this nervousness in different ways.

Some people find it helpful to practice **mental and physical relaxation techniques.** If this appeals to you, try alternately flexing and relaxing your muscles, beginning at your toes and moving up through your shoulders, neck, and arms. Meanwhile, imagine yourself in a quiet, peaceful place: at the beach, in the mountains, or just in your favorite lounge chair. Breathe deeply and evenly.

Other people like to **redirect that nervous energy** and turn it to their advantage. For them, concentrating on the task at hand and shutting everything else out of their minds is the most helpful strategy. If this is your style, you may even want to close your eyes and imagine yourself already working on the exam, thinking about how it will feel to move confidently and smoothly through the tests.

If you have the chance, try out the two approaches on some classroom tests and see which one works better for you. The important thing is to keep the ACT in perspective. Try not to let it become larger than life. Remember, it's just one part of a long academic and professional career. If you begin to feel tired during the test, check your posture to make sure you're sitting up straight. Getting enough air in your lungs is difficult when you're slouching. You'll stay more alert and confident if your brain receives a steady supply of oxygen.

You might want to practice those relaxation techniques again, too, because tension contributes to fatigue. As you start a new test, you might find it helpful to stretch your neck and shoulder muscles, rotate your shoulders, stretch back in your chair and take some long, deep breaths.

You can expect a short break (approximately 10 to 15 minutes) after the second test. During this break, it's a good idea to stand up, walk around a little, stretch, and relax. You may wish to get a drink, have a snack, or use the restroom. Keep in mind, though, that you still have work ahead of you that requires concentrated effort. Eat lightly and return to the room quickly. The third test will start promptly, and you'll need to be back at your desk and ready to go on time.

Voiding Your Answer Documents on Test Day

If you have to leave before completing all tests, you must decide whether you want your answer document scored and then inform your supervisor if you do *not* want your answer document scored; otherwise, your answer document will be scored.

Once you break the seal on your multiple-choice test booklet, you cannot request a test date change. If you do not complete all your tests and want to test again, you will have to pay the full fee for your test option again. If you want to take the ACT again, see www.actstudent.org for your options. Once you begin filling out your answer document, you cannot change from one test option to another.

Testing More Than Once

If you think you can improve your scores, you can retake the ACT. ACT may limit the number of times you take the ACT. The current retest limit can be found at www.actstudent.org. Many students take the test twice, once as a junior and again as a senior. Of the students who took the ACT more than once:

- 56% increased their Composite score
- 20% had no change in their Composite score
- 24% decreased their Composite score

You determine which set of scores are sent to colleges or scholarship programs. ACT will release only the scores from the test date (month and year) and test location (e.g., national or state) you designate. This protects you and ensures that you direct the reporting of your scores.

Our mission is helping people achieve education and workplace success. Thank you for allowing ACT to be a part of your journey and good luck on test day.

NOTES

NOTES

NOTES

NOTES

NOTES

NOTES

NOTES

NOTES

NOTES